# A Glossary of Zoning, Development, and Planning Terms

**Edited by**

FAY DOLNICK AND
MICHAEL DAVIDSON

**With Research Assistance from**

SHANNON ARMSTRONG
BARRY BAIN
JOSEPH BORNSTEIN
JEROME CLELAND
ANDREW GLICKSBERG
ANNE LOUCKS

n the 10 years since APA published *A Survey of Zoning Definitions* (Planning Advisory Service Report 421) by Tracy Burrows, the PAS staff has received numerous inquiries from our subscribers and others seeking help with definitions that were not covered in that report or in the three previous PAS Reports (Nos. 72, 233, and 322) that addressed zoning definitions and planning terms. The calls reflected a need for a more expansive glossary that contained zoning, development, and planning terms.

The editors first compiled a list of terms to be defined. Beyond the inquiries we received from PAS subscribers and the PAS Reports that were glossaries, we used a number of sources to decide on our list of terms. First, we consulted the California Planning Roundtable, the New York Planning Federation, the Iowa State University Extension Service, and the Handbook for Planning Commissioners in Missouri. More information about those sources can be found in the acknowledgments on the inside cover of this report. We also compared our list of terms with those in The *New Illustrated Book of Development Definitions* by Harvey S. Moscowitz and Carl G. Lindbloom (New Brunswick, N.J.: Center for Urban Policy Research, Rutgers, 1993), and *The Zoning Dictionary: Resource Materials for Planners* by Lehman and Associates (Barrie, Ontario, 1993). We recommend that readers consult these two publications for their definitions, which do not appear in our report.

The process of compiling the terms, researching the definitions, and culling them down into a "manageable" report turned out to be far more complex and daunting than it first appeared. What has amazed all of us involved in the process is the incredible breadth of what planners are expected to know and have to deal with on a daily basis. The definitions in this glossary clearly point the way to the intersection of planning with numerous other professions including, but not limited to (as many of the definitions are fond of saying), architecture, civil engineering, environmental science, landscape architecture, law, public works, real estate management, transportation engineering, and even philosophy (e.g., see the definition of "art, works of"). We think that everyone involved in land-use planning will find that this is not just a useful list of terms, but that spending some time with this glossary will provide quite an education about the various professions and their terminology.

Despite our efforts, we do not pretend that this glossary contains the most exhaustive list of terms and the best (or most acceptable or locally appropriate) definitions. The terms and definitions we found range from the mundane to the highly esoteric. Much of our editing has been to cut the list down to make sure that we covered the essential and contentious terms, seeking to limit any repetition of terms and definitions found in a dictionary of the English language (e.g., potable water) that did not have some special meaning or significance for planning, zoning, and development, or (often) the law of planning and zoning. Some of those still made it in, however, when we deemed them too essential to leave out. We also eliminated some local or regional terms and definitions that did not seem to fit in a national publication or incorporated those terms and definitions under our terms (e.g., see the entry for "car wash," which notes that some of the jurisdictions use quite different terms for what we think of as simply a car wash).

Despite this culling, we have erred on the side of inclusiveness and even what might be called "repetition by relatedness" (as is attested to by the volume of "See also" references). We found we could not, in good conscience, attempt to group all the definitions related to each other, often in subtle ways, under a single term. There was also the matter of the general term (e.g., retail sales establishment) versus the specific, related term (e.g., hardware store). Our reasoning was that, if communities found it necessary to use numerous terms dictated by policy, history, or local use, we were in no position to decide that the best and most suitable term was one we chose. Such a decision was impractical from an editorial standpoint as well. The decision making involved would have been overwhelming. We have, however, grouped many terms with their "main" component so that a user could easily compare, for instance, one type of sign to another, one type of street to another, or one type of elderly housing to another. In those cases and others, you will find long lists of definitions gathered in one place under a main term with qualifiers.

The end result of all this work is a glossary of 2,887 terms, with commentary and extensive "see" and "see also" cross-referencing. While we think we succeeded in creating a practical and comprehensive glossary, we fully understand that any glossary is, by necessity, a work in progress and open to all kinds of improvements. Even as this report was going to print, we continued to find terms we would have liked to add and other ways that we might have more effectively grouped terms together. Knowing that we can improve this glossary, we will continue to work at it over time, creating an in-house document that is an expanded and revised version of this report. We also invite any reader of this work to contact the PAS staff with comments and suggestions for revisions, additions, and deletions. Please send those comments via e-mail to pasreports@planning.org or in writing to Jim Hecimovich, Chief Editor, PAS Reports, 122 S. Michigan Ave., Suite 1600, Chicago, IL 60603.

We intend at some point in the next year or two to put this glossary on APA's web site where it will be a "living" document.

### Using this Glossary

Perhaps the best starting point for using this glossary is a review of the list of terms that follow this introduction. It will provide, at a glance, some idea of how things are arranged and where you might look first for the terms and definitions you need. The terms are arranged alphabetically, following the rule of word-by-word alphabetizing. All the "See" and "See also" references are noted in the list. Terms followed by an asterisk indicate that a commentary accompanies the definition.

The definitions have been taken primarily from local ordinances, although we also consulted the PAS Report series, federal documents and agencies, state documents, APA research projects (e.g., Growing Smart and the Land-Based Classification System (LBCS)), and more. In a few cases, we created our own definition. We received permission from The California Planning Roundtable, the New York Planning Federation, the Iowa State University Extension Service, and the University Extension at the University of Missouri–Columbia, to use their definitions, and we are extremely grateful for their cooperation. In many cases, we have listed more than one definition for a term; in the case of contentious terms (e.g., family), we have listed many and, in some cases, provided a commentary. As a rule of thumb, we have tried to keep the number of definitions to three or fewer, except for contentious or essential terms, where we may supply as many as five or more.

We have provided graphics from our previous PAS Report glossaries as well as photos to illustrate the terms and break up long pages of text.

The definitions in this report have been edited to save space (e.g., we deleted the word "means" if it was used to start a definition), to correct grammatical errors, and to bring the definitions more in line with PAS Report style conventions. In addition, we have used ellipses to indicate where we have removed what we considered to be extraneous material from definitions and have used brackets to "generalize" the definitions for a national audience (e.g., specific state statutes usually appear as [state law]). Terms are in boldface, followed by the definition, followed by the source of the definition in parentheses and italics. Publications that are sources (e.g., *Zoning News*) appear in regular type in parentheses. We opted to employ "bullets" to more clearly mark the terms on the page.

### What Is Good; What Is Best; What Is Necessary

Many of the terms and definitions in this report contain standards to regulate the thing being defined. For definitions that will not be used in a zoning ordinance, that's probably not a problem. But for zoning ordinances, standards more properly belong in the ordinance itself. The dangers are obvious: inconsistencies between the standards in the ordinance and the definition, or the need to constantly refer to the definitions to understand how a thing is regulated, rather than just reading the ordinance. Our attempts to provide a more complete glossary convinced us to include such definitions or we would be faced with a severe cut in the number of terms we would provide. Editing such definitions to eliminate the standards would have been somewhat dangerous; we did not want to alter meaning. Such thorough editing would also have been impossible given time and budget constraints.

We believe that all these definitions provide a good starting point for those who need to draft zoning definitions. Ideally, users will edit the definitions they find here to make them better—-eliminating regulations from the definitions and considering what is most appropriate for local circumstances. In other words, use them only as a reference to create something new and suitable; do not just copy these definitions without thought. In fact, as we always advise in PAS Reports, consult your state enabling legislation (which may, in fact, have definitions you can safely copy) and consult the attorney working for your jurisdiction before adopting any of the definitions in this report or drafting any new definition.

*The Editors*
Michael Davidson
Fay Dolnick
Jim Hecimovich

# a

abandoned vehicle *(See* motor vehicle, abandoned)

abandonment

abate

abatement

abattoir *(See* slaughterhouse, commercial)

abutting *(See also* adjacent/adjoining; contiguous)

abutting owner

access

access connection

access management

access point*

accessible route

accessory apartment

accessory banking *(See also* bank)

accessory structure

accessory use

acid rain*

acre

acreage, gross

acre, net

adaptive reuse

addition *(See also* alteration; rehabilitation; remodel)

address

adequate public facilities ordinance (APFO) *(See also* carrying capacity analysis; system capacity)

adjacent/adjoining *(See also* abutting; contiguous)

adjacent properties

administrative entity

administrative headquarters office

administrative office

adult use*

adult use, adult arcade

adult use, adult bookstore

adult use, adult cabaret

adult use, adult mini motion picture theater

adult use, adult motion picture theater

adult use, adult sauna

adult use, adult theater

adult use, hotel/motel

adult use, massage parlor *(See also* massage establishment)

adult use, modeling studio

adult use, sexual encounter establishment

adult use, sexual paraphernalia store

adult use, specified anatomical areas

adult use, specified sexual activities

adverse impact

aerial mosaic

aesthetic zoning

affected persons

affiliate

affordable housing *(See also* below-market-rate housing; housing, low-income; housing, very low-income)

affordable units

afforestation *(See also* forestry *definitions)*

agency

aggrieved party

agricultural activity

agricultural building

agricultural land, prime

agricultural preserve

agricultural processing plant

agricultural protection zoning *(See also* quarter/quarter zoning)

agricultural-related industry

agricultural sales and service

agriculture

agriculture, commercial

agriculture, home

agriculture, intensive

agriculture-related business

agriculture, specialized

air contaminant

air pollution *(See also* acid rain; ozone; smog)

air rights

air traffic pattern

aircraft

airport

airport approach areas

airport environs

airport hazard

airport-related use

airport, water-based

airport zoning

airspace

all-terrain vehicle (ATV) *(See also* off-road vehicle)

alley

alteration *(See also* addition; rehabilitation; remodel)

alteration, incidental

alteration, structural*

amateur radio tower *(See also* telecommunications definitions)

ambient

ambient noise level

amenity

amortization *(See also* nonconforming *definitions)*

amusement, commercial, indoor

amusement, commercial, outdoor *(See also* carnival)

amusement device

amusement enterprise

amusement park *(See also* carnival)

amusement park, children's

amusement ride *(See also* carnival)

anchor tenant

ancillary use *(See* accessory use)

animal

animal-at-large

animal boarding place *(See also* kennel)

animal, domestic

animal-drawn carriage

animal, exotic

animal, farm

animal grooming service

animal hospital

animal husbandry

animal, large

animal shelter

animal, small

annex

annexation

antenna *(See also* telecommunications antenna)

antenna, dish *(See* telecommunications, satellite dish antenna)

antique mall

antique shop *(See also* secondhand merchandise, retail sales; thrift store)

apartment *(See also* dwelling definitions)

apartment, garden *(See* garden apartment)

apartment, high-rise

apartment hotel

apartment, senior *(See also* elderly housing)

apiary
applicant
application
appraisal
aquaculture
aquarium
aquifer *(See also* groundwater *definitions)*
aquifer, artesian
aquifer recharge *(See* groundwater
   recharge*)*
aquifer, surficial
arborist
arcade
arcade, amusement *(See also* amusement
   park*)*
arcade, internal
arcade, street
archaeological resources
archaeological site
archery range
architectural control/architectural
   review *(See also* design control; design
   review*)*
architectural decoration
architectural features
architectural plan
architectural projection
architectural recesses
architectural review board
architecture
area classification
area plan
areawide zoning
art gallery
art, public
art, works of
artisan
artisan's workshop
artist
artist studio
as-of-right zoning *(See also* cumulative
   zoning; Euclidean zoning*)*
assembly hall *(See also* auditorium;
   meeting hall*)*
assisted living *(See* elderly housing,
   assisted living*)*
athletic field
atrium
atrium house
attic
auction house
auditorium *(See also* assembly hall;
   meeting hall*)*
automated teller machine (ATM)
automobile

automobile-accommodating
   development *(See also* pedestrian-
   oriented development*)*
automobile, compact
automobile convenience market *(See* gas
   station minimart*)*
automobile court
automobile dealership
automobile dealership, new
automobile dealership, used
automobile graveyard
automobile impound facility
automobile mall
automobile parts/supply, retail
automobile rental/leasing
automobile repair services *(See also*
   motor vehicle, general repair and
   service*)*
automobile repair services, major
automobile repair services, minor
automobile sales
automobile sales lot
auxiliary massage establishment *(See
   also* massage establishment*)*
aviary
awning
awning, fixed
awning, illuminated
awning, retractable

# b

backfill *(See also* borrow; fill*)*
bakery, retail
bakery, wholesale
balcony
balloon
bank *(See also* accessory banking;
   automated teller machine (ATM);
   financial institution*)*
banner *(See* sign, banner*)*
banquet hall
bar *(See also* tavern*)*
barber shop
barn
barnyard
base density *(See* density, base*)*
base flood
base flood elevation
base map
basement *(See also* cellar; crawlspace*)*
batching plant
bathhouse *(See also* health spa; sauna*)*
bathroom/bath
bathroom, full
bathroom, half

bathroom, three-quarter
beach
beach club
beach house
beacon
beauty salon
bed
bed-and-breakfast (B&B)
bed-and-breakfast (B&B) inn
bedrock
bedrock, exposed/shallow
bedroom* *(See also* room; sleeping room*)*
below-market-rate (BMR) housing unit
   *(See also* affordable housing*)*
benchmark
benchmarking
benefit assessment district *(See also*
   special benefit district*)*
berm
berm bank top
berth
best management practices
bicycle
bicycle facilities
big-box retail *(See also* shopping center
   *definitions)*
bike lane (Class I facility*)*
bike path (Class II facility*)*
bike path (Class III facility*)*
bike route
bike way
billboard *(See* sign, billboard*)*
bingo hall
biomass
biotic community *(See also* wildlife
   habitat*)*
blight
block
block, business
block grant *(See also* Community
   Development Block Grant (CBDG);
   target area*)*
blockface
blockfront
bluff
board of supervisors
board of zoning appeals and
   adjustments
boarder *(See also* roomer; tenant*)*
boarding house *(See also* lodging house;
   rooming house *)*
boat
boat launch/ramp
boat (large) sales and/or rental
boat livery
boat parts or accessories sales

boat repair facility
boat slip
boat yard
boatel
boathouse
body art
body-painting studio
body piercing *(See also* tattoo*)*
bonus *(See also* incentive zoning*)*
bookstore
borrow *(See also* backfill; fill*)*
borrow pit *(See also* backfill*)*
botanical gardens
bottle club
boulevard *(See* street, boulevard*)*
boundary
bowling alley
breakaway wall
breakwater *(See also* jetty*)*
breezeway
brew-on-premises store
brew pub *(See also* microbrewery*)*
brewery
bridge
brownfield
buffer
buffer strip
buffer yard
buffer zone
build out
build-out analysis
build-to line *(See also* setback *definitions)*
buildable area
buildable lands
buildable width
building
building area *(See* building coverage*)*
building bulk
building code
building coverage
building, dangerous
building, detached
building elevation
building envelope
building facade *(See* facade*)*
building footprint
building frontage *(See also* facade*)*
building group
building height
building height, maximum
building inspector
building line
building lot line *(See* lot line*)*
building official
building permit
building, principal

building, residential *(See also* dwelling *definitions)*
building, single occupancy
building site
building, vacant or unoccupied
building width
built environment
bulk
bulk envelope
bulk materials
bulk plane *(See also* daylight plane; sky exposure plane*)*
bulk regulations
bulk retail *(See* retail*)*
bulkhead *(See also* shoreline stabilization*)*
bulkhead line
bunkhouse *(See also* housing, temporary employment*)*
burial space
bus
bus bay
bus, electric trolley *(See also* transit *definitions)*
bus lane
bus lot
bus, school
bus shelter
bus, sightseeing
bus stop
bus way
business
business district
business incubator
business park *(See* office park*)*
business services
business support services
business, technology, and research district
buspool *(See also* carpool; vanpool*)*
by right
bylaws

# C

cabana
cabin/cottage *(See also* summer home*)*
cafe *(See* coffee house; restaurant *definitions)*
caliper *(See also* tree *definitions)*
camp *(See* campground *)*
camp, day or youth
camp, organized recreation
camp, recreation
campground
camping trailer
campus

canal  *(See also* channel*)*
candle/candela (cd)
candlepower *(See also* footcandle; lumen*)*
canopy
canopy, building
canopy, entrance
capacity
capacity, net
capacity, planned
capacity, zoned
capital budget
capital improvement
capital improvements budget
capital improvements element (CIE)
capital improvements program (CIP)
car shelter *(See also* carport*)*
car wash
car wash, industrial
car wash, self-service
caretaker
caretaker, property
caretaker's residence
cargo, breakbulk
cargo, containerized
carnival *(See also* amusement *definitions)*
carnival, major
carnival, minor
carpool *(See also* transportation demand management (TDM)*)*
carport
carry-out restaurant  *(See* restaurant, carry-out*)*
carrying capacity analysis *(See also* adequate public facilities ordinance (APFO); system capacity*)*
cartway
casino
catering service
catering service, industrial
cattery
cellar *(See also* basement; crawlspace*)*
cemetery *(See also* burial space; crematorium; columbarium; mausoleum*)*
cemetery, pet
census
census tract*
central business district (CBD)
certificate of appropriateness
certificate of completion
certificate of compliance
certificate of occupancy
certified
certified survey
cesspool

chainwall

change of occupancy

change of use *(See* use, change of*)*

channel *(See also* canal; diversion*)*

channel bank

channel modification

character

charitable organizations

charrette

charter

child care center* *(See also* day care definitions*)*

child day care, home

church *(See also* religious institution*)*

church, community-scale

church, neighborhood-scale

cineplex *(See* movie theater, cineplex*)*

circulation

circulation system

circus *(See also* carnival*)*

citizen action group (CAG)

city

city council

city planner *(See also* Planner *definitions)*

city planning

civic center

civil defense

civil defense forces *(See also* law enforcement officer*)*

civil engineering

classification

classroom

clear-cutting *(See also* forestry *definitions)*

clear vision area

clear vision triangle *(See also* corner clearance; sight distance triangle*)*

clear zone

clearance

clinic *(See also* health care facility; hospital; sanitarium*)*

close

club

clubhouse

cluster development

cluster, residential

cluster subdivision

code enforcement

coffee house *(See also* teahouse*)*

coffee kiosk

co-generation

co-generation facility

collection office

collective household *(See also* family*)*

college/university *(See* educational facilities, college/university*)*

co-location *(See* telecommunications *definitions)*

columbarium *(See also* cemetery; crematorium; mausoleum*)*

combining zone *(See* overlay zone*)*

commercial burn

commercial, community

commercial, convenience

commercial district

commercial purpose

commercial, retail *(See* retail establishment *definitions)*

commercial service

commercial strip *(See* shopping center, commercial strip*)*

commercial use

commercial, wholesale *(See* wholesale establishment*)*

common area

common elements

common entrance

common grounds

common ownership

communications tower *(See* telecommunications tower*)*

communications services

community

community center

Community Development Block Grant (CDBG) *(See also* block grant; target area*)*

community development corporation (CDC)

community facilities

community facilities district

community gardens

community health center

community of place

community redevelopment agency (CRA) *(See also* target area*)*

community service area

commute

commute mode

commute mode, alternative

commute, reverse

commute shed

commuter matching service *(See also* transportation demand management (TDM)*)*

commuter rail *(See also* transit, light rail (LRT)*)*

company town

compatibility

compatible

compensable/compensative regulations

compensation project *(See* wetland compensation project*)*

compensatory mitigation *(See* wetland compensatory mitigation*)*

compensatory storage *(See* floodplain compensatory storage*)*

compost

composting

composting facility *(See also* solid waste compost facility*)*

comprehensive plan *(See also* general plan; master plan*)*

computer design and development facility

concentrated animal feeding operation (CAFO) *(See* feedlot*)*

concept plan

concurrency

concurrency determination network map

concurrency management system

concurrency review process

concurrency test

condemnation *(See also* eminent domain; taking*)*

condemnation for occupancy

conditional use *(See* use, conditional*)*

conditional use permit *(See* permit, conditional use*)*

conditional zoning

condominium

condominium document

condominium project (subdivision)

condominium subdivision plan

condominium unit

conference center *(See also* convention center*)*

conforming use *(See* use, conforming*)*

congestion management plan (CMP)

congregate care facility *(See* elderly housing, congregate living facility*)*

consanguinity *(See also* family*)*

conservation

conservation, agricultural land

conservation district

conservation district, architectural

conservation district, historic

conservation district, neighborhood

conservation district, neighborhood overlay

conservation district, residential

conservation easement *(See* easement, conservation*)*

conservation element

conservation land

consignment store *(See also* secondhand merchandise, retail sales; thrift store*)*

consistency with the comprehensive
    plan
consistent
consolidation
construction
construction camp
construction envelope
construction field office
construction sales and services
construction service
construction sign (See sign,
    construction)
construction waste
construction yard
contaminant (See also pollutant)
contiguous (See also abutting;
    adjacent/adjoining)
contiguous properties
contract zoning (See also developer's
    agreement)
contractors
contractor's offices
contractor's shop
contractors, special trade
contractor's storage yard
contributing building (See also historic
    preservation definitions)
contributing site (See also historic
    preservation definitions)
convalescent center (See also elderly
    housing definitions; nursing home)
convenience goods
convenience store* (See also gas station
    minimart)
convent or monastery
convention center (See also conference
    center)
convention space
conversation/rap parlor
cooperative
copy shop (See also print shop)
corner clearance
cornice
cornice height
cornice, exterior
corporate headquarters office
corral
correctional facilities (See also custodial
    care facility; juvenile detention
    facility)
corridor
corridor, environmental
corridor, historic
corridor, mixed-use
corridor, pedestrian
corridor, scenic

corridor, transit
corridor, transportation
corridor, wildlife
cost-benefit analysis
cottage (See cabin)
cottage industry (See also home
    occupation)
council of government (COG)
county
country club (See also club)
court
court, apartment
court, bungalow
court height
court, inner
court length
court, outer
court, tourist (See also motel)
court-type development
court width
courtesy car
courtesy service
courtyard (See court)
covenant, private (See also deed
    restriction)
covenant, protective
craft shop
crawlspace (See also basement; cellar)
creek (See also spring; stream)
crematorium (See also cemetery;
    columbarium; mausoleum)
criminal justice facility
crisis center (See also shelter definitions)
critical facility
crosswalk (See also pedestrian way)
cultural center
cultural features
cultural resources
cultural services
culvert, cross drainage
culvert, stream bed
cumulative (pyramidal) zoning* (See
    also as-of-right zoning; downzoning;
    Euclidean zoning; upzoning)
curb
curb cut
curb level
curb radius
curb return
currency exchange
custodial care facility (See also
    correctional facility; juvenile
    detention facility)

# d

dairy
dam
dance hall
dance hall, public
dancing establishments
data processing facilities
day care (See also child care definitions)
day care center
day care center, large
day care center, small
day care facility, adult
day care facility, child
day care home (See also family day care
    home)
day spa (See health spa)
daylight plane (See also bulk plane; sky
    exposure plane)
decentralization (See leapfrog
    development; sprawl)
decibel A-weighted (dBA) (See also
    noise)
deck
deck, attached
deck, open
deck, roof
deck, roofed
deck, unattached
declaration of use
dedication
dedication, fee in lieu of
deed restriction (See also covenant)
defensible space
delicatessen
demolition, complete
demolition, historic district only
demolition, partial
demolition permit
demolition waste
density
density, base
density bonus
density, control of
density, employment
density, gross
density, maximum allowable
density, net
density transfer
density zoning
density zoning district
department store
deposition
design guideline

design review/design control (See also architectural control/architectural review)
design standards
destination retail
detention (See also retention)
detention area
detention basin
detention basin, extended
detention, basin, regional
detention combined public detention
detention dam/basin/pond
developable acres, net
developable land
developed property
developer
developer's agreement (See also contract zoning)
developing area
development
development approval
development coverage
development, floodplain
development, high-intensity
development impact fees
development, low-intensity
development of regional impact (DRI)
development permit
development plan
development plan review
development project
development proposal
development requirement
development rights
development standards
developmentally disabled person (See also disability; handicapped)
diameter at breast height (DBH)
dike
disability
discount membership merchandiser (See also sales establishment, bulk)
distribution center
district
disturbed area
diversion
diversity
dock
dock, commercial
dock, community boat
dock, dry
dock, private
dog run
domestic violence shelter
domicile (See also dwelling definitions)
donation collection bin

dormitory
downstream
downzoning (See also cumulative zoning; upzoning)
drainage
drainage basin
drainage system
drainage well
drainageway
dredging
drip line
drive-in
drive-in restaurant (See restaurant, drive-in)
drive-through window
drive-up window service
driveway
driveway approach
driveway, circle
driveway, common
driveway, cross access
driveway, directional
driveway, divided
driveway offset
driving range
drop box facility  (See also recycling)
drug paraphernalia
drug store (See also pharmacy)
dry cleaning and laundry pickup station
dry cleaning plant
due process of law (See also compensable zoning; taking)
dump (See also landfill, sanitary)
dumpster
dumpster, compacted
dune
duplex (See also triplex)
duplex, double
dust
dwelling (See also housing definitions)
dwelling, apartment
dwelling, duplex (See duplex)
dwelling, farm labor (See farm employee housing; housing, temporary employment)
dwelling groups
dwelling, high-rise
dwelling, mid-rise
dwelling, multifamily
dwelling, semi-detached (See also duplex; rowhouse; townhouse; triplex)
dwelling, single-family
dwelling, three-family (See also triplex)
dwelling, two-family (See also duplex)
dwelling unit*

dwelling unit, attached
dwelling unit, detached

# e

earth station (See also telecommunications definitions)
easement
easement, access
easement, affirmative
easement, agricultural conservation
easement, appurtenant
easement, aviation
easement, conservation
easement, fisherman's
easement, habitat protection
easement, maintenance
easement, negative
easement, private
easement, private access
easement, scenic
easement slope
eave
eave line
ecological impact
ecology
economic base
economic development (See also community development corporation (CDC))
economic development commission (EDC) (See also community development corporation (CDC))
ecosystem
educational facilities, college/university
educational facilities, elementary school
educational facilities, high school
educational facilities, nursery school
educational facilities, preschool
educational facilities, primary/secondary
educational facilities, private school
educational facilities, school for the arts
educational institution
efficiency unit
effluent
egress
elderly
elderly housing*
elderly housing, assisted living
elderly housing, congregate care facility
elderly housing, lifecare or continuing care services
elderly housing, residential care facility
elderly/retirement housing
electric power plants

electromagnetic field (EMF)
eleemosynary institution
emergency
emergency and protective shelter (See also crisis center; shelter definitions)
emergency housing facility
emergency operations
emergency, snow or ice
emergency vehicle
eminent domain (See also condemnation; taking)
emission
employee parking area
employee quarters
employment center
enabling act
endangered species
energy facility
energy systems, small-scale
entertainment, commercial indoor
entertainment, commercial outdoor
entertainment complex
entertainment district
entertainment, live
entry arcade
environment
environment, conservancy
environment, natural
environmental impact report (EIR)
environmental impact, significant
environmental impact, significant effect
environmental impact statement (EIS)
environmental scientists
equipment sales and rental
erected
erosion
escort services
esplanade (See also riverwalk)
essential services
establishment
Euclidean zoning* (See also as-of-right zoning; cumulative zoning)
eviction
ex parte contact
exaction
examination room
excavation
exclusionary zoning (See zoning, exclusionary)
exhibition
exhibition center (See convention center)
existing-use zoning
exotic
explosive material (See also fireworks; hazardous material)
expressway (See street, expressway)

extended-stay hotel/motel (See also hotel; motel)
exterior
exterior appliance
exterior display
externalities, side effects, spillovers, repercussion effects
extraction
extractive industry (See also mineral extraction; mining; quarry)
extraterritorial land-use controls (zoning and subdivision regulations)
exurban area

# f

facade
facade, nonprincipal
facade, principal
factory-built housing (See also manufactured housing, mobile home, modular housing; panelized housing)
fair market rent
fair market value
fair share
fairgrounds
fallout shelter
family*
family day care home (See also child care and day care definitions)
family farm
farm (See also agriculture)
farm dwelling
farm employee housing (See also housing, temporary employee)
farm, exclusive farm use
farm, fish (See aquaculture)
farm, fur
farm, poultry
farm stand (See also roadside stand; stand)
farmer
farmer's market
farming
farmland
farmland preservation property (See also agricultural preservation)
fault
feasibility study
fee-in-lieu (See dedication, fee in lieu of)
fee simple
feed store
feedlot
fence
fence, barbed-wire
fence, chain-link

fence, decorative
fence height
fence, obscuring
fence, open
fence, perimeter
fence, protective
fence, safety
fence, semi-open
fence, sharp-pointed
fence, solid
fence, stockade
fence, unsafe
fence, wire
ferry and excursion boats and water taxis
ferry and excursion boats and water taxis facility
festival
festival, community or church
festival, temporary
fill (See also backfill; borrow)
filling
filling station (See gas station, service station)
final plat (See plat, final)
financial institution (See also bank; automated teller machine (ATM))
fire, contained
fire escape
fire hazard zone
fire lane
fire-resistive
fire station
firearm
firearms dealer (See also gun shop)
firearms sales or firearms business (See also gun shop)
fireworks (See also explosive material)
fiscal impact analysis
fiscal impact report (FIR)
fishery
fitness center (See health club)
fitness studio (See also health club)
fixed area-based allowance zoning
flag
flag, business
flag lot (See lot, flag)
flag, public
flagpole
flea market* (See also auction; swap meet)
flexible regulations (See also performance zoning)
floating zone
flood
flood boundary floodway (FBFW) map

flood control

flood elevation

flood frequency

flood fringe

flood insurance rate map (FIRM)

flood insurance study

flood, National Flood Insurance
Program (NFIP)

flood, 100-year

food-prone

flood protection elevation

flood protection system

flood protection system, critical feature

flood, regional

floodlight

floodplain

floodplain compensatory storage

floodplain management

floodplain management regulations

floodproofing

floodway

floodway fringe

floor area

floor area, finished

floor area, gross*

floor area, gross (for purposes of
computing parking)

floor area, gross leasable

floor area, gross leasable (for purposes
of computing shared parking)

floor area, gross, unused

floor area, minimum

floor area, net

floor area ratio (FAR)*

floor area, usable

florist

food cooperative

footcandle (See also candle power;
lumen)

footprint

forest

forest, contiguous

forest land

forest management

forest practice

forestry

forestry operations

fortune telling (See also psychic)

foster home (See also group home for
foster care)

fraternal organization

fraternity

fraternity house

freestanding sign (See sign,
freestanding)

freeway (See street, freeway)

freeway sign corridor (See also right-of
way)

freight

freight container (See also cargo,
containerized; semi-trailer)

frontage (See lot frontage)

frontage buildout

frontage open space

frontage road (See street, frontage road)

frontage width (See lot, frontage)

fumes

funeral chapel

funeral home (See also mortuary)

# g

gallery (See art gallery)

game

game arcade

game breeding and shooting preserve
area

game center

gambling (See also lottery)

gambling device

gambling excursion

gambling, excursion boat or floating
gambling facility

gambling establishment (hotel)

gambling establishment (nonhotel)

gambling, video lottery terminal

gaming (See gambling)

garage

garage apartment

garage, joint

garage, parking

garage, private

garage, private, customer and employee

garage, public

garage sale (See also rummage sale)

garage, storage

garbage (See also litter; rubbish)

garden

garden apartment (See also dwelling
definitions)

garden center (See also nursery)

gas station (See also oil change facility;
service station)

gas station, full-service

gas station, limited-service

gas station minimart (See also
convenience store)

gated communities

gateway

gateway route

gazebo

general plan (See also comprehensive
plan; master plan)

general store

gentrification

geographic information system (GIS)

geologic review

glare

golf course

golf course, miniature

golf course, regulation or par-three

golf driving range

golf training center

government, consolidated

government or city facility

government service agency

governmental unit

grade*

grade, adjacent ground elevation

grade, established

grade, existing

grade, finish

grade, highest adjacent

grade, natural

grade, percentage of

grade, rough

grade separation

grade, street

gradient

grading

graffiti

grand opening

grandfathered

granny flat (See accessory apartment)

gravel pit

great pond (See also pond)

green

green area

greenbelt

greenfield (See also brownfield)

greenhouse (See also nursery)

greenhouse, commercial

greenhouse, industrial

greenway (See also open space
definitions; park definitions)

greywater (See also wastewater,
domestic)

grid system

grocery store (See supermarket)

gross floor area (GFA) (See floor area,
gross)

gross living area (See also floor area,
gross)

ground floor

ground floor frontage

groundcover

groundcover management

groundwater (See also aquifer definitions)
groundwater recharge
groundwater recharge area
group home* (See also halfway house; substance abuse treatment facility)
group home for foster care
group home for mentally or physically handicapped
grove (See orchard)
growth, forecasted
growth management (See also smart growth; sprawl)
guest
guest house
guest house with cooking facilities
guest, permanent
guest ranch
guest room
gun shop (See also firearms sales or firearms business)
gym (See health club)

# h

habitable rooms
habitat
habitat protection area (See also preserve; wildlife habitat; wildlife refuge)
halfway house (See also group home; substance abuse treatment facility)
halfway house, penal
hamlet (See also village)
hamlet lot
handicapped* (See also developmentally disabled person; disability)
harbor (See also port and harbor facilities)
hardware store (See also home improvement center)
haunted house
hazardous material (See also explosive material; toxic or noxious substance)
hazardous waste (See also toxic or noxious substance)
hazardous waste disposal facility
hazardous waste incinerator
hazardous waste processing facility
health care facility (See also clinic; hospital; sanitarium)
health club
health/sport club
health spa (See also bathhouse; massage establishment; sauna)
hearing examiner
heath

heavy equipment
hedge
height*
height factor
height limit
height, measurement of
heliport
heliport, limited use
heliport or helistop, private
heliport or helistop, public
heliport, unlimited use
helistop
helistop, limited use
helistop, unlimited use
high occupancy vehicle (HOV) (See also transportation demand management (TDM))
high-water mark, ordinary
highest and best use (See also taking)
highway (See street, highway)
highway-oriented business
hillside
hillside landforms
historic
historic and monument sites
historic district
historic landmark
historic landmark district
historic preservation
historic preservation significance
historic structure
historical site
holding zone
home exhibition
home improvement center (See also hardware store)
home industry
home occupation
home rule
homeless shelter (See also shelter; single room occupancy (SRO))
homeowners association
homesite
horse farm
horse track
hospice
hospital (See also clinic; health care facility; sanitarium)
hospital complex
hostel (See youth hostel)
hot tub
hotel (See also extended-stay hotel/motel; motel)
hotel, convention hotel
house of worship (See also religious institution)

household
household pet (See animal, domestic)
housekeeping unit
housing, affordable (See affordable housing)
housing, elderly (See elderly housing)
housing, low-income
housing, middle-income
housing, moderate-income
housing, short-term
housing, short-term rental
housing, temporary employment
housing, transitional (See transitional housing shelter)
housing, very low-income
human services planning (See social services definitions)
hydrant, private
hydrant, public
hydroelectric generation facility
hydropower facility, small
hypermarket (See also big-box retail; shopping center definitions)

# i

ice cream vending vehicle (See also vending cart)
image
impact (See also externalities)
impact, extraordinary
impact fee
impact fee, park
impact fee, school
impact fee, transportation
impact, minor or insignificant
impervious surface
impervious surface ratio (ISR)
implementation
impound yard (See automobile impound facility)
improvement
incentive zoning
incidental, customary, remunerative activities (See also home occupation)
incineration
incinerator facility (See also hazardous waste incinerator)
inclusionary zoning
incorporation
incubator (See business incubator)
industrial
industrial park
industrial waste
industry (See also manufacturing definitions)

industry, heavy
industry, light
industry, medium
infill
infill development
infill site
infiltration
infiltration facility (See also stormwater definitions)
inflow (See also sewer definitions)
infrastructure
ingress
inn
institution/institutional building
institutional use
integrity
intensity, land-use
interchange (See also street, highway)
interchange plan
interchange study area
interim zone of influence
interim zone or interim development controls (See also moratorium)
interjurisdictional agreement (See also joint-powers authority)
intersection (See street intersection)
inverse condemnation (See also condemnation; eminent domain; taking)
irrigation
irrigation system

# j

jetty (See also breakwater)
jet ski (See personal watercraft)
jewelry store
jobs/housing balance; jobs/housing ratio (See also linkage)
joint powers authority (See also interjurisdictional agreement)
joint use (See also mixed-use development)
junk
junk dealer
junkyard
jurisdiction
juvenile detention facilities (See also correctional facilities; custodial care facility)

# k

kennel
kennel, commercial
kennel, private

kindergarten (See educational facilities, preschool)
kiosk
kiss-and-ride (See park-and-ride facility)
kitchen
knoll

# l

labor camp (See housing, temporary employment)
laboratory
laboratory, research
laboratory, support
lake (See also pond)
land assets
land banking
land clearing
Land Evaluation and Site Assessment (LESA)
land owner (See owner)
land trust
land use
land-use action
land-use classification
land-use decision
land-use element
land-use-intensity system (LUI)
land-use inventory
land-use plan
land-use projections
land-use regulation
land value
landfill, construction/demolition
landfill, sanitary*
landing strip (See also runway)
landline communications
landmark (See historic landmark)
landscape contractor
landscape planting area
landscape waste
landscape waste composting facility (See also composting facility)
landscaped buffer (See also buffer)
landscaped visual barrier
landscaping
landscaping, interior
landscaping, perimeter
landscaping plan
landslide
large-box retail (See big-box retail)
large minimum lot-size zoning
laundromat
law enforcement officer
leapfrog development (See also growth management; smart growth; sprawl)

lease
least dimension
letter of map amendment (LOMA)
letter of map revision (LOMR)
levee
level of service (LOS)
level of service (LOS) standard
level of service (LOS) standard, traffic
library
license
light rail transit (LRT) (See transit, light rail)
light source
light source, flashing illumination
lighting (See candela; lumen; lumanaire)
lighting, artificial
lighting, neon outline
lighting, outline
lighting, pedestrian-scale
limousine
limousine service
line of sight
linkage (See also jobs/housing balance)
linkage fee
liquor
litter (See also garbage; rubbish)
live entertainment (See also amusement definitions; entertainment definitions)
live-work quarters (See also loft)
livestock (See also animal definitions)
livestock, large
livestock market
livestock, small
living quarters (See also dwelling and dwelling unit definitions)
loading berth
loading space
local agency
lodge
lodging house (See also boarding house; rooming house)
loft
loft building
logging yard and landing
long-term commercial significance
lot
lot area
lot averaging
lot-by-lot development
lot, corner
lot coverage
lot, deep
lot depth
lot, double frontage
lot, flag
lot, front

lot frontage

lot improvement

lot, interior

lot, irregular

lot, key

lot line (See also property line definitions)

lot line adjustment

lot line, front

lot line, rear

lot line, side

lot, nonconforming

lot of record

lot of record, substandard

lot, panhandle

lot, pipestem

lot, recorded

lot, reversed corner

lot, reversed frontage

lot-size requirements

lot, through

lot, undeveloped

lot width

lot, zipper

lottery (See also gambling)

lounge (See bar)

lowest floor

LULU (locally unwanted land use)

lumber yard

lumen

luminaire

luminaire, cutoff-type

# m

main building (See building, principal)

main street

maintained

maintenance

maintenance guarantee (See also performance guarantee)

mall (See also pedestrian mall; shopping mall)

mansard

manufactured housing* (See also factory-built housing; mobile home; panelized housing)

manufacturing

manufacturing, custom

manufacturing, heavy

manufacturing, light

manufacturing, medium

manufacturing, primary

manufacturing, secondary

map (See base map; concurrency determination network map; flood boundary floodway (FBFW) map; Flood Insurance Rate Map (FIRM); official map; preliminary subdivision map; subdivision map; topographic map; zoning map)

marina

marina, commercial

marina facilities (See also port and harbor facilities)

marine service station

maritime activities

market value (See fair market value)

marquee (See sign, marquee)

marsh (See also wetland definitions)

mass transit (See transit, public)

massage establishment (See also adult use, massage establishment; health spa)

master plan (See also comprehensive plan; general plan)

master site plan

mausoleum (See also cemetery; crematorium; columbarium)

maximum allowable density (See density, maximum allowable)

median

median, nonrestrictive

median, restrictive

medical support facilities

medical waste

meeting hall (See also assembly hall; auditorium)

megachurch (See also religious institution)

megaplex theater (See movie theater, megaplex)

mental health facility (See also hospital; sanitarium)

messenger service office

metes and bounds

metropolitan

Metropolitan Planning Organization (MPO)

Metropolitan Statistical Area (MSA)

mezzanine

microbrewery (See also brew pub)

microclimate

migrant agricultural labor housing (See housing, temporary employment)

mill-type factory structures (See also loft building)

mineral extraction (See also mining definitions)

mineral resource

minerals

miniature golf course (See golf course, miniature)

mini-lot development

mini-mall (See shopping center, mini-mall)

minimart (See convenience store; gas station minimart)

mining (See also extractive industry; mineral extraction)

mining, accessory use

mining, open pit

mining, strip

mining, surface

mining waste

minutes

mission (See homeless shelter)

mitigation

mitigation plan

mixed-use development

mobile home (See also manufactured housing)

mobile home park

model studio

modernization

modular housing (See also factory-built housing; manufactured housing; panelized housing)

modulation

moorage, commercial

moorage, covered

moorage, dry

moorage, open

moorage, transient

moorage walkway

moratorium (See also interim zoning or interim development controls)

mortuary (See also funeral chapel; funeral home)

mosque (See religious institution)

motel (See also extended-stay hotel/motel; hotel)

motor vehicle (See also automobile definitions; truck definitions)

motor vehicle, abandoned

motor vehicle body shop

motor vehicle, commercial

motor vehicle, general repair and service

motor vehicle, inoperable

motor vehicle, junk

motor vehicle, large

motor vehicle, limited repair and service

motor vehicle-oriented business

motor vehicle repair service, commercial, major

motor vehicle, small

motor vehicle, stored

motorcade

motorcycle

movie theater (*See also* theater)

movie theater, cineplex*

movie theater, drive-in

movie theater, megaplex (*See* movie theater, cineplex)

multi-use complex (*See also* mixed-use development)

multiple-family building (*See also* dwelling, apartment)

municipal authority

municipal services

mural (*See also* art, public; sign, painted-wall; sign, wall)

museum

museum, commercial

# n

National Register of Historic Places

native vegetation

natural condition

natural drainage

natural features

natural resource area

naturalized species

navigable waters

neighborhood

neighborhood convenience store (*See also* convenience store)

neighborhood plan

neighborhood unit

neotraditional development

new town

New Urbanism

newcomer suite

newsrack

newsstand

nightclub

NIMBY (Not In My Back Yard) (*See* LULU (locally unwanted land use))

noise

noise pollution

nonattainment

nonconforming activity (*See also* amortization)

nonconforming building

nonconforming by dimension

nonconforming feature

nonconforming location

nonconforming lot (*See* lot, nonconforming)

nonconforming sign (*See* sign, nonconforming)

nonconforming structure (*See* nonconforming building; structure, nonconforming)

nonconforming use (*See* use, nonconforming)

nonconformity

noncontributing building

nonpoint pollution (*See* pollution, nonpoint)

nonprofit organization

nonwetlands (*See also* wetlands)

notice of hearing

noxious matter

nuisance

nursery

nursery, bare root

nursery farms

nursery, retail

nursery, wholesale

nursing home (*See also* convalescent center; elderly housing *definitions*)

# o

observation room/deck

obstruction, land

obstruction, watercourse

occupancy

occupant

occupied area

odor

odorous matter

off-road vehicle

off-shore facilities

off site

office

office building

office, class A

office, class B

office, class C

office conversion (*See also* home occupation)

office, intensive

office park

office, professional

office/professional district

official map

oil change facility (*See also* automobile repair services; gas station; service station)

on site

open burning

open-front store

open land district

open space*

open space, active

open space, common

open space, detached

open space, developed

open space element

open space, natural

open space, passive

open space, private

open space ratio

open space, total

open space, usable

open space use

orchard

ordinance

organic material

origin or destination survey (*See* trip)

outbuilding (*See also* accessory structure)

outdoor advertising display (*See also* sign *definitions*)

outdoor customer dining area (*See* restaurant, outdoor customer dining area)

outdoor display area (*See also* retail sales establishment *definitions*)

outdoor recreation (*See also* recreation *definitions*)

outdoor recreation concession

outdoor storage

outdoor storage, bulk

outdoor storage, non-bulk

outdoor storage, seasonal

outfall

outlet

outlot

overlay zone

owner

owner of record

owners association

ownership, common

ownership, single

ozone

# p

panelized housing (*See also* factory-built housing; manufactured housing; modular housing)

parade

parapet

paratransit (*See also* transit *definitions*)

parcel

park

park-and-ride facility (See also transportation demand management (TDM))
park-and-ride lot
park, hybrid
park land
park, minipark
park, neighborhood
park, passive use
park, private
park, regional
parking aisle
parking area, community
parking area, public
parking bay
parking, fringe lot
parking lot
parking lot, circulation area
parking lot, commercial
parking management
parking meter
parking meter space
parking, off-street
parking, on-street
parking, preferential
parking ratio
parking, self-park
parking, shared
parking, short-term
parking space
parking space, compact
parking space, covered
parking space, dependent
parking space, enclosed
parking space, handicap
parking space, high-occupancy vehicle (HOV)
parking space, independent
parking space, long-term
parking space, short-term
parking space, standard
parking space, tandem
parking, stacked
parking structure
parking surface
parking, underground
parking, valet
parking well
parkway (See also planting strip; street, parkway)
parsonage
particulate matter
party wall
passage
pasture
path (See pedestrian walkway)

patio
patio cover
patio house (See also dwelling definitions)
pave
paved surface area
pavement width
pawnshop
pay phone (See telephone, outdoor pay)
peak hour/peak period
peak rate of discharge/peak flow
peddle
pedestrian mall
pedestrian-oriented development
pedestrian outdoor service facility
pedestrian skyway system
pedestrian walkway
pedestrian walkway, connector space
pedestrian walkway, through-block
pennant (See also sign definitions)
penthouse
performance bond
performance guarantee (See also maintenance guarantee)
performance standards
performance zoning (See flexible regulations)
perimeter
permit (See also development permit)
permit, conditional use
permit, special
permit, special use
permit, special use, temporary
person
personal property
personal services
personal watercraft
pervious surface (See also impervious surface)
pet (See animal, domestic)
pet shop
pharmacy (See also drugstore)
photography retail store
physical diversity
physical value
picnic area, group
pier (See also dock; wharf)
pier, community
pier, private
pier, recreational
pierhead line
piling
place
plan (See area plan; comprehensive plan; concept plan; congestion management plan (CMP); general plan; land-use plan; master plan;

neighborhood plan; specific plan; strategic plan; subdivision, exploratory sketch plan; subdivision, preliminary plan)
planned commercial development (See also planned unit development)
planned community (See also new town)
planned development
planned general commercial district (See also commercial district)
planned neighborhood commercial development (See also commercial district)
planned unit development (PUD)
planned unit development (PUD) plat
planned zoning district
Planner*
Planner I
Planner II
Planner III
Planner IV
planning area
planning and zoning commission
planning board
planning commission
planting strip (See also parkway)
plat
plat, abbreviated/short plat
plat, final
plat, preliminary
plat, sketch
plat, tideland
platform (See also public transit concourse; transit station)
play lot (See also playground)
playfield or athletic field (See also recreation definitions)
playground
playhouse
plaza
plot
plot, corner
plot, reversed corner
plot plan
pole barn
police power
policy
pollutant (See also contaminant)
pollution (See also air pollution)
pollution, nonpoint
pollution, point
pond (See also lake)
pool/billiard hall
population density
population projection
porch

porch depth

porch, open

porch, screened

porch, unenclosed

porch width

porous paving system (See also impervious surface; pervious surface; runoff)

port and harbor facilities

port authority

porte-cochere

post office

poultry

poverty level (See also housing definitions)

premises

preschool (See educational facilities)

present value

preserve (See also habitat protection area; wildlife habitat; wildlife refuge)

principal residence

print shop (See also copy shop)

private

private recreational facility/club (See also health club; recreation definitions)

private road (See street, private)

processing (See also industry definitions; manufacturing definitions)

processing facility

processing facility, light

productive life

profession

program

project

project improvements

project site

property

property, abandoned

property line (See lot line definitions)

property, unclaimed

provider

psychic (See also fortune telling)

public access

public art (See art, public)

public building

public celebrations (See also festival)

public entrance

public facilities

public hearing (See also public meeting)

public improvement

public lands

public meeting (See also public hearing)

public place (See also open space)

public room

public service corporation

public transit concourse (See also platform)

public transportation (See also paratransit; subway; transit definitions)

public way

public works

# q

quality of life

quarry

quarry/pit rehabilitation

quarter/quarter zoning (See also agricultural preservation zoning)

quasi-public use/quasi-public facility

queue space (See also stacking lane)

# r

racetrack

railroad

railroad crossing

railroad freight depot

railroad passenger station (See also transit station; terminal definitions)

Rails to Trails (See also trail)

railyard

raised basement

ramp

ranch

ranchette

ravine

real estate development*

real property

receiving body of water

reclamation

reconstruction

record

record of survey

recreation

recreation, active

recreation, commercial

recreation, commercial indoor

recreation, commercial outdoor

recreation, commercial outdoor, concentrated

recreation, commercial outdoor, general

recreation, commercial outdoor, light

recreation, community

recreation facilities

recreation facilities, commercial, on natural sites

recreation outdoor

recreation, passive

recreation support facilities

recreation vehicle (RV)

recreation vehicle (RV) park

recreational fire

rectory (See parsonage)

recyclable material

recyclables, household

recycling center

recycling collection center

recycling collection point

recycling plants

redevelop

redevelopment

reforestation (See also forest definitions; forestry definitions)

refuse (See also garbage; litter; rubbish; solid waste)

region

regional

regional commercial complex (See also shopping center, regional)

regional entity

regulation

rehabilitation (See also addition; alteration; historic structure, rehabilitation; remodel)

related (See also family)

religious assembly

religious institution

relocation

remediation

remodel (See also addition; alteration; rehabilitation)

rental cabin

rental, short-term

repair

repair, major

repair, minor

repair or maintenance

repair services

replacement (See also teardown)

replacement value

Request for Proposal (RFP)

Request for Qualifications (RFQ)

research and development

research and development centers

research laboratory

reservation of site

reservoir

residence (See also dwelling definitions)

resident

residential

residential burn (See also open burning)

residential care facility (See elderly housing, residential care facility)

residential complex

residential concierge services

residential storage structure (See also accessory structure)
resolution
resort
resource extraction (See extractive industry)
restaurant
restaurant, carry-out/take-out
restaurant, commercial/recreation
restaurant, drive-in
restaurant, entertainment
restaurant, family
restaurant, fast-food
restaurant, outdoor customer dining area
restaurant, sit down
restaurant, small
restrictive covenant (See also covenant; deed restriction)
retail display window
retail sales establishment
retail sales establishment, bulk merchandise
retail sales establishment, food
retail sales establishment, general merchandise
retail sales establishment, household
retail sales establishment, specialty
retail services establishment
retaining wall
retaining wall, enclosed
retention (See also detention definitions)
retention basin
retention system
retreat center
retrofitting
reversion clause
rezoning
ridesharing (See also transportation demand management (TDM))
ridge
ridge, prominent
ridgeline
riding stable/riding academy (See also horse farm; stable)
right-of-way
right-of-way line
right-of-way, railroad
right-of-way, ultimate
right-to-farm laws
Ringelmann number
riparian habitat
riparian vegetation
riprap
river
riverwalk (See also esplanade)

road (See also street definitions)
roadside
roadside stand (See also farm stand; stand)
roadside stand, accessory
roadway (See also street definitions)
roller skates or roller blades (See also skateboard definitions)
roof
roof deck (See deck, roof)
roof, flat
roof line
roof overhang
roof, pitched
room (See also bedroom; sleeping room)
room, habitable
roomer (See also boarder; tenant)
rooming house (See also boarding house; lodging house)
roundabout/traffic circle (See also traffic calming)
rowhouse (See also townhouse)
rowhouse building
rubbish (See also garbage; litter; refuse; solid waste)
rule
rummage sale (See also garage sale)
runoff (See also impervious surface)
runoff, excess
runway (See also landing strip)
rural

# S

safety service
saloon (See bar)
salvage
salvage yard
sand and gravel pit (See also mining; quarry)
sanitarium/sanitorium (See also clinic; health care facility; hospital)
satellite dish antenna (See telecommunications definitions)
sauna (See also bathhouse; health spa)
sawmill
scenic area
scenic highway corridor (See also corridor)
scenic highway/scenic route
school (See educational facilities)
school district (See also educational facilities)
screen (See berm; buffer; fence)
screening
sculpture (See also art, works of)

searchlight (See sign, searchlight)
seasonal decorations
seating capacity
seating space
seawall
second-hand merchandise, retail sales (See also antique shops; consignment store; thrift store)
security system
sediment
sedimentation
segregation
self-service storage facility (See also storage; warehouse, residential storage)
sell-through window (See also drive-through window; pedestrian outdoor service facility)
semi-trailer (See also truck definitions)
seniors
sense of place (See community of place)
sensitive areas
septage
septic system (See also sewage treatment system, private)
septic tank
servant quarters (See also accessory structure)
service lane
service-oriented shopping
service station (See also gas station; oil change facility)
setback (See also lot definitions)
setback, front
setback, front, on corner lots
setback, garage entrance
setback line
setback line, base
setback line, legal
setback, minimum setback zone
setback, rear
setback regulations
setback, side
setback, side exterior
setback, site interior
setback, side street
setback, street
setback, windbreak
settlement
sewage/sewerage
sewage treatment plant
sewage treatment system, private (See also septic system)
sewer, building
sewer, central/group

sewer, combined sewer/combination sewer

sewer, on-site (See also septic system, sewer treatment system, private)

sewer, public sewer and water system

sewer, sanitary

sewer, side

sewer, storm

screening wall (See also buffer)

shade

shade point

shared living

shed

shelter (See also domestic violence shelter; emergency and protective shelter; homeless shelter)

shipyard (See also port and harbor facilities)

shooting gallery

shooting range, indoor

shooting range, outdoor

shopping center

shopping center, commercial strip

shopping center, community

shopping center, consumer retail, medium-scale

shopping center, consumer retail, small-scale

shopping center, department store

shopping center, fashion/specialty

shopping center, mini-mall

shopping center, neighborhood center

shopping center, outlet

shopping center, power center

shopping center, regional

shopping center, superregional

shopping center, theme/festival

shopping mall (See also shopping center definitions)

shore lot line (See also high-water mark)

shoreland

shoreland alteration

shoreline

shoreline stabilization

short-term housing (See housing, short term)

shrub

sidewalk

sidewalk cafe

sidewalk cafe, enclosed

sidewalk sale (See also temporary outdoor sale)

sidewalk vendor

sidewalk vendor stand

sight distance triangle (See also clear vision triangle)

sign*

sign, abandoned

sign, advertising device

sign alteration

sign, animated or moving

sign, appurtenant

sign area

sign, auxiliary

sign, awning

sign, balloon

sign, banner

sign, banner, corporate

sign, banner, ornamental

sign, banner, promotional

sign, bench

sign, billboard

sign, billboard, back-to-back

sign, billboard, V-type

sign, blade/bracket

sign, business identification

sign, cabinet/can

sign combination

sign construction/development

sign copy

sign copy area

sign, detached

sign, directional

sign, directory

sign, double-faced

sign, electric

sign, electronic message board

sign, entry feature

sign face

sign, fascia

sign, fixed

sign, flashing

sign, flat

sign, freestanding

sign gross area

sign height

sign, highway directional

sign, home occupation

sign, identification

sign, illegal

sign, illuminated

sign, illuminated direct

sign, illuminated indirect

sign, informative

sign, instructional (See sign, informative)

sign, kiosk

sign, mansard

sign, marquee

sign, memorial

sign, menu

sign, menu board

sign, mobile

sign, monument

sign monument zone

sign, nameplate

sign, neon

sign, noncommercial

sign, nonconforming

sign, off-premise

sign, official traffic and street

sign, on-premise

sign, open house directional

sign, painted wall

sign, parapet

sign, permanent

sign, pitched roof

sign, pole

sign, political

sign, portable

sign, projecting

sign, public information (See also sign, directional; sign, informative)

sign, pylon

sign, real estate

sign, real estate, off-site

sign, real estate, on-site

sign, roof

sign, rotating or revolving

sign, searchlight (See also beacon)

sign setback

sign setback line

sign, shingle

sign, sidewalk/sandwich

sign, snipe

sign, special event

sign stacking

sign structure

sign, suspended

sign, temporary

sign, third-party

sign, V-type

sign, vehicle (See also sign, portable)

sign, wall

sign, warning

sign, wind

sign, window

single room occupancy (SRO) (See also homeless shelter)

site

site area

site area, net

site coverage

site depth

site plan

site plan, final

site plan review

site width

skateboard

skateboard, motorized

skateboard pipe

skateboard ramp

skating rink, ice or roller

ski area

ski resort

sky exposure plane or front exposure plane (See also bulk plane; daylight plane)

sky exposure plane, rear

skybuilding

skylight

skytram (See also transit, public)

slaughterhouse

slaughterhouse, agricultural

sleeping room (See also bedroom; room)

slip

slope

slope, critical

slope, cut

slope, fill

slope, percent average

slope, percent of

slope, protected

slope, steep

slope, toe of

slope, top of

slope, very steep

smart growth (See also growth management)

smog

smoke

smoke unit

snack bar/snack shop

snowmobile (See also off-road vehicle)

social service facilities

social service provider

sod

soil

soil erosion

soil erosion, accelerated

soil stabilization

soil, topsoil

soils, expansive

solar access

solar access space

solar collector

solar energy

solar energy system

solar equipment

solar feature

solar skyspace

solar skyspace easement

solar structure

solid waste (See also garbage; litter; refuse; rubbish)

solid waste collection point

solid waste compost facility (See also composting facility)

solid waste facility

solid waste management

solid waste transfer facility

sorority

sorority house

soup kitchen (See also shelter definitions; social service definitions)

source reduction

space, nonhabitable

space, occupied

special assessment

special benefit district (See also benefit assessment district)

special district

special events

special exception

special permit (See permit, special)

special use

special use permit (See permit, special use)

specialty food store

specific plan

spot zoning

sprawl (See also growth management; leapfrog development; smart growth)

spring (See also creek; stream)

square (See also plaza)

SRO (See single room occupancy)

stable (See also horse farm)

stable, commercial

stable, private

stacking lane (See also queue space)

stadium/arena/amphitheater

stage

stairs

stand (See also farm stand; newsstand; roadside stand)

standard

Standard Industrial Classification (SIC)

start of construction

statement of intent/statement of purpose

statistical area (See also Metropolitan Statistical Area (MSA))

statute

statue (See sculpture)

steamroom/bathhouse (See also bathhouse; sauna)

stem wall (See also wall)

steps at grade

stockyard

stoop

stop-work order

storage

storage, bulk

storage, outside

storage structure

store

storefront church (See also religious institution)

storm drain

stormwater detention

stormwater management

stormwater retention area

stormwater runoff

story

story, first

story, half

story, lower-half (See also raised basement)

story, upper-half (See also attic)

strategic plan

stream (See also creek; spring)

stream bank

stream corridor

stream, intermittent

stream, perennial

stream, tributary

street

street, arterial

street, boulevard

street capacity (See also volume-to-capacity ratio)

street, center line of

street, collector

street, crosswalk

street, cul-de-loop

street, cul-de-sac (See also turning circle)

street, dead-end

street dedication

street edge

street, expressway

street, freeway

street frontage

street, frontage road

street furniture

street graphics

street, gridlike pattern (or flexible grid)

street, half

street hierarchy

street, highway

street, highway auxiliary lane

street, highway, major

street, highway, noise barrier

street, highway, restricted access

street, interchange

street, intersecting

street intersection

street lamp

street line
street line, planned
street, local
street, loop
street, major
street, major arterial
street, minor (*See also* street, local)
street, minor arterial
street/alley, one-way
street opening
street, parkway
street, partial
street plan line
street, primary thoroughfare
street, private
street, public
street reservation/road reservation
street, residential
street, right-of-way (*See* right-of-way)
street, secondary thoroughfare
street, spine road
street, stub
street, through
street vista
street wall
street wall, aggregate width of
street wall line
street wall line level
street width
street yard
streetscape
strip center (*See also* shopping center *definitions*)
strip development (*See also* shopping center *definitions*)
structural alteration
structural envelope
structure
structure, detached
structure, enclosed
structure, moved
structure, nonconforming
structure, illegal nonconforming
structure, principal (*See also* building, principal)
structure, public (*See also* building, public)
structure, temporary
student center
student housing (*See also* dormitory)
studio apartment (*See* efficiency unit)
studio/multimedia production facility
subcommittee
subdivider
subdivision*
subdivision, abortive or premature

subdivision, exploratory sketch plan
subdivision, hillside
subdivision improvement agreement (*See also* developer's agreement)
subdivision, major
subdivision map
subdivision map, preliminary
subdivision, minor
subdivision plan, preliminary
subdivision regulation
subdivision review/approval
subsidize
substance abuse treatment facility, inpatient residential (*See also* halfway house)
substance abuse treatment facility, outpatient
substandard housing
substantial conformance
substantial damage
substantial improvement
substantial modification
subtenant
subway (*See also* public transportation; transit, public)
suite
summer home (*See also* cabin/cottage)
superblock (*See also* block)
supermarket
supper club
surface water (*See also* groundwater)
surfaced
sustainability
sustainable development
swale
swap meet and auction (*See also* flea market)
swimming pool
swimming pool, outdoor
swimming pool, portable
swimming pool, private
swimming pool, public
synagogue (*See* religious institution)
system capacity (*See also* adequate public facilities ordinance (APFO); carrying capacity analysis)
system integrity

#

taking (*See also* condemnation; eminent domain; inverse condemnation)
tank farm
tanning studio

target area (*See also* block grant; Community Development Block Grant (CDBG); Community Redevelopment Agency (CRA))
tattooing
tattoo parlor/body-piercing studio
tavern (*See also* bar)
tax abatement
tax credit
tax increment
tax increment base
tax increment district
tax increment financing (TIF)
tax increment fund
taxi
taxicab business
teahouse (*See also* coffee house)
teardown (*See also* infill)
teen dance center
telecommunications (*See also* amateur radio tower)
telecommunications antenna
telecommunications, cell site
telecommunications, co-location
telecommunications equipment shelter
telecommunications, satellite dish antenna
telecommunications tower
telecommunications tower, alternative design structure
telecommunications tower, alternative structure
telecommunications, wireless facility
telecommuting
telephone exchange building
telephone, outdoor pay
telework center (*See also* home office; telecommuting)
temple (*See* religious institution)
temporary emergency, construction, or repair residence (*See also* shelter)
temporary employment housing (*See* housing, temporary employee)
temporary merchant
temporary outdoor sale
temporary permit (*See* permit, temporary)
temporary portable building, construction-related
tenant (*See also* boarder; roomer; subtenant)
tennis club
tent
terminal
terminal, airport
terminal, bus

terminal, bus passenger
terminal, bus/truck
terminal, cargo
terminal, marine
terminal, mass transit
terminal, motor freight
terminal, passenger
terminal, passenger station
terminal, transportation
terrace (See patio)
theater
theatrical community center
theme park (See amusement,
    commercial outdoor; amusement
    park; carnival)
thoroughfare
thrift store (See also antique shop;
    consignment store; secondhand
    merchandise, retail sales)
through-block arcade (See also
    pedestrian walkway, through-block)
tidal and submerged land
tidelands
time-share project
time-share unit
time sharing
tire store
topographic map
topography
tot lot (See play lot)
tourism
tourism-oriented
tourist court (See court, tourist)
tourist home
tower (See also telecommunications
    definitions)
tower, temporary mobile
towing service
town (See also city; hamlet; urban center;
    village)
town center
townhouse (See also rowhouse)
toxic/noxious substance (See also
    hazardous material)
tract (See parcel)
tractor
trade/business school (See also
    educational facilities)
traditional neighborhood development
    (See also neotraditional development;
    New Urbanism)
traditional neighborhood district
traffic calming*
traffic control devices
traffic impact
traffic impact analysis

traffic impact mitigation measure
traffic model
traffic signal (See traffic control devices)
traffic zone
trail
trailer (See construction/field office;
    temporary portable building,
    construction-related)
transfer of development rights (TDR)
transfer of development rights (TDR)
    easement
transfer of development rights (TDR),
    receiving area
transfer of development rights (TDR),
    sending area
transfer station (See solid waste transfer
    facility)
transformer
transient
transit
transit area
transit-dependent
transit, light rail (LRT)
transit-oriented development (TOD)
transit, public (See also paratransit;
    public transportation; subway)
transit route
transit shuttle
transit station (See also public transit
    concourse; railroad passenger station;
    terminal definitions)
transit station development area
transit stop (See also bus stop)
transit stop, planned
transitional area
transitional housing shelter (See also
    homeless shelter)
transitional lot
transitional use (See use, transitional)
transitional zone
transmission line
transportation center, intermodal
transportation demand management
    (TDM) (See also buspool; carpool;
    high-occupancy vehicle (HOV);
    ridesharing; vanpool)
transportation facilities
transportation facilities, alternate mode
transportation management area
transportation systems
transportation systems management
    (TSM)
transportation systems, smart
    technology
trash (See garbage; litter; refuse; rubbish;
    solid waste)

trash enclosure
travel demand (See also trip generation)
travelway (See also bike lane)
tree
tree bank
tree, canopy
tree, class A
tree, class B
tree conservation
tree, crown spread
tree cutting
tree density factor
tree, dominant
tree, grand tree stands
tree, heritage
tree, landmark
tree, mature
tree ordinance
tree preservation
tree, prohibited
tree protection
tree protection zone
tree, public
tree removal
tree, replacement
tree save area
tree, shade
tree, significant
tree, street
tree, street tree plan
tree, street tree planting area
trip
trip generation (See also travel demand)
trip origination and destination survey
trip reduction
triplex (See also duplex)
truck, heavy
truck, light
truck, medium
truck plaza
truck route
truck stop
truck terminal (See terminal, motor
    freight)
turnaround
turning circle

# u

undergrounding
underlying zoning district
undevelopable
undeveloped land
unified development code (See also
    zoning code)
uniformity

unit (See also condominium unit; dwelling unit definitions)
unnecessary hardship
unrelated individuals (See also family)
upholstering shop
upzoning (See also cumulative zoning; downzoning)
urban
urban center
urban design
urban forestry plan
urban fringe
urban growth area (UGA) (See also growth management)
urban growth boundary (UGB) (See also growth management)
urban land use
urban place
urban renewal
urban reserve
urban service area (See also urban growth area (UGA); urban growth boundary (UGB))
urban services
urbanized area
use*
use, administrative
use category
use, change of
use, conditional
use, conforming
use, discontinued
use, existing
use, illegal
use, incompatible
use, nonconforming
use, nonconforming, legal
use, permitted
use, principal
use, public
use, semipublic
use, similar
use, special
use, temporary
use, transitional
utilities
utilities, communication utility facilities (See also telecommunications definitions)
utilities, large
utilities, medium
utilities, public
utilities, small
utilities, water and wastewater utility facilities
utility corridors

utility district, underground
utility pole
utility poles and lines (See also transmission lines)
utility, private or public
utility, public facility
utility room
utility services
utility services, major
utility services, minor

# V

vacant
vacation
vanpool (See also transportation demand management (TDM))
variance
variety store
vegetated shallows
vegetative buffer (See also buffer)
vegetative cover
vehicle (See also motor vehicle)
vehicle emission standard
vehicle emission testing facility
vehicle, single-occupancy
vending carts (See also stand)
vending machine
vending machine, reverse
vendor stand (See stand)
vessel, derelict
vested property right
vested right
vestibule
veterinary clinic (See animal hospital)
vibration
video rental store
view
view corridor
view-obscuring vegetation
view protection regulations
viewshed
village (See also hamlet; town)
village center (See town center)
visible
visible feature
vista
visual impact
vocational school (See trade/business school)
volume-to-capacity ratio (See also street capacity)

# W

wall
wall, wing
warehouse
warehouse, residential storage (See also self-service storage facility)
warehouse, retail
warehouse, retail, specialty
waste, bulky (See also white goods)
waste, construction/demolition
waste, domestic
waste, hazardous (See hazardous waste)
waste, yard
wastewater
wastewater, domestic (See also greywater)
wastewater, industrial
wastewater irrigation
wastewater treatment plant
watchman dwelling (See caretaker's residence)
water bodies
water-dependent use
water-enjoyment use
water-related use
water supply system
water supply system, individual
water supply system, public
water table
water taxi (See ferry and excursion boats and water taxis)
water taxi station
water treatment plan
watercourse
watercourse, artificial
watercourse, natural
watercourse, underground
waterfront
waterfront lot
waterfront, marine-boat zone
waterfront, port-ship zone
waters
waters of the [jurisdiction]
watershed
watershed-based zoning
waterway
waterway setback
way
wedding chapel, commercial
well
wellfield*
wellfield area of contribution
wellfield recharge area
wellhead protection area
wetland

wetland, artificially created
wetland buffer or wetland buffer zones
wetland, coastal
wetland compensation project
wetland compensatory mitigation
wetland creation
wetland, disturbed
wetland, emergent
wetland enhancement
wetland, forested
wetland, freshwater
wetland, in-kind compensation
wetland, isolated
wetland, margin
wetland, newly emerging
wetland, nontidal (See wetland)
wetland, off-site compensation
wetland, on-site compensation
wetland restoration
wetland, scrub-shrub
wetland, tidal (See wetland, coastal)
wharf (See also dock; pier)
white goods (See also waste, bulky)
wholesale establishment
wholesale establishment with
   warehouse
wilderness areas
wildlife
wildlife habitat (See also habitat
   protection area; preserve)
wildlife refuge  (See also habitat
   protection area; preserve)
wind energy conversion system (WECS)
wine-tasting room
workplace
workplace use
wrecker service (See motor vehicle
   wrecker service)

# x

xeriscaping (See also landscaping
   definitions)

# y

yacht, boat, and beach clubs
yachting organization
yard
yard, front
yard, interior side
yard measurement
yard, rear
yard sale
yard, side

yard trash (See also waste, yard)
youth hoste

# z

zipper lot (See lot, zipper)
zero lot line
zone or zoning district*
zoning*
zoning administrator
zoning amendment
zoning certificate
zoning code (See also unified
   development code)
zoning enforcement officer (See also
   code enforcement)
zoning lot
zoning map
zoning permit
zoo
zoo, private

■ **abandoned vehicle** (*See motor vehicle, abandoned*)

■ **abandonment**    To stop the use of property intentionally. When the use of a property has ceased and the property has been vacant for 12 months, abandonment of use will be presumed unless the owner can show that a diligent effort has been made to sell, rent, or use the property for a legally permissible use. (*Alexandria, Va.*)

■ **abate**    To end a nuisance, emergency, or nonconformance. (*Ames, Iowa*)

■ **abatement**    Any action taken to reduce, relieve, or suppress another continuing action. There are two relevant forms: a summary abatement, which is a legal action taken to suppress the continuation of an offensive land use; and a tax abatement, which is a release or forgiving of a certain tax liability for a specific period of time and under certain circumstances. (*Handbook for Planning Commissioners in Missouri*)

■ **abattoir** (*See slaughterhouse, commercial*)

■ **abutting** (*See also adjacent/adjoining; contiguous*)    Having a common border with, or being separated from such a common border by a right-of-way, alley, or easement. (*Worcester, Mass.*)

Having property or district lines in common. (*Palo Alto, Calif.*)

■ **abutting owner**    A person holding a legal interest in real property in contact with property cited in an application, petition, or request pending before a commission. (*Handbook for Planning Commissioners in Missouri*)

■ **access**    The right to cross between public and private property, allowing pedestrians and vehicles to enter and leave property. (*Ames, Iowa*)

A means of vehicular or pedestrian approach, entry to, or exit from property. (*Fairbanks North Star Borough, Alaska*)

■ **access connection**    Any driveway, street, turnout, or other means of providing for the movement of vehicles to or from the public roadway system. (*Center for Urban Transportation Research, Tampa, Fla.*)

■ **access management**    The process of providing and managing access to land development while preserving the regional flow of traffic in terms of safety, capacity, and speed. (*Woodburn, Ore.*)

■ **access point**    1. A driveway, a local street, or a collector street intersecting an arterial street; 2. A driveway or a local street intersecting a collector street; or 3. A driveway or a local street intersecting a local street. (*Grant County, Ky.*)

*Commentary: If you need terms related to access beyond those we have included here, we recommend that you consult the "Model Land Development & Subdivision Regulations that Support Access Management for Florida Cities and Counties," Center for Urban Transportation Research, University of South Florida, Tampa, Florida, January 1994.*

■ **accessible route**    A route that can be used be a disabled person using a wheelchair and that is also safe for and usable by people with other disabilities. (*Portland, Ore.*)

■ **accessory apartment**    A secondary dwelling unit established in conjunction with and clearly subordinate to a primary dwelling unit, whether a part of the same structure as the primary dwelling unit or a detached dwelling unit on the same lot. (*Blacksburg, Va. *)

A separate and complete dwelling unit that is contained on the same lot as the structure of a single-family dwelling or business. (*Asheville, N.C.*)

A permitted independent, subordinate dwelling unit contained within a single-family detached dwelling or its accessory detached garage. (*York County, Va.*)

■ **accessory banking** (*See also bank*)    A banking service(s) office, which may or may not include automated teller machines, that does not include drive-through services of any kind. (*Miami, Fla.*)

■ **accessory structure**    A subordinate structure detached from but located on the same lot as a principal building. The use of an accessory structure must be identical and accessory to the use of the principal building. Accessory structures include garages, decks, and fences. (*Ames, Iowa*)

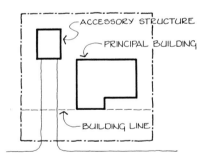

A detached subordinate structure(s), the use of which is incidental to that of the principal structure and located on the same lot therewith. (*Guilford County, N.C.*)

■ **accessory use**    A structure or use that: (1) is subordinate in area, extent, and purpose to the principal use; (2) contributes to the comfort, convenience, or necessity of the principal use; and (3) is located on the same lot and in the same zoning district as the principal use. (*Blue Springs, Mo.*)

A use incidental to and customarily associated with a specific principal use, located on the same lot or parcel. *(San Bernardino, Calif.)*

A use that is (1) customarily incidental and subordinate to the principal use of a lot or the main building thereon, and (2) located on the same lot as the principal use or building. In addition, a temporary structure or trailer used for construction administration, or real estate sales in conjunction with and during the period of development, construction, or sales within the same site or subdivision in which it is located is also an accessory use. *(Montgomery County, Md.)*

A use that is incidental and subordinate to that of the main building or use of land and that is located on the same lot and under the same ownership in all respects. *(Oxford, Conn.)*

■ **acid rain**    Air pollution produced when acid chemicals are incorporated into rain, snow, fog or mist. *(Environmental Protection Agency)*

***Commentary:*** *The "acid" in acid rain comes from sulfur oxides and nitrogen oxides, products of burning coal and other fuels and from certain industrial processes. The sulfur oxides and nitrogen oxides are related to two strong acids: sulfuric acid and nitric acid. When sulfur dioxide and nitrogen oxides are released from power plants and other sources, winds blow them far from their source. If the acid chemicals in the air are blown into areas where the weather is wet, the acids can fall to Earth in the rain, snow, fog, or mist. In areas where the weather is dry, the acid chemicals may become incorporated into dusts or smokes. Acid rain can damage the environment, human health, and property.*

■ **acre**    A land area of 43,560 square feet. *(Pima County, Ariz.)*

■ **acreage, gross**    A measure of land area. *(Manhattan Beach, Calif.)*

The acreage within the perimeter of a development tract, plus one-half the right-of-way of all adjoining streets and alleys. *(Glendale, Ariz.)*

The total area within a parcel of land. *(Mission Viejo, Calif.)*

■ **acre, net**    The area within lot boundaries of all lands comprising the building site. A net acre shall not include any portion of the abutting dedicated streets, alleys, waterways, canals, lakes, or any such dedicated right-of-way by whatever name known. *(Coral Gables, Fla.)*

A measure of developable land area after excluding existing dedicated rights-of-way and flood control and drainage easements. *(Manhattan Beach, Calif.)*

The horizontal plane area of a lot or parcel of land, exclusive of public road rights-of-way, public use area dedications, water areas, and any easement constituting a substantial impairment of the fee. *(North Miami Beach, Fla., which uses the term" acreage net")*

■ **adaptive reuse**    Rehabilitation or renovation of existing building(s) or structures for any use(s) other than the present use(s). *(Ames, Iowa)*

The conversion of obsolescent or historic buildings from their original or most recent use to a new use. For example, the conversion of former hospital or school buildings to residential use, or the conversion of an historic single-family home to office use. *(California Planning Roundtable)*

■ **addition** *(See also alteration; rehabilitation; remodel)* Any construction that increases the size of a building or structure in terms of site coverage, height, length, width, or gross floor area. *(Omaha, Nebr.)*

Any increase to the gross floor area of a structure. *(Blacksburg, Va.)*

An extension or increase in floor area or height of a building or structure. *(Corunna, Mich.)*

■ **address**    The number or other designation assigned to a housing unit, business establishment, or other structure for purposes of mail delivery, emergency services, and so forth. *(United States Census Bureau)*

■ **adequate public facilities ordinance (APFO)** *(See also carrying capacity analysis; system capacity)*    An ordinance that ties or conditions development approvals to the availability and

adequacy of public facilities. Also known as a concurrency management system. Adequate public facilities are those facilities relating to roads, sewer systems, schools, water supply and distribution systems, and fire protection that meet adopted level of service standards. *(PAS Report No. 465, Adequate Public Facilities Ordinances and Transportation Management)*

■ **adjacent/adjoining**    *(See also abutting; contiguous)* Touching or contiguous. *(Fairbanks North Star Borough, Alaska)*

Lying near or close to; sometimes, contiguous; neighboring. Adjacent implies that the two objects are not widely separated, though they may not actually touch. *(Grand Forks, N.D.)*

To be separated by common property lines, lot lines, or an alley; abutting, adjoining, contiguous, or touching. *(Carrollton, Tex.)*

Property that touches or is directly across a street from the subject property. For the purpose of height regulations, any portion of a structure that is more than 100 feet from a low-density zone is not considered to be adjoining that zone. *(Federal Way, Wash.)*

Joined contiguous to, in contact with each other, so that no third object intervenes. Lots separated by a street shall be considered adjoining, except those lots separated by an arterial or collector street shall be adjacent. *(Grand Forks, N.D.)*

■ **adjacent properties**    (This definition for purposes of site plan review notice requirements only.) All contiguous properties, with the assumption that railroads and public rights-of-way, except limited access roads, do not exist. *(Renton, Wash.)*

■ **administrative entity**    A geographic area, usually with legally defined boundaries but often without elected officials, created to administer elections and other governmental functions. Administrative areas include school districts, voting districts, ZIP Codes, and nonfunctioning MCDs such as election precincts, election districts, and assessment districts. *(United States Census Bureau)*

■ **administrative headquarters office** A use containing one or more of the day-to-day functions (e.g., management, payroll, information systems, inventory control) related to the operation of the company or affiliated corporate group. *(Renton, Wash.)*

■ **administrative office** An office establishment primarily engaged in overall management and general supervisory functions, such as executive, personnel, finance, legal, and sales activities, performed in a single location or building for other branches or divisions of the same company. *(Maryland Heights, Mo.)*

■ **adult use**

*Commentary: There are a number of difficult legal issues to consider in drafting regulations for adult uses. The ordinance definitions can be of critical importance in determining whether the regulations violate constitutional protections of free speech. Vaguely worded definitions that leave the business owner uncertain as to whether his or her business falls within the ordinance definition of adult uses are likely to be rejected by the courts. Most of the definitions provided here use the terms "specified anatomical areas" and "specified sexual activities" to make clear what the community considers to be aspects of adult use activity.*

■ **adult use, adult arcade** An establishment where, for any form of consideration , one or more motion picture projectors, slide projectors, or similar machines for viewing by five or fewer persons each are used to show films, motion pictures, video cassettes, slides, or other photographic reproductions that are characterized by an emphasis upon the depiction or description of specified sexual activities or specified anatomical areas. *(San Bernardino, Calif.)*

■ **adult use, adult bookstore** An establishment that has as a substantial portion of its stock-in-trade and offers for sale, for any form of consideration, any one or more of the following: 1) books, magazines, periodicals, or other printed matter, or photographs, films, motion pictures, video cassettes, slides, or other visual representations that are characterized by an emphasis upon the depiction

or description of specified sexual activities or specified anatomical areas; or 2) instruments, devices, or paraphernalia that are designed for use in connection with specified sexual activities. *(San Bernardino, Calif.)*

■ **adult use, adult cabaret** A nightclub, bar, restaurant, or similar establishment that regularly features live performances that are characterized by the exposure of specified anatomical areas or by specified sexual activities, or films, motion pictures, video cassettes, slides, or other photographic reproductions in which more than 10 percent of the total presentation time is devoted to the showing of material that is characterized by any emphasis upon the depiction of specified sexual activities or specified anatomical areas. . . . *(Southington, Conn.)*

■ **adult use, adult mini motion picture theater** An enclosed building with a capacity for fewer than 50 persons used for presenting material distinguished or characterized by an emphasis on matter depicting, describing, or relating to "specified sexual activities" or "specified anatomical areas.". . . *(Shelby County, Tenn.)*

A building or space with a capacity for fewer than 50 persons used for presenting material distinguished or characterized by an emphasis on matters depicting, describing or relating to specified sexual activities or specified anatomical areas as herein defined, for observation by patrons therein. The phrase "used for" in this definition shall mean a regular and substantial course of conduct and not a one-time presentation of such material. *(Bloomington, Minn.)*

■ **adult use, adult motion picture theater** An establishment where, for any form of consideration, films, motion pictures, video cassettes, slides, or similar photographic reproductions are shown, and in which a substantial portion of the total presentation time is devoted to the showing of material characterized by an emphasis on the depiction or description of specified sexual activities or specified anatomical areas. *(San Bernardino, Calif.)*

A building or space with a capacity of 50 or more persons used for presenting ma-

terial distinguished or characterized by and emphasis on matters depicting, describing, or relating to specified sexual activities or specified anatomical areas as herein defined, for observation by patrons therein. The phrase "used for" in this definition shall mean a regular and substantial course of conduct and not a one-time presentation of such material. *(Bloomington, Minn.)*

■ **adult use, adult sauna** A sauna which excludes minors by reason of age, or which provides a steam bath or heat bathing room used for the purpose of bathing, relaxation, or reducing, using steam or hot air as a cleaning, relaxing or reducing agent, if the service provided by the sauna is distinguished or characterized by an emphasis on specified sexual activities or specified anatomical areas as defined herein. *(Bloomington, Minn.)*

■ **adult use, adult theater** A theater, concert hall, auditorium, or similar establishment characterized by [activities featuring] the exposure of specified anatomical areas or by specified sexual activities. *(San Bernardino, Calif.)*

■ **adult use, hotel/motel** A hotel or motel or similar business establishment offering public accommodations for any form of consideration that (1) provides patrons with closed-circuit television transmissions, films, motion pictures, video cassettes, slides, or other photographic reproductions characterized by an emphasis upon the depiction or description of "specified sexual activities" or "specified anatomical areas"; and/or (2) rents, leases, or lets any room for less than a six-hour period, or rents, leases, or lets any single room more than twice in a 24-hour period. *(Mission Viejo, Calif.)*

A hotel, motel, or similar commercial establishment which: (1) offers accommodations to the public for any form of consideration where patrons are provided closed-circuit television transmissions, films, motion pictures, video cassettes, slides, or other photographic reproductions that are characterized by the depiction or description of specified sexual activities or specified anatomical areas and has a sign visible from the public right-of-way advertising the availability of this adult type of photographic reproductions; (2) offers a sleeping room for rent with rates for a period of time that is less than 10 hours; or (3) allows a tenant or occupant of a sleeping room to subrent the room for a period of time that is less than 10 hours. *(Hilton Head Island, S.C.)*

■ **adult use, massage parlor** *(See also massage establishment)* An establishment where, for any form of consideration, massage, alcohol rub, fomentation, electric or magnetic treatment, or similar treatment or manipulation of the human body is administered, unless such treatment or manipulation is administered by a medical practitioner, chiropractor, acupuncturist, physical therapist, or similar professional person licensed by the state. This definition does not include an athletic club, health club, school, gymnasium, reducing salon, spa, or similar establishment where massage or similar manipulation of the human body is offered as an incidental or accessory service. *(San Bernardino, Calif.)*

■ **adult use, modeling studio** An establishment whose primary business is the provision to customers of figure models who are so provided with the intent of providing sexual stimulation or sexual gratification to such customers and who engage in specified sexual activities or display specified anatomical areas while being observed, painted, painted upon, sketched, drawn, sculptured, photographed, or otherwise depicted by such customers. *(Houston, Tex.)*

■ **adult use, sexual encounter establishment** An establishment other than a hotel, motel, or similar establishment offering public accommodations, which, for any form of consideration, provides a place where two or more persons may congregate, associate, or consort in connection with specified sexual activities or the exposure of specified anatomical areas. This definition does not include an establishment where a medical practitioner, psychologist, psychiatrist, or similar professional person licensed by the state engages in sexual therapy. *(San Bernardino, Calif.)*

A companionship establishment that excludes minors by reason of age, or which provides the service for a fee of engaging in or listening to conversation, talk, or discussion between an employee of the establishment and a customer, if such service is distinguished or characterized by an emphasis on specified sexual activities or specified anatomical areas as defined herein. *(Bloomington, Minn., which uses the term "adult companionship establishment")*

A business establishment wherein the patrons thereof are invited to discuss sexual matters or engage in sexual activities with an unclothed or partially unclothed person, and who pay a fee for such discussion or activities. This definition shall not include therapy sessions conducted by physicians, therapists and counselors licensed and regulated by the state. *(Imperial Beach, Calif., which uses the term "adult use, sexual encounter studio and rap parlor")*

■ **adult use, sexual paraphernalia store** Any retail store specializing in the sale of paraphernalia, devices, or equipment distinguished or characterized by an emphasis on depicting or describing specific sexual conduct or used in connection with specified sexual conduct. *(Santa Monica, Calif.)*

■ **adult use, specified anatomical areas** As used herein specified anatomical areas means and includes any of the following: (1) less than completely and opaquely covered human genitals, pubic region, buttocks, anus, or female breasts below a point immediately above the top of the

areolae; or (2) human male genitals in a discernibly turgid state, even if completely and opaquely covered. *(San Bernardino, Calif.)*

■ **adult use, specified sexual activities** As herein, specific sexual activities means and includes any of the following: (1) the fondling or other erotic touching of human genitals, pubic region, buttocks, anus, or female breasts; (2) sex acts, normal or perverted, actual or simulated, including intercourse, oral copulation, or sodomy; (3) masturbation, actual or simulated; or (4) excretory functions as part of or in connection with any of the activities set forth in subdivisions 1 through 3 of this subsection. *(San Bernardino, Calif.)*

■ **adverse impact** A negative consequence for the physical, social, or economic environment resulting from an action or project. *(California Planning Roundtable)*

■ **aerial mosaic** A compilation of individual vertical aerial photographs joined together to provide a composite view of an entire area covered by the photographs. *(Handbook for Planning Commissioners in Missouri)*

■ **aesthetic zoning** The regulation of building or site design to achieve desirable appearance (pictured below). *(PAS Report No. 322, The Language of Zoning)*

■ **affected persons** Those owners of record of real property located within a distance of 300 feet, including public streets and other rights-of-way. *(Valdez, Alaska)*

■ **affiliate** With respect to a specific owner: (a) such owner's parents (blood or adoptive), spouse, children, or grandchildren (blood or adoptive) or any blood relative residing with such owner; (b) a trustee of a trust for the benefit of such owner or of any person identified in the immediately preceding clause; or (c) a corporation, partnership, firm, business, or entity of which the majority of the voting interest is owned by such owner or any person identified in subdivisions (a) and (b) above; or (d) a person who is an officer, director, stockholder (15 percent or more), trustee, employee, or partner of any entity or person referred to in subdivisions (a), (b) and (c) above. *(Newport, R.I.)*

■ **affordable housing** *(See also **below-market-rate housing; housing, low-income; housing, very low-income**)* Housing units where the occupant is paying no more than 30 percent of gross income for housing costs, including taxes and utilities. *(Ann Arbor, Mich.)*

Housing that has a sale price or rental amount that is within the means of a household that may occupy middle-, moderate-, or low-income housing. In the case of dwelling units for sale, housing that is affordable means housing in which mortgage, amortization, taxes, insurance, and condominium or association fees, if any, constitute no more than 28 percent of such gross annual household income for a household of the size which may occupy the unit in question. In the case of dwelling units for rent, housing that is affordable mans housing for which the rent and utilities constitute no more than 30 percent of such gross annual income for a household of the size that may occupy the unit in question. *(APA's Growing Smart project)*

(1) Housing renting for a monthly rent of not more than 30 percent of the total monthly household income of low-income households (defined to be a household earning less than 80 percent of the median annual income adjusted for household size, as determined by the United States Department of Housing and Urban Development); or (2) Housing that may be purchased with monthly payments including: principal, interest, taxes, insurance, homeowners association fees, and assessments that do not add up to more than 30 percent of the total monthly household income of low-income households (defined to be a household earning less than 80 percent of the median annual income, adjusted for household size, as determined by the United States Department of Housing and Urban Development). *(Redmond, Wash.)*

■ **affordable units** Residential dwellings that are rented or sold at a price within the range of low- to moderate-income households as established by the city council. *(Brea, Calif.)*

■ **afforestation** *(See also **forestry** definitions)* The establishment of a forest on an area on which forest cover has been absent for a long period of time; the planting of open areas that are not presently in forest cover; or the establishment of a forest according to afforestation or reforestation standards. . . . *(Maryland Department of Natural Resources)*

■ **agency** The governmental entity, department, office, or administrative unit responsible for carrying out regulations. *(California Planning Roundtable)*

■ **aggrieved party** 1. Any person or persons or entity or entities who can demonstrate that their property will be injured by a decision of either the zoning officer or the planning board or the zoning board of review or any official of the city involved in the enforcement of this zoning code; or 2. Anyone requiring notice pursuant to this zoning code. *(Newport, R.I.)*

■ **agricultural activity** Farming, including plowing, tillage, cropping, installation of best management practices, seeding, cultivating or harvesting for the production of food and fiber products (except commercial logging and timber harvesting.) *(Ft. Collins, Colo.)*

Land used exclusively as a bonafide agricultural operation by the owner or tenant. The use of land for agricultural purposes including farming, silviculture, viticulture, fish culture, animal and poultry husbandry, and the necessary accessory uses for packing, treating, or storing the produce, provided that the operation of the accessory use is clearly incidental to the agricultural activity. The business of garbage feeding of hogs, fur farms, or the raising of animals for use in medical or other tests or experiments is excluded. *(Frederick, Md.)*

■ **agricultural building** A structure on agricultural land designed, constructed, and used to house farm implements, livestock, or agricultural produce or products used by the owner, lessee, or sub-lessee or their immediate families, their employees, and persons engaged in the pick up or delivery of agricultural produce or products grown or raised on the premises. The term "agricultural building" shall not include dwellings. *(Wilton, N.H.)*

A structure designed and constructed to store farm implements or hay, grain, poultry, livestock, fruit, and other agricultural products. Controlled atmosphere and cold storage warehouses are not agricultural buildings. An agricultural building shall not be used for human habitation, processing, treating, packaging agricultural products, or as a place used by the public. *(Yakima, Wash.)*

■ **agricultural land, prime** (1) Land used actively in the production of food, fiber, or livestock. (2) All land that qualifies for rating as Class I or Class II in the Soil Conservation Service land use compatibility classifications. (3) Land that qualifies for rating 80 through 100 in the Storie Index Rating. *(California Planning Roundtable)*

■ **agricultural preserve** Land designated for agriculture or conservation. *(California Planning Roundtable)*

■ **agricultural processing plant** A facility used for the cooking, dehydrating, refining, bottling, canning, or other treatment of agricultural products which changes the naturally grown product for consumer use. May include warehousing and packaging as secondary uses. *(Dona Ana County, N. Mex.)*

A building, facility, area, open or enclosed, or any location for the refinement, treatment, or conversion of agricultural products where physical, chemical, or similar change of an agricultural product occurs. Examples of agricultural processing include, but are not limited to, fruit dehydrators, cold storage houses, hulling operations, and the sorting, cleaning, packing, and storing of agricultural products preparatory to sale and/or shipment in their natural form, including all uses customarily incidental thereto. "Agricultural processing" shall not include wineries or manufacturing of secondary products using agricultural products, such as commercial kitchens, bakeries, breweries, woodworking and wood processing plants. (*Shasta Lake, Calif.*)

■ **agricultural protection zoning** (*See also quarter/quarter zoning*) Regulations that protect the agricultural land base by limiting nonfarm uses, prohibiting high-density development, requiring houses to be built on small lots, and restricting subdivision of land into parcels that are too small to farm. (*American Farmland Trust*)

■ **agricultural-related industry** 1. Packaging plants: May include, but are not limited to, the following activities: washing, sorting, crating, and other functional operations such as drying, field crushing, or other preparation in which the chemical and physical composition of the agricultural product remains essentially unaltered. Does not include processing activities, or slaughterhouse, animal reduction yards, and tallow works. 2. Processing plants: May include, but are not limited to, those activities which involve the fermentation or other substantial chemical and physical alteration of the agricultural product. Does not include slaughterhouses or rendering plants. 3. Storage facilities: Includes controlled atmosphere and cold storage warehouses and warehouses for the storage of processed and/or packaged agricultural products. (*Yakima, Wash.*)

■ **agricultural sales and service** A use primarily engaged in the sale or rental of farm tools and implements, feed, grain, tack, animal care products, and farm supplies. This definition excludes the sale of large implements, such as tractors and combines, but includes food sales and farm machinery repair services that are accessory to the principal use. (*Blue Springs, Mo.*)

■ **agriculture** The use of land for agricultural purposes, including farming, dairying, pasturage agriculture, horticulture, floriculture, viticulture, and animal and poultry husbandry, and the necessary accessory uses for storing the products. The term shall include incidental retail sales by the producer of products raised on the farm. (*Mankato, Minn.*)

The production, keeping, or maintenance for sale or lease, of plants, including but not limited to: forages and sod crops; grains and seed crops; fruits and vegetables; and ornamental products, and unless expressly prohibited, the keeping of livestock, including but not limited to: dairy animals and dairy products; poultry and poultry products; cattle and cattle products; or horses. Agriculture does not include forest management and timber harvesting activities. (*Saco, Maine*)

The breeding, planting, nourishing, caring for, gathering, and processing of any animal or plant organism for the purpose of nourishing people or any other plant or animal organism; or for the purpose of providing the raw material for non-food products. For the purposes of this chapter, agriculture shall include the growing of flowers and other ornamental crops and the commercial breeding and caring for animals as pets. (*Kauai County, Hawaii*)

■ **agriculture, commercial** The production principally for the sale to others of plants, animals, or their products, including, but not limited to: forage and sod crops, grain and feed crops, dairy animals and dairy products; livestock, including dairy and beef cattle, poultry, sheep, swine, horses, ponies, mules and goats; including the breeding and grazing of all such animals; bees and apiary products; fruits of all kinds including grapes, nuts, and berries; vegetables; nursery, floral ornamental and greenhouse products and other commodities as described in the Standard Industrial Classification for agriculture, forestry, fishing, and trapping. Commercial agricultures shall not include poultry or swine production or animal feedlot operations. (*Randolph Township, N.J.*)

■ **agriculture, home** The production, principally for use or consumption of the property owner, of plants, animals, or their products and for sale to others where such sales are incidental, including, but not limited to: gardening, fruit production, and poultry and livestock products for household use only. (*Randolph Township, N.J.*)

■ **agriculture, intensive** Agricultural uses that include but are not necessarily limited to: (1) slaughter areas, (2) areas for the storage or processing of manure, garbage, or spent mushroom compost, (3) structures housing more than 50 animal units. Under [state law] a farm is allowed to have no more than two animal units per acre, with an animal unit defined as 1,000 pounds. (*Lancaster County, Pa.*)

■ **agriculture-related business** Feed mills, dairy supplies, poultry processing, creameries, auction yards, veterinarians, and other businesses supporting local agriculture. (*California Planning Roundtable*)

■ **agriculture, specialized** The growing, collection, or storing of any plant for ornamental or nonfood use, such as flowers and pot plants. (*Kauai, Hawaii*)

■ **air contaminant** Any smoke, soot, fly ash, dust, cinder, dirt, noxious, obnoxious acids, fumes, oxides, gases, vapors, odors, toxic or radioactive substances, waste particulates, solid, liquid or gaseous matter in the atmosphere which, when in sufficient quantities, is capable of injuring human, plant, or animal life, or depriving the enjoyment thereof. (*Edmond, Okla.*)

■ **air pollution** (*See also acid rain; ozone; smog*) Concentrations of substances found in the atmosphere that exceed naturally occurring quantities and are undesirable or harmful in some way. (*California Planning Roundtable*)

The emission of any air contaminants in such place or manner which, when by itself or combined with other air contaminants present in the atmosphere, is detrimental to or endangers the health, comfort, or safety of any person, or which may cause injury or damage to property or premises. *(Edmond, Okla.)*

■ **air rights**    The ownership or control of all land, property, and that area of space at and above a horizontal plane over the ground surface of land used for railroad or expressway purposes. The horizontal plane shall be at a height that is reasonably necessary or legally required for the full and free use of the ground surface. *(Chicago, Ill.)*

■ **air traffic pattern**    A pattern of aircraft routes set out by United States Government authorities to regulate the movements of aircraft approaching or departing an airport. *(Austin, Tex.)*

■ **aircraft**    Any contrivance now known or hereafter invented for use in or designed for navigation of or flight in air. *(North Kansas City, Mo.)*

■ **airport**    Any area of land or water designated, set aside, used or intended for use, for the landing and take-off of aircraft, and any appurtenant areas designated, set aside, used or intended for use, for airport buildings or other airport facilities, rights-of-way, or approach zones, together with all airport buildings and facilities located thereon. *(Stillwater, Okla.)*

Any area of land or water designed and set aside for the landing and take-off of aircraft, including all necessary facilities for the housing and maintenance of aircraft. *(Santa Barbara County, Calif.)*

■ **airport approach area**    An imaginary surface longitudinally centered on the runway centerline, extending outward and upward from the end of the runway, and is based upon the type of approach available or planned for that runway end. *(Thurston County, Wash.)*

■ **airport environs**    That area identified as being significantly impacted by airport noise and accident potential. *(Escambia County, Fla.)*

■ **airport hazard**    Any structure or tree or use of land that would exceed the federal obstruction standards and that obstructs the airspace required for the flight of aircraft in landing or taking off at an airport or is otherwise hazardous to such landing or taking off of aircraft. *(Escambia County, Fla.)*

■ **airport-related use**    A use that supports airport operations, including, but not limited to, aircraft repair and maintenance, flight instruction, and aircraft chartering. *(California Planning Roundtable)*

■ **airport, water-based**    A transportation facility used exclusively by aircraft that take off and land directly on the water. *(Seattle, Wash.)*

■ **airport zoning**    A particular set of controls designed to reduce the safety and noise hazards associated with aircraft flying within the airport control zone. Primarily the controls restrict the

height of buildings and trees near the landing corridors and the location of residences, schools, hospitals, and other such uses needing protection from potential aircraft hazards. *(Code of Iowa)*

A particular set of controls intended to protect the integrity of an airport, its airspace, and its environs. While the major control is on height–with permitted minimums increasing with distance from runways–airport zoning also limits electronic interference with navigational equipment and some types of uses, primarily places of assembly to reduce accident risks. Many communities have, in addition, made special provision for airport surroundings by zoning them for compatible uses (e.g., warehousing, industry, and certain commercial uses) and excluding residential uses and places of assembly (e.g., schools, stadiums, and such). *(PAS Report No. 322, The Language of Zoning)*

■ **airspace**    An area from ground up within the general operation area of an airport. *(Page, Ariz.)*

■ **all-terrain vehicle (ATV)** *(See also **off-road vehicle**)*    Any motorized, off-road vehicle 50 inches or less in ovrall width, having a dry weight of 600 pounds or less, designed to travel on three or more low-pressure tires, having a seat designed to be straddled by the operator and handle bars for steering control. *(University of Minnesota, Department of Forest Services)*

■ **alley**    A public or private way permanently reserved as a secondary means of access to abutting property (pictured below). *(San Diego, Calif.)*

An unnamed public or private right-of-way less than 22 feet wide that is primarily designed to serve as secondary access to the rear or side of those properties whose principal frontage is on some other street. *(Glendale, Calif.)*

A public thoroughfare or way 20 feet or less in width, which has been dedicated to the city of Yakima or Yakima County for public use. Alleys provide only a secondary means of access to abutting property. *(Yakima, Wash.)*

■ **alteration** *(See also **addition; rehabilitation; remodel**)*    Any change, addition, or modification in construction or occupancy of an existing structure. *(Sacramento County, Calif.)*

Any enlargement; addition; relocation; repair; remodeling; change in number of living units; development of or change in an open area; development of or change in a sign, by painting or otherwise; or other change in a facility, but excluding painting except as provided above for signs; ordinary maintenance for which no building permit is required; and demolition or removal. *(Oakland, Calif.)*

■ **alteration, incidental**    Modifications to a building or structure that are of a cosmetic nature, replacement of utilities, rearrangement of internal partitions. The replacement of load-bearing walls is not permitted. *(Nashville and Davidson County, Tenn.)*

■ **alteration, structural**    Any change in the supporting members of a building or structure, such as bearing walls, columns, beams, or girders; provided, however, that the application of any exterior siding to an existing building for the purpose of beautifying and modernizing shall not be considered a structural alteration. *(Dunedin, Fla.)*

*Commentary: Zoning codes often distinguish between superficial and substantial alterations to buildings (e.g., compare the definitions here of "alteration, incidental" and "alteration, structural"). Substantial alterations may be subject to more rigid building permit review procedures. The distinction is also important when regulating the expansion and alteration of nonconforming uses. Many codes allow alterations that enhance the appearance of the nonconforming use or structure but do not allow structural or substantial alterations to the building.*

■ **amateur radio tower** *(See also **telecommunications** definitions)*    A freestanding or building-mounted structure, including any base, tower or pole, antenna, and appurtenances, intended for airway communication purposes by a person holding a valid amateur radio (HAM) license issued by the Federal Communications Commission. *(Glendale, Ariz.)*

An amateur (HAM) radio station licensed by the Federal Communications Commission, including equipment such as but not limited to a tower or alternative tower structure supporting a single,

radiating antenna platform and other equipment. . . . *(Cape Elizabeth, Maine, which uses the term "amateur wireless telecommunications facility")*

■ **ambient**    Surrounding on all sides; used to describe measurements of existing conditions with respect to traffic, noise, air, and other environments. *(California Planning Roundtable)*

■ **ambient noise level**    The all-encompassing noise level associated with a given environment, being a composite of sounds from all sources, excluding any alleged offensive noise. In this context, the ambient noise level constitutes the normal or existing level of environmental noise at a given location. *(Oakland, Calif.)*

A change in the wording, content, or substance of this title, or change in the district boundaries on the official zoning map. *(Yakima, Wash.)*

Any change to the text of these regulations or the official zoning maps by the city council or an administrative change pursuant to this (ordinance). *(Charlotte, N.C.)*

■ **amenity**    Aesthetic or other characteristics of a development that increase its desirability to a community or its marketability to the public. Amenities may differ from development to development but may include such things as a unified building design, recreational facilities (e.g., a swimming pool or tennis courts), security systems, views, landscaping and tree preservation, or attractive site design. *(PAS Report No. 322, The Language of Zoning)*

■ **amortization** *(See also **nonconforming** definitions)*    Allows a landowner to recoup the value of a nonconforming use within a particular period of time. After that time, the community can force the owner to discontinue the use without the payment of compensation. *(Land Use Law and Zoning Digest, January 1985)*

A method of eliminating nonconforming uses by requiring the termination of the nonconforming use after a specified period of time. *(Code of Iowa)*

The process established under the zoning ordinance by which an owner of a

nonconforming use is given a reasonable period of time to continue the nonconforming use before it is terminated pursuant to the city's police power without payment of compensation. The amortization period is intended to give the owner of the nonconforming use the opportunity before the use is terminated to recoup his or her investment in the use made prior to it becoming nonconforming. *(Houston, Tex.)*

■ **amusement, commercial, indoor**    The provision of entertainment or games of skill to the general public for a fee and that is wholly enclosed in a building, including but not limited to a bowling alley or billiard parlor. This use does not include an arena. *(Nashville and Davidson County, Tenn.)*

Establishments providing multiple coin-operated amusement or entertainment devices or machines as other than an incidental use of the premises. Such devices would include pinball machines, video games, and other games of skill or scoring, and would include pool and/or billiard tables, whether or not they are coin operated. Typical uses include game rooms, billiard and pool halls, and video arcades. *(Blacksburg, Va.)*

■ **amusement, commercial, outdoor** *(See also **carnival**)*    The provision of entertainment or games of skill to the general public for a fee where any portion of the activity takes place outside of a building, including but not limited to a golf driving range, archery range, or miniature golf course. This use does not include a stadium. *(Nashville and Davidson County, Tenn.)*

Land or premises designed to be used by members of the public, for a fee, that contain outdoor amusement facilities, such as miniature golf courses, merry-go-rounds, car race tracks, and outdoor motion picture theaters. *(Kauai, Hawaii)*

■ **amusement device**    Any coin-operated, token-operated, or rented kiddie rides, music machines, skill games, or non-skill games, including pool tables, billiard tables, pinball machines, shuffle boards, shuffle bowls, ski ball, rotary merchandisers, dart boards, target games, basket loops, and other similar devices. Each coin box, token box, or player position on a machine or device with more than one such box or position shall be deemed to be a separate device. *(Glendale, Ariz.)*

Any video game, pinball, or other machines, whether mechanically or electronically operated that, upon insertion of a coin, trade-token, slug, or similar object, operates or may be operated as a game or contest of skill or amusement of any kind or description, and that contains no automatic payoff for the return of money or trade tokens, or that makes no provision whatever for the return of money to the player. An amusement device is further defined as any machine, apparatus, or contrivance that is used or that may be used as a game of skill and amusement wherein or whereby the player initiates, employs, or directs any force generated by the machine. An amusement device shall exclude billiard, pool, or bagatelle tables. *(Salt Lake County, Utah)*

■ **amusement enterprise**   Any indoor or outdoor place that is maintained or operated for the amusement, patronage, or recreation of the public to include any coin-controlled amusement device of any description, commonly known as baseball, football, pinball amusements, pool tables, miniature golf course, or driving range. *(Jefferson County, Colo.)*

■ **amusement park** *(See also **carnival**)* A commercially operated park with a predominance of outdoor games and activities for entertainment (ouctured below), including motorized rides, water slides, miniature golf, batting cages, and the like. *(Camden, Maine)*

A commercially operated park with various devices for entertainment and booths for the sale of food and drink. *(El Paso, Tex.)*

■ **amusement park, children's**   A group of not more than 12 amusement devices for children only, including pony rings, and their necessary accessory uses, located on a plot of ground with an area of not over three acres, which area shall include provisions for off-street parking. *(Kansas City, Mo.)*

■ **amusement ride** *(See also **carnival**)* A mechanical, aquatic, or other device or attraction that carries passengers over a fixed or restricted area, primarily for the passengers' amusement. *(State of Montana)*

■ **anchor tenant**   The major store or stores within a shopping center. *(Iowa State University Extension Service)*

■ **ancillary use** *(See **accessory use**)*

■ **animal**   Any vertebrate member of the animal kingdom, excluding man. *(Lincoln, Nebr.)*

Any live vertebrate creature, domestic or wild. *(Gilroy, Calif.)*

■ **animal-at-large**   [An animal] outside of a fence or other enclosure that restrains the animal to a particular premises, whether on public or private property, and not under the control, by leash or lead, of the owner or keeper. Animals tethered to a stationary object within reach of a street, sidewalk, alley, trail or other public access are deemed to be "at large." *(Ft. Collins, Colo.)*

■ **animal boarding place** *(See also **kennel**)*   Any structure, land, or combination thereof used, designed, or arranged

for the boarding, breeding or care of dogs, cats, pets, fowl, horses, or other domestic animals for profit, but exclusive of animals used for agricultural purposes. *(Mequon, Wisc.)*

■ **animal, domestic**   A domestic animal shall include dogs and cats only. *(Pomfret Township, N.Y.)*

Any dog, cat, horse, cow, sheep, goat, pig, or domestic fowl. *(Germantown, Tenn.)*

An animal that is tame or domesticated and not normally found in the wild state. Hybrids of animals normally found in the wild state are not included within the meaning of domestic animal. *(New Castle County, Del.)*

Any of various animals adopted by man so as to live and breed in a tame condition. *(Woodbury, Minn., which uses the term "domesticated animal")*

Any animal that has been bred and/or raised to live in or about the habitation of humans and is dependent on people for food and shelter. *(Ft. Collins, Colo.)*

■ **animal-drawn carriage**   Any carriage, buggy, rickshaw, or similar device drawn by one or more persons or animals in which the public, for a fee, is allowed to ride for purposes of transportation, entertainment, or amusement. *(Glendale, Ariz.)*

■ **animal, exotic**   Any member of a species of animal, reptile or bird, warm or cold blooded, that is not indigenous to the environs of the parish and/or is not classified or considered as wildlife, livestock, or domestic animal. *(Jefferson Parish, La.)*

Any wild animal not customarily confined or cultivated by man for domestic or commercial purposes but rather kept as a pet or for display. *(Manhattan Beach, Calif.)*

■ **animal, farm**   Any animal that customarily is raised for profit on farms and has the potential of causing a nuisance if not properly maintained. *(Pomfret Township, N.Y.)*

■ **animal grooming service**   Any place or establishment, public or private,

where animals are bathed, clipped, or combed for the purpose of enhancing their aesthetic value and/or health and for which a fee is charged. *(Federal Way, Wash.)*

■ **animal hospital**    An establishment for the care and treatment of small animals, including household pets. *(Kauai County, Hawaii)*

Any building or portion of a building designed or used for the care, observation or treatment of domestic animals. *(Annapolis, Md.)*

A place where animals or pets are given medical or surgical treatment and are cared for during the time of such treatment. Use as a kennel shall be limited to short-time boarding and shall be only incidental to such hospital use. *(Hemet, Calif.)*

■ **animal husbandry**    The raising of domesticated farm animals when, in the case of dairy cows, beef cattle, horse, ponies, mules, llamas, goats, and sheep, their primary source of food, other than during the winter months, is from grazing in the pasture where they are kept. *(Yakima, Wash.)*

■ **animal, large**    An animal larger than the largest breed of dogs. This term includes horses, cows, and other mammals customarily kept in corrals or stables. *(Manhattan Beach, Calif.)*

Cattle, horses, mules, sheep, goats, beasts of burden, or any other domesticated or wild animal weighing more than 20 pounds except pet animals, unusual animals, or fowl. *(Lincoln, Nebr.)*

■ **animal shelter**    Any premises designated by the county for the purpose of impounding and caring for cats and dogs found running at large or otherwise subject to impoundment in accordance with the provision of this law. *(Nags Head, N.C.)*

A facility used to house or contain stray, homeless, abandoned, or unwanted animals and that is owned, operated, or maintained by a public body, an established humane society, animal welfare society, society for the prevention of cruelty to animals, or other nonprofit organization devoted to the welfare, protec-

tion, and humane treatment of animals. *(Federal Way, Wash.)*

■ **animal, small**    Any animal, including rabbits, weighing 20 pounds or less, except pet animals, unusual animals, or fowl. *(Lincoln, Nebr.)*

An animal no larger than the largest breed of dogs. This term includes fish, birds, and mammals customarily kept in kennels. *(Manhattan Beach, Calif.)*

■ **annex**    To incorporate a land area into an existing district or municipality, with a resulting change in the boundaries of the annexing jurisdiction. *(California Planning Roundtable)*

To add territory to a governmental unit, usually an incorporated place, by an ordinance, a court order, or other legal action. *(United States Census Bureau)*

■ **annexation**    The act or process of adding land to a governmental unit, usually an incorporated place, by an ordinance, a court order, or other legal action. *(United States Census Bureau)*

The process by which cities extend their municipal services, regulations, voting privileges, and taxing authority to new territory. *(Austin, Tex.)*

The process used by a municipality to add surrounding fringe areas to the city or town. There are methods for annexing contiguous property (areas adjacent to the annexing city) as well as non-contiguous property. The main methods of annexing property are by election, petition, annexation for municipal purposes, annexation of federally owned areas, and boundary line adjustments. *(Municipal Research and Services Center)*

The traditional way a municipality expands its territorial limits and jurisdictional powers. *(Zoning News)*

The addition of territory to a city. *(Ames, Iowa)*

■ **antenna** *(See also* **telecommunications antenna***)*    Any system of wires, poles, rods, reflecting discs, or similar devices used for the transmission or reception of electromagnetic waves external to or attached to the exterior of any building. *(Cerritos, Calif.)*

■ **antenna, dish**    *(See* **telecommunications, satellite dish antenna***)*

■ **antique mall**    A building that is partitioned to provide spaces for the sale of antiques by antique dealers, for items such as clocks, lamps, clothing, rugs, toys, furniture and the like. *(Concord, Penn.)*

■ **antique shops** *(See also* **secondhand merchandise, retail sales; thrift store***)*  A place offering antiques for sale. An antique, for purposes of this chapter, shall be a work of art, piece of furniture, decorative object, or the like, of or belonging to the past, at least 30 years old. *(Prince William County, Va.)*

Any premises used for the sale or trading of articles of which 80 percent or more are over 50 years old or have collectible value. Antique shop does not include "secondhand store" *(Salinas, Calif.)*

■ **apartment** *(See also* **dwelling** *definitions)*    A room or suite of rooms, with toilet and culinary accommodations, used or designed for use as a residence by a family, located in a building containing two or more such rooms or suites or located in a building devoted primarily to nonresidential use. *(Ames, Iowa)*

A dwelling unit used exclusively for lease or rent as a residence. *(Las Cruces, N. Mex.)*

One or more rooms in a dwelling designed and intended for occupancy as a separate dwelling unit. *(Vernon Hills, Ill.)*

■ **apartment, garden** *(See* **garden apartment***)*

■ **apartment, high-rise**    A multifamily dwelling with 11 or more stories. *(Jersey City, N.J.)*

A multiple-family dwelling of six or more stories above the ground level of the principal entrance. *(Anchorage, Alaska)*

■ **apartment hotel**    A building designed for or containing both apartments and individual hotel guest rooms under resident supervision [maintaining] an inner lobby through which all tenants must pass to gain access to apartments and hotel rooms. *(Coral Gables, Fla.)*

■ **apartment, senior** *(See also **elderly housing**)* An apartment specifically designed for independent living for retired individuals or couples over the age of 55 where no meal service is provided. *(Hemet, Calif.)*

■ **apiary** A place where bee colonies are kept. *(Hemet, Calif.)*

■ **applicant** The party applying for permits or other approval required by this chapter. *(Asheville, N.C.)*

■ **application** The completed form or forms and all accompanying documents, exhibits, and fees required of an applicant by the applicable department, board, or commission of the city for development review, approval, or permitting purposes. *(Newport, R.I.)*

■ **appraisal** A systematic method of determining the market value of property. *(American Farmland Trust)*

■ **aquaculture** The hatching, raising, and breeding of fish or other aquatic plants or animals for sale or personal use. *(Asheville, N.C.)*

The growing and harvesting of plant or animal organisms in a natural or artificial aquatic situation that requires a body of water such as a pond, river, lake, estuary or ocean. *(Kauai County, Hawaii)*

■ **aquarium** An establishment where aquatic collections of living organisms are kept and exhibited. *(Burlington, Vt.)*

■ **aquifer** *(See also **groundwater** definitions)* A geologic formation, group of formations, or part of a formation capable of yielding, storing, or transmitting a usable amount of groundwater to wells or springs for domestic or animal use. *(Sioux Falls, S.D.)*

Land areas determined to overlay water saturated stratified drift deposits of sands and/or gravels capable of yielding private and public potable water supplies. *(Wilton, N.H.)*

A saturated geologic formation that will yield a sufficient quantity of water to serve as a private or public water supply. *(Yakima County, Wash.)*

■ **aquifer, artesian** Groundwater that rises to an elevation above the ground surface as a result of considerable confining pressure. *(PAS Report 476, Nonpoint Source Pollution: A Handbook for Local Governments)*

An aquifer in which water is confined under pressure between layers of impermeable material. Wells tapping into an artesian stratum will flow naturally without the use of pumps. *(California Planning Roundtable)*

■ **aquifer recharge** *(See **groundwater recharge**)*

■ **aquifer recharge area** An area in which the principal movement of water is the downward seepage of surface waters into groundwater by: (1) the infiltration of water from the surface into the soil or other rock materials that lie directly below the surface; (2) the downward movement of water through the materials that comprise the zone of aeration; and (3) the delivery of water into the zone of saturation where it becomes groundwater. *(Yakima County, Wash.)*

■ **aquifer, surficial** A water-bearing stratum which is not covered by a confining (impervious) bed and which can be replenished directly by rainfall. *(Indian River County, Fla.)*

■ **arborist** An individual trained in arboriculture, forestry, landscape architecture, horticulture, or related fields and experienced in the conservation and preservation of native and ornamental trees. This definition shall also incorporate the term urban forester. *(York County, Va.)*

■ **arcade** An area contiguous to a street or plaza that is open and unobstructed to a height of not less than 12 feet and that is accessible to the public at all times. Any portion of an arcade occupied by building columns, landscaping, statuary, pools, or fountains shall be considered part of the arcade for the purpose of computing a floor-area premium credit. The term "arcade" shall not include off-street loading areas, driveways, off-street parking areas, or open pedestrian walkways. The floor of any arcade shall be level with the adjoining street or plaza. *(Mankato, Minn.)*

■ **arcade, amusement** *(See also **amusement park**)* A building or part of a building containing four or more video, pinball, or similar player-operated amusement devices, in any combination, for commercial use. *(Prince William County, Va.)*

A business establishment offering for public use five or more of any form of game machine, instrument or apparatus operated by coin, slug, or similar medium, but not including automatic machines for vending food, soft drinks or tobacco, and outside service vending machines. *(Ocean City, Md.)*

■ **arcade, internal** A street arcade that fronts on and adjoins a plaza or other space internal to a building lot rather than the front lot line. *(Mankato, Minn.)*

■ **arcade, street** An arcade that adjoins a front lot line, is not less than 10 feet nor more than 30 feet in depth (measured perpendicular to the front lot line), and extends the full length of, or at least 50 feet along the front lot line, whichever is the greater distance; or on a corner lot, is bounded on two sides by the two intersecting street lines, and has an area of not less than 500 square feet and a minimum linear dimension of 10 feet. *(Mankato, Minn.)*

■ **archaeological resources** Any material of past human life, activities, or habitation that are of historic or prehistoric significance. Such material includes, but is not limited to, pottery, basketry, bottles, weapon projectiles, tools, structures, pit house, rock paintings, rock carving, intaglios, graves, skeletal remains, personal items and clothing, household or business refuse, printed matter, manufactured items, or any piece of the foregoing items. *(Glendale, Ariz.)*

Material evidence of past human activity found below the surface of the ground or water, portions of which may be visible above the surface. *(Asheville, N.C.)*

■ **archaeological site** A concentration of material remains of past human life or activities that is of historic or prehistoric significance, has been surveyed by a qualified archeologist where the site meets the minimum criteria in the Federal Register, 36CFR60.6, for a significant archaeological resource, and where a report by a qualified archeologist has been filed with the City of Scottsdale and/or the Arizona State Museum and/or the State Historic Preservation Office (SHPO) demonstrating the significance of the site and recommendations for treatment of the site. Examples of material remains include rock art, pottery, basketry, tools, graves, skeletal remains, structures or portions of structures, or water-control devices. *(Scottsdale, Ariz.)*

■ **archery range**　An outdoor facility that may include buildings or structures used for target practice with bows and arrows. *(McHenry County, Ill.)*

■ **architectural control/architectural review** *(See also design control/design review)*　Regulations and procedures requiring the exterior design of structures to be suitable, harmonious, and in keeping with the general appearance, historic character, and/or style of surrounding areas. A process used to exercise control over the design of buildings and their settings. *(California Planning Roundtable)*

■ **architectural decoration**　An element, design, or motif, other than an architectural feature, installed, attached, painted, or applied to the exterior of a building or structure for the purpose of ornamentation or artistic expression. *(Columbus, Ohio)*

■ **architectural features**　Ornamentation or decorative features attached to or protruding from an exterior wall (pictured at right). *(Bloomington, Ind.)*

Architectural features of a building shall include cornices, eaves, gutters, belt courses, sills, lintels, bay windows, chimneys, and decorative ornaments. *(Alma, Mich.)*

■ **architectural plan**　A plan for the construction of any structure designed by a qualified registered architect. *(Carmel, Ind.)*

■ **architectural projection**　Projections from a building that are necessary for the shading of a building or features, such as sills, cornices, and chimneys. Such projections may extend into required yards

only as allowed by the provisions of this title. *(Palm Desert, Calif.)*

Eaves, cornices, platforms, porches, or any types of structure attached to and extending from the main building. *(Ocean Shores, Wash.)*

■ **architectural recesses**　Portions of a building wall at street level which are set back from the street line so as to create articulation of the building wall and/or to provide space for windows or doors, provided such recesses are not part of the required public space or open space of a lot. *(Philadelphia, Pa.)*

■ **architectural review board**　A board composed of design professionals (e.g., architects, landscape architects), others who work with the built environment (e.g., urban planners, civil engineering), and citizens who approve or disapprove design plans for development projects. This board may be advisory only; approval of projects may, because of state legislation, still remain with an administrative or legislative body. The composition and size of the board varies by community. *(PAS Report No. 454, Design Review)*

■ **architecture**　The art and science of designing and constructing buildings adapted to their purposes, one of which is beauty. *(Coral Gables, Fla.)*

■ **area classification**　For purposes of the street standards and subdivision regulations, the area classifications "com-

mercial," "industrial," and "residential" shall mean the following:

A. Commercial: That portion of the City with designated land uses characterized by commercial office activities, services, and retail sales. Ordinarily these areas have large numbers of pedestrians and a heavy demand for parking space during periods of peak traffic or a sustained high pedestrian volume and a continuously heavy demand for off-street parking space during business hours. This definition applies to densely developed business areas outside of, as well of those that are within, the central part of the City.　B. Industrial: That portion of the City with designated land uses characterized by production, manufacturing, distribution, or fabrication activities. Ordinarily these areas have few pedestrians and a low parking turnover, but there is a large amount of truck and trailer traffic. Those portions of the City with the following zoning designations are considered for purposes of the street standards and subdivision regulations as industrial: Light Industrial, Medium Industrial, and Heavy Industrial. C. Residential: A residential development or a mixture of residential and commercial establishments characterized by a few pedestrians and a low parking demand for turnover at night. This definition includes areas with single-family homes, townhouses, and apartments. *(Renton , Wash.)*

■ **area plan**　A plan . . . that covers specific subareas of the . . . county. These plans provide basic information on the natural features, resources, and physical constraints that affect development of the planning area. They also specify detailed land-use designation used to review specific development proposals and to plan services and facilities. *(Washoe County, Nev.)*

■ **areawide zoning**　Zoning adopted for all properties within a district consistent with the comprehensive plan, rather than on a lot-by-lot basis. *(Renton, Wash.)*

■ **art gallery**　An establishment engaged in the sale, loan, or display of art books, paintings, sculpture, or other works of art. This clarification does not include libraries, museums, or non-commercial art galleries. *(Houston, Tex.)*

A room or structure in which original works of art or limited editions of original art are bought, sold, loaned, appraised or exhibited to the general public. *(Santa Monica, Calif.)*

■ **art, public**    Any visual work of art displayed for two weeks or more in an open city-owned area (pictured below), on the exterior of any city-owned facility,

within any city-owned facility in areas designated as public area, lobbies, or public assembly areas, or on non-city property if the work of art is installed or financed, either wholly or in part, with city funds or grants procured by the city. *(Palo Alto, Calif., which uses the term "art in public places")*

Any visual work of art, accessible to public view, on public or private property within the city neighborhood environs including residential, business, or industrial buildings, apartment and condominium complexes, parks, multiple-use structures, and similar facilities. The work of art may include but need not be limited to sculptures, murals, monuments, frescoes, fountains, paintings, stained glass, or ceramics. Media may include but need not be limited to steel, bronze, wood, plastic, stone, and concrete. *(Escondido, Calif.,. which uses the term "art in public places")*

A fountain, sculpture, painting, mural, or similar object that is sited within a Planned Development as a focal point

and is intended for the enjoyment of the general public. *(Champaign, Ill.)*

■ **art, works of**    All forms of original creations of visual art including but not limited to: sculpture, in any material or combination of materials, whether in the round, bas-relief, high relief, mobile, fountain, kinetic, or electronic; or painting, whether portable or permanently fixed, as in the case of murals; mosaics; photographs; crafts made from clay, fiber and textiles, wood, glass, metal, plastics, or any other material, or any combination thereof; calligraphy; mixed media composed of any combination of forms or media; unique architectural stylings or embellishments, including architectural crafts; environmental landscaping; or restoration or renovation of existing works of art of historical significance. *(Colorado State Statute)*

All forms of original creation of visual art. *(Bellevue, Wash.)*

■ **artisan**    One skilled in an applied art; a craftsman. *(San Diego, Calif.)*

■ **artisan's workshop**    An establishment, not exceeding 3,000 square feet of floor area, for the preparation, display, and sale of individually crafted artwork, jewelry, furniture, sculpture, pottery, leathercraft, hand-woven articles, and related items. *(Plano, Tex.)*

■ **artist**    A person whose major profession is the practice of an artistic discipline. *(Reno, Nev.)*

■ **artist studio**    Work space for artists or artisans, including individuals practicing one of the fine arts or skilled in an applied art or craft *(Salinas, Calif.)*

Place designed to be used, or used as, both a dwelling place and a place of work by an artist, artisan, or craftsperson, including persons engaged in the application, teaching, or performance of fine arts such as, but not limited to, drawing, vocal or instrumental music, painting, sculpture, and writing. *(St. Paul, Minn.)*

■ **as-of-right zoning** *(See also cumulative zoning; Euclidean zoning)*    Uses and development standards that are determined in advance and specifically authorized by the zoning ordinance. The ordinance, as a result, is largely self-enforcing because no flexibility is involved and no discretion occurs in its administration. For example, a single-family zone would allow single-family housing as of right so long as site development standards are met. This is the traditional Euclidean zoning system based on the earliest comprehensive ordinances and the Standard State Zoning Enabling Act. *(PAS Report No. 322, The Language of Zoning)*

■ **assembly hall** *(See also auditorium; meeting hall)*    A building or portion of a building in which facilities are provided for civic, educational, political, religious, or social purposes. *(Plano, Tex.)*

A meeting place at which the public or membership groups are assembled regularly or occasionally, including, but not limited to, schools, churches, theaters, auditoriums, funeral homes, stadiums, and similar places of assembly. *(Pine Bluff, Ark.)*

A structure for groups of people to gather for an event or regularly scheduled program. Places of public assembly include, but are not limited to, arenas, religious institutions, lecture halls, banquet facilities, and similar facilities. *(Champaign, Ill.)*

A building or a portion of a building used for gathering for such purposes as deliberation, worship, auditorium, church, or chapel, dance floor, lodge rooms, conference rooms, dining rooms, drinking establishments, exhibit rooms, or lounges. *(National City, Calif.)*

■ **assisted living** *(See elderly housing, assisted living)*

■ **athletic field**   A wide stretch of open land used for outdoor games such as baseball, football, and soccer. *(Las Cruces, N. Mex.)*

Outdoor sites, often requiring equipment, designed for formal athletic competition in field sports (e.g., softball, soccer, football). *(Guilford County, N.C.)*

■ **atrium**   A ground-level area designed for pedestrians that meets the following conditions: (a) has at least one entrance connecting to a public street, plaza, or arcade; (b) is open to the top of the building by means of a vertical open space or light well and is covered by a transparent or translucent material; (c) is open to the public during business hours; (d) has at least 25 percent of its periphery utilized by retail sales, personal services or entertainment activities; and (e) contains facilities for the public, such as benches, flower beds, fountains, etc. *(Denver, Colo.)*

A glass enclosure attached to a building on at least one of its sides. It often serves as an entry or central corridor for a building. *(Thornton, Colo.)*

■ **atrium house**   An attached dwelling unit that is designed to form a private yard through the use of building walls and fencing. *(Paramus, N.J.)*

■ **attic**   An unfinished space immediately below the roof of a main building. *(St. Paul, Minn.)*

The area between roof framing and the ceiling of the rooms below that is not habitable, but may be reached by ladder and used for storage or mechanical equipment. Improvement to habitable status shall make it a story. *(New Castle County, Del.)*

■ **auction house**   A structure or enclosure where goods and/or livestock are sold by auction. *(Yakima, Wash.)*

■ **auditorium** *(See also assembly hall; meeting hall)*   An open, partially en-

closed, or fully enclosed facility used or intended to be used primarily for spectator sports, entertainment events, expositions, and other public gatherings. Typical uses include convention and exhibition halls, sports arenas, and amphitheaters. *(Blue Springs, Mo.)*

A building or structure designed or intended for use for the gathering of people as an audience to hear music, lectures, plays, and other presentations. *(Fairbanks North Star Borough, Alaska)*

■ **automated teller machine (ATM)**   An automated device that performs banking or financial functions at a location remote from the controlling financial institution. *(Libertyville, Ill.)*

A mechanized consumer banking device operated by a financial institution for the convenience of its customers, whether outside or in an access-controlled facility. ATMs located within a building shall be considered accessory to the principal use unless the ATM is likely to be an independent traffic generator. *(Blue Spring, Mo.)*

A facility to provide banking and other electronic services that is operated by the customer. *(Nashville and Davidson County, Tenn.)*

■ **automobile**   Every vehicle, except motorcycles, designed for carrying 10 passengers or less and used for the transportation of persons. *(El Paso, Tex., which uses the term "passenger car")*

■ **automobile-accommodating development** *(See also pedestrian-oriented development)*   Development designed with an emphasis on customers who use autos to travel to the site, rather than those with an emphasis on pedestrian customers.

This type of development usually has more than the minimum required number of parking spaces. The main entrance is oriented to the parking area. In many cases, the building will have parking between the street and the building. Other typical characteristics are blank walls along much of the facade, more than one driveway, and a low percentage of the site covered by buildings. *(Portland, Ore.)*

A use of a retail area that depends on exposure to continuous auto traffic. *(California Planning Roundtable, which uses the term "automobile-intensive use")*

■ **automobile, compact**   Any vehicle less than six feet wide and 15 feet long. *(Fayetteville, Ark.)*

■ **automobile convenience mart** *(See gas station minimart)*

■ **automobile court**   A building or group of buildings attached, detached or semidetached, providing guest accommodations for transients, in which there is exterior access independently to each individual room, unit, or suite, and on which automobile storage space is provided at each unit (e.g., motel, motor lodge, motor hotel). *(Las Vegas, Nev.)*

■ **automobile dealership**   A retail business primarily housed in a structure and characterized by a mixture of related uses upon a commercial site; however, the principal use of the site shall be the marketing of new or used automobiles, whether by sale, rent, lease, or other commercial or financial means. Secondary supporting uses may also exist upon the same site, such as maintenance, repair and service areas, parts storage areas, and financial service areas. *(Nags Head, N.C.)*

Any business establishment that sells or leases new or used automobiles, trucks, vans, trailers, recreational vehicles, boats or motorcycles or other similar motorized transportation vehicles. An automobile dealership may maintain an inventory of the vehicles for sale or lease either on-site or at a nearby location and may provide on-site facilities for the repair and service of the vehicles sold or leased by the dealership. *(Santa Monica, Calif.)*

■ **automobile dealership, new** The use of any building, land area, or other premises or portion thereof, for the display, sale, or lease of new automobiles, panel trucks or vans, trailers or recreational vehicles and including any warranty repair work and other repair service conducted as an accessory use. *(Southhaven, Miss.)*

■ **automobile dealership, used** The use of land for the display or sale of used automobiles, panel truck or vans, trailers or recreational vehicles. *(Southhaven, Miss.)*

■ **automobile graveyard** The dismantling or wrecking of used motor vehicles or trailers, or the storage, sale, or dumping of dismantled or wrecked vehicles or their parts. The presence on any lot or parcel of land of tow or more motor vehicles, which for a period exceeding 30 days, have not been capable of operating under their own power and from which parts have been or are to be removed for reuse or sale, shall constitute prima-facie evidence of an automobile wrecking yard. *(Vista, Calif.)*

Any lot or place that is exposed to the weather and upon which more than five motor vehicles of any kind incapable of being operated and not currently licensed are placed, located, or found. *(Thurston County, Wash.)*

■ **automobile impound facility** A facility that provides temporary outdoor storage for Class I vehicles that are to be claimed by titleholders or their agents. No vehicle shall be stored at said facility for more than 45 days and must remain mechanically operable and licensed at all times. *(Peoria, Ill.)*

A parcel of land or a building that is used for the storage of wrecked motor vehicles usually awaiting insurance adjustment or transport to a repair shop and where motor vehicles are kept for a period of time not exceeding 14 days. *(Las Vegas, Nev.)*

■ **automobile mall** A single location that provides sales space and centralized services for a number of automobile dealers (pictured at right) and that may include such related services as auto in-

surance dealers and credit institutions that provide financing opportunities. *(California Planning Roundtable)*

■ **automobile parts/supply, retail** The use of any land area for the display and sale of new or used parts for automobiles, panel trucks or vans, trailers, or recreation vehicles. *(Plano, Tex.)*

■ **automobile rental/leasing** Leasing or renting of automobiles, motorcycles, and light load vehicles. *(Plano, Tex.)*

Rental of automobiles and light trucks and vans, including incidental parking and servicing of vehicles for rent or lease. Typical uses include auto rental agencies and taxicab dispatch areas. *(Blacksburg, Va.)*

■ **automobile repair services** *(See also **motor vehicle, general repair and service**)* Any building, structure, improvements, or land used for the repair and maintenance of automobiles, motorcycles, trucks, trailers, or similar vehicles including but not limited to body, fender, muffler or upholstery work, oil change and lubrication, painting, tire service and sales, or installation of CB radios, car alarms, stereo equipment or cellular telephones. *(Santa Monica, Calif.)*

The use of a site for the repair of automobiles, noncommercial trucks, motorcycles, motor-homes, recreational vehicles, or boats, including the sale, installation, and servicing of equipment and parts. This use includes muffler shops, auto repair garages, tire sales and installation, wheel and brake shops, body and fender shops, and similar repair and service activities, but excludes dismantling or salvage. *(Austin, Tex.)*

■ **automobile repair services, major** General repair, rebuilding, or recondi-

tioning of engines, motor vehicles or trailers, including body work, framework, welding, and major painting service. *(Eagan, Minn.)*

■ **automobile repair services, minor** The replacement of any part or repair of any part that does not require removal of the engine head or pan, engine transmission or differential; incidental body and fender work, minor painting and upholstering service. Above stated is applied to passenger automobiles and trucks not in excess of 7,000 pounds gross weight. *(Eagan, Minn.)*

■ **automobile sales** Storage and display for sale of more than two motor vehicles or any type of trailer provided the trailer is unoccupied, and where repair or body work is incidental to the operation of the new or used vehicle sales. Motor vehicles sales includes motor vehicle retail or wholesale sales. *(Cecil County, Md.)*

The use of any building or portion thereof, or other premises or portion thereof, for the display, sale, rental or lease of new motor vehicles, or used motor vehicles as an ancillary use of a zoning lot, and any warranty repair work and other repair service conducted as an accessory use. *(Schaumburg, Ill.)*

■ **automobile sales lot** Premises on which new or used passenger automobiles, trailers, mobile homes or trucks in operating condition are displayed in the open for sale or trade. *(Belmont, Calif.)*

Any such lot where vehicles are sold. Vehicles on these lots must be able to pass state vehicle inspection requirements. *(Pine Bluff, Ark.)*

■ **auxiliary massage establishment** *(See also **massage establishment**)* Any

building or tenant space in which any person, firm, association, or corporation, or any person employed by such person, firm, association, or corporation, engages, or is permitted to engage in the practice of massage as an accessory use customary and clearly incidental to a principal business and use, including but not limited to services offered by a hotel, health club or spa, or beauty salon. *(Gurnee, Ill.)*

■ **aviary**    A place for keeping birds confined for the purpose of raising, exhibiting, or selling. *(Faquier County, Va.)*

■ **awning**    A temporary hood or cover that projects from the wall of a building and that may include a type which can be retracted, folded, or collapsed against the face of a supporting building. *(Asheville, N.C. )*

A roof-like cover, often of fabric, metal, or glass designed and intended for protection from the weather or as a decorative embellishment, and which projects from a wall or roof of a structure over a window, walk, door, or the like. *(Bloomington, Minn.)*

■ **awning, fixed**    An awning constructed with a rigid frame that cannot be retracted, folded, or collapsed. *(Columbus, Ohio)*

■ **awning, illuminated**    A fixed awning covered with a translucent membrane that is, in whole or part, illuminated by light passing through the membrane from within the structure; also known as an "electric awning." *(Columbus, Ohio)*

■ **awning, retractable**    An awning that can be, retracted, folded, or collapsed against the face of the supporting building. *(Columbus, Ohio)*

■ **backfill** (*See also* **borrow; fill**) Materials used to refill a ditch or other excavation, or the process of doing so. (*McHenry County, Ill.*)

■ **bakery, retail** An establishment primarily engaged in the retail sale of baked products for consumption off site. The products may be prepared either on or off site. Such use may include incidental food service. A bakery shall be considered a general retail use. (*Santa Monica, Calif.*)

A place for preparing, cooking, baking, and selling of products on the premises. (*Plano, Tex., which uses the term "bakery & confectionary works (retail)"*)

■ **bakery, wholesale** A bakery in which there is permitted the production and/or wholesaling of baked goods, but where over-the-counter or other retail dispensing of baked goods shall be prohibited. (*Aspen, Colo., which uses the term "bakery, commercial"*)

A place for preparing, cooking, baking, and selling of products intended for off-premise distribution. (*Plano, Tex., which uses the term "bakery and confectionary works (wholesale)"*)

■ **balcony** A platform that projects from the wall of a building and is surrounded by a railing or balustrade. (*Park City, Utah*)

A platform enclosed by a railing or parapet projecting from the wall of a building for the private use of tenants or for exterior access to the above-grade living units. When a balcony is roofed and enclosed, it is considered part of the room it serves. (*Imperial Beach, Calif.*)

■ **balloon** A nonporous bag of light material filled with heated air or a gas lighter than air so as to rise and float in the atmosphere and intended to be flown in the air at the end of a cable, wire, or rope. (*Albuquerque, N. Mex.*)

■ **bank** (*See also* **accessory banking; automated teller machine (ATM); financial institution**) A freestanding building, with or without a drive-up window, for the custody, loan, or exchange of money; for the extension of credit; and for facilitating the transmission of funds. (*Redmond, Wash.*)

A financial institution that is open to the public and engaged in deposit banking, and that performs closely related functions such as making loans, investments, and fiduciary activities. (*Palm Beach Gardens, Fla.*)

■ **banner** (*See* **sign, banner**)

■ **banquet hall** A facility or hall available for lease by private parties. (*Miami, Fla.*)

■ **bar** (*See also* **tavern**) An area primarily devoted to the serving of alcoholic beverages and in which the service of food is only incidental to the consumption of such beverages. (*Blue Springs, Mo.*)

An establishment or part of an establishment used primarily for the sale or dispensing of liquor by the drink. (*Camden, Maine*)

Any place devoted primarily to the selling, serving, or dispensing and drinking of malt, vinous, or other alcoholic beverages, or any place where any sign is exhibited or displayed indicating that alcoholic beverages are obtainable within or thereon, and where such beverages are consumed on the premises. (*West Des Moines, Iowa*)

■ **barber shop** Any establishment or place of business within which the practice of barbering is engaged in or carried on by one or more barbers. (*Norfolk, Va.*)

■ **barn** A large accessory building used exclusively for the storage of grain, hay, and other farm products, and/or the sheltering of livestock or farm equipment. (*Germantown, Tenn.*)

■ **barnyard** A fenced area adjoining a barn used primarily for the keeping of animals. (*Unalaska, Alaska*)

■ **base density** (*See* **density, base**)

■ **base flood** The flood, from whatever source, having a 1 percent chance of being equaled or exceeded in any given year, otherwise commonly referred to as the 100-year flood. (*Kauai County, Hawaii*)

■ **base flood elevation** That elevation, expressed in feet above mean sea level, to which flooding can be expected to occur on a frequency of once in every 100 years, or which is subject to a 1 percent or greater chance of flooding in any given year. (*Yakima County, Wash.*)

■ **base map** A map showing the important natural and man-made features of an area. Such maps are used to establish consistency when maps are used for various purposes (e.g., reproductions of the same base map could be used to show natural resource limitations, public facilities, and land use as the basis for the official zoning map). (*PAS Report No. 322, The Language of Zoning*)

■ **basement** (*See also* **cellar; crawlspace**) That portion of a building below the first or ground-floor level and having less than four feet of clearance from its ceiling to the average finished grade of the building perimeter. A basement shall not be considered a story for the purposes of determining building height, except when it is used or suitable for habitation. (*Bloomington, Ind.*)

That portion of a building between floor and ceiling which is so located that one-half (1/2) or more of the clear height from floor to ceiling is below grade. The basement shall not be used as a habitable room. *(Coral Gables, Fla.)*

Any floor level below the first story in a building, except that a floor level in a building having only one floor level shall be classified as a basement unless such floor level qualifies as a first story as defined herein. *(Imperial Beach, Calif.)*

■ **batching plant**    A plant for the manufacture or mixing of concrete, cement, and concrete and cement products, including any apparatus and uses incident to such manufacturing and mixing. *(National City, Calif.)*

■ **bathhouse** *(See also* **health spa; sauna***)* A use or business that provides the services of baths of all kinds, including all forms and methods of hydrotherapy, unless operated or supervised by a medical or chiropractic practitioner or professional physical therapist licensed by the state. *(Blue Springs, Mo.)*

■ **bathroom/bath**    A space containing a wash basin and water closet. It may include a bathtub or shower or both. *(Albuquerque, N. Mex.)*

■ **bathroom, full**    A room or other enclosure containing a water closet, lavatory, bathtub, and shower. *(San Diego, Calif.)*

A space containing a wash basin and water closet. It may include a bathtub or shower or both. *(Albuquerque, N. Mex.)*

■ **bathroom, half**    A room or other enclosure containing only a water closet and lavatory. *(San Diego, Calif.)*

■ **bathroom, three-quarter**    A room or other enclosure containing a water closet, lavatory, and either a bathtub or shower. *(San Diego, Calif.)*

■ **beach**    The land between the edge of the sea and the first line of terrestrial vegetation (pictured above) or development or the toe of an adjacent sensitive coastal bluff or seawall, whichever is most seaward. *(San Diego, Calif.)*

The soft sand portion of land lying seaward of a seawall or line of permanent

vegetation and seaward of the mean high-water line. *(Fort Myers Beach, Fla.)*

■ **beach club**    A membership establishment, not available for use by the general public, providing for recreational and social activities related to and in close proximity to the beach. *(Indian River County, Fla.)*

■ **beach house**    A permanent structure that may contain a bathroom and other rooms, but not a kitchen or any sleeping rooms, and not used as a dwelling unit. *(Palm Beach, Fla.)*

■ **beacon**    A stationary or revolving light that flashes or projects illumination, single color or multicolored, in any manner that is intended to attract or divert attention; not including any kind of lighting device required or necessary under the safety regulations described by the Federal Aviation Agency or similar agencies. *(Clearwater, Fla.)*

■ **beauty salon**    Any commercial establishment, residence, vehicle, or other establishment, place, or event wherein cosmetology is offered or practiced on a regular basis for compensation; may include the training of apprentices under regulations of the board. *(Norfolk, Va., which uses the term "cosmetology salon")*

■ **bed**    The material extending toward the water from the ordinary high-water mark, which supports streams, lakes, and vegetated shallows. *(Yakima County, Wash.)*

■ **bed-and-breakfast (B&B)**    Formerly a single-family dwelling in the four- to five-room range, this owner-occupied establishment has an equally mixed use as home and lodging with lodging superseding home more often than not. It is located

in a legally zoned area and meets all the tax, fire, building and health requirements for this size and use of property. This establishment advertises publicly and can legally post a sign. Like the homestay or host home, because of its size, these B & Bs usually cannot support a family unit, so the B & B is often one partner's job and the other has outside income. Often the property is purchased specifically to be a B & B, but many are converted family homes. Reservations may be made directly wit the property. *(Professional Association of Innkeepers International)*

A private residence that offers sleeping accommodations to lodgers in 14 or fewer rooms for rent, in the innkeeper's (owner or operator) principal residence while renting rooms to lodgers; and serves breakfasts at no extra cost to its lodgers. For the purpose of this definition, a lodger means a person who rents a room in a bed-and-breakfast establishment for fewer than 30 consecutive days. *(Cascade Charter Township, Mich.)*

A transient lodging establishment, generally in a single-family dwelling and/or detached guesthouses, primarily engaged in providing overnight or otherwise temporary lodging for the general public and may provide meals for compensation. *(Hemet, Calif.)*

■ **bed-and-breakfast (B&B) inn**    Generally small, owner-operated businesses providing the primary financial support of the owner. Usually the owner lives on premises. The building's primary usage is for business. Inns advertise, appropriate taxes, and post signs. Breakfast is the only meal served and only to overnight guests. The inn may host events such as weddings, small business meetings, etc.

Room numbers range from 4-20 with a small, but increasing number up to 30. Reservations may be made directly with the property. *(Professional Association of Innkeepers International)*

A private, owner-occupied business with 4 to 20 guest rooms where overnight accommodations and a morning meal are provided to transients for compensation and where the bed and breakfast inn is operated primarily as a business. *(Asheville, N.C.)*

An owner-occupied building at least 50 years old designed for and used as a single-family or two-family dwelling that provides four or fewer lodging rooms or accommodating no more than eight adults, in which meals are provided to overnight guests, and that is open to the traveling public for a stay not to exceed 20 days. *(Grand Forks, ND)*

■ **bedrock**    In-place solid rock. *(Yakima County, Wash.)*

■ **bedrock, exposed/shallow**    Bedrock which is exposed or which has irregular patches of soil cover that may vary in depth or location over time. The maximum depth of the soil cover is three feet. Locations containing exposed/shallow bedrock shall be mapped if they have a minimum horizontal dimension of 40 feet or more. *(Scottsdale, Ariz.)*

■ **bedroom** *(See also* **room; sleeping room***)*

*Commentary: Some zoning codes define bedroom to include studies, dens, or family rooms. This is usually done when the code establishes the required number of off-street parking spaces based on the number of bedrooms in the dwelling unit. For example, suppose a community requires 1.3 parking spaces per dwelling unit with one bedroom or less and 1.6 parking spaces for each dwelling that has more than one bedroom. The term must be defined broadly in order to prevent developers from subverting the requirement by claiming that a two-bedroom unit is only a one-bedroom unit with a den.*

A room located within a housing unit that is used primarily for sleeping purposes by human occupants and that contains at least 70 square feet of floor area. *(Burlington, Vt.)*

That portion of a dwelling unit designed to be suitable for sleeping purposes, which may contain closets, may have access to a bathroom, and meets Uniform Building Code requirements for light and ventilation. *(Aspen, Colo.)*

A room intended for, or capable of, being used for sleeping and that is at least 70 square feet in area. A room designated on building plan submittals as a "den," "library," "study," "loft," dining room, or other extra room that satisfies the definition and is not a kitchen, living room, or bath will be considered to be a bedroom for the purpose of computing bedroom area. *(Champaign, Ill.)*

Any room used principally for sleeping purposes and does not contain separate kitchen and sanitary facilities. *(Mankato, Minn.)*

■ **below-market-rate (BMR) housing unit** *(See also* **affordable housing***)* 1. Any housing unit specifically priced to be sold or rented to low- or moderate-income households for an amount less than the fair-market value of the unit. Both the State of California and the U.S. Department of Housing and Urban Development set standards for determining which households qualify as "low income" or "moderate income." 2. The financing of housing at less than prevailing interest rates. *(California Planning Roundtable)*

■ **benchmark**    A performance-monitoring standard that allows a local government to periodically measure the extent to which the goals and policies of a local comprehensive land are being achieved. *(APA's Growing Smart project)*

Measurement of progress toward [a] vision of well-being in such terms as family stability, early childhood development, K-12 student achievement, air and water quality, housing affordability, crime, employment, and per capita income. *(Oregon Benchmarks)*

■ **benchmarking**    A public participation process that offers an integrated, comprehensive look at quality of life by defining community goals in terms of people, land, and economic assets. *(Noblesville, Ind.)*

A process to regularly collect, monitor, and analyze data on the achievement of the goals and policies of a local comprehensive plan. *(APA's Growing Smart project)*

■ **benefit assessment district** *(See also* **special benefit district***)*    An area within a public agency's boundaries that receives a special benefit from the construction of one or more public facilities. A Benefit Assessment District has no legal life of its own and cannot act by itself. It is strictly a financing mechanism for providing public infrastructure as allowed under the Streets And Highways Code. Bonds may be issued to finance the improvements, subject to repayment by assessments charged against the benefitting properties. Creation of a Benefit Assessment District enables property owners in a specific area to cause the construction of public facilities or to maintain them (for example, a downtown, or the grounds and landscaping of a specific area) by contributing their fair share of the construction and/or installation and operating costs. *(California Planning Roundtable)*

■ **berm**    An earthen mound designed to provide visual interest on a site (pic-

tured on page 31), screen undesirable views, reduce noise, or fulfill other such purposes. *(Asheville, N.C. )*

A man-made mound of earth in excess of two feet in vertical height used to shield or buffer properties from adjoining uses, highways, or noise, or to control the direction of surface water flow. *(Mequon, Wisc.)*

A mound or embankment of earth, usually two to six feet in height.

■ **berm, bank top**   The point where the upward slope of the land from the water surface or the bottom of a dry excavation intersects with the existing ground elevation or crest of berm, whichever is of higher elevation. *(Indian River County, Fla.)*

■ **berth**   A place or structure built along or at an angle from the shore of navigable water for the mooring of boats. *(Islip, N.Y., which uses the term "boat berth")*

A space within a loading facility, exclusive of driveways, aisles, maneuvering areas, ramps, columns, landscaping areas, office, and work areas, for the temporary parking of a commercial vehicle while loading or unloading goods or materials, and which abuts upon a street, alley, or other appropriate means of access. *(National City, Calif.)*

■ **best management practices**   A structural or nonstructural management-based practice used singularly or in combination to reduce nonpoint source inputs to receiving waters in order to achieve water quality protection goals. *(Guilford County, N.C. )*

Any activities, prohibitions, practices, procedures, programs, or other measures designed to prevent or reduce the discharge of pollutants directly or indirectly into waters of the United States. Shall include, but are not limited to, those measures specified in the [state authority] stormwater best management practice handbooks for municipal, industrial/commercial, and construction activity and those measures identified by the city engineer. *(Hemet, Calif.)*

That combination of conservation measures, structure, or management prac-

tices that reduces or avoids adverse impacts of development on adjoining site's land, water, or waterways, and waterbodies. *(New Castle County, Del.)*

Conservation practices or systems of practices and management measures that: (a) control soil loss and reduce water-quality degradation caused by nutrients, animal waste, toxins, and sediment; (b) minimize adverse impacts to surface water and groundwater flow, circulation patterns, and to the chemical, physical, and biological characteristics of wetlands; and (c) includes allowing proper use and storage of fertilizers/pesticides. *(Renton, Wash.)*

■ **bicycle**   Every device propelled by human power upon which any person may ride, having two tandem wheels except scooters and similar devices. *(Waukegan, Ill.)*

Any foot-propelled vehicle, irrespective of the number of wheels in contact with the ground. *(Carmel, Ind.)*

■ **bicycle facilities**   A general term denoting improvements and provisions to accommodate or encourage bicycling, including parking facilities, maps, all bikeways, and shared roadways not specifically designated for bicycle use. *(Indian River County, Fla.)*

■ **big-box retail**   *(See also shopping center definitions)*   A singular retail or wholesale user who occupies no less than 75,000 square feet of gross floor area, typically requires high parking to building area ratios (pictured above), and has a regional sales market. Regional retail/wholesale sales can in-

clude, but are not limited to, membership warehouse clubs that emphasize bulk sales, discount stores, and department stores. *(Redmond, Wash., which uses the term "large-box retail")*

■ **bike lane (Class I facility)**   A corridor expressly reserved for bicycles, existing on a street or roadway in addition to any lanes for use by motorized vehicles. *(Temecula, Calif.)*

Those bikeways on existing street rights-of-way where a portion of the roadway is set aside for exclusive bicycle use and designated by signs placed on vertical posts or stencilled on the pavement and by a painted line marking the bicycle land on the pavement. Through travel by motor vehicles or pedestrians is prohibited. Vehicular parking may or may not be allowed or it may be restricted to certain hours of each day. Cross-flows by motor vehicles and pedestrians when necessary to gain access to and from a public street or alley and/or a private driveway or other entranceway are permitted. *(Raleigh, N.C.)*

A paved route not on a street or roadway, and expressly reserved for bicycles traversing an otherwise unpaved area. Bicycle paths may parallel roads but typically are separated from them by landscaping. *(California Planning Roundtable)*

■ **bike path (Class II facility)**   A portion of a roadway or separate pathway designated for use by bicycles. *(Las Cruces, N. Mex.)*

An off-street bikeway. *(Colts Neck, N.J.)*

Those bikeways on existing street rights-of-way or on a completely separated right-of-way or easement or upon and across parks, schools, or other publicly owned lands where a path is designated for the exclusive or semi-exclusive use of bicycles. Use by pedestrians may or may not be permitted. The parking of any through traffic by motor vehicles is prohibited. Cross-flows by motor vehicles and pedestrians, when necessary to gain access to and from a public street or alley and/or a private driveway or other entranceway, are permitted. *(Raleigh, N.C.)*

■ **bike path (Class III facility)** A facility shared with motorists and identified only by signs; a bicycle route has no pavement markings or lane stripes. *(Temecula, Calfi.)*

Any road, street, path or way which in some manner is specifically designated as being open to bicycle travel, regardless of whether the facility is designed for the exclusive use of bicycles or is to be shared with other transportation modes. *(Gainesville, Fla.)*

■ **bike route** Those bikeways on existing street rights-of-way where bicycles share the roadway with motor vehicles. Bicycle routes are designed by signs placed on vertical posts or stencilled on the pavement. Parking may or may not be allowed or it may be restricted to only certain hours of each day. *(Raleigh, N.C.)*

■ **bike way** All thoroughfares that explicitly provide for bicycle travel including facilities existing within street and highway rights-of-way and facilities along separate and independent corridors. *(Raleigh, N.C.)*

■ **billboard** *(See sign, billboard)*

■ **bingo hall** A facility used primarily for the conduct of bingo games, open to the public and not in a subsidiary nature to another use. *(Virginia Beach, Va.)*

■ **biomass** Plant material, used for the production of such things as fuel alcohol and nonchemical fertilizers. Biomass sources may be plants grown especially for that purpose or waste products from livestock, harvesting, milling, or from agricultural production or processing. *(California Planning Roundtable)*

■ **biotic community** *(See also **wildlife habitat**)* A group of living organisms characterized by a distinctive combination of both animal and plant species in a particular habitat. *(California Planning Roundtable)*

■ **blight** Unsightly condition including the accumulation of debris, litter, rubbish, or rubble; fences characterized by holes, breaks, rot, crumbling, cracking, peeling or rusting; landscaping that is dead, characterized by uncontrolled growth or lack of maintenance, or damaged; and any other similar conditions of disrepair and deterioration regardless of the condition of other properties in the neighborhood. *(Lincoln, Nebr.)*

■ **block** An area of land bounded by a street, or by a combination of streets and public parks, cemeteries, railroad rights-of-way, exterior boundaries of a subdivision, shorelines of waterways, or corporate boundaries. *(Ames, Iowa)*

An area of land entirely bounded by streets. *(Blue Springs, Mo.)*

The property abutting one side of a street and lying between the two nearest intersecting streets (crossing or terminating), or between the nearest such street and railroad right-of-way, unsubdivided acreage, lake, river, or live stream, or between any of the foregoing and any other physical barrier to the continuity of development, or corporate boundary line of the municipality. *(St. Paul, Minn.)*

A block consists of two facing block fronts bounded on two sides by alleys or rear property lines and on two sides by the centerline of platted streets, with no other intersecting streets intervening. Where blocks are unusually long or short, or of unusual shape, block length shall be determined by address ranges. *(Renton, Wash.)*

A unit of land bounded by streets or by a combination of streets and public land, railroad rights-of-way, waterways, or any other barrier to the continuity of development. *(Nashville and Davidson County, Tenn.)*

■ **block, business** Frontage in any commercial or industrial district on one side of a street between the two nearest intersecting streets (or between an intersecting street and railroad right-of-way or unsubdivided acreage) 50 percent or more of which is in use for business or industrial purposes. *(Santa Clara County, Calif.)*

■ **block grant** *(See also **Community Development Block Grant (CDBG); target area**)* A grant which can be used to fund a wide range of community improvement projects or programs. It is a multipurpose grant and is not to be used for a single specific purpose. *(Handbook for Planning Commissioners in Missouri)*

■ **blockface** The properties abutting on one side of a street and lying between the two nearest intersecting or intercepting streets, or nearest intersecting or intercepting street and railroad right-of-way, unsubdivided land, watercourse, or city boundary. *(Huntington Beach, Calif.)*

The portion of a block that abuts a street. *(Houston, Tex.)*

■ **blockfront** A block front means the frontage of property along one side of a street bound on three sides by the centerline of platted streets and on the fourth side by an alley or rear property lines. *(Renton, Wash.)*

■ **bluff** A steep headland, promontory, riverbank, or cliff. *(Asheville, N.C.)*

An escarpment or steep face of rock, decomposed rock, sediment, or soil resulting from erosion, faulting, folding, or excavation of the land mass that has a vertical relief of 10 feet or more and is in the coastal zone. *(San Diego, Calif.)*

■ **board of supervisors** A county's legislative body. Board members are elected by popular vote and are responsible for enacting ordinances, imposing taxes, making appropriations and establishing county policy. The board adopts the general plan, zoning, and subdivision regulations. *(Sierra, California, Business Council)*

■ **board of zoning appeals and adjustments** A local body, appointed by the city council, whose responsibility is to hear appeals from decisions of the director of planning and development and to consider requests for variances and exceptions. *(Conyers, Ga.)*

■ **boarder** (*See also* ***roomer; tenant***) A person who occupies a bedroom or room as a lodging unit within a dwelling unit, boardinghouse, rooming house, or lodging house on a long-term residential basis for a consideration and where meals may be provided by the owner or operator. (*Maui County, Hawaii*)

■ **boarding house** (*See also* ***lodging house; rooming house***) A single-family dwelling where more than two, but fewer than six rooms are provided for lodging for definite periods of times. Meals may or may not be provided, but there is one common kitchen facility. No meals are provided to outside guests. (*Champaign, Ill., which uses the term "boarding/rooming house"*)

An establishment with lodging for five or more persons where meals are regularly prepared and served for compensation and where food is placed upon the table family style, without service or ordering of individual portions from a menu. (*Venice, Fla.*)

■ **boat** Any vehicle designed for travel on water, not exceeding 35 feet in body length and eight feet in width. (*Gainesville, Fla.*)

A vehicle for traveling in or on water, not exceeding 30 feet in body length, 8 feet in width, or 11 feet in overall height. Height includes the trailer, if the boat is mounted on a trailer. (*Albuquerque, N. Mex.*)

A vehicle designed for operation as a watercraft propelled by oars, sails, or one or more internal combustion engine(s). A boat shall not be considered as a recreational vehicle even though it has facilities for temporary living quarters. (*Indian River County, Fla.*)

■ **boat launch/ramp** Facility to launch and retrieve recreational boats from a trailer. Some are limited to hand launching of canoes. Most ramps have breakwater protection from large waves, parking lots, a courtesy dock to assist in launching, toilets, refuse containers, lighting, and telephones. (*Green Bay, Wis.*)

■ **boat (large) sales and/or rental** A marine retail sales and service use in which boats 16 feet or more in length are rented or sold. The sale or rental of smaller boats shall be defined as a major durables sales and service use. (*Seattle, Wash.*)

■ **boat livery** A commercial establishment providing boat hauling or launching facilities, rental of covered or uncovered boat slips or dock space or enclosed dry storage space, rental or sale of boats and boat motors, repair and maintenance of boats and boat motors, sale of marine fuel and lubricants, and as accessory service uses, on-shore restaurants, hotels, or motels, and sale of bait and fishing equipment. The term boat livery includes marinas but shall not be deemed to include boat yards. (*Indian River County, Fla.*)

■ **boat parts or accessories sales** A marine retail sales and service use in which goods are rented or sold primarily for use on boats and ships but excluding uses in which fuel for boats and ships is the primary item sold. Examples of goods sold include navigational instruments, marine hardware and paints, nautical publications, nautical clothing such as foul-weather gear, marine engines, and boats less than 16 feet in length. (*Seattle, Wash.*)

■ **boat repair facility** A facility (which could include a boat repair garage, boat storage yard) where boats are repaired and stored until repairs are completed. (*Valdez, Alaska*)

■ **boat slip** A space designed for the mooring of a single watercraft. Such spaces may extend from a dock or shoreline but shall not be allowed to project from a pier. (*Indian River County, Fla.*)

■ **boat yard** A premise or site used as an industrial establishment for the provision of all such facilities as are customary and necessary to the construction, reconstruction, repair, or maintenance and accessory sale of boats, marine engines, or marine equipment, supplies, or services of all kinds (pictured at left) including, but not limited to, rental of covered or uncovered boat slips, or dock space or enclosed dry storage space, lifting or launching services. The term boat yards shall include marinas and boat liveries. (*Indian River County, Fla.*)

■ **boatel** One or more buildings containing guest rooms or dwelling units that are designed, used, or intended to be used, wholly or in part, for the accommodation of boat transients or tourists and which are located near or abutting a river, lake, or ocean. (*Thousand Oaks, Calif.*)

■ **boathouse** An enclosed or partially enclosed structure designed for the use and storage of private watercraft and marine equipment. (*Traverse City, Mich.*)

Accessory structure constructed either wholly or partially over a body of water and designed primarily to provide shelter for water craft or for marine-related equipment. (*York County, Va.*)

■ **body art** The practice of physical body adornment by establishments and artists using, but not limited to, the techniques of body piercing and tattooing. This definition does not include, for the purposes of the code, ear piercing. *(Denver, Colo.)*

■ **body-painting studio** A business establishment wherein the patrons may apply paint or similar matter to another unclothed or partially clothed person. *(Imperial Beach, Calif.)*

■ **body piercing** *(See also **tattoo**)* The act of penetrating the skin to make, generally permanent in nature, a hole, mark, or scar. Body piercing does not include the use of a mechanized, pre-sterilized ear-piercing system that penetrates the outer perimeter or lobe of the ear or both. *(Ft. Myers Beach, Fla.)*

The perforation of human tissue other than an ear for a nonmedical purpose. *(Alma, Mich.)*

■ **bonus** *(See also **incentive zoning**)* Inducements given to developers under the provisions of incentive zoning. *(PAS Report No. 322, The Language of Zoning)*

■ **bookstore** A retail establishment that, as its primary business, engages in the sale, rental, or other charge-for-use of books, magazines, newspapers, greeting cards, postcards, videotapes, computer software, and/or any other printed or electronically conveyed information or media, excluding any "adult bookstore," "adult theater," "theater," or "studio theater." *(Denver, Colo.)*

■ **borrow** *(See also **backfill; fill**)* Fill material required for on-site construction and obtained from other locations. *(Guilford County, N.C.)*

■ **borrow pit** *(See also **backfill**)* An area from which soil or other unconsolidated material are removed to be used, without further processing, as fill for activities such as landscaping, building construction, or highway construction and maintenance. *(Carroll County, Md.)*

Any place or premises where dirt, soil, sand, gravel, or other material is removed below the grade of surrounding land, for any purpose other than that necessary and incidental to site grading or building construction. *(Schaumburg, Ill.)*

■ **botanical gardens** A public or private facility for the demonstration and observation of the cultivation of flowers, fruits, vegetables, or ornamental plants. *(Renton, Wash.)*

■ **bottle club** Any establishment engaged in the business of catering to patrons who bring to the establishment an alcoholic beverage to be consumed on the premises with a mixer or other beverage, ice, food, or container furnished by the establishment for a consideration, or in connection with the viewing of, entertainment for a consideration, or where admission to the premises is for a consideration. *(Boca Raton, Fla.)*

■ **boulevard** *(See **street, boulevard**)*

■ **boundary** A line, which may or may not follow a visible feature, that defines the limits of a geographic entity such as a block, block numbering area, census tract, county, or place. *(United States Census Bureau)*

■ **bowling alley** An establishment that devotes more than 50 percent of its

gross floor area to bowling lanes, equipment, and playing area. *(Austin, Tex.)*

■ **breakaway wall** A wall that is not part of the structural support of the building and is intended through its design and construction to collapse under specific lateral loading forces without causing damage to the elevated portion of the building or the supporting foundation system. *(Escambia County, Fla.)*

■ **breakwater** *(See also **jetty**)* A protective structure, usually built off-shore for the purpose of protecting the shoreline or harbor areas from wave action. *(Renton, Wash.)*

A fixed or floating off-shore structure that protects a shoreline from wave action or currents. *(Yakima County, Wash.)*

■ **breezeway** A structure for the principal purpose of connecting the main building or buildings on a property with other main buildings or accessory buildings. *(Camas, Wash.)*

■ **brew-on-premises store** A facility that provides the ingredients and equipment for a customer to use to brew malt liquor at the store. Intoxicating liquor may not be sold or otherwise provided to customers of a brew-on-premises store unless the owner of the brew-on-premises store holds the appropriate liquor license. Customers using the brew-on-premises store must be of minimum age to purchase intoxicating liquor. Intoxicating malt liquor brewed by a customer may not be sold and must be used by the customer for personal or family use. *(St. Paul, Minn.)*

■ **brew pub** *(See also microbrewery)* A restaurant that manufactures up to 5,000 barrels of fermented malt beverages per year on premises for either consumption on premises in hand-capped or sealed containers in quantities up to one-half barrel or 15 and one-half gallons sold directly to the consumer. Wholesaling shall be permitted only where authorized within the zoning code. *(Madison, Wisc.)*

An eating place that includes the brewing of beer as an accessory use. The brewing operation processes water, malt, hops, and yeast into beer or ale by mashing, cooking, and fermenting. The area used for brewing, including bottling and kegging, shall not exceed 25 percent of the total floor area of the commercial space. The brewery shall not produce more than 1,500 barrels of beer or ale per year. A barrel is equivalent to 31 gallons. *(Vail, Colo.)*

A restaurant that prepares handcrafted natural beer as an accessory use intended for consumption on the premises. Production capacity shall be limited to not more than 5,000 barrels per year. Such accessory use may occupy up to 30 percent of the gross floor area of the restaurant. *(Melbourne, Fla.)*

■ **brewery** An industrial use that brews ales, beers, meads and/or similar beverages on site. Breweries are classified as a use that manufactures more than 15,000 barrels of beverage (all beverages combined) annually. In addition, uses that manufacture 15,000 barrels of beverage or less, but which do not meet one or more of the additional requirements needed to be considered brewpubs, are breweries. *(Bloomington, Ind.)*

A facility with a capacity to manufacture more than 1 million barrels of alcoholic and nonalcoholic malt liquor a year. This definition excludes brew on premises stores as defined herein and/or small breweries operated in conjunction with a bar or restaurant defined herein as an accessory use. *(St. Paul, Minn., which uses the term "brewery, national")*

■ **bridge** A structure carrying a path, street, or railway over water, and necessary support structures. *(Seattle, Wash.)*

■ **brownfield** Abandoned, idled, or underused industrial and commercial facilities where expansion or redevelopment is complicated by real or perceived environmental contamination. *(United States Environmental Protection Agency)*

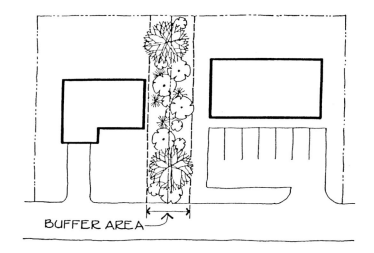

BUFFER AREA

A vacant or unoccupied site with respect to any portion of which the owner has reasonable cause to believe may, as a result of any prior commercial or industrial activity by any person, have been environmentally contaminated by the release or threatened release of a hazardous substance as defined under (chapter) in a manner that would interfere with the owner's intended use of such site. *(New Castle County, Del.)*

■ **buffer** A strip of land, fence, or border of trees, etc., between one use and another, which may or may not have trees and shrubs planted for screening purposes, designed to set apart one use area from another. An appropriate buffer may

vary depending on uses, districts, size, etc., and shall be determined by the [appropriate local board]. *Pomfret Township, N.Y.)*

An area of land, including landscaping, berms, walls, fences, and building setbacks, that is located between land uses of different character and is intended to mitigate negative impacts of the more intense use on a residential or vacant parcel. *(Dona Ana County, N. Mex.)*

A strip of land with natural or planted vegetation located between a structure and a side or rear property line intended to separate and partially obstruct the view of two adjacent land uses or properties from one another. A buffer area may include any required screening for the site. *(Charlotte, N.C.)*

■ **buffer strip** A portion of a lot or a land area used to visually separate one use from another through the use of vegetation, screening and distance; to shield or obstruct noise illumination, visual, or other incompatibilities or nuisances. A buffer is measured from the common property line of the different uses. *(Conyers, Ga.)*

■ **buffer yard** A unit of land, together with a specified type and amount of planting thereon, and any structures which may be required between land uses to eliminate or minimize conflicts between them. *(Grand Forks, N. Dak.)*

A yard containing materials used to provide sight and sound screening from adjoining properties and rights-of-way. The required height and width of the buffer yard and materials used in its construction vary according to use. *(Nags Head, N.C.)*

■ **buffer zone** An area of land separating two distinct land uses that acts to soften or mitigate the effects of one land use on the other. *(California Planning Roundtable)*

Districts established at or adjoining commercial-residential district boundaries to mitigate potential frictions between uses or characteristics of use. Such district regulations may provide for transitional uses, yards, heights, off-street parking, lighting, signs, buffering or screening. *(Miami, Fla., which uses the term "buffer district")*

■ **build out** Development of land to its full potential or theoretical capacity as permitted under current or proposed planning or zoning designations. *(California Planning Roundtable)*

Development of land to its full potential. *(Jefferson County, Colo.)*

A planner's reference to a hypothetical point in the future when all land that can be developed has been developed. *(Upper Valley Lake Sunapee Regional Planning Commission, Lebanon, N.H.)*

■ **build-out analysis** Illustrates the form and pattern that development can be expected to take under a continuation of current trends and the manner and degree to which this form and pattern are contrary to planning goals. *(State of New Jersey)*

Planning tool [u]sed to estimate the impact of cumulative growth upon a town's land area once all developable land has been consumed and converted to the uses permitted under the current regulatory framework. *(Center for Rural Massachusetts, University of Massachusetts)*

■ **build-to line** *(See also **setback** definitions)* An alignment established a certain distance from the curb line to a line along which the building shall be built. Front porches and handicap ramps shall be exempt from build-to line requirements, and must occur behind the property line. *(South Miami, Fla.)*

■ **buildable area** The area of a lot remaining after the minimum yard and open space requirements of the zoning

ordinance have been met. *(Iowa State University Extension Service)*

The portion of a lot or site, exclusive of required yard areas, setbacks, landscaping, or open space within which a structure may be built. *(Renton, Wash.)*

The space remaining on a lot after the minimum open space, offset, and setback requirements have been complied with; excepting any floodplain, wetland, or similarly designated unbuildable lands. *(Mequon, Wisc.)*

■ **buildable lands** Lands within urban and urbanizable areas that are suitable, available, and necessary for residential, commercial, and industrial uses, and include both vacant land and developed land that, in the opinion of the local planning agency, is likely to be redeveloped. *(APA's Growing Smart project)*

■ **buildable width** The width of that part of a lot not included within the open spaces herein required. *(El Paso, Tex.)*

■ **building** A structure entirely separated from any other structure by space or by walls in which there are no communicating doors, windows, or similar openings. *(Coral Gables, Fla.)*

A structure having a roof supported by columns or walls for shelter, support, or enclosure of persons, animals, or chattels. When separated by division walls from the ground up without openings, each portion of such structure shall be deemed a separate building. *(Ames, Iowa)*

A structure for the support or shelter of any use or occupancy. *(Thornton, Colo.)*

■ **building area** *(See **building coverage**)*

■ **building bulk** The visual and physical mass of a building. *(Newport Beach, Calif.)*

■ **building code** The various codes of the City that regulate construction and require building permits, electrical permits, mechanical permits, plumbing permits, and other permits to do work regulated by [city code] pertaining to building and building regulation. *(Glendale, Ariz.)*

Regulations governing building design, construction, and maintenance. *(Handbook for Planning Commissioners in Missouri)*

■ **building coverage** The horizontal area measured within the outside of the exterior walls of the ground floor of all principle and accessory buildings on the lot. *(Iowa State University Extension Service)*

A percentage figure referring to that portion of a lot covered only with principal and accessory buildings. *(Gurnee, Ill.)*

The total of areas taken on a horizontal plane at the main grade level of the principal building and all accessory buildings exclusive of uncovered porches, terraces, and steps. All dimensions shall be measured between the exterior faces of walls. *(Pomfret Township, N.Y.)*

■ **building, dangerous** All buildings or structures that have any or all of the following defects shall be deemed dangerous buildings:

A. Whenever the building or structure, or any portion thereof, because of (1) dilapidation, deterioration, or decay; (2) faulty construction; (3) the removal, movement, or instability of any portion of the ground necessary for the purpose of supporting such building; (4) the deterioration, decay, or inadequacy of its foundation; or (5) any other cause, is subject to structural failure under its design usage.

B. Whenever the building or structure has been so damaged by fire, wind, earthquake, or flood, or has become (1) an attractive nuisance to children; (2) a harbor for vagrants, criminals, or immoral persons; or as to (3) enable persons to resort thereto for the purpose of committing unlawful or immoral acts.

C. Whenever a building or structure, because of inadequate maintenance, dilapidation, decay, damage, faulty construction or arrangement, inadequate light, air or sanitation facilities, or otherwise is determined by the City or County Heath Officer to be unsanitary, unfit for human habitation or in such a condition that is likely to cause sickness or disease.

D. Whenever any building or structure, because of obsolescence, dilapidated condition, deterioration, damage, inadequate exits, lack of sufficient fire resistive construction, faulty electric wiring, gas connections or heating apparatus, or other cause is determined to be a fire hazard.

E. Whenever any portion of a building or structure remains on a site after the demolition or destruction or whenever any building or structure is vacant and open to unauthorized entry for a period in excess of six months so as to constitute such building or portion thereof an attractive nuisance or hazard to the public.

F. Whenever the exterior walls or other vertical structural members list, lean or buckle to such an extent that a plumb line passing through the center of gravity does not fall inside the middle one-third of the base.

G. Whenever the building or structure, exclusive of the foundation, shows 33 percent or more damage or deterioration of its supporting member or members, or 50 percent damage or deterioration of its nonsupporting members, enclosing or outside walls or coverings.

H. Whenever any portion thereof has been damaged by fire, earthquake, wind, flood, or by any other cause, to such an extent that the structural strength or stability thereof is materially less than it was before such catastrophe and is less than the minimum requirements of the City's Uniform Building Code, as then in force or as same may be amended from time to time, for new buildings of similar structure, purpose or location.

I. Whenever any portion or member or appurtenance thereof is likely to fail, or to become detached or dislodged, or to collapse and thereby injure persons or damage property. *(Renton, Wash.)*

■ **building, detached**   A building surrounded by open space on the same lot. *(Vernon Hills, Ill.)*

Any building or structure separated by at least five feet in horizontal distance from any other building or structure. *(Glendale, Calif.)*

■ **building elevation**   The perimeter surface of a building set approximately parallel to a lot line. Elevations are sub-

ject to setback and height restrictions. *(Orlando, Fla.)*

(1) A vertical distance above or below a fixed reference level; (2) A flat scale drawing of the front, rear, or side of a building. *(Iowa State University Extension Service)*

■ **building envelope**   That area on a lot that encompasses all development including but not limited to excavation, fill, grading, storage, demolition, structures, building heights, decks, roof overhangs, porches, patios and terraces, pools, any areas of disturbance, access ways, and parking. Approved plantings of landscape materials on natural grade and approved walkways and driveways may occur outside of a building envelope. Otherwise, all areas outside of a building envelope shall remain in pristine and untouched condition unless approved by the Community Development Director. *(Aspen, Colo.)*

The volume of space for building as defined by the minimum setbacks and the maximum allowable building height. *(Oakland, Calif.)*

The three-dimensional space within which a structure is permitted to be built on a lot and which is defined by regulations governing building setbacks, maximum height, and bulk; by other regulations; and/or any combination thereof. *(Newport, R.I.)*

The area formed by the front, side, and rear building restriction or setback lines of a lot within which the principal buildings must be located. *(Caroline County, Md.)*

■ **building facade**   *(See facade)*

■ **building footprint**   The area of a lot or site included within the surrounding exterior walls of a building or portion of a building, exclusive of courtyards. In the absence of surrounding exterior walls, the building footprint shall be the area under the horizontal projection of the roof. *(Renton, Wash.)*

The outline of the total area covered by a building's perimeter at the ground level. *(Thornton, Colo.)*

■ **building frontage**   *(See also facade)* The horizontal linear dimension designated as the primary facade of that portion of a building occupied by a single use or occupancy. A corner tenant will be permitted to use the secondary facade to determine the "building frontage." *(Thornton, Colo.)*

Those building elevations that face upon a road or parking area between the building and the road. *(Shasta Lake, Calif.)*

■ **building group**   A group of two or more main buildings and any uses accessory thereto, occupying a lot in one ownership and having any yard in common. *(Thurston County, Wash.)*

■ **building height**   The overall height of a building as measured from flood level or average sidewalk elevation, whichever is higher, to (1) the top of the roof for flat roofs, (2) the deck lines for mansard roofs, and (3) the average height between eaves and ridge for gable, hip, and gambrel roofs. *(Miami, Fla.)*

The vertical distance above a referenced datum measured to the highest point of the coping of a flat roof or to the deck line of a mansard roof or to the average height of the highest gable of a pitched or hipped roof. The reference datum shall be selected by either of the following, whichever yields a greater height of building: (a) The elevation of the highest adjoining sidewalk or ground surface within a five-foot horizontal distance of the exterior wall of the building when such sidewalk or ground surface is not more than 10 feet above lowest grade measured within a five-foot horizontal distance of the exterior wall of the building; or (b) An elevation 10 feet higher than the lowest grade when the sidewalk or ground surface described in subsection (a) above is more than 10 feet above lowest grade measured within a 5-foot horizontal distance of the exterior wall of the building. *(Renton, Wash.)*

The vertical measurement from grade to the highest point of the roof beams in flat roofs; to the highest point on the deck of mansard roofs; to a level midway between the level of the eaves and highest point of pitched roofs or hip roofs; or to a level two-thirds of the distance from the level of the eaves to the highest point of gambrel roofs. For this purpose, the level of the eaves shall be taken to mean the highest level where the plane of the roof intersects the plane of the outside wall on a side containing the eaves. *(Gorham, Maine)*

■ **building height, maximum**   A plane parallel to and measured vertically from undisturbed natural ground level above which no part of any building may extend except as provided in [another part of the code] and except that the highest part of a gable, gambrel, hip, shed, or similar pitched roof may extend up to five feet above the specified maximum building height. *(Glenwood Springs, Colo.)*

■ **building inspector**   A governmental employee charged with enforcement of the building code, and such other ordinances (zoning, signboard, housing, electrical and plumbing, for example) as may be assigned to his or her department. *(Handbook for Planning Commissioners in Missouri)*

■ **building line**   The building line is the inner edge of any required yard or required setback, and the corresponding outer edge of the buildable area. Except as specifically provided by these regulations, no portion of any building or structure may be extended to occupy any portion of a lot outside its building lines. *(Miami, Fla.)*

A line parallel to a street right-of-way line, edge of a stream, or other property line established on a parcel of land or lot for the purpose of prohibiting construction of a building or structure in the area between such building line and right-of-way, stream bank, or other property line. *(Maryland Heights, Mo.)*

A line parallel to the street right-of-way line at any story level of a building and representing the minimum distance which all or any part of the building is set back from said right-of-way line. *(Nicollet County, Minn.)*

■ **building lot line**   *(See lot line)*

■ **building official**   The city official or employee responsible for implementing and enforcing the applicable building codes and standards of the city. *(Imperial Beach, Calif.)*

■ **building permit**   A document signed by the director of the planning and building services department or their authorized representative as a condition precedent to the commencement of a use or the erection, construction, reconstruction, restoration, alteration, conversion, or installation of a building, which acknowledges that such use or building complies with the provisions of the municipal zoning ordinance . . . or an authorized variance therefrom. *(Sioux Falls, S.D.)*

A permit issued by the duly designated building official authorizing the erection, construction, reconstruction, alteration, repair, conversion, or maintenance of any building, structure, or portion thereof. Such a permit shall not be issued without the signature of the zoning enforcement officer, certifying compliance with this ordinance. *(Ames, Iowa, which uses the term "building/zoning permit")*

An official document or certification that is issued by the building official and which authorizes the construction, alteration, enlargement, conversion, reconstruction, remodeling, rehabilitation, erection, demolition, moving or repair of a building or structure. *(Mount Vernon, Wash.)*

■ **building, principal**   A building in which the primary use of the lot on which the building is located is conducted. *(Fairfax County, Va.)*

■ **building, residential** *(See also dwelling definitions)*   Any building arranged, designed, used, or intended to be used for residential occupancy by one or more families or lodgers and that includes, but is not limited to, the following types: (a) Single-family detached dwellings; (b) Two-Family dwellings; (c) Townhouse dwellings; and (d) Multiple-family dwellings. *(Gurnee, Ill.)*

■ **building, single occupancy**   A building or structure with one major enterprise, generally under one ownership. A building is considered to be "single occupancy" if it: (a) has only one occupant; (b) has no wall in common with another building; and (c) has no part of its roof in common with another building. *(Renton, Wash.)*

■ **building site**   A lot or parcel of land, in single or joint ownership, and occupied or to be occupied by a main building and accessory buildings, or by a dwelling group and its accessory buildings, together with such open spaces as are required by the terms of this title and having its principle frontage on a street, road, highway, or waterway. *(King City, Calif.)*

Land occupied or intended to be occupied by a building or interrelated buildings, together with all open space required by this title, which is located on a lot that has been lawfully created and meets all criteria of the city for the intended use. *(Shasta Lake, Calif.)*

■ **building, vacant or unoccupied**   Any building or structure that is not occupied, used, or inhabited on a regular and continuing basis by some person with a valid claim of right to posession or a fee

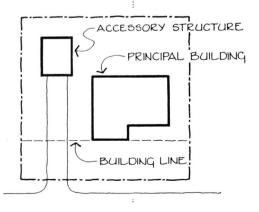

simple title. The intrusion of trespassers or squatters into such buildings on any basis shall not render such building occupied or nonvacant within the meaning of this [ordinance]. *(Newport News, Va.)*

■ **building width** The distance from the exterior face of the building siding as measured from side to side. *(Sheridan, Wyo.)*

The width of the lot left to be built upon after the side yards are provided. *(Perryville, Mo.)*

■ **built environment** The elements of the environment . . . that are generally built or made by people as contrasted with natural processes. *(Renton, Wash.)*

■ **bulk** The size and mutual relationships of a building or structure and the location of same with respect to: size and height of the building; location of exterior walls at all levels in relation to lot lines, streets, or other buildings; gross floor area of the building in relation to the lot area; all open space allocated to the building. *(Vernon Hills, Ill.)*

The size of buildings or structures, and their relationships to each other and to open areas and lot lines, and therefore includes: (1) the size of a building or structure; (2) the area of the lot upon which a building or structure is located, and the number of dwelling units within such building or structure in relation to the area of the lot; (3) the shape of a building or structure; ( 4) the location of exterior walls of a building or structure in relation to lot lines, to other walls of the same building or structure, to legally required windows, or to other buildings or structures; and (5) all open areas relating to a building or structure and their relationship thereto. *(Naperville, Ill.)*

The total volume of a structure. *(Thornton, Colo.)*

■ **bulk envelope** The three-dimensional space within which a structure is permitted to be built on a zoning lot and which is defined with respect to such bulk regulations as height, yards, building coverage, floor area ratio, bulk plane, and, in a few ordinances, land-use-intensity ratings. *(PAS Report No. 322,* The Language of Zoning*)*

■ **bulk materials** Uncontained solid matter such as powder, grain, stone, sand, etc. *(Mankato, Minn.)*

■ **bulk plane** *(See also daylight plane; sky exposure plane)* An imaginary inclined plane, rising over a lot, drawn at a specified angle from the vertical, the bottom side of which is coincidental with the lot line(s) or yard line(s) of the lot, or directly above them, and which, together with other bulk regulations and lot size requirements, delineate the maximum bulk of any improvement that may be constructed on the lot. The angle of bulk plane is established by district regulations, and no portion of any structure, with specified exceptions, is permitted to extend beyond it. Where such requirements exist, upper floors must be set back increasingly greater distances from the street or sides of the lot. New York City's familiar "wedding cake" architecture is one result. Such requirements have in some cases been replaced or supplemented by floor area ratio (FAR) requirements. Some synonyms are light plane, setback plane, or sky exposure plane. *(PAS Report No. 322,* The Language of Zoning*)*

■ **bulk regulations** Standards and controls that establish the maximum size of buildings and structures on a lot and the buildable area within which the building can be located, including coverage, setbacks, height, impervious surface ratio, floor area ratio, and yard requirements. *(Nashville and Davidson County, Tenn.)*

Controls that establish the maximum size, height, and setback of a building on its lot. *(New Castle County, Del.)*

■ **bulk retail** *(See retail)*

■ **bulkhead** *(See also shoreline stabilization)* A structure including riprap or sheet piling, constructed to separate land and water and establish a permanent shoreline. *(Imperial Beach, Calif.)*

A structure or partition placed on a bank or bluff to retain or prevent sliding of the land and protect the inland area from wave action or currents. *(Yakima County, Wash.)*

■ **bulkhead line** A line established to define the bayward limit for solid-filling or solid structures. *(Newport Beach, Calif.)*

■ **bunkhouse** *(See housing, temporary employment)*

■ **burial space** A lot or portion of a lot in any cemetery designated and maintained for the interment of a human body or bodies or remains thereof and for no other purpose. *(Waukegan, Ill.)*

■ **bus** A rubber-tired vehicle that is designed for roadway operation for public transportation service. *(Sacramento Regional Transit District)*

■ **bus bay** A bus berthing area in a facility such as a transit center or rail station. *(Sacramento Regional Transit District)*

■ **bus, electric trolley** *(See also transit definitions)* A rubber-tired bus powered by electricity that draws power from over-

head wires through a trolley pole or similar mechanism. Electric trolley buses are designed to allow the bus to maneuver in mixed traffic, over several lanes, and pick up passengers at the street curb. *(Sacramento Regional Transit District)*

■ **bus lane**   A lane of roadway intended primarily for use by buses, either all day or during specified periods. *(Sacramento Regional Transit District)*

■ **bus lot**   Any lot or land area used for the storage or layover of passenger busses or motor coaches. *(Aurora, Ill.)*

■ **bus, school**   Every motor vehicle owned by a public or governmental agency and operated for the transportation of children to or from school or privately owned and operated for compensation for the transportation of children to and from school. *(Carmel, Ind.)*

■ **bus shelter**   A small, roofed structure, usually having three walls, located near a street and designed primarily for the protection and convenience of bus passengers (pictured on page 54). *(Maryland Heights, Mo.)*

■ **bus, sightseeing**   Any motor-propelled passenger-carrying vehicle for hire (other than a vehicle operated by the San Francisco Municipal Railway), used in the conveyance, for hire, of tourists and sightseers, over the public streets, for the purpose of a sightseeing trip or tour in the visiting and viewing of places of interest. *(San Francisco, Calif.)*

■ **bus stop**   A curbside place where passengers board or alight transit. *(Sacramento Regional Transit District)*

■ **bus way**   A vehicular right-of-way or portion thereof—often an exclusive lane—reserved exclusively for buses. *(California Planning Roundtable)*

■ **business**   Any lawful commercial endeavor to engage in the manufacturing, purchase, sale, lease, or exchange of goods and/or the provision of services. *(Thornton, Colo.)*

■ **business district**   An urban downtown district . . . that has design features and a diversity of uses not found in the commercial and office districts. Such uses include government buildings, cultural facilities, hotels, apartments, retail shops, and ancillary uses. *(Peoria, Ill.)*

■ **business incubator**   A facility dedicated to the start-up and growth of small businesses, accomplished through management and facility support systems. For purposes of this definition, management support systems include access to professional advice, information on small business regulations, management, advertising, promotion, marketing, sales, inventory, employees, labor relations, and financial counseling. Facility support systems include clerical and reception staff, cleaning and building security, and access to copy and facsimile machines, computers, faxes, and other electronic equipment. *(Galesburg, Ill.)*

Retail or industrial space that is affordable to new, low-margin businesses. *(California Planning Roundtable)*

■ **business park** *(See office park)*

■ **business services**   A subcategory of commercial land use that permits establishments primarily engaged in rendering services to other business establishments on a fee or contract basis, such as advertising and mailing; building maintenance; personnel and employment services; management and consulting services; protective services; equipment rental and leasing; photo finishing; copying and printing; travel; office supply; and similar services. *(California Planning Roundtable)*

■ **business support services**   Establishments or places of business engaged in the sale, rental, or repair of office equipment, supplies, and materials, or the provision of services used by office, professional, and service establishments. Typical uses include office equipment and supply firms, small business machine repair shops, convenience printing and copying establishments, as well as temporary labor services. *(Blacksburg, Va.)*

Establishments that primarily provide goods and services to other businesses including, but not limited to, minor job printing, duplicating, binding and photographic processing, office security, maintenance and custodial services, and office equipment and machinery sales, rentals, and repairing, but no manufacturing of any products. *(Glendale, Ariz.)*

Establishments primarily engaged in rendering services to business establishments on a fee or contract basis, such as advertising and mailing, consulting services, protective services, equipment rental, leasing, and financial services. *(Mequon, Wisc.)*

■ **business, technology, and research district**   A working environment for research and development institutions, offices, and certain specialized production and assembly establishments along with other special uses, all of a non-nuisance type. *(Kalamazoo, Mich.)*

■ **buspool** *(See also carpool; vanpool)* A vehicle carrying 16 or more passengers commuting on a regular basis to and from work with a fixed route, according to a fixed schedule. *(Hermosa Beach, Calif.)*

■ **by right**   Refers to uses requiring a permit with no public hearing required. *(Pomfret Township, N.Y.)*

A use permitted or allowed in the district involved, without review by the review board, and complies with the provisions of these zoning regulations and other applicable ordinances and regulations. *(Montrose, Colo.)*

■ **bylaws**   Rules adopted by a board which govern its procedures. *(New York Planning Federation)*

■ **cabana** An accessory building or a portion of the main building used as a bathhouse or a dressing area in connection with a swimming pool or a tennis court. *(Coral Gables, Fla.)*

■ **cabin/cottage** *(See also **summer home**)* Living quarters in a building separate from and in addition to the main residential building on a lot, used for intermittent or temporary occupancy by non-paying guests; provided that the quarters have no kitchen, cooking facilities, or kitchen sink. The quarters shall be not be rented, leased, or otherwise made available for compensation of any kind. *(Jacksonville, Fla.)*

■ **cafe** *(See **coffee house; restaurant** definitions)*

■ **caliper** *(See also **tree** definitions)* A horticultural method of measuring the diameter of nursery stock. For trees less than four inches in diameter, the measurement should be taken at six inches above ground level. For trees greater than four inches in diameter up to and including 12 inches, the caliper measure-

ment must be taken at 12 inches above the ground level. For trees greater than 12 inches in diameter, the trunk is measured at breast height (diameter at breast height or DBH), which is 4.5 feet above the ground. *(Asheville, N.C.)*

■ **camp** *(See **campground**)*

■ **camp, day or youth** A camp providing facilities for groups of young people such as YMCA camps, Boy Scout camps, and Girl Scout camps. *(Gurnee, Ill.)*

Any parcel or parcels of land having the general characteristics of a camp as the term is generally understood, used wholly or in part for recreational or educational purposes, and accommodating five or more children under 28 years of age for a period of, or portions of, two days or more, including a site which is operated as a day camp or as a resident camp. *(Siskiyou County, Calif.)*

The use of a site for provision of indoor or outdoor activities for children, including sports, arts and crafts, entertainment, recreation, educational activities, swimming, fishing, horseback riding, and incidental food service. If incidental to the camp use, camp facilities may be used to provide meeting, recreation, or social facilities for a private association or group. *(Austin, Tex.)*

■ **camp, organized recreation** Land or premises containing structures designed to be used for organized camping. The structures include bunk houses, tent platforms, mess halls and cooking facilities, and playfields. Examples include Boy Scout Camps and summer camps. *(Kauai, Hawaii)*

■ **camp, recreation** An establishment consisting of a permanent building or group of permanent buildings used periodically by an association of persons where seasonal accommodations for recreational purposes are provided only to the members of such association and not to anyone who may apply. *(Brookfield, Wisc.)*

■ **campground** Temporary or permanent buildings, tents, or other structures established or maintained as a temporary living quarter, operated continu-

ously for a period of five days or more for recreation, religious, education, or vacation purposes. *(Cascade Charter Township, Mich.)*

Any area of land and/or water on which is located a cabin, tent, travel trailer, motor home, or other type of shelter suitable and intended for use in a temporary seasonal manner. For the purposes of this law, no minimum floor space shall be required for a camp structure. *(Pomfret Township, N.Y.)*

Any area that is occupied or intended or designed or improved for occupancy by transients using recreational vehicles, motor homes, or mobile trailers for dwelling, lodging, or sleeping purposes and is held out as such to the public. Campsite does not include any manufactured housing community. *(Imperial Beach, Calif., which uses the term "campsite")*

■ **camping trailer** A vehicular portable structure mounted on wheels constructed with collapsible, partial side walls of fabric, plastic, or other pliable materials for folding compactly while being transported. *(Manatee County, Fla.)*

■ **campus** A contiguous area of land constituting and making up the grounds of a college or university containing the main buildings or within the main enclosure; provided, however, that for the purpose of this definition the contiguity of any land area involved shall not be deemed to be destroyed by the presence of public rights-of-way. *(Denver, Colo.)*

■ **canal** *(See also **channel**)* An artificial channel for conveyance of water including laterals and drains. *(El Paso, Tex.)*

■ **candle/candela (cd)** Unit of luminous intensity. One candela [or candle] is one lumen per steradian. . . . *(International Dark-Sky Association)*

■ **candlepower** *(See also **footcandle; lumen**)* Luminous intensity expressed in candelas. *(International Dark-Sky Association)*

The amount of light that will illuminate a surface one foot distant from a light source to an intensity of one footcandle. Maximum (peak) candlepower is the largest amount of candlepower emitted by any lamp, light source, or luminaire. (*Williamson County, Tenn.*)

■ **canopy** A permanently roofed shelter projecting over a sidewalk, driveway, entry, window, or similar area, which shelter may be wholly supported by a building or may be wholly or partially supported by columns, poles, or braces extending from the ground. . . . [A]ny roof overhang extending more than two feet from the face of a building shall be considered a canopy. (*Traverse City, Mich.*)

With reference to structures, a rooflike cover, including an awning, that projects from the wall of a building over a door, entrance or window; or a freestanding or projecting cover above an outdoor service area, such as at a gasoline service station. A marquee is not a canopy. With reference to bufferyards, a landscape element that functions as an overhead or "ceiling," used in single or multiple plantings to create shade. (*Tippacanoe County, Ind.*)

A rooflike structure serving the purpose of protecting pedestrians from rain and sun, which structure projects from a building and the width of which ("width" being taken as the dimensions parallel to the face of the building) is not greater than one-fourth the width of the face of the building or 20 feet, whichever is lesser. Such structure must be open on three sides and, if ground-supported, supports must be confined in number and cross-section area to the minimum necessary for actual support of the canopy. (*Denver, Colo.*)

■ **canopy, building** A rigid multi-sided structure covered with fabric, metal, or other material, and supported by a building at one or more points or extremities and by columns or posts embedded in the ground at other points or extremities. Any structure that extends above any adjacent parapet or roof of supporting building is not included within the definition of building canopy. (*Renton, Wash.*)

■ **canopy, entrance** A roof-like covering over a door or an opening of a structure intended and used for the purpose

of sheltering persons or inanimate objects from the rays of the sun and from rain and weather. Entrance canopies shall be attached to the building and may be supported from the ground up; the overall width of said entrance canopies shall be a maximum of the entrance opening and framing width, plus 12 inches, and said entrance canopies shall extend out perpendicular from the building. Entrance canopies are permitted on commercial buildings only. (*Coral Gables, Fla.*)

■ **capacity** The maximum lawful level of designed use of any structure, or part thereof, as determined by the city's adopted building code and expressed in terms of occupants, seats, persons, employees, or other units specified by the building code. (*Gainesville, Fla.*)

The maximum number of persons that can avail themselves of the services (or goods) of an establishment or use at any one time, as determined by the required floor space per person established in the building code. (*Minneapolis, Minn., which uses the term "capacity in persons"*)

■ **capacity, net** Population and employment growth likely to occur under zoned capacity, minus existing infrastructure and service standard limitations. (*Renton, Wash.*)

■ **capacity, planned** Population and employment growth planned (contained in local comprehensive plans with a specified horizon) in the context of the Countywide Planning Policies. (*Renton, Wash.*)

■ **capacity, zoned** Population and employment growth permitted under current zoning, land development, and environmental regulations. (*Renton, Wash.*)

■ **capital budget** A plan of proposed capital outlay appropriations and means of financing them. (*Indian River County, Fla.*)

■ **capital improvement** Any physical asset constructed or purchased to provide, improve or replace a public facility and which is large scale and high in cost.

The cost of a capital improvement is generally nonrecurring and may require multi-year financing. (*Indian River County, Fla.*)

■ **capital improvements budget** The capital improvement program put into dollars and cents terms, indicating the prorated amount to be expended for each project listed over a given period, and including the sources of revenue. (*Handbook for Planning Commissioners in Missouri*)

■ **capital improvements element (CIE)** That portion of the . . . Comprehensive Plan which . . . guides the provision of the needed capital improvements identified in the other plan elements. (*Indian River County, Fla.*)

■ **capital improvements program (CIP)** A proposed schedule of all future projects listed in order of construction priority together with cost estimates and the anticipated means of financing each project. Included are all major projects requiring the expenditure of public funds, over and above the annual local government's operating expenses, for the purchase, construction, or replacement of the physical assets for the community. (*Park City, Utah*)

A program, administered by a city or county government and reviewed by its planning commission, which schedules permanent improvements, usually for a minimum of five years in the future, to fit the projected fiscal capability of the local jurisdiction. The program generally is reviewed annually for conformance to and consistency with the general plan. (*California Planning Roundtable*)

A community's present and near-future financial plan that matches future capital improvement costs, such as sewers, hospitals, and roads to anticipated revenues. The planning and zoning commission should be given authority to develop and review the CIP proposal, thereby linking planning to the annual budgetary process. CIPs are usually prepared for five or six years and updated annually. (*Iowa State University Extension Service*)

■ **car shelter** (*See also* ***carport***)   An accessory structure (pictured below) made of canvas, aluminum, or similar materials, or any combination thereof, on movable framing for the shade and shelter of one or two private passenger vehicles. (*Miami, Fla.*)

■ **car wash**   The use of a site for washing and cleaning of passenger vehicles, recreational vehicles, or other light duty equipment. (*Austin, Tex., which uses the term "automotive washing"*)

A building or portion thereof containing facilities for washing more than two automobiles, using production line methods. The use of personnel for one or more phases of this operation in conjunction with or without complete automatic or mechanical devices does not alter its classification. For the purpose of this ordinance, coin-operated devices . . . operated on a self-service basis shall be construed to be the same. (*Grant County, Ky., which uses the term "auto laundry"*)

Mechanical facilities for the washing or waxing of private automobiles, light trucks and vans, but not commercial fleets, as an accessory use to an automobile service station. (*Multnomah County, Ore., which uses the term "convenience car wash"*)

■ **car wash, industrial**   Mechanical facilities for the washing, waxing, and vacuuming of automobiles, heavy trucks, and buses. (*Multnomah County, Ore.*)

■ **car wash, self-service**   A car wash wherein the customer provides labor and where no self-propelled wash racks are provided. (*Glendale, Calif.*)

An establishment where washing, drying, polishing, or vacuuming of an automobile is done by the driver or the occupant. (*El Paso, Tex.*)

■ **caretaker**   A person residing in the home where a child care facility operates, whose duties include, but are not limited to, direct care, supervision and guidance. (*El Paso, Tex.*)

■ **caretaker, property**   One who is employed to maintain, repair, and protect a facility or property. (*El Paso, Tex.*)

■ **caretaker's residence**   A single-family dwelling unit accessory to an agricultural, professional, commercial, or industrial use for occupancy by the owner-caretaker. (*Yakima, Wash., which uses the term "caretaker dwelling"*)

A residence located on a premises with a main nonresidential use and occupied only by a caretaker or guard employed on the premises. (*Plano, Tex.*)

A dwelling unit on the site of a commercial, industrial, public, or semipublic use, occupied by a guard or caretaker. (*Manhattan Beach, Calif.*)

An accessory dwelling on a nonresidential premises, occupied by the person who oversees the nonresidential operation 24 hours a day, and his or her family. (*Tippacanoe, Ind.*)

■ **cargo, breakbulk**   Cargo packed in separate packages or individual pieces of cargo and loaded, stored and unloaded individually. (*Seattle, Wash.*)

■ **cargo, containerized** (*See also* ***freight container***)   Cargo packed in a large (typically eight feet by eight feet by 20

feet) trunk-like box, and loaded, stored, and unloaded as a unit. (*Seattle, Wash.*)

■ **carnival** (*See also* ***amusement*** *definitions*)   Any aggregation of shows or riding devices, games of skill or chance, or any combination of shows and riding devices, or any combination of several enterprises, such as revolving wheels, merry-go-rounds, giant swings, panoramas, musical and theatrical entertainments, or riding devices, whether carried on or engaged in or conducted in any field, park or in a building or enclosure, and whether carried on, engaged in or conducted as one enterprise or by several concessionaires, and whether one admission fee is charged for admission to all such shows or entertainments, or separate fee for admission is charged for each amusement. (*Aurora, Ill.*)

Any establishment at which a combination of attractions or exhibitions, such as rides, illusions, freak shows, eating concessions, and gaming booths, with a main attraction and/or sideshows, are available for the purpose of amusement and entertainment and where the public pays either an admission or participation fee. A carnival with more than three attractions and exhibitions shall be deemed to be a large carnival; a carnival with no more than three attractions and exhibitions shall be deemed to be a small carnival. A carnival shall be inclusive of an exhibition as defined in this section. (*Glendale Ariz., which uses the term "carnival (large or small)"*)

A traveling or transportable group or aggregation of rides, shows, games or concessions or any combination thereof. (*Fairfax County, Va.*)

■ **carnival, major**   A promotional event intended to attract people to a site where there may or may not be an admission charge, and which may include such activities as rides, entertainment, game booths, food stands, exhibitions, and animal displays. (*Scottsdale, Ariz.*)

■ **carnival, minor**   A promotional event intended to attract people to a site where there is no admission charge, and which may include up to 7 small rides, each a maximum of 15 feet in height, and such activities as entertainment, game booths, food stands, exhibitions, and animal displays. (Scottsdale, Ariz.)

■ **carpool** (See also **transportation demand management (TDM)**) A vehicle carrying two to six persons commuting together to and from work on a regular basis. (Hermosa Beach, Calif.)

A group of people in excess of some minimum number (usually two or three persons) traveling to the same or relatively nearby locations. (Renton, Wash.)

■ **carport** A roofed structure (pictured on page 59) not more than 75 percent enclosed by walls and attached to the main building for the purpose of providing shelter for one or more motor vehicles. (Coral Gables, Fla.)

A permanent roofed structure permanently open on at least two sides, designed for or occupied by private passenger vehicles. (Edmond, Okla.)

Any parking space or spaces having a roof but not enclosed by walls and accessory to a dwelling unit or units. "Carports" shall not include any parking structures. (Ames, Iowa)

■ **carry-out restaurant** (See **restaurant, carry-out**)

■ **carrying capacity analysis** (See also **adequate public facilities ordinance (APFO); system capacity**) An assessment of the ability of a natural system to absorb population growth as well as other physical development without significant degradation. (APA's Growing Smart project)

Used in determining the potential of an area to absorb development. (1) The level of land use, human activity, or development for a specific area that can be accommodated permanently without an irreversible change in the quality of air, water, land, or plant and animal habitats. (2) The upper limits of development beyond which the quality of human life, health, welfare, safety, or community character within an area will be impaired. (3) The maximum level of development allowable under current zoning. (California Planning Roundtable)

A measure of the ability of a region to accommodate the growth and development within the limits defined by existing infrastructure and natural resource capabilities. (Iowa State University Extension Service, which uses the term "current planning capacity")

■ **cartway** The hard or paved surface portion of a street customarily used by vehicles in the regular course of travel. Where there are curbs, the cartway is that portion between the curbs. (Colts Neck, N.J.)

■ **casino** A room or rooms in which legal gambling is conducted. (Jefferson Parish, La.)

■ **catering service** An establishment that serves and supplies food to be consumed off premises. (Dallas, Tex.)

A service providing meals and/or refreshments for public or private entertainment for a fee. (Bel Air, Md.)

A social or home catering service provides food and incidental service for a social affair or for a private dwelling, but does not use commercial vehicles that are equipped in any manner for the purpose of transporting food to be sold directly from such vehicles. (Miami, Fla., which uses the term "catering services, social or home")

■ **catering service, industrial** An industrial catering service uses vehicles equipped to transport food to be sold directly from such vehicles. (Miami, Fla.)

■ **cattery** A place where four or more adult cats are kept, whether by owners of the cats or by persons providing facilities and care, whether or not for compensation, but not including small animal hospitals, clinics or pet shops. An adult cat is one of either six, altered or unaltered, that has reached the age of six months. (Federal Way, Wash.)

A commercial establishment wherein any person, for profit, buys, sells, boards, breeds, or grooms cats. (Raleigh, N.C.)

■ **cellar** (See also **basement; crawlspace**) That portion of a building between floor and ceiling that is wholly or partly below grade and so located that the vertical dis-

tance from grade to the floor below is equal to or greater than the vertical distance from grade to ceiling. (Lincoln, Nebr.)

A space having more than one-half of its height below grade and which may not be occupied for dwelling purposes. (Mequon, Wisc.)

A story having more than one-half of its height below grade. A cellar is not included in computing the number of stories for the purpose of height measurement. (Wheeling, Ill.)

A storage room or rooms located under the main floor or floors of a building and which are partly or totally below ground level. (Boise City, Idaho)

■ **cemetery** (See also **burial space; crematorium; columbarium; mausoleum**) Land used or dedicated to the burial of the dead, including crematoriums, mausoleums, necessary sales, and maintenance facilities. Mortuaries shall be included when operated within the boundary of such cemetery. (Blacksburg, Va.)

A place used for interment of human or animal remains or cremated remains, including a burial park for earth interments, a mausoleum for vault or crypt interments, a columbarium for cinerary interments, or a combination thereof. (Carroll County, Md.)

Land used for the burial of the dead, and dedicated for cemetery purposes, excluding columbariums, crematories, mausoleums, and mortuaries. (Stonington, Conn.)

■ **cemetery, pet** A parcel of land, buildings, and/or structures used for the interring of animal remains. (McHenry County, Ill.)

■ **census** A complete enumeration, usually of a population, but also businesses and commercial establishments, farms, governments, and so forth. (United States Census Bureau)

■ **census tract** A small, relatively permanent statistical subdivision of a county in a metropolitan area or a selected non-metropolitan county, delineated by a local committee of census data users for the purpose of presenting decennial census data. Census tract boundaries normally follow visible features, but may follow governmental unit boundaries and other non-visible features in some instances; they always nest within counties. *(United States Census Bureau)*

*Commentary: Designed to be relatively homogeneous units with respect to population characteristics, economic status, and living conditions at the time the census data users established them, census tracts usually contain between 2,500 and 8,000 inhabitants. They may be split by any sub-county geographic entity.*

■ **central business district (CBD)**  A business, office, and residential district to provide a full range of services, and a variety of uses in a downtown atmosphere. *(Arvada/Jefferson County, Colo.)*

The major commercial downtown center of a community. General guidelines for delineating a downtown area are defined by the U.S. Census of Retail Trade, with specific boundaries being set by the local municipality. *(California Planning Roundtable)*

The major shopping area within the city usually containing, in addition to retail uses; government offices; service uses; professional, cultural, recreational, and entertainment establishments and uses; residences, hotels, and motels; appropriate industrial activities; and transportation activities. *(Iowa State University Extension Service)*

■ **certificate of appropriateness**  A permit issued by the historic architecture review board granting an applicant approval for the alteration, change, demolition, relocation, excavation, or new construction of contributing site, contributing structure, landmark, noncontributing structure, or noncontributing site in an historic district. *(Blacksburg, Va.)*

■ **certificate of completion**  A written document required prior to occupancy, issued for a use upon a developer's compliance with the provisions of this code and any applicable development agreement. *(Boulder, Colo.)*

■ **certificate of compliance**  A statement, signed by an administrative officer, setting forth that a building, structure, or use complies with the zoning ordinance and building codes and that the same may be used for the purposes stated on the permit. *(Durham, N.C.)*

■ **certificate of occupancy**  A document issued by the proper authority allowing the occupancy or use of a building and certifying that the structure or use has been constructed or will be used in compliance with all the applicable municipal codes and ordinances. *(Sioux Falls, S.D.)*

The written approval of the Zoning Administrator certifying that a newly constructed structure, addition to an existing structure, or existing structure undergoing a change in use is in full compliance with the provisions of this ordinance and that such structure is habitable and in conformance with all applicable Village building codes and regulations. *(Gurnee, Ill.)*

A document signed by the building inspector as a condition precedent to the commencement of a use after the construction/reconstruction of a structure or building which acknowledges that such use, structure, or building complies with the provisions of this ordinance. *(Muskegon, Mich.)*

■ **certified**  [A guarantee that] a facility and staff [are] qualified and able to provide certain tests and measurements relating to specific tasks and traceable to established standards. *(Renton, Wash.)*

■ **certified survey**  A survey, sketch plan, map, or other exhibit containing a written statement regarding accuracy or conformity to specified standards certified and signed by the registered surveyor under whose supervision said survey was prepared. *(Atlantic Beach, Fla.)*

■ **cesspool**  Any buried chamber including but not limited to any metal tank, perforated concrete vault or covered hollow or excavation, which receives discharges or sanitary sewage from a building sewer for the purpose of collecting solids or discharging liquids to the surrounding soil. Cesspools are not

an approved method of sewage disposal under these regulations and all existing cesspools are substandard. *(New Shoreham, R.I.)*

■ **chainwall**  The exterior foundation wall used to elevate a structure above grade and provide support for the structure's exterior walls and floor system. The chainwall extends around the periphery of the structure and shall not be construed to include such items as driveways, courtyards, and loading docks. *(Baton Rouge, La.)*

■ **change of occupancy**  A discontinuance of an existing use and the substitution therefor of a use of a different kind or class. Change of occupancy is not intended to include a change of tenants or proprietors unless accompanied by a change in the type of use. *(Boca Raton, Fla.)*

■ **change of use** *(See use, change of)*

■ **channel** *(See also canal; diversion)*  An open conduit, either naturally or artificially created, which periodically or continuously contains moving water, or which forms a connecting link between two bodies of water. *(Yakima County, Wash.)*

Any river, stream, creek, brook, branch, natural or artificial depression, ponded area, flowage, slough, ditch, conduit, culvert, gully, ravine, wash, or natural or man-made drainage way that has a definite bed and banks or shoreline, in or into which surface or groundwater flows, either perennially or intermittently. *(Schaumburg, Ill.)*

The portion of a natural stream that conveys normal flows of water, or a ditch or channel excavated for the flow of water. *(Grand Traverse County, Mich.)*

■ **channel bank**  The sloping land bordering a channel. The bank has a steeper slope than the bottom of the channel and is normally steeper than upland areas adjacent to the channel. *(Yakima County, Wash.)*

■ **channel modification**  Alteration of a channel by changing the physical dimensions or materials of its bed or banks. Channel modification includes damming, rip-rapping (or other armoring), widening, deepening, straightening, relocating, lining, and significant removal of bottom or woody vegetation. Channel modification does not include the clearing of dead or dying vegetation, debris, or trash from the channel. Channelization is a severe form of channel modification involving a significant change in the channel cross-section and typically involving relocation of the existing channel (e.g., straightening). *(Schaumburg, Ill.)*

■ **character**   Special physical characteristics of a structure or area that set it apart from its surroundings and contribute to its individuality. *(California Planning Roundtable)*

■ **charitable organizations**   Nonprofit organizations that are supported primarily by charity and whose principal function is the performance of charitable works or religious activities. This definition shall include but not be limited to churches, mosques, synagogues, or other religious institutions. Not included in this definition are social organizations and clubs. *(Durham, N.C.)*

■ **charrette**   A public design workshop in which designers, property owners, developers, public officials, environmentalists, citizens, and other persons or group of people work in harmony to achieve an agreeable [project]. *(Monroe County, Fla.)*

■ **charter**   The governing document of a municipality. *(New York Planning Federation)*

■ **child care center** *(See also day care definitions)*   Any place operated by a person, society, agency, corporation, institution, or any other group that is licensed by the state wherein are received seven or more children under 17 years of age who are not related to such person and whose parents or guardians are not residents in the same house and with such person, society, agency, corporation, or institution responsible for the control and care of children enrolled therein. *(Baton Rouge, La.)*

A facility other than a private residence, receiving one or more minor children for care for periods of less than 24 hours a

day, and where the parents or guardians are not immediately available to the child. Child care center or day care center does not include a facility that provides care for less than two consecutive weeks, regardless of the number of hours or care per day. The facility is generally described as child care center, day care center, day nursery, nursery school, parent cooperative pre-school, play group, or drop-in center. Child care center or day care center does not include a Sunday school conducted by a religious organization where children are cared for during short periods of time while persons responsible for such services are attending religious activities. *(Muskegon, Mich., which also uses the term "day care center")*

Any establishment that provides regular shelter, care, activity, and supervision (with or without academic instruction) for five or more children. *(Stonington, Conn.)*

*Commentary: A common fault of zoning codes is to treat all child care facilities as if they were large commercial operations. Zoning definitions of child care facilities should distinguish between home-based child care and larger child care centers. These distinctions should be based on the number of children to be served at the facility. When possible, the classifications should correspond to those included in state law pertaining to the licensing and regulation of child care. This same recommendation applies to care centers for people with developmental disabilities and senior citizens. Readers seeking additional information about child care center definitions and regulations should consult PAS Report No. 422, Zoning for Child Care, by Ann Cibulskis and Marsha Ritzdorf.*

■ **child day care home**   A private home in which more than six but not more than 12 minor children are given care and supervision for periods of less than 24 hours a day, unattended by a parent or legal guardian, except children related to an adult member of the family by blood, marriage, or adoption. Group day care home includes a home that gives care to an unrelated minor child for more than four weeks during a calendar year. *(Muskegon, Mich.)*

■ **church** *(See also religious institution)*   A building used for non-profit purposes

by a recognized and legally established sect solely for the purpose of worship. *(Coral Gables, Fla.)*

A building wherein persons regularly assemble for religious worship and which is maintained and controlled by a religious body organized to sustain public worship, together with all accessory buildings and uses customarily associated with such primary purpose. Includes synagogue, temple, mosque, or other such place for worship and religious activities. *(Muskegon, Mich.)*

*Commentary: Most zoning codes allow churches, either by right or as a conditional use, in residential districts. Some codes include accessory uses, such as schools, coffee houses, day care centers, bingo parlors, and halls, in the definition of church. A community, however, may want to distinguish these uses from the church itself because they are likely to have a greater impact on the surrounding residential area. Indeed, one of the problems confronting communities in the past few years is the creation of "megachurches" (see the definition of "megachurch") whose impacts far exceed those of a traditional church.*

■ **church, community-scale**   A church or religious institution with a seating capacity of greater than 600 persons in the sanctuary or main activity area. *(Denver, Colo.)*

■ **church, neighborhood-scale**   A church or religious institution with a seating capacity of 600 persons or less in the sanctuary or main activity area. *(Denver, Colo.)*

■ **cineplex** *(See movie theater, cineplex)*

■ **circulation**   Those means of transportation that carry passengers or goods to, from, over, or along a corridor. *(Renton, Wash.)*

Systems, structures and physical improvements for the movement of people, goods, fuel, water, air, sewage or power by such means as streets, highway, railways, waterways, towers, airways, pipes and conduits, and the handling of people and goods by such means as terminals, stations, warehouses and other storage buildings or transshipment points. *(Colts Neck, N.J.)*

■ **circulation system**   A network of transit, automobile, bicycle, and pedestrian rights-of-way that connect origins and destinations. *(California Planning Roundtable)*

■ **circus** *(See also carnival)*   A temporary outdoor amusement center, bazaar, or fair, either involving use of special purpose equipment or conducted by professional operators, or both, and where activities include such things as rides, exhibitions, food service, sales, or small-scale games. *(National City, Calif.)*

■ **citizen action group (CAG)**   A requirement for formalized citizen participation in the determination of where and how Community Development Blocak Grants will be spent. Since the inception of the requirement to show citizen involvement in community planning and action in the Federal Housing Act of 1954, the federal government has continued to increase its pressure for representative citizen involvement in policy determination in the use of aid money. Members of CAGs are usually appointed, although in some instances election by districts may be used. In all cases, the membership is required to be representative to all geographic, economic, and ethnic groups. *(Handbook for Planning Commissioners in Missouri)*

■ **city**   [T]he city [city name] or the area within the territorial limits of the city of [city name] and such territory outside of the city over which the city has jurisdiction or control by virtue of any constitutional or statutory provision. *(Soldotna, Alaska)*

A form of municipal government; also, the territory lying within the boundaries of such government. *(New York Planning Federation)*

An incorporated place that has combined its governmental functions with a county or sub-county entity but contains one or more other incorporated places that continue to function as local governments within the consolidated government. *(United States Census Bureau, which uses the term "consolidated city")*

■ **city council**   The legislative or governing board in most cities. *(New York Planning Federation)*

■ **city planner** *(See also Planner definitions)*   The officially designated city employee charged with the responsibility for the interpretation and administration of the zoning code, and other land development ordinances adopted by the city, including the issuance of zoning permits. . . . *(Maryland Heights, Mo.)*

■ **city planning**   The decision-making process in which goals and objectives are established, existing resources and conditions analyzed, strategies developed, and controls enacted to achieve the goals and objectives as they relate to cities and communities. *(Iowa State University Extension Service)*

Furthering the welfare of people and their communities by creating convenient, equitable, healthful, efficient, and attractive environments for present and future generations. *(The American Planning Association)*

■ **civic center**   An area developed or to be developed with any of the following public buildings or uses, including offices, libraries, playgrounds, parks, assembly halls, police stations, fire stations. *(Santa Clara County, Calif.)*

■ **civil defense**   The preparations for and the carrying out of all emergency functions, other than functions for which military forces are primarily responsible, to prevent, minimize, and repair injury and damage resulting from disasters caused by enemy attack, sabotage, or other enemy hostile action, or from fire, flood, earthquake, or other natural causes. These functions include, without limitation, fire-fighting services, police services, medical and health services, rescue, engineering, air-raid warning services, communications, radiological, chemical and other special weapons defense, evacuation of persons from stricken areas, emergency welfare services, emergency transportation, existing or properly assigned functions of plant protection, temporary restoration of public utility services, and other functions related to civilian protection, to-

gether with all other activities necessary or incidental to preparation for and carrying out of the foregoing functions. *(Rochester, Minn.)*

■ **civil defense forces** *(See also law enforcement officer)*   Any personnel employed by the city and any other volunteers or paid members of the local civil defense organization engaged in carrying on civil defense functions. *(Rochester, Minn.)*

■ **civil engineering**   The application of the knowledge of the forces of nature, principles of mechanics, and the properties of materials to the evaluation, design, and construction of civil works for the beneficial uses of mankind. *(Renton, Wash.)*

■ **classification**   A use category in the broad list of land uses in which certain uses, either individually or as to type, are identified as possessing similar characteristics or performance standards and are permitted as compatible uses in the same zone or classification. A classification, as the term is employed in this title, includes provisions, conditions, and requirements related to the location of uses. *(Ocean Shores, Wash.)*

■ **classroom**   Educational facilities of the district required to house students for its basic educational program. The classrooms are those facilities the district determines are necessary to best serve its student population. Specialized facilities as identified by the district, including but not limited to gymnasiums, cafeterias, libraries, administrative offices, and child care centers, shall not be counted as classrooms. *(Bellevue, Wash.)*

■ **clear-cutting** *(See also forestry definitions)*   Removal of an entire stand of trees and shrubs. *(St. Paul, Minn.)*

■ **clear vision area**   The area bounded by the street property lines of corner lots and a line joining points along said street lines 20 feet) from their point of intersection. *(Renton, Wash.)*

■ **clear vision triangle** *(See also corner clearance; sight distance triangle)*   The vision triangle at a street intersection or street and railroad intersection shall be formed horizontally, by measuring 40 feet along the roadway edges or roadway and railroad track edges from the intersection of the roadway edges or roadway edge and railroad track and connecting those points, and vertically by measuring between three feet and 10 feet above grade. The Clear Vision Triangle at driveway and street intersections: Where a driveway enters the street right-of-way, a vision triangle shall be formed horizontally, by measuring 10 feet into the lot as measured from the sidewalk edge that is closest to the property line (or from the property line if no sidewalk exists), and 20 feet along the sidewalk edge (or property line if no sidewalk exists) parallel to the street, and vertically by measuring between three feet and 10 feet above grade. *(Boise City, Idaho)*

An area of unobstructed vision at street intersections between three and eight feet above the gutter line and within a triangular area at the street corner, which area is bounded by: (1) The street property lines of the corner lot and a line connecting points 25 feet distant from the intersection of the property lines of such lot; or (2) The curb lines of an intersection and a line connecting points 35 feet distant from the corner of the intersection, such corner determined by projecting the curb lines out to a specific point, whichever is the lesser. *(Albuquerque, N. Mex.)*

■ **clear zone**    An area beyond the curb radius, so specified, which shall be kept clear of all objects to provide emergency vehicle clearance. *(Monroe County, Fla.)*

■ **clearance**    The vertical distance from the established grade level to the bottom of the sign or sign can. *(Baton Rouge, La.)*

■ **clinic** *(See also **health care facility; hospital; sanitarium**)*    A building, other than a hospital as herein defined, used by two or more licensed physicians for the purpose of receiving and treating patients. *(Boise City, Idaho)*

A facility providing medical, psychiatric, or surgical service for sick or injured per-

sons exclusively on an out-patient basis, including emergency treatment, diagnostic services, training, administration, and services to outpatients, employees, or visitors. The term, "clinic," includes immediate care facilities, where emergency treatment is the dominant form of care provided at the facility. *(Blacksburg, Va.)*

An establishment where human patients who are not lodged over night are admitted for examination and treatment by a group of physicians, dentists, other health care professionals, or similar professions. *(Muskegon, Mich.)*

A facility for examining and treating patients with medical problems on an outpatient basis, including ambulatory care or similar medical services that generally require a stay of less than 24 hours. *(Nashville and Davidson County, Tenn.)*

A building or portion of a building containing offices and facilities for providing medical, dental, and psychiatric services for outpatients only. *(Camas, Wash.)*

■ **close**    A small square or rectangular space providing road access to several house use lots and performing the same function as a cul-de-sac. Its landscape consists of grassy areas and benches, informal play grounds, and native trees formally disposed. A close requires high maintenance. The width of the close must correspond to the standard turning radius requirements. *(Monroe County, Fla.)*

■ **club**    Buildings and facilities, owned or operated by a corporation, association, person or persons, for a social, edu-

cational, or recreational purpose, to which membership is required for participation and not primarily operated for profit nor to render a service that is customarily carried on as a business. *(Stonington, Conn.)*

A nonprofit association of persons who are bonafide members paying annual dues, use of premises being restricted to members and their guests. *(Maple Grove, Minn.)*

An organization and its premises catering exclusively to members and their guests for social, intellectual, recreational, or athletic purposes that are conducted for profit; includes lodge. *(Albuquerque, N. Mex.)*

■ **clubhouse**    A building to house a club or social organization not conducted for private profit, as documented by state or federal records, and which is not an adjunct to or operated by or in connection with a public tavern, cafe, or other public place. *(Hartford, Conn.)*

■ **cluster development**    A development design technique (pictured below) that concentrates buildings in specific areas on a site to allow remaining land to be used for recreation, common open space, or the preservation of historically or environmentally sensitive features. *(Omaha, Nebr.)*

A residential use that divides land into not more than the number of lots permissible in a conventional subdivision of the same property in the same zone, but where the size of individual lots may be reduced in order to gain common open space. *(Deering, N.H.)*

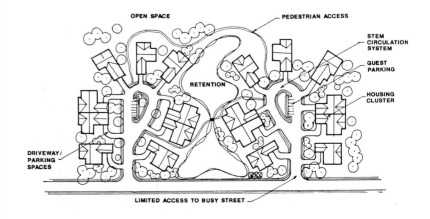

Development in which a number of dwelling units are placed in closer proximity than usual, or are attached, with the purpose of retaining an open space area. *(California Planning Roundtable)*

The site planning technique of grouping dwelling units around courts, parking areas, common open spaces and private drives as opposed to fronting all on a public street. *(North Kansas City, Mo., which uses the term "cluster housing")*

■ **cluster, residential** The placement of more than one building envelope on a single lot or parcel of land for the purpose of constructing single-family residential dwelling units in either attached or detached construction arrangement, and where the property ownership outside the building envelopes is commonly held by all single-family dwellings on that lot or parcel of land. *(Renton, Wash.)*

■ **cluster subdivision** A subdivision in which the lot sizes are reduced below those normally required in the zoning district in which the development is located, in return for the provision of permanent open space. *(Muskegon, Mich.)*

A wholly or principally residential subdivision that permits a reduction in lot area, setback, or other site development regulations, provided there is no increase in the overall density permitted for a conventional subdivision in a given zoning district, and the remaining land area is used for common space. *(Omaha, Nebr.)*

■ **code enforcement** The attempt by a government unit to cause property owners and others responsible for buildings and related land to bring their properties up to standards required by building codes, housing codes, and other ordinances. *(Handbook for Planning Commissioners in Missouri)*

■ **coffee house** *(See also tea house)* An informal restaurant (pictured above) primarily offering coffee, tea, and other beverages, and where light refreshments and limited menu meals may also be sold. *(Plymouth, Minn.)*

■ **coffee kiosk** A retail food business in a freestanding building (pictured at right) that sells coffee or other beverages

and premade bakery goods from a drive-through window to customers seated in their automobiles for consumption off the premises and that provides no indoor or outdoor seating. *(St. Paul, Minn.)*

■ **co-generation** The harnessing of heat energy that normally would be wasted to generate electricity—usually through the burning of waste. *(California Planning Roundtable)*

■ **co-generation facility** A nonutility, privately owned installation that produces useful energy, but not limited to electricity, water, thermal, and gas; or produces a service as waste disposal to create or convert to a useable energy; that is intended for sale to the public by use of a distribution system or connection to an existing system, such as a utility, which is owned by an agency which, under public franchise or ownership, or under certificate of convenience and ne-

cessity, provides the public with electricity, gas, heat, steam, communication, water, sewerage collection, or other similar services. *(Valdez, Alaska)*

■ **collection office** The business location of any person engaged in the business of collecting or receiving payment for others on any account, bill, or other indebtedness. *(Madison, Wisc.)*

■ **collective household** *(See also family)* A group of at least two, but not more than five, persons who are unrelated by blood, marriage, or adoption, living together as an independent housekeeping unit. *(Oakland, Calif.)*

■ **college/university** *(See educational facilities, college/university)*

■ **co-location** *(See telecommunications, co-location)*

■ **columbarium** *(See also cemetery; crematorium; mausoleum)* A structure or building substantially exposed above ground intended to be used for the interment of the cremated remains of a deceased person or animal. *(Durham, N.C.)*

A vault with niches for urns. *(Gurnee, Ill.)*

■ **combining zone** *(See overlay zone)*

■ **commercial burn** Burning performed for the purpose of commercial profit, land clearing, and all other burning not classified as residential burning or recreational fire. *(Hilton Head Island N.C.)*

■ **commercial, community** A mix of commercial land uses typically serving more than one residential neighborhood, usually a subarea of the city, with services and retail goods. *(Renton, Wash.)*

■ **commercial, convenience**    Small commercial areas providing limited retail goods and services, such as groceries and dry cleaning for nearby residential customers. *(Renton, Wash.)*

■ **commercial district**    Neighborhood, community, highway/tourist, and service commercial zoning designations or their equivalent specific plan zoning designation. *(Temecula, Calif.)*

■ **commercial purpose**    The growing, processing, or manufacturing of products or the provision of services for consideration and profit. *(Maui County, Hawaii)*

■ **commercial, retail** *(See retail establishment definitions)*

■ **commercial service**    Retail establishments that primarily render services rather than goods. Such services may include, but not be limited to, copy shops, printing services, package and postal services, photo processing, janitorial services, and similar operations. *(Champaign, Ill.)*

■ **commercial strip** *(See shopping center, commercial strip)*

■ **commercial use**    An occupation, employment, or enterprise that is carried on for profit by the owner, lessee, or licensee. *(Mankato, Minn.)*

A land-use classification that permits facilities for the buying and selling of commodities and services. *(California Planning Roundtable)*

A business use or activity at a scale greater than home industry involving retail or wholesale marketing of goods and services. Examples of commercial uses include offices and retail shops. *(Island County, Wash.)*

The purchase, sale, or transaction involving the disposition of any article, substance, commodity, or service; the maintenance or conduct of offices, professions, or recreational or amusement enterprises conducted for profit and also including renting of rooms, business offices, and sales display rooms and premises. *(Danville, N.Y.)*

■ **commercial, wholesale** *(See wholesale establishment)*

■ **common area**    Any portion of a development that is not part of a lot or tract and is designed for the common usage of the development. These areas include green open spaces and may include such other uses as parking lots and pedestrian walkways. Maintenance of such areas is not the responsibility of city-parish government and shall be set forth by the development association in the form of restrictive covenants, which shall guarantee the maintenance of these areas. *(Baton Rouge, La.)*

Land within a development, not individually owned or dedicated for public use, which is designed and intended for the common use or enjoyment of the residents of the development. May include complementary structures and improvements. *(Boise City, Idaho)*

A parcel or parcels of land or an area of water or a combination of land and water within the site designated for a planned unit development and designed and intended for the use or enjoyment of residents of a planned unit development. Common areas may contain such complementary structures and improvements as are necessary and appropriate for the benefit and enjoyment of residents of the planned unit development. *(Renton, Wash.)*

■ **common elements**    Land amenities, parts of buildings, central services, and utilities and any other elements and facilities owned and used be all unit owners and designated in the master deed as common elements. *(Schaumburg, Ill.)*

■ **common entrance**    Any access facility that provides passageway from the outside to a group of apartments in a garden apartment building or apartment house. *(Gurnee, Ill.)*

■ **common grounds**    Any land held in common through a homeowners' association or similar organization. *(Sioux Falls, S.D.)*

■ **common ownership**    Ownership by the same person, corporation, firm, entity, partnership, or unincorporated asso-

ciation; or ownership by different corporations, firms, partnerships, entities, or unincorporated associations, in which a stockholder, partner, or associate owns an interest in each corporation, firm, partnership, entity, or unincorporated association. *(Escambia County, Fla.)*

■ **communication tower** *(See telecommunications tower)*

■ **communications services**    Establishments primarily engaged in the provision of broadcasting and other information relay services accomplished through the use of electronic and telephonic mechanisms. Excluded are facilities classified as major utility services or broadcasting or communication towers. Typical uses include television studios, telecommunication service centers, telegraph service offices, or film and sound recording facilities. *(Blacksburg, Va.)*

■ **community**    A subarea of the city consisting of residential, institutional, and commercial uses sharing a common identity. *(Renton, Wash.)*

■ **community center**    A building to be used as a place of meeting, recreation, or social activity and not operated for profit and in which neither alcoholic beverages or meals are normally dispensed or consumed. *(Hartford, Conn.)*

A place, structure, area, or other facility used for and providing religious, fraternal, social, and/or recreational programs generally open to the public and designed to accommodate and serve significant segments of the community. May also be referred to as a convention center or civic center. *(Mankato, Minn.)*

A meeting place where people living in the same community may carry on cultural, recreational, or social activities, and possessing outdoor recreational facilities, such as golf courses, tennis courts, or polo grounds. *(Thousand Oaks, Calif.)*

■ **Community Development Block Grant (CDBG)** *(See also block grant; target area)*    A grant program administered by the U.S. Department of Housing and Urban Development (HUD) on a formula basis for entitlement communities, and by the State Department of Housing and Community Development (HCD) for nonentitled jurisdictions. This grant allots money to cities and counties for housing rehabilitation and community development, including public facilities and economic development. *(California Planning Roundtable)*

The term resulting from the passage of the Housing and Community Development Act of 1974 (Public Law 93-383). Under this legislation, the various community development programs administered by the Department of Housing and Urban Development (HUD) were consolidated into a single block grant system. Within the guidelines adopted, local governments were given greater discretion as to where the money would be used. A principal purpose was to strengthen the ability of local government to "determine the community's development needs, set priorities, and allocate resources to various activities." *(Handbook for Planning Commissioners in Missouri)*

■ **community development corporation (CDC)**  A quasi-public nonprofit corporation organized under bylaws to carry out certain public purposes. *(APA Research Department)*

■ **community facilities**  A noncommercial use established primarily for the benefit and service of the population of the community in which it is located. *(Palm Desert, Calif.)*

■ **community facilities district**  Under the Mello-Roos Community Facilities Act of 1982, a legislative body may create within its jurisdiction a special district that can issue tax-exempt bonds for the planning, design, acquisition, construction, and/or operation of public facilities, as well as provide public services to district residents. Special tax assessments levied by the district are used to repay the bonds. *(California Planning Roundtable)*

■ **community gardens**  A private or public facility for cultivation of fruits, flowers, vegetables, or ornamental plants by more than one person or family. *(Renton, Wash.)*

■ **community health center**  A public or nonprofit private medical care facility that (1) is not part of a hospital and is organized and operated to provide comprehensive primary care service; (2) is located in an area that has demonstrated need for services based on geographic and economic factors; (3) serves low-income, uninsured, minority and elderly persons; (4) makes its services available to individuals, regardless of their ability to pay; (5) employs a charge schedule with a discount based on income; (6) provides, on an ongoing basis, primary health services by physicians and, where appropriate, mid-level practitioners, diagnostic laboratory, and x-ray, or through firm arrangement; (7) has at least one-half of the full-time equivalent primary care providers as full-time members of its staff; (8) maintains an ongoing quality assurance program; (9) is a participating Title XIX and Medicare provider; (10) has a governing board of at least 9 and no more than 25 members with authority and responsibility for policy and conduct of the center, the majority of whom are active users of the center and of the nonuser board members, nor more than half may derive more than 10 percent of their annual income from the health care industry; (11) provides primary care services at least 32 hours per week; and (12) has arrangements for professional coverage during hours when the center is closed. For purposes of this chapter, none of medical institutions or organizations defined in Connecticut General Statute Section 19a-490 shall be considered a "community health center." *(Hartford, Conn.)*

A community center facility where social, recreational, welfare, health, or child care assistance is provided by a public, quasi-public, tax exempt, church, or municipal agency. *(Island County, Wash., which uses the term "community welfare or health center")*

■ **community of place**  A dynamic, diverse, compact, and efficient center that has evolved and been maintained at a human scale, with an easily accessible central core of commercial and community services, residential units, and recognizable natural and built landmarks

and boundaries that provide a sense of place and orientation. *(New Jersey State Plan)*

■ **community redevelopment agency (CRA)** *(See also **target area**)*  A local agency . . . for the purpose of planning, developing, re-planning, redesigning, clearing, reconstructing, and/or rehabilitating all or part of a specified area with residential, commercial, industrial, and/or public (including recreational) structures and facilities. The redevelopment agency's plans must be compatible with adopted community general plans. *(California Planning Roundtable)*

■ **community service area**  A geographic subarea of a city or county used for the planning and delivery of parks, recreation, and other human services based on an assessment of the service needs of the population in that subarea. *(California Planning Roundtable)*

■ **commute**  A home-to-work or work-to-home trip. *(Alameda County, Calif.)*

■ **commute mode**  The type of conveyance used in transportation, including single-occupancy motor vehicle, rideshare vehicle (carpool or vanpool), transit, bicycle, and walking. *(Tucson, Ariz., which uses the term "mode")*

■ **commute mode, alternative**  Any means of commute transportation other than that in which the single occupant motor vehicle is the dominant mode, including telecommuting and compressed work weeks if they result in reducing commute trips. *(Thurston County, Wash.)*

■ **commute, reverse**  Movement in a direction opposite to the main flow of travel, such as from the central city to a suburb during the commute hour. *(Sacramento Regional Transit District)*

■ **commute shed**  The area from which people do or might commute from their homes to a specific workplace destination, given specific assumptions about maximum travel time or distance. *(California Planning Roundtable)*

■ **commuter matching service** *(See also **transportation demand management (TDM)**)*  Any system, whether it uses computer or manual methods, which assists in matching employees for the purpose of sharing rides to reduce drive-alone travel. *(Tucson, Ariz.)*

■ **commuter rail** *(See also **transit, light rail (LRT)**)* The portion of passenger railroad operations that carries passengers within urban areas, or between urban areas and their suburbs, but differs from rail rapid transit in that the passenger cars generally are heavier, the average trip lengths are usually longer, and the operations are carried out over tracks that are part of the railroad system. *(Sacramento Regional Transit District)*

■ **company town** Employee housing and supporting commercial, office, recreational, professional, administrative, and other ancillary uses associated with the functioning of an isolated industrial, mining, energy production, utilities, resorts, or agricultural-based use. This development may occur on a single parcel or multiple parcels. *(Washoe County, Nev.)*

■ **compatibility** The characteristics of different land uses or activities that permit them to be located near each other in harmony and without conflict. It is a general but important concept which forms the basis for the separation of uses, through zoning, into districts. *(Handbook for Planning Commissioners in Missouri)*

■ **compatible** (1) Having harmony in design and/or appearance between two or more attributes of a structure; (2) Having harmony in design and/or appearance between two or more structures; (3) Having harmony in design and/or appearance between two or more attributes of a neighborhood; or (4) Having harmony in use or function between two or more attributes of a neighborhood or area. *(Thornton, Colo.)*

Capable of existing together without conflict or ill effects. *(California Planning Roundtable)*

Any property, use, or service that is capable of direct association with certain other uses because it is complementary, congruous, or otherwise nondetrimental. *(Gurnee, Ill., which uses the term "compatible use")*

■ **compensable/compensative regulations** Regulations that permit the payment of compensation to property owners when their land is severely diminished in value as a result of the regulations. Such regulations are a device to chart the middle course between police power regulations and eminent domain; that is, when there is an effective taking of the land or most of its value. They have been proposed to keep land in a relatively undeveloped state and thus have some of the same elements as the purchase of development rights. Compensable regulations have seldom been employed in actual practice. *(PAS Report No. 322, The Language of Zoning)*

■ **compensation project** *(See **wetland compensation project**)*

■ **compensatory mitigation** *(See **wetland compensatory mitigation**)*

■ **compensatory storage** *(See **floodplain compensatory storage**)*

■ **compost** A humus-like material, produced from composting, that has been stabilized to a degree that is potentially beneficial to plant growth and usable as a soil conditioner, top soil, growing medium amendment, or other similar uses to buffer the soil Ph, improve soil aggregation and tilth, reduce erosion, enhance water infiltration and retention, increase soil porosity and aeration, slow the rate of temperature change in soil, provide food for soil microorganisms, or enhance availability of micronutrients in soils. *(Boise City, Idaho)*

■ **composting** Processing waste in a controlled environment to produce a stable product by microbiologically degrading organic matter under aerobic conditions. *(State of Vermont)*

■ **composting facility** *(See also **solid waste compost facility**)* A facility where organic matter that is derived primarily from off-site is to be processed by composting and/or is processed for commercial purposes. Activities of a composting facility may include management, collection, transportation, staging, composting, curing, storage, marketing, or use of compost. *(Boise City, Idaho)*

A commercial or public solid waste processing facility where yard or garden waste is transformed into soil or fertilizer by biological decomposition. *(Blue Springs, Mo.)*

■ **comprehensive plan** *(See also **general plan; master plan**)* A plan for development of an area which recognizes the physical, economic, social, political, aesthetic, and related factors of the community involved. *(Handbook for Planning Commissioners in Missouri)*

A compilation of policy statements, goals and objectives, standards, maps, and statistical data for the physical, social, and economic development, both public and private, of [the] community. *(Las Cruces, N. Mex.)*

■ **computer design and development facility** A business primarily engaged in the development or engineering of computer software or computer hardware, but excluding retail sales, computer hardware manufacturers, and computer repair services. *(Boulder, Colo.)*

■ **concentrated animal feeding operation (CAFO)** *(See **feedlot**)*

■ **concept plan** Written and graphic documents submitted for rezoning of a tract to Planned Unit Development Concept (PUD) that indicate in a conceptual form the proposed land uses and their overall impact on the subject tract and surrounding tracts. . . . *(Baton Rouge, La.)*

■ **concurrency** Installation and operation of facilities and services needed to meet the demands of new development simultaneous with the development. *(California Planning Roundtable)*

■ **concurrency determination network** A listing of all existing and planned roadway segments . . . that comprise the roadway network to be used when evaluating the traffic impacts of a proposed development. *(Indian River County, Fla.)*

■ **concurrency management system** The process used to determine that public facilities and services needed to support development are available concurrent with the impacts of such development. *(Indian River County, Fla.)*

■ **concurrency review process** The procedures, review time frames, and appeals process pursuant to . . . the concurrency management system of the . . . land development regulations. *(Indian River County, Fla.)*

■ **concurrency test** A comparison of a development's impact on public facilities with the capacity of public facilities that are or will be available no later than the impacts of development. *(Clearwater, Fla.)*

■ **condemnation** *(See also **eminent domain; taking**)* The taking of private property by a government unit for public use, when the owner will not relinquish it through sale or other means; the owner is compensated by payment of market value. The power to take the property is based on the concept of eminent domain. *(Handbook for Planning Commissioners in Missouri)*

■ **condemnation for occupancy** An order issued by the code official prohibiting any person from occupying the dwelling unit specified in such order until it has been revoked, and further preventing anyone from being present on such premises except for the purpose of cleaning up and/or making repairs to the premises. *(St. Louis, Mo.)*

■ **conditional use** *(See **use, conditional**)*

■ **conditional use permit** *(See **permit, conditional use**)*

■ **conditional zoning** The attachment of special conditions to a rezoning that are not spelled out in the text of the zoning chapter. Conditions can include restrictions as to use, size, design, and development timing and can be stipulated by the city council as a means to mitigate potential adverse impacts that could be expected to occur without imposing such conditions. *(Conyers, Ga.)*

■ **condominium** A multiple dwelling or development containing individually owned dwelling units and jointly owned and shared areas and facilities, which dwelling or development is subject to the provisions of [state and local laws]. *(Maple Grove, Minn.)*

Real estate, portions of which are designated for separate ownership and the remainder of which is designated for common ownership solely by the owners of those portions. Real estate is not a condominium unless the undivided interests in the common elements are vested in the unit owners. *(Boise City, Idaho)*

The ownership of individual dwelling units located on a lot or lots which are owned in common by individual unit owners, or any division of the interests in real property, including easements and leases of over five years, that have the effect of permitting more than one dwelling unit on a lot without the division of the fee simple interest in said lot. *(Stonington, Conn.)*

■ **condominium document** The master deed, recorded pursuant to the [state act], as amended, and any other instrument referred to in the master deed or bylaws that affects the rights and obligations of a co-owner of the condominium. *(Muskegon, Mich.)*

■ **condominium project (subdivision)** A division of land on the basis of condominium ownership, which is not subject to the provisions of the (ordinances) or successor act. Any "condominium unit," or portion thereof, consisting of vacant land shall be equivalent to the term "lot" for the purposes of determining compliance of a condominium subdivision with the provisions of this ordinance pertaining to minimum lot size, minimum lot width, maximum lot coverage, and maximum floor area ratio. *(Muskegon, Mich.)*

■ **condominium subdivision plan** The drawings attached to the master deed for a condominium subdivision project which describe the size, location, area, horizontal and vertical boundaries, and volume of each condominium unit contained in the condominium subdivision project, as well as the nature, location, and size of common elements. *(Muskegon, Mich.)*

■ **condominium unit** That portion of a condominium project or condominium subdivision project that is designed and intended for separate ownership and use, as described in the master deed, regardless of whether it is intended for residential, office, industrial, business, recreational use as a time-share unit, or any other type of use. A condominium unit may consist of either vacant land or space that either encloses or is enclosed by a building structure. Any "condominium unit" consisting of vacant land shall be equivalent to the term "lot" for the purposes of determining compliance of a condominium subdivision project with the provisions of this ordinance pertaining to minimum lot size, minimum lot width, maximum lot coverage, and maximum floor area ratio. *(Muskegon, Mich.)*

■ **conference center** *(See also **convention center**)* A facility used for service organizations, business and professional conferences, and seminars limited to accommodations for conference attendees. The accommodations can include sleeping, eating, and recreation. A conference center is not designed to be only utilized by the general public for overnight purposes. *(Howard County, Md.)*

■ **conforming use** *(See **use, conforming**)*

■ **congestion management plan (CMP)** A mechanism employing growth management techniques, including traffic level-of-service requirements, standards for public transit, trip reduction programs involving transportation systems management and jobs/housing balance strategies, and capital improvement programming, for the purpose of controlling and/or reducing the cumulative regional traffic impacts of development. *(California Planning Roundtable)*

■ **congregate care facility** *(See **elderly housing, congregate care facility**)*

■ **consanguinity** *(See also **family**)* Only the following persons are related within the second degree of consanguinity: husbands and wives, parents and children, grandparents and grandchildren, brothers and sisters, aunts and uncles and nephews and nieces, and first cousins. These relationships may be of the whole or half blood, by adoption, or by affinity. *(Boulder, Colo.)*

■ **conservation** The management of natural resources to prevent waste, destruction, or degradation. *(California Planning Roundtable)*

■ **conservation, agricultural land**  The planting of soil-nourishing plants and trees to achieve soil conservation and environmental benefits, including but not limited to soil nourishment, prevention of soil erosion, improvement of air quality, and habitat restoration. *(Maui County, Hawaii)*

■ **conservation district**  A district that has retained an adequate amount of its historic character for interpretation, although some alterations may have occurred. *(Atlanta, Ga.)*

A district established to provide a means of conserving an area's distinctive atmosphere or character by protecting or enhancing its significant architectural or cultural attributes. *(Dallas, Tex.)*

An area . . . that contains buildings or sites within definable geographic boundaries that, while not of such historic and/or architectural significance to be designated as landmarks or included within a Historic District, nevertheless are characterized by sound housing or commercial buildings that contribute to the visual characteristics or distinctive atmosphere of the neighborhood in which such property is located. *(Champaign, Ill.)*

■ **conservation district, architectural**  Any area designated by the commission as an area containing any physical features or improvements or both that are of historical, social, cultural, architectural, or aesthetic significance to the city and cause such area to constitute a distinctive section of the city. *(Boston, Mass.)*

■ **conservation district, historic**  A local historic district established by the city council requiring architectural design review guidelines for demolition, new construction, or additions to habitable area of buildings, structures, sites, and objects in the public right-of-way and within the boundaries of the historic conservation district. *(Memphis, Tenn.)*

■ **conservation district, neighborhood**  A district, the purposes of which are (1) to conserve and protect the beauty and heritage of the city and to improve the quality of its environment through conservation and maintenance of neighborhoods

that constitute or reflect distinctive features of the architectural, cultural, political, economic, or social history of the city; (2) to resist and restrain environmental influences to this purpose; (3) to foster appropriate use and wider public knowledge and appreciation of such neighborhoods; and (4) to promote the public welfare by making the city a more attractive and desirable place in which to live and work. *(Cambridge, Mass.)*

■ **conservation district, neighborhood overlay**  A district intended to accommodate unique land use, urban design, and other distinctive characteristics of older established neighborhoods. The district, used in combination with a base district, allows variations in permitted uses and site development regulation that are adapted to the needs of a specific neighborhood. *(Omaha, Neb.)*

■ **conservation district, residential**  A zoning overlay district intended to be applied to selected areas of residential districts in order to conserve areas that retain the character of earlier periods of development, to stabilize and improve property values in such areas, to encourage rehabilitation of existing housing, and to promote new construction that is compatible with the character of the area. *(Lincoln, Neb.)*

■ **conservation easement** *(See easement, conservation)*

■ **conservation element**  One of the seven state-mandated elements of a local general plan, it contains adopted goals, policies, and implementation programs for the conservation, development, and use of natural resources, including water and its hydraulic force, forests, soils, rivers and other waters, harbors, fisheries, wildlife, minerals, and other natural resources. *(California Planning Roundtable)*

■ **conservation land**  Any parcel or area of undeveloped land conserved in its natural state for perpetuity through deeds or other legal means. *(Newport, R.I.)*

■ **consignment store** *(See also second-hand merchandise, retail sales; thrift store)*  A retail establishment engaged

in selling used merchandise, such as clothing, furniture, books, shoes, or household appliances, on consignment, or a retail establishment engaged in selling donated used merchandise that is operated by an organization granted federal tax exemption pursuant to section 501(c)(3) of the Internal Revenue Service Code as amended. Merchandise is brought to the establishment and processed by marking, cleaning, sorting, and storing as a major part of the principal use. Such stores do not include those selling vehicle, auto parts, scrap or waste. *(Iowa City, Iowa)*

An enclosed facility in which used personal items such as clothes, jewelry, and/or artifacts, and/or small furniture is resold through a broker for the owner at an agreed-upon price. *(Grand Prairie, Tex.)*

■ **consistency with the comprehensive plan**  All regulations that are used to implement the local comprehensive plans must be consistent with the recommendations and policies of the plan, and state and local funding decisions must be consistent with the local plan. *(Rhode Island Statutes)*

■ **consistent**  Free from variation or contradiction. Programs in the General Plan are to be consistent, not contradictory or preferential. State law requires consistency between a general plan and implementation measures such as the zoning ordinance. *(California Planning Roundtable)*

■ **consolidation**  A combination of two or more governmental units. The units may be at the same or different levels of government. *(United States Census Bureau)*

■ **construction**  Any act or process that requires a building permit and that adds an addition onto an existing building or erects a new principal or accessory structure on a lot which is subject to the design standards for the district in which the property is located. *(Champaign, Ill.)*

On-site erection, fabrication, installation, alteration, demolition, or removal of any structure, facility, or addition thereto, including all related activities, but not restricted to, clearing of land, earth moving, blasting and landscaping. *(Peoria, Ill.)*

■ **construction camp** Those on-site buildings and/or trailers that are temporarily used to house and feed construction workers and/or store project construction materials and/or provide office space for contractors and sub-contractors. *(Unalaska, Alaska)*

■ **construction envelope** One or more specified areas on a lot or parcel within which all structures, driveways, parking, nonnative landscaping, water surfaces, decks, walks, and improved recreation facilities are located. Underground utilities may be located outside the construction envelope. *(Scottsdale, Ariz.)*

■ **construction field office** A mobile home, travel trailer, truck trailer, and/or other structure used as an office in conjunction with a construction project. Only one construction or field office shall be allowed per construction site. *(Coral Gables, Fla.)*

■ **construction sales and services** Establishments or places of business primarily engaged in retail or wholesale sale, from the premises, of materials used in the construction of buildings or other structures, but specifically excluding automobile or equipment supplies otherwise classified herein. Typical uses include building material stores and home supply establishments. *(Blacksburg, Va.)*

■ **construction service** Any of the activities commonly referred to as construction and shall include without limiting thereby, plumbing, heating, roofing, interior remodeling, excavating. *(Cambria County, Pa.)*

■ **construction sign** *(See **sign, construction**)*

■ **construction waste** Building materials and other wastes associated with construction projects including, but not limited to, such materials as wood, concrete, drywall, masonry, roofing, siding, structural metal, wire, insulation, plastics, styrofoam, twine, baling and strapping materials, cans, buckets, packaging materials, and containers. *(Renton, Wash.)*

■ **construction yard** An area on or immediately adjacent to a major construction or demolition site used on a temporary basis for the parking and storage of equipment used in the project, and the storage and preparation of materials and other items used in the project. Such yard may include construction offices and such shops as are necessary for work on the immediate project. *(National City, Calif.)*

Any area used on a temporary basis for the storage or processing of materials and supplies used in the actual construction of a project for a limited period of time. *(Thurston County, Wash., which uses the term "construction materials yard")*

■ **contaminant** *(See also **pollutant**)* Any "regulated substance," as defined by [state law], as in effect on the date of passage of this ordinance and as amended from time to time, and all petroleum products, including gasoline, oil, waste oil, and other fuels as well as their hazardous constituents. *(Sioux Falls, S.D.)*

Any physical, chemical, biological, or radiological substance that enters then hydrological cycle through human action and may cause a deleterious effect on ground and/or surface water resources; it shall include but not limited to hazardous waste, limiting nutrients and sanitary sewage. *(New Shoreham, R.I.)*

■ **contiguous** *(See also **abutting; adjacent/adjoining**)* In contact, adjoining, or touching another object or item, as distinguished from being adjacent. *(Gurnee, Ill.)*

Next to, abutting, or touching and having a boundary, or portion thereof, which is common or coterminous. *(Valdez, Alaska)*

■ **contiguous properties** Properties sharing a property line. *(Renton, Wash.)*

Land adjoining and touching other property regardless of whether or not portions of the property have separate assessor's parcel numbers, or were purchased at different times, lie in different sections, different government lots, or are separated from each other by private road or private right-of-way. *(Island County, Wash.)*

■ **contract zoning** *(See also **developer's agreement**)* The establishment of conditions in connection with a rezoning that bind the developer and the community to its terms. Contract zoning has often been invalidated mainly because it is seldom specifically authorized in state enabling legislation. *(PAS Report No. 322, The Language of Zoning)*

■ **contractors** General contractors and builders engaged in the construction of buildings, either residences or commercial structures as well as heavy construction contractors engaged in activities such as paving, highway construction, and utility construction. *(Durham, N.C.)*

■ **contractor's offices** A room or group of rooms used for conducting business affairs that does not use any exterior storage area. *(Grand Forks, N.D.)*

■ **contractor's shop** An enclosed space used for the housing and/or operating of machinery, the provision of services, the fabrication of building-related products, and interior storage, but which does not use any exterior storage area. *(Grand Forks, N.D.)*

■ **contractors, special trade** Contractors who undertake trades of a type that are specialized to assist in building construction and remodeling. This definition includes but is not limited to heating, air conditioning, painting, plumbing, and roofing. *(Durham, N.C.)*

■ **contractor's storage yard** An unenclosed portion of the lot or parcel upon which a construction contractor maintains its principal office or a permanent business office. Designation of the lot or parcel as a contractor's storage yard would allow this area to be used to store and maintain construction equipment and other materials customarily used in the trade carried on by the construction contractor. If permitted to be used in this manner, the entire lot or parcel would then be classified as a "contractor's storage yard" and will be required to conform to all applicable zoning district standards and other legislative regulations. *(Wheeling, Ill.)*

■ **contributing building** *(See also **historic preservation** definitions)* A building, site, structure, or object that adds to the historic association, historic architectural quality, or cultural values because it was present during the period of significance, relates to the documented significance of the property, and possesses historic integrity, or is capable of yielding important information about the period. *(Champaign, Ill.)*

A building within a historic district that the city finds is consistent with the description of the characteristics of the historic district, justifying its designation and is in substantially original condition, has had minimal changes to the defining characteristics of the building, or has been appropriately restored to a substantially original condition. Contributing buildings may have been previously altered with compatible additions. *(Boulder, Colo.)*

A structure that is a part of a group of structures, designated an historic district, which together reflect a unique architectural, historic, cultural, or archaeological feature of the town, commonwealth, or nation. In order to be a contributing structure, the structure must be at least 50 years old, measured from when the determination is made, and must retain its original architectural, historic, cultural, or archaeological integrity. Contributing structure includes its curtilage, where appropriate. *(Blacksburg, Va.)*

■ **contributing site** *(See also **historic preservation** definitions)* A site that is a part of a group of structures or sites designated an historic district, which as a group reflect a unique historic, cultural, or archaeological feature of the town, commonwealth, or nation, and which is a part of an historic district. *(Blacksburg, Va.)*

■ **convalescent center** *(See also **elderly housing** definitions; **nursing home**)* A facility that provides nursing services and custodial care on a 24-hour basis for three or more unrelated individuals who for reasons of illness, physical infirmity, or advanced age, require such services. *(Durham, N.C.)*

An installation other than a hospital where two or more persons afflicted with illness, injury, or an infirmity are housed or lodged, and furnished with nursing care. *(Muskegon, Mich.)*

A building wherein for compensation, nursing care is provided for persons suffering from illness, other than mental or contagious, which is not of sufficient severity to require hospitalization, or persons requiring further institutional care after being discharged from a hospital other than a mental hospital. Occupancy of a convalescent home by any patient shall not exceed 30 days within any calendar year. *(Coral Gables, Fla.)*

■ **convenience goods** Retail items generally necessary or desirable for everyday living, usually purchased at a convenient nearby location. Because these goods cost relatively little compared to income, they are often purchased without comparison shopping. *(California Planning Roundtable)*

■ **convenience store** *(See also **gas station minimart**)* A retail store with a floor area of less than 2,500 square feet that sells groceries and may also sell gasoline; does not include automotive service stations, or vehicle repair shops. *(Durham, N.C.)*

Any retail establishment offering for sale a limited line of groceries and household items intended for the convenience of the neighborhood. *(Boulder, Colo.)*

A small retail establishment, usually located within or associated with another use, that offers for sale convenience goods, such as prepackaged food items, tobacco, periodicals, and other household goods. *(Renton, Wash.)*

*Commentary: Some zoning codes make a distinction between convenience stores and other commercial retail uses. This distinction is most commonly based on the size of the establishment—with the upper threshold for convenience stores ranging from 5,000 to 7,500 square feet. Convenience stores are regulated differently from other retail uses because their operating characteristics—traffic generation, hours of operation, noise, litter, and lighting—tend to be more intrusive to neighboring residential areas. Readers should also consult the definitions for "gas station minimart."*

■ **convent or monastery** The dwelling units of a religious order or congregation. *(Island County, Wash.)*

A facility designed to accommodate 500 or more persons and used for conventions, conferences, seminars, product displays, recreation activities, and entertainment functions, along with accessory functions including temporary outdoor displays, and food and beverage preparation and service for on-premise consumption. *(Clearwater, Fla.)*

■ **convention center** *(See also **conference center**)* A facility designed to accommodate 500 or more persons and used for conventions, conferences, seminars, product displays, recreation activities, and entertainment functions, along with accessory functions including temporary outdoor displays, and food and beverage preparation and service for on-premise consumption. *(Clearwater, Fla.)*

■ **convention space** That public area assigned to conventions and in no case includes service facilities, such as kitchens or coat check rooms. *(Reno, Nev.)*

■ **conversation/rap parlor** A building or portion of a building in which there is advertising, offering, or selling the service of engaging in or listening to conversation, talk, or discussion, regardless of whether other goods or services are also simultaneously advertised, offered, or sold, and regardless of whether those other goods or services are also required to be licensed. The term "conversation parlor" shall not include bona fide legal, medical, psychiatric, psychological, or counseling services by a person or firm appropriately licensed; or bona fide educational institutions, or panels, seminars, or other similar services offered by such institutions; or churches or synagogues. *(St. Paul, Minn.)*

■ **cooperative** A multiple-family dwelling owned and maintained by the residents. The entire structure and real property is under common ownership as contrasted to a condominium dwelling where individual units are under separate individual occupant ownership. *(Maple Grove, Minn.)*

A type of ownership characterized by collective ownership of an object by an organization whose members share in the profits or other benefits of said collective ownership. *(Carmel, Ind.)*

■ **copy shop** *(See also* **print shop***)* A business engaging in the reproduction or photographic impressions through mimeographic, electrostatic, or thermal copy process, whether wet or dry. *(El Paso, Tex.)*

■ **corner clearance** The distance from an intersection of a public or private road to the nearest access connection, measured from the closest edge of the pavement of the intersecting road to the closest edge of the pavement of the connection along the traveled way. *(Clearwater, Fla.)*

■ **cornice** Any horizontal member, structural or nonstructural, of any building, projecting outward from the exterior walls at the roof line, including eaves and other roof overhang. *(Imperial Beach, Calif.)*

■ **cornice height** The vertical distance from ground level (top of finished sidewalk) to the top of the exterior cornice. *(Clearwater, Fla.)*

■ **cornice, exterior** The uppermost horizontal molded projection or other uppermost horizontal element located at the top of a building or portion of a building. *(Clearwater, Fla.)*

■ **corporate headquarters office** A complex of buildings whose purpose is to be the administrative center of a business enterprise. Corporate headquarters may include transient residential units only for employees subject to any and all provisions of this ordinance. *(Scottsdale, Ariz.)*

■ **corral** A fence-type structure consisting of vertical posts and horizontal members, and so constructed that 75 percent or more of the vertical surface is open. Chain link or other similar types of wire fences are not intended to be included in this definition and shall be classified as a fence or wall. *(Scottsdale, Ariz.)*

The primary enclosure for confining livestock. *(Valdez, Alaska)*

■ **correctional facilities** *(See also* **custodial care facility***;* **juvenile detention facility***)* Publicly or privately operated facilities housing persons awaiting trial or persons serving a sentence after being found guilty of a criminal offense. *(Durham, N.C.)*

■ **corridor** A broad geographical band that follows a general directional flow connecting major sources of trips that may contain a number of streets, highways, and transit route alignments. *(Sacramento Regional Transit District)*

A strip of land forming a passageway between two otherwise separate parts. *(Renton, Wash.)*

■ **corridor, environmental** An area of land usually bordering a water course or wetland identified as containing unique natural features that should be preserved for environmental education and/or passive recreation. *(Green Bay, Wisc.)*

■ **corridor, historic** A right of way or an area comprising one or more landmarks, historic sites, or an historic district. *(New Jersey State Plan)*

■ **corridor, mixed-use** An area of land typically along a linear transportation route where a variety of land uses are permitted, including employment, shopping, and residential. These areas are intended to be pedestrian oriented and accessible by public transit. *(APA Research Department)*

■ **corridor, pedestrian** Areas designated in the comprehensive plan as primary routes for pedestrian use to connect subareas of the city or regional trail systems, and to provide access to public facilities. *(Renton, Wash.)*

■ **corridor, scenic** An area of land generally adjacent to and visible from a roadway that requires protective measures to ensure perpetuation of its scenic qualities, whether of an urban or rural setting. *(El Paso, Tex.)*

A right-of-way or an area visible from a highway, waterway, railway or major hiking, biking, or equestrian trail that is accessible to the public, and which provides vistas over water, across expanses of vegetation such as farmlands, woodlands or coastal wetlands, or from mountaintops or ridges. *(State of New Jersey)*

■ **corridor, transit** A broad geographic band that follows a general route alignment, such as a roadway or rail right-of-way, and includes a service area within that band that would be accessible to the transit system. *(Sacramento Regional Transit District)*

■ **corridor, transportation** A combination of principal transportation routes involving a linear network of one or more highways of four or more lanes, rail lines, or other primary and secondary access facilities which support a development corridor. *(New Jersey State Plan)*

■ **corridor, wildlife** Habitats of endangered or threatened species, or habitats of other significant wildlife communities or indicator species identified in consultation with [environmental protection organizations] or [the state's] Department of Environmental Protection, Division of Fish, Game and Wildlife. *(State of New Jersey).*

A strip of land having vegetation that provides habitat and a safe passageway for wildlife. *(Cecil County, Md.)*

■ **cost-benefit analysis** An analytic method whereby the actual and hidden costs of a proposed project are measured against the benefits to be received from the project. *(Iowa State University Extension Service)*

A quantified comparison of costs and benefits generally expressed in monetary or numerical terms. It is not synonymous with the weighing or balancing of environmental and other impacts or benefits of a proposal. *(Renton, Wash.)*

■ **cottage** *(See* **cabin***)*

■ **cottage industry** *(See also* **home occupation***)* A small, individual owned business or concern . . . that functions without altering the residential character of the neighborhood, and which does not create any negative impacts on the public health, safety, and general welfare of the adjacent property owners. *(Dona Ana County, N. Mex.)*

■ **council of government (COG)** Voluntary associations of local government officials and entities. (*Handbook for Planning Commissioners in Missouri*)

■ **county** A form of regional municipal government; also, the territory lying within the boundaries of such government. (*New York Planning Federation*)

■ **country club** (*See also* **club**) A club with recreation facilities for members, their families and invited guests. (*Germantown, Tenn.*)

■ **court** An uncovered area partly or wholly enclosed by buildings or walls and used primarily for supplying access, light, and air to abutting buildings. (*Belmont, Calif.*)

An open space that may or may not have street access, and around which is arranged a single building or group of related buildings. (*Topeka, Kans.*)

An open, unoccupied, unobstructed space, other than a yard, on the same lot as a building. Trees or shrubs may be used in a court. (*Coral Gables, Fla.*)

■ **court, apartment** One or more multifamily dwellings, occupied on a long-term residential basis, any of which may be more than one story in height and arranged around one or more sides of a court or place from which court or place any dwelling unit therein has its principal means of access. An apartment court shall be deemed to include those multifamily dwellings that contain the principal means of access to any dwelling unit therein from a court or place or side yard. (*Maui County, Hawaii*)

■ **court, bungalow** Two or more single-family detached dwellings occupied and arranged around one, two, or three sides of a court that opens onto a street. (*Maui County, Hawaii*)

A group of three or more detached one-story, one-family or two-family dwellings located on a single lot, and having a common court or yard. Each dwelling unit will have a separate entrance on the ground floor. (*National City, Calif.*)

■ **court height** Height of a court measured from the level of the windowsills of the lowest story it is required to serve. (*Rye, N.Y.*)

■ **court, inner** That portion of a lot unoccupied by any part of a building, surrounded on all sides by walls, or by walls and a lot line. (*Topeka, Kans.*)

A court bounded on all sides by the building or structure. (*Homestead, Fla.*)

■ **court length** The horizontal dimension of a court at right angles to its width. (*Rye, N.Y.*)

■ **court, outer** That portion of a lot unoccupied by any part of a building, opening onto a street, alley, or yard. (*Topeka, Kans.*)

A court extending to a street or alley or to a front, side, or rear yard. (*Coral Gables, Fla.*)

■ **court, tourist** (*See also* **motel**) A group of attached or detached buildings containing individual living or sleeping units, designed or used temporarily by automobile tourists or transients with garage attached or parking spaces conveniently located to each unit, including auto courts, motels, or motor lodges. (*Maui County, Hawaii*)

■ **court-type development** A residential-type development in which the area of the court exclusive of all required yards and off-street parking spaces shall be not less than one-half of the gross ground floor area of the buildings the court is intended to serve, and the width or diameter of the court area shall be not less than the average height of the building or buildings it is intended to serve. (*Columbus, Ohio*)

■ **court width** The width of an outer court is that horizontal dimension that is substantially parallel to the principal open end of such court. The width of an inner court is its least horizontal dimension. (*Rye, N.Y.*)

■ **courtesy car** Any motor vehicle (including electrically-powered vehicles) of any carrying capacity that is operated by a motel, hotel, parking lot, automobile rental agency, limousine service, shuttle bus service or other off-airport business for the transportation of persons and/or property to and from the airport. (*Austin, Tex.*)

■ **courtesy service** The operation of an off-airport business involving the transportation of persons and/or property to and from the airport via courtesy car, regardless of whether or not there is a fee for such service. (*Austin, Tex.*)

■ **courtyard** (*See* **court**)

■ **covenant, private** (*See also* **deed restriction**) [An agreement that] binds and restricts the land in the hands of present owners and subsequent purchasers. They are enforced only by the land owners involved and not by the city or other public agency. (*Conyers, Ga.*)

■ **covenant, protective** Contract made between private parties as to the manner in which land may be used with a view towards protecting and preserving the physical and economic integrity of an area. (*Grand Forks, N.D.*)

■ **craft shop** Any business establishment that produces on the premises articles for sale of artistic quality or effect or handmade workmanship. Examples include candle making, glass blowing, weaving, pottery making, woodworking, sculpting, painting, and other associated activities. (*Muskegon, Mich.*)

■ **crawlspace** (*See also* **basement; cellar**) An enclosed area below the first usable floor of a building, generally less than five feet in height, used for limited access to plumbing and electrical utilities. (*Racine County, Wisc.*)

■ **creek** (*See also* **spring; stream**) Those areas where surface waters flow sufficiently to produce a defined channel or bed. A defined channel or bed is indicated by hydraulically sorted sediments or the removal of vegetative litter or loosely rooted vegetation by the action of moving water. The channel or bed need not contain water year-round. This definition is not meant to include stormwater runoff devices or other entirely artificial watercourses unless they are used to store and/or convey pass-through stream flows naturally occurring prior to construction of such devices. (*Renton, Wash.*)

■ **crematorium** *(See also* ***cemetery;*** ***columbarium; mausoleum)*** A location containing properly installed, certified apparatus intended for use in the act of cremation. *(Sheridan, Wyo.)*

■ **criminal justice facility** A facility used primarily for conducting the affairs of the criminal justice system, including federal, state, county, and municipal courts, public safety departments and detention facilities, together with incidental storage and maintenance of necessary vehicles. *(Glenwood Springs, Colo.)*

■ **crisis center** *(See also* ***shelter*** *definitions)* A facility or portion thereof and premises that are used for purposes of emergency shelter, crisis intervention, including counseling, referral, hotline response, and similar human social service functions. Said facility [may] include meal preparation, distribution, or service [for residents of the center as well as nonresidents]; merchandise distribution; or shelter, including boarding, lodging, or residential care. *(Topeka, Kans.)*

■ **critical facility** Facilities housing or serving many people, which are necessary in the event of an earthquake or flood, such as hospitals, fire, police, and emergency service facilities, utility "lifeline" facilities, such as water, electricity, and gas supply, sewage disposal, and communications and transportation facilities. *(California Planning Roundtable)*

■ **crosswalk** *(See also* ***pedestrian way)*** A city-owned right-of-way (pictured below) that crosses a block and furnishes pedestrian access to adjacent streets or properties. *(St. Paul, Minn.)*

That part of a roadway at an intersection included within the connections of the lateral lines of the sidewalks on opposite sides of the highway measured from the curbs, or in the absence of curbs and sidewalks from the edges of the traversable roadway; any portion of a roadway at an intersection or elsewhere distinctly indicated for pedestrian crossing by lines or other markings on the surface. *(Bethel, Maine)*

■ **cultural center** Services to the public, such as, but not limited to museums, art galleries, and libraries by a public or private, nonprofit facility. *(Nashville and Davidson County, Tenn.)*

■ **cultural features** Human structures, such as roads or buildings, that are within view of a proposed land-use change and that affect site planning. *(Maryland Department of Natural Resources)*

■ **cultural resources** Those resources that possess qualities of significance in American, [name of state], or [name of locality] history, architecture, archaeology, and culture present in districts, sites, structures, and objects that possess integrity of location, design, setting, materials, workmanship, congruency, and association. *(San Antonio, Tex.)*

■ **cultural services** A library, museum, or similar public or quasi-public use displaying, preserving, and exhibiting objects of community and cultural interest in one or more of the arts or sciences. *(Blacksburg, Va.)*

■ **culvert, cross drainage** Pipelike or boxlike construction of wood, metal, plastic, or concrete that passes under a road to catch surface water from side ditches and direct it away from a road. *(Maine Forest Service)*

■ **culvert, stream bed** Pipelike or boxlike construction of wood, metal, plastic, or concrete that passes under a road or embankment to convey a stream under a crossing without constricting waterflow or movement of fish. *(Maine Forest Service)*

■ **cumulative (pyramidal) zoning** *(See also* ***as-of-right zoning; downzoning; Euclidean zoning; upzoning)*** A zoning scheme that begins with the most pro-

tected land use, usually the single-family home, and permits in each "lower" district all the uses above plus new ones, in a sort of pyramidal fashion. Thus, the least protected zone (e.g., the heavy industrial district) would permit all uses allowed in all other districts; such districts, in effect, are not zoned. The R-2 zone would permit all R-1 zone uses and two-family homes. And so on. There are variations on this theme. Some ordinances, for example, are cumulative only within use categories but not across them. For example, single-family houses might be allowed in multifamily districts but not in commercial or industrial districts. *(PAS Report No. 322, The Language of Zoning)*

*Commentary: Cumulative zoning has been discredited in recent years. Jurisdictions have recognized that zoning districts are not hierarchical and that a single-family home is just as out of place in an industrial zone as a factory in a residential district. Most modern zoning ordinances have dropped the cumulative feature in favor of exclusive use zoning.*

■ **curb** A stone or concrete boundary usually marking the edge of a roadway or paved area. *(Schaumburg, Ill.)*

■ **curb cut** The providing of vehicular ingress and/or egress between property and an abutting public street. *(Conyers, Ga.)*

The length of the opening along the road curb for a straight-sided (90 degree) driveway. *(Hudsonville, Mich.)*

■ **curb level** The level of the established curb in front of a building or structure measured at the center of such front. Where no curb level has been established, it shall be deemed to be the established level of the center line of the street surface in front of a building or structure measured at the center line of such front. *(North Kansas City, Mo.)*

■ **curb radius** The curved edge of the throroughfare at intersections, measured at the edge of the travel lines. Curbs at intersections shall not intrude into the intersection beyond the specified maximum curb radius. Where thoroughfares of different use categories intersect, the requirements of the higher intensity use shall govern. *(Monroe County, Fla.)*

■ **curb return**    A curved segment of curb used at each end of an opening in the roadway curb. *(Las Cruces, N. Mex.)*

■ **currency exchange**    A commercial use that exchanges common currencies, sells money orders or cashiers checks, and cashes checks as its principal business activity. This shall not include a financial institution. *(Champaign, Ill.)*

An establishment that, for compensation, engages in the business of cashing checks, warrants, drafts, money orders, or other commercial paper serving the same purpose. This classification does not include a state or federally chartered bank, savings association, credit union, or industrial loan company. Further, this classification does not include establishments selling consumer goods, including consumables, where the cashing of checks or money orders is incidental to the main purpose of the business. *(Redondo Beach, Calif., which uses the term "check-cashing business")*

Any person, except a bank, trust company, savings bank, savings and loan association, credit union, or industrial loan and thrift company, engaged in the business of cashing checks, drafts, money orders, or travelers' checks for a fee. Does not include a person who provides these services incidental to the person's primary business if the charge for cashing a check or draft does not exceed one dollar or 1 percent of the value of the check or draft, whichever is greater. *(St. Paul, Minn.)*

■ **custodial care facility** *(See also **correctional facility; juvenile detention facility**)* A facility providing custodial care and treatment in a protective living environment for persons residing voluntarily or by court placement, including, without limitation, correctional and post-correctional facilities, juvenile detention facilities, and temporary detention facilities. *(Boulder, Colo.)*

■ **dairy**    An area of land on which cows are kept for the purpose of producing dairy products in commercial quantities, as well as the related buildings, equipment, and processes. *(Dona Ana County, N. Mex.)*

■ **dam**    All obstructions, wall embankments or barriers, together with their abutments and appurtenant works, if any, constructed for the purpose of storing or diverting water or creating a pool. Underground water storage tanks are not included. *(Schaumburg, Ill.)*

■ **dance hall**    Establishments in which more than 10 percent of the total floor area is designed or used as a dance floor, or where an admission fee is directly collected, or some other form of compensation is obtained for dancing. *(Blacksburg, Va.)*

■ **dance hall, public**    Any room, place or space open to the general public patronage in which is carried on dancing wherein the public may participate, whether or not a charge for admission for dancing is made. *(St. Paul, Minn.)*

■ **dancing establishments**    Any restaurant, bar, hotel or motel, club or lodge, nightclub, or other gathering place open to the public, whether or not admission is charged, wherein dancing is allowed and participated in on a recurring basis by one or more persons, whether or not they are compensated for their dancing. This shall not include dance academies, schools, or studios where dancing is permitted only by students and instructors engaged in dancing instruction, nor shall this include public or private schools, which host dances solely for students, or adult-supervised youth organizations, city, park district, or other governmental facilities that host dances, nor shall this include motels, hotels, or restaurants or businesses that only rent enclosed banquet rooms or space for private parties. *(Thousand Oaks, Calif.)*

■ **data processing facilities**    Facilities where electronic data is processed by employees, including, without limitation, data entry, storage, conversion or analysis, subscription and credit card transaction processing, telephone sales and order collection, mail order and catalog sales, and mailing list preparation. *(Boulder, Colo.)*

■ **day care** *(See also **child care** definitions)*    The care of one or more children on a regular basis, for periods of less than 24 hours per day, in a place other than the child's own dwelling unit. Day care includes family day care, group family day care, and group day care, as hereinafter defined: (1) Family Day Care: a day care program providing care for not more than 10 children at one time, and which is licensed by the county as a family day care home. The licensed capacity must include all children of any caregiver when the children are present in the residence. (2) Group Family Day Care: a day care program providing care for no more than 14 children at any one time, of which no more than 10 are under school age and which is licensed by the county as a group family day care home. The licensed capacity must include all children of any caregiver when the children are present in the residence. (3) Group Day Care: a day care program providing care for more than six children at one

time and licensed by the state or the city as a group day care center. Group day care includes programs for children known as nursery schools, day nurseries, child care centers, play groups, day care centers for school age children, after school programs, infant day care centers, cooperative day care centers, and Head Start programs. *(St. Paul, Minn.)*

■ **day care center**    Any facility operated for the purpose of providing care, protection and guidance to 10 or more individuals during only part of a 24-hour day. This term includes nursery schools, preschools, day care centers for individuals, and other similar uses but excludes public and private educational facilities or any facility offering care to individuals for a full 24-hour period. *(Blacksburg, Va.)*

A place other than an occupied dwelling that provides for the care of children or adults; or a large care home. Those receiving care are not all related to each other by blood or marriage and are not legal wards or foster children of the attendant adults, and for which care a payment, fee, or grant is made. Of those receiving care, only dependents of a large care home operator may reside on the site. *(Durham, N.C.)*

■ **day care center, large**    A facility: (1) licensed by the state, if applicable; (2) providing care for seven or more children or adults who do not reside in the facility, are present primarily during daytime hours, and do not regularly stay overnight; and (3) which may include some instruction. *(Boulder, Colo.)*

■ **day care center, small**    A facility: (1) in a dwelling unit; (2) licensed by the state, if applicable; (3) providing care for six or fewer children or adults who (except for family members) do not reside in the facility, are present primarily during daytime hours, and do not regularly stay overnight. Family members who receive care in the facility are included in the total; and (4) which may include some instruction. *(Boulder, Colo.)*

■ **day care facility, adult**    A facility providing care for the elderly and/or funcionally impaired adults in a protective setting for a portion of a 24-hour day. (Wheaton Ill.)

■ **day care facility, child** A facility that provides nonmedical care to children under 18 years of age in need of personal services, supervision, or assistance essential for sustaining the activities of daily living or for the protection of the individual on less than a 24-hour basis. Child day care facility includes day care centers and family day care homes. (State of California Health and Safety Code)

■ **day care home** A dwelling in which a permanent occupant of the dwelling provides for the care of children or adults. Those receiving care are not all related to the occupant or to each other by blood or marriage and are not the legal wards or foster children of the attendant adults. Those receiving care and who are not dependents of the occupant, do not reside on the site. For the purpose of this ordinance, such activities shall meet all requirements for home occupations. If children are the primary clients of the use, the following standards must be met: (1) the home meets all state standards for registration and inspections; (2) the number of children does not exceed five preschool children, including the caregiver's children, and three school-age children not including the caregiver's children. (Durham, N.C.)

■ **day spa** (See **health spa**)

■ **daylight plane** (See also **bulk plane; sky exposure plane**) An inclined plane, beginning at a stated height above grade at a side or rear property line, and extending into the site at a stated upward angle to the horizontal, which may limit the height or horizontal extent of structures at any specific point on the site where the daylight plane is more restrictive than the height limit or the minimum yard applicable at such point on the site. (Newport Beach, Calif.)

■ **decentralization** (See **leapfrog development; sprawl**)

■ **decibel A-weighted (dBA)** (See also **noise**) A unit for describing the amplitude of sound as measured on a sound level meter using the A-weighting network. (Nashville and Davidson County, Tenn.)

■ **deck** A structure, without a roof, directly adjacent to a principal building, which has an average elevation of 30 inches or greater from finished grade. A deck may be constructed of any materials. (Blacksburg, Va.)

A platform, either freestanding or attached to a building, that is supported by pillars or posts. (Newport Beach, Calif.)

■ **deck, attached** A structure within six feet of the main building that may or may not have railings or access to the ground, but does not contain walls or a roof. May also be referred to as a balcony. (Mankato, Minn.)

■ **deck, open** Any deck that is unroofed. (Fairfax County, Va.)

■ **deck, roof** A structure that is constructed above the top plate line of a structure, accessed from below the top plate line, and which is designed to function as an outdoor patio or observation area. (Dana Point, Calif.)

■ **deck, roofed** Any deck that is either completely or partially roofed, even by open beams or lattice work. A roofed deck shall have no enclosure other than the side(s) of the principal building to which the deck is attached, the minimum required supports for the roof and a railing [as permitted in the ordinance]. (Fairfax County, Va.)

■ **deck, unattached** A structure six feet or more from the main building that may or may not have railings or access to the ground, but does not contain walls or a roof. (Mankato, Minn.)

■ **declaration of use** A document signed under oath and recorded against the title of land in order to provide notice that the use of the land or structure is subject to certain limitations and that the use will remain in compliance with this code and other ordinances of the city. (Boulder, Colo.)

■ **dedication** The transfer of private property to public ownership upon written acceptance. (Blacksburg, Va.)

The intentional appropriation or conveyance of land or an interest in land by the owner to the city for public use. (Steamboat Springs, Colo.)

The turning over by an owner or developer of private land for public use, and the acceptance of land for such use by the governmental agency having jurisdiction over the public function for which it will be used. Dedications for roads, parks, school sites, or other public uses often are made conditions for approval of a development by a city or county. (California Planning Roundtable)

Required under some subdivision regulations to transfer part of the developer's private land for public use. As a condition for the approval of a development by a planning and zoning commission, the developer is typically required to build streets and utility lines to specification and then to "dedicate" them, including the land, to the public. Many subdivision regulations now have been extended to include land dedication for open space, schools, and other community facilities. The dedication may be a transfer of ownership or a transfer of a portion of the development rights through an "easement." The purpose is an attempt to assess developers for some of the costs incurred by the community because of a new development. (Iowa State University Extension Service)

■ **dedication, fee in lieu of** Cash payments that may be required of an owner or developer as a substitute for a dedication of land, usually calculated in dollars per lot, and referred to as in-lieu fees or in-lieu contributions. (California Planning Roundtable)

■ **deed restriction** (See also **covenant**) A private legal restriction on the use of land, attached in the deed to a property. A deed restriction is most commonly used in the establishments of a subdivision to restrict the use of all individual lots in the development to a certain type of use (e.g., single-family dwellings). Usually the community has no control over deed restrictions. (Iowa State University Extension Service)

A restriction on the use of a lot or parcel of land that is set forth in the deed and recorded with the county register of deeds. It is binding on subsequent owners and is sometimes also known as a restrictive covenant. *(Muskegon, Mich.)*

■ **defensible space**    (1) In fire-fighting and prevention, a 30-foot area of noncombustible surfaces separating urban and wildland areas. (2) In urban areas, open spaces, entry points, and pathways configured to provide maximum opportunities to rightful users and/or residents to defend themselves against intruders and criminal activity. *(California Planning Roundtable)*

■ **delicatessen**    An establishment where food is sold for consumption off-premises and no counters or tables for on-premises consumption of food are provided, but excludes groceries and supermarkets. *(Boulder, Colo.)*

■ **demolition, complete**    Any act or process that destroys or removes 75 percent or more of the exterior walls of a structure, improvement, or object. *(Oak Park, Ill.)*

■ **demolition (historic district only)** The dismantling, razing, or neglect of all or part of any structure or landmark or the destruction of an archaeological site. *(Blacksburg, Va.)*

■ **demolition, partial**    Any act or process that destroys or removes less than 75 percent of the exterior walls of a structure, improvement, or object. *(Oak Park, Ill.)*

■ **demolition permit**    A permit that gives the applicant/owner the right to demolish a building and to ensure that no unsafe condition exists on the site when the demolition is complete. *(Edmonton, Alberta, Canada)*

■ **demolition waste**    Materials found in demolished buildings, roads, and other structures including, but not limited to, concrete, drywall, asphalt, wood, masonry, composition roofing, roofing, siding, structural metal, wire, insulation. *(Renton, Wash.)*

■ **density**    The number of dwelling units permitted per net acre of land. *(Coral Gables, Fla.)*

The number of dwelling units per gross area devoted to residential development. *(Baton Rouge, La.)*

The number of dwelling units per acre. *(Durham, N.C.)*

The number of dwelling units situated on or to be developed on a net acre (or smaller unit) of land, which shall be calculated by taking the total gross acreage and subtracting surface water, undevelopable lands (e.g., wetlands) and the area in rights-of-way for streets and roads. *(Muskegon, Mich.)*

The number of dwellings or principal buildings or uses permitted per net acre of land. Net acre of land shall not include land required for public streets. *(Mankato, Minn.)*

■ **density, base**    The maximum number of dwelling units permitted outright by a particular land-use classification. *(Island County, Wash.)*

■ **density bonus**    The allocation of development rights that allow a parcel to accommodate additional square footage or additional residential units beyond the maximum for which the parcel is zoned, usually in exchange for the provision or preservation of an amenity at the same site or at another location. Under California law, a housing development that provides 20 percent of its units for lower-income households, or 10 percent of its units for very-low-income households, or 50 percent of its units for seniors, is entitled to a density bonus. *(California Planning Roundtable)*

The granting of the allowance of additional density in a development in exchange for the provision by the developer of other desirable amenities from a public perspective (e.g., public open spaces, plazas, art, landscaping, etc.). *(Peoria, Ill.)*

■ **density, control of**    A limitation on the occupancy of land. Density can be controlled through zoning in the following ways: use restrictions, minimum lot-size requirements, floor area ratios, land use-intensity ratios, setback and yard requirements, minimum house-size requirements, ratios comparing number

and types of housing units to land area, limits on units per acre, and other means. Allowable density often serves as the major distinction between residential districts. *(California Planning Roundtable)*

■ **density, employment**    A measure of the number of employed persons per specific area (for example, employees/acre). *(California Planning Roundtable)*

■ **density, gross**    The numerical value obtained by dividing the total number of dwelling units in a development by the gross area of the tract of land (in acres) within a development. This would include all nonresidential land uses and private streets of the development, as well as rights-of-way of dedicated streets; the result being the number of dwelling units per gross acre of land. *(Gurnee, Ill.)*

The total number of dwelling units divided by the total project area, expressed as gross dwelling units per acre. *(Maryland Heights, Mo.)*

■ **density, maximum allowable**    The number of dwelling units allowed on a parcel of land based upon the gross, overall area of the parcel without any consideration for land areas required for road rights-of-way, easements, and other nonresidential uses. However, in using gross area to compute allowable dwelling units, the overall area of the parcel shall be adjusted by subtracting the area of any subparcel of unbuildable or submerged lands. In computing the maximum allowable density for any parcel, any fractional dwelling count shall be equal to zero dwelling units. *(Boca Raton, Fla.)*

■ **density, net**    The numerical value obtained by dividing the total number of dwelling units in a development by the area of the actual tract of land (in acres) upon which the dwelling units are proposed to be located and including common open space and associated recreational facilities within the area; the result being the number of dwelling units per net residential acre of land. Net density calculations exclude rights-of-way of publicly dedicated streets and private streets. *(Gurnee, Ill.)*

The total number of dwelling units divided by the net project area. In determining net density, all land area associated with and accessory to the dwelling unit, including private streets and driveways, off-street parking facilities, and common open space and recreational facilities, shall be included in the calculation. Net density calculations exclude rights-of-way of publicly dedicated streets and nonresidential structures, land uses and accessory facilities. *(Maryland Heights, Mo.)*

■ **density transfer**   A way of retaining open space by concentrating densities—usually in compact areas adjacent to existing urbanization and utilities—while leaving unchanged historic, sensitive, or hazardous areas. In some jurisdictions, for example, developers can buy development rights of properties targeted for public open space and transfer the additional density to the base number of units permitted in the zone in which they propose to develop. *(California Planning Roundtable)*

■ **density zoning**   A device for averaging residential density over an entire parcel and placing no restrictions on lot sizes or on dwelling types. Under this approach, any type of dwelling is permitted, from detached houses to apartments, anywhere on the site, so long as total density does not exceed the maximum permitted. The only development standards imposed are for distances between buildings, distance between facing windows, amount of parking, and minimum open space. Conventional setback and lot-size requirements are dropped. It is a somewhat further extension of cluster development provisions. *(PAS Report No. 322, The Language of Zoning)*

■ **density zoning district**   Synonymous with zone and means an area of the county that is characterized by economic, geographic, or geological conditions that justify the determination of a maximum density for residential land use and the application of special land-use regulations; and which is delineated on the zone map or maps. *(Thurston County, Wash.)*

■ **department store**   A business which is conducted under a single owner's name wherein a variety of unrelated merchandise and services are housed enclosed and are exhibited and sold directly to the customer for whom the goods and services are furnished. *(Maple Grove, Minn.)*

■ **deposition**   Any rock, soil, gravel, sand, or other material deposited naturally or by man into a waterbody, watercourse, floodplain, or wetland. *(Maple Grove, Minn.)*

■ **design guideline**   A standard of appropriate activity that will preserve the historic and architectural character of a structure or area. *(St. Charles, Mo.)*

■ **design review/design control** *(See also **architectural control/ architectural review**)*   The comprehensive evaluation

of a development and its impact on neighboring properties and the community as a whole, from the standpoint of site and landscape design, architecture, materials, colors, lighting, and signs, in accordance with a set of adopted criteria and standards. Design control requires that certain specific things be done and that other things not be done. Design control language is most often found within a zoning ordinance. Design review usually refers to a system set up outside of the zoning ordinance, whereby projects are reviewed against certain standards and criteria by a specially established design review board or committee. *(California Planning Roundtable)*

■ **design standards**   A set of guidelines regarding the architectural appearance of a building, or improvement, that governs the alteration, construction, demolition, or relocation of a building, or improvement. *(Champaign, Ill.)*

The specifications for the preparation of plats, both preliminary and final, indicating among other things the optimum minimum or maximum dimensions of such items as right-of-way, blocks, easements, and lots. *(Grand Forks, N.D.)*

■ **destination retail**   Retail businesses that generate a special purpose trip and that do not necessarily benefit from a high-volume pedestrian location. *(California Planning Roundtable)*

■ **detention** *(See also **retention**)*   The temporary on-site restraining of storm water. *(Gurnee, Ill.)*

■ **detention area**   An area that is designed to capture specific quantities of stormwater and to gradually release the stormwater at a sufficiently slow rate to avert flooding. *(Thornton, Colo.)*

■ **detention basin**   A structure or facility, natural or artificial (pictured above), which stores stormwater on a temporary basis and releases it at a controlled rate. A detention basin may drain completely after a storm event, or it may be a body of water with a fixed minimum and maximum water elevation between runoff events. *(Grand Traverse County, Mich.)*

■ **detention basin, extended**   Detention basin designed to provide substantial removal of suspended solids and particulates, typically achieved by holding stormwater for 24 hours or more. *(Grand Traverse County, Mich.)*

■ **detention basin, regional**   A basin to detain water flow from a number of development sites or a small watershed. *(Grand Traverse County, Mich.)*

■ **detention, combined public detention**   A stormwater detention system designed to accommodate runoff from both public streets and private property. *(Renton, Wash.)*

■ **detention dam/basin/pond**   Dams may be classified according to the broad function they serve, such as storage, diversion, or detention. Detention dams are constructed to retard flood runoff and minimize the effect of sudden floods. Detention dams fall into two main types. In one type, the water is temporarily stored and released through an outlet structure at a rate that will not exceed the carrying capacity of the channel downstream. Often, the basins are planted with grass and used for open space or recreation in periods of dry weather. The other type, most often called a retention pond, allows for water to be held as long as possible and may or may not allow for the controlled release of water. In some cases, the water is allowed to seep into the permeable banks or gravel strata in the foundation. This latter type is sometimes called a water-spreading dam or dike because its main purpose is to recharge the underground water supply. Detention dams are also constructed to trap sediment. These are often called debris dams. *(California Planning Roundtable)*

■ **developable acres, net**   The portion of a site that can be used for density calculations. Some communities calculate density based on gross acreage. Public or private road rights-of-way are not included in the net developable acreage of a site. *(California Planning Roundtable)*

The land area within a subdivision excluding areas dedicated to the public, including parks and open spaces and public rights-of-way. *(Thornton, Colo., which uses the term "net land area")*

The area within the development boundaries, not including areas for public or private streets, driveways, or utility easements. *(Champaign, Ill., which uses the term "net area")*

■ **developable land**   Land that is suitable as a location for structures and that can be developed free of hazards to, and without disruption of, or significant impact on, natural resource areas. *(California Planning Roundtable)*

Land area outside of delineated wetlands and wetland buffers that is otherwise developable, taking into consideration steep slopes, unstable soil, etc. *(Renton, Wash., which uses the term "developable area")*

■ **developed property**   Property or a lot upon which significant site improvements, such as utility installations, paving and, in many instances, the construction of one or more structures has occurred. For the purposes of sign regulation, it shall additionally mean all private property within 200 feet of an existing building. *(Thornton, Colo.)*

■ **developer**   That person who is improving a parcel of land within the city and who may or may not be the owner of the property. *(Thornton, Colo.)*

An individual who or business that prepares raw land for the construction of buildings or causes to be built physical building space for use primarily by others, and in which the preparation of the land or the creation of the building space is in itself a business and is not incidental to another business or activity. *(California Planning Roundtable)*

The legal or beneficial owner or owners of a lot or of any land included in a proposed development including the holder of an option or contract to purchase, or other persons having enforceable proprietary interests in such land. *(Iowa State University Extension Service)*

■ **developer's agreement**   *(See also **contract zoning**)*   An agreement by a developer with the city that clearly establishes the developer's responsibility regarding project phasing, the provision of public and private facilities, and improvements and any other mutually

agreed to terms and requirements. *(Thornton, Colo.)*

A legislatively approved contract between a jurisdiction and a person having legal or equitable interest in real property within the jurisdiction that "freezes" certain rules, regulations, and policies applicable to development of a property for a specified period of time, usually in exchange for certain concessions by the owner. *(California Planning Roundtable)*

■ **developing area**   An area determined by the commission to contain an average residential density less than one dwelling unit per 2.5 acres or has less than an average of 50,000 square feet of gross floor area devoted to nonresidential structures which require a certificate of occupancy. *(Thornton, Colo.)*

■ **development**   Any human-caused change to improved or unimproved real estate that requires a permit or approval from any agency of the city or county, including but not limited to, buildings or other structures, mining, dredging, filling, grading, paving, excavation or drilling operations, and storage of materials. *(Durham, N.C.)*

The construction of a new building or other structures on a zoning lot, the relocation of an existing building on another zoning lot, or the use of open land for a new use. Also means any man-made change to improved or unimproved real estate, including but not limited to parking, fences, pools, signs, temporary uses, clearing of land, mining, dredging, filling, grading, paving, excavation, or drilling operations. *(Muskegon, Mich.)*

The physical extension and/or construction of urban land uses. Development activities include: subdivision of land; construction or alteration of structures, roads, utilities, and other facilities; installation of septic systems; grading; deposit of refuse, debris, or fill materials; and clearing of natural vegetative cover (with the exception of agricultural activities). Routine repair and maintenance activities are exempted. *(California Planning Roundtable)*

■ **development approval**   Any written authorization for the city or another governmental entity party to a joint powers agreement with the city, which authorizes the commencement of a development. *(Boise City, Idaho)*

■ **development coverage** All developed surface areas within the subject property including but not limited to roof tops, concrete or asphalt paved driveways, carports, accessory buildings and parking areas. *(Renton, Wash.)*

■ **development, floodplain** Any manmade change to improved or unimproved real estate including, but not limited to, buildings or other structures, mining, dredging, filling, grading, paving, excavation or dwelling operations, or storage of equipment or materials. *(Blacksburg, Va.)*

■ **development, high-intensity** Land uses with higher impacts from density or uses (i.e., multifamily, industrial, commercial uses). *(Renton, Wash.)*

■ **development impact fees** A fee or fees imposed upon a developer to pay for the costs to the city of providing services and infrastructure required in response to a new development. *(Conyers, Ga.)*

■ **development, low-intensity** Land uses that have fewer impacts from density or uses (i.e., large-lot single family, natural open space areas). *(Renton, Wash.)*

■ **development of regional impact (DRI)** Any development that, because of its character, magnitude, or location, would have a substantial effect upon the health, safety, or welfare of citizens of more than one county. *(State of Florida)*

■ **development permit** A permit signifying compliance with the provisions of this ordinance as to design, use, activity, height, setbacks, density, site planning, special use status, and/or planned unit development status. *(Muskegon, Mich.)*

Any permit or approval under this chapter or the city's building code that must be obtained before initiating a use or development activity. *(Federal Way, Wash.)*

A permit issued by the city certifying

that a proposed development has undergone and completed the required development review procedures. The development permit may include one or more conditions, which conditions shall apply to any future development or use of the land, regardless of ownership changes, unless a new development permit is obtained. The development permit shall be recorded in the permanent records with the county clerk *(Glenwood Springs, Colo.)*

■ **development plan** A type of plan that becomes part of the zoning for a property. The plan depicts site characteristics and development information and provides guidance for site plans. *(Durham, N.C.)*

A dimensioned presentation of the proposed development of a specified parcel of land that reflects thereon the location of buildings, easements, parking arrangements, public access, street pattern, and other similar features. *(Pine Bluff, Ark.)*

■ **development plan review** The process whereby authorized officials of the city review the site plans, maps, and other documentation of a development to determine the compliance of the stated purposes and standards of this zoning code. *(Newport, R.I.)*

■ **development project** A public- or private-sector venture involving the development, structural modification, or redevelopment of commercial, industrial, residential or other properties. *(Thornton, Colo.)*

A project in which one or more lots, tracts or parcels of land are to be developed or redeveloped as a coordinated site for a complex of uses, units or structures, including, but not limited to, planned development and/or cluster development for residential, commercial, institutional, recreational, open space, and/or mixed uses. . . . *(Newport, R.I.)*

■ **development proposal** The application submitted by an owner or owner's representative, seeking approval for the development of land. *(New York Planning Federation)*

■ **development requirement** A requirement attached to a development approval or other governmental action approving or authorizing a particular development project including, but not limited to, a rezoning, which requirement compels the payment, dedication or contribution or goods, services, land, or money as a condition of approval. *(Boise City, Idaho)*

■ **development rights** The right to develop land by a land owner who maintains fee-simple ownership over the land or by a party other than the owner who has obtained the rights to develop. Such rights usually are expressed in terms of density allowed under existing zoning. For example, one development right may equal one unit of housing or may equal a specific number of square feet of gross floor area in one or more specified zone districts. *(California Planning Roundtable)*

One of a series of rights inherent in fee simple ownership of land, similar to mineral rights. Development rights represent the potential for the improvement of a parcel or unit of land measured in dwelling units. *(Island County, Wash.)*

■ **development standards** Standards established . . . for zoning lots or the placement or size of a building on the lot. *(Champaign, Ill.)*

Regulations that limit the size, bulk, or siting conditions of particular types of buildings or uses located within any designated district. *(El Paso Tex.)*

■ **developmentally disabled person** *(See also **disability; handicapped**)* A person who has a physical or mental impairment, or both, that substantially limits one or more major life activities, such as caring for oneself, performing manual tasks, walking, seeing, hearing, speaking, learning, breathing or working. A physical or mental impairment may include orthopedic, visual, speech, or hearing impairments, Alzheimer's disease, presenile dementia, cerebral palsy, epilepsy, muscular dystrophy, multiple sclerosis, cancer, heart disease, diabetes, mental retardation, autism, or emotional illness. *(El Paso, Tex.)*

*Commentary: There are a number of terms (e.g., "person with developmental disabilities") that are used to describe individuals with physical, mental, and psychological impairments. Check with your local health service to see if there is a strong preference for one term over another or for a series of terms.*

■ **diameter at breast height (DBH)** Diameter at breast height, or the diameter in inches of a tree measured at four and one-half feet above the existing grade. *(St. Paul, Minn.)*

■ **dike** An embankment to prevent flooding by a stream or other water body. A dike is also referred to as a levee. *(Yakima County, Wash.)*

■ **disability** A physical or mental impairment that substantially limits one or more of a person's major life activities, impairs their ability to live independently, or a record of having such an impairment, or being regarded as having such impairment, not to include use or addiction to a controlled substance. *(Danville, Ill.)*

■ **discount membership merchandiser** *(See also **retail sales establishment, bulk**)* Any membership-based, bulk-purchase retail establishment where membership is available to the general public subject to the payment of a membership fee, and compliance with membership criteria. Such establishments advertise and cater to the general public by providing a single pricing structure for all members irrespective of quantity purchased. Goods purveyed in discount

membership merchandisers are intended to serve the daily retail and service needs of the public. *(Miami, Fla.)*

■ **distribution center** A use where goods are received and/or stored for delivery to the ultimate customer at remote locations. *(Clearwater, Fla., which uses the term "wholesale or distribution or warehouse facility")*

■ **district** A portion of the incorporated area of the municipality within which certain regulations and requirements or various combinations thereof apply under the provisions of this zoning code. *(St. Paul, Minn.)*

A section or sections of the city for which the regulations and provisions governing the use of buildings and lands are uniform for each class of use permitted therein. *(Maple Grove, Minn.)*

■ **disturbed area** An area of land subjected to erosion due to the removal of vegetative cover and/or earthmoving activities, including filling. *(Grand Traverse County, Mich.)*

■ **diversion** A channel that intercepts surface water runoff and that changes the accustomed course of all or part of a stream. *(Maple Grove, Minn.)*

■ **diversity** Differences among otherwise similar elements that give them unique forms and qualities (e.g., housing diversity can be achieved by differences in unit size, tenure, or cost). *(California Planning Roundtable)*

■ **dock** A structure built over or floating upon the water (pictured below) and used as a landing place for boats and other marine transport, fishing, swimming, and other recreational uses. *(Yakima County, Wash.)*

A landing pier for boats; a wharf, a structure supported by piling or floats in such a manner as to allow free flow of water beneath said structure and in which any buildings constructed thereon are incidental to the use of said structure as a wharf or landing pier. *(National City, Calif.)*

■ **dock, commercial** A fixed or floating structure, including moorings, used for the purpose of berthing buoyant vessels on a commercial basis. A commercial dock does not include a marina, boat livery, or boat yard. A commercial dock may exist independently or as an incidental part of a marina, boat livery, or boat yard. *(Indian River County, Fla.)*

■ **dock, community boat** A facility for secure mooring of boats provided in conjunction with a residential development for use by residents of the development as opposed to the public at large; facilities for storage and repair of boats and sale of boating supplies and fuel are not provided for. *(Virginia Beach, Va.)*

■ **dock, dry** An upland structure used for storing watercraft. A dry dock may be part of a boat livery or boat yard but shall not be permitted as part of a marina. *(Indian River County, Fla.)*

■ **dock, private** A fixed or floating structure, including moorings, used for the purpose of berthing buoyant vessels and which does not produce income, and does not serve as an inducement to renting, purchasing, or using accompanying facilities. A dock may include a pier. *(Indian River County, Fla.)*

■ **dog run** An enclosed outdoor area intended for the exercising and/or containment of dogs and similar animals. *(Schaumburg, Ill.)*

■ **domestic violence shelter** A residential facility serving as a center to receive and house persons who are victims of domestic violence, including dependents of the victim, to provide temporary boarding, lodging, counseling, and day care. The facility shall meet all certification requirements of the state. *(Melbourne, Fla.)*

One main building, or portion thereof, on one zoning lot where adults and children who have suffered assault or battery live on a 24-hour-per-day basis for a period of time generally not to exceed 30 days and are served by a program certified by the [state] department of corrections. *(St. Paul, Minn., which uses the term "shelter for battered persons")*

Housing for adult women or men and their dependent children, if any, who are victims of domestic violence perpetrated by the spouse, domestic partner, or significant other of the adult victim. *(Federal Way, Wash.)*

■ **domicile** *(See also dwelling definitions)* A residence that is a permanent home to an individual. *(Siskiyou County, Calif.)*

■ **donation collection bin** A receptacle designed with a door, slot, or other opening that is intended to accept and store donated items (pictured below); provided, however, that the definition of donation collection bins shall not include trailers where personnel are present to accept donations. *(Miami, Fla.)*

■ **dormitory** A building intended or used principally for sleeping accommodations where such building is related to

an educational or public institution, including religious institutions. *(Coral Gables, Fla.)*

A room for sleeping purposes for more than four persons, which is rented. *(Columbia County, Wash.)*

A structure specifically designed for a long-term stay by students of a college, university, or nonprofit organization for the purpose of providing rooms for sleeping purposes. One common kitchen and some common gathering rooms for social purposes may also be provided. *(Durham, N.C.)*

■ **downstream** Lands and waters which receive stormwater runoff and other surface water flows from a designated site. Downstream lands and waters are downgradient from the designated site. *(Grand Traverse County, Mich.)*

■ **downzoning** *(See also cumulative zoning; upzoning)* A change in the zoning classification of land to a classification permitting development that is less intensive or dense, such as from multifamily to single family or from commercial to industrial to residential. A change in the opposite direction is called "upzoning." *(Handbook for Planning Commissioners in Missouri)*

■ **drainage** (1) Surface water runoff; and (2) The removal of surface water or groundwater from land by drains, grading, or other means that include runoff controls to minimize erosion and sedimentation during and after construction

or development, the means for preserving the water supply, and the prevention or alleviation of flooding. *(Siskiyou County, Calif.)*

The outflow of water or other fluid from a site, whether be natural or artificial means. *(New York Planning Federation)*

■ **drainage basin** The area from which water is carried off by a drainage system; a watershed or catchment area. *(Clark County, Nev.)*

The area defined by topographic boundaries that contributes stormwater to a drainage system, estuarine waters, or oceanic waters, including all areas artificially added to the basin. *(Volusia County, Fla.)*

■ **drainage system** All facilities, channels, and areas which serve to convey, filter, store, and/or receive stormwater, either on a temporary or permanent basis. *(Grand Traverse County, Mich.)*

A system for the removal of water from land by drains, grading, or other appropriate means. These techniques may include runoff controls to minimize erosion and sedimentation during and after construction or development, the means for preserving surface and groundwaters, and the prevention and/or alleviation of flooding. *(Newport, R.I.)*

■ **drainage well** A bed of stone or hole in the ground constructed for the purpose of trapping stormwater for infiltration into the ground. *(Grand Traverse County, Mich.)*

■ **drainageway** A ditch, levee, watercourse, or other natural or artificial condition for the removal of surplus or excess surface water collecting or accumulating on the land. *(Naperville, Ill.)*

■ **dredging** To enlarge or clean-out a waterbody, watercourse, or wetland. *(Maple Grove, Minn.)*

Removal of earth from the bed of a stream, lake, or vegetated shallows for the purpose of increasing the depth of surface water or obtaining minerals, construction aggregate, or landfill materials. *(Yakima County, Wash.)*

■ **drip line**  An imaginary vertical line that extends from the outermost branches of a tree's canopy to the ground. *(St. Paul, Minn.)*

■ **drive-in**  A business establishment so developed that its retail or service character is dependent on providing a driveway approach or parking spaces for motor vehicles so as to serve patrons while in the motor vehicle rather than within a building or structure. *(Muskegon, Mich.)*

An establishment accommodating the patron's automobile from which the occupants may receive a service or in which products purchased from the establishment may be consumed. *(Maple Grove, Minn.)*

A term used to describe an establishment designed or operated to serve a patron who is seated in an automobile. *(Stonington, Conn.)*

An establishment that dispenses products or services to patrons who remain in vehicles. *(Durham, N.C.)*

■ **drive-in restaurant** *(See restaurant, drive-in)*

■ **drive-through window**  An opening in the wall of a building or structure designed and intended to be used to provide for sales to and/or service to patrons who remain in their vehicles. *(Philadelphia, Pa.)*

■ **drive-up window service**  A building opening, including windows, doors, or mechanical devices (pictured at right), through which occupants of a motor vehicle receive or obtain a product or service. *(Albuquerque, N. Mex.)*

■ **driveway**  A private roadway providing access for vehicles to a parking space, garage, dwelling, or other structure. *(Blacksburg, Va.)*

A minor private way used by vehicles and pedestrians for common access to a single lot or facility. *(Perryville, Mo.)*

■ **driveway approach**  An area of the public right-of-way located between the roadway and property adjacent to the public right-of-way that is intended to provide access for vehicles from the roadway to the adjacent property. *(Lincoln, Nebr.)*

■ **driveway, circle**  A private drive, one-way driveway which enters and leaves private property at two points within the same frontage. *(Hudsonville, Mich.)*

■ **driveway, common**  A shared access that serves up to four separate single-family residential parcels, each having public street frontage. *(Boise City, Idaho)*

A driveway shared by adjacent property owners and privately owned and maintained. *(Steamboat Springs, Colo.)*

■ **driveway, cross access**  A service drive providing vehicular access between two or more contiguous sites so the driver need not enter the public street system. *(Clearwater, Fla.)*

■ **driveway, directional**  A driveway system so designed so that traffic leaving the road is separated from and does not conflict with traffic entering the road. Turning movements into and from the property are restricted. *(Hudsonville, Mich.)*

■ **driveway, divided**  A driveway so designed that traffic entering the driveway is separated by a traffic island from the traffic leaving the driveway. *(Hudsonville, Mich.)*

■ **driveway offset**  The minimum distance between two commercial driveways on the opposite sides of the roadway. *(Hudsonville, Mich.)*

■ **driving range**  An area equipped with distance markers, clubs, balls, and tees for practicing golf drives and putting, and which may include a snack-bar and pro-shop, but excludes miniature golf courses and "putt-putt" courses. *(Nashville and Davidson County, Tenn.)*

■ **drop box facility**  *(See also recycling)* A site used for the placement of a municipal refuse collection box including the area adjacent for necessary entrance and exit roads, and unloading and turn-around areas. Drop boxes are normally without attendants, and receive waste from off-site. *(Island County, Wash.)*

■ **drug paraphernalia**  All equipment, products, and materials of any kind that are used, intended for use, or designed for use, in planting, propagating, cultivating, growing, harvesting, manufacturing, compounding, converting, producing, processing, preparing, testing, analyzing, packaging, repackaging, storing, containing, concealing, injecting, ingesting, inhaling, or otherwise introducing into the human body marijuana and/or a controlled substance as defined in [state code]. *(Fairfax County, Va.)*

■ **drug store** *(See also pharmacy)*  An establishment engaged in the retail sale of prescription drugs, nonprescription medicines, cosmetics, and related supplies. *(King County, Wash.)*

■ **dry cleaning and laundry pickup station**    An establishment or business maintained for the pickup and delivery of dry cleaning and/or laundry without the maintenance or operation of any laundry or dry-cleaning equipment or machinery on the premises. *(Wheeling, Ill.)*

■ **dry cleaning plant**    A building, portion of a building, or premises used or intended to be used for cleaning fabrics, textiles, wearing apparel, or articles of any sort by immersion and agitation, or by immersions only, in volatile solvents including, but not by way of limitation, solvents of the petroleum distillate type, and/or the chlorinated hydrocarbon type, and the processes incidental thereto. *(Muskegon, Mich.)*

■ **due process of law** *(See also compensable zoning; taking)*    Generally, a requirement that legal proceedings be carried out in accordance with established rules and principles. Commonly, it takes two forms: procedural and substantive. Procedural due process means an assurance that all parties to a proceeding are treated fairly and equally, that citizens have a right to have their views heard, that necessary information is available for informed opinions to be developed, that conflicts of interest are avoided, and that, generally, the appearance of, as well as the fact of, corruption does not exist. The meaning of substantive due process is less precise, but it usually refers to the payment by government of just compensation to property owners when their property is condemned by government or is severely diminished in value because of government action. *(PAS Report No. 322, The Language of Zoning)*

■ **dump** *(See also landfill, sanitary)*    A lot of land or part thereof used primarily for the disposal, by abandonment, dumping, burial, burning, or any other means and for what purpose, or garbage, sewage, trash, refuse, junk, discarded machinery, vehicles or parts thereof, or waste material of any kind. *(Stonington, Conn.)*

■ **dumpster**    A container that has a hooking mechanism that permits it to be raised and dumped into a sanitation truck. *(Morgantown, W. Va.)*

■ **dumpster, compacted**    A dumpster that is mechanically compacted by either an integral or separate power unit, that results in more solid waste material, by weight, being placed in a container that is naturally filled. *(Morgantown, W. Va.)*

■ **dune**    A mound or ridge of loose sediments, usually sand-sized, lying landward of the beach, and deposited by natural or artificial means. *(Indian River County, Fla.)*

■ **duplex** *(See also triplex)*    A structure containing two dwelling units, each of which has direct access to the outside. *(Boulder, Colo.)*

■ **duplex, double**    A separate or detached four-family residence, the first and second floors of which are each designed and arranged for use by two families separated by a vertical division wall, each unit of which is heated independently of the others. Each dwelling unit shall have its own separate, private means of ingress. *(Columbus, Ohio)*

MULTIFAMILY DWELLING

■ **dust**    Fine dry pulverized particles of any material or a fine powder of any kind. *(Albuquerque, N. Mex.)*

■ **dwelling** *(See also housing definitions)* A building or part of a building, containing living, sleeping, housekeeping accommodations, and sanitary facilities for occupancy by one or more families. *(Stonington, Conn.)*

A building, or structure of portion thereof, designed for occupancy by one family for residential purposes as a single housekeeping unit. In no case shall a motor home, trailer coach, automobile chassis, tent, or portable building be considered a dwelling. *(Muskegon, Mich.)*

■ **dwelling, apartment**    A building, or portion thereof, designed for occupancy by three or more families living independently of each other. *(Columbia County, Wash.)*

■ **dwelling, farm labor** *(See farm employee housing; housing, temporary employment)*

■ **dwelling groups**    A group of two or more one-family, two-family, or multiple dwellings occupying a parcel of land in one ownership and having a yard or court in common, but not including motels. *(Santa Clara County, Calif.)*

■ **dwelling, high-rise**    A multiple-family dwelling located in a building containing eight or more stories. *(Schaumburg, Ill.)*

■ **dwelling, mid-rise**    A multiple-family dwelling located in a building containing four to seven stories. *(Schaumburg, Ill.)*

■ **dwelling, multifamily**    A building containing four or more individual dwellings with separate cooking and toilet facilities for each dwelling. *(Durham, N.C.)*

A dwelling or group of dwellings on one lot, containing separate living units for three or more families, having separate or joint entrances, and including apartments, group homes, row houses, and condominiums; also multiple dwellings. *(Stonington, Conn.)*

A building, or portion thereof, designed exclusively for occupancy by three or more families living independently of each other in individual dwelling units. *(St. Paul, Minn.)*

■ **dwelling, semi-detached** *(See also duplex; rowhouse; townhouse; triplex)* A building containing two attached dwelling units that share a common wall

ATTACHED SINGLE-FAMILY
DWELLING

at the lot line and that are on separate lots. *(Cecil County, Md)*

■ **dwelling, single-family**   A structure designed for occupancy by one family. *(Columbia County, Wash.)*

A building designed exclusively for and occupied exclusively by one family. *(Muskegon, Mich.)*

■ **dwelling, three-family** *(See also triplex)*   A building designed exclusively for or occupied exclusively by no more than three families living independently of each other in three separate dwelling units. *(St. Paul, Minn.)*

■ **dwelling, two-family** *(See also duplex)* A residence building designed for, or used as, the separate homes or residence of two separate and distinct families, having the exterior appearance of a single family dwelling house. Each individual unit in the duplex shall have all living room accessible to each other from within the unit and each individual unit is to be occupied exclusively by one family or by no more than three individuals unrelated to any other occupant, excluding servants, who are living and cooking as a single household *(Coral Gables, Fla.)*

■ **dwelling unit**   A single unit providing complete, independent living facilities for one or more persons, including permanent provisions for living, sleeping, eating, cooking, and sanitation. *(Columbia County, Wash.)*

One room or rooms connected together, constituting a separate, independent

housekeeping establishment for owner or renter occupancy, and containing independent cooking and sleeping facilities and sanitary facilities. No dwelling unit shall contain less than 300 square feet of habitable living area. *(Stonington, Conn.)*

*Commentary: The definition for dwelling unit is an essential part of the definition of density. Depending on local housing conditions, cooking and sanitary facilities in each unit may or may not be required. For example, resort areas may be less likely to require a dwelling unit to have cooking facilities since they have transient populations.*

■ **dwelling unit, attached**   Two or more dwelling units within a structure. *(Boulder, Colo.)*

■ **dwelling unit, detached**   No more than one dwelling unit within a structure. *(Boulder, Colo.)*

■ **earth station** *(See also **telecommunications** definitions)*　A facility that transmits and/or receives radio signals to and/or from a satellite. *(Tuscaloosa, Ala.)*

■ **easement**　A grant by a property owner to the use of land by the public, a corporation, or persons for specific purposes as the construction of utilities, drainage ways and roadways. *(St. Paul, Minn.)*

The right to use property owned by another for specific purposes or to gain access to another property. For example, utility companies often have easements on the private property of individuals to be able to install and maintain utility facilities. *(California Planning Roundtable)*

Authorization by a property owner for the use by another, and for a specified purpose, of a designated part of his or her property. *(Iowa City, Iowa)*

■ **easement, access**　An easement created for the purpose of providing vehicular or pedestrian access to a property. *(Renton, Wash.)*

■ **easement, affirmative**　An easement the gives the holder a right to make some limited use of land owned by another. *(Iowa State University Extension Service)*

■ **easement, agricultural conservation**　A legal agreement restricting development on farmland. Land subjected to an ACE is generally restricted to farming and open space use. *(American Farmland Trust)*

■ **easement, appurtenant**　An easement that runs with the land. *(Iowa State University Extension Service)*

■ **easement, aviation**　A right of use over property whereby an airport proprietor may operate over real property of another. *(Indian River County, Fla.)*

■ **easement, conservation**　A nonpossessory interest in real property imposing limitations or affirmative obligations, the purposes of which include retaining or protecting natural, scenic, or open space values of real property; assuring its availability for agricultural, forest, recreational, or open space use; protecting natural resources; or maintaining air or water quality. *(Muskegon, Mich.)*

■ **easement, fisherman's**　A public easement running parallel to the high water line of a creek or river for the purpose of providing access along a stream and adjacent banks for fishing and other passive nonmotorized recreation. *(Glenwood Springs, Colo.)*

■ **easement, habitat protection**　An exclusive easement intended to protect a specific plant or animal community by discouraging human intervention. Significant habitat may be identified in the River Management Plan or in site-specific reports prepared by a qualified biologist or ecologist. *(Glenwood Springs, Colo.)*

■ **easement, maintenance**　An area of a parcel of land free of structures reserved to an adjacent parcel of land to allow access to repair and maintain a structure located on the adjacent parcel. *(Maui County, Hawaii)*

■ **easement, negative**　An easement that precludes the owner of the land from doing that which the owner would be entitled to do if the easement did not exist. *(Iowa State University Extension Service)*

■ **easement, private**　A right-of-way granted but not dedicated to the city, for the limited use of private land where general use and maintenance of such right-of-way is governed by an agreement that runs with the land, is unseverable therefrom, and is recorded with the office of the county clerk. For purposes of a commercial unit development, a private easement may include certain improved portions of private land that are intended for the general use, enjoyment, convenience, and benefit of all signatories, owners or lessees, and their permittees, including but not limited to, parking areas and spaces, roadways (including roads or lateral access drives), driveways, entrances to dedicated public or private streets, sidewalks, landscaped areas, and truck loading or delivery areas. *(El Paso, Tex.)*

■ **easement, private access**　A privately owned and maintained right-of-way that provides vehicular access to each of not more than four lots. A private access easement allows the creation of no more than four lots without street frontage, each with vehicular access on the easement. The area designated for the private access easement shall be excluded in computing minimum lot areas. A private access easement shall be a part of one or more lots. At the discretion of the director of public works, based on considerations described in the city planning commission guidelines, the street entrance portion of the private access easement may be located within the public right-of-way. Private access easements shall not be named. Addresses for the dwelling units served by the easement shall conform to the address range of the street upon which the easement abuts. *(Oakland, Calif.)*

■ **easement, scenic**　A tool that allows a public agency to use an owner's land for scenic enhancement, such as roadside landscaping or vista preservation. *(California Planning Roundtable)*

■ **easement slope**　A grant by a property owner of the use of a strip of land for the purpose of constructing a slope or grade transition from the existing property grade to a new established grade. (*Grand Forks, N.D.*)

■ **eave**    The projecting lower edges of a roof overhanging the wall of a building. (*Siskiyou County, Calif.*)

■ **eave line**    The extension of a roof line beyond the vertical wall of a building. (*Nashville and Davidson County, Tenn.*)

■ **ecological impact**    A modification or change in the existing natural environment that could result in the disruption and/or loss of wildlife habitat, vegetation, air quality, soil and water resources, and/or an increase in ambient noise levels. (*Albuquerque/Bernalillo County, N. Mex.*)

■ **ecology**    The interrelationship of living things to one another and their environment; the study of such interrelationships. (*California Planning Roundtable*)

■ **economic base**    Economic base theory essentially holds that the structure of the economy is made up of two broad classes of productive effort basic activities that produce and distribute goods and services for export to firms and individuals outside a defined localized economic area, and nonbasic activities whose goods and services are consumed at home within the boundaries of the local economic area. Viewed another way, basic activity exports goods and services and brings new dollars into the area; nonbasic activity recirculates dollars within the area. This distinction holds that the reason for the growth of a particular region is its capacity to provide the means of payment for raw materials, food, and services that the region cannot produce itself and also support the nonbasic activities that are principally local in productive scope and market area. (*California Planning Roundtable*)

■ **economic development** (*See also community development corporation (CDC)*) A development that provides a service, produces a good, retails a commodity, or emerges in any other use or activity for the purpose of making financial gain. (*Renton, Wash.*)

Any change in a community that enables greater production, increased employment, and a better distribution of goods and services. (*Interstate 81 Corridor Council*)

■ **economic development commission (EDC)** (*See also community development corporation (CDC)*) An agency charged with seeking economic development projects and economic expansion at higher employment densities. (*California Planning Roundtable*)

■ **ecosystem**    An interacting system formed by a biotic community and its physical environment. (*California Planning Roundtable*)

■ **educational facilities, college/university**    An institution other than a trade school that provides full-time or part-time education beyond high school. (*Durham, N.C.*)

A post-secondary institution for higher learning that grants associate or bachelor degrees and may also have research facilities and/or professional schools that grant master and doctoral degrees. This may also include community colleges that grant associate or bachelor degrees or certificates of completion in business or technical fields. (*Federal Way, Wash.*)

An educational institution authorized by the state to award associate, baccalaureate, or higher degrees. (*Champaign, Ill.*)

An institution for post-secondary education, public or private, offering courses in general, technical, or religious education and not operated for profit. It operates in buildings owned or leased by the institution for administrative and faculty offices, classrooms, laboratories, chapels, auditoriums, lecture halls, libraries, student and faculty centers, athletic facilities, dormitories, fraternities, and sororities, but not including colleges or trade schools operated for profit. (*St. Paul, Minn., which uses the terms "college, university, or seminary"*)

■ **educational facilities, elementary school**    Serves students between the kindergarten and high school levels. (*Redmond, Wash.*)

■ **educational facilities, high school**    Ninth, tenth, eleventh, and twelfth grades. (*Redmond, Wash.*)

■ **educational facilities, nursery school**    A school that is primarily educational in nature, meets the needs of a child of three to five years [of age]. (*Goochland County, Va.*)

■ **educational facilities, preschool**    Providing day care with or without educational services for children not yet attending elementary school; includes nursery school and kindergarten. (*Palmer, Alaska*)

A school for children primarily between the ages of three and five, providing preparation for elementary school. (*Carmel, Ind., which uses the term "kindergarten"*)

■ **educational facilities, primary/secondary**    A public, private, or parochial school offering instruction at the elementary, junior, and/or senior high school levels in the branches of learning and study required to be taught in the public schools of the [state]. (*Blacksburg, Va.*)

■ **educational facilities, private school**    Any building or group of buildings, the use of which meets state requirements for primary, secondary, or higher education and which does not secure the major part of its funding from any governmental agency. (*McHenry County, Ill.*)

■ **educational facilities, school for the arts**    A school where classes in the various arts (e.g. dance, painting, sculpting, singing) are taught to four or more persons at a time. (*Gastonia, N.C.*)

■ **educational institution**    A public, parochial, or private institution that provides educational instruction to students. This definition does not include trade or business schools or colleges. (*Pine Bluff, Ark.*)

Any public, parochial, private, charitable, or nonprofit school, junior college, or university, other than trade or business schools, including instructional and recreational uses, with or without living quarters, dining rooms, restaurants, heating plants, and other incidental facilities for students, teachers and employees. (*Gurnee, Ill.*)

■ **efficiency unit** A dwelling unit that has only one combined living and sleeping room, said dwelling unit, however, may also have a separate room containing only kitchen facilities and also a separate room containing only sanitary facilities. *(Scottsdale, Ariz.)*

A dwelling unit containing only one habitable room, sometimes referred to as a studio apartment. *(Fairbanks North Star Borough, Alaska)*

■ **effluent** Sewage, water or other liquid, partially or completely treated or in its natural state, flowing out of any component of an individual sewage disposal system or flowing over the ground's surface or beneath the ground in groundwater. *(New Shoreham, R.I.)*

■ **egress** An exit. *(Champaign, Ill.)*

■ **elderly** Persons age 62 and older. *(California Planning Roundtable)*

Persons 60 years of age or older. *(El Paso, Tex.)*

■ **elderly housing** A multiple-family structure, controlled by either a public body, institutional body, or nonprofit corporation, 80 percent of whose occupants shall be 65 years of age or over, or a multiple-family structure where each unit is occupied by at least one person who is 55 years of age or over and is retired, and where the rental arrangement includes a requirement that all members of each household consume at least one meal per day in a congregate dining facility contained within the multiple-family structure. *(St. Paul, Minn.)*

Typically one- and two-bedroom apartments or condominiums designed to meet the needs of persons 62 years of age and older or, if more than 150 units, persons 55 years of age and older, and restricted to occupancy by them. *(California Planning Roundtable)*

*Commentary: We have attempted to provide a full range of elderly housing definitions here to accommodate the many types of such housing that are evolving in the United States at this time. Over time, the number of types of elderly and retirement housing is likely to grow as more specific niches and preferences for types of care are found. Please note that the ordinance provisions for elderly housing must address the issue of housing discrimination against children, which is prohibited by federal law.*

■ **elderly housing, assisted living** Services in these establishments include assistance with daily activities, such as dressing, grooming, bathing, etc. These are also referred to as board and care establishments. *(APA's Land-Based Classification Standards project)*

■ **elderly housing, congregate care facility** Funded through the 1978 Congregate Housing Services Act, many of these establishments served meals and other services in low-income and federally subsidized housing. Now, many establishments provide such services to other nonsubsidized housing facilities and the services they offer include housekeeping, laundry, transportation, recreational programs, and other convenient stores. *(APA's Land-Based Classification Standards project)*

A facility for long-term residence exclusively by persons 60 years of age or older, and which shall include, without limitation, common dining and social and recreational features, special safety and convenience features designed for the needs of the elderly, such as emergency call systems, grab bars and handrails, special door hardware, cabinets, appliances, passageways, and doorways designed to accommodate wheelchairs, and the provision of social services for residents which must include at least two of the following: meal services, transportation, housekeeping, linen, and organized social activities. *(Boulder, Colo.)*

■ **elderly housing, lifecare or continuing care services** These were the traditional church or social welfare organization run retirement centers where residents turn their entire assets in exchange for housing, personal care, convenience care, and some health care. Recently, some of these centers developed other financial arrangements (instead of turning over all assets) for those who want these services. Other terms used for such establishments are: endowment facilities, founder's care facilities, continuing care retirement centers, etc. *(APA's Land-Based Classification Standards project)*

■ **elderly housing, residential care facility** A facility that provides primarily nonmedical resident services to seven or more individuals in need of personal assistance essential for sustaining the activities of daily living, or for the protection of the individual, excluding members of the resident family or persons employed as facility staff, on a 24-hour a day basis *(Sacramento, Calif.)*

Any facility licensed by the [state] department of human services, public or private, which for gain or otherwise, regularly provides one or more persons with 24-hour per day substitute care, food, lodging, training, education, supervision, habilitation, rehabilitation, and treatment they need, but which for any reason cannot be furnished in the person's own home. Residential facilities include, but are not limited to: state institutions under the control of the (public welfare agency), foster homes, halfway houses, residential treatment centers, maternity shelters, group homes, residential programs, or schools for handicapped children. *(Plymouth, Minn.)*

Housing that provides residents with a program of assisted-living services to deal with the activities and instrumental activities of daily living. *(Cape Elizabeth, Maine)*

■ **elderly/retirement housing** A residential complex containing multifamily dwellings designed for and principally occupied by senior citizens. Such facilities may include a congregate meals program in a common dining area, but exclude institutional care such as medical or nursing care and are distinguished from life care retirement centers as elsewhere defined. *(Tulsa, Okla.)*

These offer minimal convenience services, but focus on attracting elderly residents so as to provide a social support system among the residents. *(APA's Land-Based Classification Standards project)*

■ **electric power plants** All equipment, fixtures, and personal property operated or maintained in connection with the production of electricity using any source of thermal, steam, wind, or solar energy with a generating capacity of more than 500 kilowatts and less than 50 megawatts, including all conduits, ducts, or other devices, materials, apparatus, or property used or to be used for the transmission of the electricity so produced. *(Santa Clara County, Calif.)*

■ **electromagnetic field (EMF)**   A field with two components, one electrical and the other magnetic, arising from the conduction of electricity through a medium of transmission. *(Minnetonka, Minn.)*

■ **eleemosynary institution**   Any building or group of buildings devoted to and supported by charity. *(Gurnee, Ill.)*

An organization that distributes charity or doles out relief. *(Maui County, Hawaii)*

■ **emergency**   Actions that must be undertaken immediately or within a time frame too short to allow full compliance with this [ordinance] to avoid an immediate threat to public health or safety, to prevent an imminent threat of serious environmental degradation. *(Renton, Wash.)*

A condition arising from actual or imminent failure and resulting in a substantial health or safety hazard to occupants or in substantial hazard to a dwelling. . . . *(Ames, Iowa)*

■ **emergency and protective shelter** *(See also **crisis center; shelter** definitions)*   A residential facility which provides room and board for a temporary (30 days or less) period, protection, counseling, and pre-placement screening for abused, displaced, or transient children or adults. *(Tulsa, Okla.)*

■ **emergency housing facility**   One main building, or portion thereof, on one zoning lot where persons who do not have housing live on a 24-hour-per-day basis until more permanent arrangements can be made, but generally for no longer than 30 days. *(St. Paul, Minn.)*

■ **emergency operations**   Work made necessary to restore property to a safe condition following a public calamity, or work required to protect persons or property from an imminent exposure to danger or potential danger. *(Eliot, Maine)*

■ **emergency, snow or ice**   A condition of snowfall, snow accumulation, or ice accumulation or anticipated snowfall, snow accumulation, or ice accumulation that creates or is likely to create hazardous street conditions endangering or impeding or likely to endanger or impede the movement of fire, police, emergency, or other vehicular traffic, or otherwise endanger the safety, health, or welfare of the public. *(Rochester, Minn.)*

■ **emergency vehicle**   Any vehicle legitimately participating in an emergency response to include, but not necessarily limited to crash/fire/rescue vehicles, authorized police vehicles, medical services vehicles, or tenant-operated vehicles. *(Austin, Tex.)*

Vehicles of the fire department, police vehicles, ambulances, and such emergency vehicles of municipal departments or public service corporations as are designated or authorized by the police chief. A privately owned vehicle commandeered by the fire or police chief or owned or used by a fireman, policeman, or ambulance attendant shall have the same status under this ordinance as a publicly owned authorized emergency vehicle while actually engaged in or responding to a call for public emergency service. *(Bethel, Maine, which uses the term "authorized emergency vehicle")*

■ **eminent domain** *(See also **condemnation; taking**)*   The authority of a government to take, or to authorize the taking of, private property for public use. *(Iowa State University Extension Service)*

■ **emission**   Release of pollutants into the air from a source. *(Environmental Protection Agency)*

■ **employee parking area**   The portion of total required parking at a development used by on-site employees. Unless specified in the city's zoning/building code, employee parking shall be calculated as follows: Commercial: 30 percent [devoted to employees]; Office/professional: 85 percent; Industrial/manufacturing: 90 percent. *(Hermosa Beach, Calif.)*

■ **employee quarters**   Accessory residential structures that house people employed by the residents of the principal building or owners of the property and that is not used for rental purposes. *(Germantown, Tenn.)*

■ **employment center**   An area of higher-intensity uses that typically employ thousands of people that is contained by a boundary to prevent it from encroaching on adjacent areas and/or neighborhoods. *(Renton, Wash.)*

Entities that employ 300 people or more at a particular site. *(Interstate 81 Corridor Council)*

■ **enabling act**   The legislative act authorizing a government agency to do something that previously could not be done. *(Iowa State University Extension Service)*

■ **endangered species**   A species of animal or plant is considered to be endangered when its prospects for survival and reproduction are in immediate jeopardy from one or more causes. *(California Planning Roundtable)*

■ **energy facility**   Any public or private processing, producing, generating, storing, transmitting, or recovering facility for electricity, natural gas, petroleum, coal, or other source of energy. *(Imperial Beach, Calif.)*

■ **energy systems, small-scale**   Energy production facilities that are incidental and subordinate to a principal use established on a property. These systems include, but are not limited to, solar, wind, hydrologic, and biomass systems. *(Maui County, Hawaii)*

■ **entertainment, commercial indoor**   Predominantly spectator uses conducted within an enclosed building. Typical uses include motion picture theaters and concert or music halls. *(Blacksburg, Va.)*

■ **entertainment, commercial outdoor**   Predominantly spectator uses conducted in open or partially enclosed or screened facilities. Typical uses include sports arenas, motor vehicle or animal racing facilities, and outdoor amusement parks. *(Blacksburg, Va.)*

■ **entertainment complex**   A structure or facility for the presentation of the performing arts, including indoor motion picture theaters, theaters for live performances, and indoor and outdoor concert halls. Entertainment complex includes restaurants as an accessory use. Entertainment complex does not include adult motion picture theaters or establishments featuring burlesque. *(Anne Arundel County, Md.)*

■ **entertainment district**   An area with a variety of uses that provide entertainment and supporting uses to the public, such as theaters, restaurants, plazas, outdoor cafes, kiosks, retail shops, docks, boats, and vessels moored at dock space, public areas, and ways. *(Fort Lauderdale, Fla.)*

■ **entertainment, live**   A musical, theatrical, dance, cabaret, or comedy act performed by one or more persons. Any form of dancing by patrons and guests at an eating or drinking establishment or bar is live entertainment. Live entertainment does not include the term "adult entertainment facility" or "adult entertainment establishment." *(Salinas Calif.)*

■ **entry arcade**   An arcade that provides public access to building entrances, retail space and/or public space. *(Philadelphia, Pa.)*

■ **environment**   The physical conditions which exist within the area that will be affected by a proposed project, including land, air, water, mineral, flora, fauna, noise, and objects of historic or aesthetic significance. *(California Environmental Quality Act)*

■ **environment, conservancy** This environment is characterized by very low-intensity land uses primarily related to natural resources use and diffuse recreational development, relatively low land values, relatively minor public and private capital investment, and/or relatively major biophysical development limitations. Management objectives are oriented toward establishing a balance between sustained-yield natural resource utilization and low-density recreational uses in this environment, with restriction of development in hazardous areas. *(Yakima County, Wash.)*

■ **environment, natural**   This environment is characterized by severe biophys-

ical limitations, presence of some unique natural or cultural features intolerant of intensive human use, and/or its value is retained only in its natural condition. Management objectives are oriented toward preserving unique features, restricting activities that may degrade the actual or potential value of this environment, and severely restricting development in hazardous areas. *(Yakima County, Wash.)*

■ **environmental impact report (EIR)** A report required of general plans by the California Environmental Quality Act (CEQA) that assesses all the environmental characteristics of an area and determines what effects or impacts will result if the area is altered or disturbed by a proposed action. *(California Planning Roundtable)*

■ **environmental impact, significant** (1) As used in [the State Environmental Protection Act], a reasonable likelihood of more than a moderate adverse impact of environmental quality. (2) Significance involves context and intensity and does not lend itself to a formula or quantifiable test. The context may vary with the physical setting. Intensity depends on the magnitude and duration of an impact. The severity of an impact should be weighed along with the likelihood of its occurrence. An impact may be significant if its chance of occurrence is not great, but the resulting environmental impact would be severe if it occurred. (3) [State law] specifies a process, including criteria and procedures, for determining whether a proposal is likely to have a significant adverse environmental impact. *(Renton, Wash.)*

■ **environmental impact, significant effect**   A beneficial or detrimental impact on the environment. May include but is not limited to significant changes in an area's air, water, and land resources. *(California Planning Roundtable)*

■ **environmental impact statement (EIS)**   Under the National Environmental Policy Act (NEPA), a statement on the effect of development proposals and other major actions that significantly affect the environment. *(California Planning Roundtable)*

A comprehensive report that describes the natural features and characteristics of a proposed development site, the changes that will occur as a result of the proposed development activities on the site, the anticipated environmental impacts and consequences of the proposed development, and the mitigation measures to be taken to minimize undesirable impacts to the environment. *(Cecil County, Md., which uses the term "environmental assessment")*

■ **environmental scientists**   Professionals with training or experience in areas such as environmental planning, physical geography, environmental geology, ecology, botany, soil sciences, or natural resource administration. *(Scottsdale, Ariz.)*

■ **equipment sales and rental**   Establishments primarily engaged in the sale or rental of tools, trucks, tractors, construction equipment, agricultural implements, and similar industrial equipment, and the rental of mobile homes. Included in this use type is the incidental storage, maintenance, and servicing of such equipment. *(Blacksburg, Va.)*

■ **erected**   Built, constructed, reconstructed, moved upon, or any physical operations on the premises required for building. Excavations, fill, drainage, and the like shall be considered a part of erection. *(Boca Raton, Fla.)*

■ **erosion**   The detachment and movement of soil or rock fragments, or the wearing away of the land surface by water, wind, ice, and gravity. *(Champaign, Ill.)*

The general process by which soils are removed by flowing surface or subsurface water or by wind. *(St. Paul, Minn.)*

■ **escort services**   Any business, agency, or person who, for a fee, commission, hire, reward or profit, furnishes or offers to furnish names of persons, or who introduces, furnishes or arranges for persons, who may accompany other persons to or about social affairs, entertainments or places of amusement, or who may consort with others about any place of public resort or within any private quarters. . . . *(Imperial Beach, Calif.)*

■ **esplanade** *(See also riverwalk)* Waterfront area devoted to public use, includes both upland walkways and open space. *(Tacoma, Wash.)*

■ **essential services** Services provided by public and private utilities, necessary for the exercise of the principal use or service of the principal structure. These services include underground, surface, or overhead gas, electrical, steam, water, sanitary sewerage, stormwater drainage, and communication systems and accessories thereto, such as poles, tower, wires, mains, drains, vaults, culverts, laterals, sewers, pipes, catch basins, water storage tanks, conduits, cables, fire alarm boxes, police call boxes, traffic signals, pumps, lift stations and hydrants, but not including buildings used or intended to be used for human habitation. *(Racine County, Wisc.)*

The erection, construction, alteration, or maintenance by public utilities or municipal departments of underground, surface or overhead gas, communication, electrical, steam, fuel or water transmission or distribution systems, collection, supply or disposal systems, including towers, poles, wires, mains, drains, sewers, pipes, conduits, cables, fire alarm and police call boxes, traffic signals, hydrants, and similar accessories in connection therewith but not including structures that are necessary for the furnishing of adequate service by such utilities or municipal departments for the general public health, safety, convenience, and welfare. *(Hartford, Conn.)*

■ **establishment** The headquarters of a single business. Establishment includes both the tenants and the owners of the business property they occupy. *(Anne Arundel County, Md.)*

A place of business, including the possessions and employees. *(El Paso, Tex.)*

An economic unit where business is conducted or services or industrial operations performed. *(St. Charles, Mo.)*

■ **Euclidean zoning** *(See also as-of-right zoning; cumulative zoning)* A convenient nickname for traditional as-of-right or self-executing zoning in which: district regulations are explicit; residential, commercial, and industrial uses are segregated; districts are cumulative; and bulk and height controls are imposed. *(PAS Report No. 322, The Language of Zoning)*

*Commentary: The term is derived from Euclid (Ohio) v. Ambler Realty Co., the 1926 U.S. Supreme Court decision to affirm the validity of comprehensive zoning. (The term has nothing to do with geometry; Euclid could just as well have been Cleveland.)*

■ **eviction** Any effort by a developer to remove a tenant from the premises or terminate a tenancy by lawful or unlawful means. *(Renton, Wash.)*

■ **ex parte contact** Some form of communication between one party to a proceeding (e.g., an applicant for a permit) and a public official with some responsibility for making a decision affecting that proceeding occurring outside the formal decision-making process and without the knowledge of the other party to the proceeding. Such contacts are usually prohibited or circumscribed by codes of ethics to preclude conflict of interest or the appearance of favoritism to one party in a proceeding. *(PAS Report No. 322, The Language of Zoning)*

■ **exaction** A contribution or payment required as an authorized precondition for receiving a development permit; usually refers to mandatory dedication (or fee in lieu of dedication) requirements found in many subdivision regulations. *(California Planning Roundtable)*

■ **examination room** Any room wherein special equipment may be installed for use in the examination and treatment of a patient, as distinguished from a waiting room, counseling room or office of such practitioner. *(Colts Neck, N.J.)*

■ **excavation** The mechanical removal of earth material. *(Yakima County, Wash.)*

Any breaking of ground, except common household gardening and ground care. *(St. Paul, Minn.)*

■ **exclusionary zoning** Zoning that has the effect of keeping out of a community or neighborhood certain groups, or in some cases, additional population of any kind. Techniques such as large-lot zoning or high floor area or minimum residential floor area requirements, which increase housing costs, have been challenged for their potential exclusionary effects. *(Handbook for Planning Commissioners in Missouri)*

Development regulations that result in the exclusion of low- and moderate-income and/or minority families from a community *(California Planning Roundtable)*

■ **exhibition** Any establishment at which an exhibit of animals, human beings or objects is featured for the purpose of amusement and entertainment, and at which the public pays an admission fee. *(Glendale, Ariz.)*

■ **exhibition center** *(See convention center)*

■ **existing-use zoning** A mechanism for communities to retain prevailing land use except where change serves a compelling public interest, whereby the lawful uses of each piece of land are the uses for which the parcel already is reasonably adapted. Existing-use zoning is appropriate in non-urban areas where a planning objective is to avoid dynamic changes in patterns of land use, and is suited to those relatively undisturbed locales where the normal presumption runs against active modification of current land use. *(New Jersey State Plan)*

■ **exotic** Any species of plants or animals that are not indigenous to the planning area. *(Renton, Wash.)*

■ **explosive material** *(See also fireworks; hazardous material)* Any chemical compound mixture or device, the primary and common purpose of which is to function by explosion with substantially simultaneous release of gas and heat, the resulting pressure being capable of producing destructive effects. *(National City, Calif.)*

■ **expressway** *(See street, expressway)*

■ **extended-stay hotel/motel** *(See also hotel; motel)* Any building containing six or more guest rooms intended or designed to be used, or which are used, rented, or hired out to be occupied or which are occupied for sleeping purposes for guests and contain kitchen facilities for food preparation including but not limited to such facilities as refrigerators, stoves, and ovens. *(Norcross, Ga.)*

A hotel offering suites with living, kitchen, and sleeping areas. . . . *(Aurora, Ill., which uses the term "hometel")*

A building or structure intended as, used as, maintained as, or advertised as a place where sleeping accommodations are furnished to the public as regular roomers, primarily for periods of one week or more. *(Plymouth, Minn.)*

■ **exterior** *(See also **facade**)* The front facade of any structure and any external features visible from public ways. *(Galena, Ill.)*

■ **exterior appliance** A central air-conditioning condenser unit, heat pump, or any other noise-producing mechanical system components that are typically required to be located on the exterior of a structure. *(West Bloomfield Charter Township, Mich.)*

■ **exterior display** The outdoor display of products, vehicles, equipment, and machinery for sale or lease. Exterior display is an outdoor showroom for customers to examine and compare products. There is variety or a distinction among the goods on display through different products, brands, or models. The display area does not have to be visible to the street. Examples of uses that often have exterior display are car and boat sales and plant nurseries. Exterior display does not include goods that are being stored or parked outside. It does not include damaged vehicles, vehicles or equipment being services, bulk goods and materials, and other similar products. *(Portland, Ore.)*

■ **externalities, side effects, spillovers, repercussion effects** The impacts of those other than the direct beneficiaries or targets of a course of action. Externalities may be local or widespread and may be fiscal, environmental, social, or all three. Much of the recent environmental impact legislation is based on increased understanding of the spillovers of development processes on a community's natural and human environment.

*(Handbook for Planning Commissioners in Missouri)*

■ **extraction** To draw out or forth; hence to derive as if by drawing out; removal of physical matter in a solid, liquid, or gaseous state from its naturally occurring location; the initial step in use of a natural resource; examples include petroleum and natural gas wells, shale and coal mines, gravel pits, timber cutting. *(Glenwood Springs, Colo.)*

■ **extractive industry** *(See also **mineral extraction; mining; quarry**)* The extraction of minerals, including solids, such as coal and ores; liquids, such as crude petroleum; and gases, such as natural gases. The term also includes quarrying; well operation; milling, such as crushing, screening, washing and flotation; and other preparation customarily done at the extraction site or as a part of the extractive activity. *(Newport, R.I.)*

A use involving on-site extraction of surface or subsurface mineral products or natural resources. Typical uses are quarries, borrow pits, sand and gravel operation, mining, and soil mining. Specifically excluded from this use is grading and removal of dirt associated with an approved site plan or subdivision or excavations associated with, and for the improvement of, a bona fide agricultural use. *(Blacksburg, Va., which uses the term "resource extraction")*

■ **extraterritorial land-use controls (zoning and subdivision regulations)** Authority granted to certain cities to exercise zoning and subdivision powers for two miles outside their boundaries. It is intended to protect the use of land on the edge of communities from being encroached on by incompatible activities that might degrade adjoining property of cause a nuisance. *(The Iowa Code)*

■ **exurban area** The region that lies beyond a city and its suburbs. *(California Planning Roundtable)*

■ **facade**    That portion of any exterior elevation on the building extending from grade to top of the parapet, wall, or eaves and the entire width of the building elevation. *(Peoria, Ill.)*

The exterior wall of a building exposed to public view or that wall viewed by persons not within the building. *(Iowa State University Extension Service)*

The entire area of a building facing or side extending from the roof or parapet to the ground and from one corner of the building to another but does not include any structural or nonstructural elements which extend beyond the roof of a building. *(Grand Forks, N.D.)*

■ **facade, nonprincipal**    The exterior wall(s) of a structure that do not face a public right-of-way. *(Orlando, Fla)*

■ **facades, principal**    Exterior walls of a building which are adjacent to or front on a public street, park, or plaza. *(San Francisco, Calif.)*

■ **factory-built housing** *(See also manufactured housing; mobile home; modular housing; panelized housing)*    Any structure, designed for residential use, which is wholly or in substantial part, made, fabricated, formed, or assembled in manufacturing facilities for installation or assembly and installation, on a building site. For the purpose of this chapter, factory-built homes include mobile homes, manufactured homes and modular homes and also include park trailers, travel trailers and other similar vehicles placed on a site for greater than 180 consecutive days. *(Iowa City, Iowa)*

■ **fair market rent**    The rent, including utility allowances, determined by the United States Department of Housing and Urban Development for purposes of administering the Section 8 Existing Housing Program. *(California Planning Roundtable)*

■ **fair market value**    The price at which property would change hands between a willing buyer and a willing seller, neither being under any compulsion to buy or to sell and both having reasonable knowledge of relevant facts. *(Blacksburg, Va..)*

The price in terms of money that a property will bring in a competitive and open market under all conditions of a fair sale, the buyer and seller each prudently knowledgeable, and assuming the price is not affected by undue stimulus. *(SeaTac, Wash.)*

■ **fair share**    A proportionate amount by local jurisdiction. For example, used in the context of affordable housing, fair share means that each city and county within the region works with the regional authority [or the state] to establish local and regional policies that will provide the opportunity within each jurisdiction for accommodating a portion of the region's need for affordable housing. *(Portland, Ore.)*

■ **fairgrounds**    An area of land use including, but not limited to: Agricultural related office buildings, animal shows and judging, carnivals, circuses, community meeting or recreational buildings and uses, concerts, food booths and stands, games, rides, rodeos, sales and auctions, storage, theaters. Such county fairs, exhibitions, and shows do not include racetracks or motorized contests of speed. *(Iowa City, Iowa)*

An area wherein buildings, structures, and land are used for the exhibition of livestock, farm products, etc., and/or for carnival-like entertainment. *(McHenry County, Ill.)*

■ **fallout shelter**    An accessory building and use specifically designed for the protection of life from radioactive fallout. *(Gurnee, Ill.)*

■ **family**    A person living alone, or any of the following groups living together as a single nonprofit housekeeping unit and sharing common living, sleeping, cooking, and eating facilities: (1) any number of people related by blood, marriage, adoption, guardianship, or duly-authorized custodial relationship; (2) two unrelated people; (3) two unrelated people and any children related to either of them; (4) not more than eight people who are: (a) residents of a "Family Home" as defined in the [state code] and this ordinance; or (b) "handicapped" as defined in the Fair Housing Act . . . and this ordinance. This definition does not include persons currently illegally using or addicted to a "controlled substance"; (5) three or more people who are granted a special-use permit as a "functional family" pursuant to the special use permit procedures section of this ordinance. Family does not include any society, club, fraternity, sorority, association, lodge combine, federation, coterie, or like organization; any group of individuals whose association is temporary or seasonal in nature; any group of individuals who are in a group living arrangement as a result of criminal offenses. *(Ames, Iowa)*

One or more persons occupying a single dwelling unit, as a single housekeeping unit, provided that unless all members are related by blood, marriage, or adoption, no such family shall contain over six persons, including any roomers, boarders and/or domestic servants. A home for independent living with support personnel that provides room and board, personal care and habilitation services in a family environment as a single-housekeeping unit for not more than six resident elderly or disabled persons (mentally and/or physically impaired) with at least one, but not more than two resident staff persons shall be considered a family. *(Tulsa, Okla.)*

Two or more persons related by blood, marriage, adoption, or not more than four persons not related by blood, marriage, or adoption, occupying a dwelling unit as an individual housekeeping organization. *(Boone County, Mo.)*

An individual or two or more persons related to each other by blood, marriage, or adoption, or a group of not more than four persons not all so related, together with his or their domestic servants, living in a dwelling unit. A family may include, in addition thereto, not more than two boarders, roomers, or permanent guests, whether or not gratuitous. *(Roswell, N. Mex.)*

One or two persons or parents, with their direct lineal descendants and adopted or legally cared for children (and including the domestic employees thereof) together with not more than two persons not so related, living together in the whole or part of a dwelling comprising a single housekeeping unit. Every additional group of four or fewer persons living in such housekeeping unit shall be considered a separate family for the purpose of this code. *(St. Paul, Minn.)*

Two or more persons related to each other by blood, marriage, or legal adoption living together as a single housekeeping unit; or a group of not more than three persons who need not be related by blood, marriage, or legal adoption, living together as a single housekeeping unit and occupying a single dwelling unit. *(Lake County, Ill.)*

One or more persons occupying a premises and living as a single housekeeping unit as distinguished from a group occupying a rooming house or motel. *(Gorham, Maine)*

One or more persons occupying a premise[s] and living as a single housekeeping unit as distinguished from a group occupying a boardinghouse, lodging house, or hotel as herein defined. *(Scottsdale, Ariz.)*

**Commentary***: The definition of family has been widely litigated. The definitions here define family as a single housekeeping unit rather than as persons related by blood or marriage. Several of the definitions specifically exclude a group living in a boarding house, hotel, lodging house, or rooming house. These exclusions might be extended to include a fraternity, sorority, and clubs. Many of these definitions employ restrictions on the number of unrelated persons living in a single-family housekeeping unit. Such restrictions, however, may be struck down by the courts if they limit the housing opportunities of nontraditional families, such as group homes for people with developmental disabilities. The Federal Fair Housing Act, state law, case law, and the attorney for the jurisdiction should all be consulted before adopting or drafting a definition of family.*

■ **family day care home** *(See also **child care** and **day care** definitions)*    A single family dwelling in which more than five but less than 13 individuals are received for care, protection, and guidance during only part of a 24-hour day. Individuals related by blood, legal adoption, or marriage to the person who maintains the home shall not be counted towards this total. The care of five or fewer individuals for portions of a day shall be considered as a home occupation. *(Blacksburg, Va.)*

A dwelling used to house and provide supervision and care for seven children, said total to include those preschool children under five years of age who reside in the residence. *(Tulsa, Okla.)*

■ **family farm**    A farming operation conducted by a person or persons, including a family farm corporation . . . but not a corporate farm. *(Ford County, Kans.)*

Land within areas designated as [zoning designation] which may be used by family members of the property owner for use as a permanent residence at densities higher than that permitted by the land use classification, upon approval by the (county commissioners). However, densities may not exceed one acre. This provision is intended for the perpetuation of the family farm by making it possible for family members to both work and reside on the property devoted to agricultural uses. *(Polk County, Fla.)*

■ **farm**    *(See also **agriculture**)* An area of five or more contiguous acres that is used for the production of farm crops, such as vegetables, fruit trees, cotton, or grain, and their storage, as well as raising thereon of farm animals, such as poultry or swine, on a limited basis. Farms also include dairy produce [products]. Farming does not include the commercial raising of animals, commercial pen feeding (feed lots), or the commercial feeding of garbage or offal to swine or other animals. *(Scottsdale, Ariz.)*

A parcel of land used for growing or raising agricultural products, including related structures thereon. *(Maryland Heights, Mo.)*

A parcel of land containing no less than 40 acres or a parcel of land that is a portion of a larger tract of land containing no less than 40 acres owned in fee or leased to a single legal entity and which is devoted to agriculture, pasturage, or stock or poultry raising. The term "farm" does not include: (a) truck gardens; (b) commercial tree farms; (c) sales of agricultural equipment or chemicals; (d) commercial storage of agricultural produce or chemicals; (e) commercial feedlots and poultry lots; and (f) nurseries. *(Grand Forks, N.D.)*

An area of five or more contiguous acres used for the production of farm crops such as vegetables, fruit trees, cotton or grain and their storage, as well as raising thereon of farm animals such as poultry or swine on a limited basis. Farms also include dairy produce. *(Scottsdale, Ariz.)*

No less than 40 contiguous acres of land, or one-quarter of one-quarter of a Section, as legally described and recorded, while used for agricultural purposes. Residential structures occupied by persons engaged in farm operations shall be included in the term farming as are roadside stands for the sale of farm products. *(Iowa City, Iowa)*

■ **farm dwelling**  A single-family dwelling that is located on and used in connection with a farm. (*Maui County, Hawaii*)

■ **farm employee housing** (*See also housing, temporary employment*)  A dwelling located on a farm for the purpose of housing an employee of that farm operation and his/her family. Also included in this use type would be multi-family dwelling(s) for seasonal employees in connection with an orchard or other agricultural use which relies on seasonal employees who must be housed. (*Blacksburg, Va.*)

A dwelling or lodging unit that is used exclusively by agricultural employees employed full-time or seasonally in the county, and that is located on a farm and is ancillary and secondary to agriculture. (*Maui County, Hawaii, which uses the term "farm labor dwelling"*)

Buildings or mobile homes located on land owned by the laborer's employer, inhabited solely by persons and their families while employed in agricultural activities on land owned by the laborer's employer. (*Shasta Lake, Calif., which uses the term "farm labor dwelling"*)

■ **farm, exclusive farm use**  Land zoned primarily for farming and restricting many uses that are incompatible with farming, such as rural housing. . . . (*Portland, Ore.*)

■ **farm, fish** (*See aquaculture*)

■ **farm, fur**  A tract of land devoted in whole or part to the commercial raising of animals for the fur. (*Brookfield, Wisc.*)

■ **farm, poultry**  A tract of land devoted principally to the production of poultry for eggs or meat for commercial purposes. (*Brookfield, Wisc.*)

■ **farm stand** (*See also roadside stand; stand*)  A building or structure used for the retail sales of fresh fruits, vegetables, flowers, herbs or plants. May also involve the accessory sales of other unprocessed foodstuffs, home processed food products such as jams, jellies, pickles, sauces or baked goods, and homemade handicrafts. The floor area devoted to the sales of these accessory items shall not exceed 50 percent of the total sales area. No commercially packaged handicrafts or commercially processed or packaged foodstuffs shall be sold at a roadside stand. (*Gorham, Maine, which uses the term "roadside stand"*)

■ **farmer**  An individual who normally devotes the major portion of his time to the activities of producing products of the soil, poultry, livestock, or dairy farming in such products' unmanufactured state and who normally receives not less than 50 percent of his annual gross income from any of the foregoing activities; and the term also includes an individual who is retired because of illness or age and who at the time of retirement owned and occupied as a farmer as defined above the residence in which he lives. (*Grand Forks, N.D.*)

■ **farmer's market**  The offering for sale of fresh agricultural products directly to the consumer at an open air market designated by the council as a community activity. (*Rapid City, S.D.*)

The seasonal selling or offering for sale at retail of home-grown vegetables or produce, occurring in a pre-designated area, where the vendors are generally individuals who have raised the vegetables or produce or have taken the same on consignment for retail sale. (*Ford County, Kans.*)

■ **farming**  Commercial agricultural uses in general and especially crop, dairy, stock and poultry farming; commercial greenhouses on three acres or more. (*Chandler, Ariz.*)

■ **farmland**  Land in active agricultural or horticultural use. (*Blacksburg, Va.*)

Refers to eight classifications of land mapped by the U.S. Department of Agriculture Soil Conservation Service. The five agricultural classifications defined here—except Grazing Land—do not include publicly owned lands for which there is an adopted policy preventing agricultural use. (1) *Prime Farmland.* Land which has the best combination of physical and chemical characteristics for the production of crops. It has the soil quality, growing season, and moisture supply needed to produce sustained high yields of crops when treated and managed, including water management, according to current farming methods. Prime Farmland must have been used for the production of irrigated crops within the last three years. (2) *Farmland of Statewide Importance.* Land other than Prime Farmland which has a good combination of physical and chemical characteristics for the production of crops. It must have been used for the production of irrigated crops within the last three years. (3) *Unique Farmland.* Land which does not meet the criteria for Prime Farmland or Farmland of Statewide Importance, that is currently used for the production of specific high economic value crops. It has the special combination of soil quality, location, growing season, and moisture supply needed to produce sustained high quality or high yields of a specific crop when treated and managed according to current farming methods. Examples of such crops may include oranges, olives, avocados, rice, grapes, and cut flowers. (4) *Farmland of Local Importance.* Land other than Prime Farmland, Farmland of Statewide Importance, or Unique Farmland that is either currently producing crops, or that has the capability of production. This land may be important to the local economy due to its productivity. (5) *Grazing Land.* Land on which the existing vegetation, whether grown naturally or through management, is suitable for grazing or browsing of livestock. This classification does not include land previously designated as Prime Farmland, Farmland of Statewide Importance, Unique Farmland, or Farmland of Local Importance, and heavily brushed, timbered, excessively steep, or rocky lands which restrict the access and movement of livestock. (*California Planning Roundtable*)

■ **farmland preservation property** (*See also agricultural preservation*)  A lot, tract or parcel of land, which is encumbered with a deed restriction prohibiting its use for purposes other than agriculture. (*Colt's Neck, N.J.*)

■ **fault**   A fracture in the earth's crust forming a boundary between rock masses that have shifted. *(California Planning Roundtable)*

■ **feasibility study**   An analysis of a specific project or program to determine if it can be successfully carried out. *(Iowa State University Extension Service)*

■ **fees in lieu** *(See dedication, fees in lieu of)*

■ **fee simple**   A private property land right, sometimes also referred to as a fee simple absolute, whereby a property owner unconditionally owns a specified piece of land. *(Schaumburg, Ill.)*

A form of land ownership that includes all property rights, including the right to develop land. *(American Farmland Trust)*

■ **feed store**   An establishment engaged in retail sale of supplies directly

related to the day-to-day activities of agricultural production. *(King County, Wash.)*

■ **feedlot**   A lot, yard, corral, or other area in which livestock are confined, primarily for the purposes of feeding and growth prior to slaughter. The term does not include areas which are used for raising crops or other vegetation or upon which livestock are allowed to graze. *(Iowa City, Iowa)*

A lot or building or combination of lots and buildings intended for the confined feeding, breeding, raising, or holding of

animals and specifically designed as a confinement area in which manure may accumulate, or where the concentration of animals is such that a vegetative cover cannot be maintained within the enclosure. Open lots used for feeding and rearing of poultry (poultry ranges) and barns, dairy farms, swine facilities, beef lots and barns, horse stalls, mink ranches and zoos, shall be considered to be animal feedlots. Pastures shall not be considered animal feedlots. *(Plymouth, Minn.)*

■ **fence**   An enclosure or barrier, such as wooden posts, wire, iron, etc., used as a boundary, means of protection, privacy screening or confinement, but not including hedges, shrubs, trees, or other natural growth. *(Blue Springs, Mo.)*

An artificially constructed barrier of wood, masonry, stone, wire, metal, or other manufactured material or combination of materials erected to enclose, screen, or separate areas. *(Maryland Heights, Mo.)*

A structure, solid or otherwise, which is a barrier and used as a boundary or means of protection, confinement, or concealment. *(Roswell, N. Mex.)*

■ **fence, barbed-wire**   One or more strands of wire or other material having intermittent sharp points of wire or metal that may puncture, cut, tear, or snag persons, clothing, or animals. The term "barbed wire" as used herein excludes razor ribbon. *(Palmetto, Fla.)*

■ **fence, chain-link**   An open mesh fence made entirely of wire woven in squares of approximately 1.5 inches with vertical supports not less than 1.5 inches in diameter spaced not less than six feet, and not more than eight feet, apart. *(Palmetto, Fla.)*

■ **fence, decorative**   A designed open or solid fence or wall that meets all of the following: a. It contributes to the identification and beauty of the principal use; b. It is not erected to satisfy any other provision of this code; c. It does not act as a retaining structure; d. It is made of material that typically is not found in security structures, such as chain link; e. It is not available for purchase in stores. *(Raleigh, N.C.)*

■ **fence height**   The vertical distance measured from the side of the fence that is exterior to the property or from the lowest adjacent ground level to the top of the fence material. In the case of wire fencing, height shall be measured by the width of the material used providing that when installed the material is directly adjacent to the ground level. *(Blue Springs, Mo.)*

The vertical distance between the ground, either natural or filled, directly under the fence and the highest point of the fence, excluding ornamental projections at no closer than five-foot intervals. *(Valdez, Alaska)*

■ **fence, obscuring**   A fence that is 80 percent or more opaque (pictured at left). *(St. Paul, Minn.)*

A fence that is constructed or planted in such a fashion as to cause 80 percent or more opaqueness at any angle of view through such fence. *(Ocean Shores, Wash.)*

A fence (including any gates in said fence) whose vertical surface is covered by a solid or opaque material through which no complete visual images can be seen. Openings in such fence (with its gates closed) shall not exceed 20 percent of any one square foot of vertical surface area that is more than 8 inches above grade, nor shall any opening exceed one-half inch in width. *(Vista, Calif.)*

■ **fence, open**    A fence (including any gates in said fence) that permits direct vision through at least 90 percent of any one square foot segment of vertical fence surface area (e.g., chain link or woven wire fence without slats). *(Vista, Calif.)*

A wall or fence through which clear vision is possible from one side to the other for 75 percent or more of the structure, as viewed on a horizontal plane. *(Raleigh, NC)*

A fence constructed with openings between the material used for construction, whereby the openings represent 50 percent or more of the total front face surface of the fence. *(Imperial Beach, Calif.)*

■ **fence, perimeter**    A fence located on or within six inches of a property line. *(Schaumburg, Ill.)*

■ **fence, protective**    A substantially built fence (including any gates in said fence) not less than five feet in height, above grade, which may be required as an enclosure for an "attractive" nuisance or other potential hazard to children (e.g., a swimming pool). Such a fence may be either solid (as defined herein or of other substantial construction consisting of vertical structural members with clear openings between each, not exceeding four inches, and with horizontal rails or supporting members no closer than three feet). Chain link or woven wire fencing materials, with or without slats, may also be used, provided they meet other requirements contained herein. Gates in such a fence shall be self

closing and self latching with a latch and lock not less than 4.5 feet above grade. In no case shall a fence of this classification include design features that would facilitate its ascent, or permit the passage of a child's body, as determined by the building official. *(Vista, Calif.)*

■ **fence, safety**    A solid and substantially built fence not less than eight feet in height, above grade, that shall be placed between any pedestrian way and a site containing any hazardous conditions. *(Vista, Calif.)*

■ **fence, semi-open**    A fence having a regular pattern that is between 30 percent and 80 percent permeable to both light and air when viewed perpendicular to the plane of the fence. *(Schaumburg, Ill.)*

■ **fence, sharp-pointed**    A barbed fence, a fence with spikes, other sharp points or a razor blade fence. *(Blue Springs, Mo.)*

■ **fence, solid**    A fence, including solid entrance and exit gates, that effectively conceals from viewers in or on adjoining properties, streets, alleys, or public ways, materials stored and operations conducted behind it. *(North Kansas City, Mo.)*

A fence (including any gates in said fence) constructed of solid material, wood or masonry, through which no visual images may be seen. Openings in such a fence (with its gates closed) shall not exceed 2 percent of a one-square-foot segment of vertical fence surface area more than eight inches above grade. *(Vista, Calif.)*

■ **fence, stockade**    A fence constructed of vertical wood strips, with no intervening spaces, providing a complete visual barrier. *(Carmel, Ind.)*

■ **fence, unsafe**    (1) A dilapidated, deteriorated, or decayed fence that, by reason of inadequate maintenance, obsolescence, or abandonment, poses a risk to human safety or property, or is no longer adequate to serve the purpose for which it was originally intended; or (2) A fence that, due to the manner of its construction or the materials used in its construction, poses a risk to human safety or property; or (3) A fence that incorporates razor ribbon or glass-impregnated fence tops; or an electrically charged fence; or a barbed wire fence that is not allowed under this article. *(Palmetto, Fla.)*

■ **fence, wire**    A fence whose principal material is wire. This includes, but is not limited to, chain link fences. *(Blue Springs, Mo.)*

■ **ferry and excursion boats and water taxis**    Waterborne transportation for the purposes of commuting, sight-seeing, dining, gambling, and other entertainment purposes. *(San Francisco, Calif.)*

■ **ferry and excursion boats and water taxis facility**    Primary support and ancillary facilities for waterborne transportation (e.g. commuter ferries, water taxis, hovercraft) or short-term excursions (e.g. charter boats, mini-cruises, sight-seeing, gambling, dining and entertainment on the water) including but not limited to: passenger terminals and berthing areas, storage, employee or passenger parking, administrative functions, ship servicing area, layover berths, fueling stations, and other boat or passenger services. *(San Francisco, Calif.)*

■ **festival**    The sale of ethnic specialty, regional, and gourmet foods, art and crafts, live musical entertainment, in an outdoor setting (pictured at left). *(Scottsdale, Ariz.)*

■ **festival, community or church**    A recreational, social, educational, or cultural activity, open to the public or a designated part of the public, operated by a public or nonprofit group or agency. *(Brookfield, Wisc.)*

■ **festival, temporary** The provision of rides, games, food and amusements outside of permanent structures. The use shall have a duration of no more than 10 days in a month. *(Nashville and Davidson County, Tenn.)*

■ **fill** *(See also backfill; borrow)* Earth or any other substance or material, including pilings placed or deposited for the purposes of erecting structures thereon, placed in a submerged area. *(Imperial Beach, Calif.)*

Sand, gravel, earth, or other materials of any composition whatsoever placed or deposited by humans. *(Siskiyou County, Calif.)*

Any material, such as (by way of illustration) earth, clay, sand, concrete, rubble, wood chips, bark, or waste of any kind, that is placed, stored, or dumped upon the surface of the ground resulting in an increase in the natural surface elevation. *(Yakima County, Wash.)*

■ **filling** The depositing on land, whether submerged or not, of gravel, earth, or other materials of any composition whatsoever. *(Grand Forks, N.D.)*

■ **filling station** *(See gas station; service station)*

■ **final plat** *(See plat, final)*

■ **financial institution** *(See also bank; automated teller machine (ATM))* A bank, savings and loan, credit union, mortgage office, or automated teller machine (ATM). Financial institution shall not include a currency exchange. *(Champaign, Ill.)*

Provision of financial and banking services to consumers or clients. Walk-in and drive-in services to consumers are generally provided on site. Typical uses include banks, savings and loan associations, savings banks, credit unions, lending establishments, and automatic teller machines (ATMs). *(Blacksburg, Va.)*

Any building wherein the primary occupation is concerned with such federal or state-regulated businesses as banking, savings and loans, loan companies, and investment companies. *(Carmel, Ind.)*

■ **fire, contained** Any fire contained in an incinerator, fireplace, cooking grill, or other enclosure designed for outdoor cooking or fireproof container. *(Bucks County, Pa.)*

■ **fire escape** A fireproof stairway, ladder, or chute on the outside wall of a building intended to be used to help people escape from the building in case of fire or other calamity. *(Schaumburg, Ill.)*

■ **fire hazard zone** An area where, due to slope, fuel, weather, or other fire-related conditions, the potential loss of life and property from a fire necessitates special fire protection measures and planning before development occurs. *(California Planning Roundtable)*

■ **fire lane** Path of egress whether on public roads and highways, or on private property, that is a continuous path of travel from any one point at a building or structure, to any other point along that structure, so posted and marked as a fire lane. *(Hilltown, Pa.)*

■ **fire-resistive** Able to withstand specified temperatures for a certain period of time, such as a one-hour fire wall; not fireproof. *(California Planning Roundtable)*

■ **fire station** A building used for fire equipment and firefighters (pictured below). *(Miami, Fla.)*

■ **firearm** Any device, designed to be used as a weapon, which will or is designed to or may readily be converted to expel a projectile by the action of an explosive or other form or combustion, but excluding antique firearm, "BB" gun, scuba gun, stud or nail gun used in the construction industry, or pop gun or toy gun. *(Minneapolis, Minn.)*

■ **firearms dealer** *(See also gun shop)* Any person engaged in the sale, lease, trade, or other transfer of firearms or ammunition at wholesale or retail. Firearms dealer shall not include any person engaged only in the business of repairing firearms. *(Minneapolis, Minn.)*

■ **firearms sales or firearms business** *(See also gun shop)* An establishment having at least 25 percent of its gross floor area used for the sale of firearms, ammunition and ammunition components, and hunting or shooting equipment. *(Redondo Beach, Calif.)*

■ **fireworks** *(See also explosive material)* Any substance or combination of substances or articles prepared for the purpose of producing a visible or an audible effect by combustion, explosion, deflagration, or detonation, and includes blank cartridges, toy pistols, toy cannons, toy canes, or toy guns in which explosives other than toy paper caps are used, firecrackers, torpedoes, sky rockets, Roman candles, Daygo bombs, sparklers, or other fireworks of like construction, any fireworks containing any explosive or flammable compound, or any tablet or other device containing any explosive substance. Nothing in this regulation shall be construed as applying to toy paper caps containing not more than 0.25 of a grain (16.20 milligrams) of explosive composition per cap. *(Grand Forks, N.D.)*

■ **fiscal impact analysis** A projection of the direct public costs and revenues resulting from population or employment change to the local jurisdiction(s) in which the change is taking place. Enables local governments to evaluate relative fiscal merits of general plans, specific plans, or projects. *(California Planning Roundtable)*

■ **fiscal impact report (FIR)**  A report projecting the public costs and revenues that will result from a proposed program or development. *(California Planning Roundtable)*

■ **fishery**  A parcel or building where commercial water dependent fishery facilities are located, including structures for the packing, processing, canning, or freezing of fin fish, crustaceans, molluscs, amphibians and reptiles, including related activities such as wholesale and retail sales, product storage facilities, crab shedding, off-loading docks, shellfish culture operations, and shore-based facilities necessary for aquaculture operations. *(Cecil County, Md.)*

■ **fitness center** *(See health club)*

■ **fitness studio** *(See also health club)*  A place or building where passive or active exercises and related activities are performed for the purpose of physical fitness, improved circulation or flexibility, and/or weight control. The activities shall be conducted entirely within an enclosed building. Fitness studio may include passive exercise equipment (motorized equipment which does not require physical exertion) but exclude equipment or apparatus used for weight control or muscle building, and shall exclude massage in any form. *(Scottsdale, Ariz.)*

■ **fixed area-based allowance zoning**  Ordinances that specify a certain number of units per acre. *(American Farmland Trust)*

■ **flag**  Any fabric or other flexible material attached to or designed to be flown from a flagpole or similar device. *(Clearwater, Fla.)*

■ **flag, business**  A flag displaying the name, insignia, emblem, or logo of a profit-making entity. *(Champaign, Ill.)*

■ **flag lot** *(See lot, flag)*

■ **flag, public**  A flag displaying the name, insignia, emblem, or logo of any nation, state, municipality, or noncommercial organization. *(Champaign, Ill.)*

■ **flagpole**  A freestanding structure or a structure attached to a building or to the roof of a building on a parcel of record and used for the sole purpose of displaying flags of political entities. *(Thousand Oaks, Calif.)*

■ **flea market** *(See also swap meet)*  An outdoor commercial activity, not including shopping centers, individual retail operations, or sales conducted by a nonprofit or charitable organization, that is open to the general public and composed of five or more semi-enclosed or outdoor stalls, rooms, stands, or spaces used for the purpose of display and sale, exchange, or barter of merchandise. *(El Paso, Tex.)*

An occasional or periodic market held in an open area or structure where goods are offered for sale to the general public by individual sellers from open or semi-open facilities or temporary structures. *(Schaumburg, Ill.)*

*Commentary: Flea markets are conventional profit-seeking businesses that usually operate only on weekends. As such, the definition of flea market should not include informal garage or yard sales (see the definition of "garage sales").*

■ **flexible regulations** *(See also performance zoning)*  Regulations that apply general standards to property with final decisions made shortly before development occurs. These are employed in subdivision regulations and sometimes in zoning. The intent of such devices is to widen the range of options available to developers and thereby lead to more desirable and better designs. They recognize that the appropriate use for every parcel of land cannot be predetermined; as a result, policies and criteria for decision making are established, often through performance standards, rather than specified uses and standards. Among flexible zoning devices are floating zones, overlay zones, planned unit development, bonus and incentive zoning, and conditional rezoning. The zoning devices are usually administered through special use permits, site plan review, and rezonings. *(PAS Report No. 322, The Language of Zoning)*

■ **floating zone**  An unmapped zoning district where all the zone requirements are contained in the ordinance and the zone is fixed on the map only when the application for development meeting the zone requirements is approved. *(Iowa State University Extension Service)*

A zoning district that is described in the text of the zoning ordinance but not mapped as a specific district in a specific location. When a project of sufficient size anywhere within unrestricted areas can meet certain other requirements, however, the floating zone can be anchored and the area designated on the zoning map. *(Handbook for Planning Commissioners in Missouri)*

An unmapped zoning district that is established on the zoning map only when an application for development, meeting the zoning requirements, is approved. *(Newport, R.I.)*

■ **flood**  A general and temporary inundation of normally dry land areas. *(Blacksburg, Va.)*

A general and temporary condition of partial or complete inundation of normally dry land areas from the overflow of inland or tidal waters or the unusual and rapid accumulation or runoff of surface waters from any source. *(Washington County, Ark.)*

An overflow of surface water onto lands not normally covered by water. Floods have these essential characteristics: the inundation of land is temporary and results from unusually heavy precipitation; and the land is inundated by overflow for a lake, pond, stream, and/or wetland, or is flooded by natural runoff. *(Grand Traverse County, Mich.)*

■ **flood boundary floodway (FBFW) map**  An official map delineating the floodway, floodway fringe, 100-year floodplain, and 500-year floodplain. The FBFW is prepared in conjunction with the flood insurance study (FIS). *(Columbia, Mo.)*

■ **flood control**  Any undertaking for the conveyance, control, and dispersal of flood waters. *(Renton, Wash.)*

■ **flood elevation**  The elevation flood waters would reach at a particular site during the occurrence of a specific flood period. For instance, the 100-year flood elevation is that elevation of flood waters related to the occurrence of the 100-year flood. *(Iowa City, Iowa)*

■ **flood frequency**    The probability of a flood of a certain magnitude occurring in a given year. *(Grand Traverse County, Mich.)*

■ **flood fringe**    That portion of the floodplain outside of the floodway. *(St. Paul, Minn.)*

■ **flood insurance rate map (FIRM)**  The official map on which the Federal Emergency Management Agency has delineated both the areas of special flood hazards and the risk premium zones applicable to the town. *(Gorham, Maine)*

The official map prepared as part of (but published separately from) the Flood Insurance Study which delineates both the flood hazard areas and the risk premium zones applicable to the county. *(Iowa City, Iowa)*

■ **flood insurance study**    A study initiated, funded and published by the Federal Emergency Management Agency for the purpose of evaluating in detail the existence and severity of flood hazards; providing the county with the necessary information for adopting a floodplain management program and establishing actuarial flood insurance rates. *(Iowa City, Iowa)*

■ **flood, National Flood Insurance Program (NFIP)**    A program created by the National Flood Insurance Act, passed by Congress in 1968, amended in 1969, and revised in 1973 to offer a nonstructural approach to flood damage. The program has two major objectives: (1) provide property owners in flood-prone areas with affordable flood insurance; and (2) discourage development that would be subject to flood damage. *(Department of Water Resources, Calif.)*

■ **flood, 100-year**    A flood that, on the average, is likely to occur once every 100 years (i.e., that has a one percent chance of occurring each year, although the flood may occur in any year). *(Blacksburg, Va.)*

The maximum flood expected to occur during a 100-year period. *(Renton, Wash.)*

A standard adopted by the Federal Emergency Management Agency (FEMA) to identify areas where there exists a 1 percent annual chance of a flood occurring. *(Nashville and Davidson County, Tenn.)*

■ **flood-prone**    A land area adjoining a river, stream, watercourse, or lake for which a floodway and floodplain has not been determined with respect to any specific flood frequency, but for which the potential for flooding can be identified by soils, geological evidence, or other data. *(Yakima County, Wash.)*

■ **flood protection elevation**    That elevation not less than one foot above the water surface profile associated with the regional flood, plus any increases in flood heights attributable to encroachments on the floodplain. *(St. Paul, Minn.)*

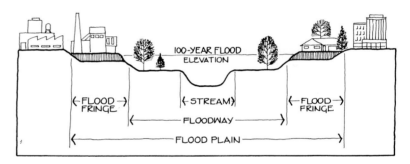

■ **flood protection system**    Those physical structural works for which funds have been authorized, appropriated, and expended and which have been constructed specifically to modify flooding in order to reduce the extent of the areas within a community subject to a "special flood hazard" and the extent of the depths of associated flooding. Such a system typically includes hurricane tidal barriers, dams, reservoirs, levees or dikes. These specialized flood-modifying works are those constructed in conformance with sound engineering standards. *(Washington County, Ark.)*

■ **flood protection system, critical feature**    An integral and readily identifiable part of a flood protection system, without which the flood protection pro-

vided by the entire system would be compromised. *(Baton Rouge, La.)*

■ **flood, regional**    A flood which is representative of large floods known to have occurred and characteristic of what can be statistically expected to occur on an average of once every 100 years and have water surface elevations equal to those filed with and made a part of the [zoning map]. *(St. Paul, Minn.)*

■ **floodlight**    Reflector type light fixture that is attached directly to a building and that is unshielded. *(Indian River County, Fla.)*

■ **floodplain**    The land area susceptible to inundation by water as a result of the flood. *(Iowa City, Iowa)*

(1) A relatively flat or low land area adjoining a river, stream, or watercourse which is subject to partial or complete inundation; or, (2) an area subject to the

unusual and rapid accumulation of runoff or surface waters from any source. *(Blacksburg, Va.)*

The areas adjoining a watercourse at or below the water surface elevation associated with the regional flood that have been or hereafter may be covered by the regional flood. *(St. Paul, Minn.)*

■ **floodplain compensatory storage**  An artificially excavated, hydraulically equivalent volume of storage . . . used to balance the loss of natural flood storage capacity when artificial fill or structures are placed within the floodplain. The uncompensated loss of natural floodplain storage can increase off-site floodwater elevations and flows. *(Schaumburg, Ill.)*

■ **floodplain management** The operation of an overall program of corrective and preventive measures for reducing flood damage, including, but not limited to, emergency preparedness plans, flood control works, and floodplain management regulations. *(Washington County, Ark.)*

An overall program of corrective and preventive measures for reducing flood damages and promoting the wise use of floodplains, including but not limited to emergency preparedness plans, flood control works, flood proofing, and floodplain management regulations. *(Iowa City, Iowa)*

■ **floodplain management regulations** Zoning ordinances, subdivision regulations, building codes, health regulations, special-purpose ordinances (such as a floodplain ordinance, grading ordinance, and erosion control ordinance) and other applications of police power. The term describes such state or local regulations, in any combination thereof, that provide standards for the purpose of flood damage prevention and reduction. *(Washington County, Ark.)*

■ **floodproofing** Any combination of structural and nonstructural additions, changes, or adjustments to structures that reduce or eliminate flood damage to real estate or improved real property, water and sanitary facilities, structures, and their contents. *(Washington County, Ark.)*

Those methods of construction . . ., which, when applied to structures or properties, will prevent or mitigate damage from floods. *(St. Paul, Minn.)*

Any combination of structural and nonstructural additions, changes or adjustments to structures, including utility and sanitary facilities, which would preclude the entry of water. Structural components shall have the capability of resisting hydrostatic and hydrodynamic loads and the effect of buoyancy. *(Columbia, Mo.)*

■ **floodway** The channel of a river or other watercourse and the adjacent land areas that must be reserved in order to discharge the base flood without cumu-

latively increasing the water surface elevation more than a designated height. *(Blacksburg, Va.)*

Channel of a river or stream and those portions of the floodplain joining the channel which are reasonably required to carry and discharge flood waters or flood flows so that confinement of flood flows to the floodway area will not result in substantially higher flood levels and flow velocities. *(Iowa City, Iowa)*

The channel of a river or other watercourse and the adjacent land areas that must be reserved in order to discharge the base flood without cumulatively increasing the water surface elevation more than a designated height. *(Washington County, Ark.)*

■ **floodway fringe** Those portions of the floodplain, other than the floodway, which can be filled, leveed, or otherwise obstructed without causing substantially higher flood levels or flow velocities. *(Iowa City, Iowa)*

That portion of a floodplain that is inundated by floodwaters but is not within a defined floodway. Floodway fringes serve as temporary storage for floodwaters. *(Yakima County, Wash.)*

■ **floor area** The sum of the horizontal areas of each floor of a building, measured from the interior faces of the exterior walls or from the centerline of walls separating two buildings. The floor area measurement is exclusive of areas of basements, unfinished attics, attached garages, or space used for off-street parking or loading, breezeways, and enclosed and unenclosed porches, elevator or stair bulkheads and accessory structures. *(St. Paul, Minn.)*

The square feet of floor space within the outside line of walls, including the total of all space on all floors of a building. Floor area shall not include porches, garages, or space in a basement or cellar. *(Iowa City, Iowa)*

The sum of the gross horizontal areas of the several floors, including basements, of a building measured from the exterior faces of the exterior walls or from the centerline of walls separating two build-

ings. Provided that for the purpose of determining compliance with the permitted floor area, the floor area of enclosed required off-street parking areas shall not be included. Provided further that floor area for outdoor display of merchandise or customer seating, whether uncovered or covered by a tent or canopy, under the provisions of [ordinance] shall mean the smallest rectangular area encompassing the display or customer seating area. *(Tulsa, Okla.)*

■ **floor area, finished** Areas excluded from the finished floor area include basements and attics. *(Blacksburg, Va.)*

■ **floor area, gross** The sum of the horizontal areas of the several stories of a building, measured from the exterior faces of exterior walls, or in the case of a common wall separating two buildings, from the centerline of such common wall. Gross floor area shall exclude basements and attics. The surface area of tennis courts, swimming pools, driveways, parking spaces, decks, and porches, is not included in the total floor area. *(Blacksburg, Va.)*

The sum of the gross areas of the several floors of a building or buildings, measured from the exterior faces of exterior walls or from the center lines of walls separating two buildings. Gross floor area shall not include: (a) underground parking space; (b) uncovered steps; (c) exterior balconies. *Scottsdale, Ariz.)*

The total area of a building measured by taking the outside dimensions of the building at each floor level intended for occupancy or storage. *(Jacksonville, N.C.)*

***Commentary:*** *The definition of gross floor area is a critical element of calculating floor area ratio (FAR) and, as noted in some definitions in this section, for calculating parking and shared parking requirements. Most ordinances define floor area as the gross floor area of the entire building measured between the exterior walls, with specified exceptions. Usually, measurement of the gross floor area includes stairwells and elevator shafts. Ordinances differ, however, in their treatment of basements, porches, attics, exterior balconies, penthouses, and parking structures. The definition might also take into ac-*

count the problem of measuring the floor area of hotels and office buildings with large atriums.

■ **floor area, gross (for purposes of computing parking)**    The sum of the horizontal areas of each floor of a building, measured from the exterior faces of the exterior walls or from the centerline of walls separating two buildings. The gross floor area measurement is exclusive of areas of unfinished basements, unfinished cellars, unfinished attics, attached garages, space used for off-street parking or loading, breezeways, enclosed and unenclosed porches and accessory structures. However, unfinished basements and unfinished cellars are counted as storage space for purposes of meeting parking requirements *(St. Paul, Minn.)*

■ **floor area, gross leasable**    The total floor area designed for tenant occupancy and exclusive use, including basements, mezzanines, and upper floors, if any; expressed in square feet and measured from the centerline of joint partitions and from outside wall faces. *(Thurston County, Wash.)*

■ **floor area, gross leasable (for purposes of computing shared parking)**    The total floor area of a building or structure designed for the tenants' occupancy and exclusive use, including basements, mezzanines, and upper floors, expressed in square feet and measured from the outside face of the exterior walls and from the centerline of common walls or joint partitions. All that area for which tenants pay rent, including sales and integral stock areas, but excluding stairwells, elevator shafts, mechanical rooms, space related to the operation and maintenance of the building, and lobbies and bathrooms located for common or public use rather than for tenant or internal use. *(St. Paul, Minn.)*

■ **floor area, gross, unused**    The amount of gross floor area remaining after the total gross floor area of all buildings and structures existing on the lot is deducted from the permitted gross floor area of the lot. *(Philadelphia, Pa.)*

■ **floor area, minimum**    That area computed for the floors in the dwelling above the lot grade line. The second floor in each case qualifying for living quarters shall have access thereto by a permanent built-in stairway. "Minimum net floor area for living quarters" excludes rooms for garage purposes, outside vestibules, and open or closed porches or verandas. "Living quarters" means that portion of the building that is constructed with ceilings and walls finished on the inside in accordance with the building code. *(Columbus, Ohio)*

■ **floor area, net**    The horizontal area of a floor or several floors of a building or structure; excluding those areas not directly devoted to the principal or accessory use of the building or structure, such as storage areas or stairwells, measured from the exterior faces of exterior or interior walls. *(Roswell, N. Mex.)*

■ **floor area ratio (FAR)**    The total floor area of all buildings or structures on a zoning lot divided by the area of said lot. *(St. Paul, Minn.)*

*Commentary: The floor area ratio (FAR) was developed as a more refined and adaptable measure of intensity than building coverage. It expresses in one measure, instead of several, the mathematical relation between volume of building and unit of land. FAR, however, cannot replace more traditional bulk controls entirely. Often it is not a sufficient height control nor does it regulate the placement of the building on the site.*

■ **floor area, usable**    That area used for or intended to be used for the sale of merchandise or services, or for use to serve patrons, clients or customers and all that area devoted to employee workspace. Such floor area which is used or intended to be used principally for the storage of merchandise, hallways, elevator or stair bulkheads or for utilities or sanitary facilities shall be excluded from this computation of "usable floor area." Measurement of usable floor area shall be the horizontal areas of the several floors of the building, measured from the exterior faces to the exterior walls. *(St. Paul, Minn.)*

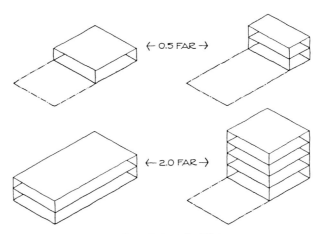

FLOOR AREA RATIO

The ratio of gross building floor area to the net lot area of the building site *(Scottsdale, Ariz.)*

The ratio of gross floor area of all structures on a lot to total lot area. *(Blacksburg, Va.)*

The floor area of a building or buildings on a lot divided by the lot area. *(Tulsa, Okla.)*

■ **florist**    Retail business whose principal activity is the selling of plants which are not grown on the site and conducting business within an enclosed building. *(St. Paul, Minn.)*

■ **food cooperative**    A nonprofit enterprise that is collectively owned and operated and is engaged in the purchase and distribution of food and produce among its members with no profit motive. The purchase of the food shall be by prior order and distribution shall occur within the same day of the arrival of the food at the residential property. The food cooperative shall be conducted solely within properties developed with single-family detached residences and shall be incidental to the primary use as a residence. Commercial vehicles are permitted for deliveries, however this activity shall not be so intense as to destroy the character and integrity of the residential neighborhood. *(Thousand Oaks, Calif.)*

■ **footcandle** *(See also* **candlepower; lumen**) A measure of illumination on a surface that is everywhere one foot from a uniform point source of light of one candle and equal to one lumen per square foot. *(Champaign, Ill.)*

■ **footprint** The horizontal area as seen in plan, measured from outside of all exterior walls and supporting columns. It includes residences, garages, covered carports, and accessory structures, but not trellises, patios, and areas of porch, deck and balcony less than 30 inches from finished grade. *(Oakland, Calif.)*

■ **forest** In a critical area, a biological community dominated by trees and other woody plants covering a land area of one acre or more. This also includes forests that have been cut but not cleared. In other areas, a biological community dominated by trees and other woody plants covering a land area of 10,000 square feet or greater. Forest includes: (a) areas that have at least 100 trees per acre with at least 50 percent of those trees having a two-inch or greater diameter at 4.5 feet above the ground and larger; and (b) forest areas that have been cut but not cleared. *(Cecil County, Md.)*

■ **forest, contiguous** A forest that connects the largest undeveloped or most vegetated tracts of land within and adjacent to a site. *(Maryland Department of Natural Resources)*

■ **forest land** Land primarily devoted to forest management activities. *(Yakima County, Wash.)*

■ **forest management** The application of business methods and forestry principles to the operation of a forest property for the purpose of maintaining forest resources and producing a continuous supply of forest products. Forest management practices include, but are not limited to, site preparation, planting, harvesting, road construction, insect and disease control, inventory and fire protection. *(Shasta Lake, Calif.)*

Timber cruising and other forest resources evaluation activities, pesticide or fertilizer application, management planning activities, timber stand improvement, pruning, regeneration of forest stands, and other similar or associated activities, exclusive of timber harvesting and construction, creation, or maintenance of roads. *(Gorham, Maine)*

Activities conducted on or directly pertaining to forest land relating to the growing, managing, harvesting, and interim storage of merchantable timber for commercial value. *(Yakima County, Wash.)*

■ **forest practice** Any activity conducted on or directly pertaining to forest land and relating to growing, harvesting, or processing timber, including but not limited to: a. Road and trail construction; b. Harvesting, final and intermediate; c. Precommercial thinning; d. Reforestation; e. Fertilization; f. Prevention and suppression of diseases and insects; g. Salvage of trees; and h. Brush control. Forest practice shall not include forest management activities. [I]ncludes preparatory work such as tree marking, surveying, and road flagging. *(Thurston County, Wash.)*

■ **forestry** Generally, a profession embracing the science, business, and art of creating, conserving, and managing forests and forest lands for the continuing use of both commodity and noncommodity benefits. *(Maryland Department of Natural Resources)*

■ **forestry operations** The use of land for the raising and harvesting of timber, pulp woods, and other forestry products for commercial purposes, including the temporary operation of a sawmill

and/or chipper to process the timber cut from that parcel or contiguous parcels. Excluded from this definition shall be the cutting of timber associated with land development approved by the [jurisdiction], which shall be considered accessory to the development of the property. *(Blacksburg, Va.)*

■ **fortune telling** *(See also* **psychic**) A use involving the foretelling of the future in exchange for financial or other valuable consideration. Fortune telling shall be limited to uses where the fortune is told through astrology, augury, card or tea reading, cartomancy, clairvoyance, clairaudience, crystal gazing, divination, magic mediumship, necromancy, palmistry, psychometry, phrenology, prophecy, spiritual reading or any similar means. Fortune telling does not include forecasting based on historical trends or patterns, religious dogma, or any of the previously listed arts when presented in an assembly of people who purchase tickets or means in exchange for the presentation at a site licensed for such purpose. *(Salinas, Calif.)*

Establishments providing advice, predictions, or interpretations of planetary effects, on or about future events or human affairs. *(Miami, Fla., which uses the terms "astrologists, fortune tellers, and spiritualists)*

■ **foster home** *(See also* **group home for foster care**) A dwelling used in whole or in part as living quarters for a household including one or more minor children, placed by a licensed child placement agency, who are not members of the family occupying said dwelling but, are under their supervision. Further, provided that a maximum of five children are allowed to reside in the home including any natural children living in the home, if any children in the home are age two or younger. If no children are under two years, the maximum number of children residing in the home is six. *(Tulsa, Okla.)*

■ **fraternal organization** A group of people formally organized for a common interest, usually cultural, religious, or entertainment, with regular meetings and formal written membership requirements. *(Schaumburg, Ill.)*

■ **fraternity**   A club or social activity officially associated with and recognized and supervised by an institution for higher education whose membership is limited exclusively to students of the said institution. *(Williamstown, Ky., which uses this definition for both terms "fraternity" and "sorority")*

■ **fraternity house**   A building used as group living quarters for students of a college, university or seminary, who are members of a fraternity that has been officially recognized by the college, university, or seminary. *(St. Paul, Minn.)*

■ **freestanding sign** *(See **sign, freestanding**)*

■ **freeway** *(See **street, freeway**)*

■ **freeway sign corridor** *(See also **right-of-way**)*   An area 400 feet in width on each side of and adjacent to the publicly acquired right-of-way of a freeway. *(Tulsa, Okla.)*

■ **freight**   Goods, merchandise, substances, materials, and commodities of any kind that may be transported or transferred from one place to another by air, rail, or motor-carrier. *(El Paso, Tex.)*

■ **freight container** *(See also **cargo, containerized; semi-trailer**)*   A standardized, reusable shipping vessel used in the transportation of freight and capable of being mounted and moved on a rail car, or mounted on a chassis or bogie for movement by truck trailer or loaded on a ship. *(Minneapolis, Minn.)*

■ **frontage** *(See **lot frontage**)*

■ **frontage buildout**   The length of a front building facade compared to the length of the front lot line, expressed as a percentage. *(Austin, Tex.)*

■ **frontage open space**   All the meaningful open space between the right-of-way line of a dedicated public street and any perimeter structure(s) within the development, except that this space may extend between structures or between a structure and a side property line to a depth of not more than one-half the width of the opening. (Scottsdale, Ariz. )

■ **frontage road** *(See **street, frontage road**)*

■ **frontage width** *(See **lot, frontage**)*

■ **fumes**   A vaporous, odorous, noxious, or corrosive exhalation. *(Albuquerque, N. Mex.)*

■ **funeral chapel**   A building used primarily for human funeral services, provided that such building shall not contain facilities for (a) embalming; (b) performance of autopsies or other similar surgical procedures; (c) cremation; or (d) storage of funeral caskets and funeral urns, except those on display on the premises; and (e) that funeral vehicles shall not be stored on the premises except in a garage or other accessory building with no direct public street frontage; and (f) that the garage or other accessory building shall not be used for other purposes. *(Thurston, Wash.)*

■ **funeral home** *(See also **mortuary**)*   A building or part thereof used for human funeral services. Such building may contain space and facilities for (a) embalming and the performance of other services used in the preparation of the dead for burial; (b) the performance of autopsies and other surgical procedures; (c) the storage of caskets, funeral urns, and other related funeral supplies; (d) the storage of funeral vehicles; and (e) facilities for cremation. . . . [W]here a funeral home is permitted, a funeral chapel shall also be permitted. *(Thurston, Wash.)*

Establishment engaged in undertaking services such as preparing the dead for burial, and arranging and managing funerals. Typical uses include funeral homes or mortuaries. *(Blacksburg, Va.)*

A building used for the preparation of the deceased for burial and display of the deceased and rituals connected therewith before burial or cremation. A funeral home, as defined for purposes of this code, includes a funeral chapel. *(Gorham, Maine)*

■ **gallery** *(See art gallery)*

■ **game**   Any banking or percentage game played with cards, dice, or any mechanical, electromechanical, or electronic device or machine for money, property, checks, credit, or any representative of value. . . . [This] does not include games played in private homes or residences for prizes or games operated by charitable or educational organizations that have been approved by the [state]. *(Reno, Nev.)*

■ **game arcade**   Any commercial building in which there are more than three amusement game machines on the premises which are available to the public. An arcade may contain commercial recreational machines or games other than amusement game machines. *(Columbia, Mo.)*

■ **game breeding and shooting preserve area**   An area licensed by the [state] that must meet certain requirements for area and operating purposes, and which is granted special hunting privileges. *(McHenry County, Ill.)*

■ **game center**   A place or facility where pinball or other similar electronic games are played for amusement only. Shall not be construed so as to include bingo games nor shall it be construed so as to include gambling devices or any other devices prohibited by law. *(Scottsdale, Ariz.)*

■ **gambling** *(See also lottery)*   To deal, operate, carry on, conduct, maintain or expose for play any game, sports book, parimutuel, or any other form of wagering. *(Reno, Nev.)*

■ **gambling device**   Any clock, tape machine, slot machine, or other machine or device for the reception of money or other thing of value on chance or skill or upon the action of which money or other thing of value is staked, hazarded, bet, won, or lost; or any mechanism, furniture, fixture, equipment or other device designed primarily for use in a gambling place. It does not include: (1) A coin-in-the-slot-operated mechanical device played for amusement that rewards the player with the right to replay such mechanical device; . . . . (2) Vending machines by which full and adequate return is made for the money invested and in which there is no element of chance or hazard. *(State of Illinois)*

■ **gambling excursion**   The time during which gambling games may be operated on an excursion gambling boat or floating facility whether docked or during a cruise. *(Cape Girardeau, Mo.)*

■ **gambling, excursion boat or floating gambling facility**   A boat, ferry, barge, or similar structure licensed by the [state commission] on which gambling games are allowed. *(Cape Girardeau, Mo.)*

■ **gambling establishment (hotel)**   A part of a hotel that is used or intended to be used for gaming activities for which a nonrestricted gaming license is required. . . . *(Las Vegas, Nev.)*

■ **gambling establishment (nonhotel)**   A building or structure, other than a hotel, that is located within one of the districts specified . . . this code and any part of which is used or intended to be used for the purpose of dealing, operating, maintaining, or conducting any

game, as defined in . . . this code, except a slot machine, as defined in . . . this code. *(Las Vegas, Nev.)*

The operation or conducting of any games played with cards, roulette wheels, dice, craps, slot machines, video lottery terminals, mechanical, electro-mechanical or electronic amusement devices or machine for money, property, checks, credit, or any representative of value including, without limiting the generality of the foregoing, baccarat, faro, monte, poker, keno, black jack, bingo, fan-tan, twenty-one, seven-and-a-half, big injun, klondike, chuck-a-luck, wheel of fortune, chemin de fer, pai gow, beat the banker, and panguingui and similar games of chance for the return of money, cash, or prizes, or anything that could be redeemed for money, cash, or prizes. This definition does not apply to games of chance operated by charitable organizations licensed under [state law]. *(Newport, R.I., which uses the term "casino-type gambling")*

■ **gambling, video lottery terminal**   Gambling by the use of any electronic computerized video game machine that, upon the insertion of cash, is available to play a video game authorized by the lottery commission, and which uses a video display and microprocessor in which, by chance, the player may receive free games or credits that can be redeemed for cash. This definition shall include any game or device that is commonly known as a video game of chance or a video gaming machine or that is commonly known as or considered to be a video gambling machine, except a video device authorized by the lottery commission to permit the sale of tickets by retailers in a game authorized [by state law] if all of the following apply: 1. The device does not determine whether the player has won a prize; 2. The device does not indicate whether the player has won a prize other than by verifying that the player's ticket or some or all of the player's symbols or numbers on the player's ticket have been selected in a chance drawing, or by verifying that the players ticket has been randomly selected by a central system computer at the time of purchase; 3. Any game that is similar to a game listed in subdivisions 1 and 2 above. *(Newport, R.I.)*

■ **gaming** *(See gambling)*

■ **garage**     A building or structure, or part thereof, used or designed to be used for the parking and storage of vehicles. *(Fairbanks North Star Borough, Alaska)*

■ **garage apartment**     A structure above a private garage in which provision is made for one dwelling unit. . . . *(Virginia Beach, Va.)*

■ **garage, joint**     A building on its own lot which serves two or more residences on separate lots and is used jointly for the storage of not more than six private automobiles belonging to the owners or tenants of the said residences. *(Tuscaloosa, Ala.)*

■ **garage, parking**     A garage, other than a private or storage garage, which is used for the short-term parking of vehicles. *(Jefferson County, Mo.)*

■ **garage, private**     A detached accessory or portion of a main building housing the automobiles of the occupants of the premises, but not commercial vehicles. *(Boone County, Mo.)*

Any accessory building or portion of a main building designed or used for the storage of not more than three motor-driven vehicles, provided that no private garage may be used or rented for the storage of commercial trucks having a capacity in excess of one ton. *(Scottsdale, Ariz.)*

A building or space used as an accessory to or a part of a main building permitted in any residential district, and providing for the storage of one or more motor vehicles and in which no business, occupation, or service for profit is in any way conducted. *(Jacksonville, N.C.)*

■ **garage, private, customer and employee**     A detached accessory building or portion of a principal building intended to be used for the parking and storage of motor vehicles operated by the customers, visitors, and employees of the premises on which the garage is located. *(Schaumburg, Ill.)*

■ **garage, public**     A building or portion thereof, other than a private or storage garage, designed or used for equipping, servicing, repairing, hiring, selling, storing, or parking motor driven vehicles. The term repairing shall not include an automotive body repair shop nor the rebuilding, dismantling, or storage of wrecked or junked vehicles. *(Boone County, Mo.)*

A building or portion thereof designed or used for servicing, repairing, equipping, hiring, selling, or storage of automobiles. *(Roswell, N. Mex.)*

■ **garage sale** *(See also rummage sale)*     The sale or offering for sale to the general public of over five items of personal property on any portion of a lot in a residential zoning district, whether within or outside any building. Sales of programs and food and beverage items at school athletic events shall not be deemed to constitute garage sales. *(Columbia, Mo.)*

■ **garage, storage**     Any building or premises, other than a private or public garage, used exclusively for the parking or storage of motor vehicles. *(Jacksonville, N.C.)*

■ **garbage** *(See also litter; rubbish)*     Rejected or waste household food, offal, and swill composed of vegetable and animal substances. It shall be taken to mean and include all table and kitchen refuse of every kind and description; also decaying vegetables and meats, or anything that will, or may, decompose and become offensive or dangerous to health. *(Gurnee, Ill.)*

The animal and vegetable waste resulting from the handling, preparation, cooking, and consumption of food. *(Ames, Iowa.)*

■ **garden**     The garden is public space which is part of a residential or hotel development where over 50 percent of the gross floor area of the building is used for residential units or hotel rooms. Such space is designed to provide visual relief for the public. Gardens need not provide for direct public access or seating, and may be open or partially or totally enclosed. *(Philadelphia, Pa.)*

■ **garden apartment** *(See also dwelling definitions)*     An apartment building located on a lot, either singly or together with other similar apartment buildings, generally having a low density of population and having substantial landscaped open space adjacent to the dwelling units. *(North Kansas City, Mo.)*

A group of detached or attached apartment houses not more than two stories in height containing dwelling units, with each unit having its own cooking facilities. For the purpose of front yard, setback, side yard and rear yard, such "garden apartments" may be treated as a single unit, provided that site plans showing the location of structures, paving facilities, drainage facilities, screening and fencing are approved by the Town Board. *(Islip, N.Y.)*

A multifamily structure two or three stories in height where apartments are grouped into separate buildings containing eight to 16 units per building with two to four units adjacent to a stairway. *(Jersey City, N.J.)*

■ **garden center** *(See also nursey)*     A place of business where retail and wholesale products and produce are sold to the consumer. These centers, which may include a nursery and/or greenhouses, import most of the items sold, and may include plants, nursery products and stock, potting soil, hardware, power equipment and machinery, hoes, rakes, shovels, and other garden and farm variety tools and utensils. *(Lake County, Ill.)*

■ **gas station** *(See also oil change facility; service station)*     Any lot or parcel of land or portion thereof used partly or entirely for storing or dispensing flammable liquids, combustible liquids, liquified flammable gas, or flammable gas into the fuel tanks of motor vehicles. *(Hartford, Conn.)*

Any building, structure, or area of land used for the retail sale of automobile fuels, oils, and accessories, where repair service, if any, is incidental, where no more than two abandoned vehicles or other motor vehicles shall be stored on the premises. May include the sale of propane or kerosene as accessory uses. *(Cecil County, Md., which uses the term "motor vehicle filling station")*

■ **gas station, full-service** A facility limited to retail sales to the public of gasoline, motor oil, lubricants, motor fuels, travel aides, and minor automobile accessories. In addition, such a facility must provide minor vehicle servicing, minor repairs, and maintenance, and may provide engine rebuilding but not reconditioning of motor vehicles, collision services such as body, frame, or fender straightening and repair, or overall painting of automobiles. *(Londonderry, N.H.)*

■ **gas station, limited-service** A facility limited to retail sales to the public of gasoline, motor oil, lubricants, motor fuels, travel aides, and minor automobile accessories. In addition, such a facility may provide minor vehicle servicing, minor repairs, and maintenance, including engine rebuilding but not reconditioning of motor vehicles, collision services such as body, frame, or fender straightening and repair, or overall painting of automobiles. *(Londonderry, N.H.)*

■ **gas station minimart** *(See also convenience store)* A facility associated with the sale of gasoline products, that also offers for sale prepackaged food items and tangible consumer goods, primarily for self-service by the consumer. Hot beverages, fountain-type beverages, and pastries may be included in the food items offered for sale, but food items that are prepared or individually proportioned on the premises shall be prohibited. *(Wheeling, Ill.)*

A place where gasoline, motor oil, lubricants, or other minor accessories are retailed directly to the public on the premises in combination with the retailing of items typically found in a convenience market or supermarket. *(St. Paul, Minn., which uses the term "automobile convenience market")*

■ **gated communities** Residential areas that restrict access to normally public spaces (pictured above). These are subdivisions of usually high-end houses

located mostly in suburbs, but some more recently in inner-city areas. The type of gates can range from elaborate guard houses to similar electronic arms. Residents may enter by electronic cards, identification stickers, codes, or remote control devices. Visitors must stop to be verified for entry. (Planning and Zoning News, *March 1999)*

■ **gateway** An arrival point followed by a zone that marks the transition between the arrival point and the objective destination (pictured below). *(Rochester, N.Y., Gateway Study)*

An entrance corridor that heralds the approach of a new landscape and defines the arrival point as a destination. (Zoning News)

■ **gateway route** A street or parkway designated on the Major Streets and Routes (MS&R) Plan map, which is a heavily traveled entrance to and through the city. These routes link major employment areas, shopping centers, and recre-

ational areas used regularly by a large number of residents and visitors and present a visual impression of [the city's] character. *(Tucson, Ariz.)*

■ **gazebo** An accessory building consisting of a detached, covered, free-standing, open-air structure not exceeding 300 square feet (pictured below at right). Such gazebo shall be of masonry construction with tile roof, and shall meet setback and ground area coverage as set forth elsewhere in this code. *(Coral Gables, Fla.)*

A freestanding structure (similar to a detached open patio cover), with a pitched roof design, having a maximum height of 15 feet, and a maximum area of 600 square feet, and shall be designed for recreational use only and not for habitation. (*Thousand Oaks, Calif., which uses the term "gazebo or pool house cabana"*)

■ **general plan** (*See also* **comprehensive plan; master plan**) A comprehensive declaration of goals, policies, and programs for the development of the city and including, where applicable, diagrams, maps, and text setting forth objectives, principles, standards, and other features, and which has been adopted by the city council. (*Imperial Beach, Calif.*)

■ **general store** A single store (pictured below), the ground floor area of which is 4,000 square feet or less and which offers for sale primarily, most of the following articles: bread, milk, cheese, canned and bottled foods and drinks, tobacco products, candy, papers and magazines, and general hardware articles. Gasoline may also be offered for sale but only as a secondary activity of a county general store. (*Goochland County, Va.*)

■ **gentrification** The rehabilitation and resettlement of low- and moderate-income urban neighborhoods by middle- and high-income professionals. (*APA Research Department*)

■ **geographic information system (GIS)** A method of storing geographic infor-mation on computers. Geographic information can be obtained from a variety of sources, including topographical maps, soil maps, aerial and satellite photographs, and remote sensing technology. (*American Farmland Trust*)

■ **geologic review** The analysis of geologic hazards, including all potential seismic hazards, surface ruptures, liquefaction, landsliding, mudsliding, and the potential for erosion and sedimentation. (*California Planning Roundtable*)

■ **glare** The effect produced by brightness sufficient to cause annoyance, discomfort, or loss in visual performance and visibility. (*Siskiyou County, Calif.*)

(1) The reflection of harsh, bright light; and (2) the physical effect resulting from high luminances or insufficiently shielded light sources in the field of view. (*Federal Way, Wash.*)

■ **golf course** A tract of land laid out with at least nine holes for playing a game of golf and improved with tees, greens, fairways, and hazards. A golf course including a clubhouse and shelters as accessory uses. (*Maryland Heights, Mo.*)

An area or course for playing golf, consisting of at least nine holes, except miniature golf, within which the playing area is not artificially illuminated. (*Pine Bluff, Ark.*)

A lot or portion of a lot used for the playing of golf and shall include pitch-and-putt courses but shall not include driving ranges, miniature golf courses, or other similar commercial enterprises. (*Thousand Oaks, Calif.*)

■ **golf course, miniature** A theme-oriented recreational facility, typically comprised of nine or 18 putting greens, each with a "cup" or "hole," where patrons in groups of one to four pay a fee to move in consecutive order from the first hole to the last. (*APA Research Department*)

■ **golf course, regulation or par-three** A facility other than a miniature golf course for the playing of golf at which there may be a clubhouse including rest rooms and locker rooms. A golf course may provide additional services custom-arily furnished such as swimming, outdoor recreation, and related retail sales that may include a restaurant and cocktail lounge if approved as a part of the required use permit. (*Scottsdale, Ariz.*)

■ **golf driving range** A limited area on which golf players do not walk, but onto which they drive golf balls from a central driving tee. (*Cecil County, Md.*)

■ **golf training center** A facility other than a miniature golf course or commercial driving range providing primarily both indoor and outdoor professional instruction in all phases of golf learning skills. Accessory uses may be allowed if approved as part of the required use permit. (*Scottsdale, Ariz.*)

■ **government, consolidated** A governmental unit that comprises two or more legal entities that have joined together to form a common government; for example, a consolidated city-county government. The combined governmental units may or may not occupy the same territory. (*United States Census Bureau*)

■ **government or city facility** A building or structure owned, operated, or occupied by governmental agency to provide a governmental service to the public. (*Maryland Heights, Mo.*)

■ **government service agency** A government service facility providing direct services to the public wherein large aggregations of people are probable, especially those such as employment offices, public assistance offices, motor vehicle registration and licensing services, and similar activities commonly accustomed to having sizeable assemblages of people queueing, tarrying, biding or waiting for service, whether pedestrian or vehicular. (*National City, Calif.*)

■ **governmental unit** A geographic entity established by legal action and for the purpose of implementing administrative or governmental functions. Most governmental units have officially recognized boundaries. All area and population of the United States are part of one or more legal units, such as American Indian reservations, states, counties, county subdivisions, and incorporated places. A governmental unit that has elected or appointed officials, raises revenues, and performs governmental activities (such as enactment of laws, provision of services, and entering into contracts). *(United States Census Bureau)*

■ **grade**    The average level of the finished surface of the ground adjacent to the exterior walls of the building. *(Boone County, Mo.)*

The elevation established for the purpose of regulating the number of stories and the height of buildings. Grade shall be the mean level of the finished surface of the ground adjacent to the exterior walls of the buildings. *(St. Paul, Minn.)*

The lowest point of elevation of the finished surface of the ground between the exterior wall of a building and a point five feet distant from said wall, or the lowest point of elevation of the finished surface of the ground between the exterior wall of a building and the property line if it is less than five feet distant from said wall. In case walls are parallel to and within five feet of a public sidewalk, alley or other public way, the grade shall be the elevation of the sidewalk, alley, or public way. *(Scottsdale, Ariz.)*

*Commentary: Grade is an essential part of height regulations since building height is usually measured from the established grade to the appropriate roof line. Most ordinances define grade as the average finished ground level of the land around the buildings. The Scottsdale, Arizona, definition takes a different approach.*

■ **grade, adjacent ground elevation**    The lowest part of elevation of the finished surface of the ground surface, paving, or sidewalk within the area between the building and the property line, or when the property line is more than five feet from the building, between the building and a line five feet from the building. *(Rapid City, S.D.)*

■ **grade, established**    The elevation of the centerline of the streets as officially established by the city authorities. *(Rapid City, S.D.)*

The elevation of the finished street at the centerline or curb as fixed by the city en-

gineer or by such authority as shall be authorized by law to determine such an elevation. *(Brookfield, Wisc.)*

■ **grade, existing**    The vertical elevation of the ground surface prior to excavating or filling. *(Renton, Wash.)*

The surface of the ground or pavement at a stated location as it exists prior to disturbance in preparation for a project regulated by this ordinance. *(Imperial Beach, Calif.)*

■ **grade, finished**    The final grade of the site that conforms to the approved plan. *(Renton, Wash.)*

The completed surfaces of lawns, walks, and roads brought to grades as shown on official plans or designs relating thereto. *(Rapid City, S.D.)*

The final elevation of the ground surface after man-made alterations, such as grading, grubbing, filling, or excavating, have been made on the ground surface. *(Maui County, Hawaii)*

■ **grade, highest adjacent**    The highest natural elevation of the ground surface prior to construction next to the proposed walls of a structure. *(Washington, Ark.)*

■ **grade, natural**    The existing grade or elevation of the ground surface that exists or existed prior to man-made alterations, such as grading, grubbing, filling, or excavating. *(Maui County, Hawaii)*

The unaltered natural surface of the ground at a stated location. *(Newport Beach, Calif.)*

The surface of the ground prior to grading for development. *(Oakland, Calif.)*

■ **grade, percentage of**    The rise or fall of a slope in feet and tenths of a foot for each 100 feet of horizontal distance. *(Grand Forks, N.D.)*

On street center line, means the distance vertically from the horizontal in feet and tenths of a foot for each 100 feet of horizontal distance. *(Buffalo, Minn.)*

■ **grade, rough**    The stage at which the grade approximately conforms to the approved plan. *(Renton, Wash.)*

■ **grade separation**    The physical development of structures or intersections that separate motor vehicles from motor vehicles; motor vehicles, pedestrians, and bicyclists from trains; motor vehicles from pedestrians and bicycles, as well as pedestrians from bicycles. *(Tempe, Ariz.)*

■ **grade, street**    The top of the curb, or the top of the edge of the pavement or traveled way where no curb exists. *(Newport Beach, Calif.)*

■ **gradient**    The difference in elevation between defined reference points divided by the horizontal distance between these points. *(Oakland, Calif.)*

The rate of vertical change of a ground surface expressed as a percentage figure and determined by dividing the vertical distance by the horizontal distance. *(National City, Calif.)*

■ **grading**    An excavating or filling or combination thereof.    A. Regular grading: Any grading that involves 5,000 cubic yards or less of material. B. Engineered Grading: Any grading that involves more than 5,000 cubic yards of material. *(Renton, Wash.)*

The act of excavation or filling or combination thereof or any leveling to a smooth horizontal or sloping surface on a property, but not including normal cultivation associated with an agricultural operation. *(Island County, Wash.)*

■ **graffiti**    Any inscription, word, figure, marking or design that is marked, etched, scratched, drawn or painted on any building, structure, fixture or other improvement, whether permanent or temporary, including by way of example only and without limitation, fencing surrounding construction sites, whether public or private, without the consent of the owner of the property or the owner's authorized agent, and which is visible from the public right-of-way. *(San Francisco, Calif.)*

Any writing, printing, marks, signs, symbols, figures, designs, inscriptions, or other drawings that are scratched, scrawled, painted, drawn, or otherwise placed on any exterior surface of a building, wall, fence, sidewalk, curb, or other permanent structure on public or private property and which have the effect of defacing the property. (*Rochester, Minn.*)

■ **grand opening**   The introduction, promotion or announcement of a new business, store, shopping center, or office, or the announcement or introduction or promotion of an established business changing ownership or location. (*Scottsdale, Ariz.*)

■ **grandfathered**   Describes the status accorded certain properties, uses, and activities that are legally existing prior to the date of adoption of the zoning ordinance or provisions of the zoning ordinance. (*Cecil County, Md.*)

■ **granny flat** (*See accessory apartment*)

■ **gravel pit** An open land area where sand, gravel, and rock fragments are mined or excavated for sale or off-tract use. (*Siskiyou County, Calif.*)

■ **great pond** (*See also pond*) Any inland body of water which in a natural state has a surface area in excess of 10 acres, and any inland body of water artificially formed or increased which has a surface area in excess of 30 acres except where artificially formed or increased inland body of water is completely surrounded by land held by a single owner. (*Gorham, Maine*)

■ **green** An open space available for unstructured recreation, its landscaping consisting of grassy areas and trees. (*Austin, Tex.*)

■ **green area**   Land shown on a development plan, master plan, or official map for preservation, recreation, landscaping, or park. (*Iowa State University Extension Service*)

■ **greenbelt**   A series of connected open spaces that may follow natural features such as ravines, creeks, or streams. (*Austin, Tex.*)

An area where measures such as fuel management, land-use planning, and development standards are applied to mitigate fire, flood, and erosion hazard. More traditionally, an irrigated landscaped buffer zone between development and woodlands, usually put to ad-

ditional uses (e.g. golf course, park, etc.). (*Washoe County, Nev.*)

An area designated in the Land Use Element of the comprehensive plan intended for open space, recreation, very-low-density residential uses, agriculture, geographic relief between land uses, or other low-intensity uses. (*Renton, Wash.*)

■ **greenfield** (*See also brownfield*)   Farmland and open areas where there has been no prior industrial or commercial activity, and therefore where the threat of contamination is much lower than in urbanized areas. (*APA Research Department*)

■ **greenhouse** (*See also nursery*)   Retail business whose principal activity is the selling of plants grown on the site and having outside storage, growing, or display. (*St. Paul, Minn.*)

A building or structure constructed chiefly of glass, glasslike or translucent material, cloth or lath, which is devoted to the protection or cultivation of flowers or other tender plants. (*Escondido, Calif.*)

An establishment where flowers, shrubbery, vegetables, trees, and other horticultural and floricultural products are grown both in open and enclosed buildings. (*Unalaska, Alaska*)

■ **greenhouse, commercial**   A building used for the growing of plants, all or part of which are sold at retail or wholesale. (*Carmel, Ind.*)

■ **greenhouse, industrial**   Wholesale business whose principal activity is the growing and selling of plants within an enclosed building. (*St. Paul, Minn.*)

■ **greenway** (*See also open space definitions; park definitions*)   A linear park, alternative transportation route, or open space conservation area approved by the metro greenways commission that provides passive recreational opportunities, pedestrian and/or bicycle paths, and/or the conservation of open spaces or natural areas, as indicated in a greenway plan adopted by the commission. (*Nashville and Davidson County, Tenn.*)

■ **greywater** (*See also wastewater, domestic*)   Wastewater obtained from domestic sinks and tubs, but excluding

that part of the plumbing waste stream that includes human wastes ("blackwater"). (*Volusia County, Fla.*)

■ **grid system**   A series of designated parallel lines one mile apart, intersecting a second set of designated parallel lines one mile apart forming approximately one square mile areas (also known as sections). (*Indian River County, Fla., which uses the term "basic grid system"*)

■ **grocery store** (*See supermarket*)

■ **gross floor area (GFA)** (*See floor area, gross*)

■ **gross living area** (*See also floor area, gross*)   The square footage of all floor areas which include finished space that is heated, excluding heated garages and out buildings which do not include living quarters. (*Jaffrey, N.H.*)

■ **ground floor**   The first floor of a building other than a cellar or basement. (*APA Research Department*)

■ **ground floor frontage**   The portion of a structure that occupies the first 20 feet of any floor that is within 10 feet above or below curb level. Ground floor frontage shall be measured from the outer structure wall which is at or within five feet of curb level in a line generally parallel to and 20 feet from any building face which fronts a public street. (*Los Angeles, Calif.*)

■ **groundcover**   Any evergreen or broadleaf evergreen plant that does not attain a mature height of more than one foot. Such plants shall be characterized by a growth habit in which the plant spreads across the ground to connect with other similar plants forming a continuous vegetative cover on the ground. Sod and seed shall also be considered as qualifying groundcover. (*Peoria, Ill.*)

Small plants, such as salal, ivy, ferns, mosses, grasses, or other types of vegetation, that normally cover the ground and includes trees of less than six inches caliper. (*Renton, Wash.*)

■ **groundcover management**   The mowing or cutting of ground cover in order to create an orderly appearing property so long as such activities do not disturb the root structures on the plants. Ground cover management shall include the removal of vegetative debris from the property. *(Renton, Wash.)*

■ **groundwater** *(See also **aquifer** definitions)* Water that occurs beneath the land surface, also called subsurface water or subterranean water. Groundwater includes water in the zone of saturation of a water-bearing formation. *(Yakima County, Wash.)*

Water found underground that completely fills the open spaces between particles of sand, gravel, clay, silt, and consolidated rock fractures. The zone of materials filled with groundwater is called the "zone of saturation." *(Newport, R.I.)*

The supply of freshwater under the surface in an aquifer or soil that forms a natural reservoir. *(Champaign, Ill.)*

■ **groundwater recharge** The natural process of infiltration and percolation of rainwater from land areas or streams through permeable soils into water-holding rocks that provide underground storage ("aquifers"). *(California Planning Roundtable)*

■ **groundwater recharge area** A catchment basin or watershed underlain by layers of alternating permeable and impermeable strata such that excess rainfall not lost by evapotranspiration or runoff is retained and stored in subterranean porous layers of soil. [Components of such a system could include ponds, wetland swales, bay forests, dunes, and marsh.] *(Nags Head, N.C.)*

■ **group home** *(See also **halfway house; substance abuse treatment facility**)* One main building, or portion thereof, on one zoning lot that is licensed by the commissioner of health as a rooming and/or boardinghouse and receives 50 percent or more of its residents under a contract or other arrangement with the state or local government human services agency. Provides lodging for people who are mentally ill or chemically dependent. *(St. Paul, Minn., which uses the term "community residential facility, health department licensed")*

*Commentary: The Federal Fair Housing Amendments Act of 1988 prohibits zoning practices that discriminate against or unnecessarily restrict community-based housing for people with developmental disabilities. Any community drafting or adapting a definition needs to consult the Act for its provisions. You may also want to consult PAS Report No. 397,* Siting Group Homes for Developmentally Disabled Persons, *by Martin Jaffe and Thomas P. Smith.*

■ **group home for foster care** Any private residence licensed by the division of family services or department of mental health to provide foster care to one or more but less than seven children who are unrelated to either foster parent by blood, marriage, or adoption. *(St. Paul, Minn.)*

■ **group home for mentally or physically handicapped** Any home in which eight or fewer mentally or physically handicapped persons reside, and may include two additional persons acting as houseparents or guardians who need not be related to each other or to any of the mentally or physically handicapped persons residing in the home. *(St. Paul, Minn.)*

■ **grove** *(See orchard)*

■ **growth, forecasted** Current estimate of population and employment growth for King County, prepared by the Puget Sound Regional Council based on defined assumptions and generally accepted scientific methods. *(Renton, Wash.)*

■ **growth management** *(See also **smart growth; sprawl**)* The use by a community of a wide range of techniques in combination to determine the amount, type, and rate of development desired by the community and to channel that growth into designated areas. Growth management policies can be implemented through growth rates, zoning, capital improvement programs, public facilities ordinances, urban limit lines, standards for levels of service, and other programs. *(California Planning Roundtable)*

The use by a community of a wide range of techniques in combination to permit it to determine its own amount, type, and rate of growth, and channel it into desig-

nated areas. *(Handbook for Planning Commissioners in Missouri)*

■ **guest** Any person other than the family occupying or hiring a room for living or sleeping purposes. *(Maui County, Hawaii)*

Any person hiring or occupying a room for living or sleeping purposes. *(Imperial Beach, Calif.)*

■ **guest house** An attached or detached building that provides living quarters for guests and (a) contains no kitchen or cooking facility; (b) is clearly subordinate and incidental to the principal residence on the same building site; and (c) is not rented or leased, whether compensation be direct or indirect. *(Shasta Lake, Calif.)*

An attached or detached accessory building used to house guests of the occupants of the principal building, and which is never rented or offered for rent. *(Scottsdale, Ariz.)*

■ **guest house with cooking facilities** An attached or detached accessory building equipped to operate major appliances requiring 220 volts electric for the purposes of housing guests of the occupants of the principal building, and which is never rented or offered for rent. *(Scottsdale, Ariz.)*

■ **guest, permanent** A person who occupies or has the right to occupy a residence or dwelling accommodation for a period of 30 days or more. *(North Kansas City, Mo.)*

■ **guest ranch** A use incorporating two or more guest rooms, other than a boardinghouse, hotel, or motel, and including outdoor recreational facilities, such as, but not limited to, horseback riding, swimming, tennis courts, shuffleboard courts, barbecue and picnic facilities, and dining facilities intended primarily for use by the guests of the guest ranch. Bars and restaurants that cater primarily to those other than guests of the guest ranch are not permitted. *(Scottsdale, Ariz.)*

A recreational facility where lodging and horses for riding are furnished for compensation. *(Boone County, Mo.)*

■ **guest room**   A sleeping room intended to serve no more than two transient guests per night. *(Peoria, Ill.)*

Any room in a dormitory or boarding or lodging house used for and maintained to provide sleeping accommodations for not more than two persons. *(Valdez, Alaska)*

Any room or rooms used or intended to be used by a guest for sleeping purposes. Every 100 square feet of superficial floor area in a dormitory shall be considered a guestroom. *(Imperial Beach, Calif.)*

■ **gun shop** *(See also firearms sales or firearms business)*   Any premises or portion thereof used for the sale, vending, dealing, exchange or transfer, within a 12- month period, of two or more handguns as defined in [city ordinance] or short-barreled handguns as defined in [city ordinance]. *(Madison, Wisc.)*

■ **gym** *(See health club)*

the habitats of threatened and endangered species and species in need of conservation; (iv) anadromous fish propagation waters; and (v) plant and wildlife habitats, including: (1) colonial water bird nesting sites; (2) historic waterfowl staging and concentration areas; (3) riparian forests 300 feet or more in width; (4) large forested areas (100 acres or more); (5) natural heritage areas; (6) plant and wildlife habitats of local significance; (7) wildlife corridors; and (8) nontidal wetlands. *(Anne Arundel County, Md.)*

The site where a protected species of flora or fauna lives and grows. [H]abitat is limited to areas that are critical to breeding, rearing, and nesting. *(Island County, Wash., which uses the term "habitat for protected species")*

■ **halfway house** *(See also **group home; substance abuse treatment facility**)*   A licensed home for inmates on release from more restrictive custodial confinement or initially placed in lieu of such more restrictive custodial confinement, wherein supervision, rehabilitation, and counseling are provided to mainstream residents back into society, enabling them to live independently. *(Peoria, Ill.)*

A place where persons are aided in readjusting to society following a period of imprisonment, hospitalization, or institutionalized treatment. *(Jefferson City, Mo.)*

■ **halfway house, penal**   One or more resident is: (1) on probation; (2) on parole; or (3) participating in a penal institution's pre-release program. *(Jefferson City, Mo.)*

■ **hamlet (***See also **village***)   An existing or planned settlement, predominantly residential, that accommodates development in a more compact form than might occur otherwise in scattered clusters and single-tract, standard-design subdivisions on nearby individual tracts of lands. *(New Jersey State Plan)*

■ **hamlet lot**   A small residential lot located in a contiguous group, with adjacent and fronting lots oriented toward each other in some ordered geometric way–as on a street, a green, or a paved

square–and forming a distinct boundary with the surrounding countryside. Such lots are subject to certain lesser minimum lot standards than otherwise provided in the [district] regulations. No fewer than five and nor more than 25 hamlet lots may be grouped together as a rural hamlet. Hamlet lots may consist of two categories of land–one designated for development, called the building area, and another that is permanent open space. *(Loudon County, Va.)*

■ **handicapped** *(See also **developmentally disabled person; disability**)*

*Commentary: There are a number of terms (e.g., "person with developmental disabilities" ) that are used to describe individuals with physical, mental, and psychological impairments. Check with your local health service to see if there is a strong preference for one term over another or for a series of terms.*

A person determined to have a physical impairment or mental disorder expected to be of long or indefinite duration. Many such impairments or disorders are of such a nature that a person's ability to live independently can be improved by appropriate housing conditions. *(California Planning Roundtable)*

A person having (1) a physical or mental impairment that substantially limits one or more of such person's major life activities so that such person is incapable of living independently; (2) a record of having such an impairment; or (3) being regarded as having such an impairment. However, "handicapped" shall not include current illegal use of or addiction to a controlled substance, nor shall it include any person whose residency in the home would constitute a direct threat to the health and safety of the other individuals. *(Schaumburg, Ill.)*

■ **harbor** *(See also **port and harbor facilities**)*   Shelter for recreational boats from damaging storm waves. Usually an enclosure of water protected by either breakwaters, a natural small bay, or within the mouth of a navigable river. *(Green Bay, Wisc.)*

■ **hardware store** *(See also **home improvement center**)*   A facility of 30,000 or fewer square feet gross floor area, pri-

■ **habitable rooms**   Rooms designed and used for living, sleeping, eating, or cooking, or combinations thereof. Bathrooms, toilet compartments, closets, halls, storage rooms, laundry and utility spaces, basement recreation rooms, and similar areas are not considered habitable rooms. *(Miami, Fla.)*

Any room for sleeping or living purposes, excluding such enclosed places as closets, bath or toilet rooms, connecting corridors, unfinished attics, foyers, storage spaces, utility rooms, spaces used exclusively for cooking or eating, and similar spaces. *(Palm Desert, Calif.)*

■ **habitat**   The physical location or type of environment in which an organism or biological population lives or occurs. *(California Planning Roundtable)*

■ **habitat protection area** *(See also **preserve; wildlife habitat; wildlife refuge**)*   Those areas of state and local significance that are identified by using the habitat assessment methodology found in the habitat assessment manual and that include: (i) buffers; (ii) wetlands; (iii)

marily engaged in the retail sale of various basic hardware lines, such as tools, builders' hardware, plumbing and electrical supplies, paint and glass, housewares and household appliance, garden supplies and cutlery; if greater than 30,000 square feet, such a facility is a Home Improvement Center. *(Prince William County, Va.)*

■ **haunted house** Temporary structures that house booths, displays, and live performances related to Halloween themes. *(Scottsdale, Ariz.)*

Any establishment that is represented or advertised to the public as a haunted house or establishment or in which the public, for a fee, is directed through walkways, corridors, or other paths in a building, tent, or other structure and which contains a combination of displays, acts, exhibits, or other attractions intended to entertain or amuse patrons through the use of scary, spooky, or Halloween images. *(Glendale, Ariz.)*

■ **hazardous material** *(See also **explosive material; toxic or noxious substance**)* Any substance that, because of its quantity, concentration, or physical or chemical characteristics, poses a significant present or potential hazard to human health and safety or to the environment if released into the workplace or the environment. The term includes, but is not limited to, hazardous substances and hazardous wastes. *(California Planning Roundtable)*

Any substances or materials that by reason of their toxic, caustic, corrosive, abrasive, or otherwise injurious properties, may be detrimental or deleterious to the health of any person handling or otherwise coming into contact with such material or substance. *(Oakland Park, Fla., which uses the term "hazardous substances")*

■ **hazardous waste** *(See also **toxic or noxious substance**)* Any refuse or discarded material or combinations of refuse or discarded materials in solid, semisolid, liquid, or gaseous form which cannot be handled by routine waste management techniques because they pose a substantial present or potential hazard to human

health or other living organisms because of their chemical, biological, or physical properties. Categories of hazardous waste include, but are not limited to, explosives, flammables, oxidizers, poisons, irritants, and corrosives. Hazardous waste does not include sewage sludge and source, special nuclear, or by-product material as defined by the Atomic Energy Act of 1954, as amended. *(St. Paul, Minn.)*

■ **hazardous waste disposal facility** All structures, other appurtenances, and improvements on the land used for treating, storing, or disposing of hazardous waste, including all operations or storage areas, diked overflow, or emergency spillway areas. A hazardous waste disposal facility may consist of several treatment, storage, or disposal operational units; it includes all areas where hazardous waste may be received, stored, handled, or processed. *(Cecil County, Md.)*

■ **hazardous waste incinerator** An enclosed device using controlled flame combustion, the primary purpose of which is to thermally break down hazardous waste. Examples of incinerators are rotary kiln, fluidized bed, and liquid injection incinerators. *(Cecil County, Md.)*

■ **hazardous waste processing facility** Any commercial facility, as defined [state rules] for which a [state] pollution control agency permit is required, treating hazardous waste generated at any off-site location, that is designed and operated to modify the chemical composition or chemical, physical, or biological properties of a hazardous waste by means such as reclamation, distillation, precipitation, or other similar processes, which neutralizes the waste or renders it nonhazardous, safer for transport, amenable for recovery, storage, or reduced in volume, excepting "elementary neutralizing units" and "pretreatment units," as defined in [state] rules. Hazardous waste processing does not include incineration or disposal. *(St. Paul, Minn.)*

■ **health care facility** *(See also **clinic; hospital; sanitarium**)* A facility or in-

stitution, whether public or private, principally engaged in providing services for health maintenance, diagnosis or treatment of human diseases, pain, injury, deformity or physical condition, including, but not limited to, a general hospital, diagnostic center, treatment center, rehabilitation center, extended care center, nursing home, intermediate care facility, outpatient laboratory, or central services facility serving one or more such institutions. . . . *(Schaumburg, Ill.)*

■ **health club** A facility where members or nonmembers use equipment or space for the purpose of physical exercise. *(Blue Springs, Mo.)*

■ **health/sport club** A building or portion of a building designed and equipped for the conduct of sports, exercise, leisure time activities, or other customary and usual recreational activities, operated for profit or not-for-profit and which can be open only to bona fide members and guests of the organization or open to the public for a fee. *(St. Paul, Minn.)*

■ **health spa** *(See also **bathhouse; massage establishment; sauna**)* A place or building where active exercise and related activities are performed utilizing weight control or muscle building equipment or apparatus for the purpose of physical fitness. Also, a place or building that provides massage, exercise, and related activities with or without such equipment or apparatus. . . . *(Scottsdale, Ariz.)*

■ **hearing examiner** A public official who usually has authority to hold public hearings in connection with applications for variances, special use permits, and small parcel rezonings, and, occasionally, has the authority to make approval or denial decisions. The purpose of the office is to professionalize the making of such decisions and free the process from political pressures. *(PAS Report No. 322, The Language of Zoning)*

■ **heath** A public tract available for unstructured recreation, located at the edge of the village or along the water boundaries. Its landscape is somewhat naturalistic, consisting of native plants growing unchecked, and requiring minimal maintenance. (*Monroe County, Fla.*)

■ **heavy equipment**  A movable or transportable vehicle or other apparatus commonly used in commercial, industrial, or construction enterprises, such as, but not limited to, trucks, trailers, bulldozers, cranes, backhoes, rollers, loaders, lifts, having a gross weight of 2.5 tons or more. (*Bensalem Township, Pa.*)

■ **hedge**  A row of closely planted shrubs, bushes, or any kind of plant forming a boundary or fence. (*Grand Forks, N.D.*)

Any group of shrubs planted in line or in groups that forms a compact, dense, living barrier that protects, shields, separates, or demarcates an area from view; any similar plant material, or similar plant material in conjunction with a structure, which is 80 percent opaque within 12 months after planting. (*Newport Beach, Calif.*)

■ **height**  The vertical distance to the highest point of the roof for flat roofs; to the deck line of mansard roofs; and to the average height between eaves and the ridge for gable, hip, and gambrel roofs, measured from the curb level if the building is not more than 10 feet from the front lot line or from the grade in all other cases. (*Fairfax County, Va.*)

*Commentary: There are various methods of measuring building height. Some definitions require that the measurement be taken from the average grade level adjoining the building, while others allow measurements from the highest adjoining sidewalk. Definitions also vary in their measurement of terraced buildings and gabled roofs. Some allow measurement to the average height of the gables or terraces, while other measure to the maximum height of any segment of the building.*

■ **height factor**  The height factor of a building is equal to the total floor area of the building divided by its lot coverage. If two or more buildings are located on the same zoning lot, their height factor is the sum of their floor areas divided by the sum of their lot coverages. The height factor is, therefore, equal to the number of stories if the building were erected without setbacks. In computing a height factor, a fraction of .5 or more may be considered a whole number, and smaller fractions shall be disregarded. (*New York, N.Y.*)

■ **height limit**  A vertical distance fixed in certain districts contained herein and measured from the average ground level at the base of the structure. (*Philadelphia, Pa.*)

■ **height, measurement of**  Measured from existing grade at all points of the site to a warped plan an equal height above all points on the site. (*Imperial Beach, Calif.*)

■ **heliport**  An area designed to be used for the landing or takeoff of helicopters including operations facilities, such as maintenance, loading and unloading, storage, fueling, or terminal facilities. (*St. Paul, Minn.*)

An area used or intended to be used for the landing and takeoff of helicopters, and may include any or all of the areas of buildings appropriate to accomplish these functions. (*Scottsdale, Ariz.*)

■ **heliport, limited use**  Any landing area used for the landing and taking off of helicopters, including all necessary passenger and cargo facilities, fueling, and emergency service facilities. (*Federal Aviation Administration*)

■ **heliport or helistop, private**  A heliport or helistop not open to the general public and requiring prior permission of the owner or operator to land. (*St. Paul, Minn.*)

■ **heliport or helistop, public**  A heliport or helistop open to use by any helicopter. (*St. Paul, Minn.*)

■ **heliport, unlimited use**  Any landing area used by helicopters which, in addition, includes all necessary passenger and cargo facilities, maintenance and overhaul, fueling, service, storage, tiedown areas, hangars, and other necessary buildings and open spaces. (*Federal Aviation Administration*)

■ **helistop**  An area designed to be used for the landing or takeoff of one helicopter, the temporary parking of one helicopter, and other facilities as may be required by federal and state regulations, but not including operation facilities such as maintenance, storage, fueling, or terminal facilities. (*St. Paul, Minn.*)

■ **helistop, limited use**  Any landing area used for the taking off or landing of private helicopters for the purpose of picking up and discharging of passengers or cargo. This facility is not open to use by any helicopter without prior permission having been obtained. (*Federal Aviation Administration*)

■ **helistop, unlimited use**  Any landing area used for the landing and taking off of helicopters for the purpose of picking up or discharging of passengers or cargo. No fueling, refueling, or service facilities. (*Federal Aviation Administration*)

■ **heritage, corridor**  [An area of land that] represents large, identifiable, and diverse landscapes [that may have] many significant environmental, cultural, agricultural, historic, recreation, and economic resources and themes. (*National Park Service*)

■ **high occupancy vehicle (HOV)** (*See also **transportation demand management (TDM)**)*  A vehicle carrying more than some minimum number of people (usually two or three persons). (*Renton, Wash.*)

■ **high-water mark, ordinary**  That mark on lakes and streams that will be found by examining the bed and banks and ascertaining where the presence and action of waters are so common and usual, and so long continued in ordinary years, as to mark upon the soil a character distinct from that of the abutting upland. (*Yakima County, Wash.*)

The line between upland and bottomland that persists through successive changes in water levels, below which the presence and action of the water is so common or recurrent that the character of the land is marked distinctly from the upland and is apparent in the soil itself, the configuration of the surface of the soil and the vegetation. On an inland lake which has a level established by law, it means the high established level.

Where water returns to its natural level as the result of the permanent removal or abandonment of a dam, it means the natural ordinary high water mark. *(Grand Traverse County, Mich.)*

■ **highest and best use** *(See also **taking**)* The use of property that will bring to its owner the greatest profit if offered for sale. In theory, the economics of the real estate market establish a maximum value for each parcel of land at any given time. Ordinances are sometimes challenged as they apply to particular sites because they prevent the highest and best use. Where the ordinance is found to be a valid exercise of the police power (viz., it accomplishes a demonstrable public purpose and is based on a plan), such arguments are seldom decisive. But where a court does not find in the ordinance a public benefit overriding the loss to the property owner of the highest and best use, the court may find that there has been a taking of property without due process of law and declare the provisions of the ordinance invalid. *(PAS Report No. 322,* The Language of Zoning*)*

The use of land in such a way that its development will bring maximum profit to the owner. It's a theoretical real estate concept that does not take into account the externalities from such a use of lands. Thus, public regulations often limit land use to some activity that will provide the owners with less than maximum profits in order to minimize spillover costs to other properties and the public at large. *(Handbook for Planning Commissioners in Missouri)*

■ **highway** *(See **street, highway**)*

■ **highway-oriented business** A use dependent upon both a large flow of traffic and convenient access. It includes such uses as motels, restaurants, automobile service stations, and produce stands. *(Thurston County, Wash.)*

Land uses that cater to the traveling public, both auto and truck (e.g., gas stations, restaurants, motels, truck stops). *(Interstate 81 Corridor Council, which uses the term "highway commercial use")*

■ **hillside** Land that has an average percent of slope equal to or exceeding 15

percent. *(California Planning Roundtable)*

■ **hillside landforms** The more elevated, deeper and rugged landforms which tend to divide broad desert valleys or separate the lower deserts from higher plateau regions, to the north and east. These landforms include mountains, hills, buttes, or escarpments predominantly composed of bedrock materials. Typical bedrock materials include volcanics such as basalt and tuff; intrusives such as granite; and metamorphics such as diorites, quartzites, and schists. Locally, slopes may be covered by colluvium comprised of upslope bedrock materials or by thin veneers of in-situ soils. Land slopes are usually above 15 percent and in most cases are over 35 percent, but may be as little as 5 percent in isolated pockets, typically atop ledges or near ridge tops. Drainageways are relatively poorly defined on the slopes but collect into deep canyon bottom courses strewn with large-sized rubble. Hazards that may be present include boulder rolling, rock falls, debris movement, and general slope instability. The surface movement of materials occurs as a result of both gravity and water transport. The surface material size includes larger boulders, rocks and gravel, as well as grainy soil materials. *(Scottsdale, Ariz.)*

■ **historic** Includes, but is not limited to, cultural, artistic, social, economic, ethnic, or political heritage. *(Champaign, Ill.)*

■ **historic and monument sites** Those locations set aside for no other purpose

than to commemorate a historical event, activity, or person. *(Hartford, Conn.)*

■ **historic district** An area designated as an "Historic District" by ordinance and which contains within definable geographic boundaries, properties, or buildings, that may or may not be landmarks but which contribute to the overall historic character of the designated area. *(Champaign, Ill.)*

■ **historic landmark** An individual structure or group of structures on a single lot, a site, an area, a district, or combination thereof, having a special historical, architectural, cultural, or aesthetic value (pictured below). *(Santa Clara County, Calif.)*

A property, structure, or building designated as a "landmark" by ordinance of the city council that is worthy of rehabilitation, restoration, and preservation because of its historic and/or architectural significance. *(Champaign, Ill.)*

An individual site or feature (which may or may not be a structure), or a site with a structure or structures on it, of particular importance because of its unique architectural, historical, cultural, or archaeological features, designated an historic district and eligible for designation on the National Register of Historic Places. *(Blacksburg, Va.)*

■ **historic landmark district** A geographically defined area possessing a significant concentration, linkage, or continuity of landmarks, improvements,

or landscape features united by historic events or aesthetically by plan or physical development, and which area has been designated as an Historic Landmark District pursuant to procedures of the city code and in accordance with this ordinance. Said district may have within its boundaries non-contributing buildings or other structures that, while not of such historic and/or architectural significance to be designated as landmarks, nevertheless contribute to the overall visual character of the district. *(Coral Gables, Fla.)*

■ **historic preservation**　The preservation of historically significant structures and neighborhoods until such time as, and in order to facilitate, restoration and rehabilitation of the building(s) to a former condition. *(California Planning Roundtable)*

■ **historic preservation, significance**　A term ascribed to buildings, sites, objects, or districts that possess exceptional value or quality for illustrating or interpreting the cultural heritage of the community when evaluated in relation to other properties and property types within a specific historic theme, period, and geographical setting. A principal test of significance is "integrity." *(California Planning Roundtable)*

■ **historic structure**　Any structure that is: (a) listed individually in the National Register of Historic Places (a listing maintained by the Department of Interior) or preliminarily determined by the Secretary of the Interior as meeting the requirements for individual listing on the National Register; (b) certified or preliminarily determined by the Secretary of the Interior as contributing to the historical significance of a registered historic district or a district preliminarily determined by the Secretary to qualify as a registered historic district; (c) individually listed on a state inventory of historic places in states with historic preservation programs that have been approved by the Secretary of Interior; or (d) individually listed on a local inventory of historic places in communities with historic preservation programs that have been certified either: (1) by an ap-

proved state program as determined by the Secretary of the Interior; or (2) directly by the Secretary of the Interior in states without approved programs. *(Washington County, Ark.)*

Any antique structure or building existing contemporaneously with and commonly associated with an outstanding event or period of history, and any structure or building in which the relics and/or mementos of such event or period are housed and preserved. *(Rapid City, S.D., which uses the term "historic and monument structures")*

Any structure that is: (1) listed individually in the National Register of Historic Places (maintained by the Department of Interior) or preliminarily determined by the Secretary of the Interior as meeting the requirements for individual listing on the National Register; (2) certified or preliminarily determined by the Secretary of the Interior as contributing to the historical significance of a registered historic district or a district preliminarily determined by the Secretary to qualify as a registered historic district; or (3) designated by the city as a heritage preservation site. *(St. Paul, Minn.)*

■ **historic structure, rehabilitation**　The act or process of returning a structure or landmark to a state of utility through repair or alteration which renders possible an efficient contemporary use while preserving those portions or features significant to its architectural, historic, cultural, or archaeological value. *(Blacksburg, Va.)*

■ **historical site**　One or more parcels, structures, or buildings that is either: included on a city listing of historic properties covered by the city's historic property overlay zoning district, included on the state register of historic properties, designated on the National Register of Historic Places, or authenticated as historic in a survey and report by a registered architect or an architectural historian and the report accepted by the city. The historic survey and report includes: dating the property from a specified period, associating the property with significant events or outstanding past people or groups, determining the distinguishing architectural characteristics or

style of the buildings, and demonstrating the role of the building in the community's heritage. *(Scottsdale, Ariz.)*

■ **holding zone**　A zone established in the zoning ordinance on a temporary basis awaiting applications for rezoning to desired uses. These are usually very low-density zones; their purpose may be made explicit in the ordinance's statement of purpose or left implicit. *(PAS Report No. 322, The Language of Zoning)*

■ **home exhibition**　A one-time display of homes including furnishing and accessories in an unoccupied subdivision. The exhibition may include live entertainment, food sales, street closures, and other activities. *(Scottsdale, Ariz.)*

■ **home improvement center** *(See also hardware store)*　A facility of more than 30,000 square feet gross floor area, engaged in the retail sale of various basic hardware lines, such as tools, builders hardware, paint and glass, housewares and household appliances, garden supplies, and cutlery. *(Prince William County, Va.)*

An establishment selling various household goods, tools, and building materials, durable household goods (e.g., refrigerators, lawn care machines, washing machines), electronic equipment, household animal supplies, nursery products, etc. Retail stock (e.g., nursery items, lumber goods) may be kept outdoors. All such stock (except plant materials) shall be screened in accordance with (city ordinance). At least 75 percent of all indoor floor-good space shall be for retail sales. Likely examples of such uses include "Lowe's," "Home Depot," etc. *(Gastonia, N.C., which uses the term "home center")*

The retail sale of a diverse range of hardware and related materials generally used in the maintenance, repair, or construction of buildings or other structures, including lawn and garden supplies. *(Nashville and Davidson County, Tenn.)*

■ **home industry**　A commercial or light industrial use of a scale greater than home occupation but which is still secondary to the residential use, but not including agricultural or horticultural activities. *(Island County, Wash.)*

■ **home occupation** An occupation carried on in a dwelling unit by the resident thereof; provided that the use is limited in extent and incidental and secondary to the use of the dwelling unit for residential purposes and does not change the character thereof. (*St. Paul, Minn.*)

An occupation or profession that is: accessory to a residential use and is customarily carried on in a dwelling unit or in a building or other structure accessory to a dwelling unit; carried on by a member of the family residing in the dwelling unit; clearly incidental and secondary to the use of the dwelling unit for residential purposes; conforms with the following conditions: (1) the occupation or profession shall be carried on wholly within the principal building or within a building or other structure accessory thereto; (2) not more than two people outside the family shall be employed in the home occupation, and there shall be no stock in trade; (3) there shall be no exterior display, no exterior sign (except as expressly permitted by the district regulations of this chapter), no exterior storage of materials and no other exterior indication of the home occupation or variation from the residential character of the principal building; (4) no nuisance, offensive noise, vibration, smoke, dust, odors, heat, glare, or electrical disturbance shall be generated; (5) no traffic shall be generated by such home occupation in greater volumes than would normally be expected in the neighborhood; (6) in addition to the off-street parking provided to meet the normal requirements of the dwelling, adequate off-street parking shall be provided for the vehicles of each employee and the vehicles of the maximum number of users the home occupation may attract during peak operating hours; (7) the home occupation shall not utilize more than 20 percent of the total floor area of the dwelling unit. A home occupation shall include, but not be limited to, the following: art studio, day care home, dressmaking shop, hairdressing shop, teaching or tutoring facilities, office of a physician, dentist, optometrist, lawyer, engineer, architect, or accountant, office of a real estate broker or agent, office of an insurance agent or broker. A home occupation shall not be interpreted to include the following: facilities for the repair of motor vehicles, day care center. (*Gorham, Maine*)

■ **home rule** The principle under which local governments are broadly authorized by the State Legislature to enact laws, rules, and regulations relating to their own property, affairs, and government. (*New York Planning Federation*)

■ **homeless shelter** (*See also* **shelter; single room occupancy (SRO)**) A facility providing temporary housing to indigent, needy, homeless, or transient persons; may also provide ancillary services such as counseling, vocational training, etc. (*Prince William County, Va.*)

An activity providing personal assistance on a nonprofit basis to individuals of an indigent status. Such assistance must include food and/or shelter and may, in addition, include religious instruction, counseling, and other incidental services customarily provided by missions. (*Rapid City, S.D., which uses the term "mission"*)

A facility providing, without charge, single night, temporary lodging, with or without meals, for people with no ordinary or regular home or residence address, such as cold night shelter. Such shelters shall not provide lodging on a regular basis and shall not continually provide shelter for the same individuals. Temporary shelters shall operate no more than a total of 30 days per year, a year being the period July 1 through June 30. A temporary overnight shelter shall be used only as an accessory use to a church or nonprofit agency that has been established for a period of at least 12 consecutive months and where specifically permitted in this code and shall meet the following requirements: (1) Any temporary overnight shelter for the homeless shall comply fully with the requirements of applicable state, county and city codes, ordinances and regulations; and (2) Any temporary overnight shelter for the homeless shall be contained within the structure of, and operated by, a not-for-profit corporation or charitable organization. (*Melbourne, Fla.*)

A structure used for temporary housing of persons in a dormitory-style setting in which each resident lives at the shelter for a period not to exceed 60 consecutive days. (*Champaign, Ill.*)

■ **homeowner's association** An incorporated nonprofit organization operating under recorded land agreements through which: (a) each lot and/or home owner in a planned unit or other described land area is automatically a member; (b) each lot is automatically subject to a charge for a proportionate share of the expenses for the organization's activities, such as maintaining a common property; and (c) the charge if unpaid becomes a lien against the property. (*Edmond, Okla.*)

An incorporated nonprofit organization operating under recorded land agreements through which: (a) each lot owner is automatically a member; and (b) each lot is automatically subject to a proportionate share of the expenses for the organization's activities, such as maintaining common property. (*Renton, Wash.*)

■ **homesite** That portion of any lot or parcel of land covered by any structure including but not limited to septic systems and reserve area, wells, buildings, pools, and driveways. (*Newtown, Conn.*)

■ **horse farm** A building or structure and/or land whose operator keeps equines primarily for breeding and boarding (pictured on page 123) and which operation may or may not be incidental to the owner's primary occupation. (*McHenry County, Ill.*)

■ **horse track** A circular, elliptical, rectangular, oblong, or similarly shaped endless accessory structure either enclosed or outside, usually constructed of earth, used for the exercise and/or training of horses and/or driver and riders on a farm. (*Colt's Neck, N.J.*)

■ **hospice** One main building, or portion thereof, on one zoning lot in which terminally ill persons live in order to receive appropriate Medicare-certified hospice services. (*St. Paul, Minn.*)

■ **hospital** (*See also* **clinic; health care facility; sanitarium**) An institution, li-

censed by the state department of health, providing primary health services and medical or surgical care to persons, primarily in-patients, suffering from illness, disease, injury, deformity and other abnormal physical or mental conditions, and including as an integral part of the institution, related facilities such as laboratories, outpatient facilities or training facilities. *(St. Paul, Minn.)*

An establishment providing physical or mental health services, in-patient or overnight accommodations, and medical or surgical care of the sick or injured. Includes sanitariums. *(Boone County, Mo.)*

An institution where sick or injured persons are given medical care and, in the course of same, are housed overnight, fed, and provided nursing and related services. This definition shall not include drug rehabilitation facilities, halfway houses, convalescent or nursing homes, institutions for mentally ill individuals, or other similar facilities. *(Pine Bluff, Ark.)*

■ **hospital complex** One or more buildings, one of which must be a hospital (defined as an institution to provide medical and surgical care to the sick or injured, including operating room facilities and beds for overnight stay). A hospital complex may also include a cafeteria or restaurant, medically related heliports, nursing homes, extended care clinics, physical therapy/employee exercise facilities, employee housing, temporary patient/patient family housing, and shops for medical equipment, pharmaceutical supplies, gifts, books, magazines, toiletries, flowers, candy, or similar items, provided such uses are primarily for the benefit of patients, staff, and visitors, and are located so as not to normally to attract other retail customers. A hospital complex may also include, in the same building as the hospital or in separate buildings, other health care and health-care-related services, which may include, but shall not be limited to, the following: health centers and child care centers, . . . optical facilities, and medical office buildings. *(Steamboat Springs, Colo.)*

■ **hostel** *(See youth hostel)*

■ **hot tub** An artificial container of water with a liquid capacity greater than 100 gallons and designed with a mechanical air injection system and/or recirculating device. These devices may filter and/or disinfect the water for reuse and are not intended to be drained between uses. *(Illinois Department of Public Health)*

■ **hotel** *(See also extended-stay motel/hotel; motel)* A building in which lodging is provided and offered to the public for compensation, and which is open to transient guests and is not a rooming or boarding house as herein defined. *(Boone County, Mo.)*

■ **hotel, convention hotel** Any facility that provides a variety of services designed predominately to serve the needs of the convention business. The facility shall be permitted to have 100 square feet of floor space for associated related uses for every 100 square feet of room space. A convention hotel shall have a minimum of 150 rooms and shall provide such facilities as restaurants, lounges, meeting rooms, and similar related retail uses. A minimum of 20 percent of the rooms shall be business suites. *(Rapid City, S.D.)*

■ **house of worship** *(See also religious institution)* A structure owned and/or used by a religious organization for worship, religious training, or education. A house of worship, . . . may include, in addition to the principal structure, accessory structures and/or dwelling units for religious organization personnel located within an accessory structure that is used primarily for religious training or educational purposes. *(Palm Beach, Fla.)*

■ **household** A family living together in a single dwelling unit with common access to, and common use of, all living and eating areas and all areas and facilities for the preparation and storage of food within the dwelling unit. *(Siskiyou County, Calif.)*

■ **household pets** *(See animal, domestic)*

■ **housekeeping unit** An individual or group of persons occupying a dwelling unit that has a single kitchen. *(Santa Clara County, Calif.)*

■ **housing, affordable** *(See affordable housing)*

■ **housing, elderly** *(See elderly housing)*

■ **housing, low-income** Housing that is affordable, according to the U.S. Department of Housing and Urban Development, for either home ownership or rental, and that is occupied, reserved, or marketed for occupancy for households with a gross household income that does not exceed 50 percent of the median gross household income for households of the same size within the housing region in which the housing is located. *(APA Growing Smart project)*

■ **housing, middle-income** Housing that is affordable, according to the U.S. Department of Housing and Urban Development, for either home ownership or rental, and that is occupied, reserved or marketed for occupancy by households with a gross household income that is greater than 80 percent but does not exceed [specify a number within a range of 95-120] percent of the median gross household income for households pf the same size within the housing region in which the housing is located. *(APA Growing Smart project)*

■ **housing, moderate-income**   Housing that is affordable, according to the U.S. Department of Housing and Urban Development, for either home ownership or rental, and that is occupied, reserve, or marketed for occupancy by households with a gross household income that is greater than 50 percent but does not exceed 80 percent of the median gross household income for households of the same size within the housing region in which the housing is located. *(APA Growing Smart project)*

■ **housing, short-term**   A structure that contains one or more individual sleeping rooms, and where tenancy of all rooms may be arranged for periods of less than one month. The short-term housing facility may or may not have food preparation facilities, and shower or bath facilities may or may not be shared. The facility is managed by a public or nonprofit agency to provide short-term housing, with or without a fee. Examples include transitional housing and emergency shelter where individual rooms are provided. Where individual rooms are not provided, the facility may be a mass shelter. *(Portland, Ore.)*

■ **housing, short-term rental**   Any dwelling or portion thereof that is available for use or is used for accommodations or lodging of guests paying a fee or other compensation for a period of less than 30 consecutive days; a short-term rental shall not contain more than four bedrooms. . . . *(Salt Lake County, Utah)*

■ **housing, temporary employment**   Any living quarters . . . permanently maintained in connection with any farm work for the housing of five or more farm employees. *(Fresno, Calif., which uses the term "labor camp, permanent farm")*

Dwelling units, including mobile homes, for use by full-time, temporary, or permanent employees engaged in agricultural pursuits. *(McHenry County, Ill.,*

*which uses the term "migrant agricultural labor housing")*

Housing for employees of an isolated industrial, mining, highway, utilities, or agricultural use where those employees occupy the housing on a seasonal basis not more than six months per year. This development may occur on a single parcel or multiple parcels. *(Washoe County, Nev.)*

■ **housing, transitional** *(See transitional housing shelter)*

■ **housing, very low-income**   Housing that is affordable, according to the U.S. Department of Housing and Urban Development, for either home ownership or rental, and that is occupied, reserved, or marketed for occupancy by households with a gross household income equal to 30 percent or less of the median gross household income for households of the same size within the housing region in which the housing is located. *(APA Growing Smart Project)*

■ **human services planning** *(See social service definitions)*

■ **hydrant, private**   A fire hydrant situated and maintained to provide water for firefighting purposes with restrictions as to use. The location may be such that it is not readily accessible for immediate use by the fire authority for other than certain private property. *(Renton, Wash.)*

■ **hydrant, public**   A fire hydrant situated and maintained to provide water for fire fighting purposes without restriction as to use for that purpose. The location is such that it is accessible from immediate use of the fire authority at all times. *(Renton, Wash.)*

■ **hydroelectric generation facility**   An establishment for the generation of electricity using water sources. *(King County, Wash.)*

■ **hydropower facility, small**   Machinery, including related structures and equipment, that generates electricity from turbines powered by water diverted from the natural flow of a creek, stream, or river, which may be impounded by a dam or other diversion

structure to create a reservoir, and that is capable of producing not more than 30 megawatts of electricity. "Small hydropower facility" includes the site at which the facility is located. *(Shasta Lake, Calif.)*

■ **hypermarket** *(See also big-box retail; shopping center definitions)*   A large-scale (minimum of roughly 100,000 square feet) self-service retail store selling food, drugs, household merchandise, clothing, and a variety of other retail goods. The store may, in some cases, include limited medical services, such as a dentist's office. *(Peoria, Ill.)*

**ice cream vending vehicle** *(See also vending cart)* Every motor vehicle in which ice cream, popsicles, ice sherbets, or frozen desserts of any kind are carried for the purposes of selling at retail sale on the city streets. *(Rochester, Minn.)*

**image** The mental picture or impression of a city or place taken from memory and held in common by members of the community. *(California Planning Roundtable)*

**impact** *(See also externalities)* The effect of any direct man-made actions or indirect repercussions of man-made actions on existing physical, social, or economic conditions. *(California Planning Roundtable)*

The effect on the local public facilities in a given area produced by the additional population attracted by development. *(Boise City, Idaho)*

**impact, extraordinary** An impact that is reasonably determined . . . to result in the need for system improvement, the cost of which will significantly exceed the sum of the development impact

fees to be generated from the project of the sum agreed to be paid pursuant to a development agreement . . . or result in the need for system improvements that are not identified in the capital improvements plan. *(Boise City, Idaho)*

**impact fee** A payment of money imposed by city on development activity pursuant to this chapter as a condition of granting development approval and/or a building permit in order to pay for the planned facilities needed to serve new growth and development activity. "Impact fee" does not include a reasonable permit fee, an application fee, the administrative fee for collecting and handling impact fees, the cost of reviewing independent fee calculations, or the administrative fee required for an appeal. . . . *(Mount Vernon, Wash.)*

A fee, also called a development fee, levied on the developer of a project by a city, county, or other public agency as compensation for otherwise-unmitigated impacts the project will produce. [State code] specifies that development fees shall not exceed the estimated reasonable cost of providing the service for which the fee is charged. To lawfully impose a development fee, the public agency must verify its method of calculation and document proper restrictions on use of the fund. *(California Planning Roundtable)*

A fee levied on the developer or builder of a project by the county or other public agency as compensation for otherwise unmitigated impacts the project will produce. *(Jefferson County, Colo.)*

A fee charged by local governments to developers as a total or partial reimbursement for the cost of providing additional facilities or services needed as a result of new development (e.g., wider roads, new sewers, etc.). *(Homestead, Fla.)*

**impact fee, park** The impact fee designated to pay for publicly owned parks, open space, and recreational facilities. *(Mount Vernon, Wash.)*

**impact fee, school** The impact fee designated to assist in the funding for acquisition and development of school facilities needed to serve new growth and

development, to be owned and operated by school district. *(Puyallup, Wash.)*

**impact fee, transportation** The impact fee designated to pay for public streets and roads. *(Mount Vernon, Wash.)*

A payment of money required from development, as a condition of development approval, to pay for transportation facilities needed to serve new growth and development, and that is reasonably related to the new development that creates additional demand and need for transportation facilities, that is a proportionate share of the cost of the public facilities, and that is used for facilities that reasonably benefit the new development. A transportation impact fee may be used to pay for system improvement costs previously incurred by the city, to the extent that new growth and development will be served by the previously constructed improvements, provided such fee shall not be imposed to make up for any system improvement deficiencies. A transportation impact fee does not include a reasonable permit or application fee. *(Redmond, Wash.)*

**impact, minor or insignificant** Development or redevelopment activities in the Critical Area District that result in little or no land disturbance such as second-story additions, maintenance of existing structures, or interior renovations or remodeling. *(Cecil County, Md.)*

**impervious surface** Any hard-surfaced, man-made area that does not readily absorb or retain water, including but not limited to building roofs, parking and driveway areas, graveled areas, sidewalks, and paved recreation areas. *(Lake County, Ill.)*

Any nonvertical surface artificially covered or hardened so as to prevent or impede the percolation of water into the soil mantle, including but not limited to roof tops excepting eaves, swimming pools, paved or graveled roads, and walkways or parking areas and excluding landscaping, surface water retention/detention facilities, access easements serving neighboring property, and driveways to the extent that they extend beyond the street setback due to location

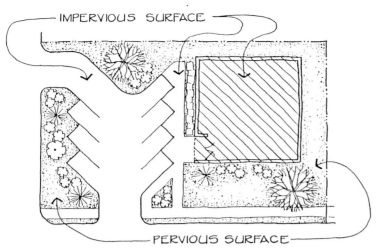

IMPERVIOUS SURFACE — PERVIOUS SURFACE — LOT COVERAGE

within an access panhandle or due to the application of [county] requirements to site features over which the applicant has no control. *(King County, Wash.)*

Surfaces that do not absorb water. Examples of such surfaces include buildings and concrete or asphalt parking areas, roads, sidewalks, or driveways. *(Island County, Wash.)*

■ **impervious surface ratio (ISR)** A measure of the intensity of land use, determined by dividing the total of all impervious surfaces on a site by the gross site area. *(Island County, Wash.)*

A ratio derived by dividing the amount of the site that is covered by any material that substantially reduces or prevents the infiltration of stormwater by the total horizontal area of the lot. Impervious surfaces include, but are not limited to, roofs, streets, sidewalks, and parking lots paved with asphalt, concrete, compacted sand, compacted gravel, or clay. *(Nashville and Davidson County, Tenn.)*

■ **implementation** Actions, procedures, programs, or techniques that carry out policies. *(California Planning Roundtable)*

■ **impound yard** *(See automobile impound facility)*

■ **improvement** Any building, structure, bridge, work of art, area, parking facility, public facility, fence, gate, wall, landscaping, or other object constituting a

physical addition to real property, or any part of such addition. *(Champaign, Ill.)*

Alterations to any structure that: do not change the intensity of its use; do not increase either the gross floor area, height, or bulk of the structure by more than 10 percent; do not block or impede public access; and do not result in a seaward encroachment by the structure. *(Imperial Beach, Calif.)*

■ **incentive zoning** The awarding of bonus credits to a development in the form of allowing more intensive use of land if public benefits—such as preservation of greater than the minimum required open space, provision for low- and moderate-income housing, or plans for public plazas and courts at ground level—are included in a project. *(California Planning Roundtable)*

The process whereby a developer may be granted additional development capacity in exchange for the developer's provision of a public benefit or amenity as may be specified in this zoning code. *(Newport, R.I.)*

■ **incidental, customary, remunerative activities** *(See also home occupation)* Incidental gainful activities which are customarily carried on in the home by its bona fide residents, but not rising to the level of a home occupation, such as baby sitting, giving individual music lessons, the operation of a day care home as defined herein, and the like, as interpreted

by the zoning officer. In the event that the zoning officer later concludes that the activity goes beyond the bounds of an incidental, customary, remunerative activity, or in the event that any citizen objects to the operation of a day care home, then the matter shall be referred to the zoning board of adjustment, and the particular use thus questioned shall henceforth be permitted only if approved as a home occupation by the zoning board of adjustment. *(Tuscaloosa, Ala.)*

■ **incineration** The burning of refuse at high temperatures to reduce the volume of waste. *(California Planning Roundtable)*

■ **incinerator facilities** *(See also hazardous waste incinerator)* A site under one ownership with one or more incinerators that uses thermal combustion processes to destroy or alter the character or composition of medical waste, sludge, soil or municipal solid waste (not including animal or human remains). *(Anchorage, Alaska)*

■ **inclusionary zoning** Regulations that increase housing choice by providing the opportunity to construct more diverse and economical housing to meet the needs of low- and moderate-income families. Often such regulations require a minimum percentage of housing for low- and moderate- income households in new housing developments and in conversions of apartments to condominiums. *(California Planning Roundtable)*

■ **incorporation** Creation of a new city. *(California Planning Roundtable)*

■ **incubator** *(See business incubator)*

■ **industrial** Activity including resource extraction, manufacturing, warehousing, storage, distribution, shipping, and other related uses. *(Valdez, Alaska)*

A business use or activity at a scale greater than home industry involving manufacturing, fabrication, assembly, warehousing, and/or storage. Examples of industrial uses include sawmills and boat building. *(Island County, Wash.)*

■ **industrial park** A planned, coordinated development of a tract of land with two or more separate industrial buildings. Such development is planned, designed, constructed, and managed on an integrated and coordinated basis with special attention given to on-site vehicular circulation, parking, utility needs, building design, orientation, and open space. *(Mankato, Minn.)*

A special or exclusive type of planned industrial area designed and equipped to accommodate a community of industries, providing them with all necessary facilities and services in attractive surroundings among compatible neighbors. Industrial parks may be promoted or sponsored by private developers, community organizations, or government organizations. *(Pine Bluff, Ark.)*

A tract of land, the control and administration of which are vested in a single body, suitable for industrial use because of location, topography, proper zoning, availability of utilities, and accessibility to transportation. The uses permitted may be regulated by protective minimum restrictions (covenants), including the size of the site, parking, and loading regulations, and building setback lines from front, side, and rear yards that may be more restrictive than this chapter. *(Perryville, Mo.)*

■ **industrial waste**   Any material resulting from a production or manufacturing operation having no net economic value to the source producing it. *(Anchorage, Alaska)*

■ **industry**   *(See also **manufacturing definitions**)* The manufacture, fabrication, processing, reduction, or destruction of any article, substance or commodity, or any other treatment thereof in such a manner as to change the form, character, or appearance thereof, and includes storage elevators, truck storage yards, warehouses, wholesale storage, and other similar types of enterprise. *(Palm Desert, Calif.)*

■ **industry, heavy**   Manufacturing or other enterprises with significant external effects (pictured above), or which pose significant risks due to the involvement of explosives, radioactive materials, poisons, pesticides, herbi-

cides, or other hazardous materials in the manufacturing or other process. *(Blacksburg, Va.)*

A use engaged in the basic processing and manufacturing of materials or products predominately from extracted or raw materials, or a use engaged in storage of or manufacturing processes using flammable or explosive materials, or

storage or manufacturing processes that potentially involve hazardous or commonly recognized offensive conditions. *(Easton, Md.)*

■ **industry, light**   Research and development activities, the manufacturing, compounding, processing, packaging, storage, assembly, and/or treatment of finished or semi-finished products from previously prepared materials, which activities are conducted wholly within an enclosed building. Finished or semi-finished products may be temporarily stored outdoors pending shipment. *(Cecil Co., Md.)*

A use engaged in the manufacture, predominately from previously prepared materials, of finished products or parts, including processing, fabrication, assembly, treatment, packaging, incidental storage, sales, and distribution of such products, but excluding basic industrial processing. *(Easton, Md.)*

Enterprises engaged in the processing, manufacturing, compounding, assembly, packaging, treatment, or fabrication of materials and products, from processed or previously manufactured

materials. Light industry is capable of operation in such a manner as to control the external effects of the manufacturing process, such as smoke, noise, soot, dirt, vibration, odor, etc. A machine shop is included in this category. Also included is the manufacturing of apparel, electrical appliances, electronic equipment, camera and photographic equipment, ceramic products, cosmetics and toi-

letries, business machines, fish tanks and supplies, food, paper products (but not the manufacture of paper from pulpwood), musical instruments, medical appliances, tools or hardware, plastic products (but not the processing of raw materials), pharmaceuticals or optical goods, bicycles, any other product of a similar nature. *(Blacksburg, Va. )*

■ **industry, medium**   Enterprises in which goods are generally mass produced from raw materials on a large scale through use of an assembly line or similar process, usually for sale to wholesalers or other industrial or manufacturing uses. Medium industry produces moderate external effects such as smoke, noise, soot, dirt, vibration, odor, etc. *(Blacksburg, Va.)*

■ **infill**   Development or redevelopment of land that has been bypassed, remained vacant, and/or is underused as a result of the continuing urban development process. Generally, the areas and/or sites are not particularly of prime quality, however they are usually served by or are readily accessible to the infrastructure (services and facilities) provided by the applicable local governmental entity. Use of such lands for new housing and/or other urban development is considered a more desirable alternative than to continue to extend the outer development pattern laterally and horizontally thus necessitating a higher expenditure for capital improvements than would be required for infill development. The use of infill development, among others, promotes the best use of resources and also will tend to have a positive impact upon the tax and other fiscal policies. *(Topeka, Kans.)*

■ **infill development**   Development of vacant, skipped-over parcels of land in otherwise built-up areas. Local governments are showing increasing interest in infill development as a way of containing energy costs and limiting costs of extending infrastructure into newly developing areas. Infill development also provides an attractive alternative to new development by reducing loss of critical and resource lands to new development and by focusing on strengthening older neighborhoods. *(King County, Wash.)*

Construction on an existing vacant lot on an existing street in an existing neighborhood. *(Lexington, Mass.)*

The construction of a building on a vacant parcel located in a predominately built up area. The local zoning regulations determine whether the new building fits harmoniously into the neighborhood. *(New York City, N.Y.)*

The use of vacant land, the reuse or change of use of a previously-developed parcel or group of parcels, or the intensification of use or change of use by remodeling or renovating an entire structure. Infill development can be on land having one or more of the following characteristics: (1) Was platted or developed more than 25 years ago; (2) Is in a subdivision that is more than 80 percent built out and that was platted more than 15 years ago; (3) Is bounded on two or more sides by existing development; (4) Is within a Historic Preservation District; (5) Is within an unplatted area that contains lots of two and one-half acres or less where 80 per-

cent or more of the lots or tracts are developed and have been for at least 15 years; (6) Is within a blighted area as defined by state law; (7) Contains an original structure or use that is no longer viable or which is not economically feasible to renovate; (8) Contains an existing structure that does not comply with current building and/or zoning code requirements; (9) The lot does not comply with current zoning code requirements or is in an area with inadequate or antiquated platting; (10) Is in an area that is currently served by inadequate infrastructure for its planned reuse. *(Tulsa, Okla.)*

■ **infill site**   Any vacant lot or parcel within developed areas of the city, where at least 80 percent of the land within a 300-foot radius of the site has been developed, and where water, sewer, streets, schools, and fire protection have already been developed and are provided. Annexed areas located on the periphery of the city limits shall not be considered as infill sites. *(Boise, Idaho)*

■ **infiltration**   The downward movement or seepage of water from the surface to the subsoil and/or groundwater. The infiltration rate is expressed in terms of inches per hour. *(Grand Traverse County, Mich.)*

■ **infiltration facility**   *(See also **stormwater** definitions)*   A structure or area that allows stormwater runoff to gradually seep into the ground (e.g. french drains, seepage pits, infiltration basin, dry well, or perforated pipe). *(Grand Traverse County, Mich.)*

■ **inflow**   *(See also **sewer** definitions)*   Water, other than wastewater, that enters a sewer system (including sewer service connections) from sources such as, but not limited to, roof leaders, cellar drains, yard drains, area drains, drains from springs and swamping areas, manhole covers, cross connections between storm sewers and sanitary sewers, catch basins, cooling towers, stormwaters, surface runoff, street wash waters or drainage. *(Indian River County, Fla.)*

■ **infrastructure**   Facilities and services needed to sustain industry, resi-

dential, commercial, and all other land-use activities, including water, sewer lines, and other utilities, streets and roads, communications, and public facilities such as fire stations, parks, schools, etc. *(Redmond, Wash.)*

The basic facilities such as roads, schools, power plants, transmission lines, transportation, and communication systems on which the continuance and growth of a community depends. *(Washoe County, Nev.)*

Streets, water and sewer lines, and other public facilities necessary to the functioning of a community. *(Handbook for Planning Commissioners in Missouri)*

■ **ingress**   Access or entry point or entrance. *(Champaign, Ill.)*

■ **inn**   Any building or group of buildings in which there are five or less guest rooms, used for the purpose of offering public lodging on a day-to-day basis, not including a bed and breakfast home. *(Valdez, Alaska)*

■ **institution/institutional building**   Public and public/private group use of a nonprofit nature, typically engaged in public service (e.g., houses of worship, nonprofit cultural centers, charitable organizations). *(Palm Beach, Fla.)*

A facility that provides a public service and is operated by a federal, state, or local government, public or private utility, public or private school or college, church, public agency, or tax-exempt organization. *(Island County, Wash.)*

■ **institutional use**   A nonprofit or quasi-public use, such as a religious institution, library, public, or private school, hospital, or government-owned or government-operated structure or land used for public purpose. *(Champaign, Ill.)*

■ **integrity**   As used in historic preservation, the degree to which authenticity of a property's historic identity has been maintained, evidenced by the survival of substantial physical characteristics that existed during the property's historic period. *(California Planning Roundtable)*

■ **intensity, land-use** The range or scale or concentration of findings, often measured by floor area ratios or building coverage. *(Elbert County, Colo.)*

The magnitude of activity affecting the development of densities, traffic flow, commercialism, tourism, and land use. *(Palm Desert, Calif.)*

Any ratio that assesses the relative level of activity of a land use, including, but not limited to, a floor area ratio, building coverage ratio, or impervious surface ratio. *(APA's Growing Smart project)*

■ **interchange** *(See also **street, highway**)* The road improvement providing transfer of motor vehicles from one roadway to another. *(Interstate 81 Corridor Council)*

■ **interchange plan** The plan that contains official policies developing the interchange study area. *(Interstate 81 Corridor Council)*

■ **interchange study area** A potential interchange area studied for its features and characteristics, suggesting development because of its critical economic and overall impact in the local community and region. *(Interstate 81 Corridor Council)*

■ **interim zone of influence** A procedure for the exchange of information on certain proposed land uses between a city or town and the county, and for the resolution of conflicts between the plans, policies, and development standards of such jurisdictions, pursuant to interlocal agreement. If this procedure is used, it shall be for a specified period not to exceed 18 months to permit the participating jurisdictions to establish a zone of influence. *(Island County, Wash.)*

■ **interim zone or interim development controls** *(See also **moratorium**)* A device to freeze or severely restrict development for a short period during which a comprehensive plan for an area or a new set of zoning regulations is prepared. Interim zoning has three main purposes: it permits planning and ordinance writing to proceed relatively free of development pressures; it prevents uses that will not conform to the adopted ordinances; and it engenders public debate on the issues. When the controls have been found to be a subterfuge for a more-or-less permanent effort to halt growth, the courts have thrown them out. *(PAS Report No. 322, The Language of Zoning)*

In a community that has not been zoned, the use of a stop-gap zoning ordinance is sometimes used to preserve the existing pattern of land development, usually by limiting new commercial or industrial uses to areas where such uses are already found. *(Handbook for Planning Commissioners in Missouri)*

A zoning designation that temporarily reduces or freezes allowable development in an area until a permanent classification can be fixed; generally assigned during General Plan preparation to provide a basis for permanent zoning. *(California Planning Roundtable)*

■ **interjurisdictional agreement** *(See also **joint-powers authority**)* A contractual or other formal agreement between two or more political jurisdictions that results in a cooperative action or activity. *(New Jersey State Plan)*

■ **intersection** *(See **street intersection**)*

■ **inverse condemnation** *(See also **condemnation; eminent domain; taking**)* The effective taking or reduction in value of a property as a result of public action, in contrast to a direct taking through eminent domain. For example, by building a dam that inundates a property, the public will have destroyed its value, and the law requires that the landowner be reimbursed for the amount of the loss. *(PAS Report No. 322, The Language of Zoning)*

■ **irrigation** The methods of supply and application of water other than natural rainfall. *(Indian River County, Fla.)*

■ **irrigation system** A permanent, artificial watering system designed to transport and distribute water to plants. *(Indian River County, Fla.)*

■ **jetty** *(See also **breakwater**)*   An artificial barrier perpendicular to the shoreline used to change the natural littoral drift to protect inlet entrances from clogging by excess sediment, or to protect a harbor area from storm waves. *(Seattle, Wash.)*

■ **jet ski** *(See **personal watercraft**)*

■ **jewelry store**   Shops that sell new merchandise primarily and some used merchandise from estate sales or reconstitute precious metals they purchase into jewelry forms that are sold at retail on the premises. *(Las Vegas, Nev.)*

■ **jobs/housing balance; jobs/housing ratio** *(See also **linkage**)*   The availability of affordable housing for employees. The jobs/housing ratio divides the number of jobs in an area by the number of employed residents. A ratio of 1.0 indicates a balance. A ratio greater than 1.0 indicates a net in-commute; less than 1.0 indicates a net out-commute. *(California Planning Roundtable)*

■ **joint powers authority** *(See also **interjurisdictional agreement**)*   A legal arrangement that enables two or more units of government to share authority in order to plan and carry out a specific program or set of programs that serves both units. *(California Planning Roundtable)*

■ **joint use** *(See also **mixed-use development**)*   The development of two or more adjacent zoning lots located in the same zoning district and used for a single, unified project or development. *(Maui County, Hawaii)*

■ **junk**   Scrap or waste material of whatsoever kind or nature collected or accumulated for resale, disposal, or storage. *(Homestead, Fla.)*

Worn-out, cast-off, or discarded articles or materials that have been collected or stored for salvage, destruction, or conversion to some use, but not including articles or material that, unaltered and unchanged and without further reconditioning, can be used for its original purpose as readily as when new. *(Quincy, Mass.)*

■ **junk dealer**   Any person who buys, exchanges, collects, receives, stores, or sells any article defined as junk or salvage. *(Columbus, Ohio)*

■ **junkyard**   A building structure, or parcel of land, or portion thereof, used for collecting, storage, or sale of waste paper, rags, scrap metal, rubber tires, bottles, or discarded material. Where such materials are a byproduct of a permitted use, such activity shall be considered outdoor storage. *(Jefferson County, Colo.)*

Any space for storage, abandonment or sale of junk, scrap material or similar waste, including the dismantling, demolition or abandonment of automobiles, other vehicles, machinery or parts. Junkyard shall be synonymous with salvage yard. *(Washoe County, Nev.)*

Any business and any place of storage or deposit, whether in connection with another business or not, which has stored or deposited two or more unregistered motor vehicles that are no longer intended or in condition for legal use on the public highways, or used parts of motor vehicles or old iron, metal, glass, paper, cordage, or other waste or discarded or secondhand material which has been a part, or intended to be a part, of any motor vehicle, the sum of which parts or material shall be equal in bulk to two or more motor vehicles. Such terms shall also include any place of business or storage or deposit of motor vehicles purchased for the purpose of dismantling the vehicles for parts or for use of the metal for scrap and where it is intended to burn materials that are parts of a motor vehicle or cut up the parts thereof. *(Hartford, Conn.)*

■ **jurisdiction**   Any governmental unit or political division or subdivision including, but not limited to: township, village, borough, parish, city, county, state, commonwealth, province, freehold, district, or territory over which the governmental unit exercises power and authority. *(San Diego, Calif.)*

■ **juvenile detention facility** *(See also **correctional facility; custodial care facility**)*   A public facility or institution exclusively for the incarceration of people under 21 years of age awaiting trial or sentencing or serving a court imposed sentence. *(Thurston County, Wash.)*

An institution, home, or other facility operated as a place for juvenile detention . . . for children alleged or adjudicated as delinquent, unruly, dependent, neglected, abused, or juvenile traffic offenders. *(Cincinnati, Ohio)*

■ **kennel**   Any premises, except where accessory to an agricultural use, where domestic animals, such as dogs and cats, are boarded, trained, or bred. *(Jefferson County, Colo.)*

Any place where four or more dogs, cats, or other animals over three months of age are kept, raised, sold, boarded, bred, shown, treated, or groomed. *(Woodbury, Minn.)*

■ **kennel, commercial**   The boarding, breeding, raising, grooming or training of two or more dogs, cats, or other household pets of any age not owned by the owner or occupant of the premises, and/or for commercial gain. *(Blacksburg, Va.)*

A facility for the keeping, boarding or maintaining of four or more dogs four months of age or older that are not owned by the kennel owner for commercial purposes, except for dogs in pet shops or animal hospitals. *(San Luis Obispo County, Calif.)*

■ **kennel, private**   The keeping, breeding, raising, showing or training of four or more dogs over six months of age for personal enjoyment of the owner or occupants of the property, and for which commercial gain is not the primary objective. *(Blacksburg, Va.)*

■ **kindergarten** *(See educational facilities, preschool)*

■ **kiosk**   A freestanding structure upon which temporary information and/or posters, notices, and announcements are posted, or a freestanding building with one or more open sides from which commercial activities are conducted. *(Clark Co, Nev.)*

A temporary or semi-permanent structure having one or more open air sides, operating on either private property or public rights-of-way and plazas, generally no larger than six feet wide by 10 feet long. Operated for the purpose of vending food, drink, or retail goods. *(Redmond, Wash.)*

A structure that may be constructed somewhere other than the lot on which it is placed or which is comprised of parts that are constructed elsewhere and assembled on a lot, and which is designed and intended to be used primarily for retail sale, display, and accessory advertising of food or merchandise. *(Philadelphia, Pa.)*

■ **kiss-and-ride facility** *(See park-and-ride facility)*

■ **kitchen**   Any room principally used, intended or designed to be used for cooking or the preparation of food. The presence of a range or oven, or utility connections suitable for servicing a range or oven, shall normally be considered as establishing a kitchen. *(Clark Co, Nev.)*

Any room in a building which is used, intended or designed to be used for cooking or preparation of food. *(Pima County, Ariz.)*

Any room or part of a room designed, built, used, or intended to be used for food preparation and dishwashing, but not including a bar, butler's pantry, or similar room adjacent to or connected with a kitchen. *(Imperial Beach, Calif.)*

■ **knoll**   A small natural round hill or mound. *(Brea, Calif.)*

■ **labor camp** (*See housing, temporary employment*)

■ **laboratory** A building or group of buildings in which are located facilities for scientific research, investigation, testing, or experimentation, but not facilities for the manufacture or sale of products, except as incidental to the main purpose of the laboratory. (*North Kansas City, Mo.*)

■ **laboratory, research** A facility for scientific laboratory research in technology-intensive fields. Examples include biotechnology, pharmaceuticals, genetics, plastics, polymers, resins, coatings, fibers, fabrics, films, heat transfer, and radiation research facilities. (*Blacksburg, Va.*)

■ **laboratory, support** A facility for scientific laboratory analysis of natural resources, medical resources, and manufactured materials. The scientific analysis is generally performed for an outside customer, to support the work of that customer. This category includes environmental laboratories for the analysis of air, water, and soil; medical or veterinary laboratories for the analysis of blood, tis-

sue, or other human medical or animal products. Forensic laboratories for analysis of evidence in support of law enforcement agencies would also be included in this category. (*Blacksburg, Va.*)

■ **lake** (*See also pond*) Natural or artificial bodies of water of two or more acres and/or where the deepest part of the basin at low water exceeds two meters (6.6 feet). Artificial bodies of water with a recirculation system approved by the Public Works Department are not included in this definition. (*Renton, Wash.*)

A permanent body of open water five acres or more in size. (*Grand Traverse County, Mich.*)

■ **land assets** Those infrastructure investments under public ownership, or maintained for public benefit, that are necessary to support development and redevelopment and to protect the public health, safety, and environment by providing for the preservation and public control of existing land resources that are sensitive to, and necessary to support, growth, and development in other locations, and include, but not limited to parks, open space, and farmland retention. (*New Jersey State Plan*)

■ **land banking** The purchase of land by a local government for use or resale at a later date. Banked lands have been used for development of low- and moderate-income housing, expansion of parks, and development of industrial and commercial centers. Federal railbanking law allows railroads to bank unused rail corridors for future rail use while allowing interim use as trails. (*California Planning Roundtable*)

■ **land clearing** Any activity that removes the vegetive ground cover. (*Cecil Co., Md*)

The removal of vegetation from any site, parcel or lot except when land is cleared and cultivated for bona fide agricultural or garden use in a district permitting such use. Mowing, trimming, pruning, or removal of vegetation to maintain it in a healthy, viable condition is not considered clearing. (*Muskegon, Mich.*)

The act of removal or destruction of vegetation by mechanical or chemical means, but does not include normal cultivation associated with an agricultural operation. (*Island County, Wash.*)

■ **Land Evaluation and Site Assessment (LESA)** A numerical system that measures the quality of farmland. It is generally used to select tracts of land to be protected or developed. (*American Farmland Trust*)

■ **land owner** (*See owner*)

■ **land trust** A private, nonprofit conservation organization formed to protect natural resources, such as productive farm and forest land, natural areas, historic structures, and recreational areas. Land trusts purchase and accept donations of conservation easements. They educate the public about the need to conserve land and some provide land-use and estate planning services to local governments and individual citizens. (*American Farmland Trust*)

■ **land use** The occupation or use of land or water area for any human activity or any purpose. . . . (*California Planning Roundtable*)

A description of how land is occupied or utilized. (*Schaumburg, Ill.*)

A use of land that may result in an earth change, including but not limited to subdivision, residential, commercial, industrial, recreational, agricultural practices, or other development, private and public highway, road and stream construction, and drainage construction. (*Grand Traverse County, Mich.*)

■ **land-use action** The decision made by the review authority on a land-use application, including appropriate findings, environmental determination, and conditions of approval, where applicable. (*San Bernardino, Calif.*)

■ **land-use classification** A system for classifying and designating the appropriate use of properties. (*California Planning Roundtable*)

■ **land-use decision** A final determination by a city body or officer with the highest level of authority to make the determination, including those with authority to hear appeals on: (a) an application for a project permit or other governmental approval required by law before real property may be improved, developed, modified, sold, transferred or used, but excluding applications for permits or approvals to use, vacate, or transfer streets, parks, and other similar types of public property, excluding applications for legislative approval such as areawide rezones and annexations, and excluding applications for business licenses; (b) an interpretive or declaratory decision regarding the application to a specific property of zoning or other ordinances or rules regulating the improvement, development, modification, maintenance, or use of real property; (c) the enforcement by the city of codes regulating improvement, development, modification, maintenance, or use of real property. *(Renton, Wash.)*

■ **land-use element**    A required element of the General Plan that uses text and maps to designate the future use or reuse of land within a given jurisdiction's planning area. The land-use element serves as a guide to the structuring of zoning and subdivision controls, urban renewal and capital improvements programs, and to official decisions regarding the distribution and intensity of development and the location of public facilities and open space. . . . *(California Planning Roundtable)*

A plan or scheme designating the location and extent of use for agriculture, timber production, housing, commerce, industry, recreation, open spaces, public utilities, public facilities, and other land uses as required by the [state's] Growth Management Act. *(Renton, Wash.)*

■ **land-use-intensity system (LUI)**  An organized and comprehensive system for determining or controlling the intensity with which land is developed, replacing conventional fixed yard, height, spacing, etc., and density (i.e., lot area per dwelling unit) controls with more sensitive regulatory devices. The heart of the system is a land-use-intensity scale that establishes ratios to be applied to gross land area in determining

maximum residential floor area, minimum total livability and recreation open space requirements, and ratios based on number of dwelling units to determine parking requirements. Developed in the mid-1960s by the U.S. Federal Housing Administration, LUI has been adapted as a control device for the planned residential development provisions of some zoning ordinances. Partly because of its complexity, but also because of its unconventional innovations, its use has been very limited. *(PAS Report No. 322, The Language of Zoning)*

■ **land-use inventory**    A study of how land is currently being used within the community. The study catalogs the types, extent, distribution, and intensity of the uses or activities found on parcels of land or in spaces within a building. For example, the land may be used for residential or commercial activity. Office, retail, and residential uses may all be found within different areas of the same building. Knowing what activities currently occur in different locations in a community and the relations between those different uses or activities is essential information for planning future land use. *(Washington State Growth Management Program)*

■ **land-use plan**    A basic element of the comprehensive plan. It designates the future use or reuse of the land within a given jurisdictions' planning area, and the policies and reasoning used at arriving at the decisions in the plan. The land-use plan serves as a guide to official decisions regarding the distribution and intensity of private development, as well as public decisions on the location of future public facilities and open spaces. It is also a basic guide the zoning and subdivision controls, urban renewal, and capital improvement programs. *(Handbook for Planning Commissioners in Missouri)*

The relevant portion of the city's general plan that is sufficiently detailed to indicate the kinds, location, and intensity of land uses, the applicable resource protection and development policies, and, where necessary, a listing of implementing actions. *(Imperial Beach, Calif.)*

■ **land-use projections**    A description of the service area and projections of land uses, densities, intensities, and population in the service area over at least a 20-year period. *(Boise City, Idaho, which uses the term "land-use assumptions")*

■ **land-use regulation**    A term encompassing the regulation of land in general and often used to mean those regulations incorporated in the General Plan, as distinct from zoning regulations (which are more specific). *(California Planning Roundtable)*

■ **land value**    The value of land as established for the tax base by the property appraiser's office prior to any or all exemptions. *(Palm Beach County, Fla.)*

■ **landfill, construction/demolition**    The disposal of nonbiodegradable waste resulting from road building, construction, remodeling, repair, or demolition of structures. *(Nashville and Davidson County, Tenn.)*

■ **landfill, sanitary**    *(See also **dump**)*  The burial of nonhazardous and nonmedical farm, residential, institutional, commercial, or industrial waste. *(Nashville and Davidson County, Tenn.)*

***Commentary:*** *A sanitary landfill should not be confused with a dump. Solid waste at a dump site is disposed of without being compacted and covered. A sanitary landfill presents fewer health and aesthetic problems, and has the potential of being reclaimed for other uses. Hazardous or radioactive waste disposal is not permitted in a sanitary landfill. See the definitions for "hazardous waste processing facility" for a definition for those types of facilities.*

■ **landing strip**    *(See also **runway**)*  The area of the airport used for the landing, the taking-off, or taxiing of aircraft. *(Huntsville, Ala.)*

A specified area on an airport or airfield prepared for landing and takeoff of aircraft. *(York County, Va., which uses the term "runway")*

■ **landline communications**    A system for the transmission of information by wire or fiber. *(Cincinnati, Ohio)*

■ **landmark** *(See historic landmark)*

■ **landscape contractor** A business principally engaged in the decorative and functional alteration, planting, and maintenance of grounds. Such a business may engage in the installation and construction of underground improvements but only to the extent that such improvements (e.g., drainage facilities) are accessory to the principal business and are necessary to support or sustain the landscaped surface of the ground. *(Lake County, Ill.)*

■ **landscape planting area** An area that is permanently devoted and maintained to the growing of shrubbery, grass, and other plant material or by the use of such materials as crushed stone, lava rock, or similar materials. *(El Paso, Tex.)*

The installation and permanent maintenance of an area with trees, shrubs, lawn, or planted ground cover to present an attractive, well-kept appearance. (i) Landscaped areas shall not be surfaced in part or whole with concrete, asphalt, or other surface material, but shall contain earth, and may contain organic mulch, inorganic fillers such as wood shavings, bark, volcanic rock, or other similar mulch material. (ii) A portion of such landscaped treatment may consist of decorative planters, stone work, brick work, and the like; any such landscaping treatment shall not exceed three feet in height. Elements of ornamentation, such as an archway, piece of statuary, lamp post, and the like, provided as part of the landscaping in a required front or street side yard, may exceed three feet in height. (iii) Each landscaped area shall be surrounded with a six-inch, raised, concrete curbing or planning division-approved equivalent. (iv) An irrigation system shall be installed and maintained in working order in each separate planter area. *(Santa Clara County, Calif., which uses the term "landscaped areas")*

■ **landscape waste** All accumulations of grass or shrubbery cuttings, leaves, tree limbs, and other materials accumulated as the result of the care of lawns, shrubbery, vines and trees. *(Lake County, Ill.)*

■ **landscape waste composting facility** *(See also composting facility)* An establishment for the composting of waste materials accumulated as the result of the care of lawns, shrubbery, vines, and trees. However, property on which the principal use is residential and on which composting of such materials, accumulated exclusively on-site, is conducted, shall not be considered a landscape waste composting facility. *(Lake County, Ill.)*

■ **landscaped buffer** *(See also buffer)* An area of landscaping separating two distinct land uses, or a land use and a public right-of-way, and acts to soften or mitigate the effects of one land use on the other. *(Washoe County, Nev.)*

■ **landscaped visual barrier** Evergreen trees, and/or evergreen shrubs providing equivalent buffering, planted to provide a year-round dense screen within three years from the time of planting. *(Renton, Wash.)*

■ **landscaping** The bringing of the soil surface to a smooth finished grade, installing sufficient trees, shrubs, ground cover and grass to soften building lines, provide shade and generally produce a pleasing visual effect of the premises (pictured below). *(North Kansas City, Mo.)*

The area within the boundaries of a given lot that consists of planting materials, including, but not limited, to trees, shrubs, ground covers, grass, flowers, decorative rock, bark, mulch, and other similar materials. At least 50 percent of the landscaping area must be covered by live plant material at the time of plant maturity. *(Fayetteville, Ark.)*

The modification of the landscape for an aesthetic or functional purpose. It includes the preservation of existing vegetation and the continued maintenance thereof together with grading and installation of minor structures and appurtenances. *(Kauai, Hawaii)*

■ **landscaping, interior** A landscaped area or areas within the shortest circumferential line defining the perimeter or exterior boundary of the parking or loading area, or similar paved area, excluding driveways or walkways providing access to the facility (as applied to parking and loading facilities or to similar paved areas). *(Newport Beach, Calif.)*

■ **landscaping, perimeter** A landscaped area adjoining and outside the shortest circumferential line defining the perimeter or exterior boundary of the parking or loading area, or similar paved area, excluding driveways or walkways providing access to the facility (as applied to parking and loading facilities or to similar paved areas). *(Newport Beach, Calif.)*

■ **landscaping plan** A plan, drawn to scale, showing dimensions and details for revegetating an area 2,500 square feet or greater in size and at least 35 feet wide, including maintenance and protection measures. *(Maryland Department of Natural Resources)*

■ **landslide** Rock, earth, or debris flows on slopes due to gravity. Also known as mud flows, debris flows, earth failures, slope failures, etc., a landslide can be triggered by rains, floods, earthquakes, and other natural causes, as well as human-made causes, such as grading, terrain cutting and filling, excessive or inappropriate development, etc. Because the factors affecting a landslide can be geophysical or human-made, a landslide can occur in developed areas, undeveloped areas, or any area where the terrain was altered for roads, houses, utilities, and even for lawns. Landslides occur in all 50 states; more than half of the states have rates sufficient to be classified as a significant natural hazard. (*APA's Land-Based Classification Standards project*)

■ **large-box retail** (*See big-box retail*)

■ **large minimum lot-size zoning** Ordinances that require a certain number of acres for every nonfarm dwelling; typically at least 20 acres in the eastern United States or at least 35 acres in other regions. (*American Farmland Trust*)

■ **laundromat** A facility where patrons wash, dry, or dry clean clothing or other fabrics in machines operated by the patron. (*Clark County, Nev.*)

A business that provides washing, drying, and/or ironing machines for hire to be used by customers on the premises. (*Dry Ridge, Ky.*)

■ **law enforcement officer** Any person who is appointed or employed by the city, who is vested with authority to bear arms and make arrests, and whose primary responsibility is the prevention and detection of crime or the enforcement of the criminal or traffic laws of the state. (*Clearwater, Fla.*)

■ **leapfrog development** (*See also growth management; smart growth; sprawl*) New development separated from existing development by substantial vacant land. (*California Planning Roundtable*)

Development that occurs well beyond the existing limits of development and thus leaves intervening vacant land behind. This bypassing of the next-in-line lands at the urban fringe results in the haphazard shotgun pattern of urbanization known as "sprawl." (*Handbook for Planning Commissioners in Missouri*)

■ **lease** A contractual agreement by which an owner of real property (the lessor) gives the right of possession to another (a lessee) for a specified period of time (term) and for a specified consideration (rent). (*California Planning Roundtable*)

■ **least dimension** The shortest lineal dimension of [a] yard. If two opposite sides of a yard are not parallel, such "least dimension" shall be deemed to be the shorter distance of the two measurements. (*Columbus, Ohio*)

■ **letter of map amendment (LOMA)** Official determination by Federal Emergency (FEMA) that a specific structure is not in a [flood hazard area]; amends the effective Flood Hazard Boundary Map (FHBM) or Flood Insurance Rate Map (FIRM). (*Lake County, Ill.*)

■ **letter of map revision (LOMR)** Letter that revises base flood elevations, flood insurance rate zones, flood boundaries, or floodways as shown on an effective flood insurance rate map. (*Jefferson County, Colo.*)

A letter issued by FEMA or IDOT/DWR that revises base flood elevations, flood insurance rate zones, flood boundaries, or regulatory floodways as shown on an effective Flood Hazard Base Map or Flood Insurance Rate Map. (*Lake County, Ill.*)

■ **levee** A man-made structure, usually an earthen embankment, designed and constructed in accordance with sound engineering practices to contain, control, or divert the flow of water so as to provide protection from temporary flooding. (*Washington County, Ark.*)

■ **level of service (LOS)** The quality and quantity of existing and planned public facilities. . . . (*Jefferson County, Colo.*)

A measure of the relationship between service capacity and service demand for public facilities. (*Boise City, Idaho*)

■ **level of service (LOS) standard** A standard used by government agencies to measure the quality or effectiveness of a municipal service, such as police, fire, or library, or the performance of a facility, such as a street or highway. (*California Planning Roundtable*)

■ **level of service standard (LOS), traffic** A scale that measures the amount of traffic that a roadway or intersection can accommodate, based on such factors as maneuverability, driver dissatisfaction, and delay. Level of Service A indicates a relatively free flow of traffic, with little or no limitation on vehicle movement or speed. Level of Service B describes a steady flow of traffic, with only slight delays in vehicle movement and speed. All queues clear in a single signal cycle. Level of Service C denotes a reasonably steady, high-volume flow of traffic, with some limitations on movement and speed, and occasional backups on critical approaches. Level of Service D designates the level where traffic nears an unstable flow. Intersections still function, but short queues develop and cars may have to wait through one cycle during short peaks. Level of Service E represents traffic characterized by slow movement and frequent (although momentary) stoppages. This type of congestion is considered severe, but is not uncommon at peak traffic hours, with frequent stopping, longstanding queues, and blocked intersections. Level of Service F describes unsatisfactory stop-and-go traffic characterized by "traffic jams" and stoppages of long duration. Vehicles at signalized intersections usually have to wait through one or more signal changes, and "upstream" intersections may be blocked by the long queues. (*California Planning Roundtable*)

A quantitative measure of traffic congestion identified by a declining letter scale (A-F) as calculated by the methodology contained in the 1985 Highway Capacity Manual Special Report 209 or as calculated by another method approved by the department of public works. Level of Service (LOS) indicates free flow of traffic with no delays, while LOS indicates jammed conditions or extensive delay. (*King County, Wash.*)

■ **library**   A public facility for the use, but not sale, of literary, musical, artistic, or reference materials. *(Redmond, Wash.)*

■ **license**   Any form of written permission given to any person, organization, or agency to engage in any activity, as required by law or agency rule. A license includes all or part of an agency permit, certificate, approval, registration, charter, or plat approvals or re-zones to facilitate a particular proposal. The term does not include a license required solely for revenue purposes. *(Renton, Wash.)*

■ **light rail transit (LRT)**   *(See transit, light rail)*

■ **light source**   A single artificial point source of luminescence that emits measurable radiant energy in or near the visible spectrum. *(Myrtle Beach, S.C.)*

■ **light source, flashing illumination**   A light source or other image which in whole or in part physically changes in light intensity or gives the appearance of such change. *(Tulsa, Okla.)*

■ **lighting**   *(See candela; lumen; luminaire)*

■ **lighting, artificial**   Any fixed source of light emanating from a manmade device, including but not limited to, incandescent mercury vapor, metal halide, or sodium lamps, spotlights, street lights, construction or security lights. *(Indian River County, Fla., which uses the term "artificial light")*

■ **lighting, neon outline**   Outline lighting formed in whole or part with neon. *(Columbus, Ohio)*

■ **lighting, outline**   An arrangement of incandescent lamps or electric discharge tubing that outlines or calls attention to certain features of a building, such as its shape or the decoration of a window. *(Columbus, Ohio)*

■ **lighting, pedestrian-scale**   Light standards or placements no greater than 14 feet in height located along walkways. *(Ashland, Ore.)*

■ **limousine**   Any motor vehicle, other than a taxi, offered to the public by a public limousine business for the purpose of carrying or transporting passengers for a fixed charge or fee, or an hourly rate. *(Columbus, Mo.)*

■ **limousine service**   The business of offering the public motor vehicles for carrying or transportation of passengers between airports and points within the city for a fixed charge or fee, or offering a vehicle with driver for a fixed charge or fee, or offering a vehicle with driver for transportation of passengers at an hourly rate. *(Columbus, Mo.)*

■ **line of sight**   A visual path emanating from an average eye level adjudged to be five feet above the ground level. *(Palm Desert, Calif.)*

■ **linkage**   *(See also jobs/housing balance)* With respect to jobs/housing balance, a program designed to offset the impact of employment on housing need within a community, whereby project approval is conditioned on the provision of housing units or the payment of an equivalent in-lieu fee. The linkage program must establish the cause-and-effect relationship between a new commercial or industrial development and the increased demand for housing. *(California Planning Roundtable)*

■ **linkage fee**   The requirement by local governments that developers provide low- and moderate-income housing, day care or social activity centers, or funds to provide such housing or services, in relation to the demand created by their development. *(New Jersey State Plan)*

■ **liquor**   Spirituous or intoxicating liquor, including wine and beer. *(Santa Clara County, Calif.)*

■ **litter**   *(See also garbage; rubbish)*   All garbage, rubbish, garden trash, and all waste materials, including, but not limited to, bottles, glass, cans, scrap metal, junk, paper, disposable packages or containers and all other similar materials, and any substance of any kind or nature whatsoever that creates a public health, safety or fire hazard or a public nuisance. *(Indian River County, Fla.)*

■ **live entertainment**   *(See also amusement definitions; entertainment definitions)*   Any musical act (including karaoke), theatrical act (including stand-up comedy), play, revue, scene, dance act, or song and dance act, or any combination thereof, performed by one or more persons, whether or not they are compensated for the performance, in a privately owned premises that is open to the public, whether or not admission is charged. *(Thousand Oaks, Calif.)*

■ **live-work quarters**   *(See also loft)* Buildings or spaces within buildings that are used jointly for commercial and residential purposes (pictured below) where the residential use of the space is secondary or accessory to the primary use as a place of work. *(California Planning Roundtable)*

A structure or portion of a structure combining a residential living space for a group of persons including not more than four adults with an integrated work space principally used by one or more of the residents. *(San Francisco, Calif.)*

■ **livestock**   *(See also animal definitions)* Generally accepted outdoor farm animals (i.e., cows, goats, horses, pigs, barnyard fowl, etc.) not to include cats, dogs, and other house pets. *(Valdez, Alaska)*

(1) All cattle or animals of the bovine species; (2) all horses, mules, burros and asses or animals of the equine species; (3) all goats or animals of the caprine species; (4) all swine or animals of the

porcine species; and (5) all sheep or animals of the ovine species. *(Washoe County, Nev.)*

Grazing animals kept either in open fields or structures for training, boarding, home use, sales, or breeding and production, including but not limited to: cattle; riding and draft horses; hogs, excluding pigs weighing under 120 pounds and standing 20 inches or less at the shoulder which are kept as pets or small animals; sheep; and goats. *(King County, Wash.)*

■ **livestock, large**   Livestock 250 pounds and over, and older than 12 months. *(Valdez, Alaska)*

Cattle, horses, and other livestock generally weighing over 500 pounds. *(King County, Wash.)*

■ **livestock market**   A commercial establishment wherein livestock is collected for sale or auctioning. *(Cecil Co., Md.)*

■ **livestock, small**   Livestock under 250 pounds and older than six months. *(Valdez, Alaska)*

Hogs, excluding pigs weighing under 120 pounds and standing 20 inches or less at the shoulder which are kept as household pets or small animals, sheep, goats, miniature horses, llamas, alpaca, and other livestock generally weighing under 500 pounds. *(King County, Wash.)*

■ **living quarters** *(See also **dwelling** and **dwelling unit** definitions)*   One or more rooms in a building designed for occupancy by one or more persons for living or sleeping quarters. *(Maui County, Hawaii)*

■ **loading berth**   A space within a building or on the premises providing for the standing, loading or unloading, and together with apron space for maneuvering of vehicles, trucks and semi-tractor trailers. *(El Paso, Tex.)*

■ **loading space**   An off-street space on the same lot with a building or group of buildings for temporary parking of a commercial vehicle while loading and unloading merchandise or materials. *(Homestead, Fla.)*

■ **local agency**   Any political subdivision, regional governmental unit, district, municipal or public corporation, including cities, towns, and counties and their legislative bodies. The term encompasses but does not refer specifically to the departments within a city or county. *(Renton, Wash.)*

■ **lodge**   A membership organization that holds regular meetings and that may, subject to other regulations controlling such uses, maintain dining facilities, serve alcohol, or engage professional entertainment for the enjoyment of dues paying members and their guests. There are no sleeping facilities. This definition shall not include fraternities or sororities. *(Champaign, Ill.)*

■ **lodging house** *(See also **boarding house; rooming house**)*   A building or place where lodging is provided (or which is equipped regularly to provide lodging by prearrangement for definite periods), for compensation, for three or more, but not exceeding 12 individuals, not open to transient guests, in contradistinction to hotels open to transients. *(Peoria, Ill.)*

■ **loft**   The floor placed between the roof and the floor of the uppermost story within a single-family detached dwelling, the floor area of which is not more than one-third of the floor area of the story or room in which it is placed. *(Kauai, Hawaii)*

■ **loft building**   Multistoried industrial building, often with higher ceilings and wider columns than a comparable office building (pictured above). They are popular structures for rehabilitation to residential activities. Other rehabilitation adaptations include art galleries, selling books, computer data centers, mail order centers, and general office space. *(APA's Land-Based Classification Standards project)*

A dwelling unit established in an existing nonresidential building. *(Cincinnati, Ohio, which uses the term "loft dwelling unit")*

■ **logging yard and landing**   Areas to which wood is hauled by skidder or other extraction equipment for temporary storage before transfer to trucks. *(Maine Forest Service)*

■ **long-term commercial significance**   The growing capacity, productivity, and soil composition of land that makes it suitable for long-term commercial production, in consideration with the land's proximity to population areas, and the possibility of more intense uses of land. *(Yakima County, Wash.)*

■ **lot**   A parcel of land occupied or intended for occupancy by a use permitted in this chapter, including one main building, together with any accessory buildings, open spaces, and parking spaces required by this chapter and having its principal frontage upon a street or upon an officially approved place. *(Perryville, Mo.)*

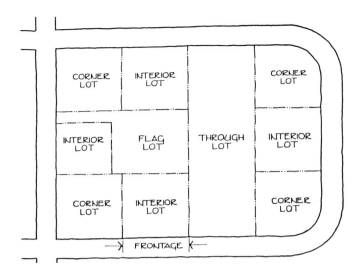

A parcel of land recorded in the Office of the Clerk of the Court, or a parcel described by metes and bounds, the description of which has been so recorded. *(Cecil Co., Md.)*

A contiguous parcel of land in identical ownership throughout, bounded by other lots or streets, and used or set aside and available for use as the site of one or more buildings or other definite purpose. For the purpose of this title, a lot may or may not coincide with a lot of record. *(Quincy, Mass.)*

■ **lot area**    The horizontal area within the exterior lines of the lot, exclusive of any area in a public or private way open to public uses. *(Quincy, Mass.)*

■ **lot averaging**    The design of individual adjoining lots within a residential subdivision in which the average lot equals the minimum prescribed area for the [zoning district]. To maintain an average, some lots may be reduced to a maximum of 10 percent below the minimum lot size, while a corresponding number of lots shall each maintain a lot area of at least 10 percent above the minimum lot size. Allowable density shall be within the prescribed maximums. *(San Bernadino, Calif.)*

■ **lot-by-lot development**    The conventional approach to development in which each lot is treated as a separate development unit conforming to all land-use, density, and bulk requirements. Usually, it is contrasted with cluster development or planned unit development. Lot-by-lot development, especially for larger tracts, has tended to

become discredited for straitjacketing design by producing "little boxes all in a row." *(PAS Report No. 322,* The Language of Zoning*)*

■ **lot, corner**    A lot located at the intersection of two or more streets. *(Blacksburg, Va.)*

(1) A lot located at the junction of two or more intersecting streets, having an interior angle of less than 135 degrees, with a boundary line thereof bordering on two of the streets; (2) The point of intersection of the street lot lines. *(Pima Co., Ariz.)*

■ **lot coverage**    A measure of intensity of land use that represents the portion of a site that is impervious (i.e. does not absorb water). This portion includes, but is not limited to, all areas covered by buildings, parked structures, driveways, roads, sidewalks, and any area of concrete asphalt. In the case of lumberyards, areas where lumber is stored also constitutes impervious surfaces. *(Washoe County, Nev.)*

■ **lot, deep**    A lot whose depth is excessive in relation to its frontage. *(PAS Report No. 322,* The Language of Zoning*)*

■ **lot depth**    The mean (average) horizontal distance between the front and the rear lot lines. *(Perryville, Mo.)*

The mean horizontal distance between the front and rear lot lines measured in the mean direction of the side lot lines. *(Quincy, Mass.)*

The horizontal distance for the midpoint of the front-lot line to the midpoint of the rear-lot line, or to the rear most point of the lot where there is no rear-lot line. *(Newport Beach, Calif.)*

■ **lot, double frontage**    A lot having frontage on two nonintersecting streets, as distinguished from a corner lot. *(Perryville, Mo.)*

An interior lot having frontage on more than one street or a corner lot having frontage on more than two streets. Each street frontage of an interior lot and the two shortest street frontages of a corner lot shall be deemed a front lot line. *(Newport Beach, Calif.)*

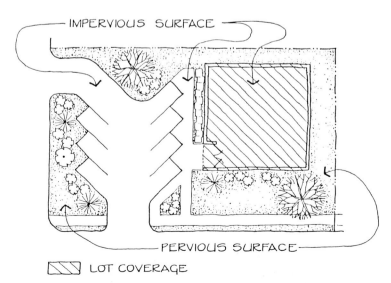

A lot abutting on two streets at their juncture, when the interior angle formed is less than 135 degrees. *(Lake County, Ill.)*

■ **lot, flag**    A lot not fronting or abutting a public roadway and where access to the public roadway is limited to a narrow private right-of-way. *(Schaumburg, Ill.)*

■ **lot front**    The side of a lot that abuts a public street is the front of the lot. For corner lots, the shortest side fronting upon a street shall be considered the front of the lot. Where buildings exist on the lot, the frontage may be established by the orientation of the buildings, or of the principal entrance, if building orientation does not clearly indicate lot frontage. Where no other method determines conclusively the front of a lot, the administrator shall select one frontage on the basis of traffic flow on adjacent streets, so that the lot is considered to front on the street with the greatest traffic flow. *(Blacksburg, Va.)*

■ **lot frontage**    That part of a lot (a lot line) abutting on a street or way; except that the ends of incomplete streets, or streets without a turning circle, shall not be considered frontage. *(Quincy, Mass.)*

The horizontal distance between the side lot lines measured at the point where the side lot lines intersect the street right-of-way. All sides of a lot that abuts a street shall be considered frontage. On curvilinear streets, the arc between the side lot lines shall be considered the lot frontage. *(Blacksburg, Va.)*

■ **lot improvement**    a building, structure, place, work of art, or other object, or improvment of the land on which they are situated constituting a physical betterment of real property, or any part of such betterment. *(Buffalo, Minn.)*

■ **lot, interior**    A lot other than a corner lot. *(Blacksburg, Va.)*

A lot other than a corner or reversed corner lot. *(Cecil Co., Md.)*

■ **lot, irregular**    A lot of such a shape or configuration that technically meets the area, frontage and width to depth requirements of this ordinance but meets these requirements by incorporating un-

usual elongations, angles, curvilinear lines unrelated to topography or other natural land features. *(Blacksburg, Va.)*

■ **lot, key**    A lot with a side lot line that abuts the rear lot line of one or more adjoining lots. *(Newport Beach, Calif.)*

A lot: (1) abutting along the entire length of at least one of its side lot lines, either directly or across an alley, the rear lot line of any other lot; or (2) situated between two such key lots. *(Pima Co., Ariz.)*

The first interior lot to the rear of a reversed corner lot. *(Sacramento, Calif.)*

■ **lot line**    Any line bounding a lot as herein defined. Lot lines for unusual lot configurations may be determined by the planning director. *(Clark County, Wash.)*

The property lines bounding the lot. *(Cecil Co., Md.)*

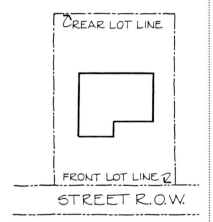

■ **lot line adjustment**    A lot line adjustment is the adjusting of common property line(s) or boundaries between adjacent lots, tracts, or parcels for the purpose of accommodating a transfer of land, rectifying a disputed property line location, or freeing such a boundary from any difference or discrepancies. The resulting adjustment shall not create any additional lots, tracts, or parcels, and all reconfigured lots, tracts, or parcels shall contain sufficient area and dimension to meet minimum requirements for zoning and building purposes. *(Renton, Wash.)*

■ **lot line, front**    In the case of an interior lot, a line separating the lot from a

street or place; and in the case of a corner lot, a line separating the narrowest frontage of the lot from street. *(Perryville, Mo.)*

A line connecting the foremost points of the side lot lines and dividing the lot from the access right-of-way. *(Cecil Co., Md.)*

■ **lot line, rear**    (1) The lot line that is opposite and most distant from the front lot line; (2) The rear lot line of an irregular, triangular, or gore lot shall, for the purpose of this code, be a line entirely within the lot at least 10 feet long and parallel to and most distant from the front lot line. *(Pima Co., Ariz.)*

A line connecting the rearmost points of the side lot line. *(Cecil Co., Md.)*

■ **lot line, side**    (1) Any lot line not a front lot line or a rear lot line; (2) A side lot separating a lot from a street is a street lot line; (3) A side lot line separating a lot from another lot is an interior side lot line. *(Pima Co., Ariz.)*

Any boundary of a lot that is not a front lot line nor a rear lot line. *(Cecil Co., Md.)*

Any boundary of a lot that is not a front lot line, a street lot line, a shore lot line, or a rear lot line. *(Delafield, Wisc.)*

■ **lot, nonconforming**    A lot lawfully existing at the effective date of this chapter, or any subsequent amendment thereto, which is not in conformity with all provisions of this chapter. Notwithstanding the minimum lot area requirements, in any district in which structures are permitted, a structure may be erected on a lot which was a lot of record, even though such lot fails to meet the present requirements for frontage or area, or both, that are applicable for that use in the district allowed; provided, however, that such lot is not contiguous with another lot or lots in the same ownership, provided that the property is either on town sewer or the property owner obtains a state and/or municipal septic permit, and further provided that the zone's minimum front, side and back yard setbacks are satisfied. *(Hudson, N.H.)*

A lot that lawfully existed prior to the enactment of the requirements of this chapter, but which does not meet the minimum lot size or lot width requirements of the zoning district in which it is located. *(Champaign, Ill.)*

A lot or parcel of land that was of record and lawfully established and maintained but which, because of the enactment of this [code], no longer conforms to the land-use standards or use regulations of the zone in which it is located. *(Island County, Wash.)*

■ **lot of record**    A lot that is part of a recorded subdivision or a parcel of land that has been recorded at the county recorder's office containing property tax records. *(California Planning Roundtable)*

A lot that is a part of a subdivision, the map or plat of which has been recorded in the office of the county recorder . . .; or a lot or parcel of land, the deed of which has been recorded in the office of the county recorder. . . . *(Perryville, Mo.)*

■ **lot of record, substandard**    Any lot lawfully existing at the time of adoption or amendment of this zoning code and not in conformance with the dimensional and/or area provisions of this zoning code. *(Newport, R.I.)*

■ **lot, panhandle**    A polygonal-shaped lot with the appearance of a frying pan or flag and staff in which the handle is most often used as the point of access. . . . The handle, when less than the minimum width for a building lot in the zoning district in which it is located, is not to be used in computing the minimum required lot area or delineating the minimum required building envelope. The width of the handle at any point must not be less than the minimum required frontage. *(Cecil Co., Md.)*

■ **lot, pipestem**    A "panhandle" or "flag"-shaped lot with its widest point set back from the road at the rear of another lot (called the pipe), and having a thin strip of land connecting to the road to provide legal access and frontage (called the stem). Pipestem lots are also referred to as panhandle lots or flag lots. *(Blacksburg, Va.)*

■ **lot, recorded**    A lot designed on a subdivision plat or deed, duly recorded pursuant to statute in the Recorder's Office. A recorded lot may or may not coincide with a zoning lot. *(Lake County, Ill.)*

■ **lot, reversed corner**    A corner lot, the side street line of which is substantially a continuation of the front lot line of the first lot to its rear. *(Redding, Calif.)*

A corner lot, the side street of which is substantially a continuation of the front lot line upon which the rear of said reverse corner lot abuts. *(Santa Clara County, Calif.)*

■ **lot, reversed frontage**    A key lot or the first lot to the rear of a corner lot, the front lot line of which is a continuation of the side lot line of the corner lot and fronting on the street that intersects the street upon which the corner lot fronts and/or that faces the street upon which the side of a corner lot abuts. *(Newport Beach, Calif.)*

■ **lot-size requirements**    Restrictions controlling the minimum area and minimum width of lots and the density of residential development in terms of dwelling units per acre. *(Wheeling, Ill.)*

■ **lot, through**    A lot having a pair of opposite lot lines along two more or less parallel public streets and which is not a corner lot. On a through lot, both street lines shall be deemed front lot lines. Unless circumstances specifically indicate the contrary, the front yard of a waterfront lot is the yard facing the waterway. A waterway for purpose of this definition is considered to be any body of water or wetland affected by tidal action. *(Cecil Co., Md.)*

■ **lot, undeveloped**    A platted lot or parcel of land upon which no structure exists. *(Renton, Wash.)*

■ **lot width**    The horizontal distance between side lines measured along a line that is parallel to the front lot line and located the minimum exterior setback distance from the front lot line. *(Blue Springs, Mo.)*

The horizontal distance between side lot lines measured at the required front setback *(Blacksburg, Va.)*

The horizontal distance between the side lot lines, measured at right angles to the lot depth at a point midway between the front and rear lot lines. *(Staunton, Va.)*

The distance between side lot lines. In an open space residential development, the distance between side lot lines shall be measured at the street lot line. In a conventional residential development and for nonresidential developments, the distance between side lot lines shall be measured parallel to, and at a distance equal to the required street yard from the street lot line. When a lot has more than one street lot line, the required lot width shall be measured along the narrowest street lot line. *(Lake County, Ill.)*

■ **lot, zipper**    A division of property using smaller lots with offset rear lot lines to allow a usable rear yard. *(Renton, Wash.)*

■ **lottery** *(See also **gambling**)*    Any scheme or procedure whereby one or more prizes are distributed by chance among persons who have paid or promised consideration for a chance to win such prizes, whether such scheme or procedure is called a lottery, raffle, gift, sale, or some other name. *(State of Illinois)*

■ **lounge** *(See **bar**)*

■ **lowest floor**    The lowest floor of the lowest enclosed area (including basement). An unfinished or flood-resistant enclosure, usable solely for parking of vehicles, building access, or storage in an area other than a basement area is not considered a building's lowest floor, provided that such enclosure is not built so as to render the structure in violation of the applicable nonelevation design requirements. . . . *(Pulaski, Tenn.)*

■ **LULU (locally unwanted land use)** A term that has been applied to projects that have historically generated intense local opposition to their siting. It is often used in referring to such land uses as prisons, hazardous waste facilities, landfills, power plants, and other uses perceived by the public as posing a health or safety risk. *(Volusia County, Fla.)*

■ **lumber yard**    An area used for the storage, distribution, and sale of finished or rough-cut lumber and lumber products, but not including the manufacture or fabrication of lumber, lumber products, or firewood. *(Siskiyou County, Calif.)*

An establishment where lumber and other building materials such as brick, tile, cement, insulation, roofing materials, and the like are sold at retail. The sale of items, such as heating and plumbing supplies, electrical supplies, paint, glass, hardware, and wallpaper is permitted at retail and deemed to be customarily incidental to the sale of lumber and other building materials—retail. *(Hartford, Conn., which uses the term "lumber and other building material, retail")*

■ **lumen**    A unit of luminous flux. One footcandle is one lumen per square foot. For the purposes of these regulations, the lumen-output values shall be the initial lumen output ratings of a lamp. *(Ames, Iowa)*

A unit of measure of the quantity of light that falls on an area of one square foot every point of which is one foot from the source of one candela. A light source of one candela emits a total of 12.57 lumens. *(Eatontown, N.J.)*

A unit of luminous flux. One footcandle is one lumen per square foot. For the purposes of this ordinance, the lumen output values shall be the initial lumen output ratings of a lamp. *(Kennebunkport, Maine)*

■ **luminaire**    A complete lighting unit consisting of a light source and all necessary mechanical, electrical, and decorative parts. *(Champaign, Ill.)*

A complete lighting unit consisting of one or more lamps, together with the components designed to distribute the light, to position and protect the lamps, and to connect the lamps to the electrical power supply; also called the lighting fixture. *(Juneau, Alaska)*

■ **luminaire, cutoff-type**    A luminaire with elements such as shields, reflectors, or refractor angles that direct and cut off the light at a cutoff angle less than 90 degrees. *(Lake County, Ill.)*

■ **main building** (See *building, principal*)

■ **main street**   A neighborhood shopping area . . . sometimes having a unique character that draws people from outside the area. *(Portland, Ore.)*

■ **maintained**   Preserved in a condition or state of equivalent quality to that which was approved or required by the city. Unless the context demands otherwise, the term is synonymous and is interchangeable with the term "permanently maintained." *(Santa Clara County, Calif.)*

■ **maintenance**   In reference to a graphic, cleaning, painting, repair, or replacement of defective parts in a manner that does not alter the basic copy, design, or structure. *(Columbus, Ohio)*

■ **maintenance guarantee** (See also *performance guarantee*)   A guarantee of facilities or work to ensure the correction of any failures of any improvements required pursuant to this ordinance and regulation, or to maintain same. *(Easton, Md.)*

■ **mall** (See also *pedestrian mall; shopping mall*)   (1) A shaded walk or public promenade; (2) A shopping center where stores front on both sides of a pedestrian way that may be enclosed or open. *(Iowa State University Extension Service)*

■ **mansard**   An extension of an exterior wall or roof projection of a building that is architecturally integrated into the building design. *(Clearwater, Fla.)*

■ **manufactured housing** (See also *factory-built housing; mobile home; panelized housing*)   Single-family detached housing that is built to the National Manufactured Housing Construction and Safety Standards Act of 1974. . . . *(Aurora, Colo.)*

A factory-built, single-family structure that is manufactured under the authority of 42 U.S.C. Sec. 5401, the National Manufactured Home Construction and Safety Standards Act, is transportable in one or more sections, is built on a permanent chassis, and is used as a place of human habitation; but which is not constructed with a permanent hitch or other device allowing transport of the unit other than for the purpose of delivery to a permanent site, and which does not have wheels or axles permanently attached to its body or frame. *(Cedar Rapids, Iowa)*

*Commentary: Manufactured housing is a generic term that describes housing that is manufactured in a factory rather than on site. As defined above, manufactured housing includes all housing built to the "HUD Code," which is cited in the definitions. Some zoning codes still refer to manufactured housing that is built to the HUD Code as a mobile home. However, manufactured housing is the correct term.*

■ **manufacturing**   The mechanical or chemical transformation of materials or substances into new products, including the assembling of component parts, the manufacturing of products, and the blending of materials, such as lubricating oils, plastics, resins, or liquors. *(Siskiyou County, Calif.)*

■ **manufacturing, custom**   Establishments primarily engaged in the on-site production of goods by hand manufacturing, within enclosed structures, involving the use of hand tools, or the use of mechanical equipment commonly associated with residential or commercial uses, or a single kiln. *(Blacksburg, Va.)*

■ **manufacturing, heavy**   The manufacture or compounding process of raw materials. These activities or processes would necessitate the storage of large volumes of highly flammable, toxic matter or explosive materials needed for the manufacturing process. These activities may involve outdoor operations as part of their manufacturing process. *(Nashville and Davidson County, Tenn.)*

■ **manufacturing, light**   The manufacture, predominantly from previously prepared materials, of finished products or parts, including processing, fabrication, assembly, treatment and packaging of such products, and incidental storage, sales, and distribution of such products, but excluding basic industrial processing and custom manufacturing. *(Nashville and Davidson County, Tenn.)*

■ **manufacturing, medium**   The processing and manufacturing of materials or products predominately from extracted or raw materials. These activities do not necessitate the storage of large volumes of highly flammable, toxic matter or explosive materials needed for the manufacturing process. *(Nashville and Davidson County, Tenn.)*

■ **manufacturing, primary**   Establishments engaged in the initial processing or treatment of raw material or manufacturing of products that require additional processing, fabrication, or assembly for ultimate use by the consumer. *(Jefferson County, Colo.)*

■ **manufacturing, secondary**   Establishments engaged in the manufacture of products for final use or consumption. This usually involves the secondary processing, fabrication, or assembly of semifinished products from a primary manufacturing industry. *(Jefferson County, Colo.)*

■ **map** (See *base map; concurrency determination network map; flood boundary floodway (FBFW) map; Flood Insurance*

*Rate Map (FIRM); official map; preliminary subdivision map; subdivision map; topographic map; zoning map)*

■ **marina**　A dock or basin where slips, moorings and often supplies, repairs, and other services are available for craft. *(Quincy, Mass.)*

Any facility for the mooring, berthing, storing, or securing of watercraft (pictured at right), but not including community piers and other non-commercial boat docking and storage facilities. A marina may include boat sales, boat fuel sales, boat construction, boat repair, marine equipment sales, or promotional events, boat and jet ski rental, and other uses clearly incidental to watercraft activities. *(Cecil Co., Md.)*

An establishment providing docking, moorage space, and related activities limited to the provisioning or minor repair of pleasure boats and yachts, and accessory facilities including, but not limited to showers, toilets, and self-service laundries. *(King County, Wash.)*

■ **marina, commercial**　A facility for secure mooring of boats, including facilities for storage and repair of boats and sale of boating supplies and fuel, for use by the owner or resident of the lot, and those other than the owner or resident of the lot, upon which the facility is located. *(Virginia Beach, Va.)*

■ **marina facilities** *(See also **port and harbor facilities**)*　A use of land involved in the operation of a marina including structures and activities normally integral to the operation of a marina, such as servicing, fueling, pumping-out, chartering, launching, and dry-storage of boats and boating equipment. *(Clearwater, Fla.)*

■ **marine service station**　A marine retail sales and service use in which fuel for boats is sold, and where accessory uses including but not limited to towing or minor vessel repair may also be provided. *(Seattle, Wash.)*

■ **maritime activities**　Activities required for, supportive of, or commonly associated with the construction, repair, operation, storage, loading, and unload-

ing of boats, waterfront dock and port facilities, marinas, navigation aids, boat fuel and equipment supply, ground-level parking incidental to such uses, and other activities the primary purpose of which is to facilitate maritime trade. *(Portland, Maine)*

■ **market value** *(See **fair market value**)*

■ **marquee** *(See **sign, marquee**)*

■ **marsh** *(See also **wetland** definitions)* Any area designated as marsh or swamp on the largest-scale United States Geologic Survey topographic map most recently published. A marsh usually is an area periodically or permanently covered with shallow water, either fresh or saline. *(California Planning Roundtable)*

■ **mass transit** *(See **transit, public**)*

■ **massage establishment** *(See also **adult use, massage establishment; health spa**)* Any building, room, place, or establishment other than a regularly licensed and established hospital or dispensary where non-medical or non-surgical manipulative exercises or devices are practiced upon the human body manually or otherwise by any person other than a licensed physician, surgeon, dentist, occupational or physical therapist, chiropractor or osteopath with or without the use of therapeutic, electrical, mechanical, or bathing devices. Shall also include any bathing establishment. *(Gurnee, Ill.)*

Any establishment having a fixed place of business where any person, firm, association, or corporation engages in or carries on or permitted to be engaged in or carried on the activity of massage, defined as any method of pressure on or

friction against or stroking, kneading, rubbing, tapping, pounding, vibrating, or stimulating of the external soft parts of the body with the hands of with the aid of any mechanical or electrical apparatus or appliance with or without such supplementary aids as rubbing alcohol, liniments, antiseptics, oils, powders, creams, lotions, ointments, or other similar preparations commonly used in this practice by a certified massage therapist. *(Schaumburg, Ill.)*

■ **master plan** *(See also **comprehensive plan; general plan**)*　A comprehensive long-range plan intended to guide growth and development of a community or region and one that includes analysis, recommendation, and proposals for the community's population economy, housing, transportation, community facilities, and land use. *(Iowa State University Extension Service)*

A land-use plan focused on one or more sites within an area that identifies site access and general improvements and is intended to guide growth and development over a number of years, or in several phases. *(Renton, Wash.)*

A comprehensive long-range plan intended to guide the growth and development of the community or region, and one that includes analysis, recommendations and proposals for the community's population, economy, housing, transportation, community facilities, and land use. The term master plan shall include the terms comprehensive plan and land-use plan. *(Sheridan, Wyo.)*

■ **master site plan**　A conceptual site plan indicating the physical and functional interrelationships between uses and facilities on a site for those projects, series of projects, phased developments or developments occurring over a period of five years or longer, or which are such a size and complexity or duration as to make independent site plan review burdensome, difficult, or inclined to lead to segmented and inconsistent conditions and approvals. Examples include public and private developments with a number of unconnected buildings on the same site as well as development where buildings may be occurring on geographically separated parcels within the city. *(Renton, Wash.)*

■ **mausoleum** *(See also cemetery; crematorium; columbarium)*  A building containing above-ground tombs. *(Southaven, Miss.)*

■ **maximum allowable density** *(See density, maximum allowable)*

■ **median**  An area in the approximate center of a city street or state highway that is used to separate the directional flow of traffic, may contain left-turn lanes, and is demarcated by curb and guttering, having painted or thermally applied stripes or other means of distinguishing it from the portion of the roadway used for through traffic. *(Thornton, Colo.)*

■ **median, nonrestrictive**  A painted centerline that does not provide a physical barrier between center traffic turning lanes or traffic lanes traveling in opposite directions. This includes roadways with continuous center turn lanes and undivided roads. *(Orlando, Fla.)*

■ **median, restrictive**  The portion of a divided roadway or divided driveway separating vehicular traffic traveling in opposite directions. Restrictive medians include physical barriers that prohibit movement of traffic across the median, such as a concrete barrier, a raised concrete curb and/or island, and a grassed or swaled median. *(Orlando, Fla.)*

■ **medical support facilities**  Uses and facilities such as, but not limited to: on-site medical waste storage and disposal; warehousing and storage of medical related equipment and supplies; garages;

and other facilities commonly associated with medical institutions. *(Renton, Wash.)*

■ **medical waste**  A facility used to store and/or repackage medical waste for transportation to a processing facility. *(Nashville and Davidson County, Tenn.)*

Any solid waste that is generated in the diagnosis, treatment, or immunization of human beings or animals, in research pertaining thereto, or in the production or testing of biologicals, but does not include any hazardous waste, radioactive waste, or those substances excluded from the definition of solid waste. *(Alamance County, N.C.)*

■ **meeting hall** *(See also assembly hall; auditorium)*  A building designed for public assembly, containing at least one room having an area equivalent for four square feet per dwelling unit or 2,400 gross square feet, whichever is greater. *(Monroe County, Fla.)*

■ **megachurch** *(See also religious institution)*  A large, specialized type of house of worship that includes such nontraditional accessory uses as retail sales, residential uses, amusement parks, and sports and entertainment facilities, as an integrated part of the development. *(Easton, Md.)*

■ **megaplex theater** *(See movie theater, megaplex)*

■ **mental health facility** *(See also hospital; sanitarium)*  A facility or institution for diagnosing, treating, caring for, or counseling people requiring mental health services in confinement. *(Palmer, Alaska)*

■ **messenger service office**  A place wherein communications or other items are taken for eventual delivery to another place, or have been already delivered from another place to be received at said place, but in no event does said definition include a place where wagers or bets are placed for delivery to other places or where receipts from wagers or bets have been delivered from other places. *(Wheeling, Ill.)*

■ **metes and bounds**  A series of lines around the perimeter of an area: "metes"

means bearing and distances and "bounds" refers to monuments both physical and legal. *(Jefferson County, Colo.)*

A description of land prepared by a state-registered land surveyor providing measured distances and courses from known or established points on the surface of the earth. *(Cecil Co., Md.)*

A system of describing and identifying land by measures (metes) and direction (bounds) from an identifiable point of reference such as a monument or other marker, the corner of intersecting streets, or, in rural areas, a tree or other permanent feature. It is the most precise of the three most common forms of urban land description (the others are by street number of house and by blocks and lots in tract subdivision). *(Handbook for Planning Commissioners in Missouri)*

■ **metropolitan**  Of, relating to, or characteristic of a large important city. *(California Planning Roundtable)*

■ **metropolitan planning organization (MPO)**  A local governmental unit that has legal jurisdiction over a geographic area for government service planning such as transportation and land-use planning. *(United States Census Bureau)*

■ **metropolitan statistical area (MSA)**  A county with a central city or adjoining central cities totaling 50,000 or more in population, and the surrounding suburbs or counties that are strongly linked economically and socially. The Bureau of the Census established the definition, which is more complex than the above. *(Handbook for Planning Commissioners in Missouri)*

A geographic entity . . . based on the concept of a core area with a large population nucleus, plus adjacent communities having a high degree of economic and social integration with that core. Qualification of an MSA requires the presence of a city with 50,000 or more inhabitants, or the presence of an urbanized area and a total population of at least 100,000 (75,000 in New England). *(United States Census Bureau)*

■ **mezzanine**  An intermediate floor placed in any story or room. When the total area of any such mezzanine floor exceeds 33.3 percent of the total floor area in the room or story in which the mezzanine floor occurs, it shall be considered as constituting an additional story. The clear height above or below a mezzanine floor construction shall be not less than seven feet. (*Coral Gables, Fla.*)

An intermediate or fractional story between the floor and ceiling of a main story, used for a purpose accessory to the principal use. A mezzanine is usually just above the ground or main floor and extending over only part of the main floor. The floor area of a mezzanine is included in calculating the floor area ratio of a structure. (*Gurnee, Ill.*)

■ **microbrewery** (*See also **brew pub***)   A facility for the production and packaging of malt beverages of low alcoholic content for distribution, retail, or wholesale, on or off premise, with a capacity of not more than 15,000 barrels per year. The development may include other uses such as a standard restaurant, bar or live entertainment as otherwise permitted in the zoning district. (*Kalamazoo, Mich.*)

A facility at which beer, fermented on the premises, is bottled and sold. The volume of production of such facility may not exceed 200 gallons a day. (*Dona Ana County, N. Mex.*)

■ **microclimate**   The climate of a small, distinct area, such as a city street or a building's courtyard; can be favorably altered through functional landscaping, architecture, or other design features.   (*California Planning Roundtable*)

■ **migrant agricultural labor housing** (*See **housing, temporary employment***)

■ **mill-type factory structures** (*See also **loft bulding***)   Older multistory factories, common in many older industrial areas, and supported by large wood beams and columns. These are popular structures for rehabilitation to activities that are not industrial (art galleries, book selling, computer data centers, mail order centers, etc.). (*APA's Land-Based Classification Standards project*)

■ **mineral extraction** (*See also **mining definitions***)   The extraction of metallic and nonmetallic minerals or materials, including rock crushing, screening, and the accessory storage of explosives. (*Nashville and Davidson County, Tenn.*)

The excavation or extraction of any earth products of natural mineral deposit, except where such excavation is for purposes of grading for a building lot or roadway, where grass sod is removed to be used for landscaping, or where materials are excavated from a lot for use on that same lot by the owner of the property. (*Cecil County, Md.*)

■ **mineral resource**   Land on which known deposits of commercially viable mineral or aggregate deposits exist. This designation is applied to sites determined by the State Division of Mines and Geology as being a resource of regional significance, and is intended to help maintain the quarrying operations and protect them from encroachment of incompatible land uses. (*California Planning Roundtable*)

Rock, sand, gravel, clay, oil, gas, minerals, or similar non-renewable substances occurring in their natural state on or below the surface of the earth, the utilization of which requires some form of excavation. (*Cecil County, Md.*)

■ **minerals**   Gravel, sand, and metallic and nonmetallic substances of commercial value. (*Yakima County, Wash.*)

■ **miniature golf course** (*See **golf course, miniature***)

■ **mini-lot development**   A comprehensively designed development containing lots that do not meet the minimum size or other requirements applying to individual lots in the zone where it is located. (*Oakland, Calif.*)

■ **mini-mall** (*See **shopping center, mini-mall***)

■ **minimart** (*See **convenience store; gas station minimart***)

■ **mining** (*See also **extractive industry; mineral extraction***)   All or any part of the process involved in the mining of minerals by removing overburden and mining directly from the mineral de-

posits, open pit mining or minerals naturally exposed, mining by auger method, dredging and quarrying, underground mining and surface work incidental to an underground mine. (*Shasta Lake, Calif.*)

The development or extraction of a mineral from its natural occurrences on affected land. (*Jefferson County, Colo.*)

■ **mining, accessory use**   Uses customarily incidental, appropriate, and subordinate to mining located on the same site, such as stockpiling, sorting, screening, washing, crushing, batching, recycling of concrete, asphalt, and related construction materials, maintenance facilities, and contractors' service and storage yards, and concrete products manufacturing that make use of the products produced from the subject mining site. (*Ventura County, Calif.*)

■ **mining, open pit**   Strip mining, except that open pit mining is more often deeper with less horizontal area than strip mining. (*El Paso, Tex.*)

■ **mining, strip**   A type of open mining in which overburden is removed from the mineral to be mined. The mineral is then dug out directly by shovels, loaders, scrapers, or by other means. (*El Paso, Tex.*)

■ **mining, surface**   Processes for the commercial removal of minerals from the surface of the earth. (*Siskiyou County, Calif.*)

■ **mining waste**   Accumulations of waste material and overburden placed on the land surface, whether above or below water. (*Island County, Wash.*)

■ **minutes**   The chronological record of the proceedings of a public body. (*New York Planning Federation*)

■ **mission** (*See **homeless shelter***)

■ **mitigation**   For the purposes of administering . . . Sensitive Areas, mitigation includes: (1) avoiding the impact altogether by not taking a certain action or parts of actions; (2) minimizing impacts by limiting the degree or magnitude of the action and its implementation; (3) rectifying the impact by repairing, rehabilitating, or restoring the affected environment; (4) reducing or eliminating the impact over time by preservation and maintenance operations during the life of the action; (5) compensating for the impact by replacing or providing substitute resources or environments. While monitoring without additional actions is not considered mitigation for the purposes of these regulations, it may be part of a comprehensive mitigation program. *(Redmond, Wash.)*

Measures taken to eliminate or minimize damages from development activities, such as construction in wetlands or regulatory floodplain filling, by replacement of the resource or other means of compensation. *(Lake County, Ill.)*

■ **mitigation plan**   A strategy developed by the property owner, planning department staff, and the zoning board of appeals to eliminate as many nonconforming aspects of a nonconforming use as possible and to alleviate or mitigate any negative impacts of the use on surrounding properties. *(Champaign, Ill.)*

■ **mixed-use development**   A single building containing more than one type of land use or a single development of more than one building and use, where the different types of land uses are in close proximity, planned as a unified complementary whole, and functionally integrated to the use of shared vehicular and pedestrian access and parking areas. *(Jefferson County, Colo.)*

A tract of land or building or structure developed for two or more different uses such as, but not limited to, residential, office, manufacturing, retail, public, or entertainment. *(Schaumburg, Ill.)*

■ **mobile home** *(See also manufactured housing)*   A transportable structure suitable for year-round single-family occupancy and having water, electrical, sewage connections similar to those of conventional dwellings. This definition applies only to units constructed prior to June 15, 1976. Compare with manufactured home. *(Pima Co., Ariz.)*

■ **mobile home park**   A parcel of land under one ownership that has been planned and improved for the placement of two or more mobile homes for rental

purposes for nontransient use. *(Monterey County, Calif.)*

■ **model studio**   A business establishment wherein the patrons may view, paint, draw, or photograph a live model who is unclothed or partly clothes. *(Imperial Beach, Calif.)*

■ **modernization**   The replacement and upgrading of existing facilities that increases the productive input or output, updates the technology, or substantially lowers the unit cost of the operation. Modernization may result from the construction, alteration, or installation of buildings, structures, or fixed machinery or equipment. It shall not be for the purpose of reconditioning, refurbishing, or repairing to meet local, state, or federal regulations. *(Houston, Tex.)*

■ **modular housing** *(See also factory-built housing; manufactured housing; panelized housing)*   A dwelling unit constructed on-site in accordance with the [state or municipal] code and composed of components substantially assembled in a manufacturing plant and transported to the building site for final assembly on a permanent foundation. *(Blacksburg, Va.)*

■ **modulation**   A measured setback or offset. *(Renton, Wash.)*

■ **moorage, commercial**   A marine retail sales and service use in which a system of piers, buoys, or floats is used to provide moorage, primarily for commercial vessels, except barges, for sale or rent, usually on a monthly or yearly basis. Minor vessel repair, haul-out, dry boat storage, tugboat dispatch offices, and other services are also often accessory to or associated with the use. *(Seattle, Wash.)*

■ **moorage, covered**   A pier or system of floating or fixed accessways covered with a roof, to which boats on water may be secured. *(Seattle, Wash.)*

■ **moorage, dry** *(See also boat yard)*   A marine retail sales and service use, in which space on a lot on dry land or inside a building over-water or on dry land, is rented or sold to the public or to members of a yacht, boat, or beach club for the purpose of storing boats. *(Seattle,*

*Wash., which uses the term "dry storage of boats")*

■ **moorage, open**   An uncovered pier or system of floating or fixed accessways to which boats on water may be secured. *(Seattle, Wash.)*

■ **moorage, transient**   Moorage available to the public, generally for a fee, on a short-term basis. Transient moorage may be available on an hourly, daily, or weekly basis. *(Seattle, Wash.)*

■ **moorage walkway**   The pier, float(s), or combination of pier and float(s) designed and used to give pedestrian access from the land to floating home sites at a floating home moorage. Ramps that provide access to individual floating homes are not moorage walkways. *(Seattle, Wash.)*

■ **moratorium** *(See also interim zone or interim development controls)*   A temporary halting or severe restriction on specified development activities. *(PAS Report No. 322, The Language of Zoning)*

A freeze on all new development pending the completion, adoption, or revision of a comprehensive plan. *(Handbook for Planning Commissioners in Missouri)*

■ **mortuary** *(See also funeral chapel; funeral home)*   An establishment providing services such as preparing the human dead for burial and arranging and managing funerals, and may include limited caretaker facilities. This classification excludes cemeteries, crematoriums, and columbariums. *(Redondo Beach, Calif.)*

A place for the storage of human bodies prior to their burial or cremation. *(Siskiyou County, Calif.)*

A facility in which dead bodies are prepared for burial or cremation and where funeral services may be conducted. *(Clark Co, Nev.)*

■ **mosque** *(See religious institution)*

■ **motel** *(See also extended-stay motel/hotel; hotel)*   A building (or group of buildings) containing living or sleeping accommodations used only for transient occupancy. *(Londonderry, N.H.)*

A building or group of buildings in which lodging is provided to transient guests, offered to the public for compensation, and in which access to and from each room or unit is through an exterior door. *(Cecil County, Md.)*

■ **motor vehicle** *(See also automobile and truck definitions)* Any self-propelled vehicle designed primarily for transportation of persons or goods along public streets or alleys, or other public ways. *(North Kansas City, Mo.)*

Every vehicle that is self-propelled. *(El Paso, Tex.)*

■ **motor vehicle, abandoned** A vehicle that does not bear a current license plate unless said vehicle is stored within a completely enclosed building or unless it is stored on a bona fide sales lot and is in a satisfactory operating condition. *(Conyers, Ga.)*

A vehicle shall be presumed abandoned under any of the following circumstances: 1) The vehicle is physically inoperable and/or is missing parts so that it is not maintained for driving, and 2) The vehicle does not bear any or all of the following: (a) A valid registration plate, or (b) A current certificate of inspection. Vehicles with a Commonwealth Certificate of Salvage and that are stored at a salvor or salvage program awaiting to be destroyed dismantled, salvaged, or recycled shall not be included in the definition. *(York, Pa.)*

Any vehicle as defined herein that has remained for a period of more than 48 hours on public property illegally or lacking vital component parts; or has remained for a period of more than 48 hours on private property without the consent of the person in control of such property; or is in an inoperable condition such that it has no substantial potential use consistent with its usual functions unless it is kept in an enclosed garage or storage building. It shall also mean a motor vehicle voluntarily surrendered by its owner to and accepted by the [city]. Any motor vehicle coming into possession of the [city] by seizure, confiscation or other means and such vehicle has remained unclaimed after notice

to the last registered owner hereinafter provided shall be deemed to have been abandoned *(Chaska, Minn.)*

■ **motor vehicle body shop** Any building or portion thereof used for the repair or straightening of a motor vehicle body or frame or painting of motor vehicles. Maintenance, service, and engine repair may be performed as an ancillary function of the body work. *(Schaumburg, Ill.)*

■ **motor vehicle, commercial** Any vehicle used or designed to be used for business or commercial purposes that infringes on the residential character of residential districts and includes, but is not necessarily limited to: a bus, cement truck, commercial tree-trimming equipment, construction equipment, dump truck, garbage truck, panel truck, semi-tractor, semi-trailer, stake bed truck, step van, tank truck, tar truck, or other commercial type vehicle licensed by the [state] as a commercial vehicle or truck. *(Columbus, Ohio)*

■ **motor vehicle, general repair and service** The business of repairing, overhauling, removing, adjusting, replacing, assembling, or disassembling parts of any motor vehicle. *(Hartford, Conn.)*

A building or establishment where the following activities may occur: general repair, engine rebuilding, reconditioning of motor vehicles, collision repair, painting, general maintenance, and where no more than two abandoned vehicles shall be stored on the premises. *(Cecil County, Md.)*

Any building or portion thereof used for the repair or replacement of engines, transmissions, differentials, drive trains, or any parts thereof, in addition to the replacement of parts, service, and incidental repairs to motor vehicles. *(Schaumburg, Ill.)*

■ **motor vehicle, inoperable** Any motorized vehicle incapable of immediately being driven and not properly licensed or inspected for safety in accordance with state law. *(Conyers, Ga.)*

■ **motor vehicle, junk** Any motor vehicle, trailer, or semitrailer that is inoperable and which, by virtue of its condi-

tion, cannot be economically restored to operable condition; provided, that such vehicle, trailer or semitrailer shall be presumed to be a junk vehicle if no license plates are displayed or if the license plates displayed have been invalid for more than 60 days. *(Thurston County, Wash.)*

■ **motor vehicle, large** Motor vehicles including, but not limited to, trucks, recreational vehicles, buses, boats, and heavy equipment, and similar size vehicles which have gross vehicle weights greater than 10,000 pounds, but excluding airplane or aircraft. *(Renton, Wash.)*

■ **motor vehicle, limited repair and service** The business of minor repairs to any motor vehicle, including repairs and replacement of cooling, electrical, fuel and exhaust systems, brake adjustments, relining and repairs, wheel alignment and balancing, and repair and replacement of shock absorbers. *(Hartford, Conn.)*

■ **motor vehicle-oriented business** Any commercial business which, by design, type of operation, or nature of business, has as one of its functions the provision of services to a number of motor vehicles or its occupants in a short time span, or the provision of services to the occupants of motor vehicles while they remain in a vehicle. Businesses included in this category shall have one or more of the following facilities: one or more pump islands for retail sale of gasoline; one or more drive-thru lanes/service windows for distribution of products or other transactions; or an automated car wash facility. *(Maryland Heights, Mo.)*

■ **motor vehicle repair services, major** Repair of construction equipment, commercial trucks, agricultural implements and similar heavy equipment, including automobiles, where major engine and transmission repairs are conducted. Typical uses include automobile and truck repair garages, transmission shops, radiator shops, body and fender shops, equipment service centers, machine shops, and other similar uses where major repair activities are conducted. *(Blacksburg, Va.)*

■ **motor vehicle, small**    Motor vehicles including, but not limited to, motorcycles, passenger cars, light trucks, vans, and similar size vehicles that have gross vehicle weights less than 10,000 pounds. *(Renton, Wash.)*

Any motor vehicle having an engine cubic centimeter displacement of less than 1,000, including but not limited to, riding lawn mowers, farm equipment, motorcycles, mini-bikes, all-terrain vehicles, and snowmobiles. *(Wheeling, Ill.)*

■ **motor vehicle, stored**    With reference to vehicles or vehicle parts, means allowed to remain in one place for more than 72 consecutive hours. *(Las Vegas, Nev.)*

■ **motorcade**    An organized procession containing 25 or more vehicles upon any public street, sidewalk, or alley. *(Escondido, Calif.)*

■ **motorcycle**    Every motor vehicle having a saddle for the use of the rider and designed to travel on not more than three wheels in contact with the ground, but excluding a tractor. *(El Paso, Tex.)*

■ **movie theater** *(See also **theater**)*    A specialized theater for showing movies or motion pictures. The primary structural difference between a theater and a movie theater is the projection screen. However, many movie theaters can easily be adapted for stage performances and many stages have folding screens for movie projections. Although screen shapes are mostly rectangular, they come in a variety of shapes. Also, some special-purpose multimedia movie theaters use multiple screens, one on each wall face, or the entire ceiling surface, which are sometimes curved or geodesic in shape. *(APA's Land-Based Classification Standards project)*

Consists of audience seating, one or more screens and auditoriums, and a lobby and refreshment stand. *(Redmond, Wash.)*

■ **movie theater, cineplex**    Complex structures with multiple movie theaters, each theater capable of providing performances independent of the others in the complex. Structurally, theaters in a cineplex are grouped in a manner that allows them to share box or ticket offices, parking facilities, lobby areas, restrooms, concession stands, signs and marquee displays, and other service and maintenance facilities. These structures first started appearing in shopping centers and malls, sometimes integrated with the layout of the mall. *(APA's Land-Based Classification Standards project)*

*Commentary: Historically, a cineplex meant a theater with two or more movie theaters. Popular configurations have 9 or 12 theaters. But as structures evolved to accommodate 20 or more theaters, the movie theater industry started using such terms as multiplex, megaplex, and megatheater to differentiate these newer configurations from the older cineplex layout. But there is no clear distinction between a cineplex and a megaplex. The distinction between a cineplex and a megaplex has been further blurred because developers sometimes retrofit cineplexes with more screens, often smaller, within the existing structure.*

■ **movie theater, drive-in**    An open lot or part thereof, with its appurtenant facilities, devoted primarily to the showing of moving pictures on a paid admission basis to patrons seated in automobiles. *(Clarksville, Tenn.)*

■ **movie theater, megaplex** *(See **movie theater, cineplex**)*

■ **multi-use complex** *(See also **mixed-use development**)*    A group of separate buildings operating under a common name or management; a single building containing multiple uses where there are specific exterior entrance ways for individual uses; or a group of uses on separate but adjoining properties that request treatment as a multi-use complex. *(Federal Way, Wash.)*

■ **multiple-family building** *(See also **dwelling, apartment**)*    A detached building designed and used exclusively as a dwelling by three or more families occupying separate suites. *(California Planning Roundtable)*

■ **municipal authority**    A special municipal corporation, usually organized to perform a single proprietary function, which exists as an organized entity. Assumes a governmental character, and enjoys substantial autonomy. For example, a municipal housing authority. *(Handbook for Planning Commissioners in Missouri)*

■ **municipal services**    Services traditionally provided by local government, including water and sewer, roads, parks, schools, and police and fire protection. *(California Planning Roundtable)*

■ **mural** *(See also **art, public**; **sign, painted wall**; **sign, wall**)*    A graphic displayed on the exterior of a building (pictured below), generally for the purposes of decoration or artistic expression, including, but not limited to, painting, fresco, or mosaic. *(Columbus, Ohio)*

Artwork applied to the wall of a building that covers all or substantially all of the wall and depicts a scene or event of natural, social, cultural, or historic significance. *(Clearwater, Fla.)*

■ **museum**    A building having public significance by reason of its architecture or former use or occupancy or a building serving as a repository for a collection of natural, scientific, or literary curiosities

or objects of interest, or works of art, and arranged, intended, and designed to be used by members of the public for viewing, with or without an admission charge, and which may include as an accessory use the sale of goods to the public as gifts or for their own use. *(Newport, R.I.)*

■ **museum, commercial** A commercial establishment for preserving and exhibiting artistic, historical, scientific, natural, or man-made objects of interest. Such activity may include the sale of the objects collected and memorabilia, the sale of crafts work and artwork, boutiques, and the holding of meetings and social events. *(Denver, Colo.)*

■ **National Register of Historic Places**
The listing maintained by the U.S. National Park Service of areas that have been designated as historically significant. The Register includes places of local and state significance, as well as those of value to the nation in general. *(Washoe County, Nev.)*

■ **native vegetation**   Any indigenous tree, plant, or shrub adapted to soil and climatic conditions occurring on site. *(Nashville and Davidson County, Tenn.)*

Plant communities that develop in the absence of human activities. *(Cecil County, Md.)*

Vegetation comprised of plant species, other than noxious weeds, that are indigenous to the coastal region of the Pacific Northwest and that reasonably could have been expected to naturally occur on the site. *(King County, Wash.)*

■ **natural condition**   That condition that arises from or is found in nature and not modified by human intervention; not to include artificial or manufactured conditions. *(Yakima County, Wash.)*

■ **natural drainage**   Channels formed in the existing surface topography of the earth prior to changes made by unnatural causes. *(Westchester County, N.Y.)*

■ **natural features**   Components and processes present or produced by nature (pictured below), including soil types, geology, slopes, vegetation, surface water, drainage patterns, aquifers, recharge areas, climate, floodplains, aquatic life, and wildlife. *(Anne Arundel County, Md.)*

Physical characteristics of the subject property that are not man made. *(Federal Way, Wash.)*

■ **natural resource area**   Following are considered natural resource areas: *Archaeological Resource*: Any significant evidence of human activity from prehistoric periods including, but not limited to, occupation sites and work areas, evidence of farming, hunting, gathering, burials, and other funeral remains and aboriginal artifacts and structures. This definition also includes, for the purpose of convenience, paleontological specimens and sites; *Historical Resource*: Sites, districts, structures or other evidence of human activities existing for more than 50 years that represent facets of history in the locality, state, or nation which have been officially included in the National or State Register of Historic Places or in the [county] inventory of historical sites; *Mineral Resource*: An area in which minerals are located in sufficient concentration in veins, deposits, bodies, beds, seams, fields, pools or otherwise,

John West

as to be capable of economic recovery. *(Jefferson County, Colo.)*

■ **naturalized species**   Non-native species of vegetation that are adaptable to the climatic conditions of the coastal region of the Pacific Northwest. *(King County, Wash.)*

■ **navigable waters**   Waterways used or susceptible of being used in their natural or ordinary condition as highways for commerce over which trade and travel are or may be conducted in customary modes of trade and travel on water. *(Riverhead, N.Y.)*

■ **neighborhood**   An area of a community with characteristics that distinguish it from other community areas and that may include schools, or social clubs, or boundaries defined by physical barriers, such as major highways and railroads, or natural features, such as rivers. *(Iowa State University Extension Service)*

A subarea of the city in which the residents share a common identity focused around a school, park, community business center, or other feature. *(Renton, Wash.)*

The smallest sub-area in planning, defined as a residential area whose residents have public facilities and social institutions in common, and generally within walking distance of their homes. *(Handbook for Planning Commissioners in Missouri)*

■ **neighborhood convenience store** *(See also convenience store)*   Establishments primarily engaged in the provision of frequently or recurrently needed goods for household consumption, such as prepackaged food and beverages and limited household supplies and hardware. Convenience stores shall not include fuel pumps or the selling of fuel for motor vehicles. Typical uses include neighborhood markets and country stores. *(Blacksburg, Va.)*

■ **neighborhood plan**   The master plan for a particular neighborhood or district that provides specific design standards and guidelines regulating the development and use of the property. *(Orlando, Fla.)*

■ **neighborhood unit** The neighborhood unit should be the basic building block of the city. It is based around the elementary school, with other community facilities located at its center and arterial streets at its perimeter. The distance from the school to the perimeter should be a comfortable walking distance for a school-age child; there would be no through traffic uses. Limited industrial or commercial would occur on the perimeter where arterials intersect. This was the model for American suburban development after World War II. *(California Planning Roundtable)*

■ **neotraditional development** An approach to land-use planning and urban design that promotes the building of neighborhoods with a mix of uses and housing types, architectural variety, a central public gathering place, interconnecting streets and alleys, and edges defined by greenbelts or boulevards. The basic goal is integration of the activities of potential residents with work, shopping, recreation, and transit all within walking distance. *(California Planning Roundtable)*

■ **new town** Moderately sized planned communities that offer residents an alternative to congestion and sprawl through a livable and pedestrian-friendly development pattern. A new town may contain community centers, housing, employment, retail, recreation, open space, and public facilities. Examples include Columbia, Maryland, and Reston, Virginia. *(APA Research Department)*

■ **New Urbanism** The process of reintegrating the components of modern life—housing, workplace, shopping and recreation—into compact, pedestrian-friendly, mixed-use neighborhoods linked by transit and set in a larger regional open space framework. Initially dubbed "neotraditional planning," the principles that define new urbanism can be applied successfully to infill and redevelopment sites within existing urbanized areas. *(Congress for the New Urbanism)*

■ **newcomer suite** A dwelling unit in an apartment complex that is available, when specifically authorized by the zoning board of adjustment as a special ex-

ception, for rent for periods as short as one week to persons newly arriving in the community for temporary use while they search for permanent housing. *(Tuscaloosa, Ala.)*

■ **newsrack** Any type of unmanned device for the vending or free distribution of news periodicals (pictured above). *(Coral Gables, Fla.)*

Any self-service or coin-operated box, container, storage unit, or other dispenser installed, used, or maintained for the display and sale of newspapers or news periodicals. *(Burbank, Calif.)*

■ **newsstand** A temporary structure, manned by a vendor, that sells newspapers, magazines, and other periodicals. (pictured below). *(APA Research Department)*

■ **nightclub** A commercial establishment dispensing alcoholic beverages for consumption on the premises and in which dancing and musical entertainment are permitted. *(Maryland Heights, Mo.)*

An establishment operated as a place of entertainment, characterized by any or all of the following as a principal use: (1) live, recorded, or televised entertainment, including but not limited to performance by magicians, musicians or comedians; (2) dancing. *(Las Vegas, Nev.)*

■ **NIMBY (not in my back yard)** *(See LULU (locally unwanted land use))*

■ **noise** The intensity, duration, and character of sound from any and all sources. *(Federal Way, Wash.)*

Any sound that is undesirable because it interferes with speech and hearing, or is intense enough to damage hearing, or is otherwise annoying. Noise, simply, is "unwanted sound." *(California Planning Roundtable)*

Any sound that is unwanted or that causes or tends to cause an adverse psychological or physiological effect on human beings. . . . *(Jefferson County, Colo.)*

■ **noise pollution**   Continuous or episodic excessive noise in the human environment. *(Siskiyou County, Calif.)*

■ **nonattainment** *(See also air pollution)* The condition of not achieving a desired or required level of performance. Frequently used in reference to air quality. *(California Planning Roundtable)*

■ **nonconforming activity** *(See also amortization)*   An activity that, under the zoning regulations, is not itself a permitted activity where it is located or does not conform to the off-street parking or loading requirements, performance standards, or other requirements applying to activities. However, an activity of the character described above shall not be deemed a nonconforming activity to the extent that it has been or is hereafter authorized by a subsisting conditional use permit, variance, or other special zoning approval. *(Oakland, Calif.)*

■ **nonconforming building**   The lawful use of a building or structure or portion thereof, existing at the time this title or amendments thereto take effect, and which does not conform to all the height, area, and yard regulations prescribed in the district in which it is located. *(Clark Co, Nev., which uses the term "legal nonconforming building or structure")*

A structure or building, the size, dimensions, or location of that was lawful prior to the adoption of, revision, or amendment to a zoning ordinance, but which fails by reason of such adoption, revision, or amendment to conform to the present requirements of the zoning district. *(Iowa State University Extension Service)*

A building or part thereof lawfully existing which does not comply with one or more of the regulations of this chapter. *(Staunton, Va.)*

■ **nonconforming by dimension**   A building, structure or parcel of land not in compliance with the dimensional regulations of this zoning code. Dimensional regulations include all regulations of this zoning code, other than those pertaining to the permitted uses. A building or structure containing more dwelling units than are permitted by the use regulations of this zoning code shall be nonconforming by use; a building or structure containing a permitted number of dwelling units by the use regulations of this zoning code, but not meeting the lot area per dwelling unit regulations, shall be nonconforming by dimension. *(Newport, R.I.)*

■ **nonconforming feature**   A characteristic of a building or property, such as signs, parking, loading, landscaping, performance standards, or condition of a special/provisional use that lawfully existed prior to the enactment of the requirements of this chapter, but does not comply with the current requirements of this chapter. *(Champaign, Ill.)*

■ **nonconforming location**   A use that lawfully existed prior to the enactment of the requirements of this chapter and is permitted in the zoning district, but does not meet the location requirements of the district. *(Champaign, Ill.)*

■ **nonconforming lot** *(See lot, nonconforming)*

■ **nonconforming sign** *(See sign, nonconforming)*

■ **nonconforming structure** *(See nonconforming building; structure, nonconforming)*

■ **nonconforming use** *(See use, nonconforming)*

■ **nonconformity**   Any nonconforming aspect of a structure, land, or use. . . . *(Champaign, Ill.)*

■ **noncontributing building**   A building, site, structure, or object that does not add to the historic architectural qualities, historic association, or cultural values of the area because it was not present dur-

ing the period of significance or does not relate to the documented significance of the property due to alterations, disturbances, additions, or other changes, or because it no longer possesses historic integrity nor is capable of yielding important information about the period. *(Champaign, Ill.)*

■ **nonpoint pollution** *(See pollution, nonpoint)*

■ **nonprofit organization**   Any person(s), partnership, association, corporation or other group whose activities are conducted for unselfish, civic, or humanitarian motives, or for the benefit of others, and not for the gain of any private individual or group and may include, but shall not be limited to, patriotic, philanthropic, social service, welfare, benevolent, educational, civic, fraternal, cultural, charitable, scientific, historical, athletic, or medical activities. *(Glendale, Ariz.)*

■ **nonwetlands** *(See also wetlands)* Uplands and lowland areas that are neither deep water aquatic habitats, wetlands, nor other special aquatic sites. They are seldom or never inundated or, if frequently inundated, they have saturated soils for only brief periods during the growing season, and, if vegetated, they normally support a prevalence of vegetation typically adapted for life only in aerobic soil conditions. *(Island County, Wash.)*

■ **notice of hearing**   A legal document announcing the opportunity for the public to present their views to an official representative or board of a public agency concerning an official action pending before the agency. *(California Planning Roundtable)*

■ **noxious matter** *(See toxic/noxious substance)*

■ **nuisance**   An interference with the enjoyment and use of property. *(Siskiyou County, Calif.)*

■ **nursery**   Any land used to raise trees, shrubs, flowers, and other plants for sale or for transplanting. *(Jefferson County, Colo.)*

An enterprise that conducts the retail and/or wholesale of plants grown on the premises, as well as accessory items (but not power equipment, such as gas or electric lawn mowers and farm implements) directly related to their care and maintenance. *(Cecil County, Md.)*

An establishment for the growth, display, and/or sale of plants, shrubs, trees, and materials used in indoor or outdoor planting, conducted within or without an enclosed building. *(Clark County, Nev.)*

■ **nursery, bare root** An area for the cultivation and propagation of trees, shrubs, and plants that are grown in the ground and not in containers. *(Thurston County, Wash.)*

■ **nursery farms** An operation for the cultivating, harvesting, and sale of plants, bushes, trees, and other nursery items grown on site or established in the ground prior to sale, and for related accessory sales and uses. *(Anne Arundel County, Md.)*

The use of land for the growing of trees, shrubs, or ornamental plants that are to be transported to another location for replanting. *(Edmond, Okla., which uses the term "plant nursery")*

■ **nursery, retail** *(See also **garden center; green house**)* The retail handling of any article, substance, or commodity related to the planting, maintenance, or harvesting of garden plants, shrubs, trees, packaged fertilizers, soils, chemicals, or other nursery goods and related products in small quantities to the consumer. *(Shasta Lake, Calif.)*

■ **nursery, wholesale** The growing, storage, and sale of garden plants, shrubs, trees, or vines for resale, including incidental retail sales conducted from within a building not exceeding 20 percent of the combined wholesale and retail sales volume during any year. *(Shasta Lake, Calif.)*

■ **nursing home** *(See also **convalescent center; elderly housing** definitions)* A home licensed by the [state] for the aged or chronically or incurably ill persons in which five or more such persons not of the immediate family are provided with food and shelter or care for compensa-

tion, but not including hospitals, clinics, or similar institutions devoted primarily to the diagnosis and treatment of the sick or injured. *(Jefferson County, Colo.)*

A home for the aged or infirm in which three or more persons not of the immediate family are received, kept, or provided with food and shelter, or care for compensation; but not including hospitals, clinics, or similar institutions devoted primarily to the diagnosis and treatment of the sick or injured. *(Boone County, Mo.)*

A use providing bed care and in-patient services for persons requiring regular medical attention but excluding a facility providing surgical or emergency medical services and excluding a facility providing care for alcoholism, drug addiction, mental disease, or communicable disease. *(Blacksburg, Va.)*

A facility established for profit or nonprofit, which provides nursing care and related medical services on a 24-hour per day basis to two or more individuals because of illness, disease, or physical or mental infirmity. Provides care for those persons not in need of hospital care. *(Kauai, Hawaii)*

■ **observation room/deck**    Space designed and intended to be used by the public that may be within a building or in the open air and that is maintained so as to be open and available to the public during the hours the building is open to the public, provided, such space must be located at or above the highest occupied floor of a building or at or above the 30th floor of a building 30 stories or more in height. *(Philadelphia, Pa.)*

■ **obstruction, land**    Any building, structure, apparatus, mechanical equipment, fence, or other construction of a long-term nature placed above or on the ground within a required yard, setback, or buffer area. *(Champaign, Ill.)*

■ **obstruction, watercourse**    Any dam, wall, wharf, embankment, levee, dike, pile, abutment, projection, excavation, channel, rectification, bridge conduit, culvert, building, wire fence, rock gravel, refuse, fill, structure, or matter in, along, across, or projecting into any channel, watercourse, or regulatory flood hazard area that may impede, retard, increase, or change the direction of the flow of

water, either in itself or by catching or collecting debris carried by such water, or that is placed where the flow of water might carry the same downstream to the damage of life or property. *(Rapid City, S.D.)*

■ **occupancy**    The use of land, buildings or structures. Change of occupancy is not intended to include change of tenants or proprietors. *(Quincy, Mass.)*

The residing of an individual overnight in a dwelling unit or the installation, storage, or use of equipment, merchandise, or machinery in any public, commercial, or industrial building. *(Siskiyou County, Calif.)*

■ **occupant**    Tenant or person in actual possession. *(Champaign, Ill.)*

Any person who holds a written or an oral lease of or who actually occupies the whole or a part of such building or land, either alone or with others. *(Peoria, Ill., which uses the term "occupant or tenant applied to a building or land")*

■ **occupied area**    The total of the areas of all buildings on the lot. The area of each building is the area of a horizontal section of such building on any floor at or above ground level taken at its greatest outside dimensions, including all structures, except fences. *(Philadelphia, Pa.)*

■ **odor**    Stimulus affecting the olfactory nerves. *(Federal Way, Wash.)*

■ **odorous matter**    Material that is gas, liquid, or solid that causes an odor sensation to a human being. *(Aurora, Ill.)*

Any matter that yields an odor that is offensive in any way. *(Gurnee, Ill.)*

Material suspended in the atmosphere that produces an olfactory response in normal human beings. *(National City, Calif.)*

■ **off-road vehicle**    Any motorized vehicle designed for or capable of cross-country travel on or immediately over land, water, sand, snow, ice, swampland, or other natural terrain, except that such terms exclude (a) registered motorboats, (b) military, fire, emergency, and law enforcement vehicles when used for emer-

gency purposes, and (c) any vehicle whose use is expressly authorized by [the jurisdiction]. *(Executive Order 11644, Use of Off-Road Vehicles on the Public Lands)*

■ **off-shore facilities**    Any facilities, seaward of the outer harbor line, floating or supported on a pier or piers, used to transfer or assemble materials or for construction purposes, except aquacultural facilities and structures, research and scientific monitoring facilities. *(Seattle, Wash.)*

■ **off site**    Outside the limits of the area encompassed by the tract area or the parcel of record on which the activity is conducted. *(Maryland Department of Natural Resources)*

■ **office**    A room or group of rooms used for conducting the affairs of a business, profession, service industry, or government. *(Miami, Fla.)*

A room or a suite of rooms or portion of a building used for the practice of a profession or for the conduct of a business that involves the accessory sale of goods from the premises. If the goods or merchandise are sold for delivery on or from the premises, and constitutes a portion greater than 20 percent of the gross revenue from the office, then the premises shall be considered to be a store rather than an office. *(Champaign, Ill.)*

Administrative, executive, professional, research, or similar organizations, and laboratories having only limited contact with public, provided that no merchandise or merchandising services are sold on the premises, except such as are incidental or accessory to the principal permissible use. *(Grand Forks, N.D.)*

■ **office building**    A building used primarily for offices that may include ancillary services for office workers, such as a restaurant, coffee shop, newspaper, or candy stand. *(Champaign, Ill.)*

■ **office, Class A**    A principal building that is not necessarily the only building on the lot on which it is situated; it may be attached to another building. It is not limited in floor area by definition (although it may be so limited by bulk regulations). Class A office may include separate office buildings, supporting uses, and open space designated, planned, constructed, and managed on an integrated and coordinated basis. *(Cecil County, Md.)*

■ **office, Class B**    A principal building that is not attached to any other building and is the only building on the lot on which it is situated. *(Cecil County, Md.)*

■ **office, Class C**    A principal building originally constructed as a one-family or two-family detached dwelling and then converted to office use without any external enlargement for the purpose of creating office space or otherwise accommodating office use. For the purpose of this definition, enclosure of a porch does not constitute external enlargement. *(Cecil County, Md.)*

■ **office conversion** *(See also home occupation)*    A single-family residential structure occupied by or converted for an office use. *(Champaign, Ill.)*

■ **office, intensive**    Mid-rise (six stories) to high-rise (over six stories) office development, including structured parking. *(Renton, Wash.)*

■ **office park**    A development that contains a number of separate office buildings, supporting uses, and open space designed, planned, constructed, and managed on an integrated and coordinated basis. *(Champaign, Ill.)*

A large tract of land that has been planned, developed and operated as an integrated facility for a number of separate office buildings and supporting ancillary uses with special attention to circulation, parking, utility needs, aesthetics, and compatibility. *(Schaumburg, Ill.)*

■ **office, professional**    The office of a member of a recognized profession maintained for the conduct of that profession. A profession is a vocation, calling, occupation, or employment requiring training in the liberal arts or sciences, or combination thereof, requiring advanced study in a specialized field; any occupation requiring licensing by the state and maintenance of professional standards applicable to the field. *(Sheridan, Wyo.)*

■ **office/professional district**    [The district that includes] the less intensive office and professional center land uses including low-rise office parks, single freestanding office buildings, depository facilities, such as banks, and residential structures converted to office use. Office land uses tend to be single-use oriented and have less intensive employee/acre ratios. *(DeKalb County, Ill.)*

■ **official map**    A legally adopted map that conclusively shows the location and width of proposed streets, public facilities and public areas, and drainage rights-of-way. *(Iowa State University Extension Service)*

A map, adopted by a legislative body through a resolution or ordinance, showing existing streets and approved proposed streets, parks, and other public places. *(Handbook for Planning Commissioners in Missouri)*

■ **oil change facility** *(See also automobile repair services; gas station; service station)*    Operations that provided lubrication and/or checking, changing, or additions of those fluids and filters necessary to the maintenance of a vehicle. It is intended that these services will be provided while customers wait, generally within a 15- to 20-minute time period. *(Myrtle Beach, S.C., which uses the term "speedy/fast lube operations")*

■ **on site**    Within the limits of the area encompassed by the tract area or parcel of record on which the activity is conducted. *(Maryland Department of Natural Resources)*

■ **open burning**    The burning of any matter in such manner that the products of combustion resulting from the burning are emitted directly into the atmosphere without passing through an approved stack, duct, vent, or chimney but does not refer to the operation of safety flares for the purpose of protecting human life. *(Anchorage, Alaska)*

■ **open-front store**    A business establishment other than a restaurant, bank, or gasoline station, so developed that service to the portion may be extended beyond the walls of the building, not requiring the patron to enter the building. *(West Bloomfield, Mich.)*

■ **open-land district**    A zoning classification that limits the allowable uses to agriculture, recreation, parks, reservoirs, and water supply lands. Open Land Districts are most commonly used for publicly owned lands, but are also used in areas subject to flooding (floodplain zones) and other natural hazards. *(Handbook for Planning Commissioners in Missouri)*

■ **open space**    Any land or area, the preservation of which in its present use would: (1) conserve and enhance natural or scenic resources; or (2) protect streams or water supply; or (3) promote conservation of soils, wetlands, beaches, or tidal marshes; or (4) enhance the value to the public of abutting or neighboring parks, forests, wildlife preserves, nature reservations, or sanctuaries; or (5) enhance recreation opportunities. *(Redmond, Wash.)*

Land and water areas retained for use as active or passive recreation areas or for resource protection in an essentially undeveloped state. *(Cecil County, Md.)*

Land used for recreation, resource protection, amenity, and/or bufferyards. In no event shall any area of a lot constituting the minimum lot area of said lot nor any part of an existing or future road or right-of-way be counted as constituting open space except that bufferyard areas may be included in the area of a lot constituting the minimum lot area. *(Lake County, Ill.)*

*Commentary: Many zoning codes establish minimum open space ratios—the portion of the site that is devoted to open space—to regulate the intensity of development and to preserve natural areas. The definition of open space is critical to the calculation of this ratio. Some codes allow balconies, terraces, and roof areas to be included under the definition of open space as long as these areas are available for use by all of the occupants of the building.*

■ **open space, active**    Open space that may be improved and set aside, dedicated, designated, or reserved for recreational facilities such as swimming pools, play equipment for children, ball fields, court games, picnic tables, etc. *(Redmond, Wash.)*

■ **open space, common**   An open space within a residential development reserved for the exclusive use of residents of the development and their guests. *(Newport Beach, Calif.)*

The total land area, not individually owned or dedicated for public use, which is designed and intended for the common use or enjoyment of the residents or occupants of a development. Common open space includes swimming pools, putting greens, and other recreational-leisure facilities; areas of scenic or natural beauty and habitat areas; hiking, riding, or off-street bicycle trails; and landscaped areas adjacent to roads that are in excess of minimum required rights-of-way. *(Washoe County, Nev.)*

Land within or related to a development, not individually owned or dedicated for public use, that is designed and intended for the common use or enjoyment of the residents of the development and may include such complementary structures and improvements as are necessary and appropriate. *(Schaumburg, Ill.)*

■ **open space, detached**   Required open space that is not on the same lot(s) as the dwellings for which the open space is required. *(Albuquerque, N. Mex.)*

■ **open space, developed**   Open space substantially free of structures but possibly containing improvements that are part of a development plan or are appropriate for the residents of any residential development. *(Palm Desert, Calif.)*

■ **open space element**   An inventory of privately and publicly owned open-space lands, and adopted goals, policies, and implementation programs for the preservation, protection, and management of open space lands. *(California Planning Roundtable)*

■ **open space, natural**   Any parcel of land or water that is essentially unimproved and devoted to an open space use. *(Palm Desert, Calif.)*

An open space area not occupied by any structure or impervious surface. *(Siskiyou County, Calif.)*

■ **open space, passive**   Open space that is essentially unimproved and set aside, dedicated, designated, or reserved for public or private use or for the use and enjoyment of owners or occupants. *(Redmond, Wash.)*

■ **open space, private**   A usable open space adjoining and directly accessible to a dwelling unit, reserved for the exclusive use of residents of the dwelling unit and their guests. *(Newport Beach, Calif.)*

The outdoor living area directly adjoining a dwelling unit or building, intended for the private enjoyment of the residents or occupants of the dwelling unit or building and defined in such a manner that its boundaries are evident. *(Washoe County, Nev.)*

■ **open space ratio**   A measure of the intensity of land use, determined by dividing the total of all open space areas contained within a site by the gross site area. *(Island County, Wash.)*

■ **open space, total**   The sum of private open space and shared open space. *(Newport Beach, Calif.)*

■ **open space, usable**   Outdoor or unenclosed area on the ground, or on a roof, balcony, deck, porch, or terrace designed and accessible for outdoor living, recreation, pedestrian access, or landscaping, but excluding parking facilities, driveways, utility or service areas, or any required front or street side yard, and excluding any space with a dimension of less than six feet in any direction. *(Newport Beach, Calif.)*

■ **open space use**   The current employment of land, the preservation of which use would conserve and enhance natural or scenic resources, protect streams and water supplies, or preserve sites designated as historic pursuant to law, provided such land has a greater value for another use than for open space use. *(Washoe County, Nev.)*

■ **orchard**   The establishment, care, and harvesting of more than 25 fruit bearing trees, such as persimmon, guava, banana, or papaya, for the purpose of selling the fruit to others. *(Kauai, Hawaii)*

A group of fruit or nut trees, either small and diverse and grown for home use, or large and uniform (i.e., of one variety) and cultivated for revenue. Such a collection must be planted, managed, and renewed by the householder or farmer and should not be confused with a naturally occurring grove. Citrus and nut plantations are customarily called groves. *(California Planning Roundtable)*

■ **ordinance**   A law or regulation set forth and adopted by a governmental authority, usually a city or county. *(Jefferson County, Colo.)*

■ **organic material**   A material or substance composed of chemical compounds of carbon in combination with other chemical elements (often hydrogen) and generally manufactured in the life processes of plants and animals. Organic substances include paper, wood, food and plastic, as well as the waste products of these and similar materials. *(Gurnee, Ill.)*

■ **origin and destination survey** *(See* **trip***)*

■ **outbuilding** *(See also* **accessory structure***)*   A separate accessory building or structure not physically connected to the principal building. *(Siskiyou County, Calif.)*

■ **outdoor advertising display** *(See also* **sign** *definitions)*   A fixed or portable appliance, structure, or surface, including the supporting structure made necessary thereby, erected upon the ground, on the wall of a building, or above the roof of a building, and used and erected for the public display of posters, painted displays, electrical displays, pictures, or other pictorial or reading matter for the benefit of a person, organization, business, or cause not residing or located on the lot or in the building where the appliance, structure, or surface is erected. *(Orrville, Ohio)*

■ **outdoor customer dining area** *(See* **restaurant, outdoor customer dining area***)*

■ **outdoor display area** *(See also* **retail sales establishment** *definitions)*   An area of designated size used for the display of merchandise or tangible property normally vended within the contiguous

159

business or organization. Multiple items may be displayed on a rack but shall not be stacked upon each other. *(Melbourne, Fla.)*

The placement of goods for sale or for advertisement, outside of the building or structure, including but not limited to vehicles, garden supplies, gas, tires, motor oil, food and beverages (vending machines), boats and farm equipment, motor homes and clothes. *(Hudson, N.H., which uses the term "outside display")*

■ **outdoor recreation** *(See also recreation definitions)* Uses and facilities pertaining primarily to recreation activities that are carried on primarily outside of structures. *(Kauai, Hawaii)*

A privately or publicly owned or operated use providing facilities for outdoor recreation activities. *(California Planning Roundtable)*

■ **outdoor recreation concession** Uses and facilities ancillary to outdoor recreation uses, such as gasoline pumps at piers and marinas, and boat rental and food and beverage facilities at public beaches. *(Kauai, Hawaii)*

■ **outdoor storage** The keeping of personal or business property or motor vehicles in a required open parking space or any other area outside of a building for a period of time exceeding 72 consecutive hours. *(Santa Clara, Calif.)*

The storage of any material for a period greater than 24 hours, including items for sale, lease, processing, and repair (including vehicles) not in an enclosed building. *(Redmond, Wash.)*

■ **outdoor storage, bulk** Goods for sale, storage, or display that have a large size, mass, or volume and are not easily moved or carried, such as railroad ties, large bags of feed, or fertilizer, wood, etc. *(Redmond, Wash.)*

■ **outdoor storage, non-bulk** Goods for sale, storage, or display that are distinguished from bulk items by being small in size or volume and not requiring a mechanical lifting device to move them. Includes such items as bikes, light weight furniture, lawn accessories, and other items that can easily be moved in-

doors during close of business. *(Redmond, Wash.)*

■ **outdoor storage, seasonal** Outdoor storage of items for retail sale that are, by their nature, sold during a peak season, including such items as fruits, vegetables, Christmas trees, pumpkins, lawn accessories, bedding plants, etc. *(Redmond, Wash.)*

■ **outfall** The point where water flows out from a conduit, drain, or stream. *(Grand Traverse County, Mich.)*

■ **outlet** A stream or facility receiving the flow from a basin, drain, or other stormwater management facility. *(Grand Traverse County, Mich.)*

■ **outlot** A lot remnant or parcel of land left over after platting, which is intended as open space or other use, for which no building permit shall be issued. *(Buffalo, Minn.)*

A platted lot which is unbuildable and held in common ownership by a homeowners association or which is transferred to a public agency or utility. *(Polk County, Iowa)*

■ **overlay zone** Provides for the possibility of superimposing certain additional requirements upon a basic use zoning district without disturbing the requirements of the basic use district. In the instance of conflicting requirements, the stricter of the conflicting requirement shall apply. *(Racine County, Wisc.)*

A district established by ordinance to prescribe special regulations to be applied to a site in combination with the underlying or base district. *(Blacksburg, Va.)*

A land-use designation on the land-use map or a zoning designation on a zoning map that modifies the basic underlying designation in some specific manner. *(Jefferson County, Colo.)*

Zoning districts that extend on top of more than one base zoning district and are intended to protect certain critical features and resources. Where the standards of the overlay and base zoning district are different, the more restrictive standards shall apply. *(Hilton Head, S.C.)*

■ **owner** Any person, agent, firm, corporation, or partnership that alone, jointly or severally with others: (1) has legal or equitable title to any premises, dwelling or dwelling unit, with or without accompanying actual possession thereof; or (2) has charge, care, or control of any premises, dwelling or dwelling unit, as agent of the owner or as executor, administrator, trustee, or guardian of the estate of the beneficial owner. The person shown on the records of the recorder of deeds of the county to be the owner of a particular property shall be presumed to be the person in control of that property. *(Peoria, Ill.)*

The legal or beneficial owner or owners of the land. The holder of an option or contract to purchase, a lessee having a remaining term of not less than 50 years in duration, or other person having an enforceable proprietary interest. . . . *(Nashville and Davidson County, Tenn.)*

■ **owner of record** One who has complete dominion over particular property and who is the one in whom legal or equitable title rests; when applied to a building or land, owner means any part owner, joint owner, owner of a community or partnership interest, trust, estate, life tenant in common, or joint tenant, of the whole or part of such building or land. *(Champaign, Ill.)*

■ **owners association** The nonprofit corporation or association created to own, lease, or provide management, maintenance, preservation, and control of the contiguous or noncontiguous lots, parcels, areas, or improvements owned in common or the lots, parcels, areas, or improvements separately owned or, in which there is a right to exclusive occupancy, or both types of ownership, common and separate, or any portion of or interest in them. *(Santa Clara County, Calif.)*

■ **ownership, common** 1. Ownership by one or more individuals or entities in any form of ownership of two or more contiguous lots; or 2. Ownership by any association (such ownership may also include a municipality) of one or more lots under specific development techniques. *(Newport, R.I.)*

■ **ownership, single**  Holding record title, possession under a contract to purchase, or possession under a lease, by a person, firm corporation, or partnership, individually, jointly, in common, or in any other manner where the property is or will be under unitary or unified control. *(Newport Beach, Calif.)*

■ **ozone**  A gas that is a variety of oxygen. The oxygen gas found in the air consists of two oxygen atoms stuck together; this is molecular oxygen. Ozone consists of three oxygen atoms stuck together into an ozone molecule. Ozone occurs in nature; it produces the sharp smell you notice near a lightning strike. High concentrations of ozone gas are found in a layer of the atmosphere—the stratosphere—high above the Earth. Stratospheric ozone shields the Earth against harmful rays from the sun, particularly ultraviolet B. Smog's main component is ozone; this ground-level ozone is a product of reactions among chemicals produced by burning coal, gasoline, and other fuels, and chemicals found in products including solvents, paints, hairsprays, etc. *(Environmental Protection Agency)*

■ **panelized housing** *(See also factory-built housing; manufactured housing; modular housing)* Panelized housing consists of factory-produced wall panels constructed approximately eight feet high and four feet to 40 feet in length; the home is of open or closed construction and does not involve a permanent steel chassis. Open wall panels are wall sections containing exterior sheathing only, with necessary plumbing, electrical, heating, air conditioning, insulation, and interior sheathing installed at the building site. Closed wall panels are shipped from the factory as complete wall units containing necessary electrical, plumbing, heating, air conditioning, insulation, interior, and exterior sheathing installed and connected at the site. All service systems and connections must comply with all local and state codes. *(Danville, Ill.)*

■ **parade** Any march or procession consisting of people, animals, or vehicles, or any combination thereof, except funeral processions, upon any public street, sidewalk, alley, jogging trail, or bike path which does not comply with normal and usual traffic regulations or controls. *(Rochester, Minn.)*

■ **parapet** That portion of a wall which extends above the roof line. *(Coral Gables, Fla.)*

■ **paratransit** *(See also **transit** definitions)* A form of public transportation characterized by the flexible routing and scheduling of small vehicles (taxis, vans, or small buses) to provide shared occupancy, doorstep, or curbside personalized transportation service. *(Sacramento Regional Transit District)*

Forms of public passenger transportation that are distinct from conventional transit and can operate over the highway and street system. Examples of paratransit include shared-ride taxis, carpools, rental cars, and subscription bus clubs. *(New Jersey State Plan)*

Refers to transportation services that operate vehicles, such as buses, jitneys, taxis, and vans for senior citizens, and/or mobility impaired. *(California Planning Roundtable)*

■ **parcel** Any legally described piece of land designated by the owner or developer as land to be used or developed as a unit, or that has been developed as a unit. *(Clearwater, Fla.)*

A tract or plot of land of any size that may or may not be subdivided or improved. *(Tumwater, Wash.)*

A lot or contiguous group of lots in single ownership or under single control, usually considered a unit for purposes of development. *(Jefferson County, Colo.)*

A piece of land created by a partition, subdivision, deed, or other instrument recorded with the appropriate recorder. This includes a lot, a lot of record, or a piece of land created through other methods. *(Portland, Ore.)*

■ **park** A noncommercial, not-for-profit facility designed to serve the recreation needs of the residents of the community. Such facilities include subdivision recreation facilities (neighborhood parks), community parks, regional parks and special use facilities, all as described in the recreation and open space element of the [comprehensive plan]. Such facilities may also include but shall not be limited to school and religious institution ballfields, football fields and soccer fields, if they meet the above definition. Commercial amusement facilities, such as water slides, go-cart tracks, and miniature golf courses shall not be considered parks. *(Melbourne, Fla.)*

Any public or private land available for recreational, educational, cultural, or aesthetic use. *(Mankato, Minn.)*

An open space with natural vegetation and landscaping; may include recreational facilities. *(Austin, Tex.)*

An area reserved for recreational, educational, or scenic purposes. *(Beaufort County, S.C.)*

Any area that is predominately open space, used principally for active or passive recreation, and not used for a profit-making purpose. Any area designated by the city as a park. *(Cumberland, Md.)*

■ **park-and-ride facility** *(See **also** transportation demand management (TDM))* A facility designed for parking automobiles, the occupants of which transfer to public transit to continue their trips (pictured on page 164). *(Elbert County, Colo.)*

An off-street parking facility designed or intended to provide peripheral collection and storage of vehicles to accommodate commuter traffic into or out from the community, including accessory structures such as passenger shelters. *(Chapel Hill, N.C.)*

A publicly owned, short-term, parking facility for commuters. *(Bedford County, Va.)*

■ **park-and-ride lot** The temporary storage of automobiles on a daily basis for persons traveling together to and from work either through carpools, vanpools, buspools, or mass transit. *(Nashville and Davidson County, Tenn.)*

■ **park, hybrid** An open space used for storm drainage, water retention, and unstructured recreation. Its landscape consists of naturalistically disposed native trees, grassy areas, and other vegeta-

tion that can absorb all the nutrients from stormwater. Any park, greenbelt, green, or close, may be utilized as a hybrid park. *(Monroe County, Fla.)*

■ **park land**　Land that is publicly owned or controlled for the purpose of providing parks, recreation, or open space for public use. *(California Planning Roundtable)*

■ **park, minipark**　Small neighborhood park of approximately one acre or less. *(California Planning Roundtable)*

■ **park, neighborhood**　City- or county-owned land intended to serve the recreation needs of people living or working within one-half mile radius of the park. *(California Planning Roundtable)*

■ **park, passive use**　A park featuring passive recreation pursuits, such as interpretive programs and trail systems that take advantage of geological, biological, or scenic resources located within the park but not including recreational facilities, such as swimming pools, gyms, and playing fields. *(Island County, Wash.)*

■ **park, private**　A tract of land presently owned or controlled and used by private or semi-public persons, entities, groups, etc. for active and/or passive recreational purposes. *(Plymouth, Minn.)*

■ **park, regional**　A park typically 150 to 500 acres in size focusing on activities and natural features not included in most other types of parks and often based on a specific scenic or recreational opportunity. *(California Planning Roundtable)*

■ **parking aisle**　An area within a parking facility intended to provide ingress and egress to parking spaces. *(Orlando, Fla)*

The clear space for either one- or two-way traffic movement and maneuvering between rows of parking stalls. *(Pittsburgh, Pa.)*

■ **parking area, community**　A parking area used exclusively by the residents of the neighborhood or customers or persons engaged in the conduct of establishments in the immediate vicinity of its location, or by those for whom such establishments are conducted. *(Pittsburgh, Pa.)*

■ **parking area, public**　An open area, excluding a street or other public way, used for the parking of automobiles and available to the public, whether for free or for compensation. *(California Planning Roundtable)*

An open space, other than a street or way, used for the parking of only automobiles. *(Pittsburgh, Pa.)*

■ **parking bay**　The clear space containing one or two rows of parking stalls and a parking aisle. *(Pittsburgh, Pa.)*

■ **parking, fringe lot**　Parking located on the immediate periphery of the central business district and is usually associated with a shuttle service. *(Portland, Ore.)*

■ **parking lot**　An off-street, surfaced, ground level open area, for the temporary storage of five or more motor vehicles. *(Fayetteville, Ark.)*

An authorized area not within a building where motor vehicles are stored for the purpose of temporary, daily, or overnight off-street parking. *(Richfield, Minn.)*

An open, hard-surfaced area, other than street or public way, to be used for the storage, for limited periods of time, of operable passenger automobiles and commercial vehicles, and available to the public, whether for compensation, free, or as an accommodation to clients or customers. *(Belmont, Calif.)*

An area provided for self-parking by employees, visitors, and/or patrons of any office of state or local government, any public accommodations, commercial or industrial establishments, or any other business open to the general public. Also includes the area provided for self-parking by residents, visitors or employees of an apartment building available to the general public. *(Las Cruces, N. Mex.)*

■ **parking lot, circulation area**　All of the area within a parking lot exclusive of driveways or off-street parking or loading spaces, which is provided for vehicular maneuvering, pedestrian movement, or other accessory or incidental purposes. *(Columbus, Ohio)*

■ **parking lot, commercial**　A parcel of land or portion thereof used for the parking or storage of motor vehicles as a commercial enterprise for which any fee is charged independently of any other use of the premises. *(Newport, R.I.)*

■ **parking management**　An evolving Transportation Demand Management (TDM) technique designed to obtain maximum use from a limited number of parking spaces. Can involve pricing and preferential treatment for HOVs, non-peak period users, and short-term users. *(California Planning Roundtable)*

■ **parking meter**   Any mechanical device or meter installed on public streets for the purpose of regulating the parking on such streets, and operated by the insertion of U.S. coins therein. *(Rochester, Minn.)*

■ **parking meter space**   The space adjacent to a parking meter designated for the parking of a single vehicle by lines painted or otherwise marked on the curbing or on the surface of the roadway. *(Rochester, Minn.)*

■ **parking, off-street**   Space occupied by automobiles on premises other than streets. *(Ellington, Conn.)*

A space adequate for parking a motor vehicle with room for opening doors on both sides, together with properly related access to a public street or alley and maneuvering room. *(Londonderry, N.H.)*

■ **parking, on-street**   The storage space for an automobile that is located within the street right-of-way. *(Hilton Head, S.C.)*

■ **parking, preferential**   Parking spaces designated or assigned, through use of a sign or painted space markings, for carpool and vanpool vehicles carrying commute passengers on a regular basis that are provided in a location more convenient to a place of employment than parking spaces provided for single-occupant vehicles. *(Hermosa Beach, Calif.)*

■ **parking ratio**   The number of parking spaces provided per 1,000 square feet of floor area. *(California Planning Roundtable)*

■ **parking, self-park**   Parking of vehicles other than valet parking. *(Pittsburgh, Pa.)*

■ **parking, shared**   A public or private parking area used jointly by two or more uses. *(California Planning Roundtable)*

■ **parking, short-term**   Parking having a duration of four hours or less. *(Portland, Ore.)*

■ **parking space**   An off-street space available for the parking of one motor vehicle conforming to the typical parking lot standards. *(Southington, Conn.)*

Usable space within a public or private parking area, or a building of sufficient size and area, exclusive of access drives, aisles or ramps, for the storage of one properly spaced passenger automobile or commercial vehicle. *(Belmont, Calif.)*

An area for the purpose of parking one automobile, having a minimum width of 10 feet and a minimum length of 22 feet, surfaced with concrete or asphalt, with access to a public street or alley. *(Sheridan, Wyo.)*

■ **parking space, compact**   A space in a garage or parking area, not less than 7.75 feet wide clear dimension and 16 feet long clear dimension, reserved for the parking of only one compact automobile. *(Pittsburgh, Pa.)*

■ **parking space, covered**   A building or portion of a building, open or enclosed by walls or doors on not more than two sides, that is designed or used to shelter a parking space. *(Newport Beach, Calif.)*

■ **parking space, dependent**   A parking space that can only be accessed by driving across another parking space. *(Oakland, Calif.)*

■ **parking space, enclosed**   A building or portion of a building, completely enclosed by walls or doors on three or more sides, that is designed or used to shelter a parking space. *(Newport Beach, Calif.)*

■ **parking space, handicap**   A space in a garage or parking area not less than 13 feet wide and 19 feet long clear dimension, reserved exclusively for an automobile registered with the [state] with handicapped license plates or displaying an official city- or [state]-issued handicapped placard. *(Pittsburgh, Pa.)*

■ **parking space, high-occupancy vehicle (HOV)**   A space intended for the parking of vehicles with three or more occupants sharing a vehicle four or more days per week on the average and priced and managed to achieve the use. *(Pittsburgh, Pa.)*

■ **parking space, independent**   A parking space that can be accessed without driving across another parking space. *(Oakland, Calif.)*

■ **parking space, long-term**   A space intended for the primary use of vehicles parked for a duration of four hours or more and neither priced nor managed to encourage turnover of vehicles. *(Pittsburgh, Pa.)*

■ **parking space, short-term**   A space intended for the primary use of vehicles parked for less than four hours duration and priced and managed to encourage turnover of vehicles. *(Pittsburgh, Pa.)*

■ **parking space, tandem**   A parking space within a group of two or more parking spaces arranged one behind the other. *(Newport Beach, Calif.)*

An arrangement of parking spaces such that one or more spaces must be driven across in order to access another space or spaces. . . . *(Oakland, Calif.)*

■ **parking, stacked**   The parking of cars in a parallel line, one in back of the other. *(Steamboat Springs, Colo.)*

■ **parking structure**   A structure or portion thereof composed of one or more levels or floors used exclusively for the parking or storage of motor vehicles (pictured on page 166). A parking structure may be totally below grade (as in an underground parking garage) or either partially or totally above grade with those levels being either open or enclosed. *(Richfield, Minn.)*

A structure designed to accommodate vehicular parking spaces that are fully or partially enclosed or located on the deck surface of a building. This definition includes parking garages, deck parking and underground or under-building parking areas. *(Beaufort County, S.C.)*

A structure of two or more stories, whether privately or publicly owned, used for parking more than four automobiles. *(Tumwater, Wash.)*

A covered structure or portion of a covered structure that provides parking areas for motor vehicles. Parking on top

of a structure—where there is gross building area below the parking, but nothing above it—is structured parking. The structure can be the primary structure for a commercial parking facility or be accessory to multidwelling residential, commercial, employment, industrial, institutional, or other structures. A structure that is accessory to a single-dwelling residential structure (including houses, attached houses, duplexes, mobile homes, or houseboats) is a garage and is not included as structured parking. *(Portland, Ore.)*

■ **parking, surface**  A parking area for motor vehicles where there is no gross building area below the parking area and no gross building area or roof above it. Area occupied by small, permanent buildings, such as booths used by parking attendants, is not parking area. Temporary vending carts are not gross building area. *(Portland, Ore.)*

■ **parking, underground**  Below-grade parking facilities (pictured at right) which typically include ventialtion systems where motor vehicles are parked, stored, or allowed to remain, and where the owner or person storing or parking the vehicle is charged a fee. *(APA Research Department)*

■ **parking, valet**  Parking of vehicles by an attendant provided by the establishment for which the parking is provided. *(Pittsburgh, Pa.)*

■ **parking well**  A paved parking area where each parking space has direct access to a public or private street. *(St. Charles, Mo.)*

■ **parkway**  *(See also* ***planting strip; street, parkway)***  The area, excluding the sidewalk, if any, between the property line and the curb or, in the absence of a curb, between the property line and the nearest edge of the street paving. *(El Paso, Tex.)*

A piece of land located between the rear of a curb and the front of a sidewalk, usually used for planting low ground cover and/or street trees, also known as "planter strip." *(California Planning Roundtable)*

■ **parsonage**  The permanent place of residence of the pastor or minister of a church. *(Valdez, Alaska)*

■ **particulate matter**  Material, other than water, that is suspended in or discharged into the atmosphere in a finely divided form as a liquid or solid. *(Gurnee, Ill.)*

■ **party wall**  A wall common to but dividing contiguous buildings; such a wall contains no openings and extends from its footing below the finished ground grade to the height of the exterior surface of the roof. *(North Kansas City, Mo.)*

■ **passage**  A pedestrian-only connector not more than five-feet wide that cuts between buildings. Passages provide shortcuts through long blocks, or connect rear parking areas with street frontages. *(Monroe County, Fla.)*

■ **pasture**  A fenced grazing area. . . . *(Jacksonville, Fla.)*

■ **path**  *(See* ***pedestrian walkway****)*

■ **patio**  A level surfaced area directly adjacent to a principal building which has an average elevation of not more than 30 inches, and without walls or a roof. A patio may be constructed of any materials. *(Bedford County, Va.)*

A level, surfaced area directly adjacent to a principal building at or within three feet of the finished grade, without a permanent roof intended for outdoor lounging, dining, and the like. *(Plymouth, Minn.)*

An attached roofed structure, open on one or more sides, whose principal use shall be for indoor-outdoor living and recreation. *(National City, Calif.)*

■ **patio cover**  A solid or open roof structure not exceeding 12 feet in height

and covering a patio, platform, or deck area. Patio covers may be detached or attached to another structure. Patio covers may be enclosed and used for recreational and outdoor living purposes, but do not include structures used as carports, garages, storage rooms, or habitable rooms. *(Newport Beach, Calif.)*

■ **patio house** *(See also **dwelling** definitions)* A detached, single-family unit typically situated on a reduced-size lot that orients outdoor activity within rear or side yard patio areas for better use of the site for outdoor living space. *(California Planning Roundtable)*

■ **pave** The act or result of applying . . . cement concrete or asphaltic concrete to any ground surface in such manner as to present a uniform surface over a large area. *(Maryland Heights, Mo.)*

■ **paved surface area** Ground surface covered with cobblestones, clay-fired bricks, concrete precast paver units (including, but not limited to, grasscrete), poured concrete with or without decorative surface materials, blacktop, or other asphaltic or rubber mixture which may include sand or gravel as an ingredient and which creates a hard surface. A graded natural surface or one covered with rolled stone or overlaid with loose gravel is not considered a paved surface. *(St. Charles, Mo.)*

■ **pavement width** Width of paved driving and parking surface, including gutters as measured from face of curb to face of curb, or from edge of pavement where there are no curbs. *(Renton, Wash.)*

■ **pawnshop** Any business that loans money on deposit of personal property or deals in the purchase or possession of personal property on condition of selling the same back again to the pledger or depositor, or loans or advances money on personal property by taking chattel mortgage security thereon, and takes or receives such personal property. *(Clark County, Nev.)*

■ **pay phone** *(See **telephone, outdoor pay**)*

■ **peak hour/peak period** For any given roadway, a daily period during which traffic volume is highest, usually occurring in the morning and evening commute periods. *(California Planning Roundtable)*

■ **peak rate of discharge/peak flow** The maximum calculated rate of stormwater flow at a given point in a channel, watercourse, or conduit resulting from a predetermined frequency storm or flood, measured in cubic feet per second (cfs). *(Grand Traverse County, Mich.)*

■ **peddle** Selling, offering for sale, or soliciting orders for goods or services or distributing, disseminating, or gathering information by written or spoken word upon the streets, sidewalks, or alleys of the city, or by going from place to place whether by foot or by other means of transportation. *(Reno, Nev., which uses the term "peddle or solicit")*

■ **pedestrian mall** An area of street-like proportions given over entirely to pedestrian traffic. Such an area usually forms a line in the regular street plan of a city where the need for a vehicular right-of-way is not great and such traffic can be routed around the mall area. *(Ocean Shores, Wash., which uses the term "mall")*

■ **pedestrian-oriented development** Development designed with an emphasis primarily on the street sidewalk and on pedestrian access to the site and building, rather than on auto access and parking areas. The building is generally placed close to the street and the main entrance is oriented to the street sidewalk. There are generally windows or display cases along building facades which face the street. Typically, buildings cover a large portion of the site. Although parking areas may be provided, they are generally limited in size and they are not emphasized by the design of the site. *(Portland, Ore.)*

■ **pedestrian outdoor service facility** A use involving direct sales or provision of services to pedestrians who line up in areas outside a totally enclosed building. *(Santa Clara County, Calif., which uses the term "outdoor walk-up service facility")*

■ **pedestrian skyway system** Any system of providing for pedestrian traffic circulation, mechanical or otherwise elevated above ground, within or without the public rights-of-way, and through or above private property and buildings, and including overpasses, bridges, passageways, walkways, concourses, hallways, corridors, arcades, courts, plazas, malls, elevators, escalators, heated canopies and access, and all fixtures, furniture, signs, equipment, facilities, services and appurtenances. . . . A pedestrian skyway system shall include stairways and escalators leading from or into the skyway system from private buildings and areas under stairs and escalators connecting the concourse corridors to public streets or other public property. *(Rochester, Minn.)*

A walkway in an elevated structure used exclusively for pedestrian traffic that passes over a right-of-way. This skyway shall not be used for any occupancy. *(Reno, Nev.)*

■ **pedestrian walkway** A surfaced walkway, separate from the traveled portion of the roadway (pictured on page 168), usually of crushed rock or asphalt, and following the existing ground surface. *(Renton, Wash.)*

A public or private right-of-way across a block or within a block to provide access to be used by pedestrians. *(Grand Forks, N.D., which uses the term "pedestrian way")*

As a surrogate for a sidewalk in rural areas or rural centers where there is no curb, this is a hard-surfaced pedestrian facility adjacent to a public roadway but protected from vehicular traffic or setback behind a planting strip. *(Clackamas County, Ore.)*

A right-of-way for pedestrians, free from vehicular traffic and including access ramps, stairs, and mechanical lifts and routes through buildings which are available for public use. *(National City, Calif., which uses the term "pedestrian way")*

■ **pedestrian walkway, connector space** Public space within a lot that may be open or enclosed and which is designed and/or intended to be used by the pub-

lic to pass from or through the lot to a public sidewalk, a public transit concourse, a transit station, other public space within the lot, the public space of another lot, entrances to the building or entrances to the retail spaces on a lot, or other public space. *(Philadelphia, Pa.)*

■ **pedestrian walkway, through-block** A walkway or corridor designed and intended to be used by the public that provides public access through a building's public space, which is bounded on both sides by active space or public space, and which connects two parallel streets. . . . *(Philadelphia, Pa.)*

■ **pennant** *(See also **sign** definitions)* Any lightweight plastic, fabric, or other material, whether or not containing a message of any kind, suspended from a rope, wire, or string, usually in a series, designed to move in the wind. *(Cranberry Township, Pa.)*

■ **penthouse** An enclosed structure above the roof of a building, other than a roof structure or bulkhead, occupying more than one-third of the roof area. A penthouse, bulkhead, or any other similar projection above the roof shall not be used for purposes other than shelter of mechanical equipment or shelter of vertical shaft openings in the roof. *(Germantown, Tenn.)*

An enclosed roofed structure extending not more than 12 feet above the roof of a building and having an area not exceeding more than 25 percent of the area of the floor immediately below. A pent-

house shall not be construed as a story. . . . *(Coral Gables, Fla.)*

■ **performance bond** A document issued by a surety, in return for a fee or premium, guaranteeing the performance of the terms and conditions of a development approval. *(New York Planning Federation)*

■ **performance guarantee** *(See also **maintenance guarantee**)* Any security that may be accepted my a municipality as a guarantee that improvements required as part of an application for development are satisfactorily completed. *(Iowa State University Extension Service )*

A financial deposit to ensure that all improvements, facilities, or work required will be completed in conformance with the approved plan. *(Mankato, Minn.)*

■ **performance standards** Zoning regulations that permit uses based on a particular set of standards of operation rather than on particular type of use. Performance standards provide specific criteria limiting noise, air pollution, emissions, odors, vibration, dust, dirt, glare, heat, fire hazards, wastes, traffic impacts, and visual impact of a use. *(California Planning Roundtable)*

A set of criteria or limits relating to nuisance elements that a particular use or process may not exceed. *(Iowa State University Extension Service)*

Criterion established to control and limit the impacts generated by, or inherent in, uses of land or buildings. *(Delafield, Wisc.)*

■ **performance zoning** *(See also **flexible regulations**)* Zoning regulations that permit uses based on a particular set of standards rather than on particular type of use. *(Jefferson County, Colo.)*

■ **perimeter** The aggregate of the frontage lines of the surrounding lots. *(Monroe County, Fla.)*

■ **permit** *(See also **development permit**)* A document issued by [county or city] and/or [department of building inspections] allowing a person to begin an activity provided for in this ordinance. *(Bedford County, Va.)*

A document issued by the proper authority authorizing the applicant to undertake certain activities. *(Cumberland, Md.)*

■ **permit, conditional use** A permit issued by the city or city and county planning commissions stating that the conditional use complies with the conditions and standards set forth in this title and authorized by the planning commission. *(Sioux Falls, S.D.)*

The documented evidence of authority granted by the board of adjustment to locate a conditional use at a particular location. *(Ocean Shores, Wash.)*

A permit issued as a flexibility device to enable the city council to assign dimensions to a proposed use or conditions surrounding it after consideration of adjacent uses and their functions and the special problems which the proposed use presents. *(Maple Grove, Minn.)*

■ **permit, special** A use of a structure or lot or any action upon a premises that may be permitted under this ordinance only upon application to, and the approval of, the board of appeals, planning board, or city council and in accordance with provisions of this ordinance. *(Newburyport, Mass.)*

A use that would not be appropriate generally or without restriction throughout a zoning district but which, if controlled as to number, area, location, or relation to the neighborhood, would promote the public health, safety, morals, order, comfort, convenience, appearance, prosperity, or general welfare. *(Fall River, Mass.)*

■ **permit, special use**    A permit issued by the proper governmental authority that must be acquired before a special exception use can be constructed. *(Iowa State University Extension Service)*

A permit issued by the board of adjustment (with the exception of planned unit developments, telecommunication towers, and planned neighborhood developments) that authorizes the recipient to make use of property in accordance with the requirements of this ordinance as well as any additional requirements imposed by the board of adjustment. *(Indian Trail, N.C.)*

A specific approval for a use that has been determined to be more intense or to have a potentially greater impact than a permitted or conditional use within the same zoning district. *(Las Vegas, Nev.)*

■ **permit, special use, temporary**    A variance of a type that is for a special purpose, granted to a purchaser of property that is the subject of an existing special use permit, for a limited period of time and under the same conditions and restrictions set out in the original special use permit. *(Homestead, Fla.)*

■ **person**    Any individual, partnership, corporation, joint stock association or any city or state or any subdivision thereof; and includes any trustee, receiver, assignee or personal representative thereof. *(Peoria, Ill.)*

An individual, partnership, organization, association, trust, or corporation. When used in a penalty provision, "person" shall include the members of such partnership, the trustees of such trust, and the officers and members of such organization, association, or corporation. *(Cumberland, Md.)*

■ **personal property**    Any money, goods, movable chattels, things in action, evidence of debt, all objects, and rights that are capable of ownership, and every other species of property except real property. *(Champaign, Ill.)*

■ **personal services**    An establishment or place of business primarily engaged in the provision of frequent or recurrent needed services of a personal nature.

Typical uses include, but are not limited to, beauty and barber shops, shoe repair shops, and tailor shops. *(Champaign, Ill.)*

Establishments primarily engaged in providing individual services generally related to personal needs, such as a tailor shop. *(Valdez, Alaska)*

■ **personal watercraft**    A small . . . vessel that uses an outboard motor or an inboard motor powering a water jet pump as its primary source of motive power and that is designed to be operated by a person sitting, standing, or keeling on, or being towed behind the vessel, rather than in the conventional manner of sitting or standing inside the vessel. *(State of Florida)*

■ **pervious surface** *(See also impervious surface)*    A surface that presents an opportunity for precipitation to infiltrate into the ground. *(New Castle County, Del.)*

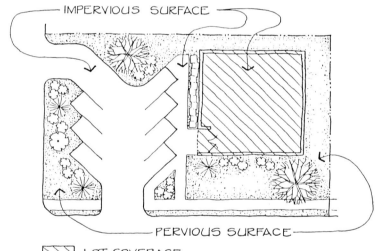

■ **pet** *(See animal, domestic)*

■ **pet shop**    A retail sales establishment primarily involved in the sale of domestic animals, such as dogs, cats, fish, birds, and reptiles, excluding exotic animals and farm animals such as horses, goats, sheep, and poultry. *(Miami, Fla.)*

A retail shop primarily engaged in the business of selling animals and maintaining, keeping, or possessing any animal for which a permit may be issued by the city clerk under this article at any time during the calendar year or any part thereof. *(Stillwater, Okla.)*

■ **pharmacy** *(See also drugstore)*    A place where drugs and medicines are prepared and dispensed. *(Valdez, Alaska)*

■ **photography retail store**    A facility primarily engaged in the retail sale, lease, and service of photography equipment and supplies, including limited on-site processing or development. *(Prince William County, Va.)*

■ **physical diversity**    A quality of a site, city, or region in which are found a variety of architectural styles, natural landscapes, and/or land uses. *(California Planning Roundtable)*

■ **physical value**    The replacement cost minus depreciation [of a building or structure] as determined by the director of inspections. *(Quincy, Mass.)*

■ **picnic area, group**    Two or more picnic tables reserved for use by 10 or more persons equipped with picnic tables, barbecue stands, and may be provided with a roofed shelter. *(California Planning Roundtable)*

■ **pier** *(See also dock; wharf)*    A general term including docks and similar structures consisting of a fixed or floating platform extending from the shore over the water. *(Renton, Wash.)*

Any fixed or floating structure for securing vessels, loading or unloading persons or property, or providing access to the water, including wharfs, docks, floats, or other landing facilities, and dry docks. (*Newport Beach, Calif.*)

A structure built out over the water and supported by pillars, piles or floats; used as a landing place, pleasure pavilion, etc. including tie-out piles. (*Kent County, Md.*)

■ **pier, community**    A boat-docking facility associated with a subdivision or similar residential area or with condominiums, apartments, or other multi-family dwelling units. Community pier does not include a private pier or a mooring. (*Anne Arundel County, Md.*)

■ **pier, private**    A structure, fixed or floating, generally referred to as a pier, dock, or wharf, including pilings, buoys, and similar facilities for wet storage of water craft, no more than four of which may be more than 16 feet in length, that is used: (1) solely by the owner or occupant of the lot or parcel of real estate from which the facility extends; and (2) during visits by the guests, for temporary docking of water craft owned by and registered to guests visiting the owner or occupant of the lot or parcel of real estate from which the facility extends. (*Anne Arundel County, Md.*)

■ **pier, recreational**    A pier, dock, or wharf used by a residential community, including guests, for crabbing, fishing, sunning, swimming, and similar activities, but not for boating. (*Anne Arundel County, Md.*)

■ **pierhead line**    A line established to define the bayward limit for piers and float-type structures. (*Newport Beach, Calif.*)

■ **piling**    Vertical poles, concrete bars, or other materials forming the structural support of a water access structure. (*Southwest Florida Water Management District*).

■ **place**    An open, unoccupied space, other than a street or alley, permanently reserved as the principal means of access to abutting property. (*Cape Girardeau, Mo.*)

■ **plan** (*See area plan; comprehensive plan; concept plan; congestion management plan (CMP); general plan; land-use*

plan; master plan; neighborhood plan; specific plan; strategic plan; subdivision, exploratory sketch plan; subdivision, preliminary plan)

■ **planned commercial development** (*See also planned unit development*) An area of minimum contiguous size, as specified by ordinance, to be planned, developed, operated, and maintained as a single entity containing one or more structures to accommodate commercial areas and other uses incidental to the predominant uses. (*Iowa State University Extension Service*)

■ **planned community** (*See also new town*)    A large-scale development whose essential features are a definable boundary; a consistent, but not necessarily uniform, character; overall control during the development process by a single development entity; private ownership of recreation amenities; and enforcement of covenants, conditions, and restrictions by a master community association. (*California Planning Roundtable*)

■ **planned development**    A contiguous land area of a minimum size, as specified by district regulation, to be planned and developed using a common master zoning plan, and containing one or more uses and appurtenant common areas. (*Prince William County, Va.*)

An area of land under single ownership containing any combination of two or more principal uses permitted by right or as a conditional use in the district in which the development is proposed, provided that conditional use approval must be obtained for any proposed use so listed in the regulations of the district in which the development is proposed. (*Cumberland, Md.*)

Land, under unified control, to be planned and developed as a whole in a single development operation or a definitely programmed series of development operations or phases. May include principal and accessory structures and those uses substantially related to the character and purposes of the planned development. (*Garrett, Ind.*)

■ **planned general commercial district**

(*See also commercial district*)    A land area under unified control designed and planned to be developed in a single operation of by a series of prescheduled development phases according to an officially approved site development plan to accommodate more than one commercial use of a more intensive nature beyond that of the neighborhood convenience type and limited to those uses allowed in the general commercial district. (*Palm Beach County, Fla.*)

■ **planned neighborhood commercial development** (*See also commercial district*)    A land area under unified control designed and planned to be developed in a single operation by a series of prescheduled development phases according to an officially approved Site Development Plan to accommodate more than one commercial use of a neighborhood/convenience nature as allowed in the Neighborhood Commercial District. (*Palm Beach County, Fla.*)

■ **planned unit development (PUD)** A description of a proposed unified development, consisting at a minimum of a map (pictured on page 171) and adopted ordinance setting forth the regulations governing, and the location and phasing of all proposed uses and improvements to be included in the development. (*California Planning Roundtable*)

An area of minimum contiguous size, as specified by ordinance, to be planned and developed as a single entity containing one or more residential clusters or planned unit residential developments and one or more public, quasi-public, commercial, or industrial areas in such ranges of ratios, and nonresidential uses to residential uses as shall be specified. (*Iowa State University Extension Service*)

A tract of land developed as a unit under single ownership or unified control, which includes one or more principal buildings or uses and is processed under the Planned Unit Development provisions of this ordinance. Also, a parcel of land planned as a single unit, rather than as an aggregate of individual lots, with design flexibility from traditional siting regulations (such as side yards, setbacks, and height limitations) or land-use re-

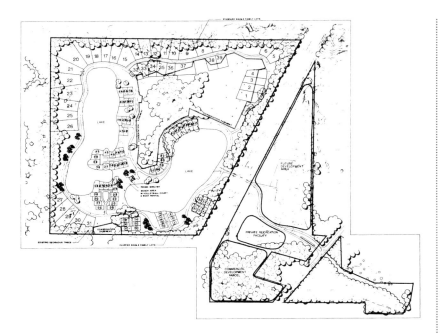

strictions (such as prohibitions against mixing land uses within a development). The greater flexibility in locating buildings and in combining various land uses often makes it possible to achieve certain economics in construction, as well as the preservation of open space and the inclusion of many amenities. *(Gurnee, Ill.)*

An area for which a unitary development plan has been prepared indicating, but not being limited to, the following land uses: open space, on-site circulation for both pedestrians and vehicles, parking, setbacks, housing densities, building spacings, land coverage, landscaping, relationships, streets, building heights, accessory uses, and architectural treatment. A Planned Unit Development also includes "cluster developments," which are a development design technique that concentrates buildings in a specific area on a site to allow the remaining land to be used for recreation, common open space, or preservation of environmentally sensitive areas. *(Mankato, Minn.)*

A large, integrated development adhering to a comprehensive plan and located on a single tract of land or on two or more tracts of land that may be separated only by a street or other right-of-way. *(Oakland, Calif.)*

■ **planned unit development (PUD) plat**  A drawing or map made to measurable scale upon that is presented a de-

scription and definition of the way in which the design requirements of the Planned Unit Development are to be met and intended for recording [with the appropriate office]. *(Gurnee, Ill.)*

■ **planned zoning district**  The zoning designation of a lot or tract to permit that development as is specifically depicted on plans approved in the process of zoning that lot or tract. *(North Kansas City, Mo.)*

■ **Planner**  Under general supervision, performs journey-level professional duties in current or long-range planning and performs related work as required. *(Washoe County , Nev.)*

***Commentary****: This definition is, of course, actually a job description. This job description and those for Planner I, II, III, and IV are illustrative only and will need to be adapted to local circumstances.*

■ **Planner I**  Performs routine professional work in the handling of a variety of assignments in the Planning and Development Department; does related work as required. Work is performed under the regular supervision of a senior planner. *(High Point, N.C.)*

Researches and analyzes technical data in the field of city planning and assists the public in applying planning and zoning regulations and information to construction and land-use problems; does related work as required. *(Phoenix, Ariz.)*

Under supervision, to perform the less complex professional planning duties involving data collection and analysis, public contract, report preparation, and related duties. *(Pittsburg, Calif.)*

Performs beginning-level professional studies pertaining to current planning problems in the city; does related work as required. *(Aurora, Ill.)*

■ **Planner II**  Performs responsible professional work in the handling of a variety of assignments in the Planning and Development Department; does related work as required. Work is performed under the general supervision of a senior planner. Supervision may be exercised over subordinate professional, technical, and clerical personnel. *(High Point, N.C.)*

Provides advance analysis of technical data and major project work in the field of city planning; does related work as required. *(Phoenix, Ariz.)*

This is intermediate-level professional work in urban planning. An employee in this class is responsible for the design and implementation of planning studies with the aim of guiding orderly development in the country and the subareas and communities therein. An employee in this class may conduct a variety of general and specialized planning studies depending upon the office to which he is assigned. Work involves the identification of problems; the development of goals and objectives; the design of programs and alternatives thereto meet the objectives and the implementation, monitoring and evaluation of programs. General direction is provided in completing assigned projects, and work is reviewed through conferences, reports, and observations of results obtained. A planner at this level is expected to require only a moderate level of supervision and to exercise a degree of independent latitude and initiative in the performance of his duties. *(Los Angeles, Calif.)*

■ **Planner III**  Performs difficult professional and responsible administrative work in conducting major activities, special projects, or programs in the Planning and Development Department; does related work as required. Work is performed under the general supervision of the Director of Planning and Development. Supervision is exercised over all subordinate professional, technical and clerical personnel. *(High Point, N.C.)*

Supervises a section of a planning division in a program of current planning or advanced planning; does related work as required. *(Phoenix, Ariz.)*

This is responsible professional work in urban planning. An employee in this class prepares and implements planning studies designed to promote the orderly growth and development of the country as a whole and of the various subareas and communities contained within its boundaries. Work involves the identification and analysis of problems; the development of goals and objectives; the design of programs and alternatives thereto meet the objectives and the implementation, monitoring, and evaluation of programs. Work is performed with considerable latitude for independent judgement and action within the scope of office programs and policies. General direction is received in performing projects, and work is reviewed through conferences, reports, and observations of results. *(Los Angeles, Calif.)*

■ **Planner IV**    Performs complex professional and responsible administrative work in conducting major activities, special projects, or programs in the Planning and Development Department; does related work as required. Work is performed under the general supervision of the Director of Planning and Development. Supervision is exercised over all subordinate professional, technical and clerical personnel. *(High Point, N.C.)*

This is highly responsible professional work in urban planning. An employee in this class is responsible for the design and implementation of planning studies designed to promote the orderly growth and development of the county as a whole and of subareas and communities contained within its boundaries. Work involves the identification and analysis of problems; the development of goals and objectives; the design of programs

and alternatives thereto meet the objectives and implementation, monitoring and evaluation of programs. Work is performed with considerable latitude for independent initiative and action within the scope of office programs and policies. The Planner IV is expected to perform highly responsible assignments with only general supervision and to coordinate the work of less experienced planners. *(Los Angeles, Calif.)*

■ **planning area**    The area directly addressed by the general plan. A city's planning area typically encompasses the city limits and potentially annexable land within its sphere of influence. *(California Planning Roundtable)*

■ **planning and zoning commission** A body of persons who recommends the boundaries of zoning districts and determines appropriate requirements relative to site plan review. *(St. Charles, Mo.)*

■ **planning board**    A public body of a local government, appointed pursuant to state statutes relating to planning boards, having the powers and duties set forth in those statutes. *(New York Planning Federation)*

■ **planning commission**    A body, usually having five or seven members, created by a city or county in compliance with California law, . . . [which] requires the assignment of the planning functions of the city or county to a planning department, planning commission, hearing officers, and/or the legislative body itself, as deemed appropriate by the legislative body. *(California Planning Roundtable)*

A group of people appointed by the city council that administer planning and land-use regulations for the city and provide recommendations on a wide array of land-use and land-use policy issues. *(Kennewick, Wash.)*

The administrative body, appointed by the city council, charged with the development of the General Plan and formulation and administration of the zoning map and ordinance. *(Walnut Creek, Calif.)*

■ **planting strip**    *(See also parkway)* A section of land not less than 10 feet in

width intended to contain plant materials and for the purpose of creating a visual separation between uses or activities. *(Carmel, Ind.)*

■ **plat**    (1) A map representing a tract of land, showing the boundaries and location or individual properties and streets; (2) a map of a subdivision or a site plan. *(Iowa State University Extension Service)*

A document, prepared by a registered surveyor or engineer, that delineates property lines and shows monuments and other landmarks for the purpose of identifying property. *(Prince William County, Va.)*

A map or plan with written provisions that is prepared in compliance with the Land Development Regulation which, when approved by the County, is recorded. *(Jefferson County, Colo.)*

The schematic representation of land divided or to be divided. *(Bedford County, Va.)*

■ **plat, abbreviated/short plat**    A plat that is generally simple in design that will subdivide a single lot into not more than four lots or combine not more than two lots into one, has required access, and does not require vacation or dedication activities. *(Unalaska, Alaska)*

■ **plat, final**    The final map of all of a portion of a subdivision or site plan that is presented to the proper review authority for final approval. *(Iowa State University Extension Service)*

■ **plat, preliminary**    A map of a subdivision of land showing . . . required features . . . that is submitted to the platting authority for purposes of preliminary consideration and approval. Preliminary approval may be given to typical land subdivision, abbreviated, right-of-way acquisition, and tideland plats. *(Unalaska, Alaska)*

■ **plat, sketch**    A rough sketch map of a proposed subdivision or site plan of sufficient accuracy to be used for the purpose of discussion and classification. *(Iowa State University Extension Service)*

■ **plat, tideland**    A plat created for the purpose of subdividing or platting tide or submerged lands, or tidelands in conjunction with adjacent uplands. *(Unalaska, Alaska)*

■ **platform** *(See also **public transit concourse; transit station**)*   That portion of the station directly adjacent to the tracks at which trains stop to load and unload passengers. *(Sacramento Regional Transit District)*

■ **play lot** *(See also **playground**)*   A small area developed especially for preschool or elementary school aged children. It may contain such facilities as sandboxes, slides, teeters, swings, climbing apparatus, and the like. *(Hartford, Conn.)*

An improved and equipped play area for small children, usually no older then elementary school age. *(Schaumburg, Ill., which uses the term "tot lot")*

■ **playfield or athletic field** *(See also **recreation** definitions)*   A developed recreation area that may contain a playground as well as fields for competitive sports such as baseball, football, or soccer. Bleachers or grandstands may be provided. *(Hartford, Conn.)*

Grounds and facilities for open air games. *(Valdez, Alaska)*

■ **playground**   A publicly owned area for recreational use primarily by children. *(Palmer, Alaska)*

An area developed for active play and recreation that may contain courts for such games as basketball or tennis. *(Hartford, Conn.)*

■ **playhouse**   A freestanding structure, exclusively for the use of children, with a

maximum height of 12 feet and an area not to exceed 120 square feet. *(Thousand Oaks, Calif.)*

■ **plaza**   An open space that may be improved, landscaped, or paved usually surrounded by buildings or streets (pictured below). *(Miami, Fla.)*

An area generally open to the public on a controlled basis and used for passive recreational activities and relaxation. Plazas are paved areas typically provided with amenities, such as seating, drinking and ornamental fountains, art, trees, and landscaping, for use by pedestrians. *(Portland, Ore.)*

A public open space at ground level wholly or partly enclosed by a building or buildings. It is continuously accessible to the public and has openings to the sky. *(Davis, Calif.)*

■ **plot**   Land occupied or to be occupied by a building or use, and its accessory buildings and accessory uses, together with such yards and open spaces as are required. . . . A plot may consist of one or more or portions of a platted lot or unplatted land. *(Boca Raton, Fla.)*

(1) A single unit parcel of land; (2) a parcel of land that can be identified and referenced to a recorded plat or map. *(Iowa State University Extension Service)*

■ **plot, corner**   A plot of which at least two adjacent sides abut for their full length upon streets, provided that such two sides intersect at any interior angle of not more than 135 degrees. Where a plot is on a curve, if tangents through the intersections of the lot lines with the

street lines make an interior angle of not more than 135 degrees, such a plot is a corner plot. In the case of a corner plot with a curved street line, the corner shall be considered to be that point on the street line nearest to the point of intersection of the tangents herein described. *(Boca Raton, Fla.)*

■ **plot, reversed corner**   A corner plot the side street line of which is substantially a continuation of the front plot line of the first plot to its rear. *(Boca Raton, Fla.)*

■ **plot plan**   A plat of a lot, drawn to scale, showing the actual measurements, the size and location of any existing structures or structures to be erected, the location of the lot in relation to abutting streets, and other such information. *(Newport Beach, Calif.)*

■ **pole barn**   A typically metal clad structure most often utilizing wooden poles and trusses for support with unfinished, insulated interiors. Such structures are normally used for agricultural purposes, for construction trade storage, or for general storage and not intended for human inhabitation. *(Duquoin, Ill.)*

■ **police power**   The right of government to regulate personal conduct and the use of land in order to protect that public health, safety, and welfare. The use of police power by a unit of government must follow "due process" and be "reasonable," but the government does not have to pay compensation for related losses. In this last respect, it differs from the government's use of eminent domain (where just compensation is mandatory). *(Iowa State University Extension Service)*

■ **policy**   A specific statement of principle or of guiding actions that implies clear commitment but is not mandatory. A general direction that a governmental agency sets to follow in order to meet its goals and objectives before undertaking an action program. *(California Planning Roundtable)*

■ **pollutant** *(See also **contaminant**)*   Any introduced gas, liquid, or solid that makes a resource unfit for its normal or usual purpose *(California Planning Roundtable)*

■ **pollution** (*See also* **air pollution**) The presence of matter or energy whose nature, location, or quantity produces undesired environmental effects. (*California Planning Roundtable*)

■ **pollution, nonpoint** Sources for pollution that are less definable and usually cover broad areas of land, such as agricultural land with fertilizers that are carried from the land by runoff, or automobiles. (*California Planning Roundtable*)

■ **pollution, point** In reference to water quality, a discrete source from which pollution is generated before it enters receiving waters, such as a sewer outfall, a smokestack, or an industrial waste pipe. (*California Planning Roundtable*)

■ **pond** (*See also* **lake**) Any inland body of water that in its natural state has a surface area of 1,000 square feet or more, and any body of water artificially formed or increased that has a surface area of 1,000 square feet or more. (*Cape Elizabeth, Maine*)

A permanent or temporary body of open water which is more than one acre in size and less than five acres in size. (*Grand Traverse County, Mich.*)

■ **pool/billiard hall** A business establishment containing more than two pool or billiard tables for the use of patrons. (*Imperial Beach, Calif.*)

■ **population density** A numerical method of expressing the extent to which people are clustered within a specific geographic area, usually in terms of people per square mile or per square kilometer. The population density of an area is derived by dividing the total population of the entity by the total land area of the entity. (*United States Census Bureau*)

■ **population projection** A prediction of a future demographic condition that will occur if the assumptions inherent in the projection technique prove true. (PAS Memo, *February 2000*)

■ **porch** A covered but unenclosed projection from the main wall of a building that may or may not use columns or other ground supports for structural purposes. (*Chandler, Ariz.*)

A roofed structure not more than 75 percent enclosed by walls and attached to the main building for the purpose of sheltering from the rays of the sun and from rain and weather, exclusive of vehicles, either persons or inanimate objects. (*Coral Gables, Fla.*)

A covered platform, usually having a separate roof, at an entrance to a dwelling, or an open or enclosed gallery or room, which is not heated or cooled, that is attached to the outside of a building. (*Newport Beach, Calif.*)

■ **porch depth** The dimension of a porch or arcade measured forward from the facade. (*Orlando, Fla.*)

■ **porch, open** A porch open on three sides except for wire screening. A porch shall not be considered open if enclosed by either permanent or detachable glass sash. (*Hartford, Conn.*)

A roofed structure attached to a building and open on two or more sides. A screened-in porch shall not be considered open. (*Cape Girardeau, Mo.*)

■ **porch, screened** A roofed structure not more than 75 percent enclosed by walls and attached to the main building provided, however, the remainder of the screened porch may be enclosed with insect screening or metal, fiberglass, or other approved insect screening. The insect screening shall have at least 50 percent of open area per inch enclosed by walls and attached to the building for the

purpose of sheltering from the rays of the sun, exclusive of vehicles, either persons or inanimate objects. (*Coral Gables, Fla.*)

■ **porch, unenclosed** A unheated, open-air stoop that may be partially enclosed with a roof on top, and railings or walls on the sides not exceeding 40 inches in height from the porch floor. The area between the roof and the railings or walls may be covered with screening or netting material only, and cannot be enclosed with windows or other material. (*Grand Forks, N.D.*)

■ **porch width** The dimension of a porch or arcade measures as a percentage of the facade lot width. (*Orlando, Fla.*)

■ **porous paving system** (*See also* **impervious surface; pervious surface; runoff**) A system providing erosion control, softening hard surfaces, reducing storm water/snow-melt runoff, and/or providing green space. The system includes concrete, plastic, or other systems that may incorporate grass or other landscaped surfaces. (*Glenwood Springs, Colo.*)

■ **port and harbor facilities** Those facilities generally associated with a port or harbor (pictured below), such as docks, piers, floats, and the harbor master structure. (*Valdez, Alaska*)

Those improvements and their appurtenant areas . . . that are adapted to the purpose of securing and/or servicing vessels. The term includes, but is not lim-

ited to, docks, mooring devices, floats, fingers, stalls, gridirons, and other appurtenances. *(Unalaska, Alaska)*

■ **port authority**    A special governmental agency of the locality, county, or state [which] is authorized or established by state law to tightly control development of [a] port. *(The Zoning Report)*

■ **porte-cochere**    A structure attached to a residence and erected over a driveway, not exceeding one story in height, and open on two or more sides. *(Homestead, Fla.)*

A porch or cover, under which a vehicle may be driven temporarily to protect the occupants when alighting. A porte cochere shall not be construed to be a "carport." *(Champaign, Ill.)*

■ **post office**    Houses service windows for mailing packages and letters, post office boxes, offices, vehicle storage areas, and sorting and distribution facilities for mail. *(Redmond, Wash.)*

■ **poultry**    Domestic fowl, chickens, ducks, geese, and similar fowl, but specifically excluding turkeys and guinea fowl. *(Thousand Oaks, Calif.)*

■ **poverty level** *(See also **housing** definitions)*    As used by the U.S. Census, families and unrelated individuals are classified as being above or below the poverty level based on a poverty index that provides a range of income cutoffs or "poverty thresholds" varying by size of family, number of children, and age of householder. The income cutoffs are updated each year to reflect the change in the Consumer Price Index. *(California Planning Roundtable)*

■ **premises**    A building lot with the required front, side, and rear yards for a dwelling. *(Grand Forks, N.D.)*

A lot, together with all buildings and structures thereon. *(El Paso, Tex.)*

■ **preschool** *(See **educational facilities**)*

■ **present value**    The total current monetary value of past, present, or future payments, contributions, or dedications of goods, services, materials, construction, or money. *(Boise City, Idaho)*

■ **preserve** *(See also **habitat protection area; wildlife habitat; wildlife refuge**)*    An area in which beneficial uses in their present condition are protected; for example, a nature preserve or an agricultural preserve. *(California Planning Roundtable)*

Open space that preserves or protects endangered species, a critical environmental feature, or other natural feature. *(Austin, Tex.)*

■ **principal residence**    The place where a person resides seven months or more in a 12-month period. *(Danville, Ill.)*

■ **print shop** *(See also **copy shop**)*    A facility for the custom reproduction of written or graphic materials on a custom order basis for individuals or businesses. Typical processes include, but are not limited to, photocopying, blueprint, and facsimile sending and receiving, and including offset printing. *(Clark County, Nev.)*

■ **private**    Belonging to, or restricted for the use or enjoyment of particular persons. *(Palm Desert, Calif.)*

■ **private recreational facility/club** *(See also **health club; recreation** definitions)*    Recreational center for the exclusive use of members and their guests with facilities usually including swimming pools and/or tennis courts, but specifically excluding golf courses. *(Williamson County, Tenn.)*

A building in which members of a community or association may gather for social, educational, or cultural activities. *(Tumwater, Wash.)*

A recreation facility open only to bona fide members and guests of the private organization operating the facility. *(Garrett, Ind.)*

■ **private road** *(See **street, private**)*

■ **processing** *(See also **industry** definitions; **manufacturing** definitions)*    To subject to some special process or treatment, as in the course of manufacture; change in the physical state or chemical composition of matter; the second step in use of a natural resource; examples include petroleum refining, oil shale crush-

ing, retorting and refining, ore smelting, coal crushing and cleaning, saw mill, alfalfa pellet mills, food canning or packing, creation of glass, ceramic or plastic materials, gravel crushing, cement manufacture, concrete batch plants. *(Glenwood Springs, Colo.)*

■ **processing facility**    A building or an enclosed space used for the collection and processing of recyclable material. "Processing" means the preparation of material for efficient shipment, or to an end-user's specifications, by such means as baling, briquetting, compacting, flattening, grinding, crushing, mechanical sorting, shredding, cleaning, and remanufacturing. *(El Paso, Tex.)*

■ **processing facility, light**    Occupies an area of less than 45,000 square feet of gross collection, processing and storage area. Light processing facilities are limited to baling, briquetting, crushing, compacting, grinding, shredding, and sorting of source-separate recyclable material and repairing of reusable material. A light processing facility shall not shred, compact, or bale ferrous metals other than food and beverage containers. *(El Paso, Tex.)*

■ **productive life**    The number of years a property improvement is expected to be in service in a facility. *(Jefferson County, Tex.)*

■ **profession**    An occupation involving the dispensation of a service that involves either some skill or knowledge, or that requires connections to other business not easily or readily available to the general public (examples are doctors, lawyers, architects, financial services, stockbrokers, detective agencies, engineers, etc.). A distinction is made between purveyors of professions and purveyors of merchandise or repair of articles. *(Ocean Shores, Wash.)*

■ **program**    An action, activity, or strategy carried out in response to adopted policy to achieve a specific goal or objective. Policies and programs establish the "who," "how" and "when" for carrying out the "what" and "where" of goals and objectives. *(California Planning Roundtable)*

■ **project**    A particular development on an identifiable parcel of land. *(Boise City, Idaho)*

■ **project improvements**    Site improvements and facilities that are planned and designed to provide for a particular development project and that are necessary for the use and convenience of the occupants or users of the project. *(Boise City, Idaho)*

■ **project site**    That portion of any lot, parcel, tract, or combination thereof that encompasses all phases of the total project proposal. *(Yakima County, Wash.)*

■ **property**    Includes real and personal property. *(Peoria, Ill.)*

■ **property, abandoned**    Personal property of any type the owner of which has failed to make satisfactory claim and proof of ownership within 60 days after notice has been provided. *(Rochester, Minn.)*

■ **property line** *(See lot line definitions)*

■ **property, unclaimed**    Personal property of any type where the owner or his or her whereabouts is unknown, or which is unclaimed for more than seven days. *(Rochester, Minn.)*

■ **provider**    A person residing in the home where a personal care facility operates, whose duties include, but are not limited to, direct care, supervision, and guidance of personal care recipients. *(El Paso, Tex.)*

■ **psychic** *(See also fortune telling)*    Pertaining to predictions of the future based on intuitive or mental powers or supernatural influences and not statistical or otherwise empirical evidence. *(Wheeling, Ill.)*

■ **public access**    A means of physical approach to and along the shoreline available to the general public. This may also include visual approach. *(Renton, Wash.)*

■ **public art** *(See art, public)*

■ **public building**    Any building held, used, or controlled exclusively for public purposes by any department or branch of government, state, county, or munici-

pal, without reference to the ownership of the building or of the realty upon which it is situated. A building belonging to or used by the public for the transaction of public or quasi-public business. *(Grand Forks, N.D.)*

Structures principally of an institutional nature and serving a public need, such as churches, hospitals, schools, libraries, museums, post offices, police and fire stations, public utilities, and other public services, but not including the operation of a public bar, restaurant or recreational facility as a commercial enterprise. *(Brookfield, Wisc.)*

■ **public celebrations** *(See also festival)* An event or series of events scheduled in observance of a state, federal, or religious holiday, or conducting organized activities for a historical, cultural, or a special theme held for a limited period of time and where such events or activities are not being held solely for profit. *(Siskiyou County, Calif.)*

■ **public entrance**    The entranceway of a residence or other building closest to the public street or sidewalk or one which would be reasonably perceived by the public to be the entrance to the dwelling available for public use. *(Springfield, Ill.)*

■ **public facilities**    A use conducted by, or a facility or structure owned or managed by, the government of the United States, the State of Hawaii or the County of Maui that provides a governmental function, activity, or service for public benefit. *(Maui County, Hawaii, which uses the terms "public facility" or "public use")*

■ **public hearing**    *(See also public meeting)* A meeting, announced and advertised in advance and open to the public, in which members of the public have an opportunity to participate. *(Clark County, Nev.)*

A formal meeting held pursuant to public notice by the supervisors or planning agency, intended to inform and obtain public comment, prior to taking action in accordance with this act. *(Cranberry Township, Pa.)*

■ **public improvement**    Any improvement, facility, or service together with its associated public site or right-of-way necessary to provide transportation, drainage, public utilities, cable television, or similar essential services. *(Champaign, Ill.)*

■ **public lands**    Any land area within the planned development that has been dedicated or reserved for use as streets, alleys, public ways, parks, playgrounds, schools, community buildings, ways for public service facilities, sidewalks, stormwater or floodwater runoff channels, detention basins, or other public uses. *(Wheeling, Ill.)*

■ **public meeting** *(See also public hearing)*    An informal meeting, hearing, workshop, or other public gathering of people to obtain comments from the public or other agencies on a proposed project permit prior to the local government's decision. The proceedings at a public meeting may be recorded and a report or recommendation may be included in the county's project permit application file. *(Whatcom County, Wash.)*

■ **public place** *(See also open space)* Open space, including any park, lake, stream, stadium, athletic field, playground, school yard, street, avenue, plaza, square, bus, train or railroad depot, station, terminal, cemetery, open space adjacent thereto, or any other place commonly open to the public, including but not limited to, areas on private property commonly open to the view by the public. *(Champaign, Ill.)*

■ **public room**    Public space that is totally within a building, but which allows for year-round, climate controlled use by the public and which has direct access to the public street, transit concourses, and/or transit stations. *(Philadelphia, Pa.)*

■ **public service corporation**    A city- or state-owned enterprise or corporation providing services essential to the general public convenience or safety. . . . All projects proposed by the public service corporations must be reviewed and approved by the city administration through the site plan review chapter of the zoning code. In addition, in the case [the transit authority], any facility that would be permitted must be adjacent to a state highway. A public charitable corporation incorporated under the laws of the state, . . . exempt from income taxation under the provisions of Section 501 (c) (3) of the Internal Revenue Code, may also be considered a public service corporation in those instances where the following conditions are met: 1. The corporation owns and manages property that has been purchased by the corporation directly from the city; . . . 2. The corporation's primary purpose is the preservation and restoration of historic structures; and 3. The standards established in . . . this zoning code are complied with. *(Newport, R.I.)*

■ **public transit concourse** *(See also **platform**)* The network of interconnected spaces below the street level which provide ingress and egress to public transit and/or railway stations from street level and/or buildings. *(Philadelphia, Pa.)*

■ **public transportation** *(See also **paratransit; subway; transit** definitions)* Services provided for the public on a regular basis by vehicles such as bus or rail on public ways, using specific routes and schedules, and usually on a fare-paying basis. *(Sacramento Regional Transit District)*

■ **public way** Any street or sidewalk *(Champaign, Ill.)*

Any street, alley, pedestrian way, pathway, channel, viaduct, subway, bridge, easement, right-of-way or other way in which the public has a right of use. *(Palm Desert, Calif.)*

■ **public works** A. All production, storage, transmission, and recovery facilities for water, sewerage, telephone, and other similar utilities owned or operated by any public agency or by any utility subject to the jurisdiction of the Public Utilities Commission, except for energy facilities. B. All public transportation facilities, including streets, roads, highways, public parking lots and structures, ports, harbors, airports, railroads, and mass transit facilities and stations, bridges, trolley wires and other related facilities. C. All publicly financed recre-

ational facilities, all projects of the State Coastal Conservancy, and any development of a special district. *(Imperial Beach, Calif.)*

■ **quality of life**    The attributes or amenities that combine to make an area a good place to live. Examples include the availability of political, educational, and social support systems; good relations among constituent groups; a healthy physical environment; and economic opportunities for both individuals and businesses. *(Indianapolis, Ind.)*

■ **quarry**    A lot or land or part thereof used for the purpose of extracting stone, sand, gravel, or top soil for sale and exclusive of the process of grading a lot preparatory to the construction of a building for which application for a building permit has been made. *(Farragut, Tenn.)*

An open pit from which building stone, sand, gravel, mineral, or fill is taken to be processed for commercial purposes. *(El Paso, Tex.)*

■ **quarry/pit rehabilitation**    To provide slopes that will be covered with a layer of soil and revegetated where prac-

tical. It applies to the rehabilitation of all kinds of sand, gravel, and rock excavations to obtain fill or construction materials and from which no further removal of materials is intended, as well as to resource extraction. Rehabilitation is intended to minimize the hazardous and unsightly nature of abandoned pits, and if practical, to return the area to some productive use. *(Unalaska, Alaska)*

■ **quarter/quarter zoning** *(See also agricultural protection zoning)*    A quarter of a quarter-section of land (1/16 of 640 acres or 40 acres). A nonexclusive, density-based zoning method designed to preserve farmland indefinitely. A limited number of nonfarm homes are allowed for every 40 acres of land. This technique is most appropriate in rural areas with large farming operations and moderate growth pressures where average parcel sizes exceed 40 acres. *(Michigan Townships Association)*

■ **quasi-public use/quasi-public facility**    A use conducted by, or a facility or structure owned or operated by, a nonprofit, religious, or eleemosynary institution that provides educational, cultural, recreational, religious, or other similar types of public services. *(Maui County, Hawaii)*

Institutional, academic, governmental, and community service uses, either owned publicly or operated by nonprofit organizations, including private hospitals and cemeteries. *(California Planning Roundtable)*

■ **queue space** *(See also stacking lane)*    A temporary waiting area for motor vehicles obtaining a service or other activity. *(Newport Beach, Calif.)*

■ **racetrack**   A measured course where animals or machines are entered in competition against one another or against time, including tracks used only in the training of animals. *(Kent County, Md.)*

■ **railroad**   A public or private right-of-way on which tracks for trains are constructed. Railroad yards and stations shall be classified as cargo or passenger terminals. *(Seattle, Wash.)*

■ **railroad crossing**   A place where a public road or right-of-way intersects with railroad lines or tracks and one crosses over the other. This term shall include the entire width of the right-of-way of the public road and the entire width of the railroad right-of-way at the place of crossing. *(Boone County, Ky.)*

■ **railroad freight depot**   A heavy rail facility for freight pick-up or distribution; may include intermodal distribution facilities for truck or shipping transport. *(Prince William County, Va.)*

■ **railroad passenger station** *(See also transit station; terminal definitions)* A facility, either light or heavy rail, for the boarding of passengers and related ticketing sales and offices. *(Prince William County, Va.)*

■ **Rails To Trails** *(See also trail)*   A federal act to give interested parties (governments) the opportunity to use railroad rights-of-way, which might otherwise be abandoned, for recreational use. *(Green Bay, Wisc.)*

■ **railyard**   An area of land, a portion of which is covered by a system of tracks (pictured below), that provides for the making up of trains by one or more railroads or private industry concerns. Necessary functions of a railyard include, but are not limited to, the classifying, switching, storing, assembling, distributing, consolidating, moving, repairing, weighing or transferring of cars, trains, engines, locomotives and rolling stock. *(El Paso, Tex.)*

An area for storing and switching of freight and passenger rolling stock. *(Prince William County, Va.)*

■ **raised basement**   A semi-underground story serving to raise the principal floor level not more than five feet above the sidewalk. A raised basement shall not count against the story height limitations. *(Howard County, Md.)*

■ **ramp**   A structure attached to a principal or accessory building that is constructed at a slope that meets the

Uniform Building Code requirements for the purposes of providing access to a building. *(Mankato, Minn.)*

■ **ranch**   A lot used primarily for the breeding of horses; raising of livestock; individual training or training of small groups of eight or fewer students; practice polo courses and arenas not used for scheduled, public, or club events; boarding only of horses, mules, or ponies directly involved with current breeding or training activities; and ancillary sales and previews of livestock and occasional weekend seminars and clinics. Permanent housing for ranch employees shall be permitted as an accessory use to the ranch. No feed lot shall be permitted. . . . *Scottsdale, Ariz.)*

A place where livestock is bred or raised. *(Siskiyou County, Calif.)*

■ **ranchette**   A single dwelling unit occupied by a nonfarming household on a parcel of 2.5 to 20 acres that has been subdivided from agricultural land. *(California Planning Roundtable)*

■ **ravine**   Any natural land area with a steep-sided, wooded valley typically with continual or intermittent running water at its base, that has a drop in elevation from the top ravine edge equal to or greater than two feet vertical for every 10 feet horizontal. . . . A ravine shall not include: (i) mere depressions, gullies, or streams that do not have adjacent, larger, wooded steep-sided areas; (ii) the upper reaches or secondary reaches of a steep sided,

wooded valley, that has been extensively filled or extensively graded; . . . or (iii) the extreme upper reaches or secondary reaches of a steep-sided, wooded valley, that is less than 150 feet in length and that is isolated from all primary ravine areas as a result of man-made improvements, such as roads or other structures. *(Lake Bluff, Ill.)*

■ **real estate development**

*Commentary: There are many complex terms related to real estate. Due to space constraints, we opted not to define them all; rather, we are directing readers to Appendix A of PAS Report 380,* Analyzing the Economic Feasibility of a Development Project: A Guide for Planners *by Richard J. Roddewig and Jared Schlaes, or contact your PAS representative for a xeroxed copy of that appendix.*

■ **real property**    Lands, tenements, and hereditaments and . . . all chattels real. *(Peoria, Ill.)*

■ **receiving body of water**    Any lake, pond, stream, wetland, or groundwater into which stormwater runoff is directed. *(Grand Traverse County, Mich.)*

Creeks, streams, rivers, lakes, storm sewers, wetlands, and other bodies of water into which surface waters are directed, either naturally or in man-made ditches, or open and closed system. *(Renton, Wash.)*

■ **reclamation**    The reuse of resources, usually those present in solid wastes or sewage. *(California Planning Roundtable)*

■ **reconstruction**    As used in historic preservation, the process of reproducing by new construction the exact form and detail of a vanished structure, or part thereof, as it appeared during a specific period of time. Reconstruction is often undertaken when the property to be reconstructed is essential for understanding and interpreting the value of an historic district and sufficient documentation exists to insure an exact reproduction of the original. *(California Planning Roundtable)*

■ **record**    A document kept in the ordinary course of business by a governmental unit. Also, the written expression

of the proceedings of a public body. Meeting minutes are one form of record. *(New York Planning Federation)*

■ **record of survey**    A map prepared by a professional land surveyor that re-establishes survey controls, boundaries, locations of improvements, or the alignment of right-of-ways for recording. *(Unalaska, Alaska)*

■ **recreation**    The refreshment of body and mind through forms of play, amusement, or relaxation. The recreational experience may be active, such as boating, fishing, and swimming, or may be passive, such as enjoying the natural beauty of the shoreline or its wildlife. *(Renton, Wash.)*

■ **recreation, active**    Leisure activities, usually performed with others, often requiring equipment and taking place at prescribed places, sites, or fields. The term active recreation includes, but is not limited to, swimming, tennis, and other court games, baseball and other field sports, golf and playground activities. *(Tumwater, Wash.)*

Recreation requiring some constructed facilities and organized activities. *(Jefferson County, Colo.)*

■ **recreation, commercial**    Any establishment whose main purpose is to provide the general public with an amusing or entertaining activity and where tickets are sold or fees are collected for the activity. Includes, but not limited to, skating rinks, water slides, miniature golf courses, arcades, bowling alleys, and billiard halls, but not movie theaters. *(Durham, N.C.)*

■ **recreation, commercial indoor**    A commercial recreational land use conducted entirely within a building, including arcade, arena, art gallery and studio, art center, assembly hall, athletic and health clubs, auditorium, bowling alley, club or lounge, community center, conference center, exhibit hall, gymnasium, library, movie theater, museum, performance theater, pool or billiard hall, skating rink, swimming pool, tennis court. *(Glenwood Springs, Colo.)*

■ **recreation, commercial outdoor**    Predominantly participant uses conducted in

open or partially enclosed or screened facilities. Typical uses include driving ranges, miniature golf, swimming pools, tennis courts, outdoor racquetball courts, motorized cart and motorcycle tracks, and motorized model airplane flying facilities. *(Blacksburg, Va.)*

■ **recreation, commercial outdoor, concentrated**    A recreational land use conducted outside of a building, characterized by potentially substantial impacts on traffic, the natural environment, and the surrounding neighborhood, including aerial tramway; alpine or water slide; amphitheater; amusement ride; auto, cycle and go-cart race track; campgrounds without recreational vehicles; coliseum, stadium; drive-in theater; horse, dog racing track; pack station; shooting range; stable; zoo. *(Glenwood Springs, Colo.)*

■ **recreation, commercial outdoor, general**    A recreational land use conducted outside of a building, characterized by potentially moderate impacts on traffic, the natural environment, and the surrounding neighborhood, including athletic fields; miniature golf; skateboard park; swimming, bathing, wading and other therapeutic facilities; tennis, handball, basketball courts; batting cages, trampoline facilities. *(Glenwood Springs, Colo.)*

■ **recreation, commercial outdoor, light**    A commercial recreational land use conducted outside of a building, characterized by minimal impact on traffic, the natural environment, or the surrounding neighborhood, including arboretum, botanical garden, bridle trails, country club, golf course, historic site. *(Glenwood Springs, Colo.)*

■ **recreation, community**    A private recreational facility for use solely by the residents and guests of a particular residential development, planned unit development, or residential neighborhood, including indoor and outdoor facilities. These facilities are usually proposed or planned in association with development and are usually located within or adjacent to such development. *(Blacksburg, Va.)*

■ **recreation facilities** Country clubs, riding stables, golf courses, and other private noncommercial recreation areas and facilities, or recreation centers, including private swimming pools. *(Rapid City, S.D.)*

■ **recreation facilities, commercial, on natural sites** Commercial recreation premises consisting of woodlands, water courses, and fields used for active recreational activities that do not require modifying the existing setting, including but not limited to, paintball, laser tag, and orienteering. *(Durham, N.C.)*

■ **recreation, outdoor** Recreational uses conducted almost wholly outdoors, including golf driving ranges (not associated with a golf course), miniature golf, firing ranges, water parks, amusement parks, and similar uses. *(Renton, Wash.)*

■ **recreation, passive** Recreational activities that generally do not require a developed site. This generally includes such activities as hiking, horseback riding, and picnicking. *(Durham, N.C.)*

Recreation that involves existing natural resources and has a minimal impact. *(Jefferson County, Colo.)*

Nonmotorized recreation not requiring "development," as defined, nor requiring any alteration of existing topography, nor any activity regulated pursuant to this section. Such passive recreation shall include, but not be limited to, hiking, hang gliding, bicycling, picnicking, and birdwatching. *(Middlefield, Conn.)*

■ **recreation support facilities** Those facilities used exclusively for the preparation, maintenance, and storage of equipment used in recreational activities; business operations and nonresidential shelter facilities for persons engaged in said activities; for example, trailers housing field offices for rafting companies. *(Glenwood Springs, Colo.)*

■ **recreation vehicle (RV)** Any building, structure, or vehicle designed and/or used for living or sleeping and/or recreational purposes and equipped with wheels to facilitate movement from place to place, and automobiles when used for living or sleeping

purposes and including pick-up coaches (campers), motorized homes, boats, travel trailers, and camping trailers not meeting the specifications required for a manufactured home or mobile home. *(Clark County, Nev.)*

A vehicle built on a single chassis, containing 400 square feet or less when measured at the largest horizontal projections and designed to be self propelled or towed by another vehicle. A recreational vehicle is not designed or intended for use as a permanent dwelling, but as temporary living quarters for recreational camping, travel, or seasonal use. This definition includes vehicles such as travel trailers, motor homes, boats, house boats, and campers. *(Fort Wayne, Ind.)*

A vehicular-type unit primarily designed as temporary living quarters for recreational, camping, or travel use, which either has its own motive power or is mounted on or drawn by another vehicle. . . . *(Jacksonville, Fla.)*

■ **recreation vehicle (RV) park** Any lot or parcel of land used or intended to be used for the accommodation of two or more recreational vehicles for transient dwelling purposes. *(Clark County, Nev.)*

A commercial use providing space and facilities for motor homes or other recreational vehicles for recreational use or transient lodging. There is no minimum required stay in a recreational vehicle park. Uses where unoccupied recreational vehicles are offered for sale or lease, or are stored, are not included. *(Portland, Ore.)*

A parcel of land reserved for the location of recreational vehicles, including buildings and sites set aside for group camping and similar recreational vehicles. *(Clearwater, Fla.)*

■ **recreational fire** A fire contained within a pit, barrel, or other noncombustible enclosure for the purpose of pleasure, religious, ceremonial, or other similar purposes. *(Hilton Head Island, N.C.)*

■ **rectory** (See *parsonage*)

■ **recyclable material** Residential, commercial, and industrial materials or

byproducts that are set aside, handled, packaged, or offered for collection separate from garbage for the purpose of being processed and then returned to the economic mainstream in the form of commodities or products. *(Oakland, Calif.)*

Reusable materials including, but not limited to, metals, glass, plastic, wood, and paper that are intended for remanufacturing or reconstitution. Recyclable materials do not include junk, rubbish, refuse, or hazardous waste. *(Boulder County, Colo.)*

■ **recyclables, household** Waste material from normal household operations accepted at recycling centers, including, but not limited to, glass, plastic, aluminum, tin, newspaper, cardboard, lawn clippings, leaves and tree branches. *(Rapid City, S.D.)*

■ **recycling center** A building in which recyclable material only is collected, processed, and/or baled in preparation for shipment to others who will use those materials to manufacture new products. *(Clark County, Nev.)*

A building or an area where the primary activity is the separation of materials prior to shipment for remanufacture into new materials. This shall not include junk yards or wrecking yards. *(Durham, N.C.)*

A facility designed to be a collection point where only recyclable materials are sorted and/or temporarily stored prior to delivery to a permanent disposal site, or shipment to others for reuse, and/or processing into new products. This facility can be a temporary and/or mobile, profit or not-for-profit operation, not accessory to the principal permitted use or a permanent installation that is the principal permitted use. *(Jefferson County, Colo., which uses the term "recycling station")*

A facility where recyclable materials, such as newspapers, magazines, books, and other paper products, glass, metal cans, and other products are recycled, reprocessed, and treated in order to return such products to a condition where they may be reused. *(Fort Wayne, Ind.)*

A building or enclosed area used for the collection and processing of recyclable materials. Processing means the preparation of material for shipment, or an end-user's specifications, by such means as baling, briquetting, compacting, flattening, grinding, crushing, mechanical sorting, shredding, cleaning and remanufacturing. Processing facilities include storage and loading areas located entirely on the processing center site. *(Chico, Calif.)*

■ **recycling collection center**    A center for the acceptance by donation, redemption, or purchase of recyclable materials from the public. Collection centers include: reverse vending machines or groups of reverse vending machines occupying more than 75 square feet, a mobile recycling unit, kiosk-type units that may include permanent structures, unattended containers placed for the donation of recyclable materials. *(Chico, Calif.)*

A building and/or site in which source-separated recoverable materials, such as newspapers, glassware, and metal cans are collected, stored, flattened, crushed, or bundled prior to shipment to others who will use those materials to manufacture new products. The materials are stored on-site in bins or trailers for shipment to market. *(Blue Springs, Mo.)*

A collection point for small recyclable items and materials, such as cans, bottles, newspapers, secondhand goods, and used motor oil. Activities of a recycling collection center are limited to sorting, compacting, and transferring. *(Tumwater, Wash.)*

A recycling facility used for the acceptance by donation, redemption, or purchase of recyclable materials from the public. A collection facility includes (1) reverse vending machine facilities, (2) small collection facilities that occupy an area of not more than 500 square feet, (3) large collection facilities that may occupy an area of more than 500 square feet and that may include permanent structures. *(Walnut Creek, Calif., which uses the term "recycling collection facility")*

■ **recycling collection point**    A facility for the drop-off and temporary holding of materials such as paper, cardboard, glass, metal, plastic, batteries, and motor oil. Processing of materials is limited to glass breaking and separation. Recycling materials are not sold to a recycling drop-off center. A recycling drop-off center is intended for household or consumer use. Use by commercial or industrial establishments is not included. Unattended drop-off stations for single materials, such as newsprint, are also not included. *(Portland, Ore.)*

An accessory use, structure, or enclosed area that serves as a neighborhood drop-off point for temporary storage of recyclable materials. A recycling collection point may also include a facility for the temporary collection of used clothing and household goods. *(Fort Wayne, Ind.)*

An incidental use that serves as a neighborhood drop-off point for temporary storage of recoverable materials. No permanent storage or processing of such items would be allowed. This facility would generally be located in a shopping center parking lot or in other public/quasi-public areas, such as in churches or schools. *(Jacksonville, N.C.)*

A convenient location not within a public right-of-way where mobile depots or drop boxes may be sited as a recyclable material collection point for nearby residents prior to delivery to a broker or user of such materials. *(Clackamas County, Ore., which uses the term "recycling drop-off station or site")*

■ **recycling plants**    A facility that is not a salvage yard and in which recoverable resources, such as newspapers, magazines, books, and other paper products, glass; metal cans, and other products, are recycled, reprocessed, and treated to return such products to a condition in which they may again be used for production. *(Jacksonville, N.C.)*

■ **redevelop**    To demolish existing buildings or to increase the overall floor area existing on a property; or both, irrespective of whether a change occurs in land use. *(California Planning Roundtable)*

■ **redevelopment**    Any proposed expansion, addition, or major facade change to an existing building, structure, or parking facility. *(Wheeling, Ill.)*

■ **reforestation** *(See also **forest and forestry** definitions)*   Replanting or planting of forest plant materials. Also includes planting in areas not originally forested for mitigation purposes. *(Beaufort County, S.C.)*

The creation of a biological community dominated by trees or other woody plants containing at least 100 live trees per acre with at least 50 percent of those trees having the potential of attaining a two-inch or greater diameter measured at 4.5 feet above the ground within seven years. Reforestation includes landscaping of areas under an approved landscaping plan. *(Maryland Department of Natural Resources)*

■ **refuse** *(See also **garbage; litter; rubbish; solid waste**)*   The term shall be synonymous with municipal solid waste (MSW) and shall mean and include all accumulations of waste matters discarded as of no further value to the owner, such as kitchen and table waste, wrappings and small discarded containers, and small dead animals weighing not over 15 pounds, but shall exclude all manure, sewage, large dead animals, petroleum products, cleanings from public and private catch basins, washracks or sumps, white goods, bulky waste, recyclables, yard waste, and special or hazardous wastes. *(Renton, Wash.)*

■ **region**    An area encompassing land in more than one municipality that is bound together by shared characteristics. *(New Jersey State Plan)*

■ **regional**    Pertaining to activities or economies at a scale greater than that of a single jurisdiction, and affecting a broad geographic area. *(California Planning Roundtable)*

■ **regional commercial complex** *(See also **shopping center, regional**)*   A large commercial development with retail, entertainment, and service uses of a scale and function to serve a regional market, that: (i) has primary and ancillary structures in an integrated development with an overall site plan approved by the Department; (ii) contains at least 750,000 square feet of floor area within the primary structure; (iii) provides vehicular and pedestrian access from ancillary structures within the complex to the primary structure; and (iv) is adjacent and accessible to a limited access highway. *(Anne Arundel County, Md.)*

■ **regional entity**    A governmental or quasi-governmental agency that performs planning for land development for an area encompassing land in more than one county. *(New Jersey State Plan)*

■ **regulation**    A rule or order prescribed for managing government. *(California Planning Roundtable)*

■ **rehabilitation** *(See also addition; alteration; historic structure, rehabilitation; remodel)*    The repair, preservation, and/or improvement of substandard housing. *(California Planning Roundtable)*

■ **related** *(See also family)*    The following relationships by marriage, blood, or legal adoption: parent, grandparent, brother, sister, stepparent, stepsister, stepbrother, uncle, aunt; it also means the relationship of a legal guardian or ward. *(Valdez, Alaska)*

A child, parent, grandparent, brother, or sister, and such relationships resulting from adoption or remarriage (stepparent, stepchild, stepbrother, stepsister, etc.). *(Eliot, Maine)*

■ **religious assembly**    A site used by a bona fide religious group primarily or exclusively for religious worship and related religious services, including a place of worship, retreat site, or religious camp. *(Blue Springs, Mo.)*

A use located in a permanent building and providing regular organized religious worship and related incidental activities, except primary or secondary schools and day care facilities. *(Blacksburg, Va.)*

■ **religious institution**    A church of place of worship or religious assembly (pictured at right) with related facilities such as the following in any combination: rectory or convent; private school, meeting hall, offices for administration of the institution, licensed child or adult daycare, playground, cemetery. *(Prince William County, Va.)*

A building, together with its accessory buildings and use, where persons regularly assemble for religious purposes and related social events and which building, together with its accessory buildings and uses, is maintained and controlled by a religious body organized to sustain religious ceremonies and purposes. *(Plymouth, Minn.)*

A building used for public worship by a congregation, excluding buildings used exclusively for residential, educational, recreational or other uses not normally associated with worship. Includes churches, chapels, cathedrals, temples, and similar designations. *(Concord, Pa.)*

■ **relocation**    Any repositioning of a building on its site or moving it to another site. *(Champaign, Ill.)*

■ **remediation**    The action or measures taken, or to be taken, to lessen, clean-up, remove, or mitigate the existence of hazardous materials existing on the property to such standards, specifications, or requirements as may be established or required by federal, state, or county statute, rule or regulation. *(Jefferson County, Colo.)*

■ **remodel** *(See also addition; alteration; rehabilitation)*    Any improvement to the exterior or interior of a building that requires an electrical, plumbing, or HVAC permit and that is not a structural alteration, new construction, or enlargement. *(Champaign, Ill.)*

As used in historic preservation, making over or rebuilding all or part of an historic structure in a way that does not necessarily preserve its historical, architectural, and cultural features and character. *(California Planning Roundtable)*

■ **rental cabin**    A single-family dwelling that does not exceed 700 square feet in total area and contains no more than one sleeping room or area, and is available for rent on a limited or long-term basis. *(Valdez, Alaska)*

■ **rental, short-term**    A transient vacation rental or use in which overnight accommodations are provided in dwelling units to guests for compensation, for periods of less than 30 days. *(Maui County, Hawaii)*

■ **repair**    Any change that does not require a building permit, that is not construction, relocation, or alteration. *(Champaign, Ill.)*

■ **repair, major**    The repair or replacement of nonbearing walls, fixtures, wiring, roof, or plumbing which exceeds 20 percent of the replacement value of the building or structure. *(Champaign, Ill.)*

■ **repair, minor**    The repair or replacement of nonbearing walls, fixtures, wiring, roof, or plumbing to an extent not exceeding 20 percent of the replacement value of the building or structure. *(Champaign, Ill.)*

■ **repair or maintenance**    An activity that restores the character, scope, size, or design of a serviceable area, structure, or land use to its previously existing, authorized, and undamaged condition. Activities that change the character, size, or scope of a project beyond the original design and drain, dredge, fill, flood, or otherwise alter additional regulated wetlands are not included in this definition. *(Renton, Wash.)*

■ **repair services**    Establishments primarily engaged in the provision of repair services to individuals and households, rather than businesses, but excluding automotive and equipment repair use types. Typical uses include appliance repair shops, shoe repair, watch or jewelry repair shops, or repair of musical instruments. *(Blacksburg, Va.)*

■ **replacement** *(See also **teardown**)* Construction on an existing street in an existing neighborhood in which the existing house on the lot is torn down and replaced by a new house. *(Lexington, Mass.)*

■ **replacement value** The current construction cost for replacement of an existing building, structure, or portion thereof, including accessory facilities and other parts of an established use. *(Santa Clara County, Calif.)*

■ **request for proposal (RFP)** Usually issued by a public agency and disseminated to consulting or development firms, a good RFP contains a description of: the project or program (what is supposed to be accomplished and for whom); what services are required; the amount budgeted to accomplish the work; the type of contract (e.g., fixed price or time-and-expense); qualifications required (unless using the two-part RFQ/RFP process); evaluation criteria; what to do to submit the RFP properly. APA recommends a two-part process in which agencies first issue a request for qualifications (RFQ) (see below) and then solicit proposals. *(PAS Report No. 443, Selecting and Retaining a Planning Consultant)*

■ **request for qualifications (RFQ)** A statement of qualifications prepared by a consultant and submitted to a community seeking assistance in a project. The RFQ should ideally contain contact information; a description of the form of the organization (e.g., is it a partnership or corporation); resumes of key personnel; a statement of qualifications (e.g., a narrative describing work done on similar projects); availability (e.g., notable time constraints or other commitments); a list of projects completed by the firm; and references. *(PAS Report No. 443, Selecting and Retaining a Planning Consultant)*

■ **research and development** A business that engages in research, or research and development, of innovative ideas in technology-intensive fields. Examples

include research and development of computer software, information systems, communication systems, transportation, geographic information systems, multi-media and video technology. Development and construction of prototypes may be associated with this use. *(Blacksburg, Va.)*

■ **research and development centers** Research, development, and testing laboratories that do not involve the mass manufacture, fabrication, processing, or sale of products. Such uses shall not violate any odor, dust, smoke, gas, noise, radiation, vibration, or similar pollution standard as specified herein. *(Jefferson County, Colo.)*

A structure or complex of structures designed or used primarily for research development functions related to industry and similar fields of endeavor. *(Cranberry Township, Pa.)*

■ **research laboratory** (1) An administrative, engineering, scientific research, design, or experimentation facility; (2) Includes research on such things as electronic components, optical equipment, etc., but not research requiring the use of animal husbandry (including dogs, poultry, or monkeys), heavy equipment (such as construction equipment); and (3) Shall be free of dust, smoke, fumes, odors, or unusual vibrations or noise. The waste from such facilities shall meet the requirements of the appropriate health authority. *(Pima County, Ariz.)*

A structure or group of structures used primarily for applied and developmental research, where product testing is an integral part of the operation and goods or products may be manufactured as necessary for testing, evaluation, and test marketing. *(Londonderry, N.H.)*

■ **reservation of site** The withholding of land, in a subdivision plan, for later purchase for public purposes such as schools or parks. *(Handbook for Planning Commissioners in Missouri)*

■ **reservoir** Any impoundment of surface waters designed to provide drinking water to the public. *(York, Va.)*

■ **residence** *(See also **dwelling** definitions)* A place where a person resides; particularly a house. *(Grand Forks, N.D.)*

A home, abode, or place where an individual is actually living at a specific point in time. *(Siskiyou County, Calif.)*

The general term implying place of human habitation and embracing both residential and apartment residential district classifications. *(Columbus, Ohio)*

A structure or part of a structure containing dwelling units or rooming units, including single-family or two-family houses, multiple dwellings, boarding or rooming houses, or apartments. Residences do not include: such transient accommodations as transient hotels, motels, tourist cabins, or trailer courts; dormitories, fraternity or sorority houses; in a mixed-use structure, that part of the structure used for any nonresidential uses, except accessory to residential uses; recreational vehicles. *(Londonderry, N.H.)*

■ **resident** One who lives and usually works in the vicinity; not a visitor or transient. *(Whatcom County, Wash.)*

■ **residential** Land designated in the city or county general plan and zoning ordinance for buildings consisting only of dwelling units. May be improved, vacant, or unimproved. *(California Planning Roundtable)*

■ **residential burn** *(See also **open burning**)* Open burning performed with the approval of the fire chief at the site of a one- or two-family dwelling unit for the purpose of disposing of natural vegetation generated at that location. *(Hilton Head Island, N.C.)*

■ **residential care facility** *(See **elderly housing, residential care facility**)*

■ **residential complex** A residential development with 15 or more dwelling units situated on the same tax parcel. *(Columbus, Ohio)*

■ **residential concierge services** The operation of an establishment that provides pick-up and delivery service, personal services such as laundry and dry cleaning drop off and pick up, packaging and shipping drop off, ground transportation, travel and entertainment-booking services and similar convenience services for occupants of the residential development. *(Cincinnati, Ohio)*

■ **residential storage structure** *(See also accessory structure)*　A structure to be used, or intended to be used, for the private noncommercial, nonindustrial storage uses by the property owner prior to the construction of a residence on the property. *(Siskiyou County, Calif.)*

■ **resolution**　The recorded expression of the will of a public body. *(New York Planning Federation)*

■ **resort**　A group or groups of buildings containing more than five dwelling units and/or guest rooms and providing outdoor recreational activities that may include golf, horseback riding, swimming, shuffleboard, tennis and similar activities. A resort may furnish services customarily furnished by a hotel, including a restaurant, cocktail lounge, and convention facilities. *(Scottsdale, Ariz.)*

A building or group of buildings containing guest rooms, with a large portion of the site devoted to recreational activities, such as tennis, horseback riding, swimming, and golf. *(Pima County, Ariz.)*

■ **resource extraction** *(See extractive industry)*

■ **restaurant**　A structure in which the principal use is the preparation and sale of food and beverages. *(Prince William County, Va.)*

A commercial establishment where food and beverages are prepared, served, and consumed primarily within the principal building and where food sales constitute more than 80 percent of the gross sales receipts for food and beverages. *(Delafield, Wisc.)*

Any establishment, however designated, at which food is sold for consumption on the premises to patrons seated within an enclosed building, or elsewhere on the premises. However, a snack bar or refreshment stand at a public, semipublic or community swimming pool, playground, playfield, or park operated by the agency or group of an approved vendor operating the recreational facilities and for the convenience of the patrons of the facility shall not be deemed to be a restaurant. *(Danville, N.Y.)*

An establishment engaged in the preparation of food and beverages containing more than 2,000 gross square feet and characterized primarily by table service to customers in non-disposable containers. *(Bedford County, Va.)*

An establishment where food and/or beverages are prepared, served, and consumed, and whose principal method of operation includes one or both of the following characteristics: (1) customers are normally provided with an individual menu and served their food and beverages by a restaurant employee at the same table or counter where the items are consumed; or (2) a cafeteria-type operation where food and beverages generally are consumed within the restaurant building. *(Cumberland, Md.)*

■ **restaurant, carry-out/take-out**　Establishments where food is usually ordered by telephone and prepared on the premises for consumption off the premises, with no seating or other area provided on the premises for consumption. The establishment may deliver food to the customer, or the customer may pick food up. *(Richfield, Minn.)*

A retail food service business that sells ready-to-eat foods, usually in bulk quantities, primarily for consumption off the premises. A carry-out restaurant that has more than limited seating (12 or fewer seats) or 75 square feet of patron area, shall be deemed to be a restaurant for zoning purposes. *(St. Paul, Minn.)*

A restaurant where food, frozen dessert, or beverages are primarily sold in a packaged, ready-to-consume state, intended for ready consumption by the customer on or off the premises. *(St. Louis, Mo.)*

■ **restaurant, commercial/recreation**　Any establishment providing as a principal use the combination of family-oriented recreation and on-premises dining where neither the recreation nor the on-premises dining is clearly accessory or incidental to the operation of the other.

Recreation may include but is not limited to television and motion pictures; sound and sight systems; mechanical-and/or electronic-operated games; animated mechanical devices and/or rides; and live entertainment. *(Fairfax County, Va.)*

■ **restaurant, drive-in**　A building and adjoining parking area used for the purpose of furnishing food, soft drinks, ice cream, and similar confections to the public normally for consumption outside the confines of the principal permitted building, or in vehicles parked upon the premises, regardless of whether or not, in addition thereto, seats or other accommodations are provided inside for the patrons. Services are effected principally while patrons remain in their vehicles. *(Concord, Pa.)*

An establishment whose primary business is serving food to the public for consumption on the premises by order from and service to vehicular passengers outside the structure, where revenues from the sale of food equal at least 40 percent of the gross revenue. *(Scottsdale, Ariz.)*

An establishment deriving more than 50 percent of gross revenue from the sale of food and drink not including alcoholic beverages, and which functions as a retail outlet where food or beverages are sold and delivered to patrons in parked motor vehicles. *(Jefferson City, Mo.)*

■ **restaurant, entertainment**　An establishment where food and drink are prepared, served, and consumed, within a structure that includes, as an integral component of the facility, electronic or mechanical games of skill, simulation, and virtual reality, play areas, video arcades, or similar uses, billiards, and other forms of amusement. *(Maryland Heights, Mo.)*

■ **restaurant, family**　An establishment serving food in or on nondisposable dishes to be consumed primarily while seated at tables or booths within a building and which has no on-sale liquor service (on-sale beer and wine permitted as regulated by the [city] code). *(Maple Grove, Minn.)*

■ **restaurant, fast-food** Restaurants where most customers order and are served their food at a counter or in a motor vehicle in packages prepared to leave the premises, or able to be taken to a table or counter to be consumed. *(Richfield, Minn.)*

An establishment engaged primarily in the business of preparing food and purveying it on a self-serve or semi self-serve basis. Customer orders and/or service may be by means of a walk-up counter or window designed to accommodate automobile traffic. Consumption may be either on or off the premises. *(Glendale, Calif.)*

Any restaurant whose design or principal method of operation includes four or more of the following characteristics: (1) 45 percent or more of the floor area is devoted to food preparation, employee work space, and customer service area; (2) a permanent menu board is provided from which to select and order food; (3) if a chain or franchised restaurant, standardized floor plans are used over several locations; (4) customers pay for food before consuming it; (5) a self-service condiment bar is provided; (6) trash receptacles are provided for self-service bussing; (7) furnishing plan indicates hard-finished, stationary seating arrangements; and (8) most main course food items are prepackaged rather than made to order. *(St. Paul, Minn.)*

■ **restaurant, outdoor customer dining area** A dining area with seats and/or tables located outdoors of a restaurant, coffee shop, or other food service establishment, and which is (a) located entirely outside the walls of the subject building, (b) enclosed on two sides or less by the walls of the building with or without a solid roof cover, or (c) enclosed on three sides by the walls of the building without a solid roof cover. *(Thousand Oaks, Calif.)*

An area of designated size used as a seating area with tables and chairs for the contiguous restaurant. This seating may be in addition to the indoor seating or it may be the only seating available for the restaurant. *(Melbourne, Fla.)*

■ **restaurant, sit-down** An establishment maintained, operated, and/or advertised or held out to the public as a place where food and beverage are served to the public on demand from a menu during stated business hours, served in and on reusable containers and dinnerware, to be consumed on the premises primarily inside the building at tables, booths or counters, with chairs, benches or stools. This use may include incidental delivery service using no more than two delivery vehicles. *(Redondo Beach, Calif.)*

■ **restaurant, small** An establishment engaged in the preparation of food and beverages containing no more than 2,000 gross square feet and characterized primarily by table service to customers in nondisposable containers. Typical uses include cafes, coffee shops, and small restaurants. *(Blacksburg, Va.)*

■ **restrictive covenant** *(See also covenant; deed restriction)* A written agreement executed by and between a property owner and the city . . . whereby the property owner for a specified consideration by the city agrees to certain conditions, restrictions, and/or limitations on the use, maintenance, or sale of his property. Such restrictive covenant shall be recorded in the public record . . . and shall run with the land and shall be binding upon the property owner, his successors, and assigns. *(Coral Gables, Fla.)*

A restriction on the use of land set forth in a formal binding agreement. Restrictive covenants run with the land and are binding upon subsequent owners of the property. *(Renton, Wash.)*

■ **retail display window** A window or opening in the exterior wall of any portion of a building used for business purposes (pictured above), through which merchandise, services, or business are displayed or advertized. A window glazed with transparent glass in the business portion of a building, any part of which window is less than six feet above the sidewalk or the established sidewalk grade beneath the window. *(New York, N.Y., which uses the term "show window")*

■ **retail sales establishment** A commercial enterprise that provides goods and/or services directly to the consumer, where such goods are available for immediate purchase and removal from the premises by the purchaser. *(Federal Way, Wash.)*

Sale or rental with incidental service of commonly used goods and merchandise for personal or household use but excludes those classified more specifically by definition. *(Bedford County, Va.)*

Establishments engaged in selling commodities or goods in small quantities to ultimate customers or consumers. *(Burlingame, Calif.)*

A business having as its primary function the supply of merchandise or wares to the end consumer. Such sales constitute the "primary function" of the business when such sales equal at least 80 percent of the gross sales of the business. *(Maple Grove, Minn.)*

The retail sale of any article, substance, or commodity within a building but not including the sale of lumber or other building materials. *(King City, Calif., which uses the term "retail business")*

■ **retail sales establishment, bulk merchandise**   A retail establishment engaged in selling goods or merchandise to the general public as well as to other retailers, contractors, or businesses, and rendering services incidental to the sale of such goods. Bulk retail involves a high volume of sales of related and/or unrelated products in a warehouse setting and may include membership warehouse clubs (i.e., "big box" retail). Bulk retail is differentiated from general retail by any of the following characteristics: items for sale include large, categorized products (e.g., lumber, appliances, household furnishings, electrical and heating fixtures and supplies, wholesale and retail nursery stock, etc.) and may also include a variety of carry out goods (e.g., groceries, household, and personal care products). *(Federal Way, Wash.)*

■ **retail sales establishment, food**   Any establishment selling food or beverages for consumption off-premises either immediately or with further preparation. Such establishments may include, but not be limited to, supermarket, grocery store, bakery, candy store, butcher, delicatessen, convenience store, and similar establishments. *(Champaign, Ill.)*

■ **retail sales establishment, general merchandise**   Establishments that are retail operations that carry an assortment of merchandise from all the other categories. Such establishments may include, but are not limited to, department store, discount store, farm store, and similar establishments. *(Champaign, Ill.)*

■ **retail sales establishment, household**   Establishments are retail operations that sell goods for furnishing or improving housing units. These establishments may include, but are not limited to, furniture store, home improvement center, electronic store, appliance store, and similar establishments. *(Champaign, Ill.)*

■ **retail sales establishment, specialty**   Retail operations that specialize in one type or line of merchandise. Such stores may include, but are not limited to, apparel stores, jewelry stores, bookstores, shoe stores, stationary stores, antique stores, and similar establishments. *(Champaign, Ill.)*

■ **retail services establishment**   Establishments providing services or entertainment, as opposed to products, to the general public for personal or household use, including eating and drinking places, hotels and motels, finance, real estate and insurance, personal service, motion pictures, amusement and recreation services, health, educational, and social services, museums, and galleries. *(Maryland Heights, Mo.)*

■ **retaining wall**   A wall or similar structure devise used at a grade change to hold the soil on the up-hillside from slumping, sliding, or falling. *(Beaufort County, S.C.)*

Any fence or wall built or designed to retain or restrain lateral forces of soil or other materials, said materials being similar in height to the height of the wall. *(Fort Wayne, Ind.)*

A wall or terraced combination of walls used to retain more than 18 inches of material and not used to support, provide a foundation for, or provide a wall for a building or structure. *(Beverly Hills, Calif.)*

■ **retaining wall, enclosed**   A retaining wall located on a lot such that it is visually shielded by other permanent structures and cannot be seen from public streets and adjacent lots. *(Oakland, Calif.)*

■ **retention** *(See also **detention** definitions)*   The permanent on-site maintenance of stormwater. *(Gurnee, Ill.)*

■ **retention basin**   A wet or dry stormwater holding area, either natural or manmade, which does not have an outlet to adjoining watercourses or wetlands other than an emergency spillway. *(Grand Traverse County, Mich.)*

■ **retention system**   A stormwater facility that is designed to accept runoff from a developed site and discharge it at a limited rate. Flows exceeding the limited rate are stored until they can be released at the limited rate (when the runoff rate into the system drops below the limited rate). A specified volume is stored indefinitely (retained) until it is displaced by runoff from another storm. *(Redmond, Wash.)*

■ **retreat center**   A facility used for professional, educational, or religious conclaves, meetings, conferences, or seminars and which may provide meals, housing, and recreation for participants during the period of the retreat or program only. Such centers may not be utilized by the general public for meals or overnight accommodations. Housing for participants may be in lodges, dormitories, sleeping cabins (with or without baths), or in such other temporary quarters as may be approved, but kitchen and dining facilities shall be located in a single centrally located building or buildings. *(Carroll County, Md.)*

■ **retrofitting**   To improve or reconstruct an existing facility with the intent of bringing it into compliance (or where that is not feasible, more nearly into compliance) with modern standards for such facilities. . . . *(Volusia County, Fla.)*

■ **reversion clause**   A requirement that may accompany special use permit approval or a rezoning that returns the property to its prior zoning classification if a specified action, (such as taking out a building permit or beginning construction) does not begin in a specified period of time, say, one year.   *(Handbook for Planning Commissioners in Missouri)*

■ **rezoning**   An amendment to the map and/or text of a zoning ordinance to effect a change in the nature, density, or intensity of uses allowed in a zoning district and/or on a designated parcel or land area. *(California Planning Roundtable)*

■ **ridesharing** *(See also **transportation demand management (TDM)**)* Transportation of more than one person for commute purposes, in a motor vehicle, with or without the assistance of a commuter matching service. *(Tucson, Ariz.)*

A travel mode other than driving alone, such as buses, rail transit, carpools, and vanpools. *(California Planning Roundtable)*

■ **ridge** A relatively narrow elevation that is prominent because of the steep angle at which it rises; an elongated crest, or series of crests, with or without individual peaks, significantly higher than the adjoining ground. *(Scottsdale, Ariz.)*

A hill that is proportionally longer than it is wider, generally with steeply sloping sides. *(Whatcom County, Wash.)*

■ **ridge, prominent** A ridge location that is visible from a major arterial, secondary, or collector street, which is seen as a distinct edge against a backdrop of land. Said ridge locations are designated on the city map of prominent ridges. *(Brea, Calif.)*

■ **ridgeline** A line connecting the highest points along a ridge and separating drainage basins or small-scale drainage systems from one another. *(California Planning Roundtable)*

■ **riding stable/riding academy** *(See also **horse farm; stable**)* An establishment where horses are boarded and cared for, and where instruction in riding, jumping, and showing is offered, and where horses may be hired for riding. *(Garrett, Ind.)*

■ **right-of-way** A strip of land acquired by reservation, dedication, prescription, or condemnation and intended to be occupied by a street, trail, water line, sanitary sewer, and/or other public utilities or facilities. *(Clark County, Nev.)*

The line determining the street or highway public limit or ownership. *(Danville, N.Y.)*

A public or private area that allows for the passage of people or goods. Right-of-way includes passageways such as freeways, streets, bike paths, alleys, and walkways. A public right-of-way is a right-of-way that is dedicated or deeded to the public for public use and under the control of a public agency. *(Portland, Ore.)*

An area of land not on a lot that is dedicated for public or private use to accommodate a transportation system and necessary public utility infrastructure (including, but not limited to, water lines, sewer lines, power lines, and gas lines.) In no case shall a right-of-way be construed to mean an easement. *(Beaufort County, S.C.)*

■ **right-of-way line** The limit of publicly owned land or easement encompassing a street or alley. *(Columbus, Ohio)*

■ **right-of-way, railroad** A public or private right-of-way, for the purpose of allowing rail travel. *(Portland, Ore.)*

A roadway not exceeding 200 feet in width occupied by a main track or other trackage including, but not limited to, land as may be reasonably needed for the purpose of cuttings and embankments necessary for the proper construction and security of its tracks, and any and all rights and appurtenances authorized by state or federal law. *(El Paso, Tex.)*

■ **right-of-way, ultimate** The right-of-way shown as ultimate on an adopted precise plan of highway alignment; or the street rights-of-way shown within the boundary of a recorded tract map, a recorded parcel map, or a recorded development plan. The latest adopted or recorded document in the cases mentioned in this section shall take precedence. If none of these exist, the ultimate right-of-way shall be considered the right-of-way required by the highway classification as shown on the master plan of arterial highways. In all other instances, the ultimate right-of-way shall be considered to be the existing right-of-way. *(Palm Desert, Calif.)*

■ **right-to-farm laws** State right-to-farm laws are intended to protect farm-

ers and ranchers from nuisance lawsuits. Every state in the nation has at least one right-to-farm law. Some statutes protect farms and ranches from lawsuits filed by neighbors who moved in after the agricultural operation was established. Others protect farmers who use generally accepted agricultural and management practices and comply with federal and state laws. Twenty-three right-to-farm laws also prohibit local governments from enacting ordinances that would impose unreasonable restrictions on agriculture. *(American Farmland Trust)*

■ **Ringelmann number** The number appearing on the Ringelmann Chart ascribed by the observer to the density of the smoke emission. Where the density of light obstructing capacity of the smoke as observed falls between two consecutive Ringelmann Numbers, the lower Ringelmann Number shall be considered the density of the smoke observed. *(Gurnee, Ill.)*

■ **riparian habitat** A habitat that is strongly influenced by water and that occurs adjacent to streams, shorelines, and wetlands. *(Anne Arundel County, Md.)*

Riparian lands are comprised of the vegetative and wildlife areas adjacent to perennial and intermittent streams. Riparian areas are delineated by the existence of plant species normally found near freshwater. *(California Planning Roundtable, which uses the term "riparian lands")*

A natural plant community dependent upon a water body or water course. *(Monterey County, Calif.)*

■ **riparian vegetation** An association of plant species growing adjacent to freshwater water courses, including perennial and intermittent streams, lakes, and other bodies of fresh water. *(San Luis Obispo County, Calif.)*

■ **riprap** A layer, facing, or protective mound of rubble or stones randomly placed to prevent erosion, scour, or sloughing of a structure or embankment; also the stone used for this purpose. *(Yakima County, Wash.)*

■ **river**    A free-flowing body of water including its associated floodplain wetlands from that point at which it provides drainage for a watershed of 25 square miles to its mouth. *(Gorham, Maine)*

■ **riverwalk** *(See also **esplanade**)*    A publicly owned or privately owned way, generally open to the sky and unobstructed by buildings, that runs along the river edge and is open to the public during specified times. It may include, without limitation, any combination of open space, paved areas, landscaped areas, pedestrian paths, and pedestrian furnishings. *(Chicago, Ill.)*

■ **road** *(See also **street** definitions)*    All property dedicated or intended for public or private road, street, alley, highway, freeway, or roadway purposes or to public easements therefore. *(Johnson County, Iowa)*

■ **roadside**    A general term denoting the area adjoining the outer edge of the roadway. Extensive areas between the roadways of a divided highway may also be considered roadside. *(Dona Ana County, N. Mex.)*

■ **roadside stand** *(See also **farm stand; stand**)*    A structure erected for the display and sale of agricultural products and may or may not be located on a zoning lot where the principal use is agricultural. Requires appropriate commercial zoning; and must comply with all site and structure provisions of the applicable zoning district and may sell up to five products not of an agricultural nature. Products sold are generally grown off the zoning lot where such stand is located. *(Gurnee, Ill.)*

A temporary structure not permanently affixed to the ground and is readily removable in its entirety, which is used solely for the display or sale of farm products produced on the premises upon which such roadside stand is located. No roadside stand shall be more than 300 square feet in ground area and there shall not be more than one roadside stand on any one premise. *(Madison, Wisc.)*

■ **roadside stand, accessory**    A structure erected for the display and sale of agricultural products no more than one story in height and 500 square feet in retail floor area and located on a zoning lot where the principal use is agricultural. *(Gurnee, Ill.)*

■ **roadway** *(See also **street** definitions)* That portion of a highway improved, designed, or ordinarily used for vehicular travel. If a highway includes two or more separate roadways, the term "roadway" shall refer to any such roadway separately but not to all such roadways collectively. *(Shreveport, La.)*

■ **roller skates or roller blades** *(See also **skateboard** definitions)*    Any footwear or device that may be attached to the foot or footwear to which wheels are attached, including wheels that are "in line" and where such wheels may be used to aid the wearer in moving or propulsion. *(Mission Veijo, Calif.)*

■ **roof**    The cover of any building, including the eaves and similar projections. *(Jefferson County, Colo.)*

A structural covering over any portion of a building or structure including projections beyond the walls or supports of the building or structure. *(Tumwater, Wash.)*

A part of a building completely covering any portion of such building and permanently attached but excluding chimneys, antennas, vents, and mechanical equipment. *(Glendale, Calif.)*

An overhead structure used for protection or shielding from the sun, rain, or other elements of weather. *(Las Cruces, N. Mex.)*

■ **roof deck** *(See **deck, roof**)*

■ **roof, flat**    A roof having a pitch of not more than 1.5 inches in 12 inches. *(Coral Gables, Fla.)*

■ **roof line**    The highest point on any building where an exterior wall encloses usable floor space. The term "roof line" includes the top of any parapet wall, providing said parapet wall extends around the entire perimeter of the building at the same elevation. However, the top of the parapet wall extending along one or more building elevations or a portion of one or more building elevations may be considered to be the roof line in

those instances where the parapet wall improves the architectural appearance of a building or shields rooftop mechanical equipment. *(Jefferson County, Colo.)*

In the case of a flat roof, the uppermost line of the roof of a building; in the case of a pitched roof, the lower edge of the eave; or in the case of an extended facade or parapet, the uppermost height of said facade or parapet. *(Columbus, Ohio)*

A horizontal line intersecting the highest point or points of a roof. *(Nashville and Davidson County, Tenn.)*

■ **roof overhang**    A projecting area at the crown of an architectural composition. *(Monroe County, Fla.)*

■ **roof, pitched**    A shed, gabled, or hipped roof having a slope or pitch of at least one-foot rise for each four feet of horizontal distance in the direction of the slope or pitch of the roof. *(Renton, Wash.)*

■ **room** *(See also **bedroom; sleeping room**)* An unsubdivided portion of the interior of a dwelling unit, excluding bathrooms, closets, hallways, and service porches. *(Redding, Calif.)*

■ **room, habitable**    A room occupied or designed to be occupied by one or more persons for living, sleeping, eating, or cooking, including kitchens serving a dwelling unit, but not including bathrooms, toilet compartments, laundries, pantries, cellars, attics for storage, and other similarly approved spaces that are not used frequently or for extended periods. *(Champaign, Ill.)*

■ **roomer** *(See also **boarder; tenant**)* A person who resides in a dwelling who is not a member of the family unit that is the primary occupant of the dwelling and who pays for or performs services in exchange for such occupancy. A "roomer" does not include a person who has separate cooking facilities made available to him. *(Cape Girardeau, Mo.)*

■ **rooming house** *(See also **lodging house; boarding house**)*    A residential building with three or more sleeping rooms for lodgers, and wherein no dining facilities are maintained for the lodger, as distinguished from a boarding house. *(Homestead, Fla.)*

A building in which three or more rooms are rented and in which no table board is furnished. *(Danville, N.Y.)*

A building with not more than five guest rooms where lodging is provided for compensation pursuant to previous arrangements, but not open to public or overnight guests. The term includes a lodging house. *(Belmont, Calif.)*

■ **roundabout/traffic circle** *(See also traffic calming)* A raised island (pictured above) that is usually landscaped and located at the intersection of two streets used to reduce traffic speeds and accidents without diverting traffic onto adjacent residential streets. *(PAS Report No. 456, Traffic Calming)*

■ **rowhouse** *(See also townhouse)* A multifamily dwelling structure consisting of attached dwelling units owned individually and not in common by one owner. *(Camas, Wash.)*

A group of attached residences, separated by vertical fire walls, in which each residence has its own front and rear yards, and has appropriated to it the entire building between the fire walls. *(Columbus, Ohio)*

■ **rowhouse building** A building containing a row of two or more attached rowhouses, each rowhouse being separated from the adjoining rowhouse in each story by fire resistive walls without openings and each rowhouse having independent access to the exterior of the building in the ground story. *(Cincinnati, Ohio)*

■ **rubbish** *(See also garbage; litter; refuse; solid waste)* Any waste material except garbage. *(Ames, Iowa)*

The miscellaneous waste materials resulting from housekeeping, mercantile enterprises, trades, manufacturing and offices, including other waste matter, such as slag, stone, broken concrete, fly ash, ashes, tin cans, glass, scrap metal, rubber, paper, rags, chemicals or any similar or related combinations thereof. *(Franklin, Mich.)*

■ **rule** An enactment which governs action or a course of conduct. *(New York Planning Federation)*

■ **rummage sale** *(See also garage sale)* The sale by a corporation, trust, church, association, community chest, fund or foundation, organized and operated for religious, charitable, scientific, community, or educational purposes, of tangible personal property to obtain money for some charitable purpose. *(Hampton Va.)*

■ **runoff** *(See also impervious surface)* Precipitation leaving a site due to the force of gravity. *(New York Planning Federation)*

The rainfall, snowmelt, or irrigation water flowing that has not evaporated or infiltrated into the soil, but flows over the ground surface. *(Beaufort County, S.C.)*

That portion of the precipitation from a drainage area or watershed that is discharged from the area in stream channels or by overland flow; types include surface runoff, groundwater runoff, or seepage. *(Conemaugh Township, Pa.)*

■ **runoff, excess** Surface runoff that cannot be accommodated satisfactorily by the natural or planned drainage systems. *(Grand Traverse County, Mich.)*

■ **runway** *(See also landing strip)* The paved surface of the airport landing strip. *(Huntsville, Ala.)*

■ **rural** A sparsely developed area where the land is primarily used for farming, forestry, resource extraction, very low-density residential uses (one unit per 10 acres or less) or open space uses. *(Renton, Wash.)*

■ **safety service**   The conduct of publicly owned safety and emergency services, such as, but not limited to, fire stations, police stations, and emergency medical and ambulance service. *(Nashville and Davidson County, Tenn.)*

■ **saloon** *(See bar)*

■ **salvage**   Any article or material that is to be or intended to be reclaimed or saved from destruction. *(Palm Desert, Calif.)*

■ **salvage yard**   A facility or area for storing, keeping, selling, dismantling, shredding, compressing, or salvaging scrap or discarded material or equipment. . . . Scrap or discarded material includes, but is not limited to, metal, paper, rags, tires, bottles, motor vehicle parts, machinery, structural steel, equipment and appliances. The term includes facilities for separating trash and debris from recoverable resources, such as paper products, glass, metal cans, and other products which can be returned to a condition in which they may again be used for production. *(Clark County, Nev.)*

Any lot or parcel, or part thereof, including automobile graveyards, where a salvage vehicle, or parts thereof, are located for the purposes of resale as parts or parts as salvage only. *(Bedford County, Va.)*

A parcel of land on which wastes or used secondhand materials are bought, sold, exchanged, stored, processed, or handled. Materials include but are not limited to: scrap iron and other ferrous metals, paper; rags, rubber tires, bottles, discarded goods, machinery, or two or more inoperable motor vehicles. *(Jacksonville, Fla.)*

■ **sand and gravel pit**   *(See also mining; quarry)* A type of open pit mine, or strip mine, from which the mineral removed is restricted to sand and gravel. *(El Paso, Tex.)*

■ **sanitarium/sanitorium** *(See also clinic; health care facility; hospital)*   A health station, retreat, or an institution for the recuperation and treatment of persons suffering from physical or mental disorders. *(Jefferson County, Colo.)*

A building and premises, other than a hospital, intended for the care and housing of more than five sick, injured, or infirm persons for compensation. *(Belmont, Calif.)*

A health station or retreat or other place where patients are housed, and where treatment is given, but excluding mental institutions, or institutions for treatment of persons addicted to the use of drugs. *(Menlo Park, Calif.)*

■ **satellite dish antenna** *(See telecommunications definitions)*

■ **sauna** *(See also bathhouse; health spa)* A steam bath or heated bathing room used for the purpose of bathing, relaxation, or reducing utilizing steam or hot air as a cleaning, relaxing, or reducing agent. *(Rochester, Minn.)*

■ **sawmill**   A facility where logs or partially processed cants are sawn, split, shaved, stripped, chipped, or otherwise processed to produce wood products, not including the processing of timber for use on the same lot by the owner or resident of that lot. *(Kent County, Md.)*

■ **scenic area**   Any area of particular scenic beauty or historical significance as determined by the United States, the state, or the city, and including any interests in land that have been acquired for the restoration, preservation, and enhancement of scenic beauty. *(El Paso, Tex.)*

■ **scenic highway corridor** *(See also corridor)*   The area outside a highway right-of-way that is generally visible to persons traveling on the highway. *(California Planning Roundtable)*

■ **scenic highway/scenic route**   A highway, road, drive, or street that, in addition to its transportation function, provides opportunities for the enjoyment of natural and man-made scenic resources and access or direct views to areas or scenes of exceptional beauty or historic or cultural interest. The aesthetic values of scenic routes often are protected and enhanced by regulations governing the development of property or the placement of outdoor advertising. . . . *(California Planning Roundtable)*

■ **school** *(See educational facilities)*

■ **school district** *(See also educational facilities)*   The territory administered by the elected or appointed authorities of a state, county, or other local governmental unit to provide educational services to a resident population. A school district typically includes several school buildings, teachers, and related staff. *(United States Census Bureau)*

■ **screen** *(See berm; buffer; fence)*

■ **screening**   (1) A method of visually shielding or obscuring one abutting or nearby structure or use from another by fencing, walls, berms, or densely planted vegetation; and (2) The removal of relatively coarse floating and/or suspended solids by straining through racks or screens. *(Siskiyou County, Calif.)*

■ **sculpture** *(See also art, works of)* A three-dimensional construction or form, generally executed for the purposes of decoration or artistic expression; and displayed in any place accessible to the public. *(Columbus, Ohio)*

An object fashioned, shaped, and formed by hand or machine into a work of art, including but not limited to contemporary, modern, classical and/or abstract design, and that which may or may not be a likeness of a person or thing. *(Palm Beach, Fla.)*

■ **searchlight** *(See sign, searchlight)*

■ **seasonal decorations** Any structure, not displaying numbers or letters, used to display holiday symbols or insignias or themes, such as, but not limited to, decorated Christmas trees, air-filled balloons or figures, wood figures, cutouts and similar constructions. *(Colt's Neck, N.J.)*

■ **seating capacity** The actual seating capacity of an area based upon the number of seats or one seat per 24 inches of bench or pew length. For other areas where seats are not fixed, the seating capacity shall be determined as indicated by the Uniform Building Code. *(Roswell, N. Mex.)*

■ **seating space** A seating space in a place of public assembly shall be considered as a fixed permanent seat; provided, in the case of bleachers, benches or the flat tops of walls, seating shall be 18 inches wide and 16 inches deep; provided, that seating 30 inches or more in depth shall count double when access is provided to both sides; further provided, in the case of open floor area used for temporary seating purposes, an area of nine square feet per seat. *(Philadelphia, Pa.)*

■ **seawall** A wall or embankment designed to halt the encroachment of a waterbody. *(Southwest Florida Water Management District).*

■ **secondhand merchandise, retail sales** *(See also antique shops; consignment store; thrift store)* Retail sales of previously used merchandise, such as clothing, household furnishings or appliances, sports/recreational equipment. This classification does not include secondhand motor vehicles, parts, or accessories. *(Hermosa Beach, Calif.)*

■ **security system** An electronic security system and all equipment related thereto for early warning of fire, smoke, intrusion, etc. Such security system shall

be connected to the permanent building power source. *(Conyers, Ga.)*

■ **sediment** Mineral or organic solid particulate matter that has been removed from its site of origin by (a) soil erosion; (b) suspension in water; and/or (c) wind or water transport. *(Grand Traverse County, Mich.)*

■ **sedimentation** The process of forming and depositing of suspended matter carried in suspension in water through the action of gravity. It is usually accomplished by reducing the velocity of the water below the point where it can transport the suspended material. *(Naperville, Ill.)*

■ **segregation** Division of land into lots or tracts each of which is 1/128 of a section of land or larger, or five acres or larger if the land is not capable of description as a fraction of a section of land. *(Renton, Wash.)*

■ **self-service storage facility** *(See also storage; warehouse, residential storage)* A building or group of buildings divided into separate compartments used to meet the temporary storage needs of small businesses, apartment dwellers and other residential uses (pictured below); and may include refrigerated facilities. *(Prince William County, Va.)*

A building or group of buildings consisting of individual, self-contained units leased to individuals, organizations, or businesses for self-service storage of personal property. *(Fort Wayne, Ind.)*

A building used for the storage of personal property where individual owners control individual storage spaces. *(Clearwater, Fla.)*

A facility used only for the storing of household and personal property (no commercial storage) with no commercial transactions permitted other than the rental of the storage units. *(Pima County, Ariz.)*

A structure containing separate storage spaces, which may be of various sizes, leased or rented on an individual basis. *(Santa Monica, Calif.)*

■ **sell-through window** *(See also drive-through window; pedestrian outdoor service facility)* An opening in the wall of a building or structure designed and intended to be used to provide for sales to and/or service to patrons who remain outside of the building or structure. *(Philadelphia, Pa.)*

■ **semi-trailer** *(See also truck definitions)* Every vehicle without motive power designed for carrying persons or property and for being drawn by a motor vehicle and so constructed that some part of its weight and that of its load rests upon or is carried by another vehicle. *(Rochester, Minn.)*

■ **seniors** Persons age 62 and older. *(California Planning Roundtable)*

An individual over the age of 60 years. *(Cape Girardeau, Mo.)*

■ **sense of place** *(See community of place)*

■ **sensitive areas** Areas not suitable for development that are included within the city's greenbelt, geologically hazardous, wetlands, or floodplain regulations. *(Renton, Wash.)*

Any area in which plant or animal life or their habitats are either rare or especially valuable because of their special nature or role in an ecosystem and which could be easily disturbed or degraded by human activities and developments. *(Imperial Beach, Calif., which uses the term "environmentally sensitive area")*

Those portions of the shoreline that (1) contain or substantially contribute to the maintenance of endangered or valuable forms of life and (2) have unstable or potentially hazardous topographic, geologic, or hydrologic features (such as steep slopes, marshes). *(Renton, Wash., which uses the term "unique and fragile areas")*

■ **septage**    The solid and liquid wastes removed from private sewage disposal systems. *(Illinois Department of Public Health)*

Waste, refuse effluent, sludge, and any other materials from septic tanks, cesspools, and any other similar facilities. . . . *(Bethel, Maine)*

■ **septic system** *(See also **sewage treatment system, private**)*    A sewage-treatment system that includes a settling tank through which liquid sewage flows and in which solid sewage settles and is decomposed by bacteria in the absence of oxygen. Septic systems are often used for individual home waste disposal where an urban sewer system is not available. *(California Planning Roundtable)*

■ **septic tank**    A watertight receptacle which receives the discharge of sewage and is designed and constructed to permit the deposition of settled solids, the digestion of the matter deposited, and the discharge of the liquid portion into a leaching system. *(New Shoreham, R.I.)*

■ **servant quarters** *(See also **accessory structure**)*    Living quarters, which may include kitchen facilities, that are either attached or detached from the principal residence, used as a residence by persons employed to provide domestic services to the occupants of the principal residence. *(Shasta Lake, Calif.)*

■ **service lane**    A vehicular passageway providing secondary and/or service access to the sides or rear of building lots. Posted speed shall not exceed 15

miles per hour. Service lanes are rural in character, with only a narrow strip of paving at the center, or may be left unpaved. Service lanes are not necessary on wide lots and front loaded garages. *(Monroe County, Fla.)*

■ **service-oriented shopping**    Those shops that primarily sell services on site. The distinction is in the physical attributes of activities associated with services, such as hairdressing. Business services, such as accounting, legal services, advertising, etc., belong in the office category. *(APA's Land-Based Classification Standards project)*

■ **service station** *(See also **gas station; oil change facility**)*    An establishment where gasoline and other petroleum products are sold as the principal use of the property. Light maintenance activities such as engine tune-ups, lubrication, and minor repairs may also be provided if incidental to such principal use. Service stations do not include premises where retail sales space exceeds 25 percent of the total building area or 500 square feet of gross floor area, whichever is less. Service stations do not include premises where heavy automobile maintenance activities, such as engine overhauls, automobile painting, and body work, are conducted. *(Richfield, Minn.)*

Any commercial building or structure, premises or other place used to supply motor fuels (including alternative fuels such as natural gas or hydrogen), lubricants, tires, batteries, and other small accessories to motor vehicles, and where repair work is not done. Automobile maintenance is permitted in conjunction with a service station. *(Clark County, Nev.)*

Any building, structure or land used primarily for the dispersal, sale, or offering for sale of automotive fuels, oils or accessories, including lubrication of automobiles and replacement or installation of minor parts and accessories, but not including major repair work, such as motor replacement or rebuilding, body and fender repair, or painting. *(Danville, N.Y.)*

■ **setback** *(See also **lot** definitions)*    The minimum distance by which any building or structure must be separated from a street right-of-way or lot line. *(Blacksburg, Va.)*

The required distance between every structure and the lot lines of the lot on which it is located. *(Doylestown, Ohio)*

The distance between a street line and the front building line of a principal building or structure, projected to the side lines of the lot and including driveways and parking areas, except where otherwise restricted by this ordinance. *(Duluth, Ga.)*

■ **setback, front**    A setback extending across the full width of a lot between the front lot line and the foremost point of any swimming pool, tennis court, or like structure, and the foremost building excluding steps. *(Wolfeboro, N.H.)*

A yard area of which the width is measured the entire length of the front property line between the side property lines; and the depth is measured as the distance between the street right-of-way line and the required front setback line. *(Las Vegas, Nev.)*

The minimum allowable distance from the street right-of-way line to the closest point of the foundation of a building or projection thereof, parking lot, or detention pond. *(Ogden, N.Y.)*

■ **setback, front, on corner lots**    The front setback of a corner lot shall be measured from the side of the lot designated as the "front." On a corner lot only one street line shall be considered as a front line, which shall be the shorter street frontage. *(Henderson, Nev.)*

■ **setback, garage entrance**    A setback measured from a street lot line to the entrance to a garage or carport. It is essentially a minimum driveway length. *(Portland, Ore.)*

■ **setback line**    A line within a lot parallel to a corresponding lot line, which is the boundary of any specified front, side, or rear yard, or the boundary of any public right-of-way whether acquired in fee, easement, or otherwise, or a line otherwise established to govern the location of buildings, structures or uses. Where no minimum front, side, or rear yards are specified, the setback line shall be coterminous with the corresponding lot line. *(Henderson, Nev.)*

The distance as measured perpendicularly from either the front, side, or rear property line to the building. *(Vicksburg, Miss.)*

■ **setback line, base**   The ultimate street line . . . from which all required setbacks shall be computed. *(Brookfield, Wisc.)*

■ **setback line, legal**   The line established by ordinance beyond which no building may be built. A legal setback line may be a property line. *(Renton, Wash.)*

■ **setback, minimum setback zone** The area around a community water supply well established and described on a map that is available for inspection in the office of the city clerk. *(Champaign, Ill.)*

■ **setback, rear**   Extends across the full width of a site, the depth of which is the minimum horizontal distance between the rear property line and a line parallel thereto on the site, except that on a corner lot the rear yard shall extend only to the side yard abutting the street. *(Henderson, Nev.)*

A setback extending across the full width of lot between the rear lot line and the rearmost point of any swimming pool, tennis court, or like structure and/or building nearest the rear setback. *(Wolfeboro, N.H.)*

The shortest distance between the building line and the rear lot line. *(Jupiter, Fla.)*

■ **setback regulations**   The requirement that a building be set back a certain distance from the street or lot line, whether on the street level or at a prescribed height. The aim is to allow more room for the pedestrian or to reduce the obstruction to sunlight reaching the streets and lower stories of adjoining buildings. *(Handbook for Planning Commissioners in Missouri)*

■ **setback, side**   A setback extending from the required front setback to the re-

quired rear setback, or to the front and/or rear property lines where no front and/or rear setback is required by the provisions of this chapter, the minimum and average dimensions of which are determined by the standards of property development of the zone in which such lot is located. *(Redondo Beach, Calif.)*

The shortest distance between the building line and the side lot line. *(Jupiter, Fla.)*

A setback between a side lot line and the nearmost point of the nearest building, swimming pool, tennis court, or like structure to it, extending from the required front setback to the required rear setback. *(Wolfeboro, N.H.)*

■ **setback, side exterior**   A side setback abutting a street. *(Redondo Beach, Calif.)*

■ **setback, side interior**   A side setback on that portion of a lot that is not adjacent to a private or public street. It extends from the rear line of the required front yard, or the front property line of the site where no front yard is required, to the front line of the required rear yard, or the rear property line of the site where no rear yard is required, the width of which is the horizontal distance between the side property line and a line parallel thereto on the site, except that the corner side yard shall extend to the rear lot line. *(Henderson, Nev.)*

■ **setback, side street**   The side setback applied to that side of a lot that has a side yard facing a private or public street or access corridor that serves more than one lot. *(Redmond, Wash.)*

A side setback on that portion of a lot that is adjacent to a private or public street. It extends from the rear line of the required front yard, or the front property line of the site where no front yard is required, to the front line of the required rear yard, or the rear property line of the site where no rear yard is required, the width of which is the horizontal distance between the side property line and a line parallel thereto on the site, except that the corner side yard shall extend to the rear lot line. *(Henderson, Nev.)*

■ **setback, street**   A setback that is measured from a street lot line. *(Portland, Ore.)*

■ **setback, windbreak**   The distance from the street right-of-way to the street side edge of a growth of trees or shrubs, serving to break the force of the wind. *(Scott County, Minn.)*

■ **settlement**   (1) The drop in elevation of a ground surface caused by settling or compacting. (2) The gradual downward movement of an engineered structure due to compaction. Differential settlement is uneven settlement, where one part of a structure settles more or at a different rate than another part. *(California Planning Roundtable)*

■ **sewage/sewerage**   All effluent carried by sewers, whether sanitary sewage, residential, commercial, or industrial wastes, or stormwater runoff. Also, the entire system of sewage collection, conveyance, treatment, and disposal. *(Concord Township, Pa.)*

The total of organic waste and wastewater generated by residential, industrial, commercial, institutional, or other establishments. *(Concord Township, Pa.)*

Refuse liquids or waste matter typically carried off site by a sewer system or treated on site by a septic system. *(Boulder County, Colo.)*

Any water-carried domestic waste, exclusive of footing and roof drainage of any residence, industry, agricultural, or commercial establishment, whether treated or untreated, including the liquid wastes produced by bathing, laundry, and culinary operation, and from toilets and floor drains associated with these sources. Raw sewage is sewage that has not been subjected to any treatment process. *(Scott County, Minn.)*

■ **sewage treatment plant**   Any facility designed for the treatment of sewage that serves in excess of two structures or dwelling units. *(Delafield, Wisc.)*

A facility designed for the collection, removal, treatment, and disposal of waterborne sewage generated within a given service area. *(Topeka, Kans., which uses the term "sewage system")*

■ **sewage treatment system, private** *(See also **septic system**)*   On-site means for disposing and treating human and domestic waste, such as a septic tank and soil absorption system or other system, allowed by state and city regulations; used where authorized by the city when access to the municipal sewer system is not required or feasible. *(Plymouth, Minn.)*

■ **sewer, building** That part of the horizontal piping of a drainage system that extends from the end of the building drain, receives the discharge of the building drain, and conveys it to a public sewer, private sewer, individual sewage disposal system, or other point of disposal. The building sewer commences five feet outside the building foundation wall. *(Illinois Department of Public Health)*

The pipe that begins outside the building wall and extends to any place or mechanism of sewage disposal, including, but not limited to a cesspool, leaching chamber, septic tank, or pressure gravity sewer leading to a leaching system. *(New Shoreham, R.I.)*

■ **sewer, central/group** A central sewage treatment facility for a single development, community, or region with an accompanying collection network. Must be designed to properly provide for the safe treatment and disposal of the generated raw sewage. Subject to the approval by the appropriate sanitation and health officials. *(Grant County, Ky.)*

■ **sewer, combined sewer/combination sewer** A sewerage system that carries both sanitary sewage and stormwater runoff. *(California Planning Roundtable)*

■ **sewer, on-site** (*See also* **septic system; sewer treatment system, private**) A septic tank or similar installation on an individual lot that uses an aerobic bacteriological process or equally satisfactory process for the elimination of raw sewage. Subject to the approval of the appropriate health and sanitation officials. *(Grant County, Ky.)*

■ **sewer, public sewer and water system** Any system, other than an individual septic tank, tile field, or individual well, which system is operated by a municipality, governmental agency, or utility for the collection, treatment, and

disposal of wastes and the furnishing of potable water. *(Siskiyou County, Calif.)*

Any system, other than septic tank or individual well, operated by a municipality for the disposal of wastes and the furnishing of water, or either, to residential, industrial and/or commercial users. *(Wheeling, Ill.)*

■ **sewer, sanitary** A system of subterranean conduits that carries refuse liquids or waste matter to a plant where the sewage is treated, as contrasted with storm drainage systems (that carry surface water) and septic tanks or leech fields (that hold refuse liquids and waste matter on-site). *(California Planning Roundtable)*

■ **sewer, side** A side sewer is that portion of a sewer from the point of connection to a public sewer to a point of demarcation that shall be the front face of a curb or a curbline of record in a public street, alley, or place, or the boundary line of record in an easement for public sewers, except that the point of demarcation shall be the first intersection of a private sewer that serves more than one building, lot, or premises. In the absence of a curb or line of record, the Director shall establish a point of demarcation based on like public streets, alleys, or places, or easements for public sewers. Also known as lateral sewer. *(San Francisco, Calif.)*

■ **sewer, storm** A sewer that carries storm, surface, and ground water drainage but excludes sewage and residential, commercial, and industrial wastes. *(Concord Township, Pa.)*

■ **screening wall** (*See also* **buffer**) A wall made of fieldstone, brick, stucco, wrought-iron (or equivalent to wrought-iron), or wood picket excluding round industrial railing and chain link fence. The wall shall create a visual buffer and be at least 50 percent solid and be three to four feet long. *(Gainesville, Fla.)*

■ **shade** For the purposes of the solar access regulations, a shadow cast by the shade point of a structure or regulated vegetation. *(Portland, Ore.)*

■ **shade point** For the purpose of the solar access regulations, the part of a

structure or regulated vegetation that casts the longest shadow onto the adjacent lots. *(Portland, Ore.)*

■ **shared living** The occupancy of a dwelling unit by persons of more than one family in order to reduce housing expenses and to provide social contact, mutual support, and assistance. *(Larkspur, Calif.)*

■ **shed** A subordinate structure or building used primarily for storage purposes, of a height no greater than seven feet, and the total square footage of which does not exceed 120 square feet. *(Chandler, Ariz.)*

■ **shelter** (*See also* **domestic violence shelter; emergency and protective shelter; homeless shelter**) A facility providing temporary protective sanctuary for victims of crime or abuse, including emergency housing during crisis intervention for individuals, such as victims of rape, child abuse, or beatings. *(Blacksburg, Va.)*

■ **shipyard** (*See also* **port and harbor facilities**) An area where ships, boats, or vessels are built, repaired, and stored. *(Miami, Fla.)*

■ **shooting gallery** Any establishment which is open to the public and at which firearms are rented for firing upon the immediate premises for the purpose of amusement. *(Glendale, Ariz.)*

■ **shooting range, indoor** The use of a structure for archery and/or the discharging of firearms for the purposes of target practice or temporary competitions. *(Blacksburg, Va.)*

A facility designed or used for shooting at targets with rifles, pistols, or shotguns, and which is completely enclosed within a building or structure. *(McHenry County, Ill.)*

■ **shooting range, outdoor** The use of land for archery and/or the discharging of firearms for the purposes of target practice, skeet and trap shooting, mock war games, or temporary competitions, such as turkey shoots. Excluded from this use type shall be general hunting and unstructured and nonrecurring discharging of firearms on private property with the property owner's permission. *(Blacksburg, Va.)*

A facility designed or used for shooting at targets with rifles, pistols, or shotguns, and which is completely enclosed within a building or structure *(McHenry County, Ill.)*

■ **shopping center**  A group of commercial establishments planned, constructed, and managed as a total entity with customer and employee parking provided on-site, provision for goods delivery separated from customer access, aesthetic considerations, and protection from the elements. *(Iowa State University Extension Service)*

A group of retail and other commercial establishments that is planned, owned, and managed as a single property. On-site parking is provided. The center's size and orientation are generally determined by the market characteristics of the trade area served by the center. The two main configurations of shopping centers are malls and open-air strip centers. *(International Council of Shopping Centers)*

A group of stores planned and designed for the site on which it is built, functioning as a unit, with off-street parking, landscaped areas, and pedestrian malls or plazas provided on the property as an integral part of the unit. *(Scottsdale, Ariz.)*

A single piece of real estate containing more than three commercial establishments and a total business space of more than 3,200 square feet planned, constructed, and managed as a total entity with customer and employee parking provided on site. *(Wolfeboro, N.H.)*

■ **shopping center, commercial strip**  Commercial development, usually one store deep, that fronts on a major street for a distance of one city block or more. Includes individual buildings on their own lots, with or without on-site parking, and small linear shopping centers with shallow on-site parking in front of the stores. *(California Planning Roundtable)*

■ **shopping center, community**  A center that typically offers a wider range of apparel and other soft goods than the neighborhood center does. Among the more common anchors are supermarkets, super drugstores, and discount department stores. Community center tenants sometimes contain off-price retailers selling such items as apparel, home improvements/furnishings, toys, electronics, or sporting goods. The center is usually configured as a strip, in a strip line, or L or U shape. Of the eight center types, community centers encompass the widest range of formats. For example, certain centers that are anchored by a large discount department store refer to themselves as discount centers. Others with a high percentage of square footage allocated to off-price retailers can be termed off-price centers. *(International Council of Shopping Centers)*

A group of two or more business establishments containing more than 40,000 square feet gross floor area designed as a large-scale commercial center offering a shopping environment for the general public. *(Ocean City, Md.)*

■ **shopping center, consumer retail, medium-scale**  Establishments of more than 10,000 square feet and not greater than 30,000 square feet of gross floor area engaged in the sale or rental of goods for consumer or household use; excluding, however, animal sales or service; building materials and/or supplies, sales, or rental; and food sales or markets. Typical uses include sale of consumer goods or art or craft objects, flower shops, gift shops, and boutiques. *(Denver, Colo.)*

■ **shopping center, consumer retail, small-scale**  Establishments of 10,000 square feet or fewer of gross floor area engaged in the sale or rental of goods for consumer or household use; excluding, however, animal sales or service; building materials and/or supplies, sales or rental; and food sales or markets. Typical uses include sale of consumer goods or art or craft objects, flower shops, gift shops, and boutiques. *(Denver, Colo.)*

■ **shopping center, department store**  A general merchandising store offering a full line of goods and having 50,000 square feet or more of floor space. *(Hilton Head, S.C.)*

■ **shopping center, fashion/specialty**  A center composed mainly of upscale apparel shops, boutiques, and craft shops carrying selected fashion or unique merchandise of high quality and price. These centers need not be anchored, although sometimes restaurants or entertainment can provide the draw of anchors. The physical design of the center is very sophisticated, emphasizing a rich decor and high-quality landscaping. These centers usually are found in trade areas having high income levels. *(International Council of Shopping Centers)*

A retail establishment that specializes in offering a single product or a specific variety of products for sale. Specific uses classified as specialty retail establishments are: arts and crafts shops or galleries; antique stores; appliance stores; automobile/pleasure craft dealerships; bakeries or confectioneries; book or stationery stores; butchers; retail or rental clothing; computer sales and service; electronics store; feed or farming store; flower shop; furniture sales, production or stripping; hardware store; hobby, collector or gift shops; home accessory store; jewelry sales or repair; large equipment rental and sale; machine shop; handicrafts manufacturing; mobile homes sales and service; notions and fabric stores; nursery or greenhouse; packing liquor sales; pet sales, grooming and obedience; pharmaceuticals; drug stores; printing, publishing, and photocopying; radio and television production and sales; repair shops; shoe sales, repair and shine; sporting goods stores; and video rental tape. *(Taos, N. Mex., which uses the term "speciality retail establishments")*

■ **shopping center, mini-mall**  A shopping center of between 80,000 and 150,000 square feet on a site of 8 to 15 acres where tenants are located on both sides of a covered walkway with direct pedestrian access to all establishments from the walkway. *(Iowa State University Extension Service)*

■ **shopping center, neighborhood center**  A center designed to provide convenience shopping for the day-to-day needs of consumers in the immediate neighborhood. Roughly half of these centers are anchored by a supermarket, while about a third have a drugstore anchor. These anchors are supported by stores offering drugs, sundries, snacks, and personal services. A neighborhood center is usually configured as a straight-line strip with no enclosed walkway or mall area, although a canopy may connect the storefronts. *(International Council of Shopping Centers)*

A group of two or more business establishments designed to provide primarily for retail shopping, personal service uses, and indoor recreational activities to meet the daily needs of residents and vacationers in the vicinity of their neighborhood. *(Ocean City, Md.)*

A shopping center having 15,000-100,000 square feet, with no individual building any larger than 29,000 square feet. *(Williamson County, Tenn.)*

■ **shopping center, outlet**    Usually located in rural or occasionally tourist locations, outlet centers consist mostly of manufacturers' outlet stores selling their own brands at a discount. These centers are typically not anchored. A strip configuration is most common, although some are enclosed malls, and others can be arranged in a "village cluster." *(International Council of Shopping Centers)*

■ **shopping center, power center**    A center dominated by several large anchors, including discount department stores, off-price stores, warehouse clubs, or "category killers," (i.e., stores that offer tremendous selection in a particular merchandise category at low prices). The center typically consists of several freestanding (unconnected) anchors and only a minimum number of small tenants. *(International Council of Shopping Centers)*

■ **shopping center, regional**    A retail shopping area in excess of 30 acres (divided by no interior public streets) containing at least one major retail store of over 100,000 square feet of gross leasable area and additional retail area. *(Jefferson County, Colo.)*

A center that provides general merchandise (a large percentage of which is apparel) and services in full depth and variety. Its main attraction are anchors: traditional, mass merchandise, or discount department stores or fashion or specialty stores. A typical regional center is usually enclosed with an inward orientation of the stores connected by a common walkway and parking surrounds the outside perimeter. *(International Council of Shopping Centers)*

A group of commercial establishments offering a wide range of retail and service uses planned, constructed, and managed as a total entity with customer and employee parking provided on site, occupies a minimum of 30 acres of land, has at least one or more anchor stores, and contains over 400,000 square feet of gross leasable space. *(Schaumburg, Ill.)*

A group of commercial establishments planned, developed, and managed as a unit, related in location, size, and type of shops to the trade area that the unit serves, and which provides off-street parking in definite relationship to the types and sizes of stores. A regional shopping center provides for complete comparison shopping goods in depth and variety and typically includes, although not limited to, general merchandise, apparel, furniture, and home furnishings establishments that serve a trade area population of a minimum of 375,000 people. *(Chicago, Ill.)*

■ **shopping center, superregional**    Similar to a regional center, but because of its larger size, a superregional center has more anchors and a deeper selection of merchandise, and draws from a larger population base. As with regional centers, the typical configuration is as an enclosed mall, frequently with multiple levels. *(International Council of Shopping Centers)*

A group of commercial enterprises offering a range of retail commercial goods and services in an aggregate of 1,400,000 square feet or more of gross floor area that (1) is designed as a single commercial group, whether or not located on the same lot; (2) is under one common ownership or management, or having one common arrangement for the maintenance of the grounds; (3) is connected by party walls, partitions, covered canopies, or other structural members to form one continuous structure; (4) shares a common parking area; and (5) otherwise presents the appearance of one continuous commercial area. *(Fairfax County, Va.)*

■ **shopping center, theme/festival**    A shopping center that employs a unifying theme carried out by the individual shops in their architectural design and, to an extent, in their merchandise. The biggest appeal of these centers is to tourists. Center can be anchored by restaurants and entertainment facilities. These centers, generally located in urban areas, tend to be adapted from older, sometimes historic buildings, and can be a part of mixed-use projects. *(International Council of Shopping Centers)*

■ **shopping mall** *(See also **shopping center** definitions)*    A facility with five or more stores for retail goods and services, which are structurally designed in an integrated fashion around or along both sides of a promenade, walkway, concourse, or courtyard. Primary individual store entrances front onto this promenade. The mall may include offices and satellite or unattached structures that are served by the mall road network. This definition applies only to a facility in which 85 percent or more of the gross floor area is accessed from enclosed promenades, walkways, concourses, or courtyards. *(Prince William County, Va.)*

Malls are typically enclosed, with a climate-controlled walkway between two facing strips of stores. The term represents the most common design mode for regional and superregional centers and has become an informal term for these types of centers. *(International Council of Shopping Centers)*

■ **shore lot line** *(See also **high-water mark**)*    The ordinary high-water line of the lake or stream that the lot abuts. *(Delafield, Wisc.)*

■ **shoreland**    Land located within the following distances from public waters: 1,000 feet from the normal high-water mark of a lake, pond, or flowage, and 300 feet from a river or stream, or the landward extent of a floodplain designated by ordinance on such a river or stream, whichever is greater. The practical limits of shorelands may be less than the statutory limits whenever the waters involved are bounded by natural topographic divides that extend landward from the waters for lesser distances, as determined by the [state] Department of Natural Resources. *(St. Paul, Minn.)*

Those lands extending landward for 200 feet in all directions, as measured on a horizontal plane from ordinary high-water mark; floodways, and contiguous floodplain areas landward 200 feet from such floodways; and all marshes, bogs, swamps, and river deltas, associated with streams, lakes, and tidal waters which are subject to the provisions of the State Shorelines Management Act. For purposes of determining jurisdictional area, the boundary will be either 200 feet from the ordinary high-water mark, or 200 feet from the floodway, whichever is greater. *(Renton, Wash.)*

■ **shoreland alteration**   Grading and filling in shoreland areas or any alteration of the natural topography where the slope of the land is toward a public water or a watercourse leading to a public water. *(Scott County, Minn.)*

■ **shoreline**   All of the water areas of the state regulated by the city, including reservoirs and their associated shorelands, together with the lands underlying them, except: (1) shorelines of statewide significance; (2) shorelines on segments of streams upstream of a point where the mean annual flow is 20 cubic feet per second or less and the wetlands associated with such upstream segments; (3) shorelines on lakes less than 20 acres in size and wetlands associated with such small lakes. *(Renton, Wash.)*

■ **shoreline stabilization**   The construction or modification of bulkheads, retaining walls, dikes, levies, riprap, and other structures along the shoreline, for the purpose of controlling stream undercutting or stream erosion. *(Yakima County, Wash.)*

■ **short-term housing** *(See housing, short-term)*

■ **shrub**   A woody plant that usually remains low and produces shoots or trunks from the base; it is not usually tree-like or single stemmed. *(Coral Gables, Fla.)*

A woody plant with a multiple stem capable of growing to a height of no more than 15 feet. *(Nashville and Davidson County, Tenn.)*

A woody plant usually greater than 3 feet but less than 20 feet tall that generally exhibits several erect, spreading, or prostrate stems and has a bushy appearance. *(Columbia River Gorge, Wash.)*

■ **sidewalk**   An improved pedestrian surface that is typically located adjacent to a roadway. *(Farragut, Tenn.)*

Any strip or section of concrete, stone, or macadam a minimum of four feet in width, the prime purpose of which is a walkway. *(Bensalem, Township, Pa.)*

■ **sidewalk cafe**   A portion of an eating or drinking place, located on a public sidewalk, that provides waiter or waitress service and is either an enclosed or unenclosed sidewalk cafe as defined. No portion of a sidewalk café shall be used for any purpose other than dining and circulation therein. *(New York, N.Y.)*

Any outdoor dining area located in any public sidewalk or right-of-way that is associated with a restaurant or other eating and drinking establishment on a contiguous adjacent parcel. *(Santa Monica, Calif.)*

■ **sidewalk cafe, enclosed**   A sidewalk cafe contained within a one-story structure constructed predominately of light materials such as glass, slow burning plastic, or lightweight metal. All materials must be approved by the department of buildings. Sidewalk cafes are permitted only upon the granting of revocable consent by the Board of Estimate and as such only nonpermanent structures are permitted. *(New York, N.Y.)*

■ **sidewalk sale** *(See also temporary outdoor sale)*   Outdoor sale, conducted by the proprietor, of products normally sold inside a retail establishment. *(Scottsdale, Ariz,)*

A promotional sales event conducted outside the confines of the commercial or manufacturing structure in which such business is normally conducted and which occurs on a paved or concrete area on the same lot as the structure. *(Las Vegas, Nev., which uses the term "sidewalk/parking lot sale")*

A seasonal or occasional sale held on the sidewalk or other structure along the front or side of a particular store or establishment where goods are offered for sale to the public, typically at a discounted price. *(Concord Township, Penn.)*

■ **sidewalk vendor**   Any person engaged in the selling, or offering for sale, of food, beverages, merchandise, or services for immediate delivery from a vendor stand or from his or her person that is not located in, or in association with, a building. *(Clearwater, Fla.)*

■ **sidewalk vendor stand**   Any portable table, showcase, bench, rack, pushcart, or similar device used for the displaying, storing, or transporting of articles offered for sale by a sidewalk vendor. *(Clearwater, Fla.)*

■ **sight distance triangle** *(See also clear vision triangle)*   The triangular area formed by a diagonal line connecting two points located on intersecting street right-of-way lines (or a right-of-way line and the curb or edge of a driveway). *(Baton Rouge, La.)*

The area of a corner lot bounded by the right-of-way lines and a line connecting the two points on the property lines 30 feet from the intersection of the property lines. *(Maryland Heights, Mo.)*

■ **sign**   Any device (including, but not limited to, letters, words, numerals, figures, emblems, pictures, or any part or combination) used for visual communication intended to attract the attention of the public and visible to the public right-of-way or other properties. The term "sign" shall not include any flag, badge, or insignia or any governmental unit, nor shall it include any item of merchandise normally displayed within a show window of a business. *(Glendale, Ariz.)*

A communication device, structure, or fixture that incorporates graphics, symbols, or written copy intended to promote the sale of a product, commodity, or service, or to provide direction or identification for a premises or facility. (Redmond, Wash.)

Any words, lettering, figures, numerals, emblems, devices, trademarks, or trade names, or any combination thereof, by which anything is made known and which is designed to attract attention and/or convey a message. (Doylestown, Ohio)

Any writing (including letter, word, or numeral), pictorial presentation (including illustration or decoration), emblem (including device, symbol, or trademark), flag (including banner or pennant), or any other figure of similar character, that: (1) is a structure or any part thereof, or is attached to, painted on, or in any other manner represented on a building or other structure; (2) is used to announce, direct attention to, or advertise; and (3) is visible from outside a building. A sign includes writing, representation, or other figures of similar character, within a building, only when illuminated and located in a window. However, nonilluminated signs containing solely noncommercial copy with a total surface area not exceeding 12 square feet on any zoning lot, including

memorial tablets or signs displayed for the direction or convenience of the public, shall not be subject to the provisions of this resolution. (New York, N.Y.)

*Commentary: The definition of sign should be broad enough to include all signs, without regard to physical appearance or content. Following this rule of thumb, the definitions of sign we offer here do not have a detailed list of the possible physical attributes of a sign and its supporting structure, nor do they say anything about the content of the sign message. Instead, the emphasis is on what a sign does. Since various types of signs are regulated differently, the zoning ordinance will necessarily provide definitions for each, and we have provided a long list of sign definitions here describing a number of types of signs. Planners must consult their municipal attorney when drafting sign definitions and regulations. PAS Report No. 489/490, Aesthetics, Community Character, and the Law, by Christopher J. Duerksen and R. Matthew Goebel has a chapter specifically devoted to an analysis of case law regarding what communities can and cannot do in the regulation of signs.*

■ **sign, abandoned**　A sign or sign structure on a site where all buildings have been demolished or removed. (Portland, Ore.)

Any sign that advertises a business, lessor, owner, product, service, or activity that is no longer located on the

premises where the sign is displayed. (Inyo County, Calif.)

A sign that no longer identifies or advertises a bona fide business, lessor, service, owner, product, or activity and/or for which no legal owner can be found. (Concord Township, Pa.)

■ **sign, advertising device**　Any advertising sign, billboard, statuary or poster that directs attention to a business, commodity, service, or entertainment not exclusively related to the premises where such sign is located or to which it is affixed, but does not include those advertising signs, billboards, or poster panels that direct attention to the business on the premises or to a brand name of a product or commodity with which the business is specifically identified and which is sold on the premises. (Doylestown, Ohio)

A sign that has as its purpose to promote, advertise, or sell a product or service obtainable on the premises upon which the sign is located, and not to identify the premises. (Duluth, Ga., which uses the term "sign marketing")

■ **sign alteration**　Any change of copy, sign face, color, size, shape, illumination, position, location, construction, or supporting structure of any sign. (Inyo County, Calif.)

■ **sign, animated or moving**　Any sign or part of a sign that changes physical position by any movement or rotation or that gives the visual impression of such movement. (Iowa State University Extension Service)

A sign with action, motion, or changing colors which require electrical energy. This does not include signs that indicate only time, temperature, or date. (Duluth, Ga.)

A sign that uses movement, lighting, or special materials to depict action or create a special effect to imitate movement. A flashing sign shall not be considered an animated or moving sign. (Inyo County, Calif.)

Any sign that, through the use of moving structural elements, flashing or sequential lights, lighting elements, or other automated method, results in movement, the appearance of movement, or change of sign image or text. Changing image signs do not include otherwise static signs where illumination is turned off and back on not more than once every 24 hours. *(Portland, Ore., which uses the term "changing image sign")*

■ **sign, appurtenant** A sign incidental, appropriate, and subordinate to a permitted use of the lot or building upon which the sign is located. *(Redding, Calif.)*

■ **sign area** The entire area within a continuous perimeter, enclosing the extreme limits of sign display, including any frame or border. Curved, spherical, or any other shaped sign face shall be computed on the basis of actual surface area. The copy of signs composed of individual letters, numerals, or other devices shall be the sum of the area of the smallest rectangle or other geometric figure encompassing all of said letters or devices. The calculation for a double-faced sign shall be the area of one face only. Double-faced signs shall be constructed so that the perimeter of both faces coincide and are parallel and not more than 24 inches apart. *(Prince William County, Va.)*

The entire face of a sign including the advertising surface and any framing, trim, or molding, but not including the supporting structure. *(Iowa State University Extension Service)*

The area within a continuous perimeter enclosing the limits of writing, representation, emblem, or any figure or similar character, together with any frame or other material or color forming an integral part of the display or used to differentiate this sign from the background against which it is placed, excluding the necessary supports or uprights on which this sign is placed: provided, however, that any open space contained within the outer limits of the display face of a sign, or between any component, panel, strip or figure of any kind composing the display face shall be included in the computation of the sign whether this open space be enclosed or not by a frame or border. For projecting or double-faced signs, only one display face shall be measured in computing sign area which the

sign faces are parallel, or where the interior angle formed by the faces is 60 degrees or less, provided that it is a common attached structure. If the two faces of a double-faced sign are of unequal area, the area of the sign shall be taken as the area of the larger face. *(Duluth, Ga., which uses the term "sign, surface area")*

■ **sign, auxiliary** A sign pertaining to the safe and efficient movement of pedestrians and vehicular traffic into and out of a building, parking area, and premises. *(El Paso, Tex.)*

■ **sign, awning** A sign incorporated into or attached to an awning. *(Portland, Ore.)*

A sign that is either attached to, affixed to, or painted on an awning or canopy (pictured below) and not exceeding 50 square feet in sign area. *(Inyo County, Calif.)*

Any nonilluminated sign painted on or applied to a structure made of cloth, canvas, metal or similar material that is affixed to a building and projects therefrom. Such signs may or may not be fixed or equipped with a mechanism for raising and holding an awning in a retracted position against the building. *(Concord Township, Penn.)*

Any sign attached to or constructed on the face of a permanent, rooflike shelter, extending from part or all of the building face and constructed of some durable material. *(Gillette, Wyo.)*

■ **sign, balloon** One or more balloons used as a permanent or temporary sign or as a means of directing attention

to any business or profession, or to a commodity or service sold, offered, or manufactured, or to any entertainment. *(Redondo Beach, Calif.)*

■ **sign, banner** A sign with or without characters, letters, illustrations, or ornamentations applied to cloth, paper, flexible plastic, or fabric of any kind with only such material for backing (pictured below, at right). *(Duluth, Ga.)*

A sign having characters, letters or illustrations applied to cloth, paper or fabric of any kind, with only such nonrigid material for background. *(Concord Township, Pa.)*

■ **sign, banner, corporate** The emblem or standard of a for-profit or not-for-profit corporation, or other similar entity. *(Columbus, Ohio)*

■ **sign, banner, ornamental**　A banner that uses any of a variety of images or colors of an ornamental nature, and that displays no on-premises or off-premises copy. *(Columbus, Ohio)*

■ **sign, banner, promotional**　A banner that displays on-premises or off-premises copy. *(Columbus, Ohio)*

■ **sign, bench**　A sign located on the seat or back of a bench or seat placed on or adjacent to a public right-of-way. *(Concord Township, Pa.)*

■ **sign, billboard**　A sign that directs attention to a business, commodity, service, or entertainment conducted, sold or offered at a location other then the premises on which the sign is located. *(Iowa State University Extension Service)*

A board, panel, or tablet used for the display of posters, printed or painted advertising matter, either illuminated or nonilluminated, that directs attention to goods, merchandise, entertainment, or services offered elsewhere than the premises where the sign is located. *(Gillette, Wyo.)*

■ **sign, billboard, back-to-back**　A structure with two parallel sign faces oriented in opposite directions. *(Cape Girardeau, Mo.)*

■ **sign, billboard, V-type**　A structure or structures with two sign faces, forming the shape of the letter "V" when viewed from above, with an angle between the two faces of not more than 60 degrees. *(Cape Girardeau, Mo.)*

■ **sign, blade/bracket**　A small, pedestrian-oriented sign (i.e., less than four square feet) that projects perpendicular from a structure (blade sign) or is hung beneath a canopy (bracket sign). *(Inyo County, Calif.)*

■ **sign, business identification**　Any sign identifying a specific business, either retail, wholesale, or industrial, or a profession and is located upon the subject property. *(Plymouth, Minn.)*

A sign displaying information pertaining to goods, services, or entertainment offered or produced by the business located on the same property as the business sign, but not including advertising devices or advertising displays. *(Malibu, Calif.)*

■ **sign, cabinet/can**　A sign that contains all the text and/or logo symbols within a single enclosed cabinet and may or may not be illuminated. *(Inyo County, Calif.)*

■ **sign, combination**　A sign incorporating any combination of the features of freestanding, projecting, and roof signs. *(St. Paul, Minn.)*

■ **sign, construction/development**　A temporary sign providing information about future development or current construction on a site and the parties involved in the project. *(Glendale, Ariz.)*

A temporary sign identifying an architect, engineer, contractor, subcontractor, and/or material supplier who participates in construction on the property on which the sign is located. *(Concord Township, Pa.)*

■ **sign copy**　Any combination of letters or numbers which is intended to inform, direct or otherwise transmit information. *(Boise City, Idaho)*

■ **sign copy area**　The area of the sign occupied by copy. It is computed by measuring the area enclosed by straight lines drawn to enclose the extremities of the letters or numbers. *(Boise City, Idaho)*

■ **sign, detached**　A sign not attached to or painted on a building, but which is permanently affixed to the ground. A sign attached to a flat surface such as a fence or wall and not a part of a building shall be considered a detached sign. *(Baton Rouge, La.)*

■ **sign, directional**　Any on-premises sign that includes information assisting in the flow of pedestrian or vehicular traffic such as enter, exit, and one-way. *(Glendale, Ariz.)*

A sign whose message is exclusively limited to guiding the circulation of motorists or pedestrians on the site. *(Portland, Ore.)*

■ **sign, directory**　A sign, other than an identification sign, listing the names, uses, or locations of the various businesses or activities conducted within a building or group of buildings, that is centrally located and intended to provide on-site directions. *(Glendale, Ariz.)*

A sign or group of signs attached to a building or freestanding which identifies the business, owner, address, or occupation of a group of businesses, but contains no advertising. *(Scott County, Minn.)*

■ **sign, double-faced**　A sign with two display areas against each other or where the interior angle formed by the display areas is 60 degrees or less, where one face is designed to be seen from one direction and the other side from another direction. *(Duluth, Ga.)*

A sign constructed to display its message on the outer surfaces of two identical and opposite parallel planes. *(Inyo County, Calif.)*

A sign with two faces. *(Concord Township, Pa.)*

■ **sign, electric**　Any sign containing or using electrical wiring, but not including signs illuminated by an exterior light source. *(Renton, Wash.)*

■ **sign, electronic message board**　A sign with a fixed or changing display/message composed of a series of lights that may be changed through electronic means. A time and/or temperature sign shall not be considered an electronic graphics sign. *(Inyo County, Calif.)*

Signs whose alphabetic, pictographic, or symbolic informational content can be changed or altered on a fixed display screen composed of electrically illuminated segments. *(Renton, Wash.)*

■ **sign, entry feature**　A permanent on-premises sign identifying a vehicular entrance to a residential subdivision (pictured on page 204), residential complex, or institutional use. *(Columbus, Ohio)*

A type of wall sign identifying an entrance or an exit to a building, or used to direct functions within the building, such as day care, gymnasium, etc. *(El Paso, Tex., which uses the term "entryway identification sign")*

■ **sign face**　The area or display surface used for the message. *(Prince William County, Va.)*

The part of the sign that is or can be used to identify, advertise, or communicate information or for visual representation that attracts the attention of the public for any purpose. The frame or structural members may be considered as part of the sign face if it is so designed with lighting or other ornamentation that is incorporated for the sign design. *(Jacksonville, N.C.)*

■ **sign, fascia**  A sign mounted against the horizontal piece covering the joint between the top of a wall and the projecting eaves of the roof. *(Glendale, Ariz.)*

A single-faced sign attached flush to a building. *(Portland, Ore.)*

■ **sign, fixed**  Any lighter-than-air or gas-filled balloon attached by means of a rope or tether to a definite or fixed location. *(Reno, Nev.)*

■ **sign, flashing**  Any illuminated sign on which the artificial light is not maintained stationary or constant in intensity and color at all times when such is in use. Any moving, illuminated sign shall be considered a "flashing sign." Such signs shall not be deemed to include time and temperature signs or public message displays using electronic switching. *(Doylestown, Ohio)*

A sign that contains an intermittent or sequential flashing light source. An animated or moving sign shall not be considered as a flashing sign. *(Inyo County, Calif.)*

A sign that exhibits artificially changing light or color effects visible from the right-of-way or adjoining properties. *(Champaign, Ill.)*

■ **sign, flat**  Any sign which is attached directly, in rigid manner, and parallel to the building wall. *(Grant County, Ky.)*

■ **sign, freestanding**  Any sign supported wholly or in part by some structure other than the building or buildings housing the business to which the sign pertains, or any sign which projects more than five feet from the side of the building to which it is attached. *(Doylestown, Ohio)*

A sign that is attached to, erected on, or supported by some structure (such as a pole, mast, frame, or other structure) that is not itself an integral part of or attached to a building or other structure whose principal function is something other than the support of a sign. *(Duluth, Ga.)*

■ **sign gross area**  The entire area within a single continuous perimeter enclosing the extreme limits of a sign. However, this perimeter shall not include any structural elements lying outside of the limits of the sign and not forming an integral part of the display. *(Doylestown, Ohio)*

■ **sign height**  The vertical distance measured from the lowest adjacent grade to the highest point of the sign or sign structure. *(Blacksburg, Va.)*

The vertical distance from the uppermost point used in measuring the area of a sign to the average grade immediately below and adjoining the sign. *(Inyo County, Calif.)*

Height shall be measured from sign base, provided that if the ground at the base is

augmented in a manner that adds height to the sign but not the surrounding buildings, the height shall be measured from the nearest paved travel way. Where such traveled way is to be enlarged or otherwise altered in the future, the measurement is to be made from the projected grade of the anticipated traveled way at final buildout. *(Henderson, Nev.)*

■ **sign, highway directional**  An official highway directional sign or other official sign authorized by a city, state, or federal agency. *(Philadelphia, Pa.)*

■ **sign, home occupation**  A sign containing only the name and occupation of a permitted home occupation. *(Iowa State University Extension Service)*

■ **sign, identification**  A sign giving the nature, logo, trademark, or other identifying symbol; address; or any combination of the name, symbol, and address of a building, business, development, or establishment on the premises where it is located. *(Iowa State University Extension Service)*

A sign used to display only the name, address, crest, or trademark of the business, individual, family, organization, or enterprise occupying the premises, the profession of the occupant or the name of the building on which the sign is displayed. Also, a permanent sign announcing the name of a subdivision, shopping center, tourist home, group housing project, church, school, park, or public or quasi-public structure, facility, or development and the name of the owners or developers. *(Doylestown, Ohio)*

■ **sign, illegal**  Any of the following: (1) a sign erected without first obtaining a permit and complying with all regulations in effect at the time of its construction or use; (2) a sign that was legally erected but whose use has ceased because the business it identifies is no longer conducted on the premises; (3) a nonconforming sign for which the amortization period has expired; (4) a sign that was legally erected but which later became nonconforming and then was damaged to the extent of 50 percent or more of its current replacement value; (5) a sign that is a danger to the public or is unsafe; or (6) a sign that pertains to a specific event that has not been removed within five days after the occurrence of the event. *(Inyo County, Calif.)*

■ **sign, illuminated** A sign designed to give forth artificial light directly or through transparent or translucent material from a source of light within this sign, including, but not limited to, neon and exposed lamp signs, or a sign illuminated by external light directed primarily toward this sign and so shielded that no direct rays from the light are visible elsewhere than on the lot where the illumination occurs. An illuminated sign that indicates only the time, temperature, or date shall not be considered a flashing sign. *(Duluth, Ga.)*

A sign lighted by or exposed to artificial lighting either by lights on or in the sign or directed toward the sign. *(Iowa State University Extension Service)*

Any sign directly lighted by any electrical light source, internal or external, except light sources specifically and clearly operated for the purpose of lighting the general area in which the sign is located rather than the sign itself. *(Tulsa, Okla.)*

■ **sign, illuminated direct** A sign whose light source is either located in the interior of the sign so that the rays go through the face of the sign, or which is attached to the face of the sign and is perceived as a design element of the sign. *(Inyo County, Calif.)*

Illumination of a sign that is effected by a source of light contained within the sign itself. Any sign in which light becomes visible by shining through a translucent surface shall be considered a sign in which internal illumination is used. *(Peoria, Ill.)*

■ **sign, illuminated indirect** A sign illuminated primarily by light directed toward or across it or by backlighting from a source not within it. Sources of illumination for such signs may be in the form of gooseneck lamps, spotlights, or luminous tubing. Reflectorized signs depending on automobile headlights for an image in periods of darkness shall be construed to be indirectly illuminated signs. *(Miami, Fla.)*

Illumination of a sign that is effected by a source of light not contained within the sign itself. *(Peoria, Ill.)*

■ **sign, informative** Any on-premise sign containing no other message, copy, announcement, or decoration other than instruction or direction to the public. Such signs include but are not limited to the following: identifying rest rooms, public telephones, walkways, entrance and exit drives, freight entrances, and traffic direction. *(Jacksonville, N.C.)*

A sign that provides a service, direction, or courtesy information intended to assist the public and is not displayed for the general purpose of advertising products or services. Information signs shall include the location of business facilities (e.g. store entrances, walk-up windows, self-service operations) and courtesy information (hours of operation, menus, "credit cards accepted," restrooms, "no solicitors"). Information signs shall not include fuel price signs or traffic directional signs, nor shall they be part of any sign whose primary function is business identification. *(Redondo Beach, Calif.)*

A sign stating the hours of operation of a business, emergency telephone numbers, credit card usage, or other information of a similar nature. *(Malibu, Calif.)*

■ **sign, instructional** *(See sign, informative)*

■ **sign, kiosk** A sign consisting of three to five sides that lists names of businesses located on a property or in a building. *(Duluth, Ga.)*

A freestanding bulletin board having more than two faces. *(Miami, Fla.)*

■ **sign, mansard** A sign permanently affixed to a wall or surface designed to protect the edge of a roof, such surface being no more than 30 degrees from vertical. *(Glendale, Ariz.)*

■ **sign, marquee** A sign designed to have changeable copy, either manually or electronically. Marquee signs may be a principal identification sign, a freestanding sign, or a wall sign. Also known as a "readerboard sign." *(Duluth, Ga.)*

A rooflike structure of a permanent nature that projects from the wall of a building or its supports and may overhang the public way. *(Cecil Co., Md.)*

A permanent rooflike structure extending from part of the wall of a building but not supported by the ground and constructed of a durable material such as metal or glass. *(Schaumburg, Ill.)*

■ **sign, memorial** A sign, tablet or plaque memorializing a person, event, structure or site. . . . *(Inyo County, Calif.)*

■ **sign, menu** A temporary sign used to inform the public of the list of entrees, dishes, foods, and entertainment available in a restaurant. *(Glendale, Ariz.)*

■ **sign, menu board** A permanently mounted sign displaying the bill of fare for a drive-through restaurant *(Glendale, Ariz.)*

A portable or freestanding sign displaying the type and price of food and beverages sold in connection with permitted outdoor dining, or a freestanding sign permanently affixed to the ground in connection with drive-through restaurant service. This definition is not meant to apply to signs displaying menu information that are attached to buildings (such signs are included within definitions for wall or projecting signs, as the case may be). *(Redondo Beach, Calif.)*

■ **sign, mobile** A sign attached to, mounted, pasted, painted, or drawn on any vehicle, whether motorized or drawn, that is placed, parked, or maintained at one particular location for the express purpose and intent of promotion or conveying an advertising message. *(Duluth, Ga.)*

■ **sign, monument** A freestanding sign supported primarily by an internal structural framework or integrated into landscaping or other solid structural features other than support poles. *(Prince William County, Va.)*

A freestanding sign where the base of the sign structure is on the ground or a maximum of 12 inches above the adjacent grade. The width of the top of the sign structure can be no more than 120 percent of the width of the base. *(Portland, Ore.)*

■ **sign monument zone**    An area of a site dedicated or permitted to the erection of a sign or sign cluster usually less than six feet in height, often lighted and planted with low, brightly colored seasonal flowers. *(Louisiana State University)*

■ **sign, nameplate**    A sign indicating the name and address of a building; or the name of an occupant thereof, and the practice of a permitted occupation therein. *(Gurnee, Ill.)*

■ **sign, neon**    A sign containing glass tube lighting in which a gas and phosphors are used in combination to create a colored light. *(Inyo County, Calif.)*

An illuminated sign affected by a colorless, odorless light source consisting of a neon or gas tube that is bent to form letters, symbols, or other shapes. *(Malibu, Calif.)*

■ **sign, noncommercial**    A sign that does not contain information or advertising for any business, commodity, service, entertainment, product, or other attraction. *(Glendale, Ariz.)*

■ **sign, nonconforming**    A sign lawfully erected and maintained prior to the adopting of this ordinance that does not conform with the requirements of this ordinance. *(Glendale, Ariz.)*

A lawfully erected sign that, on the effective date of this article, fails to comply with requirements of this ordinance. *(Duluth, Ga.)*

An advertising structure or sign that was lawfully erected and maintained prior to the adoption of this ordinance, and which has subsequently come under the requirements of this ordinance, but does not now completely comply therewith. *(Inyo County, Calif.)*

■ **sign, off-premise**    A sign that directs attention to a business, commodity, service, or entertainment not exclusively related to the premises where such sign is located or to which it is affixed. *(Doylestown, Ohio)*

A sign advertising a use, facility, service, or product that is not located, sold, or manufactured on the same premises as the sign. *(Inyo County, Calif., which uses the term "sign, off-site advertising")*

Any sign advertising goods, products, or services, not located or sold on the premises on which the sign is located. *(Gillette, Wyo.)*

■ **sign, official traffic and street**    Any sign installed within public right-of-way by a political subdivision to direct or control vehicular, pedestrian, and bicycle traffic, identify streets, parks, historical events, or provide other information deemed appropriate. *(Grand Forks, N.Dak.)*

■ **sign, on-premise**    Any sign identifying or advertising a business, person, activity, goods, products, or services, located on the premises where the sign is installed and maintained. *(Gillette, Wyo.)*

A sign relating in its subject matter to the premises on which it is located, or to products, accommodations, services, or activities on the premises. On-site signs shall not be construed to include signs erected by the outdoor advertising industry in the conduct of the outdoor advertising business. *(Miami, Fla.)*

■ **sign, open house directional**    A temporary sign used to advertise the sale of a house and direct traffic to the house for sale. *(Glendale, Ariz.)*

■ **sign, painted wall**    A sign applied to a building wall with paint and which has no sign structure. *(Portland, Ore.)*

■ **sign, parapet**    A sign attached to that portion of a building's exterior wall that projects above the plate line of a building *(Glendale, Ariz.)*

■ **sign, permanent**    A sign attached to a building, structure, or the ground in some manner that requires a permit from the buildings department and which is made of materials intended for long-term use. *(Portland, Ore.)*

A sign constructed of durable materials and intended to exist for the duration of time that the use or occupant is located on the premises. *(Inyo County, Calif.)*

■ **sign, pitched roof**    A sign attached to a roof with a pitch of one-to-four or greater and placed parallel to the building wall. *(Portland, Ore.)*

■ **sign, pole**    A sign that is mounted on a freestanding pole or other support (pictured below) so that the bottom edge of the sign face is six feet or more above grade. *(Iowa State University Extension Service)*

A freestanding sign that is affixed, attached, or erected on a pole that is not itself an integral part of or attached to a building or structure. *(Jacksonville, N.C.)*

■ **sign, political**    A sign identifying and urging voter support for a particular election issue, political party, or candidate for public office. *(Duluth, Ga.)*

■ **sign, portable**    A sign whose principal supporting structure is intended, by design and construction, to be used by resting upon the ground for support and may be easily moved or relocated for reuse. Portable signs shall include, but are not limited to, signs mounted upon a trailer, bench, wheeled carrier, or other nonmotorized mobile structure with or without wheels. *(Duluth, Ga.)*

A sign that is not permanently affixed to a structure or the ground (e.g., A-frame or sandwich-board signs) and does not exceed 12 square feet in sign area per sign face. *(Inyo County, Calif.)*

A sign designated or intended to be moved easily that is not permanently embedded in the ground or affixed to a building or other structure, including any sign that rests upon the ground, a frame, a building, or other structure. Including but not limited to the following signs: trailer signs (with or without wheels), menu and sandwich boards, hot air or gas-filled balloons or umbrellas used for advertising, signs mounted for advertising purposes on a vehicle that is parked and visible from the public right-of-way (except signs identifying the related business when the vehicle is being used in the normal day-to-day operation of that business), sidewalk or curb signs, and A-frame signs. *(Jacksonville, N.C.)*

■ **sign, projecting**    A sign attached to a building or other structure and extending in whole or in part more than 14 inches beyond the building (pictured below). *(Glendale, Ariz.)*

A sign attached to a wall and projecting away from that wall more than 12 inches, but not more than five feet. *(Doylestown, Ohio)*

A sign attached to and projecting out from a building face or wall, generally at right angles to the building. Projecting signs include signs that are totally in the right-of-way, partially in the right-of-way, or fully on private property. *(Portland, Ore.)*

■ **sign, public information** *(See also* **sign, directional; sign, informative***)*    A sign, usually erected and maintained by a public agency, that provides the public

with information and in no way relates to a commercial activity. Includes, but not limited to, speed limit signs, stop signs, city limit signs, street name signs, and directional signs. *(Doylestown, Ohio)*

Any sign erected and maintained by public officials or public agencies, or approved and authorized for use by state or local governmental authorities. *(Duluth, Ga., which uses the term "sign, public service")*

■ **sign, pylon**    A freestanding sign other than a pole sign, permanently affixed to the ground by supports, but not having the appearance of a solid base. *(Redondo Beach, Calif.)*

■ **sign, real estate**    A temporary sign that relates to the sale, lease, or rental of property or buildings, or to construction activities on a site. *(Portland, Ore.)*

A sign indicating that a property or any portion thereof is available for inspection, sale, lease, rent, or directing people to a property, but not including temporary subdivision signs. *(Inyo County, Calif.)*

Signs used solely for the purpose of offering the property on which they are displayed, for sale, rent, lease, or inspection or indicating that the property has been sold, rented, or leased. Such signs shall be nonilluminated and limited in content to the name of the owner or agent, an address and/or telephone number for contact, and an indication of the area and general classification of the property. Real estate signs are distinguished in these regulations from other forms of advertising signs and are permitted in certain districts and locations from which other forms of advertising signs are excluded. *(Miami, Fla.)*

■ **sign, real estate, off-site**    A readily removable sign announcing the proposed sale or rental of property other than the property upon which the sign is located and providing directions to the subject property. *(Federal Way, Wash.)*

■ **sign, real estate, on-site**    A sign announcing the sale or rental of the property upon which the sign is located. *(Federal Way, Wash.)*

■ **sign, roof**    A sign erected on a roof or signs that project above the highest point of the roof line, parapet, or fascia of the building. *(Glendale, Ariz.)*

A sign displayed above the eaves of a building. *(Doylestown, Ohio)*

A sign erected upon and above a roof structure and wholly supported by the roof structure placed upon a roof. *(Duluth, Ga.)*

A sign on a roof that has a pitch of less than one-to-four. *(Portland, Ore.)*

A sign that is mounted on the roof of a building or that is wholly dependent upon a building for support and projects above the highest point of a building with a flat roof, the eave line of a building with a gambrel, gable, or hip roof, or the deck line of a building with a mansard roof. *(Inyo County, Calif.)*

■ **sign, rotating or revolving**    A sign which in its entirety or in part moves in a revolving or similar manner. Such motion does not include methods of changing copy. *(Concord Township, Pa.)*

A sign or sign part that rotates or revolves. *(Tulsa, Okla.)*

An animated sign that revolves or turns or has external sign elements that revolve or turn at a speed greater than six revolutions per minute. Such sign may be power-driven or propelled by the force of wind or air. *(Miami, Fla.)*

■ **sign, searchlight** *(See also* **beacon***)* Searchlights shall be considered signs that are used to announce, direct attention to, or advertise businesses. *(Champaign, Ill.)*

■ **sign setback**    The minimum distance required between any property line and any portion of a sign or sign structure. *(Blacksburg, Va.)*

■ **sign setback line**    The spacing between a sign and a lot line or two signs. *(Nashville and Davidson County, Tenn.)*

■ **sign, shingle**    A sign suspended from and located entirely under a covered porch, covered walkway, or an awning. *(Glendale, Ariz.)*

A projection or wall sign not over six square feet in area, constructed of metal or other noncombustible material attached securely to a building and not projecting more than 24 inches over public property. *(Jacksonville, N.C.)*

■ **sign, sidewalk/sandwich**  A movable sign not secured or attached to the ground or surface upon which it is located. *(Duluth, Ga., which uses the term "sign, sandwich board/A-frame")*

An advertising or business ground sign constructed in such a manner as to form an "A" or a tent-like shape, hinged or not hinged at the top; each angular face held at an appropriate distance by a supporting member. *(Gillette, Wyo.)*

■ **sign, snipe**  An off-premises sign that is tacked, nailed, posted, pasted, glued, or otherwise attached to trees, poles, stakes, fences, or to other objects. *(Clearwater, Fla.)*

■ **sign, special event**  A sign advertising display that is temporary in nature, is not permanently attached to the ground or sign surface, and is used for special events, such as, but not limited to, grand openings, seasonal sales, liquidations, going-out-of-business sales, fire sales, and promotions. *(Duluth, Ga.)*

A sign advertising or announcing a special communitywide event or activity conducted by, or sponsored by, or on behalf of a unit of local government, the University of Illinois, a charitable organization, or a not-for-profit corporation. A special communitywide event or activity is one that occurs not more than twice in any 12-month period and seeks to attract donations, participants, or customers throughout the city. *(Champaign, Ill.)*

■ **sign stacking**  The placing of one sign above another at the same location. *(El Paso, Tex.)*

■ **sign structure**  The supports, uprights, bracing, or framework of any structure exhibiting a sign, be it single-faced, double-faced, or v-type or otherwise. *(Blacksburg, Va.)*

A structure for the display or support of signs. In addition, for purposes of these regulations, and notwithstanding the definition of structure generally applicable in these zoning regulations, any trailer or

other vehicle and any other device that is readily movable and designed or used primarily for the display of signs (rather than with signs as an accessory function) shall be construed to be a sign structure, and any signs thereon shall be limited in area, number, location, and other characteristics in accordance with general regulations and regulations applying in the district in which displayed. *(Miami, Fla.)*

■ **sign, suspended**  A sign that is suspended, parallel, or perpendicular from a building wall, roof, facade, canopy, marquee, or porch by means of brackets, hooks, or chains and the like. *(Blacksburg, Va.)*

■ **sign, temporary**  A sign not intended or designed for permanent display. *(Glendale, Ariz.)*

Any sign, banner, pennant, or advertising display intended to be displayed for a limited time period. Easily removed signs attached to windows are considered temporary signs. *(Redmond, Wash.)*

An attached on-premises sign made of nonrigid material, designed and displayed for a seasonal or brief activity such as, but not limited to, sales, specials, promotions, holidays, auctions, business grand openings, and signs advertising the lease or vacancy or rental units in multi-unit residential developments. Symbols, figures, balloons, and other similar items shall be considered temporary signs. *(Blacksburg, Va.)*

■ **sign, third-party**  Any sign identifying an enterprise and including a sponsoring advertisement, such as Coca Cola or 7-Up. *(Redmond, Wash.)*

■ **sign, V-type**  For purposes of computing surface area, is two separate signs if the angle between the two outer surfaces exceeds 240 degrees; otherwise the wings shall be considered one sign. *(Grand Forks, N.Dak.)*

Two separate sign faces at one location that are at an angle of 45 degrees or less to each other; one or two structures may be used. *(El Paso, Tex.)*

■ **sign, vehicle**  *(See also sign, portable)* A sign that is attached to or painted on a vehicle that is parked on or adjacent to

any property, the principal purpose of which is to attract attention to a product sold or business located on the property. *(Inyo County, Calif.)*

A portable sign affixed to or inside a vehicle for the purpose of directing people to a business in close proximity to where the vehicle is parked. *(Malibu, Calif., which uses the term "vehicle-related portable freestanding sign")*

■ **sign, wall**  A sign mounted flat against and projecting less than 14 inches from, or painted on the wall of, a building or structure with the exposed face of the sign in a plane parallel to the face of the wall. This does not include window signs. *(Glendale, Ariz.)*

A sign attached to a wall and not projecting away from the wall more than 12 inches. *(Doylestown, Ohio)*

A sign attached to or painted on the exterior wall of a building. The total lettering on one facade of a building or structure shall constitute one wall sign. *(Duluth, Ga.)*

■ **sign, warning**  A sign limited to a message of warning, danger, or caution. *(Siskiyou County, Calif.)*

A sign located on a property posting such property for warning or prohibitions on parking, trespassing, hunting, fishing, swimming, or other activity. . . . *(Clearwater, Fla.)*

■ **sign, wind**  Any display or series of displays, banners, flags, balloons, or other objects designed and fashioned in such a manner as to move when subjected to wind pressure. *(Reno, Nev.)*

■ **sign, window**  A sign affixed to the interior or exterior of a window or placed immediately behind a window pane so as to attract the attention of persons outside the building. *(Glendale, Ariz.)*

A sign posted, painted, placed, or affixed in or on a window exposed to public view. An interior sign that faces a window exposed to public view and located within three feet of the window is considered a window sign for the purpose of calculating the total area of all window signs. *(Inyo County, Calif.)*

Any type of sign or outdoor advertising device that is attached to a window of any building, but does not extend past the limits of said window. . . . The word "window" shall be construed to mean any glass that comprises part of the surface of the wall, regardless of its movability. *(Grant County, Ky.)*

■ **single room occupancy (SRO)** *(See also homeless shelter)*　A residential facility in which furnished rooms are rented on a weekly or monthly basis and which provides common facilities and services for laundry, cleaning, and meals. *(Las Vegas, Nev.)*

Multifamily residential buildings containing housing units with a minimum floor area of 150 square feet and a maximum floor area of 375 square feet which may have kitchen and/or bathroom facilities. Each housing unit is restricted to occupancy by no more than two persons and is offered on a monthly rental basis or longer. *(Santa Monica, Calif.)*

■ **site**　Any geographical area. *(Blacksburg, Va.)*

A parcel of land or portion thereof with frontage on a street, devoted to or intended for a use or occupied by a structure or a group of structures. *(Cotati, Calif.)*

A lot or group of contiguous lots not divided by an alley, street, other right-of-way, or city limit, that is proposed for development in accord with the provisions of this code and is in a single ownership or has multiple owners, all of whom join in an application for development. *(Newport Beach, Calif.)*

■ **site area**　The total horizontal area, included within the property lines of a site, that contains more than one use or principal structure. *(Jupiter, Fla.)*

■ **site area, net**　The area of the tract of land in question, less the area of all dedicated public lands or those lands required to be dedicated. . . . *(Wheeling, Ill.)*

■ **site coverage**　That portion of a site, expressed as a percentage, occupied by all buildings or structures that are roofed or otherwise covered and that extend more than three feet above the surface ground level. *(Jupiter, Fla.)*

■ **site depth**　The horizontal length of a straight line, drawn from the midpoint of the front property line to the midpoint of the rear property line, of a site that contains more than one use or principal structure. *(Jupiter, Fla.)*

■ **site plan**　A plan, to scale, showing uses and structures proposed for a parcel of land as required by the regulations (pictured above). Includes lot lines, streets, building sites, reserved open space, buildings, major landscape features–both natural and manmade–and,

depending on requirements, the locations of proposed utility lines. *(Handbook for Planning Commissioners in Missouri)*

A required submission, prepared and approved, that is a detailed engineering drawing of the proposed improvements required in the development of a given lot. *(Prince William County, Va.)*

A plan (to scale) showing uses and structures proposed for a parcel of land as required by the regulations involved. Its purpose is to show how the intended use relates to the major landscape features, the sun and weather, and the surrounding area. *(Iowa State University Extension Service)*

A plan, to scale, of non-single-family residential, commercial or industrial projects, showing uses and structures proposed for a parcel of land as required by the regulations involved. Includes lot lines, streets, building sites, reserved open space, buildings, major landscape features—both natural and man-made—and, depending on requirements, the location of proposed utility lines. *(Doylestown, Ohio)*

■ **site plan, final**　A plan which may be submitted for all or part of the land area shown on an approved preliminary site plan for a planned office park or planned business park. *(Southaven, Miss.)*

■ **site plan review**　The review of the site plan of any public or private project by the department of planning or the planning commission. *(Unalaska, Alaska)*

■ **site width**　The horizontal distance between the side property lines measured at right angles to the site depth, midway between the front and rear property lines, of a site that contains more than one use or principal structure. *(Jupiter, Fla.)*

■ **skateboard**　A foot board mounted upon four or more wheels and is usually propelled by the user who sometimes stands, sits, kneels, or lays upon the device while it is in motion. *(Walla Walla, Wash.)*

A wheeled device designed to transport a rider in a standing position; this device is not otherwise secured to a rider's feet or shoes. *(Rochester, Minn.)*

■ **skateboard, motorized**   The same as a skateboard in all respects except that it is designed to be or can be self-propelled by motorized power. *(Selma, Calif.)*

■ **skateboard pipe**   All outdoor structures commonly known as pipes, with a shape of a half circle or oval, that are designed and principally intended to permit persons on skateboards to move continuously from one side to the other. *(Kentwood, Mich.)*

■ **skateboard ramp**   All outdoor structures commonly known as ramps, with an upward inclined surface, essentially one of the two sides of a pipe, which are designed and principally intended to permit persons on skateboards to move from horizontal to vertical and back to horizontal. *(Kentwood, Mich.)*

■ **skating rink, ice or roller**   An establishment that provides facilities for participant skating. *(Hermosa Beach, Calif.)*

■ **ski area**   An area developed for snow skiing, with trails and lifts, and including ski rentals and sales, instruction, and eating facilities. *(Siskiyou County, Calif.)*

An establishment for cross-country or downhill ski runs and including, but not limited to, chairlifts; warming huts; and supporting services. *(King County, Wash.)*

■ **ski resort**   A ski area that also includes sales, rentals, and services of related equipment and accessories, eating places, residences, and hotels and motels. *(Siskiyou County, Calif.)*

■ **sky exposure plane or front exposure plane** *(See also **bulk plane; daylight plane**)*   An imaginary inclined plane: (1) beginning above the street line (or, where so indicated, above the front yard line) at a height set forth in the district regulations; and (2) rising over a zoning lot at a ratio of vertical distance to horizontal distance set forth in the district regulations. *(New York City, N.Y.)*

■ **sky exposure plane, rear**   An imaginary inclined plane: (1) beginning above a line at a distance from and parallel to

the street line and at a height set forth in the district regulations; and (2) rising over a zoning lot at a ratio of vertical distance to horizontal distance set forth in the district regulations. *(New York City, N.Y.)*

■ **skybuilding**   An elevated, occupiable structure, located over a right-of-way, used for occupancies that are not considered hazardous. *(Reno, Nev.)*

■ **skylight**   That portion of a roof which is glazed to admit light, and the mechanical fastening required to hold the glazing, including a curb not exceeding 10 inches in height to provide a weatherproofing barrier. *(Santa Monica, Calif.)*

■ **skytram** *(See also **transit, public**)*   An automated conveyance associated with an elevated structure, located over a right-of-way, used for the movement of people, and material that is not hazardous, as defined by the uniform building and fire code. *(Reno, Nev.)*

■ **slaughterhouse**   A facility for the slaughtering and processing of animals and the refining of their byproducts. *(Sioux Falls, S.Dak.)*

A building used for the for-profit slaughtering of animals that are either raised or transported to the building and the processing and storage of animal products and waste that results from a slaughtering process. *(Washoe County, Nev.)*

■ **slaughterhouse, agricultural**   A building used as an ancillary structure on a farm or ranch for the nonprofit slaughtering of animals raised on site and the processing and storage of animal products and waste that results from a slaughtering process. *(Washoe County, Nev.)*

■ **sleeping room** *(See also **bedroom; room**)*   A fully enclosed portion of a building, designed or intended to be used for sleeping purposes. For purposes of measurement, where a sleeping room contains more than two beds, every unit of two beds or fraction thereof, shall be counted as a separate sleeping room. *(Pittsburgh, Pa.)*

■ **slip**   That area of the waterway contained within the tie-off pilings and a

pier or bulkhead, covered or not. *(Rock Hall, Md.)*

■ **slope**   The degree of deviation of a surface from the horizontal, usually expressed in percent or degrees. *(Elbert County, Colo.)*

■ **slope, critical**   Any slope of 25 percent but less than 40 percent. *(Iowa City, Iowa).*

■ **slope, cut**   The exposed ground surface resulting from the excavation of material on the natural terrain. *(Henderson, Nev.)*

■ **slope, fill**   The exposed ground surface resulting from the placement of excavated material on the natural terrain. *(Henderson, Nev.)*

■ **slope, percent average**   The percent average slope calculated for property within the planned mountain development district, and within the boundaries of a subdivision plat, which is determined using the following equation: $S = .0023 \ IL/A$, where $S$ = Percent average slope; $I$ = Contour interval in feet; $L$ = Contour length in feet; and $A$ = Parcel area in acres. *(El Paso, Tex.)*

■ **slope, percent of**   The ratio of vertical rise or fall to horizontal distance of terrain measured perpendicular to the contour lines at horizontal intervals of more than 10 feet . . . *(Taos, N. Mex.)*

■ **slope, protected**   Any slope of 40 percent or steeper. *(Iowa City, Iowa)*

■ **slope, steep**   Slopes of 40 percent gradient or steeper. *(Redmond, Wash.)*

A grade of 25 percent or more for a distance of 50 feet or more.*(Blacksburg, Va.)*

Those areas of land characterized by a change in elevation of 15 percent or more but not exceeding 25 percent over the specified distance or contour as specified in [the ordinance]. *(Concord Township, Pa.)*

Land where agricultural activity or development is either not recommended or described as poorly suited due to slope steepness and the site's soil characteristics, as mapped and described in available county soil surveys or other technical reports, unless appropriate design and construction techniques and farming practices are used in accordance with the provisions of this ordinance. Where specific information is not available, steep slopes are lands having slopes over 12 percent, as measured over horizontal distances of 50 feet or more, that are not bluffs. *(Plymouth, Minn.)*

■ **slope, toe of**    A point or line of a slope in an excavation or cut where the lower surface changes to horizontal or meets the existing ground slope. *(Renton, Wash.)*

■ **slope, top of**    A point or line on the upper surface of a slope where it changes to horizontal or meets the original surface. (1) Top of Excavation or Cut: the upper surface point where the excavation meets the original ground surface; (2) Top of Embankment: the upper surface point or line to which side slope changes to horizontal or meets original ground surface. *(Renton, Wash.)*

The higher point of a 50-foot segment with an average slope of at least 20 percent. *(Minnetonka, Minn.)*

■ **smart growth** *(See also **growth management**)*    Planning, regulatory, and development practices and techniques founded upon and promoting the following principles: (1) using land resources more efficiently through compact building forms, infill development, and moderation in street and parking standards in order to lessen land consumption and preserve natural resources; (2) supporting the location of stores, offices, residences, schools, recreational spaces, and other public facilities within walking distance of each other in compact neighborhoods that are designed to provide alternate opportunities for easier movement and interaction; (3) providing a variety of housing choices so that the young and old, single persons and families, and those of varying economic ability may find places to live; (4) supporting walking, cycling, and transit as attractive alternatives to driving; providing alternative routes that disperse, rather than concentrate, traffic congestion; and lowering traffic speeds in neighborhoods; (5) connecting infrastructure and development decisions to

minimize future costs by creating neighborhoods where more people use existing services and facilities, and by integrating development and land use with transit routes and stations; and (6) improving the development review process and development standards so that developers are encouraged to apply the principles stated above. *(APA's Growing Smart project)*

Development that enhances existing communities, that is compatible with the natural environment, and that uses tax dollars efficiently while attracting private investment. *(A Smart Growth Agenda for Illinois, Campaign for Sensible Growth, 1999)*

■ **smog**    A mixture of pollutants, principally ground-level ozone, produced by chemical reactions in the air involving smog-forming chemicals. A major portion of smog-formers come from burning of petroleum-based fuels such as gasoline. Other smog-formers, volatile organic compounds, are found in products such as paints and solvents. Smog can harm health, damage the environment, and cause poor visibility. Major smog occurrences are often linked to heavy motor vehicle traffic, sunshine, high temperatures, and calm winds or temperature inversion (weather condition in which warm air is trapped close to the ground instead of rising). Smog is often worse away from the source of the smog-forming chemicals, since the chemical reactions that result in smog occur in the sky while the reacting chemicals are being blown away from their sources by winds. *(Environmental Protection Agency)*

■ **smoke**    Small gas-borne particles resulting from incomplete combustion, consisting predominantly but not exclusively of carbon, ash, and other combustible material that form a visible plume in the air. *(Aurora, Ill.)*

A suspension in a gas of solid particles, the gaseous products of burning organic material. *(Albuquerque, N. Mex.)*

■ **smoke unit**    The number obtained when the smoke density in the Ringelmann Number is multiplied by the time of emission in minutes. For the

purpose of this calculation: (1) a Ringelmann density reading shall be made at least once a minute during the period of observation; (2) each reading is then multiplied by the time in minutes during which it is observed; and (3) the various products are then added together to give the total number of smoke units observed during the entire observation period. *(Burr Ridge, Ill.)*

■ **snack bar/snack shop**    An establishment that serves a snack usually for consumption between meals; specifically, items such as donuts, ice cream, yogurt, or cookies are considered snacks, and the planning commission may consider additional items as snacks. *(Hermosa Beach, Calif.)*

An establishment similar to a restaurant, but limited to the extent that no food is cooked on the premises other than heating by microwave oven, no drive-through windows exist on the premises, and seating for customers does not exceed 25. *(Champaign, Ill.)*

■ **snowmobile** *(See also **off-road vehicle**)*    A self-propelled vehicle designed for travel on snow or ice or a natural terrain steered by wheels, skis or runners. *(Rochester, Minn.)*

■ **social service facilities**    Facilities other than offices providing a social service directly to the adjacent community, such as food banks, blood banks, emergency shelters, crisis centers, etc. *(Renton, Wash.)*

One main building, or portion thereof, on one zoning lot where one or more children or persons with mental retardation or related conditions, mental illness, chemical dependency, or physical handicaps reside on a 24-hour-per-day basis under the auspices of a program licensed by the Minnesota Department of Human Services to provide lodging in conjunction with monitoring, supervision, treatment, rehabilitation, habilitation, education, or training of the residents of the facility. This definition does not include: (1) foster homes or freestanding foster homes; (2) residential treatment programs physically located on hospital grounds; (3) regional treatment centers operated by the commissioner of human services; (4) licensed semi-independent living services for persons with mental retardation or related conditions or mental illness, if the license holder is not providing, in any manner, direct or indirect, the housing used by persons receiving the service. (*St. Paul, Minn., which uses the term "community residential facility, licensed human service"*)

■ **social service provider**  A facility that provides assistance to persons with limited ability for self-care, but for whom medical care is not a major element. The term includes a facility that provides assistance concerning psychological problems, employment, learning disabilities, or physical disabilities, but does not include a rescue mission or homeless shelter. (*Las Vegas, Nev.*)

■ **sod**  The grass-covered surface of the ground and the soil below the surface only to the depth of the roots of the grass. (*Delafield, Wisc.*)

■ **soil**  The natural or processed, unconsolidated, mineral, and organic material on the immediate surface of the earth that does or is suitable to serve as a natural medium for the growth of land plants. (*Redmond, Wash.*)

All unconsolidated mineral and organic material of whatever origin that overlies bedrock and can be readily excavated. (*Elbert County, Colo.*)

■ **soil erosion**  The removal of soil through the actions of water or wind. (*APA Research Department*)

■ **soil erosion, accelerated**  The increased movement of soils that occurs as a result of human activities and development. (*Grand Traverse County, Mich.*)

■ **soil stabilization**  Measures that protect soil from the erosive forces of raindrop impact and flowing water and include, but are not limited to, vegetative establishment, mulching, and the early application of gravel base on areas to be paved. (*Westchester County, N.Y.*)

■ **soil, topsoil**  The top layer of native soil. The term is also used to describe good soil imported for landscaping. (*Las Vegas, Nev.*)

Generally, the top layer of soil, characterized by having a high organic matter content and by being optimal for the growth of plants. (*Delafield, Wisc.*)

■ **soils, expansive**  Soils that swell when they absorb water and shrink as they dry. (*California Planning Roundtable*)

■ **solar access**  The provision of direct sunlight to an area specified for solar energy collection by natural forces that serves as a natural medium for growing land plants. (*Larkspur, Calif.*)

Access to sunlight to protect active or passive solar energy systems from shadows blocking exposure to the sun during hours of high isolation, from 9:20 a.m. to 3:20 p.m. local time. (*Tucson, Ariz.*)

The ability to receive sunlight across real property for any solar energy device. (*Boulder County, Colo.*)

■ **solar access space**  That airspace above all lots within the zoning district necessary to prevent any improvement, vegetation, or tree located on said lots from casting a shadow upon any solar collector located within said zone greater than the shadow case by a hypothetical vertical wall 10 feet high located along the property lines of said lots between hours of 9:30 a.m. and 2:30 p.m., Central Standard Time on December 21. This shall not apply to any improvement or tree that casts a shadow upon a solar collector at the time of the installation of said collector, or to vegetation existing at the time of installation of said solar collector. (*Scott County, Minn.*)

■ **solar collector**  A device or combination of devices, structure, or part of a device or structure that transforms direct solar energy into thermal, chemical, or electrical energy and that contributes significantly to a structure's energy supply. (*Scott County, Minn.*)

■ **solar energy**  Radiant energy (direct, diffuse, and reflected) received from the sun. (*Scott County, Minn.*)

■ **solar energy system**  Includes: (1) A design using natural and architectural features to cool or heat a structure, or (2) a mechanical assembly that may include a solar collector, storage facility, and any

other components needed to cool or heat a structure. (*Tucson, Ariz.*)

A complete design or assembly consisting of a solar energy collector, an energy storage facility (where used), and components to the distribution of transformed energy (to the extent they cannot be used jointly with a conventional energy system). To qualify as a solar energy system, the system must be permanently located for not less than 90 days in any calendar year beginning with the first calendar year after completion of construction. (*Scott County, Minn.*)

■ **solar equipment**  Any solar collector, skylight, or other solar energy device whose primary purpose is to provide for the collection, storage, and distribution of solar energy for space heating, cooling, water heating, or for power generation. (*Newport Beach, Calif.*)

■ **solar feature**  A device or combination of devices or elements that does or will use direct sunlight as a source of energy for such purposes as heating or cooling a structure, heating or pumping water, or generating electricity. Examples of a solar feature include: a solar greenhouse, solar panels, a solar hot water heater, and a south-facing window that contains a total of at least 20 square feet of glazing. Solar features may serve as a structural member of the structure. A south-facing wall without solar features is not a solar feature. (*Portland, Ore.*)

■ **solar skyspace**  The space between a solar energy collector and the sun that must be free of obstructions that shade the collector to an extent that precludes its cost-effective operation. (*Scott County, Minn.*)

■ **solar skyspace easement**  A right, expressed as an easement, covenant, condition, or other property interest in any deed or other instrument executed by or on behalf of any landowner, which protects the solar skyspace of an actual, proposed, or designated solar energy collector at a described location by forbidding or limiting activities or land uses that interfere with access to solar energy. The solar skyspace must be described as the three-dimensional space in which obstruction is prohibited or limited, or as the times of day during which direct sunlight to the solar collector may not be obstructed, or as a combination of the two methods. *(Scott County, Minn.)*

■ **solar structure**    A structure designed to utilize solar energy as an alternative for, or supplement to, a conventional energy system. *(Scott County, Minn.)*

■ **solid waste** *(See also* ***garbage; litter; refuse; rubbish)***    Any garbage, refuse, rubbish, or other discarded materials, that may be in solid, liquid, or gaseous form. *(Boulder County, Colo.)*

Sludge from air or water pollution control facilities, demolition, construction debris, and residential, industrial, and commercial wastes. *(Tonawanda, N.Y.)*

■ **solid waste collection point**    In multiple-family residences, commercial, industrial and other nonresidential developments, the exterior location designation for garbage and recyclables collection by the city's contractor or other authorized haulers. *(Renton, Wash.)*

■ **solid waste compost facility** *(See also* ***composting facility)***    A site that has been approved by the city, county, and the state pollution control agency for the storage, transfer or composting of specifically identified types of solid waste materials. *(St. Paul, Minn.)*

■ **solid waste facility**    Establishment for the disposition of unwanted or discarded material, including garbage with insufficient liquid content to be free flowing. *(Miami, Fla.)*

Any land used for the disposal or storage of solid waste material, including garbage, sewage, trash, rubble, construction debris, and all other kinds of organic or inorganic refuse by abandonment, discarding, dumping, reduction, burial, incineration, or any other similar means. *(Anne Arundel County, Md., which uses the term "solid waste disposal facility")*

■ **solid waste management**    The activities that result in the storage, transportation, treatment, or disposal or solid waste. *(State of Vermont)*

■ **solid waste transfer facility**    A fixed facility where solid waste from collection vehicles is consolidated and temporarily stored for subsequent transport to a permanent disposal site. This does not include an infectious waste incineration facility. *(Sioux Falls, S. Dak.)*

A place or facility where nonhazardous solid waste materials are taken from a collection vehicle, temporarily stored or stockpiled, and ultimately placed in a transportation unit for movement to another facility *(Anne Arundel County, Md.)*

Any storage or collection facility that is operated as a relay point for municipal solid waste that ultimately is to be transferred to a landfill. *(Blacksburg, Va)*

A facility at which refuse awaiting transportation to a disposal site is transferred from one type of collection vehicle to another. Refuse may be sorted and repackaged at a transfer station. *(Aurora, Colo.)*

■ **sorority**    A club or social activity officially associated with and recognized and supervised by an institution for higher education whose membership is limited exclusively to students of the said institution. *(Williamstown, Ky., which uses this definition for both terms "fraternity" and "sorority")*

■ **sorority house**    A building used as group living quarters for students of a college, university, or seminary, who are members of a sorority that has been officially recognized by the college, university, or seminary. *(St. Paul, Minn.)*

■ **soup kitchen** *(See also* ***shelter*** *definitions;* ***social service*** *definitions)*    A food service use that provides free meals for consumption on site. *(Tucson, Ariz.)*

Any building or structure or portion thereof that contains a fully equipped kitchen in operating condition. This facility must be used to prepare and serve food on a regular basis either without cost or at a low cost insufficient to generate a profit. Soup kitchens shall not be considered to be restaurants. *(Melbourne, Fla.)*

■ **source reduction**    Any action that avoids the creation of waste by reducing waste at the source, including redesign-

ing of products or packaging so that less material is used; voluntary or imposed behavioral changes in the use of materials (e.g.: two-sided copying or a ban on certain products or packaging), or increased durability or reusability of materials (e.g.: performance warrantees, deposit legislation). *(State of Vermont)*

■ **space, nonhabitable**    Space used as a pantry, laundry room, closet, bathroom, toilet room, restroom, dressing room, locker room, storage room, utility room, heater room, or boiler room, and other spaces used only for service and maintenance of a building and those spaces used for access and vertical travel between stories. *(Champaign, Ill.)*

■ **space, occupied**    Space in a building other than a habitable room wherein people normally work, assemble, or remain for a period of time. *(Champaign, Ill.)*

■ **special assessment**    A charge that state and local governments can impose on landowners whose land benefits from the construction of roads or sewer lines adjacent to their property. The amount of the special assessment is usually the pro rata share of the cost of installing the improvement. *(American Farmland Trust)*

■ **special benefit district** *(See also* ***benefit assessment district)***    A subarea of a community designated by city ordinance to assess payments for construction or installation of public facilities that primarily benefit the property owners within the district. *(Renton, Wash.)*

■ **special district**    A district established to accommodate a narrow or special set of uses or for special purposes. The term can signify any district beyond the conventional residential, commercial, industrial, and agricultural districts. Examples include open space districts, hotel/motel districts, planned development districts, transit impact districts, historic preservation districts, etc. The establishment of special districts must have an appropriate police power basis, and there should be a reasonable market demand for the uses permitted to avoid charges of excessive and unlawful restrictions on the uses of the property.

*(PAS Report No. 322, The Language of Zoning)*

■ **special events**    Circuses, fairs, carnivals, festivals, or other types of special events that (1) run for longer than one day but not longer than two weeks, (2) are intended to or likely to attract substantial crowds, and (3) are unlike the customary or usual activities generally associated with the property where the special event is to be located. *(Indian Trail, N.C.)*

A temporary outdoor use on private property that extends beyond the normal uses and standards allowed by the zoning ordinance of the city. Except as otherwise specifically provided, only those events held on commercial-zoned property are subject to the provisions of this ordinance. Special event includes, but is not limited to, art shows, sidewalk sales, pumpkin and Christmas tree sales, haunted houses, carnivals (major and minor), special auto sales, grand openings, festivals, home exhibitions, and church bazaars. *(Scottsdale, Ariz.)*

■ **special exception**    A special exception is a use that would not be appropriate generally or without restrictions throughout the zoning division or district but which, if controlled as to number, area, location, or relation to the neighborhood, would promote the public health, safety, welfare, morals, order, comfort, convenience, appearance, prosperity or general welfare. Such uses may be permitted in such zoning division or district as special exceptions, if specific provisions for such special exceptions are made in this ordinance. *(Goochland County, Va.)*

■ **special permit** *(See permit, special)*

■ **special use**    A use of property specifically authorized by a zoning ordinance, but not permitted unless certain stated conditions have been met. *(Handbook for Planning Commissioners in Missouri)*

■ **special use permit** *(See permit, special use)*

■ **specialty food store**    A food store of less than 10,000 square feet primarily en-

gaged in selling food stuffs associated with a particular nationality, religious observance, dietary practices, or cuisine. *(Prince William County, Va.)*

■ **specific plan**    A detailed policy plan or regulation that implements the comprehensive plan or any of the elements of that plan. Specific Plans include area and neighborhood plans . . . the land-use code . . . and any other similar plan. *(Tucson, Ariz.)*

A definite statement adopted by ordinance of policies, standards, and regulations, together with a map or description defining the location where such policies, standards, and regulations are applicable pursuant to the requirements of the . . . state. *(Palm Desert, Calif.)*

■ **spot zoning**    [A] change in district boundaries, variances, and other amendments to the zoning code and use and area maps that violate sound principles of zoning and are characterized by the following: (a) Individuals seek to have property rezoned for their private use. (b) Usually the amount of land involved is small and limited to one or two ownerships. (c) The proposed rezoning would give privileges not generally extended to property similarly located in the area. (d) Applications usually show little or no evidence of, or interest in, consideration of the general welfare of the public, the effect on surrounding property (including adequate buffers), whether all uses permitted in the classification sought are appropriate in the locations proposed, or conformity to the comprehensive plan or to comprehensive planning principles (including alterations to the population density patterns and increase of load on utilities, schools, and traffic.) *(Coral Gables, Fla.)*

■ **sprawl**    *(See also growth management; leapfrog development; smart growth)*    Low-density land-use patterns that are automobile-dependent, energy and land consumptive, and require a very high ratio of road surface to development served. *(Michigan State Planning Officials, Patterns on the Land, Trend Future Project, final report, September 1995)*

Haphazard growth or outward extension of a city resulting from uncontrolled or poorly managed development. *(California Planning Roundtable)*

Urban development or uses that are located in predominantly rural areas, or rural areas interspersed with generally low-intensity or low-density urban uses, and which are characterized by one or more of the following conditions: (a) The premature or poorly planned conversion of rural land to other uses; (b) The creation of areas of urban development or uses that are not functionally related to land uses which predominate the adjacent area; or (c) The creation of areas of urban development or uses that fail to maximize the use of existing public facilities or the use of areas within which public services are currently provided. Urban sprawl is typically manifested in one or more of the following land use or development patterns: Leapfrog or scattered development; ribbon or strip commercial or other development; or large expanses of predominantly low-intensity, low-density, or single-use development. *(Martin County, Fla.)*

■ **spring** *(See also creek; stream)*    Includes areas where permanent or ephemeral flows or ponding of water naturally occur. Such sites may include mountainous or canyon conditions where water flows or seeps out from water-bearing geologic structures or tanks and rock-bottomed washes where water typically collects for extended periods of time. *(Scottsdale, Ariz,)*

■ **square** *(See also plaza)*    Open space that may encompass an entire block, is located at the intersection of important streets, and is set aside for civic purposes, with landscaping consisting of paved walks, lawns, trees, and civic buildings. *(Austin, Tex.)*

An outdoor public civic tract whose area is defined by streets or adjacent buildings. Squares shall include streets on at least three sides and shall be surrounded by shopfront, rowhouse, or civic use lots on at least 60 percent of their perimeter. No more than 40 percent of the square may be used for parking. Squares shall have a length to width ratio no greater than 3:1. *(Gainesville, Fla.)*

■ **SRO** (*See* **Single Room Occupancy**)

■ **stable** (*See also* **horse farm**)    A building in which horses are sheltered; may be accessory to a residential or other use or a freestanding principal use. (*Prince William County, Va.*)

Any structure and/or land used, designed, or arranged for the maintenance or rental of horses, mules, ponies, or donkeys either with or without a bridle path or riding area, but excluding structures and/or land used, designed, or arranged for the maintenance of horses or mules used exclusively for agricultural purposes. (*Delafield, Wisc., which uses the term "riding stable"*)

An accessory building having stalls or compartments where animals, excluding dogs and cats, are sheltered and fed. (*Germantown, Tenn.*)

■ **stable, commercial**    A lot that may be used for commercial riding stable open to the general public; boarding of livestock not involved with current breeding or training; training involving large groups of eight or more students; polo fields or arenas used for scheduled, public, or club events; and those uses permitted on a ranch. No feed lot shall be permitted. A commercial stable shall meet the provisions of the applicable zoning district and the conditions of (ordinance section). (*Scottsdale, Ariz.*)

A building where horses and ponies are sheltered, fed, and/or kept for hire. (*Concord Township, Pa., which uses the term "public stable"*)

A structure and/or land use in or on which equines are kept for sale or hire to the public. Breeding, boarding, or training of equines may also be conducted. (*Lake County, Ill., which uses the term "public stable"*)

■ **stable, private**    A detached accessory building for the keeping of horses, mules, or ponies owned by the occupants of the premises and not kept for remuneration, hire, or sale. (*Scottsdale, Ariz.*)

An accessory structure and/or land use that is designed, arranged, used, or intended to be used for the keeping of equines for the private use of the occupants of a principal dwelling and their guests, but in no event for hire. (*Lake County, Ill.*)

■ **stacking lane** (*See also* **queue space**)    An area for temporary queuing of motor vehicles. (*Las Vegas, Nev.*)

A paved surface designed to accommodate a motor vehicle waiting for entry to any drive-in facility or auto-oriented use, which is located in such a way that a parking space or access to a parking space is not obstructed, and which is at least nine feet in width and 19 feet in length. (*Topeka, Kans.*)

The space specifically designated as a waiting area for vehicles whose occupants will be patronizing a drive-in business. Such space is considered to be located directly alongside a drive-in window, facility, or entrance used by patrons and in lanes leading up to and away from the business establishment. (*Renton, Wash., which uses the term "stacking space"*)

■ **stadium/arena/amphitheater**    A large building with tiers of seats for spectators at sporting or other recreational events. (*Dona Ana County, N. Mex.*)

A large open or enclosed space used for games or major events, and partly or completely surrounded by tiers of seats for spectators. (*Garrett, Ind., which uses the term "stadium or coliseum, non-school"*)

A commercial structure with tiers of seats rising around a field or court, intended to be used primarily for the viewing of athletic events. Sports arena may also be used for entertainment and other public gathering purposes, such as conventions, circuses, or concerts. (*Lake County, Ill., which uses the term "sports arena"*)

A building or outdoor area or structure specifically designed and used as a place of assembly. (*Miami, Fla., which uses the term "auditoriums or amphitheaters"*)

■ **stage**    A part of a timetable for development of a planned residential development over a period of years. (*Concord Township, Pa.*)

■ **stairs**    Interconnected treads constructed above grade and typically supported by piers and a framework system and typically employing handrails. (*Lake Bluff, Ill.*)

■ **stand** (*See also* **farm stand; newsstand; roadside stand**)    A structure for the display and sale of products with no space for customers within the structure itself. (*Ocean Shores, Wash.*)

Any cart, table, equipment or apparatus which is not a structure, which is designed and intended so as to not be a permanent fixture on a lot, and which is used for the retail sale, display, and accessory advertising of merchandise or food. (*Philadelphia, Pa.*)

■ **standard**    (1) A rule or measure establishing a level of quality or quantity that must be complied with or satisfied. Examples of standards might include the number of acres of park land per 1,000 population that the community will attempt to acquire and improve, or the intersection Level of Service (LOS) that the plan hopes to attain. (2) Requirements in a zoning ordinance that govern building and development as distinguished from use restrictions—for example, site-design regulations such as lot area, height limit, frontage, landscaping, and floor area ratio. (*Larkspur, Calif.*)

■ **Standard Industrial Classification (SIC)**    A classification pursuant to the SIC manual issued by the federal Office of Management and Budget (OMB). (*Henrico County, Va.*)

■ **start of construction**    For other than new construction or substantial improvements under the Coastal Barrier Resources Act (Pub. L. 97-348)), includes substantial improvement and means the date the building permit was issued, provided the actual start of construction, repair, reconstruction, rehabilitation, addition, placement or other improvement was within 180 days of the permit date. The actual start means either the first placement of permanent construction of a structure on a site, such as the pouring of slab or footings, the installation of piles, the construction of columns, or any work beyond the stage of excavation; or the placement of a manufactured home on a foundation. Permanent construction does not include land preparation, such as clearing, grading and filling; installation of streets and/or walkways; excavation for basement, footings, piers or foundations; erection of temporary forms; or installation on the property of accessory buildings such as garages or sheds not occupied as dwelling units or not part of the main structure. For the substantial improvement, the actual start of construction means the first alteration of any wall, ceiling, floor, or other structural part of a building, whether or not that alteration affects the external dimensions of the building. *(Washington County, Ark.)*

The point in time commemorating the breaking of ground for the construction of a development or structure. *(Carmel, Ind., which uses the term "commencement of construction")*

■ **statement of intent/statement of purpose**    A statement of policy or objectives, often incorporated in a zoning ordinance, that outlines the broad purpose of the ordinance and its relationship to the comprehensive plan; frequently, a statement preceding regulations for individual districts that helps to characterize the districts and their legislative purpose. When the application of particular district requirements is challenged in court, the courts rely on the intent statement in deciding whether the application is reasonable and related to a defensible public purpose. *(PAS Report No. 322, The Language of Zoning)*

■ **statistical area** *(See also **Metropolitan Statistical Area (MSA))***    A geographic planning area defined by the land use element of the general plan delineating intensity and/or density limits and major land-use policies. *(Newport Beach, Calif.)*

■ **statute**    An act of wither the United States Congress or the State Legislature. *(New York Planning Federation)*

■ **statue** *(See sculpture)*

■ **steam room/bathhouse** *(See also **bathhouse; sauna***)    A building or portion of a building used for providing a steam bath or heat bathing room used for the purpose of pleasure, bathing, relaxation, or reducing, using steam or hot air as a cleaning, relaxing, or reducing agent. *(St. Paul, Minn.)*

■ **stem wall** *(See also **wall***)    A wall, usually less than two feet high, used to divert or direct storm water flows within an area specified by the department of public works. *(Las Vegas, Nev.)*

■ **steps at grade**    Noninterconnected treads at grade typically consisting of individual pieces of stone, slate, timbers, or other similar material. *(Lake Bluff, Ill.)*

■ **stockyard**    An enclosure with pens, sheds, and other buildings or structures for the temporary keeping of livestock. *(McHenry County, Ill.)*

■ **stoop**    A structure that is less than 12 square feet in area, intended to provide ingress and egress to a building. *(Delafield, Wisc.)*

An exterior floor typically, but not necessarily, constructed of concrete and/or masonry, with a finished floor elevation at least six inches higher than the adjacent ground level, and utilized primarily as an access platform to a building. *(Lake Bluff, Ill.)*

■ **stop-work order**    A written document issued be an enforcement official, which requires the cessation of an activity, usually construction. *(New York Planning Federation)*

■ **storage**    A space or place where goods, materials, or personal property is placed and kept for more than 24 consecutive hours. *(Las Vegas, Nev.)*

■ **storage, bulk**    The storage of chemicals, petroleum products, or hazardous materials in above ground or below ground storage containers designed for wholesale distribution or mass consumption. *(Champaign, Ill.)*

The holding or stockpiling on land of material and/or products where such storage constitutes 40 percent of the developed site area and the storage area is at least one acre, and where at least three of the following criteria are met by the storage activity: (1) in a bulk form or in bulk containers; (2) under protective cover to the essential exclusion of other uses of the same space due to special fixtures or exposed to the elements; (3) in sufficient numbers, quantities, or spatial allocation of the site to determine and rank such uses as the principal use of the site; (4) the major function is the collection and/or distribution of the material and/or products rather than processing; and (5) the presence of fixed bulk containers or visible stockpiles for a substantial period of a year. . . .    *(Renton, Wash.)*

■ **storage, outside**    Exterior depository, stockpiling, or safekeeping of materials, products, vehicles, trailers, and the like. Outside storage may be enclosed by a structure that includes a roof, but no side walls, in which case the structure shall be deemed outside storage; outside storage may involve fencing or screening without a roof in which case fencing or screening shall be deemed outside storage. Parking lots do not qualify for outside storage. Outside storage does not involve any product representation or signage except for those emergency or safety-related signs specifically approved by the city. Vending machines accessory to allowable uses do not constitute outside storage. The parking or storage of vehicles, equipment, and merchandise for a period of less than 96 hours does not constitute outside storage. *(Plymouth, Minn.)*

The storage, collection or display for more than three consecutive days, or any part of a day for three consecutive days, of any products, materials, equipment, appliances, vehicles not in service, and/or personal property of any kind on an unenclosed, uncovered area. *(Vicksburg, Miss.)*

The storage of any materials outside the principal or accessory buildings on a property. *(Renton, Wash.)*

■ **storage structure**    Any structure that is used for storage and does not have a door or other entranceway into a dwelling unit and that does not have water fixtures within its confines, the use of which is limited solely to storage of inanimate objects. *(Ocean City, Md.)*

■ **store** A use devoted exclusively to the retail sale of a commodity or commodities. *(Topeka, Kans.)*

■ **storefront church** *(See also religious institution)* A store or similar structure not typically used for religious activities that is used as a meeting place for a congregation (pictured below). *(APA's Land-Based Classification Standards project)*

■ **storm drain** A conduit, pipe, natural channel, or human-made structure that serves to transport stormwater runoff. *(Grand Traverse County, Mich.)*

A sewer that carries storm surface water, subsurface water, and drainage. *(Renton, Wash.)*

A conduit that carries natural storm and surface water drainage but not sewage and industrial wastes, other than unpolluted cooling water. *(Bethel, Maine)*

■ **stormwater detention** Any storm drainage technique that retards or detains runoff, such as a detention or retention basin, parking lot storage, rooftop storage, porous pavement, dry wells, or any combination thereof. *(Champaign, Ill.)*

■ **stormwater management** Any stormwater management technique, apparatus, or facility that controls or manages the path, storage, or rate of release of stormwater runoff. Such facilities may include storm sewers, retention or detention basins, drainage channels,

drainage swales, inlet or outlet structures, or other similar facilities. *(Champaign, Ill.)*

The collecting, conveyance, channeling, holding, retaining, detaining, infiltrating, diverting, treating, or filtering of surface water, ground water, and/or runoff, together with applicable managerial (nonstructural) measures. *(Redmond, Wash.)*

■ **stormwater retention area** An area designed by a licensed professional and approved by the county to retain water to control the flow of stormwater. *(Scott County, Minn.)*

■ **stormwater runoff** Surplus surface water generated by rainfall that does not seep into the earth but flows overland to flowing or stagnant bodies of water. *(Larkspur, Calif.)*

Waters from rains falling within a tributary drainage basin, flowing over the surface of the ground or collected in channels, watercourses, or conduits, measured in depth of inches. *(Grand Traverse County, Mich.)*

■ **story** A space in a building between the surface of any floor and the surface of the next floor above, or if there is no floor above, then the space between such floor and the ceiling or roof above; provided, however, that where the floor level of the first story is at least five feet below the adjoining finished grade, the space shall be considered a basement and not counted as a story. *(Glendale, Ariz.)*

That portion of a building included between the upper surface of any floor and the upper surface of the floor next above, except that the topmost story shall be that portion of a building included between the upper surface of the topmost floor and the ceiling or roof above. If the finished floor level directly above a usable or unused under floor space is more than six feet above grade as defined herein for more than 50 percent of the total perimeter or is more than 12 feet above grade as defined herein at any point, such usable or unused under floor space shall be considered a story. *(Redmond, Wash.)*

That portion of a building, other than a basement, included between the surface of any floor and the surface of the floor next above it, or if there is no floor above it, then the space between the floor and the ceiling above the floor of such story. *(Ford County, Kans.)*

The vertical distance from top to top of two successive tiers of beams or finished floor surfaces; and, for the topmost story, from the top of the floor finish to the top of the ceiling joists, or, where there is not a ceiling, to the top of the roof rafters. *(Prince William County, Va.)*

■ **story, first** The lowest story in a building that qualifies as a story, except that a floor level in a building having only one floor level shall be classified as a first story, provided such floor level is not more than four feet below grade for more than 50 percent of the total perimeter, or not more than eight feet below grade at any point. *(Salt Lake County, Utah)*

■ **story, half** A story under a gable, hip, or gambrel roof of which the wall plates on at least two opposite exterior walls are not more than two feet above the floor of such story. *(Ford County, Kans.)*

A half-story is that part of a building between the eaves and the ridge line of pitched roofs, not for human occupancy. *(Madison, Wisc.)*

(1) That portion of a building under a sloping roof, the wall plates of which, on at least two opposite exterior walls, are

not more than four and one-half feet above the floor of such story, or (2) A basement but only when half or more of the floor to ceiling height of a basement (over more than half of the floor area) is above grade; when more than half of the floor to ceiling height of a basement (over more than half of the floor area) is below grade, the basement shall not be counted as either a story or half story. *(Libertyville, Ill.)*

■ **story, lower-half** *(See also raised basement)*   A portion of a building located partly underground, but having half or less of its floor to ceiling height below the average grade of the adjoining ground; a half-story shall be counted as a full story. *(Grand Forks, N. Dak.)*

■ **story, upper-half** *(See also attic)*   A space under a sloping roof that has the line of intersection of roof decking and wall face not more then two feet above the floor level of such story. A half-story containing independent apartment or living quarters shall be counted as a full story. *(Grand Forks, N. Dak.)*

■ **strategic plan**   A plan articulating desirable characteristics to be used in structured, on-going, decisions that are intended to influence outcomes. *(Interstate 81 Corridor Council)*

■ **stream** *(See also creek; spring)*   Those areas where surface waters produce a defined channel or bed. A defined channel or bed is an area that demonstrates clear evidence of the passage of water and includes, but is not limited to, bedrock, channels, gravel beds, sand and silt beds, and defined-channel swales. The channel or bed need not contain water year-round. This definition is not meant to include artificially created irrigation ditches, canals, storm or surface water runoff devices, or other entirely artificial water courses unless they are used by salmonid or created for the purposes of stream mitigation. *(Redmond, Wash.)*

A body of water flowing in a natural surface channel. Flow may be continuous or only during wet periods. *(Indian Trail, N.C.)*

A free-flowing body of water from the outlet of a great pond or the confluence of two perennial streams as depicted on the most recent edition of a United States Geological Survey 7.5-minute series topographic map, or if not available, a 15-minutes series topographic map, to the point where the body of water becomes a river. *(Gorham, Maine)*

■ **stream bank**   The usual boundaries, not the flood boundaries, of a stream channel. *(Grand Traverse County, Mich.)*

■ **stream corridor**   Any river, stream, pond, lake, or wetland, together with adjacent upland areas, that support protective bands of vegetation that line the waters' edge. *(New Jersey State Plan)*

■ **stream, intermittent**   Channels that naturally carry water part of the year and are dry the other part. This definition does not include streams that are intermittent because of irrigation diversion or other man-made diversions of the water. *(Yakima County, Wash.)*

■ **stream, perennial**   Stream channels that carry water the year round. *(Yakima County, Wash.)*

■ **stream, tributary**   A channel between defined banks, created by the action of surface water, whether intermittent or perennial, and which is characterized by the lack of upland vegetation or presence of aquatic vegetation and by the presence of a bed devoid of topsoil containing waterborne deposits of exposed soil, parent material or bedrock, and which flows to a water body or wetland as defined. This definition does not include the term "stream" as defined elsewhere in (the ordinance), and only applies to that portion of the tributary stream located within the shoreland zone of the receiving water body or wetland. *(Gorham, Maine)*

■ **street**   A public thoroughfare, including road, highway, drive, lane, avenue, place, boulevard, and any other thoroughfare that affords the principal means of access to abutting property. *(Glendale, Ariz.)*

Any vehicular way that: (1) is an existing state or municipal roadway: or, (2) is shown on a plat approved pursuant to law; or, (3) is approved by other official

action. The term street shall include road and highway. Unless otherwise indicated, the term street shall refer to both public and private streets. *(Blacksburg, Va.)*

A public thoroughfare (street, drive, avenue, boulevard) that has been or is intended to be dedicated for public use and has been accepted or is acceptable into the state system. *(Prince William County, Va.)*

A small-scale, low-speed, local thoroughfare. Streets provide frontage for shop front use, small house use, and work shop use. A street is urban in character, with raised curbs, closed drainage, wide sidewalks, parallel parking, trees in individual planters, and buildings aligned on short setbacks. *(Monroe County, Fla.)*

■ **street, arterial**   A major way used for fast or heavy traffic. *(Taos, N. Mex.)*

A street designed to carry large volumes of traffic and providing for efficient vehicular movement between large areas of the city as designated on the Functional Street Classification Map in the City's Comprehensive Plan. *(Roswell, N. Mex.)*

Serves the major traffic movements within the city such as between the central business district and the outlying commercial and residential areas. Serves a major portion of the vehicular traffic entering and leaving the city. *(Garrett, Ind.)*

A major street for carrying a large volume of through traffic in the area; normally controlled by traffic signs and signals. *(Concord Township, Pa.)*

Medium-speed (30-40 mph), medium-capacity (10,000-35,000 average daily trips) roadway that provides intra-community travel and access to the county-wide highway system. Access to community arterials should be provided at collector roads and local streets, but direct access from parcels to existing arterials is common. *(California Planning Roundtable)*

■ **street, boulevard**   A broad thoroughfare with landscape, sidewalk, or pedestrian improvements, often with a landscaped median or center divider (pictured below), that functions as a linear open space. *(Renton, Wash.)*

■ **street capacity** *(See also volume-to-capacity ratio)* The maximum number of vehicles which have a reasonable expectation of passing over a given section of a lane or a roadway in one direction, or in both directions for a two-lane, or four-lane highway, during a given time period under prevailing traffic conditions. In the absence of a modifier, capacity is based upon hourly volumes. *(Citrus County, Fla., which uses the term "road capacity")*

■ **street, center line of** A right-of-way, as defined or surveyed by the state department of transportation or the city engineering department. *(Durham, N.C.)*

An imaginary line that is equidistant from the boundaries of the street. *(Boulder, Colo., which uses the terms "center" or "centerline")*

A line halfway between the street right-of-way lines. *(Baton Rouge, La.)*

■ **street, collector** Relatively-low-speed (25-30 mph), relatively-low-volume (5,000-20,000 average daily trips) street that provides circulation within and between neighborhoods. Collectors usually serve short trips and are intended for collecting trips from local streets and distributing them to the arterial network. *(California Planning Roundtable)*

A minor street with a minimum right-of-way width of 60 feet which connects

major streets in a more or less direct line, or that has or will obtain, through future projection, potential use capacity of more than 300 vehicles per hour. *(Las Vegas, Nev.)*

A street carrying traffic from local streets to the major system of arterial streets and highways and including the principal entrance streets to a residential development and principal streets for circulation within such a development. *(Taos, N. Mex.)*

A street designed to carry moderate volumes of traffic from local streets to arterial streets or from arterial to arterial as designated on the Functional Street Classification Map in the City's comprehensive plan. *(Roswell, N. Mex.)*

Collects traffic from local streets and channels it to other areas of the city and to arterial streets. Has higher traffic volume than a local street. Provides through access, or relatively few stop yield signs, for traffic. *(Garrett, Ind.)*

■ **street, crosswalk** A public right-of-way, within a block, 10 feet or more in width, intended primarily for pedestrians, but may include utilities where necessary, and from which motor-propelled vehicles are excluded. *(Vernon Hills, Ill.)*

■ **street, cul-de-loop** A street that turns into and reconnects with its main axis, with the center or island used for parking or open space purposes. *(Carmel, Ind.)*

■ **street, cul-de-sac** *(See also turning circle)* A street with a single common

ingress and egress and with a turn-around at the end. *(Henderson, Nev.)*

A local street having one end open to vehicular traffic and the other end permanently closed with a vehicular turn-around. *(Tallmadge, Ohio)*

■ **street, dead-end** A local street open at one end only and without a special provision for vehicles turning around. *(Kentland, Ind.)*

A street that is connected to another street at one end, but which is intended to ultimately connect with another street at the closed end. *(Thornton, Colo.)*

■ **street dedication** The designation by plat, certified survey map, or written deed of a certain area to be used for public street purposes. . . . A dedication transfers title to the dedicated area from the private landowner to the public domain. *(Delafield, Wisc.)*

■ **street edge** The vertical face formed by building facades, street trees and screening walls that is aligned along a street and forms a comfortable people-scaled space. *(Gainesville, Fla.)*

■ **street, expressway** A divided highway with a 150-foot-wide minimum right-of-way and classified as "limited access"; a high-speed road with at-grade, cross-traffic intersections. *(Las Vegas, Nev.)*

A divided arterial highway for through traffic with full or partial control of access and generally with grade separations at major intersections. *(Grant County, Ky.)*

A divided arterial street or highway with full or partial control of access and with or without grade separated intersections. *(Racine County, Wisc.)*

A divided highway of four lanes or more that provides a high degree of service to through traffic, is designed with no direct access to individual uses on abutting properties, and may have some intersections at grade with traffic signal controls. *(Anne Arundel County, Md.)*

■ **street, freeway** A divided highway with 150-foot-wide minimum right-of-way and classified as "controlled access";

a high-speed road with grade-separated interchanges. *(Las Vegas, Nev.)*

A divided multi-lane highway for through traffic with all crossroads separated in grades and with full control of access. *(Grant County, Ky.)*

A divided highway of four lanes or more that provides the highest service in terms of mobility for through traffic on a regional level, is designed with no access to abutting properties, and has no at-grade interchanges. *(Anne Arundel County, Md.)*

■ **street frontage**   The distance along which a property line of a lot adjoins a public or private street. *(Las Vegas, Nev.)*

All the property on one side of a street between two intersecting streets (crossing or terminating), or, if the street is dead-ended, then all of the property abutting on one side between an intersecting street and the dead end of the street. *(Jupiter, Fla.)*

■ **street, frontage road**   A street adjacent to a freeway, expressway, or arterial street separated therefrom by a dividing strip (pictured above) and providing access to abutting properties. *(Grant County, Ky.)*

A local street or road auxiliary to and located on side of an arterial for service to abutting property and adjacent areas, and for control of access. Sometimes also called a "marginal access street." *(Kentland, Ind.)*

A minor street, parallel to and adjacent to an arterial street, whose primary purpose is providing access to abutting properties. *(Belmont, Calif.)*

■ **street furniture**   Those features associated with a street that are intended to enhance that street's physical character and use by pedestrians, such as benches, trash receptacles, kiosks, lights, newspaper racks, etc. *(Larkspur, Calif.)*

■ **street graphics**   The form of art such as but not limited to murals and sculptures, that shall not constitute any type of outdoor advertising of a commercial message. *(Blacksburg, Va.)*

■ **street, gridlike pattern (or flexible grid)**   A street system based upon a standard grid pattern (i.e., checkerboard blocks); however, offset intersections, loop roads, and cul-de-sacs as well as an-

gled or curved road segments may also be used on a limited basis. The block pattern is characterized by regular (i.e., rectangular or trapezoidal) blocks and irregular polygons do not predominate. *(Renton, Wash.)*

■ **street, half**   [Streets with] half the required width of the required right-of-

way on the bounding edge of a tract being subdivided. This term excludes marginal access full-width streets and frontage roads along arterial streets and limited access major streets. *(The Zoning Report)*

■ **street hierarchy**   A street layout that separates traffic routes passing through an area from streets that provide access to people living within the area (pictured below). The hierarchy forms the basis for an ordered classification system and appropriate design standards. *(Bucks County, Pa.)*

The system by which roads are classified according to their purpose and the travel demand they serve. *(New Jersey State Plan)*

■ **street, highway**   A term applied to streets and roads that are under the jurisdiction of the state highway commission. *(Kentland, Ind.)*

■ **street, highway auxiliary lane**   The portion of the roadway adjoining the traveled way for speed change, turning, storage for turning, weaving, truck climbing, or for other purposes. *(State of North Carolina)*

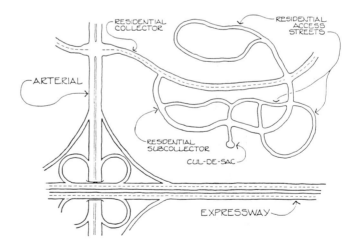

■ **street, highway, major**   A multi-lane highway, whether divided or undivided, that: (1) is a major artery of the county circulation network; (2) serves a high volume of traffic for both long and short trips; (3) allows turning movements at intersecting roads; and (4) is designed with access to abutting properties under some degree of control and safe standards of design. *(Anne Arundel County, Md.)*

■ **street, highway, noise barrier** A high wall, typically made of concrete, which parallels a major thoroughfare and is intended for the extensive screening of both visual and audio impacts from vehicular travel (pictured below) along that throughfare. *(APA Research Department)*

■ **street, highway, restricted access** A major traffic thoroughfare or part thereof that, when open to public use, is: (1) constructed or maintained pursuant to the Federal Aid Highway Act of 1956, or any amendment or supplement thereto, as an interstate highway; or (2) a limited access highway under the (state highway act), as amended ; or (3) designated from time to time as restricted access highway on the basis of being a primary or urban route on the state highway system, a primary route on the county highway system approved by the county planning commission; or a primary route on the city highway system approved by the city planning commission, and, in addition to meeting one of the above three criteria, having either a minimum width of four lanes, or 51 percent or more of the total affected frontage in one or more of the following categories: (1) public park; (2) publicly owned or controlled land; (3) redevelopment or renewal area wherein advertising signs are prohibited by the redevelopment or renewal proposal approved by the council; (4) land so located that the construction of the highway or the

regulation thereof prevents private or public vehicular access thereto; (5) land within 350 feet of the center line of any highway or interchange ramps thereof covered by (subsections). *(Pittsburgh, Pa.)*

■ **street, interchange** A grade separated intersection with one or more turning lanes for travel between intersection legs. *(Racine County, Wisc.)*

■ **street, intersecting** Any street that joins another street at an angle, whether or not it crosses the other. *(Edmond, Okla.)*

■ **street intersection** The point of crossing or meeting of two or more streets. *(Grand Forks, N. Dak.)*

The junction of any two public rights-of-way crossing at grade. *(El Paso, Tex.)*

■ **street lamp** A light standard not to exceed 15 feet in height. *(Monroe County, Fla)*

A light standard between eight and 14 feet in height equipped with an incandescent or metal halide light source (pictured at right). *(Howard County, Md.)*

■ **street line** The line between the street right-of-way and abutting property. *(Doylestown, Ohio)*

A lot line separating a street from other land. *(Shelby County, Tenn.)*

The dividing line, also known as the street right-of-way line, between a lot and the outside boundary of a public street, road, or highway, legally open or officially plotted by the township or higher governmental authority, or between a lot and a private street, road, or way over which the

owners or tenants of two or more lots held in single and separate ownership have the right-of-way. In no case shall the street line be considered to be less than 25 feet from the center of the existing street. *(Bensalem Township, Pa.)*

■ **street line, planned** The planned right-of-way for a major or secondary highway or traffic collector street. A yard abutting such a highway or street shall be measured from this planned right-of-way line. *(Palm Desert, Calif.)*

■ **street, local** Those streets that have an existing or projected traffic volume of 999 or less average daily trips. *(Jefferson County, Colo.)*

A street designed to provide vehicular access to abutting property and to discourage through traffic *(Iowa State University Extension Service)*

A street connecting blocks within neighborhoods and designed for short trips at low speeds. *(St. Paul, Minn.)*

A street with a minimum right-of-way width of 50 feet that is designed to carry residential traffic between collector or other streets or highways and abutting properties. *(Las Vegas, Nev.)*

■ **street, loop** A short, independent street that usually terminates along the same collector street of its origin. *(Maryland Heights, Mo.)*

■ **street, major**    The transportation network that includes a hierarchy of freeways, arterial, and collectors to service through traffic. *(Larkspur, Calif.)*

Routes serving predominately through traffic that connect major urban areas *(Taos, N. Mex., which uses the term "street, principal arterial")*

■ **street, major arterial**    A street with access control, channelized intersections, and restricted parking that collects and distributes traffic to and from minor arterials. *(Iowa State University Extension Service)*

Major arterials provide higher speed travel and mobility for long distance trips. These roads function within the region or community to carry large volumes of traffic to minor arterials and collector routes. Access may be limited by medians. U.S. Highway 70 is a major arterial. *(Dona Ana County, N. Nex.)*

■ **street, minor** *(See also **street, local**)* Local streets not shown on the circulation plan, map, or diagram, whose primary intended purpose is to provide access to fronting properties. *(Larkspur, Calif.)*

■ **street, minor arterial**    A street with signals at important intersections and stop signs on the side streets that collects and distributes traffic to and from collector streets. *(Iowa State University Extension Service)*

Routes with linkages to cities, larger towns, and other traffic generators that attract travel over similarly long distances. They provide an interconnecting network between most larger cities and towns. *(Taos, N. Mex.)*

Minor arterials serve a mobility function for longer-distance trips but handle moderate volumes of traffic at moderate speeds. Minor arterials provide connections to collector routes, which serve communities and local areas. Access from some major traffic generators is allowed to minor arterials. *(Dona Ana County, N. Mex.)*

■ **street/alley, one-way**    A street or alley designated and sign-posted for one-way traffic and on which all vehicles are required to move in one indicated direction. *(Rochester, Minn.)*

■ **street opening**    A curb break, or a place or way provided for the purpose of gaining vehicular access between a street and abutting property. *(Palm Desert, Calif.)*

■ **street, parkway**    A divided major thoroughfare having controlled access to adjoining property and designated as such on the transportation plan. *(Chandler, Ariz.)*

A highway for noncommercial traffic, with full or partial control of access. They are located within a park or within a ribbon or parklike development. *(Hartford, Conn.)*

■ **street, partial**    A dedicated right-of-way that provides only a portion of the required street width. *(Belmont, Calif.)*

■ **street plan line**    A precise line that establishes future rights-of-way along any portion of an existing or proposed street or highway and that is depicted on a map showing the streets and lot line or lines and the proposed right-of-way lines, and the distance thereof from the established centerline of the street or highway, or from existing or established property lines. *(California Planning Roundtable)*

Official lines established by law in accordance with the master street and highway plan of the city for the purpose of establishing the width of public streets in accordance with their projected design as provided in the master street and highway plan of the city. Buildings or other structures erected thereafter must be located outside the lines establishing the width of public streets and alleys. *(Redding, Calif.)*

■ **street, primary thoroughfare**    A street or highway that has a minimum right-of-way width of 100 feet and an existing potential design capacity of two or more travel lanes of traffic in each direction, divided when possible. *(Las Vegas, Nev.)*

■ **street, private**    Any road or street that is not publicly owned and maintained and used for access by the occupants of the development, their guests, and the general public. *(Doylestown, Ohio)*

Any right-of-way or area set aside to provide vehicular access within a development that is not dedicated or intended to be dedicated to the city and that is not maintained by the city. *(Duluth, Ga.)*

A street privately owned and maintained that is used as the principal means of access to abutting lot or lots or to more than two dwellings on a lot on which a private way is exclusively located. *(Concord Township, Pa.)*

A private roadway affording access to abutting property for private users of such property. For the purposes of density calculations, a private street shall constitute the areas of its paved surface and sidewalks or the private right-of-way if designated on the recorded plat. *(Grant County, Ky.)*

■ **street, public**    A public roadway, constructed within the boundaries of an officially deeded and accepted public right-of-way, which affords principal means of access to abutting property. For purposes of density calculations, a public street shall constitute all of the area within the public right-of-way. *(Grant County, Ky.)*

A street under the control of and kept by the public, established by regular governmental proceedings for the purpose or dedicated by the owner of the land and accepted by the proper authorities which are responsible for the maintenance of said street. *(Kentland, Ind.)*

■ **street reservation/road reservation** The designation by plat, certified survey map, or written deed of a certain area reserved for possible future public street purposes. A reservation does not transfer title of the reserved area to the public domain unless the area is accepted by the Town Board for public street purposes. *(Delafield, Wisc.)*

■ **street, residential**    Any local street as defined in the city comprehensive plan, where the primary land use of lots with frontage on both sides of the street within the block is residential. *(Champaign, Ill.)*

■ **street right-of-way** *(See right-of-way)*

■ **street, secondary thoroughfare**   A street or highway with a minimum right-of-way width of 80 feet and an existing or potential design capacity of two travel lanes of traffic in each direction. *(Las Vegas, Nev.)*

■ **street, spine road**   The main streets located within a residential subdivision. Such streets connect less traveled streets located deeper within the subdivision to the subdivision's entrance(s). *(Farragut, Tenn.)*

■ **street, stub**   A nonpermanent dead-end street intended to be extended in conjunction with the subdivision and development of the adjacent unplatted land. Access from the stub street shall be permitted only along the frontage of such street to the lots in the subdivision containing the stub street. *(Topeka, Kans.)*

A portion of a street or cross access drive used as an extension to an abutting property that may be developed in the future. *(Center for Urban Transportation Research, University of South Florida, Tampa Fla., which uses the term "stub-out")*

■ **street, through**   A major collector or arterial street that serves more than one neighborhood, or carries traffic between neighborhoods proper. *(Gainesville, Fla.)*

Streets that extend continuously between other major streets in the community. *(Larkspur, Calif.)*

■ **street vista**   A view through or along a thoroughfare centerline that is not less than 200 feet in length. *(Monroe County, Fla.)*

■ **street wall**   A wall or portion of a wall of a building facing a street. *(New York, N.Y.)*

The wall or part of the building nearest to the street line. *(Tulsa, Okla.)*

The main wall of a structure, that is closest to and most nearly parallel with an adjacent street; in case of unit group building where a structure is not adja-

cent to a street, that main wall having similar relationship to the equivalent access facility. *(Pittsburgh, Pa.)*

■ **street wall, aggregate width of**   The sum of the maximum widths of all street walls of a building within 50 feet of a street line. The width of a street wall is the length of a street line from which, when viewed directly from above, lines perpendicular to the street line may be drawn to such street wall. *(New York, N.Y.)*

■ **street wall line**   That portion of a line drawn parallel to a front line lot at a distance equal to the shallowest depth between the street wall of a building and the front lot line, from which, when viewed directly from above, lines perpendicular to the front lot line may be drawn to a street wall. *(New York, N.Y.)*

■ **street wall line level**   The mean level of the natural grade at the street wall line. On corner lots, street wall line level is the average of the mean levels of the natural grade of each street wall line. On through lots, street wall line level is determined separately for each street frontage to a distance midway between such streets. *(New York, N.Y.)*

■ **street width**   The shortest distance between the lines delineating the right-of-way of a street. *(Plymouth, Minn.)*

The width of the right-of-way, measured at right angles to the centerline of the street. *(Scott County, Minn.)*

■ **street yard**   The area between the right-of-way/property line and the principal structure. *(Jacksonville, N.C.)*

■ **streetscape**   An area that may either abut or be contained within a public or private street right-of-way or accessway that may contain sidewalks, street furniture, landscaping or trees (pictured below), and similar features. *(Prince William County, Va.)*

Portion of a lot's net area and improvements that is exposed to view from the street. *(Temecula, Calif.)*

The visual image of a street, including the combination of buildings, parking, signs, and other hardscape and street furniture. *(Las Vegas, Nev.)*

■ **strip center** *(See also shopping center definitions)*   An attached row of stores or service outlets managed as a coherent retail entity, with on-site parking usually located in front of the stores (pictured on page 224). Open canopies may connect the store fronts, but a strip center does not have enclosed walkways linking the stores. A strip center may by configured in a straight line or have an "L" or "U" shape. *(International Council of Shopping Centers)*

An area occupied by businesses that are engaged in auto-oriented commercial activity and are arranged in a line, usually along an arterial street. *(Renton, Wash., which uses the term "strip commercial uses")*

■ **strip development** *(See also shopping center definitions)* Commercial zoning/development immediately adjacent and parallel to a collector or arterial street that is generally less than 250 feet in depth. *(Jefferson County, Colo.)*

Commercial, retail, or industrial development, usually one lot deep, that fronts on a major street. *(Elbert County, Colo.)*

A mix of development, usually commercial, extending along both sides of a major street. In zoning terms, a strip zone may refer to a district consisting of a ribbon of highway commercial uses fronting both sides of a major arterial route. *(Handbook for Planning Commissioners in Missouri, which uses the term "strip zone")*

■ **structural alteration** Any change in the supporting members of a building, such as bearing walls, columns, beams, or girders except for repair or replacement. *(Doylestown, Ohio)*

Any change in either the supporting members of a building such as load bearing walls, columns, beams or girders or in the roof and exterior walls. *(Duluth, Ga.)*

Any change other than incidental repairs that would prolong the life of the supporting members of a building, such as bearing walls, columns, beams, girders, or foundations. *(Madison, Wisc.)*

■ **structural envelope** The three-dimensional space enclosed by the exterior surfaces of a building or structure. *(San Diego, Calif.)*

■ **structure** Anything constructed or erected that requires location on the ground or attached to something having location on the ground. *(Glendale, Ariz.)*

That which is built or constructed, an edifice or building of any kind, or any piece of work artificially built or composed of parts joined together in come definite manner. *(Redmond, Wash.)*

Anything constructed or erected that requires location on the ground (excluding swimming pools, fences, and walls used as fences). *(Larkspur, Calif.)*

Any piece of work constructed or erected, the use of which requires a location on the ground or attached to something having a location on the ground, but not including a tent, vehicle, trailer coach or mobile home. *(Scottsdale, Ariz.)*

(1) A combination of materials forming an edifice or building of any kind, or any piece of work artificially built up or composed of parts joined together in some definite manner, but excluding the following: retaining walls; fences not over six feet high; platforms or decks not more than 30 inches above grade and not over any basement or story below; utility mains, lines, and underground facilities; and yard and play

equipment. (2) A permanent structure is built of materials in a manner that would commonly be expected to remain useful for a substantial period of time. (3) A temporary structure is built of materials in a manner that would commonly be expected to have relatively short useful life, or is built for a purpose that would be expected to be relatively short-term in duration. *(Boulder County, Colo.)*

■ **structure, detached** A structure with no common or party wall with another structure. *(Redmond, Wash.)*

■ **structure, enclosed** A structure with a solid roof and a minimum of three exterior walls shall be considered an enclosed structure, provided that there shall be no more than a 25 percent opening along the perimeter of the structure calculated by using the total lineal footage of the sides of the portion of the structure in question. The three exterior walls, excluding windows, must provide a visual screen of the activities or items displayed within the enclosed structure. The structure must be constructed consistent with all requirements of the building code. The three walls must be of a solid material and permanently connected to the overhead structure. Wood, concrete, aluminum, glass, or other materials approved by the building official are permissible. Screening, shade cloth, plastic sheeting, or canvas are not permissible. When a use is to be in an enclosed structure because the use could be detrimental to the adjacent properties, an enclosed structure may be required to have completely opaque walls on all sides of the structure, excluding windows and doors. Such uses of a detrimental nature may include but are not limited to automotive repair, storage, general repair services, and manufacturing activities. *(Melbourne Fla.)*

■ **structure, moved** Any structure that is moved into or moved within the county. *(Scott County, Minn.)*

■ **structure, nonconforming** A structure, or a portion thereof, that no longer conforms to the site area, coverage, setback or other open space, height, or other regulations prescribing physical development standards for the district in which such structure is located. *(Los Altos, Calif.)*

A structure that legally existed prior to the adoption date of this ordinance, but which is not in compliance with the requirements of this ordinance for the district in which the structure is located. *(Scott County, Minn.)*

■ **structure, illegal nonconforming** A structure that did not legally exist prior to the adoption of this ordinance and does not conform with the current ordinance requirements for the district in which it is located. *(Scott County, Minn.)*

■ **structure, principal** *(See also **building, principal**)* A structure in which is conducted the principal use of the lot on which it is located. *(Champaign, Ill.)*

The main building on a parcel of land. *(Scott County, Minn.)*

■ **structure, public** *(See also **building, public**)* An edifice or building of any kind, or any piece of work artificially built up or composed of parts joined together in some definite manner that is owned or rented and operated by a federal, state, or local government agency. *(Plymouth, Minn.)*

■ **structure, temporary** Any piece of work that is readily movable and used or intended to be used for a period not to exceed 90 consecutive days. Such structure shall be subject to all applicable property development standards for the district in which it is located. *(Scottsdale, Ariz.)*

A structure without any foundation or footing and removed when the designated time period, activity, or use for which the temporary structure was erected has ceased. *(Santa Monica, Calif.)*

■ **student center** A building or structure devoted to active or passive recreational facilities for students of a college or university and operated by an agent of the college or university. *(Virginia Beach, Va.)*

■ **student housing** *(See also **dormitory**)* A building available to at least three and not more than eight students enrolled in a trade or business school. *(Garrett, Ind.)*

■ **studio apartment** *(See **efficiency unit**)*

■ **studio/multimedia production facility** A facility for the staging and recording of video or audio productions such as, but not limited to, music commercials, programs, and motion pictures. *(Nashville and Davidson County, Tenn.)*

Space in an outdoor or indoor area, building, part of a building, structure, or a defined area, that is used primarily for the creation of film, television, music video, multi-media, or other related activities. *(El Segundo, Calif.)*

■ **subcommittee** A body comprising a portion of the membership of a public body, usually constituted or appointed for a particular purpose. *(New York Planning Federation)*

■ **subdivider** Any individual, firm, association, syndicate, partnership, corporation, trust, or any other legal entity commencing proceedings . . . to effect a subdivision of land hereunder for the owner of record or for another, with consent of the owner of record. *(Colt's Neck, N.J.)*

■ **subdivision** The division or redivision of land into 10 or more lots, tracts, parcels, sites, or divisions for the purpose of sale, lease, or transfer of ownership. *(Redmond, Wash.)*

The process of laying out a parcel of raw land into lots, blocks, streets, and public areas. In most states, a subdivision is defined as the division of a tract of land into five or more lots. *(Handbook for Planning Commissioners in Missouri)*

The division of land into two or more lots. A development consisting of subdivided lots. *(Duluth, Ga.)*

The division of a tract of land into two or more lots, building sites, or other divisions for the purpose of sale or building development (pictured below) (whether immediate or future) and including all divisions of land involving the dedication of a new street or a change in existing streets; but the following shall not be included within this definition nor be subject to the regulations of this ordinance applicable strictly to subdivisions: (1) the combination or recombination of portions of previously platted lots where the total number of lots is not increased and the resultants lots are equal to or exceed the minimum standards set forth in this ordinance; (2) the division of land into parcels greater than 10 acres where no street right-of-way dedication is involved; or (3) the public acquisition by purchase of strips of land for widening or opening streets; or (4) the division of a tract in single ownership whose entire area is no greater than two acres into not more than three lots, where no street right-of-way dedication is involved and where the resultant lots are equal to or exceed the minimum standards set forth in this ordinance, or (5) in residential districts only, the division of one lot into two lots so as to create one new lot. *(Indian Trail, N.C.)*

***Commentary:*** *Planners should consult appropriate state enabling legislation when drafting the ordinance definition of subdivision. Most enabling statutes include a definition of the term, particularly specifying how many parcels must be created, at a minimum, to constitute a subdivision of land. Ordinances also vary in the types of land division that they exclude from consideration as subdivisions.*

■ **subdivision, abortive or premature** A subdivision that is not built on and is unlikely to be built on for an indefinite time. An abortive subdivision is one that never should have been subdivided because it is unlikely to be built on in the foreseeable future; a premature subdivision is on that is laid out considerably in advance of development. Where there have been scattered lot sales (and owners retain title), reassembly of land for development later becomes difficult, and leapfrog development may result, contributing to urban sprawl. *(PAS Report No. 322, The Language of Zoning)*

■ **subdivision, exploratory sketch plan** An informal plan indicating salient existing features of a tract and its surroundings, including the general layout of a proposed subdivision or land development. *(New Castle County, Del.)*

■ **subdivision, hillside** A subdivision in which the average slope is 20 percent or in which any street in the subdivision has grades greater than 15 percent at any point. *(Renton, Wash.)*

■ **subdivision improvement agreement** *(See also **developer's agreement**)* An agreement between the [municipality] and developer whereby the developer agrees to construct any required public street, drainage, and other improvements, for a subdivision and to provide security for completion of the subdivision improvements. *(Douglas County, Colo.)*

■ **subdivision, major** Any subdivision that does not meet the requirements of a minor subdivision. *(Tallmadge, Ohio)*

■ **subdivision map** Any map that is filed for the purpose of subdividing property; may be a final map or a parcel map. *(San Diego, Calif.)*

■ **subdivision map, preliminary** A developer's first formal submission is usually a map with accompanying documents providing the information about the proposed subdivision required by ordinance. The preliminary map contains a variety of information including the name of the subdivision, its location, acreage, owner, and engineer or surveyor. *(Handbook for Planning Commissioners in Missouri)*

■ **subdivision, minor** Any subdivision that does not result in the creation of more than five lots out of a single tract or does not require the construction of new streets, roads, public water or sewer facilities, sidewalks, or similar facilities. *(Indian Trail, N.C.)*

A division of a parcel of land along an existing public street or road, not involving the opening, widening, or extension of any street or road, and involving not more than five lots, any one of which is less than five acres, after the original tract has been completely subdivided. *(Tallmadge, Ohio)*

■ **subdivision plan, preliminary** A plan of a subdivision or of a land development, including all required supplementary data, showing the approximate proposed street and lot or site layout, or a plan of existing private streets to be dedicated to public use, as a basis for consideration by the department and the technical advisory committee prior to the preparation of a record plan. *(New Castle County, Del.)*

■ **subdivision regulation** The control of the division of a tract of land by requiring development according to design standards and procedures adopted by local ordinance. *(Handbook for Planning Commissioners in Missouri)*

■ **subdivision review/approval** The procedure governed by state statutes and by a set of local regulations for the review of, and decision on, a subdivision plat application. *(New York Planning Federation)*

■ **subsidize** To assist by payment of a sum of money or by the granting of terms or favors that reduce the need for monetary expenditures. Housing subsidies may take the forms of mortgage interest deductions or tax credits from federal and/or state income taxes, sale or lease at less than market value of land to be used for the construction of housing, payments to supplement a minimum affordable rent, and the like. *(California Planning Roundtable)*

■ **substance abuse treatment facility, inpatient residential** *(See also **halfway house**)* Structures and land used for

the treatment of alcohol or other drug abuse where one or more patients are provided with care, meals, and lodging. *(Jefferson, Mo.)*

■ **substance abuse treatment facility, outpatient** Structures and land used for the treatment of alcohol or other drug abuse where neither meals nor lodging is provided. *(Jefferson, Mo.)*

■ **substandard housing** Residential dwellings that, because of their physical condition, do not provide safe and sanitary housing. *(California Planning Roundtable)*

■ **substantial conformance** The situation in which a revision to a development that was approved through a permit or tentative map complies with the objectives, standards, guidelines, and conditions, for that permit or tentative map. *(San Diego, Calif.)*

■ **substantial damage** Damage of any origin sustained by a structure whereby the cost of restoring the structure to its before-damaged condition would equal or exceed 50 percent of the market value of the structure before the damage occurred. *(Blacksburg, Va.)*

■ **substantial improvement** Any repair, reconstruction, or improvement of a structure, the cost of which equals or exceeds 50 percent of the market value of the structure either (1) before the improvement or repair is started, or (2) if damaged, the value of the structure to be restored prior to being damaged. *(Redmond, Wash.)*

Any reconstruction, rehabilitation, addition, or other improvement of a structure, the cost of which equals or exceeds 50 percent of the market value of the structure before the start of construction of the improvement. Includes structures that have incurred "substantial damage" regardless of the actual repair work performed. The term does not, however, include either: (1) any project for improvement of a structure to correct existing violations of state or local health, sanitary, or safety code specifications that have been identified by the local code enforcement official and that are the minimum necessary to assure safe living conditions; or (2) any alteration of a "historic structure," provided that the alteration will not preclude the structure's continued designation as a "historic structure." *(Blacksburg, Va.)*

(1) Any improvement, repair, or reconstruction to an existing structure in a Flood Hazard District having a construction cost of more then 50 percent of the structure's assessed value immediately prior to improvement, or (2) the addition, extraction, or movement of any dirt, rock, or other material, or any new structure that will result in a volume larger than the volume required to increase the elevation of the property by a total height of six inches. *(Multnomah County, Ore.)*

■ **substantial modification**    A change that significantly alters the impacts and/or character of a structure, development, or activity. *(Boulder County, Colo.)*

■ **subtenant**    A person or persons whose rights to occupy a dwelling are derived from the tenant rather than from the property owner or his or her agent. *(San Francisco, Calif.)*

■ **subway** *(See also **public transportation; transit, public**)*    An urban public transportation system that uses below-ground right-of-way. Also used to refer to that portion of a transportation system that is constructed beneath the ground surface. *(Sacramento Regional Transit District)*

■ **suite**    One or a group of connected living or sleeping rooms, without cooking facilities. For purpose of measurement, where a suite contains more than two sleeping rooms, each two sleeping rooms shall be counted as a two-bedroom suite, and any remaining shall be counted as a one-bedroom suite. *(Pittsburgh, Pa.)*

■ **summer home** *(See also **cabin/cottage**)*    A dwelling designed and intended to be used only for a few months each year, principally during the warm months of the year. *(Delafield, Wisc.)*

A single-family dwelling, including boats or house boats, intended for seasonal or temporary occupancy only, and not permanently occupied as a family residence during any entire year. *(Johnson County, Iowa which uses the term "summer cottage")*

■ **superblock** *(See also **block**)*    A continuous area, either in single or multiple ownerships, that includes a vacated street and has a total gross site area in private property of at least 75,000 square feet. *(Portland, Ore.)*

■ **supermarket**    Food markets, or combination food markets and department stores with more than 4,000 square feet of floor area. *(Hermosa Beach, Calif.)*

■ **supper club**    A restaurant and bar operation with alcoholic beverage sales wherein: (1) the bar area is separated from the restaurant area by a barrier sufficient to prevent access to the bar by minors; (2) the actual seating available at all times within the restaurant area will accommodate at least 125 persons; (3) wherein alcoholic beverages are served in the restaurant area only in conjunction with the service of food; (4) full-course meals are available during all hours the bar area is open to the public; (5) a cook and food server, other than a bartender, are available at all times the bar area is open to the public; and (6) the restaurant operation is the principal portion of the business. *(Las Vegas, Nev.)*

■ **surface water** *(See also **groundwater**)*    Water on the earth's surface exposed to the atmosphere such as rivers, lakes, and creeks. *(Elbert County, Colo.)*

■ **surfaced**    A road, driveway, approach, or parking lot consisting of gravel, crushed rock, limerock, bituminous surface, concrete surface, or other similar material. *(Scott County, Minn.)*

■ **sustainability**    Community use of natural resources in a way that does not jeopardize the ability of future generations to live and prosper. *(California Planning Roundtable)*

The finite capacity of any place to support human activities, given a set of impacts that those activities have on the place. Once capacity is reached, the impacts of additional growth or activities harm the integrity of the place and im-

pair its ability to function as intended. *(New Jersey State Plan)*

■ **sustainable development**    Development that maintains or enhances economic opportunity and community well-being while protecting and restoring the natural environment upon which people and economies depend. Sustainable development meets the needs of the present without compromising the ability of future generations to meet their own needs. *(State of Minnesota)*

■ **swale**    A linear depression in land running downhill or having a marked change in contour direction in which sheet runoff would collect and form a temporary watercourse. *(Williamson County, Tenn.)*

A natural depression or wide shallow ditch used to temporarily store, route, or filter runoff. *(Holyoke, Mass.)*

Low-lying grassed area with gradual slopes which transports stormwater, either on-site or off-site. *(Grand Traverse County, Mich.)*

■ **swap meet and auction** *(See also **flea market**)*    Occasional or periodic commercial activities held in an open area or enclosed structure where: (1) groups of sellers rent space on a short-term basis to display, barter, or sell goods to the public; or (2) one or more sellers bring goods for auctioning to the public. A swap meet is composed of semi-closed or outdoor stalls, stands, or spaces, at least 50 percent of which do not occupy the same allotted area on an uninterrupted, continuous, daily basis for the purpose of display and sale, exchange, or barter of merchandise, exclusive of occasional craft fairs and benefit sales held on public property. *(Tucson, Ariz.)*

Any indoor or outdoor place, location, or activity where new or used goods or secondhand personal property is offered for sale or exchange to the general public by a multitude of individual licensed vendors, usually in compartmentalized spaces; and where a fee may be charged to prospective buyers for admission, or a fee may be charged for the privilege of offering or displaying such merchandise. The term swap meet is interchangeable with and applicable to: flea markets, auctions, open air markets, farmers markets, or other similarly named or labeled activities; but the term does not include the usual supermarket or department store retail operations. *(Redondo Beach, Calif.)*

■ **swimming pool**  A pool or tub constructed either above or below grade and having a capacity of 5,000 or more gallons. *(St. Paul, Minn.)*

A structure, whether above or below grade level, designed to hold water more than 30 inches deep to be used for recreational purposes. *(Delafield, Wisc.)*

A receptacle for water, or artificial basin of water, either above ground, below ground, or partly above and partly below ground, not wholly enclosed within a building, having a depth at any point in excess of 18 inches or a surface area exceeding 150 square feet and intended for use by persons for the purpose of immersion, partial immersion, or swimming, and including all appurtenant equipment. *(Lake Bluff, Ill.)*

Any portable pool or permanent structure containing a body of water 18 inches or more in depth and 250 square feet or more of water surface area and intended for recreational purposes, including a wading pool, but not including an ornamental reflecting pool or fish pond or other type of pool, located and designed so as not to create a hazard or be used for swimming or wading. *(Ocean City, Md.)*

■ **swimming pool, outdoor**  Any structure or device of any kind that is intended for swimming purposes, including but not limited to: any pool or tank of any material or type of construction, any depression or excavation in any natural or constructed material, any dike or berm of any material or type of construction, all appurtenances to such structure or device intended to cause, or would cause if completely filled, the retaining of water to a greater depth than 18 inches at any point. Any such structure or device shall be deemed to be included within the meaning of the term "structure" as used in this ordinance. Outdoor swimming pools shall be deemed to consist of the following classes: private,

semi-public, public and commercial, as follows. Private: when consisting of an accessory structure appurtenant to a one-family or a two-family dwelling and used only as such by persons residing on the same lot and their private guests. Semi-public: when consisting of an accessory structure appurtenant to a multiple dwelling, hotel, motel, church, school, club, etc., and used only as such by persons who reside or are housed on the same lot or who are regular members of such organizations. Public: a swimming pool operated by a unit of government for the general public. Commercial: a swimming pool operated for profit, open to the public upon payment of a fee. *(Grant County, Ky.)*

■ **swimming pool, portable**  Portable pools shall not be subject to the pool requirements of this chapter and are those pools which are not permanently installed; do not require water filtration, circulation and purification; do not exceed 18 inches in depth; do not exceed a water surface of 100 square feet; and do not require braces or supports. *(Colt's Neck, N.J.)*

■ **swimming pool, private**  A recreation facility designed and intended for water contact activities that serves a single family dwelling(s), duplex dwellings and/or multi-family dwellings, or combinations thereof, including pools owned and/or controlled by a neighborhood club or similar organization. *(Duluth, Ga.)*

■ **swimming pool, public**  A recreation facility designed and intended for water contact activities that is operated as a business or as a club unless such club is associated with a neighborhood club or similar organization. *(Duluth, Ga.)*

The same as private pool but operated as a commercial business. Public swimming pools shall conform to county health department requirements. *(Scottsdale, Ariz.)*

Any swimming pool other than a private swimming pool, including publicly and privately owned pools open to the general public and pools owned and oper-

ated in conjunction with membership organizations, motels, hotels, and other similar uses. *(Concord Township, Pa., which uses the term "swimming pool, public or semipublic")*

■ **synagogue** *(See religious institution)*

■ **system capacity** *(See also adequate public facilitites ordinance (APFO); carrying capacity anaylsis)*  The ability of natural, infrastructure, social, and economic systems to accommodate growth and development without degrading or exceeding the limits of those systems, as determined by a carrying capacity analysis. *(New Jersey State Plan)*

■ **system integrity**  The ability of an infrastructure system to function throughout its extent at a given level of service. It refers to the condition and capacity of the entire system or network, and the effect that changes to a part of the system have on the function of the whole. *(New Jersey State Plan)*

■ **taking** *(See also condemnation; eminent domain; inverse condemnation)* To take, expropriate, acquire, or seize property without compensation. *(Iowa State University Extension Service )*

A real estate term traditionally used to mean acquisition by eminent domain but broadened by the U.S. Supreme Court to mean any government action that denies economically viable use of property. More recent federal and state legislative proposals would consider any government program causing a "substantial" reduction in property values to be a taking. *(California Planning Roundtable)*

■ **tank farm** An open air facility containing a number of above-ground, large containers for the bulk storage in liquid form of petroleum products. *(Sioux Falls, S. Dak)*

■ **tanning studio** Any business that uses artificial lighting systems to produce a tan on an individual's body. This use specifically excludes spas, gymnasiums, athletic clubs, health clubs, and any

exercise equipment. *(Salt Lake County, Utah)*

■ **target area** *(See also block grant; Community Redevelopment Agency (CRA))* Specifically designated sections of the community where loans and grants are made to bring about a specific outcome, such as the rehabilitation of housing affordable by very low- and low-income households. *(California Planning Roundtable)*

■ **tattooing** Any method of placing permanent designs, letters, scrolls, figures, symbols or any other marks upon or under the skin with ink or any other substance, by the aid of needles or any other instruments designed to touch or puncture the skin, resulting in either the coloration of the skin, or the production of scars or scarring, other than by branding. *(Alma, Mich.)*

■ **tatoo parlor/body-piercing studio** An establishment whose principle business activity, either in terms of operation or as held out to the public, is the practice of one or more of the following: (1) placing of designs, letters, figures, symbols, or other marks upon or under the skin of any person, using ink or other substances that result in the permanent coloration of the skin by means of the use of needles or other instruments designed to contact or puncture the skin; (2) creation of an opening in the body of a person for the purpose of inserting jewelry or other decoration. *(Las Vegas, Nev.)*

■ **tavern** *(See also bar)* Any place in which fermented malt beverages or intoxicating liquors are sold for consumption upon said premises. *(Madison, Wisc.)*

An establishment used primarily for the serving of alcoholic beverages by the drink to the general public and where food or packaged alcoholic beverages may be served or sold only as accessory to the primary use. *(Ocean City, Md.)*

An establishment serving alcoholic beverages in which the principal business is the sale of such beverages at retail for consumption on the premises and where sandwiches and snacks may be available for consumption on the premises. *(Burr Ridge, Ill.)*

■ **tax abatement** The full or partial exemption from ad valorem taxes of certain real and/or personal property in a reinvestment zone designated for economic development purposes. *(Houston, Tex.)*

■ **tax credit** A dollar amount that may be subtracted from the amount of taxes owed. *(California Planning Roundtable)*

■ **tax increment** Additional tax revenues that result from increases in property values within a development area. [California] law permits the tax increment to be earmarked for redevelopment purposes but requires at least 20 percent to be used to increase and improve the community's supply of very low- and low-income housing. *(California Planning Roundtable)*

Generally, the incremental tax revenues, determined with reference to the tax increment base, resulting from the increase in property values or from the increase in commercial activity as a result of a project. More specifically, the term includes the following: (1) The incremental tax revenues resulting from an increase in the total market value of taxable real property situated in a tax increment district and an increase in the business use and occupancy of such taxable real property. (2) The payment in lieu of taxes assigned to or agreed to be paid by governmental entities or nonprofit organizations with property situated or otherwise assignable to a tax increment district. Whether all or only a portion of this payment is to be considered part of the tax increment shall be determined at the time the tax increment district is created. (3) The incremental tax revenues resulting from an increase in total taxable sales and rentals of tangible personal property and in the rendition of taxable services by vendors located in a tax increment district. (4) The incremental tax revenues resulting from an increase in total gross receipts or gross or net profits or income realized by persons or entities from business conducted in a tax increment district. *(Johnstown, Pa., Redevelopment Authority)*

■ **tax increment base** (1) The aggregate market value of all taxable real property located within a tax increment district on the date the district is created. (2) In a district where the governing body has levied a tax on the business use and occupancy of real estate, the average aggregate market value of real property located within the district and used or occupied for business purposes during the last available 12-month period preceding the date of creation of the district. (3) In a district where the governing body has levied a sales tax, the total amount of taxable sales, rentals and services subject to the sales tax of the [state] and occurring within the district during the last calendar year or the last available 12-month period preceding the date of creation of the district. (4) In a district where the governing body has levied a mercantile license tax, business privilege tax, net profits tax or similar tax for the privilege of engaging in business within the district, the total amount of taxable gross receipts, net income or net profits, as the case may be, realized by taxpayers at locations within the district during their last taxable period which ended before the date of creation of the district. *(Johnstown, Pa., Redevelopment Authority)*

■ **tax increment district**    A contiguous geographic area within a redevelopment area defined and created by resolution or ordinance of the governing body of the municipality. . . . *(Johnstown, Pa., Redevelopment Authority)*

■ **tax increment financing (TIF)**    A tool used by cities and other development authorities to finance certain types of development costs. The public purposes of TIF are the redevelopment of blighted areas, construction of low- and moderate-income housing, provision of employment opportunities, and improvement of the tax base. With TIF, a city "captures" the additional property taxes generated by the development that would have gone to other taxing jurisdictions and uses the "tax increments" to finance the development costs. *(Minnesota Office of the Legislative Auditor)*

A real-estate development technique applicable to industrial, commercial, and residential projects to cover the costs of publicly provided project improve-

ments. TIF uses anticipated increases in real estate tax revenues resulting from increased property values to pay off bonds sold to finance qualifying redevelopment costs. TIF allows the financing of land acquisitions and redevelopment improvements with tax-free borrowing, thereby reducing interest costs. In addition, use of TIF allows businesses to purchase renovated sites and buildings at less than market costs. *(State of Kansas)*

A . . . tool that enables local governments to finance the redevelopment of a designated blighted area [using the tax increment]. *(El Paso, Tex.)*

■ **tax increment fund**    A fund into which are paid all tax increments and into which are deposited all revenues front the sale of tax increment finance bonds or notes, revenues from the sale of any property acquired as part of a project plan or revenues to be used in the district, and from which money is distributed to pay project costs for the district or to satisfy claims of holders of tax increment bonds or notes issued for the district. *(Johnstown, Pa., Redevelopment Authority)*

■ **taxi**    Any motor vehicle other than a limousine offered to the public by a public taxicab business for the purpose of carrying or transporting passengers for a charge or a fee. *(Columbus, Mo.)*

■ **taxicab business**    A service that offers transportation in passenger automobiles and vans to persons including those who are handicapped in return for remuneration. The business may include facilities for servicing, repairing, and fueling the taxicabs or vans. *(Madison, Wisc.)*

■ **teahouse** *(See also coffee house)*    A public house or restaurant where tea and light refreshments are served, generally during midday. *(Galesburg, Ill.)*

■ **teardown** *(See also infill)*    The construction or remodeling of single-family homes to the maximum allowable size permitted by land-use and zoning regulation in neighborhoods distinctly characterized by considerably smaller homes. *(Glendale, Calif.)*

■ **teen dance center**    An enclosed or unenclosed structure open to persons from 15 through 20 years of age unaccompanied by adults at which music is furnished for the purpose of social dancing, and at which a person 15 through 20 years of age pays an admission, membership dues, or a minimum fee or cover charge, whether or not admission is limited to members only. "Teen dance center" shall include the enclosed or unenclosed structure and the surrounding premises used for parking or any activity related to the dancing operation. *(Scottsdale, Ariz.)*

A building, a part of a building, a room or a premises wherein entertainment, either live or recorded, vocal or instrumental, is provided, with or without dancing by customers or patrons, for persons between the ages of 13 and 19 years. A teen club may provide such other activities for teens or preteens as approved by the city council. A teen club does not include uses operated by public agencies or private eleemosynary or charitable organizations, such as church youth centers, the boys' and girls' club, or youth community centers provided for recreation or congregation *(Aurora, Colo., which uses the term "teen club")*

A private club providing dances primarily for persons between the ages of 14 and 18, admission for which may be gained by membership card and the payment of an admission fee or charge. *(Madison, Wisc., which uses the term "teen dance club")*

Any place or location that is not a cultural performance venue where an underage dance is conducted, operated, or maintained for more than six days in a calendar year, and includes the business premises in which an underage dance is conducted, operated, or maintained, including but not limited to hallways, bathrooms, and other areas readily open and accessible to the patrons of the underage dance, such as parking lots and other adjoining areas. *(Anchorage, Alaska, which uses the term "teen nightclub")*

■ **telecommunications** *(See also amateur radio tower)*    The transmission, between or among points as specified by the user, of information of the user's choosing, without change in the form or content of the information as sent and received. *(Southaven, Miss.)*

■ **telecommunications antenna**   Any system of wires, poles, rods, reflecting discs, or similar devices used for the transmission or reception of electromagnetic waves when such system is either external to or attached to the exterior of a structure. Antennas shall include devices having active elements extending in any direction, and directional beam-type arrays having elements carried by and disposed from a generally horizontal boom that may be mounted upon and rotated through a vertical mast or tower interconnecting the boom and antenna support, all of which elements are deemed to be part of the antenna. Antennas shall include cellular on wheels (COWs) and cellular on light trucks (COLTs) facilities; as well as dispatch carriers for Specialized Mobile Radio (SMR) services and Enhanced SMR (ESMR). *(Petaluma, Calif.)*

A specific device, the surface of which is used to transmit and/or receive radio-frequency signals, microwave signals, or other signals transmitted to or from other antennas for commercial purposes *(Bothell, Wash.)*

The surface from which wireless radio signals are sent and received by a personal wireless service facility. *(Cape Cod Commision, Mass.)*

Any structure or device used for the purpose of collecting or radiating electromagnetic waves; including but not limited to, directional antennas, such as panels, microwave dishes, and satellite dishes, and omni directional antennas, such as whip antennas, which are located on the exterior of, or outside of, any building, or structure. A single, radiating antenna platform, which includes one or more antennas, shall be regulated as a single antenna. *(Cape Elizabeth, Maine)*

The surface from which wireless radio signals are sent from and received by a personal wireless facility: A. Whip antenna is a long and thin device that transmits and/or receives radio frequency signals in a 360 degree radial pattern. B. Panel antenna is a relatively flat rectangular device that transmits and or receives radio frequency signals in a directional pattern of less than 360 degrees. C. Dish antenna is a bowl-shaped device for the reception and/or transmission radio frequency communications signals in a specific directional pattern. *(Scottsdale, Ariz.)*

■ **telecommuncations, cell site**   A tract or parcel of land that contains the cellular communications antenna, its support structure, accessory buildings, and parking and may include other uses associated and ancillary to cellular communications transmissions. *(Southhaven, Miss.)*

■ **telecommunications, co-location**   [Wireless communication facilities] equipment affixed to or erected upon existing freestanding or remote freestanding [wireless communication facilities] or other communication towers. *(Thurston County, Wash.)*

The use of a wireless telecommunication support facilities by more than one wireless telecommunication provider. *(Muskegon, Mich.)*

■ **telecommunications equipment shelter**   A cabinet or building located at the base of or near a wireless communication facility within which are housed, among other things, batteries and electrical equipment. This equipment is connected to the antenna by cable. *(Glendale, Ariz.)*

■ **telecommunications, satellite dish antenna**   A round parabolic antenna intended to receive signals from orbiting satellites and other sources. *(Colton, Calif.)*

Any antenna in the shape of a shallow dish, and appurtenant equipment, used for the reception of communications (television and otherwise) from orbiting satellites or ground transmitters. This definition includes satellite dish antennas of all sizes including those satellite dish antennas less than one meter in diameter. *(Dana Point, Calif.)*

An earth station antenna of parabolic or spherical design for the reception or transmission of satellite or terrestrial communication services. *(Farragut, Tenn.)*

■ **telecommunications tower**   A tower, pole, or similar structure that supports a telecommunications antenna operated for commercial purpose above ground in a fixed location, freestanding, guyed, or on a building or other structures. *(Baton Rouge, La.)*

A mast, pole, monopole, guyed, or freestanding framework, or other vertical elements that act as an antenna or to that an antenna is affixed or attached. *(Tucson, Ariz.)*

Any ground-mounted pole, spire, structure, or combination thereof, including supporting lines, cables, wires, braces, masts, intended primarily for the purpose of mounting an antenna or similar apparatus above ground. *(Plymouth, Minn.)*

A structure designed and constructed to support one or more antennas used by commercial wireless telecommunication facilities and including all appurtenant devices attached to it. A tower can be freestanding (solely self-supported by attachment to the ground) or supported (attached directly to the ground and with guy wires), of either lattice or monopole construction. *(Hudson, N.H.)*

■ **telecommunications tower, alternative design structure**   Artificial trees, clock towers, and similar nontraditional structures that are compatible with the existing setting or structures and camouflage or partially conceal the presence of antennas or towers. This includes any antenna or antenna array attached to the alternative design structure. *(Glendale, Ariz.)*

■ **telecommunications tower, alternative structure**   Ball field light poles, street lights, electric utility poles, water towers (pictured on page 232), and similar existing structures. This includes any antenna or antenna array attached to the alternative tower structure. *(Glendale, Ariz.)*

■ **telecommunications, wireless facility**   A facility that transmits and/or receives

electromagnetic signals for the purpose of transmitting analog or digital voice or data communications. It includes antennas, microwave dishes, horns and other types of equipment for the transmission or receipt of such signals, telecommunication towers or monopoles, or similar structures supporting said equipment, equipment buildings, shelters or cabinets, and other accessory development. Includes Personal Wireless Services as defined in the federal Telecommunications Act of 1996, and as subsequently amended, but shall not include the following: federally-licensed amateur radio stations and facilities used exclusively for receive-only antennas. *(Glendale, Calif.)*

A facility that transmits and/or receives electromagnetic signals. It includes antennas, microwave dishes, horns, and other types of equipment for the transmission or receipt of such signals, telecommunication towers, or similar structures supporting said equipment, equipment buildings, parking area, and other accessory development. *(Shererville, Ind.)*

A facility for the provision of personal wireless services as defined by the Telecommunications Act of 1996, and any amendments thereto. Personal wireless service facilities are composed of two or more of the following components: A. Antenna; B. Mount; C. Equipment Cabinet; D. Wall or Security Barrier. *(Scottsdale, Ariz.)*

Any freestanding facility, building, pole, tower or structure used to provide only wireless telecommunication services, and which consists of, without limitation, antennae, equipment and storage and other accessory structures used to provide wireless telecommunication services *(Fort Collins, Colo.)*

■ **telecommuting**    The relocation of work activities to a home or satellite work site to eliminate or reduce the distance traveled in a commute trip by at least half. Telecommunications, computers, and other supporting activities may be employed during telecommuting. *(Redmond, Wash.)*

Engaging in a gainful occupation or profession by a member or members of a family within his, her, or their, dwelling, while maintaining periodic communication with a principal office outside of the dwelling by the use of a computer modem. *(Delafield, Wisc.)*

An arrangement in which a worker is at home or in a location other than the primary place of work and communicates with the workplace and conducts work via wireless or telephone lines, using modems, fax machines, or other electronic devices in conjunction with computers. *(California Planning Roundtable)*

■ **telephone exchange building**    A building used exclusively for the transmission and exchange of telephone message, but the term shall not include wireless service towers. *(Philadelphia, Pa.)*

■ **telephone, outdoor pay**    A telephone for hire located on private property, not within a building used for additional purposes with controlled access by means of a door or doors that may be locked. *(St. Louis, Mo.)*

■ **telework center** *(See also home office; telecommuting)*    Satellite work facility incorporating sufficient technology to permit employees to reduce their commute trip, or to work closer to home. The goal of such centers is to reduce the distance traveled in a commute trip by at least half the distance. *(Redmond, Wash.)*

■ **temple** *(See religious institution)*

■ **temporary emergency, construction, or repair residence** *(See also shelter)*    A residence (which may be a mobile home) that is: (i) located on the same lot as a residence made uninhabitable by fire, flood, or other natural disaster and occupied by the persons displaced by such disaster; or (ii) located on the same lot as a residence that is under construction or undergoing substantial repairs or reconstruction and occupied by the persons intending to live in such permanent residence when the work is completed; or (iii) located on a nonresidential construction site and occupied by persons having construction or security responsibilities over such construction site. *(Indian Trail, N.C.)*

■ **temporary employment housing** *(See housing, temporary employment)*

■ **temporary merchant**    Any person who engages in the business of selling, offering for sale, or soliciting orders for goods or services from a single location of a period of seven days or less. Temporary merchant shall not include any person who has been issued a street vendor license. *(Reno, Nev.)*

■ **temporary outdoor sale** *(See also sidewalk sale)*    Any sale made by a person, firm, or corporation engaging in the temporary business of selling goods, wares, or merchandise from a tent, truck, vending cart, or other area outside of a permanent structure on property owned or leased by the person, firm, or corporation. The temporary outdoor sales, except those conducted by charitable organizations as defined, must be secondary to or incidental to the principal permitted use or structure existing on the property, and not incompatible with the intent of the district. The outdoor sale of Christmas trees is exempt from this definition. *(Jefferson County, Colo.)*

■ **temporary permit** *(See permit, temporary)*

■ **temporary portable building, construction-related**    A temporary portable unit for office use that is designed to be transported, after fabrication, on its own wheels or on a flatbed or other trailer, or have detachable wheels. *(Glen-*

*dale, Ariz., which uses the term "temporary office or construction trailer")*

■ **tenant** *(See also **boarder; roomer; subtenant**)* The lessee of facility space at an applicable development project. *(El Segundo, Calif.)*

Applied to a building or land, means any person who occupies the whole or a part of such building or land, whether alone or with others. *(Omaha, Neb.)*

Any person who occupies or has a leasehold interest in a rental unit under a lawful rental agreement, whether oral or written, express or implied. *(Renton, Wash.)*

■ **tennis club** A commercial or noncommercial establishment that provides facilities for playing tennis on a membership basis only. "Membership basis" means that the establishment sells memberships making its facilities available to members and their guests for periods of not less than one month at a time and that such facilities are not open to use by the general public. *(El Paso, Tex.)*

A commercial facility for the playing of tennis at which there is a clubhouse including rest rooms. A tennis facility may provide additional services customarily furnished by a club, such as swimming, outdoor recreation, and related retail sales, and may include a restaurant and cocktail lounge if approved as a part of the required use permit. *(Scottsdale, Ariz.)*

■ **tent** Any temporary structure or enclosure, the roof of which and/or one-half or more of the sides are constructed of silk, cotton, canvas, fabric, or a similar pliable material. *(Burr Ridge, Ill.)*

Any structure, enclosure, or shelter constructed of fabric or other pliable material supported by any manner except by air or the contents protected by the material. The horizontal area covered by the fabric or other pliable material shall be considered building floor area. In a residential district a tent shall be considered a detached accessory building. *(Tulsa, Okla.)*

■ **terminal** A facility for the transfer, pickup, or discharge of people or goods

without the long-term storage of such items. *(Clark County, Wash., which uses the term "transportation terminal")*

■ **terminal, airport** The building on the airport designated by the city for the use of the public and the certificated airlines to process, enplane, and deplane airplane passengers and to provide space for various concessions, services, supplies, and convenience for the public. *(Rochester, Minn., which uses the term "terminal building")*

■ **terminal, bus** Any premises for the transient housing or parking of motor-driven buses, and the loading and unloading of passengers. *(Philadelphia, Pa.)*

■ **terminal, bus passenger** A place where the transfer of people between modes of transportation takes place. *(Sioux Falls, S. Dak.)*

■ **terminal, bus/truck** An area and building where buses, trucks, and cargo are stored, where loading and unloading is carried on regularly, and where minor maintenance of these types of vehicles is performed. *(Sioux Falls, S. Dak.)*

■ **terminal, cargo** Transportation facility in which quantities of goods or container cargo are stored without undergoing any manufacturing processes, transferred to other carriers, or stored outdoors in order to transfer them to other locations. *(Seattle, Wash.)*

■ **terminal, marine** A facility comprising one or more berths, slips, piers, wharves, loading and unloading areas, warehouses, and storage yards used for transfer of people or cargo between waterborne carriers and land. Marine terminals do not include marinas and boatyards. *(San Francisco, Calif.)*

■ **terminal, mass transit** A place where people transfer from or to mass transit trains. *(Miami, Fla.)*

■ **terminal, motor freight** Any premises used by a motor freight company regulated by the public utility commission and/or the Interstate Commerce Commission as a carrier of goods, which is the origin and/or destination point of goods being transported, for the purpose of storing, transferring, loading, and un-

loading goods. *(Pittsburgh, Pa.)*

A building or area in which freight brought by motor truck is assembled and/or stored for routing in intrastate shipment by motor truck. *(Gurnee, Ill.)*

A facility for the receipt, transfer, short-term storage, and dispatching of goods transported by truck. Included in the use type would be express and other mail and package distribution facilities, including such facilities operated by the U.S. Post Office. *(Blacksburg, Va., which uses the term "truck terminal")*

Storage and distribution facilities having more than five heavy trucks (having a rating of more than 10,000 pounds and/or an unladen weight of more than 6,000 pounds) on the premises at any one time, but excluding trucking accessory to another industrial use on the site. *(Redondo Beach, Calif., which uses the term "truck terminal")*

The premises used for loading or unloading of trucks upon which storage of cargo is incidental to the primary function of motor freight shipment or shipment point and which is designed to accommodate the simultaneous loading or unloading of five or more trucks. *(Champaign, Ill., which uses the term "truck terminal")*

■ **terminal, passenger** A facility or location where the principal use is the handling, receiving and transfer of passenger traffic, and may include as an accessory use the loading, unloading, storing, receiving, assembling, dispatching, weighing, consolidating, classifying, switching, distribution, movement, or transfer of freight, as well as all equipment and facilities used to accomplish the foregoing activities. For purposes of this definition, a facility that handles the transport of passengers, by any vehicle type, for any public, private, or parochial school shall not be considered to be a passenger terminal. *(El Paso, Tex.)*

■ **terminal, passenger station** A type of passenger terminal that receives and discharges passengers by rail, and at which facilities and equipment required for their operation are provided. *(El Paso, Tex.)*

■ **terminal, transportation**　A type of passenger terminal at which passengers are loaded and unloaded from or onto a motor-carrier. A transportation terminal shall be categorized as follows: type A is a facility having a total land area of no more than 4,000 square feet and any building proposed within the land area is no larger than 2,000 square feet in gross floor area; type B is a facility having a total land area greater than 4,000 square feet or where a building proposed within the land area exceeds a gross floor area of 2,000 square feet. *(El Paso, Tex.)*

A facility that serves primarily as a transfer point for changing from one mode of transportation to another, or for transferring shipped materials from one vehicle to another, with associated storage area. *(Thurston County, Wash.)*

■ **terrace** *(See patio)*

■ **theater**　A structure used for dramatic, operatic, motion pictures, or other performance, for admission to which entrance money is received and no audience participation or meal service allowed. *(Topeka, Kans.)*

An outdoor or indoor area, building, part of a building, structure, or defined area utilized primarily for rehearsal or research and development related to the presentation of film, television, music video, multimedia, or other related activities that in the opinion of the director of planning and building safety are similar. Such areas may or may not be open to the general public. *(El Segundo, Calif., which uses the term "theater and performance space")*

A building or part of a building devoted to showing motion pictures, or for dramatic, dance, musical, or other live performances. *(Garrett, Ind., which uses the term "theater, indoor")*

An establishment for the performing arts with open-air seating for audiences. Such establishments may include related services such as food and beverage sales and other concessions. *(King County, Wash., which uses the term "outdoor performance center")*

■ **theatrical community center**　A building or a portion thereof used by a non-profit organization chartered by the state that has as its purposes the promotion, instruction, study, and production of the theater as an art form. Any single room within said theatrical community center used for theatrical purposes shall provide for a capacity of less than 300 persons and shall meet all requirements of the municipal code. *(Chicago, Ill.)*

An enclosed space suitable for a variety of cultural arts performances, permanently available, and managed and promoted on a nonprofit basis; principal use of the space shall be for public performing arts presentations, although incidental use for private meetings, exhibits and presentations shall be permitted. *(Miami, Fla., which uses the term "community theater")*

■ **theme park** *(See amusement, commercial; amusement park, outdoor; carnival)*

■ **thoroughfare**　Public vehicular infrastructure composed of avenues, streets, roads, and drives. *(Monroe County, Fla.)*

■ **thrift store** *(See also antique shop; consignment store; secondhand merchandise)*　A profit or nonprofit business or organization that engages in or specializes in the sale or resale of previously owned or used goods and merchandise from an area greater than 25 percent of the total floor area devoted to retail sales and whose merchandise is donated or principally donated. A specialty retail store that sells used merchandise not donated for sale, including but not limited to used record stores, used book stores, used furniture stores, and sports trading card stores, shall not be considered a thrift store for the purpose of this ordinance. *(Glendale, Ariz.)*

A shop that deals primarily in second-hand wearing apparel. All such merchandise shall be displayed and stored in an enclosed building. *(Las Vegas, Nev.)*

An establishment primarily engaged in the sale of used clothing, household goods, furniture, or appliances. This classification does not include antique shops. *(Redondo Beach, Calif.)*

A shop operated by a charitable organization that sells donated used merchandise only. All such merchandise shall be displayed and/or stored in an enclosed building. *(Las Vegas, Nev., which uses the term "thrift shop, nonprofit")*

■ **through-block arcade** *(See also pedestrian walkway, through-block)*　A continuous area within a building connecting one street with another street, residential plaza, urban plaza, or arcade adjacent to the street (pictured below). This area may be enclosed in whole or in part and must have a minimum width of 20 feet and a minimum average height of 20 feet. Such a through-block arcade shall, at either end, be at the same level as the street, residential plaza, urban plaza, or arcade that it adjoins. *(New York, N.Y.)*

■ **tidal and submerged land**　That water-covered area affected by the influence of the tidal action and those lands that are always submerged beneath the water. *(Unalaska, Alaska)*

■ **tidelands**    Lands that are located between the lines of mean high tide and mean low tide. *(Imperial Beach, Calif.)*

■ **time-share project**    A project in which a purchaser receives the right in perpetuity, for life, or for a term of years to the recurrent, exclusive use or occupancy of a lot, parcel, unit, or segment of real property, annually or on some other periodic basis, for a period of time that has been or will be allotted from the use or occupancy periods into which the project has been divided, or a project in which a license or contractual or membership right of occupancy is not coupled with an estate in the real property; except that a project in which such right to exclusive use or occupancy is available only for intervals of more than 30 days shall not be considered a timeshare project. *(Scottsdale, Ariz.)*

■ **time-share unit**    The actual and promised accommodations, and related facilities that are the subject of a time-share plan. *(Kauai, Hawaii)*

■ **time sharing**    Concept of property ownership involving either interval ownership or fractional fee interests as may be determined by the town council. "Time-sharing" shall not include a time-share license or use. *(Telluride, Colo.)*

■ **tire store**    A place where the principal business is the sale or installation of new, used, or retread tires and tubes. *(Glendale, Calif.)*

Any business where 100 or more new or used tires are collected, stored, maintained, altered, repaired, changed, prefabricated, or disposed. *(Chicago, Ill.)*

■ **topographic map**    A map showing all principal physical features of an area, including elevations. *(Handbook for Planning Commissioners in Missouri)*

■ **topography**    The physical land surface relief describing the terrain elevation and slope. *(Interstate 81 Corridor Council)*

In its broadest sense, topography includes land forms, water and other drainage features, and features such as gravel pits and mine tailings. A single feature (such as a mountain or valley) is called a topographic feature. *(United States Census Bureau)*

The configuration of a surface area showing relative elevations. *(Iowa State University Extension Service )*

The existing configuration of the earth's surface including the relative relief, elevations, and position of land features. *(Cecil County, Md.)*

■ **tot lot** *(See **play lot**)*

■ **tourism**    The business of providing services for persons traveling for pleasure, tourism contributes to the vitality of the community by providing revenue to local business. Level of tourism can be measured through changes in the transient occupancy tax or restaurant sales. *(California Planning Roundtable)*

■ **tourism-oriented**    Applied as an adjective to businesses and commercial establishments, means those catering primarily to transient visitors staying on the island for two weeks or less. If an establishment could equally cater to either tourists or island residents, it is included within this definition. *(Hilton Head, S.C.)*

■ **tourist court** *(See **court, tourist**)*

■ **tourist home**    An establishment used for dwelling purposes in which rooms, with or without meals, are offered to transient guests for compensation, including establishments known as bed and breakfasts. *(Jefferson, Mo.)*

A building in which not more than five guest rooms are used to provide or offer overnight accommodations to transient guests for compensation. *(Garrett, Ind.)*

A licensed dwelling in which overnight accommodations are provided or offered for up to a maximum of seven transient guests for compensation. A tourist house shall not be considered an accessory use or as a home occupation. *(Concord Township, Pa.)*

A building, or part thereof, other than a motel or hotel, where sleeping accommodations are provided for transient guests, with or without meals, and which also serves as the residence of the operator. *(Boca Raton, Fla.)*

■ **tower** *(See also **telecommunications** definitions)*    A portion of a building that is higher than the remainder of the building, or a tall structure of small dimension separate from the building it accompanies such as the campanile of a church. *(Ocean Shores, Wash.)*

■ **tower, temporary mobile**    Any mobile tower, pole, or structure located on a trailer, vehicle, or temporary platform intended primarily for the purpose of mounting an antenna or similar apparatus for personal wireless services, also commonly referred to as Cellular on Wheels (COW). *(Plymouth, Minn.)*

■ **towing service**    Establishment that provides for the removal and temporary storage of vehicles but does not include disposal, permanent disassembly, salvage, or accessory storage of inoperable vehicles. *(Miami, Fla.)*

The removing of a motor vehicle by towing, carrying, hauling, or pushing from public or private property when such vehicle has been ordered to be impounded to a public or private impound lot. This shall not include an "automotive service" use that has a tow truck and repairs vehicles on-site. *(Nashville and Davidson County, Tenn., which uses the term "motor vehicle wrecker service")*

■ **town** *(See also **city; hamlet; urban center; village**)*    A center that has an urban density (over 1,000 persons per square mile) and interrelated mixed uses. This term does not necessarily refer to the form of incorporation of a municipality. *(New Jersey State Plan)*

A form of municipal government. Also, the territory lying within the boundaries of such government. *(New York Planning Federation)*

■ **town center**    A center that has a high investment in public facilities and services, several neighborhoods with a highly diverse housing stock and a central core or retail, office, and community facilities (pictured on page 236). As described in the [state] plan, towns are New Jersey's traditional centers of commerce and government. This term does not necessarily refer to the form of incorporation of a municipality. *(New Jersey Office of State Planning)*

An optional and accessory use to traditional neighborhood development that provides for larger scale commercial shopfront uses in buildings that front a plaza. The town center buildings shall surround the plaza on at least 35 percent of its perimeter. *(Gainesville, Fla.)*

A location within the city containing an orderly mix of land uses that meets the daily needs of area residents. This mix is intended to contain convenience retail, food services, personnel, and business service uses; community facilities including parks, schools, libraries, and places of worship; and residential uses of a density and location that would accommodate direct pedestrian linkages to the non-residential facilities. These should be arranged in a manner that is focused around a central open space. *(Noblesville, Ind., which uses the term "village center")*

An area designated on the general plan as a village center or that has been rezoned with the application of the village center overlay zoning district. A village center designation is intended to create a mixture of land uses with pedestrian orientation, plazas, open spaces, and mass transit opportunities. *(Temecula, Calif., which uses the term "village center.")*

■ **townhouse** *(See also rowhouse)*  A one-family dwelling unit, with a private entrance, which is part of a structure whose dwelling units are attached horizontally in a linear arrangement, and having a totally exposed front and rear wall to be used for access, light, and ventilation. *(St. Paul, Minn.)*

■ **toxic/noxious substance** *(See also hazardous material)*  Any solid, liquid, or gaseous matter including but not limited to gases, vapors, dusts, fumes, and mists containing properties that by chemical means are inherently harmful and likely to destroy life or impair health or capable of causing injury to the well-being of persons or damage to property. *(Schaumburg, Ill.)*

■ **tract** *(See parcel)*

■ **tractor**  Every motor vehicle designed and used primarily for drawing other vehicles, equipment, or implements of husbandry, and not so constructed as to carry any load thereon other than part of the weight of the load being drawn. *(El Paso, Tex.)*

■ **trade/ business school** *(See also educational facilities)*  A secretarial school or college, or business school or college, when not public and not owned or conducted by or under the sponsorship of a religious or charitable organization; school conducted as commercial enterprise for teaching instrumental music, dancing, barbering, or hairdressing, or for teaching industrial skills in which machinery is employed as a means of instruction. This definition shall not be deemed to include "educational institution." *(Pine Bluff, Ark.)*

A specialized instructional establishment that provides on-site training of business, commercial, and/or trade skills such as accounting, data processing, and computer repair. This classification excludes establishments providing training in an activity that is not otherwise permitted in the zone. Incidental instruc-

tional services in conjunction with another primary use shall not be considered a business and trade school. *(Redondo Beach, Calif.)*

■ **traditional neighborhood development** *(See also neotraditional development; New Urbanism)*  A development that exhibits several of the following characteristics: alleys, streets laid out in a grid system, buildings oriented to the street, front porches on houses, pedestrian-orientation, compatible, mixed land uses, village squares and greens. *(Henderson, Nev.)*

■ **traditional neighborhood district**  A district that encourages mixed-use, compact development that is sensitive to the environmental characteristics of the land and facilitates the efficient use of services. A traditional neighborhood district diversifies and integrates land uses within close proximity to each other, and it provides for the daily recreational and shopping needs of the residents. A traditional neighborhood district is a sustainable, long-term community that provides economic opportunity and environmental and social equity for the residents. Its design adopts the urban conventions which were the norm in the United States from colonial times until the 1940s. *(Austin, Tex.)*

■ **traffic calming**  A concept fundamentally concerned with reducing the adverse impact of motor vehicles on built-up areas. Usually involves reducing vehicle speeds, providing more space for pedestrians and cyclists, and improving the local environment. *(University of Leeds, Institute for Transportation, UK)*

Reducing motorist speed, decreasing motor vehicle volumes, and increasing safety for pedestrians and nonmotorized vehicles. *(University of Hawaii at Manoa, Department of Urban and Regional Planning)*

***Commentary:*** *Traffic calming involves a number of techniques and devices that we have not defined individually in this report. The reader is directed to PAS Report No. 456, Traffic Calming, by Cynthia Hoyle for definitions and illustrations of such devices as* semi-diverters, chokers, chicanes, neck-downs, and roundabouts.

■ **traffic control devices** All signs, signals, parking meter instruction plates, markings, and devices not inconsistent with this chapter placed or erected by authority of a public body or official having jurisdiction, for the purpose of regulating, warning, or guiding traffic. (*Rochester, Minn.*)

■ **traffic impact** An adverse traffic impact as represented be an increase in congestion, worsening or level of service, or reductions in safety and efficiency. (*DuPage County, Ill.*)

■ **traffic impact analysis** An analysis of the effect of traffic generated be a development on the capacity, operations, and safety of the public street and highway system. (*DuPage County, Ill.*)

■ **traffic impact mitigation measure** Any measure or improvement taken by, or required of the developer in order to lessen, abate, or reduce the traffic impact of the development on the public street and highway system. (*DuPage County, Ill.*)

■ **traffic model** A mathematical representation of traffic movement within an area or region based on observed relationships between the kind and intensity of development in specific areas. Many traffic models operate on the theory that trips are produced by persons living in residential areas and are attracted by various nonresidential land uses. (*California Planning Roundtable*)

■ **traffic signal** (See *traffic control devices*)

■ **traffic zone** In a mathematical traffic model the area to be studied is divided into zones, with each zone treated as producing and attracting trips. The production of trips by a zone is based on the number of trips to or from work or shopping, or other trips produced per dwelling unit. (*California Planning Roundtable*)

■ **trail** A way designed for and used by equestrians, pedestrians, and cyclists using nonmotorized bicycles. (*Palm Desert, Calif.*)

■ **trailer** (See *construction field office; temporary portable building, construction-related*)

■ **transfer of development rights (TDR)** The conveyance of development rights by deed, easement or other legal instrument authorized by local law to another parcel of land and the recordation of that conveyance among the land records of [the muncipality]. (*Montgomery County, Md.*)

A program that can relocate potential development from areas where proposed land use or environmental impacts are considered undesirable (the "donor" site) to another ("receiver") site chosen on the basis of its ability to accommodate additional units of development beyond that for which it was zoned, with minimal environmental, social, and aesthetic impacts. (Also known as "Transfer of Development Credits") (*California Planning Roundtable*)

A certificate issued by Thurston County development services which represents a unit of density derived from a TDR sending area parcel. Such rights may be (a) severed from the TDR sending area parcel and used in a TDR receiving area in accordance with the TDR receiving area regulations of the applicable Thurston County jurisdiction; or (b) attached to a TDR sending area parcel when required. Transfer means the action of transferring credited development rights from a parcel or parcels in a TDR sending area to a parcel or parcels in a TDR receiving area by a deed of transfer. Transfer includes any intermediate transfers to or among transferees. (*Thurston County, Wash.*)

■ **transfer of development rights (TDR) easement** A legal covenant that protects the subject land in perpetuity from development beyond any development rights reserved subject to the underlying zone at the time the covenant is signed and grants enforcement of the covenant to the county. (*Thurston County, Wash.*)

■ **transfer of development rights (TDR), receiving area** The area within which development rights transferred from a TDR sending area can be used. (*Thurston County, Wash.*)

■ **transfer of development rights (TDR), sending area** The area from which TDRs can be transferred. (*Thurston County, Wash.*)

■ **transfer station** (See *solid waste transfer facility*)

■ **transformer** A device for changing the voltage of electrical energy. (*Washington State Department of Health*)

■ **transient** Any visitor or person who owns, rents, or uses a lodging or dwelling unit, or portion thereof, for less than 180 days and whose permanent address for legal purposes is not the lodging or dwelling unit occupied by the visitor. This definition shall not apply to nonpaying guests of the family occupying the unit and to patients or clients in health care facilities, full-time students, employees who receive room and/or board as part of their salary or compensation, military personnel, low-income renters receiving rental subsistence from state or federal governments whose rental periods are for durations shorter than 60 days, or lodging provided by nonprofit corporations or associations for religious, charitable, or education purposes, provided that no rental income is produced. (*Maui County, Hawaii*)

■ **transit** The conveyance of persons or goods from one place to another by means of a local, public transportation system. (*California Planning Roundtable*)

■ **transit area** (1) The area within a one-quarter mile radius of either public streets identified by (maps and ordinances) as having the location, mix of densities, mix of uses, and development patterns that can generate sufficient bus ridership to support a frequent and consistent level of bus service (as typified by a 10 to 15-minute frequency of service); or, (2) existing and proposed trolley stops and major bus transfer centers that have been approved for development by the transit development board with identified, available funding. (*San Diego, Calif.*)

■ **transit-dependent** Refers to persons unable to operate automobiles or other motorized vehicles, or those who do not own motorized vehicles. Transit-dependent citizens must rely on transit, para-transit, or owners of private vehicles for transportation. Transit-dependent citizens include the young, the handicapped, the elderly, the poor, and those with prior violations in motor vehicle laws. *(California Planning Roundtable)*

■ **transit, light rail (LRT)**    "Street cars" or "trolley cars" that typically operate entirely or substantially in mixed traffic and in nonexclusive, at-grade rights-of-way. Passengers typically board vehicles from the street level (as opposed to a platform that is level with the train) and the driver may collect fares. Vehicles are each electrically self-propelled and usually operate in one or two-car trains. *(California Planning Roundtable)*

■ **transit-oriented development (TOD)** Moderate and high-density housing concentrated in mixed-use developments located along transit routes . . . The location, design, and mix of uses in a TOD emphasize pedestrian-oriented environments and encourages the use of public transportation. *(Community Green Line Planning Project, "Putting Neighborhoods on the Right Track" 12/30/94 —Chicago, Ill.)*

A mixed-use community within an average 2000-foot walking distance of a transit stop and core commercial area. TODs mix residential, retail, office, and public uses in a walkable environment, making it convenient for residents and employees to travel by transit, bicycle, foot, or car. *(California Planning Roundtable)*

■ **transit, public** *(See also paratransit; public transportation; subway)* A system of regularly-scheduled buses and/or trains available to the public on a fee-per-ride basis (pictured above). Also called "mass transit." *(California Planning Roundtable)*

■ **transit route** An existing or planned route for public intracity or intraurban transit service in the local or regional transportation plan or the plan of the relevant transit service provider. Does not include temporary routes or

routes which are planned to be replaced or relocated in the relevant plans. *(Oregon Chapter of APA)*

■ **transit shuttle** Transit service that travels over a short route or one that connects two transportation systems or centers. Frequently operated using a minibus or van. *(Sacramento Regional Transit District)*

A supplement to transit [which] improves circulation between locations of available parking supply and final downtown destination. *(Portland, Ore.)*

■ **transit station** *(See also public transit concourse; railroad passenger station; terminal definitions)* A building, structure, or area designed and used for persons changing transportation modes (pictured below). *(Miami, Fla.)*

■ **transit station development area** An area near a metro transit station, not located within a central business district, that has been designated as a transit station development area by an approved and adopted master plan or sector plan. *(Montgomery County, Md.)*

■ **transit stop** *(See also bus stop)* Improvements and facilities at selected points along transit routes for passenger pickup, drop off, and waiting. Facilities and improvements may include shelters, benches, signs, structures, and other improvements to provide security, protection from the weather, and access to nearby services. *(Oregon Chapter of APA)*

■ **transit stop, planned** A location designated for use as a transit stop in a local or regional transportation plan or a plan adopted be the relevant transit service provider. *(Oregon Chapter of APA)*

■ **transitional area** An area in the process of changing from one use to another or an area which functions as a buffer between land uses of different types or intensity. *(Minnetonka, Minn.)*

■ **transitional housing shelter** *(See also homeless shelter)* Shelter provided to the homeless for an extended period, often as long as 18 months, and generally integrated with other social services and counseling programs to assist in the transition to self-sufficiency through the acquisition of a stable income and permanent housing. *(California Planning Roundtable*

One main building, or portion thereof, on one zoning lot where persons who may or may not have access to traditional or permanent housing but are capable of living independently within a reasonable period of time, generally about 18 months, reside on a 24-hour-per-day basis for at least 30 days and participate in appropriate program activities designed to facilitate independent living. (*St. Paul, Minn., which uses the term "transitional housing facility"*)

A multifamily residential facility developed in an individual dwelling unit format that does not restrict occupancy to six months or less and that provides temporary accommodations to low- and moderate-income persons and families for periods of up to three years, and which also may provide meals, counseling, and other services, as well as common areas for residents of the facility. (*Santa Monica, Calif., which uses the term "transitional housing"*)

A community-based residential facility that provides short-term (120 days or less) room and board in a supervised living environment utilizing counseling and rehabilitation services for persons with a history of juvenile delinquency, behavioral disorders, alcoholism, or drug abuse. (*Tulsa, Okla., which uses the term "transitional living center"*)

■ **transitional lot**   A specified lot, or lots, adjoining a specified lot, or lots, in another district. The "transitional" identification is used when special transitional regulations are applied to deal with possible conflicts of uses at district boundaries. Transitional yard requirements may be imposed at these locations to act as a sort of buffer zone. (*PAS Report No. 322, The Language of Zoning*)

■ **transitional use** (*See* **use, transitional**)

■ **transitional zone**   An area consisting of a lot, lots, or parts of lots, within any residential district, having side lot lines abutting a boundary of a commercial or industrial district, and extending not more than 100 feet from such boundary into the residential district. (*Multnomah County, Ore.*)

(1) Land that is in the process of changing from one predominant use to another, successional use or from one common social, economic, or ethnic characteristic to another; (2) land that acts as a buffer between uses of different density or intensity and compatibility. (*Martin County, Fla.*)

■ **transmission line**   An electric line used for the bulk transmission of electricity between generating or receiving plants and major subdivisions or delivery points, having a voltage rating greater than 12,500 volts. (*Glendale, Ariz.*)

■ **transportation center, intermodal**   A major parking garage, open to the public, designed to have the effect of reducing automobile traffic on local streets in the immediate and adjacent districts by incorporating all of the following features as integral parts of the development and not as mere connections: (1) a minimum of 500 parking stalls; (2) a transit stop or station; (3) separate or partially separate rights of way creating direct access to the parking stalls from a major traffic thoroughfare. (*Pittsburgh, Pa.*)

■ **transportation demand management (TDM)** (*See also* **buspool; carpool; high-occupancy vehicle (HOV); ridesharing; van pool**)   The implementation of programs, plans, or policies designed to encourage changes in individual travel behavior. TDM can include an emphasis on alternative travel modes to the single occupant vehicle (SOV) such as carpools, vanpools, and transit, reduction or elimination of the number of vehicle trips, or shifts in the time of vehicle commutes to other than the peak period. (*Brea, Calif.*)

A strategy for reducing demand on the road system by reducing the number of vehicles using the roadways and/or increasing the number of persons per vehicle. TDM attempts to reduce the number of persons who drive alone on the roadway during the commute period and to increase the number in carpools, vanpools, buses, and trains or walking, and biking. TDM can be an element of transportation systems management (TSM). (*California Planning Roundtable*)

Programmatic strategies designed to make efficient use of the existing transportation system. Specifically, demand management strategies attempt to increase transit ridership, vehicle occupancy, walking and bicycling, and to reduce the lengths of some trips, move them to off-peak hours, or eliminate them altogether. Implementation of demand management strategies can reduce dependence on the single-occupant vehicle, thereby reducing traffic congestion, vehicle emissions, and fuel consumption. (*1995 Update of the Metropolitan Transportation Plan for the Central Puget Sound Region, State of Washington*)

The alteration of travel behavior, usually on the part of commuters, through programs of incentives, services and policies. TDM addresses alternatives to single-occupant vehicles such as carpooling and vanpooling, and changes in work schedules that move trips out of peak period or eliminate them altogether (as in the case in telecommuting or compressed work weeks). (*Hermosa Beach, Calif.*)

■ **transportation facilities**   Individual modal or multimodal conveyances and terminals; within a corridor, facilities may be of local, regional. or statewide importance. Examples of facilities are highways, rail transit lines, transit stations, bicycle paths, airports and sea or river ports. (*Oregon Department of Transportation*)

■ **transportation facilities, alternate mode**   Any mode of commute transportation other than the single-occupancy motor vehicle. (*Tucson, Ariz.*)

■ **transportation management area**   A special designation given to all urbanized areas with a population greater than 200,000 (or other area when requested by the governor and Metropolitan Planning Organization (MPO)); these areas must comply with special transportation planning requirements regarding congestion management systems, project selection and certification. . . . (*1,000 Friends of Florida*)

■ **transportation systems**   Networks of transportation links, services and facilities which collectively are of statewide importance though these individual corridors, facilities or services which make up the system may be of only local or regional significance. Examples include highways, rail, public transportation, aviation and bicycle systems. *(Oregon Department of Transportation)*

■ **transportation systems management (TSM)** A comprehensive strategy developed to address the problems caused by additional development, increasing trips, and a shortfall in transportation capacity. Transportation Systems Management focuses on more efficiently utilizing existing highway and transit systems rather than expanding them. TSM measures are characterized by their low cost and quick implementation time frame, such as computerized traffic signals, metered freeway ramps, and one-way streets. *(California Planning Roundtable)*

Any of several different operational or management strategies for reducing the peak-hour traffic demand generated by a development, including but not limited to carpooling, vanpooling, flex-time, staggered work hours, and mass transportation. *(DuPage County, Ill.)*

■ **transportation systems, smart technology** Transportation systems that include computer-based interactive management elements that provide information to motorists and/or are responsive to changing demands, maximizing the efficiency of the existing system. *(New Jersey State Plan)*

■ **trash** *(See garbage; litter; refuse; rubbish; solid waste)*

■ **trash enclosure** An accessory use of a property where trash and/or recyclable material containers, or any other type of waste or refuse container is stored (pictured at right). *(Mankato, Minn.)*

■ **travel demand** *(See also trip generation)* The number of person trips taken during a given period in a specified geographic location. *(Sacramento Regional Transit District)*

■ **travelway** *(See also bike lane)* That portion of a public right-of-way that is improved for use by self-propelled vehicles or bicycles, including paved or gravel areas and any other area intended for vehicle movement. *(Nashville and Davidson County, Tenn.)*

■ **tree** A plant having at least one well-defined stem or trunk and normally attaining a mature height of at least 15 feet, with an average mature spread of 15 feet, and having a trunk that shall be kept clear of leaves and branches at least six feet above grade at maturity. *(Santa Monica, Calif.)*

A woody perennial plant having one well-defined main stem or trunk which, when mature, is not less than six inches in diameter at a point 4.5 feet above surrounding grade. *(Clear Lake Shores, Tex.)*

Any woody plant that normally grows to a mature height greater than 20 feet and has a diameter of four inches or more at a point four and one-half feet above the ground. *(Newbury, N.H.)*

■ **tree bank** A fund established by a city to provide an opportunity to make a cash payment to the city in lieu of providing required landscape stock on a site. *(Altamonte Springs, Fla.)*

■ **tree, canopy** Any self-supporting woody plant of a species that normally achieves an overall height at maturity of 30 feet or more. *(Nashville and Davidson County, Tenn.)*

■ **tree, class A** Any self-supporting woody plant of a species that normally grows to an overall height of at least 50 feet, usually with one main stem or trunk and many branches. May appear to have several stems or trunks, as in several varieties of oaks. *(Covington, La.)*

■ **tree, class B** Any self-supporting woody plant of a species that normally grows to an overall height of at least 25 feet, usually with one main stem or trunk and many branches. May appear to have several stems or trunks; for example, crape myrtle. *(Covington, La.)*

■ **tree conservation** Providing for optimum overall tree coverage and specific tree placement by a combination of retaining certain existing trees and planting new ones, as appropriate (in contrast to Tree Preservation). *(Beaufort, S.C.)*

■ **tree, crown spread** The typical circumference of a tree at maturity. *(Boulder, Colo.)*

■ **tree cutting** The removal, felling or destruction of 50 percent or more of a tree, but does not include trimming branches for tree maintenance purposes. *(Portland, Ore.)*

■ **tree density factor** A number based on the basal area derived from the combination of the density of trees remaining on a site and the density of additional trees to be planted. *(Nashville and Davidson County, Tenn.)*

■ **tree, dominant** Trees with crowns extending above the general level of the

crown cover and receiving full sunlight from above and partly from the side; larger than the average tree in the stand. *(Maryland Department of Natural Resources)*

■ **tree, grand tree stands**    A contiguous grouping of grand trees that has been determined to be of exceptional value. Determination is based on the following criteria: A relatively mature even-aged stand, a stand with a purity of species composition or of a rare or unusual nature, a stand with historical significance, and a stand with exceptional aesthetic beauty. *(Wildwood, Mo.)*

■ **tree, heritage**    A tree planted by a group of citizens or by the city or county in commemoration of an event or in memory of a person figuring significantly in history. *(California Planning Roundtable)*

■ **tree, landmark**    A tree whose size, visual impact, or association with a historically significant structure or event have led the city or county to designate them as landmarks. *(California Planning Roundtable)*

■ **tree, mature**    Any tree with a trunk with a diameter of 10 inches or more, measured 24 inches above existing grade. *(Newport Beach, Calif.)*

■ **tree ordinance**    A public law developed to organize a municipal urban forestry program, formulate a tree commission, and control the planting, removal, and care of public and/or private trees. *(Louisiana State University)*

■ **tree preservation**    (1) Retaining an existing tree on site. (2) An orientation to provide for maximum tree coverage on site by retaining existing trees, especially those of high value, rather than by replanting or a combination (in contrast to tree conservation). *(Beaufort, S.C.)*

■ **tree, prohibited**    Any tree that, by the nature of its fruit, root system, brittleness of wood, or susceptibility to disease, is not allowed as a replacement tree. *(Nashville and Davidson County, Tenn.)*

■ **tree protection**    Measures taken, such as, but not limited to, temporary fencing and the use of tree wells, to protect existing trees from damage or loss during and after project construction. *(Martin County, Fla.)*

■ **tree protection zone**    An area surrounding the base of a tree, generally circular in shape, within which neither construction activity nor physical development is permitted. *(Beaufort, S.C.)*

The area around a tree corresponding to the drip line or 10 feet in all directions from the trunk. *(Hilton Head Island, S.C.)*

■ **tree, public**    Any tree located on city-owned or controlled property including parks, street right-of-ways, parkways, etc. *(Wildwood, Mo.)*

■ **tree removal**    The destruction of any tree by cutting, girdling, interfering with the water supply, applying chemicals, or regrading around the base of the trunk. *(Contra Costa County, Calif.)*

■ **tree, replacement**    Those trees required to be planted based on the difference between the required tree density factor and the actual tree density factor following all approved tree removal. *(Nashville and Davidson County, Tenn.)*

■ **tree save area**    An area composed of closely grouped trees designated for preservation *(Beaufort, S.C.)*

■ **tree, shade**    A woody plant, usually deciduous, that normally grows with one main trunk and has a canopy that screens and filters the sun in the summer and winter, respectively. *(Delaware County, Pa.)*

■ **tree, significant**    Trees that are (1) six inches or greater in diameter at breast height (dbh); (2) in good health; (3) and of preferred species: (a) evergreen; (b) deciduous; (c) other such as trees with significant visual impact on the surrounding area or "landmark" trees. *(Redmond, Wash.)*

Trees that are healthy, measure a minimum of eight inches in diameter at a distance of 54 inches above ground, and are a minimum of four inches in diameter for conifers. *(Plymouth, Minn.)*

■ **tree, street**    A tree that is currently located or proposed for planting along streets or highways. Such tree can be located on private property or on publicly held land. Street trees are typically planted in a linear fashion and provide spatial enclosure as well as other technical and aesthetic benefits. *(Wildwood, Mo.)*

Trees, shrubs, bushes, and all other woody vegetation on land lying between the property lines on either side of all streets, avenues, or ways within a city/village. *(State of Nebraska)*

Trees strategically planted—usually in parkway strips, medians, or along streets—to enhance the visual quality of a street. *(California Planning Roundtable)*

■ **tree, street tree plan**    A comprehensive plan for all trees on public streets that sets goals for solar access and standards for species selection, maintenance, and replacement criteria. The plan also addresses planting trees in patterns that will define neighborhood character while avoiding monotony or maintenance problems. *(California Planning Roundtable)*

■ **tree, street tree planting area**    The area of a development site that lies between the street right-of-way line and the edge of the street curb parallel to the street. This land is publicly owned but is often used for street tree planting and maintenance. *(Louisiana State University)*

■ **trip**    A one-way journey that proceeds from an origin to a destination via a single mode of transportation; the smallest unit of movement considered in transportation studies. Each trip has one "production end," (or origin—often from home, but not always) and one "attraction end," (destination). *(California Planning Roundtable)*

■ **trip generation**    *(See also **travel demand**)*    The dynamics that account for people making trips in automobiles or by means of public transportation. Trip generation is the basis for estimating the level of use for a transportation system and the impact of additional development or transportation facilities on an existing, local transportation system. Trip generations of households are correlated with destinations that attract household members for specific purposes. *(California Planning Roundtable)*

■ **trip, origin or destination survey**    A survey designed to measure the purpose and movement of vehicular traffic. It can be used to gather information on trip purposes, define lines, rate of flow, and interval demands, and to suggest what streets and highways would best serve the requirements of the driving public. *(Handbook for Planning Commissioners in Missouri)*

■ **trip reduction**    Reduction in the number of work-related trips made by single occupant vehicles. *(Hermosa Beach, Calif.)*

■ **triplex** *(See also* **duplex***)*    A building containing three individual dwellings. Accessory dwelling units are not included in this definition. *(Durham, N.C.)*

A detached residential structure containing three and only three dwelling units, designed for occupancy by not more than three families living independently of each other. *(Duluth, Ga.)*

■ **truck, heavy**    Heavy trucks are trucks, including truck tractors, and similar vehicles with two or more rear axles. *(Portland, Ore.)*

■ **truck, light**    Light trucks are trucks and similar vehicles with single rear axles and single rear wheels. *(Portland, Ore.)*

■ **truck, medium**    Medium trucks are trucks and similar vehicles, other than truck tractors, with single rear axles and dual rear wheels. Truck tractors are in the Heavy Truck category. *(Portland, Ore.)*

■ **truck plaza**    A site in excess of two acres providing specialized facilities for retail fueling services for large trucks; the site may include related facilities including, but not limited to, restaurants, and overnight parking. *(Bernalillo County, N.M.)*

■ **truck route**    A path of circulation required for all vehicles exceeding set weight or axle limits, a truck route follows major arterials through commercial or industrial areas and avoids sensitive areas. *(California Planning Roundtable)*

■ **truck stop**    A facility intended to provide services to the trucking industry, including but not limited to the following activities: dispensing of fuel, repair shops, automated washes, restaurants and motels; all as part of the facility. *(Temecula, Calif.)*

A site in excess of two acres providing specialized facilities for retail fueling services for large trucks; the site may include related facilities including but not limited to restaurants and overnight parking. *(Bernalillo County, N. Mex., which uses the term "truck plaza")*

■ **truck terminal** *(See* **terminal, motor freight***)*

■ **turnaround**    A space on private property that permits the turning around of any passenger vehicle without the necessity of using any public right-of-way to turn around. *(Carmel, Ind.)*

■ **turning circle**    A street segment forming a circle at the closed end of a cul-de-sac street, with a curve radius of 100 feet as measured to the outside line of the right-of-way. *(Gorham, Maine)*

■ **undergrounding**   The placement of utility lines below ground, with the removal of above-ground poles, wires and structures as applicable. *(Glendale, Ariz.)*

■ **underlying zoning district**   An underlying district is the term referring to a zoning district . . . when it is affected by an overlay district. *(Peoria, Ill.)*

■ **undevelopable**   Specific areas where topographic, geologic, and/or surficial soil conditions indicate a significant danger to future occupants and a liability to the city or county and are so designated by the city or county. *(California Planning Roundtable)*

An area that cannot be used practicably for a habitable structure because of natural conditions such as slopes exceeding 20 percent in a direction greater than 45 degrees east or west of true south, severe topographic relief, water bodies or conditions, or conditions that isolate one portion of a property under another portion so that access is not practicable to the unbuildable portion; or manmade

conditions such as existing development restrictions that prohibit development of a given area of a lot by law or private agreement; or existence or absence of easements or access rights that prevent development of a given area. *(Clark County, Wash.)*

■ **undeveloped land**   Land in its natural state. *(Temecula, Calif.)*

■ **unified development code** *(See also **zoning code**)*   The combining of development regulation and procedures, including but not limited to, zoning and subdivision codes, sign and floodplain regulations, historic preservation provisions, administrative and hearings procedures, and commission bylaws, into a single unified code. *(APA Research Department)*

■ **uniformity**   A basic premise of zoning that all properties in the same zoning district are subject to the same regulations. Attacks on certain zoning actions, such as spot zoning or attaching extra conditions to a rezoning as in conditional rezoning, often are based on violation of uniformity provisions. *(PAS Report No. 322, The Language of Zoning)*

■ **unit** *(See **condominium unit; dwelling unit** definitions)*

■ **unnecessary hardship**   A hardship that is unnecessary in the sense that the preservation of the spirit and intent of this [ordinance or chapter] does not depend on the denial of the variance. *(Jefferson, Mo.)*

Arduous restrictions upon the uses of a particular property that are unique and distinct from that of adjoining property owners in the same zoning district. *(Coral Gables, Fla.)*

A hardship by reason of exceptional shape of a lot, exceptional topographic conditions, or other exceptional physical conditions of a parcel of land. Unnecessary hardship shall not include personal or financial hardship or any other hardship that is self-imposed. *(El Paso, Tex.)*

■ **unrelated individuals** *(See also **family**)*   Two or more individuals who are not related by blood, marriage, or adoption. For the purposes of this Chapter, "related

by blood" shall mean whole or half relation between a common ancestor or descendant, brother or sister, uncle or aunt, niece or nephew, or first cousin. *(Mankato, Minn.)*

■ **upholstering shop**   A business that repairs and replaces upholstery to household and office furnishings; does not include motor vehicle upholstering or repair. *(Hermosa Beach, Calif.)*

■ **upzoning** *(See also **cumulative zoning; downzoning**)*   Changing the zoning designation of an area to allow so-called less restrictive uses (e.g., from residential to commercial) or allowing higher densities. Its opposite is downzoning. *(PAS Report No. 322, The Language of Zoning)*

A change in the zoning for a particular area that results in higher residential densities. For example, a change from a zoning ordinance that requires 100 acres per dwelling to an ordinance that requires 25 acres per dwelling is an upzoning. *(American Farmland Trust)*

■ **urban**   Of, relating to, characteristic of, or constituting a city. Urban areas are generally characterized by moderate and higher density residential development (i.e., three or more dwelling units per acre), commercial development, and industrial development, as well as the availability of public services required for that development, specifically central water and sewer, an extensive road network, public transit, and other such services (e.g., safety and emergency response). Development not providing such services may be "non-urban" or "rural." *(California Planning Roundtable)*

All population and territory within the boundaries of urbanized areas and the urban portion of places outside of urbanized area that have a decennial census population of 2,500 or more. *(United States Census Bureau)*

■ **urban center**   An [area] of statewide importance; a large settlement that has a high intensity of population and mixed land uses, including industrial, commercial, residential, and cultural uses; the historical focus for growth in the major urban areas of [the state]. *(New Jersey State Plan)*

■ **urban design**    The attempt to give form, in terms of both beauty and function, to selected urban areas or to whole cities. Urban design is concerned with the location, mass, and design of various urban components and combines elements of urban planning, architecture, and landscape architecture. *(California Planning Roundtable)*

■ **urban forestry plan**    A five-year or more projection of urban forestry activities approved annually by a public authority, such as the city council or the office of public works, for tree planting programs, planting, or removal of horticulture products, beautification projects, and educational horticultural programs affecting property owned by the municipality. *(Springfield, Ill.)*

■ **urban fringe**    Land at the edge of an urban area usually made up of mixed agricultural and urban land uses. This is probably the most critical area within an urban area and requires adequate controls wisely administered by a coordinated effort of city and county officials. *(Iowa State University Extension Services)*

Surrounding the core area is the fringe, containing uses in different proportions, and at a lesser density. Higher density residential uses are intended to comprise a greater proportion of the total development in the fringe than in the core, with lower densities in the fringe. *(Aurora, Colo.)*

The closely settled territory adjacent to the central place(s) of an urbanized area. The census blocks that constitute the urban fringe generally have an overall population density of at least 1,000 people per square mile of land area. *(United States Census Bureau)*

■ **urban growth area (UGA)**    *(See also growth management)*    An area delineated in an adopted regional or county comprehensive plan [in accordance with goals, policies, and guidelines in the state land development plan], prepared pursuant to [ordinance or law section] within which urban development is encouraged by delineation of the area, compatible future land-use designations, and implementing actions in a local com-

prehensive plan, and outside of which urban development is discouraged. An urban growth area shall allow existing or proposed land uses at minimum densities and intensities sufficient to permit urban growth that is projected for the region or county for the succeeding 20-year period and existing or proposed urban services to adequately support that urban growth. *(APA's Growing Smart project)*

A line separating urban and rural areas, representing a predesignated limit to urban development and usually designed to protect open space, resource lands, or other natural amenities. It is important that areas needing protection are found within and outside the UGA. A growth boundary usually defines the limit within which the full range of urban services will be provided. No such services are provided beyond the growth boundary. The purpose is to promote compact urban development within and adjacent to existing urban areas so as to ensure efficient utilization of land resources and to facilitate the economic provision of urban services. *(Washington State Department of Community Development)*

■ **urban growth boundary (UGB)**    *(See also growth management)*    A perimeter drawn around an urban growth area. *(APA's Growing Smart project)*

The boundary or line marking the limit between the urban growth areas and other areas such as rural and resource areas where urban growth is not encouraged, as designated by the county in consultation with cities, under the requirements of the GMA. *(King County, Wash.)*

UGBs provide for an orderly and efficient transition from rural to urban land use. UGBs shall be established to identify and separate urbanizable land from rural land. Establishment and change of the boundaries shall be based upon considerations of the following factors: (1) Demonstrated need to accommodate lang-range urban population growth requirements consistent with LCDC (Land Conservation and Development Commission) goals; (2) Need for housing, employment opportunities, and livability; (3) Orderly and economic provi-

sion for public facilities and services; (4) Maximum efficiency of land uses within and on the fringe of the existing urban area; (5) Environmental, energy, economic, and social consequences; (6) Retention of agricultural land with four levels of priority; (7) Compatibility of the proposed urban uses with nearby agricultural activities. *(Oregon's State-wide Planning Goals)*

A boundary, sometimes parcel-specific, located to mark the outer limit beyond which urban development will not be allowed. It has the aim of discouraging urban sprawl by containing urban development during a specified period, and its location may be modified over time. *(California Planning Roundtable, which uses the term "urban limit line")*

■ **urban land use**    Residential, commercial, or industrial land use in areas where urban services are available. *(California Planning Roundtable)*

■ **urban place**    Any place with a decennial census population of 2,500 or more, whether incorporated or census designated, and any place regardless of population located within an urbanized area. Some urban places contain territory that is not designated as urban. *(United States Census Bureau)*

■ **urban renewal**    A governmental program generally aimed at the renovation of blighted urban areas, using public expenditures for replacing lesser economic uses with higher or more profitable uses. *(Handbook for Planning Commissioners in Missouri)*

■ **urban reserve**    An area outside of an urban service area but within an urban growth boundary, in which future development and extension of municipal services are contemplated but not imminent. *(California Planning Roundtable)*

■ **urban service area**    *(See also urban growth area (UGA); urban growth boundary (UGB))*    A defined area, not always coincidental with a municipality's corporate boundaries, that defines the geographical limits of government-supplied public facilities and services. *(Elbert County, Colo.)*

(1) An area in which urban services will be provided and outside of which such services will not be extended. (2) Developed, undeveloped, or agricultural land, either incorporated or unincorporated, within the sphere of influence of a city, which is served or will be served during the first five years of an adopted capital improvement program by urban facilities, utilities, and services. The boundary around an urban service area is called the "urban service area boundary" and is to be developed in cooperation with a city and adopted by a Local Agency Formation Commission (LAFCO). *(State of California)*

■ **urban services**    Utilities (such as water, gas, electricity, and sewer) and public services (such as police, fire, schools, parks, and recreation) provided to an urbanized or urbanizing area. *(California Planning Roundtable)*

■ **urbanized area**    An area consisting of a central place(s) and adjacent urban fringe that together have a minimum residential population of at least 50,000 people and generally an overall population density of at least 1,000 people per square mile of land area. *(United States Census Bureau)*

■ **use**

***Commentary:*** *We have opted to list here only those uses that we considered to be administrative. Actual land uses (e.g., accessory use; institutional use; etc.) are listed under the name of the use.*

Any purpose for which a lot, building, or other structure or a tract of land may be designated, arranged, intended, maintained, or occupied; or any activity, occupation, business, or operation carried on or intended to be carried on in a building or other structure or on a tract of land. *(Jefferson County, Colo.)*

The conduct of an activity or the performance of a function or operation, on a site or in a building or facility. *(Blue Springs, Mo.)*

Any functional, social, or technological activity that is imposed or applied to land or to structures on the land. *(Pine Bluff, Ark.)*

The employment or occupation of a building, structure, or land for a person's service, benefit, or enjoyment. *(Carmel, Ind.)*

■ **use, administrative**    A use permitted after receiving an administrative occupancy permit from the department of planning and development. Application for said permit shall be made on forms provided by the department. An administrative occupancy permit shall be granted by the department if the proposed use conforms to all applicable provisions of this chapter. *(Danville, Ill.)*

■ **use category**    A group of similar use types that are associated with each other to such an extent that they perform a specific land-use function. Use categories are: civic, commercial, essential public facilities, office/business, industrial, residential, resource, and utilities. *(Edgewood, Wash.)*

■ **use, change of**    Substitution of one thing for another specifically regarding use of land or use of a building. *(Sioux Falls, S.D.)*

Any alteration in the primary use of a lot for zoning purposes that may entail the need for additional parking or loading facilities. *(Columbus, Ohio)*

■ **use, conditional**    A use or occupancy of a structure, or a use of land, permitted only upon issuance of a conditional use permit and subject to the limitations and conditions specified therein. *(Belmont, Calif.)*

A use which, because of special problems of control the use presents, requires reasonable, but special, unusual and/or extraordinary limitations peculiar to the use for the protection of the public welfare and the integrity of the municipal land-use plan. *(Maple Grove, Minn.)*

A use that, because of special requirements or characteristics, may be allowed in a particular zoning district only after review by the commission and granting of conditional use approval imposing such conditions as necessary to make the use compatible with other uses permitted in the same zone or vicinity. Conditional uses are issued for uses of

land and may be transferable from one owner of the land to another. *(Boise City, Idaho)*

■ **use, conforming**    Any use of a structure or land that is a permitted or approved provisional or special use in the district in which the structure or land is situated and which conforms to the regulations of that district and all other regulations of this chapter. *(Champaign, Ill.)*

Any building or structure which: (a) complies with all the regulations of this ordinance or of any amendment hereto governing bulk for the zoning district in which such building or structure is located; or (b) is designed or intended for a conforming use. *(Gurnee, Ill., which uses the term "conforming building or structure")*

A building, or other structure, that is designed or intended for a conforming use and that complies with all the regulations of this title, or of any amendment hereto, governing use, lot size, building bulk, and off-street parking and loading for the zoning district in which such building or structure is located. *(Wheeling, Ill., which uses the term "conforming building or structure")*

■ **use, discontinued**    A use that is interrupted or in which there is a break in continuity regardless of the intent of the owner or operator. *(Island County, Wash.)*

■ **use, existing**    The use of a lot or structure at the time of the enactment of a zoning ordinance. *(Siskiyou County, Calif.)*

■ **use, illegal**    An activity or facility that does not enjoy a legal conforming or legal nonconforming status, as defined in the zoning regulations. A minor illegal use is an illegal use that can be legalized by any means other than by major variance. *(Oakland, Calif.)*

■ **use, incompatible**    A use or service that is incapable of direct association with certain other uses because it is contradictory, incongruous, or discordant. *(Gurnee, Ill.)*

■ **use, nonconforming**    A use that was valid when brought into existence, but by subsequent regulation becomes no longer conforming. This may be a structure, use, or parcel of land. *(Jefferson County, Colo.)*

A use that was valid when brought into existence but, by subsequent regulation, becomes no longer conforming. Nonconforming use is a generic term and includes (1) nonconforming structures (by virtue of size, type of construction, location on land, or proximity to other structures), (2) nonconforming use of a conforming building, (3) nonconforming use of a nonconforming building, and (4) nonconforming use of land. Thus, any use lawfully existing on any piece of property that is inconsistent with a new or amended General Plan, and that in turn is a violation of a zoning ordinance amendment subsequently adopted in conformance with the General Plan, will be a nonconforming use. Typically, nonconforming uses are permitted to continue for a designated period of time, subject to certain restrictions. *(California Planning Roundtable)*

A use that lawfully occupied a building or land on the effective date of this ordinance and that does not conform to the use regulations of the district in which it is located. *(Staunton, Va.)*

■ **use, nonconforming, legal** Areas lawfully occupied by a building or land use at the time this title or amendments thereto take effect, and which does not conform with the use regulations of the district in which it is located. *(Clark County, Nev.)*

■ **use, permitted** A use permitted in a district without the need for special administrative review and approval, upon satisfaction of the standards and requirements of this ordinance. *(Multnomah County,Ore.)*

Any use listed as a principal permitted use or as an accessory use. The term further includes a conditional use, as listed for the particular district, provided a conditional use permit is obtained. *(Temecula, Calif.)*

■ **use, principal** The primary use of any lot. *(Ann Arbor, Mich.)*

The main use to which the premises is devoted and the primary purpose for which the premises exists. *(Multnomah County County, Ore.)*

■ **use, public** A use by any agency or department of the city, county, state, or federal government. This shall also include public utilities or uses by any organization that receives funding either all or in part from any agency or department of the city, county, state, or federal government. This shall also include buildings and premises used in the operation of the public use. *(Pine Bluff, Ark.)*

Public parks, schools, and administrative, cultural, and service buildings not including public land or buildings devoted solely to the storage and maintenance of equipment and material. *(Rapid City, S.D.)*

■ **use, semipublic** Philanthropic and charitable uses, including YMCAs, YWCAs, Salvation Army, churches, and church-related institutions, orphanages, humane societies, private welfare organizations, nonprofit lodges and fraternal orders, Red Cross, and other general charitable institutions. This shall also include all buildings and premises used in the operation of the semipublic use. *(Pine Bluff, Ark.)*

■ **use, similar** A use that has the same characteristics as the specifically cited uses in terms of the following: trip generation and type of traffic, parking and circulation, utility demands, environmental impacts, physical space needs, and clientele. *(Las Vegas, Nev.)*

■ **use, special** A use that meets the intent and purpose of the zoning district but which requires the review and approval of the appropriate planning commission in order to ensure that any adverse impacts on adjacent uses, structures, or public services and facilities that may be generated by the use can be, and are, mitigated. *(Maui County, Hawaii)*

■ **use, temporary** Those land uses and structures that are needed or are in place for only short periods of time. *(Colorado Springs, Colo.)*

■ **use, transitional** A use, allowed in a transitional area, intended to create a gradual change in uses from industrial and commercial areas to residential areas. *(Multnomah County, Ore.)*

■ **utilities** Infrastructure services, including those in the Basic Utility Use category, and structures necessary to deliver those services. These services may be provided by a public or a private agency. Examples include water, sanitary sewer, electricity, natural gas, and telephone. *(Portland, Ore.)*

All lines and facilities related to the provision, distribution, collection, transmission, or disposal of water, storm and sanitary sewage, oil, gas, power, information, telecommunication and telephone cable, and includes facilities for the generation of electricity. *(Renton, Wash.)*

■ **utilities, communication utility facilities** *(See also **telecommunications** definitions)* Facilities that provide for the transmission, transfer, and distribution of telephone service and related activities that are not a minor or major utility facility. Facilities include, but shall not be limited to, communications exchanges, mini-huts, maxi-huts and other similar facilities. *(El Paso, Tex.)*

■ **utilities, large** Large-scale facilities serving the entire city or region, such as microwave substations, radio/television antennas, 230-kv power transmission lines, natural gas transmission lines, water storage tanks and reservoirs, major water transmission lines or sewer collectors and interceptors over 30 inches in diameter, solid waste disposal or processing, sewage or wastewater treatment plants, and generating facilities. *(Renton, Wash.)*

Uses or structures providing utility services that have potential major impact by virtue of their appearance, noise, size, traffic generation, or other operational characteristics, which include, but which are not limited to, 46-kilovolt transmission substations, power plants, base yards, water and wastewater treatment facilities, but not including private, individual cesspools, septic tanks, or individual household water supplies. *(Maui County, Hawaii, which uses the term "major utility facilities")*

■ **utilities, medium** Moderate-scale facilities serving a subarea of the city, including power lines, water transmission lines, wireless base stations, sewer collectors and pump stations, subregional switching stations (115 kv), and similar structures. *(Renton, Wash.)*

■ **utilities, public** Any person, firm, corporation, municipal department, or board duly authorized to furnish, and furnishing under state or municipal regulations to the public, electricity, gas, steam, communication, telegraph, transportation, or water. *(Rapid City, S.D.)*

The use of land for public utility purposes by an entity providing pipeline, gas, electrical, telephone, telegraph, water or sewage service that is subject to the jurisdiction of the California Public Utilities Commission. "Public utility" also includes the use of land for utility purposes, whether or not owned, controlled, or operated by a public entity, whose services are performed for or commodities delivered to the public or any portion thereof. Private energy production, transmission relay, repeater, translator, radio and television towers and equipment and cable television facilities are also considered public utilities. "Public utility" does not include airports or television, radio or community television antenna system administration offices or other types of administrative offices or maintenance yards. *(Shasta Lake, Calif.)*

■ **utilities, small** Small-scale facilities serving a local area, including power lines, water and sewer lines, storm drainage facilities, transformers, pump stations and hydrants, switching boxes, and other structures normally found in a street right-of-way to serve adjacent properties. *(Renton, Wash.)*

■ **utilities, water and wastewater utility facilities** Water and wastewater utility facilities shall include facilities providing service, maintenance, or repair of essential public utilities to one or more developments including, but not limited to, wells, pumping stations, boosters, reservoirs, repeaters, water storage tanks, lift stations, regulators, and other similar facilities; and

which are not a minor or major utility facility. *(El Paso, Tex.)*

■ **utility corridors** Rights-of-way or easements for utility lines on either publicly or privately owned property. *(California Planning Roundtable)*

■ **utility district, underground** An area . . . within which poles, overhead wires, and associated overhead structures are prohibited. *(Del Mar, Calif.)*

■ **utility pole** A structure which is owned by a governmental agency or utility company and which is used to support illumination devices or lines and other equipment carrying electricity or communications. *(Minnetonka, Minn.)*

■ **utility poles and line** *(See also **transmission lines**)* The poles, structures, wire, aerial cables and related facilities used in the distribution and transmission of electricity, telephone, data, telegraph, radio, television, or telecommunications. *(Glendale, Ariz.)*

■ **utility, private or public** Any closely regulated agency which, under public franchise or ownership, or under certificate of convenience and necessity, provides the public with electricity, gas, heat, steam, communication, rail transportation, water, sewage collection, or other similar service. *(Temecula, Calif.)*

■ **utility, public facility** A building or structure used or intended to be used by any public utility, including, but not limited to any gas treatment plant reservoir, tank or other storage facility, water treatment plant, well, reservoir, tank, or other storage facility, electric generating plant, distribution, or transmission substation, telephone switching or other communications plant, earth station, or other receiving or transmission facility, any storage yard for public utility equipment or vehicles, and any parking lot for parking vehicles or automobiles to serve a public utility. *(Redondo Beach, Calif.)*

■ **utility room** A room or space, located other than in the basement, specifically designed and constructed to house any home utilities, such as major home appliances (furnace, water heater, pump). *(St. Charles, Mo.)*

■ **utility services** The generation, transmission, or distribution of electricity, gas, or steam; water, irrigation, and sanitary systems used for the collection and disposal of garbage, sewage, and other wastes by means of destroying or processing these materials; transportation systems; and communication or other similar services. *(Maui County, Hawaii)*

A service essential to the health, safety, and general welfare of the public, such as the generation, transmission, and/or distribution of electricity, gas, steam, communications, and water; the collection and treatment of sewage and solid waste; the collection, storage or diversion of surface waters from land; and the provision of mass transportation. *(El Paso, Tex., which uses the term "public utility service")*

■ **utility services, major** Services of a regional nature that normally entail the construction of new buildings or structures such as generating plants and sources, electrical switching facilities, and stations or substations, community waste water treatment plants, and similar facilities. Included in this definition are also electric, gas, and other utility transmission lines of a regional nature that are not otherwise reviewed and approved by the state All overhead service, distribution and transmission lines are included in this definition. *(Blacksburg, Va. )*

■ **utility services, minor** Services that are necessary to support development within the immediate vicinity and that involve only minor structures. Included in this use type are small facilities such as transformers, relay and booster devices, and well, water, and sewer pump stations. Also included are wireless communication antennas attached to an existing building or structure, including but not limited to utility poles, signs, broadcasting or communication facilities, and water towers, and that do not increase the height of such building or structure by more than 10 feet. *(Blacksburg, Va. )*

■ **vacant**    Lands or buildings that are not actively used for any purpose. *(California Planning Roundtable)*

■ **vacation**    The termination of, or termination of interest in, an easement, right-of-way, or public dedication of land. *(Unalaska, Alaska)*

■ **vanpool** *(See also **transportation demand management (TDM)**)*    A vehicle carrying seven or more persons commuting together to and from work on a regular basis, usually in a vehicle with a seating arrangement designed to carry seven to 15 adult passengers, and on a prepaid subscription basis. *(Hermosa Beach, Calif.)*

A vehicle occupied be seven to 15 people traveling together for their commute trip that results in the elimination of at least one motor vehicle trip. A vanpool counts as zero vehicle trips. *(Thurston County, Wash.)*

■ **variance**    A departure from any provision of the zoning requirements for a specific parcel, except use, without changing the zoning ordinance or the underlying zoning of the parcel. A variance usually is granted only upon demonstration of hardship based on the peculiarity of the property in relation to other properties in the same zone district. *(California Planning Roundtable)*

Permission to depart from this development code when, because of special circumstances applicable to the property, strict application of the provisions of this development code deprives such property of privileges enjoyed by other property in the vicinity that is under identical zoning. *(Temecula, Calif.)*

An adjustment in the application of the specific regulations of this title to a particular piece of property, which property, because of special circumstances applicable to it, is deprived of privileges commonly enjoyed by other properties in the same vicinity and zone and which adjustment remedies such disparity in privileges. *(Ocean Shores, Wash.)*

*Commentary: There are two types of zoning variances–area variances and use variances. An area variance allows a deviation from the dimensional (i.e., height, bulk, yard) requirements of the ordinance. A use variance authorizes the property owner to establish a use of land that is otherwise prohibited in that zoning district. Use variances are not an adequate substitute for the rezoning process and should generally not be permitted. Indeed, many states do not allow them. Others require more substantial proof of unnecessary hardship for use variances than for area variances.*

■ **variety store**    A retail store that sells a wide variety of relatively small and inexpensive items. *(Valdez, Alaska)*

■ **vegetated shallows**    Permanently inundated areas that under normal conditions support communities of rooted aquatic vegetation. *(Yakima County, Wash.)*

■ **vegetative buffer**    *(See also **buffer**)* An area extending landward from the ordinary high-water mark of a lake or stream and/or from the edge of wetland that provides adequate soil conditions and native vegetation for the performance of the basic functional properties of a stream corridor and other hydrolog-ically related critical areas. . . . *(Yakima County, Wash.)*

■ **vegetative cover**    Grasses, shrubs, trees, and other vegetation which hold and stabilize soils. *(Grand Traverse County, Mich.)*

■ **vehicle** *(See also **motor vehicle**)* Every device in, upon, or by which any person or property is or may be transported upon a highway, except devices moved exclusively by human power or used exclusively upon stationary rails or tracks. *(El Paso, Tex.)*

■ **vehicle emission standard**    The maximum amount of pollutant legally permitted to be discharged from a single source, either mobile or stationary. *(California Planning Roundtable)*

■ **vehicle emission testing facility**    A specifically designated lot or parcel upon which a testing facility maintains a permanent business office. Designation of the lot or parcel for vehicle emission testing facility would allow this area to be used for testing of vehicles for compliance with air-quality standards. The entire lot or parcel containing the use as approved by the village board would then be required to conform to all applicable zoning district standards and other legislative regulations. *(Wheeling, Ill.)*

■ **vehicle, single-occupancy**    A motor vehicle occupied by one employee for commute purposes, excluding motorcycles, unipeds, and other two-wheeled vehicles. *(Alameda County, Calif.)*

■ **vending carts** *(See also **stand**)* Any box or container with wheels that is not propelled or moved by an engine. Trailers of any type are not vending carts. *(Jefferson County, Colo.)*

■ **vending machine**    Any unattended self-service device that, upon insertion of a coin, coins, or token, or by similar means, dispenses anything of value including food, beverage, goods, wares, merchandise or services. *(Newport Beach, Calif.)*

■ **vending machine, reverse**    An automated mechanical device that accepts at least one or more types of empty beverage containers, including but not limited to aluminum cans and glass or plastic bottles and that issues a cash refund or a redeemable credit, provided that the entire process is enclosed within the machine. A reverse vending machine may be designed to accept more than one container at a time, paying by weight instead of by container. *(Aurora, Colo.)*

■ **vendor stand** *(See stand)*

■ **vessel, derelict**    Any vessel moored or otherwise located in the boundaries of the port or at port facilities that is forsaken, abandoned, deserted, or cast away; or that by appearance gives evidence of being forsaken, abandoned, deserted, or cast away, or that is unsound, unseaworthy, and unfit for its trade or occupation, and that by any substantial evidence of neglect may be considered abandoned. *(Unalaska, Alaska, which uses the term "derelict")*

■ **vested property right**    The right to undertake and complete the development and use of property under the terms and conditions of a development agreement. Unless otherwise specified in the development agreement, a property right shall remain vested for a period of three years. *(Boulder County, Colo.)*

■ **vested right**    A right that has become fixed. Vested rights are often established by showing that some development permit has been obtained and substantial construction started on the project. *(Handbook for Planning Commissioners in Missouri)*

A right that has been legally established and cannot be revoked by subsequent conditions or changes in law without due process of law. *(Temecula, Calif.)*

■ **vestibule**    A passage, hall or room between the outer door and the interior of a building. Also known as a lobby. *(Perryville, Mo.)*

■ **veterinary clinic** *(See animal hospital)*

■ **vibration**    A motion that repeatedly reverses itself. A continuously reversing motion, such as is produced by a machine (for example, a compressor or a fan) is known as steady-state vibration.

Vibration may also result from suddenly applied force that produces a reversing motion of decreasing intensity. Such vibrations are known as impact vibrations and are produced by forge hammers, punch presses, and other impact machinery. *(Aurora, Ill.)*

The periodic displacement of earth caused by an oscillating movement, measured in inches. *(Gurnee, Ill.)*

■ **video rental store**    An establishment primarily engaged in the retail rental or lease of video tapes, films, CD-ROMs, laser discs, electronic games, cassettes, or other electronic media (pictured above). Sales of film, video tapes, laser discs, CD-ROMs, and electronic merchandise associated with VCRs, video cameras, and electronic games are permitted accessory uses. *(Prince William County, Va.)*

■ **view**    A range of sight including pleasing vistas or prospects or scenes (pictured below). Views include, but are not limited to, the sight of geologic features, bays, oceans, skylines, bridges, and distant cities. *(Contra Costa County, Calif.)*

■ **view corridor**    The line of sight identified as to height, width, and distance of an observer looking toward an object of significance to the community (e.g., ridgeline, river, historic building, etc.); the route that directs the viewer's attention. *(California Planning Roundtable)*

■ **view-obscuring vegetation**    A screen of live plant material that is opaque from the ground to a height of at least six feet, intended to exclude visual contact between uses and to create a strong impression of spacial separation during all seasons of the year. At maturity, the screen

shall be considered to be view obscuring if there are no openings of greater than one square foot. *(Fayetteville, Ark.)*

■ **view protection regulations**    Regulations that protect the view of or from particular points, usually via height limitations. *(PAS Report No. 322, The Language of Zoning)*

■ **viewshed**    The area within view from a defined observation point. *(California Planning Roundtable)*

■ **village** *(See hamlet; town)*    A small, compact center of predominantly residential character but with a core of mixed-use commercial, residential, and community services. It often incorporates local-scale economic and social functions that are integrated with housing. A village typically has a recognizable center, discrete physical boundaries, and a pedestrian scale and orientation. This term does not necessarily refer to the form of incorporation of a municipality and is often smaller than a municipality. *(New Jersey State Plan)*

■ **village center** *(See town center)*

■ **visible**    Likely to be noticed by a person of average height walking on a street or sidewalk. *(Newport Beach, Calif.)*

■ **visible feature**    A feature that can be seen on the ground, such as a street or road, railroad track, power line, stream, shoreline, fence, ridge, or cliff. *(United States Census Bureau)*

■ **vista** *(See view)*

■ **visual impact**    A modification or change that could be incompatible with the scale, form, texture, or color of the existing natural or man-made landscape. *(Albuquerque N. Mex)*

■ **vocational school** *(See trade/business school)*

■ **volume-to-capacity ratio**    *(See also street capacity)*    A measure of the operating capacity of a roadway or intersection, in terms of the number of vehicles passing through, divided by the number of vehicles that theoretically could pass through when the roadway or intersection is operating at its designed capacity. Abbreviated as "v/c." At

a v/c ratio of 1.0, the roadway or intersection is operating at capacity. If the ratio is less than 1.0, the traffic facility has additional capacity. Although ratios slightly greater than 1.0 are possible, it is more likely that the peak hour will elongate into a "peak period." *(California Planning Roundtable)*

■ **wall** A constructed solid barrier of concrete, stone, brick, tile, wood, or similar type of material that closes, marks, or borders a field, yard, or lot, and that limits visibility and restricts the flow of air and light. *(Maui County, Hawaii)*

A solid fence. *(San Diego, Calif.)*

Any structure or device forming a physical barrier that is constructed so that the vertical surface is closed, thus preventing the passage of light, air, and vision in a horizontal plane. The material of which a wall is constructed may be masonry, brick, concrete, metal, wood, or other similar materials. Measurement of height shall be from the high ground. *(El Paso, Tex., which uses the term "screening wall")*

■ **wall, wing** An architectural feature in excess of six feet in height that is a continuation of a building wall projecting beyond the exterior walls of a building. *(Palm Desert, Calif.)*

■ **warehouse** Facilities characterized by extensive warehousing, frequent heavy trucking activity, open storage of material, or nuisances such as dust, noise, and odors, but not involved in manufacturing or production. *(Baton Rouge, La.)*

A use engaged in storage, wholesale, and distribution of manufactured products, supplies, and equipment, excluding bulk storage of materials that are inflammable or explosive or that present hazards or conditions commonly recognized as offensive. *(California Planning Roundtable)*

■ **warehouse, residential storage** *(See also self-service storage facility)* An enclosed storage facility containing independent, fully enclosed bays that are leased to individuals exclusively for long-term storage of their household goods or personal property. *(Blue Springs, Mo.)*

■ **warehouse, retail** An off-price or wholesale retail/warehouse establishment exceeding 70,000 square feet of gross floor area and offering a full range of general merchandise to the public. *(Redondo Beach, Calif.)*

■ **warehouse, retail, specialty** An off-price or wholesale retail/warehouse establishment exceeding 30,000 square feet of gross floor area and offering a limited range of merchandise, serving both wholesale and retail customers. *(Redondo Beach, Calif.)*

■ **waste, bulky** *(See also white goods)* Items the large size of which precludes or complicates their handling by normal collection, processing, or disposal methods. *(Siskiyou County, Calif.)*

■ **waste, construction/demolition** Building materials and rubble resulting from construction, remodeling, repair, and demolition operations. *(Siskiyou County, Calif.)*

■ **waste, domestic** Wastes originating from bathrooms, kitchens, showers, toilets, or other sanitary facilities, public or private, regardless of the degree of treatment. *(State of Vermont)*

■ **waste, hazardous** *(See hazardous waste)*

■ **waste, yard** Plant clippings, prunings, and other discarded materials from yards and gardens. *(Siskiyou County, Calif.)*

■ **wastewater** Water carrying waste from domestic, commercial, or industrial facilities together with other waters which may inadvertently enter the sewer system through infiltration and inflow. *(Edgewood, Wash.)*

■ **wastewater, domestic** *(See also greywater)* The liquid and waterborne wastes derived from the ordinary living processes in a dwelling unit, said wastes being of such character as to permit satisfactory disposal, without special treatment, into a public sewer or by means of a private disposal system. *(San Diego, Calif.)*

■ **wastewater, industrial** All wastewater excluding domestic wastewater to include all wastewater from any producing, manufacturing, processing, institutional, commercial, service, agricultural, or other operation. These may also include wastes of human origin similar to domestic wastewater. *(San Diego, Calif.)*

■ **wastewater irrigation** The process by which wastewater that has undergone appropriate treatment is used to irrigate land. *(California Planning Roundtable)*

■ **wastewater treatment plant** The facility or group of units used for the treatment of industrial or domestic wastewater for sewer systems and for the reduction and handling of solids and gases removed from such wastes, whether or not such facility or group of units is discharging into state waters. Wastewater treatment plant specifically excludes and facility or group of units used for pretreatment, treatment, or handling of industrial water, wastewaters, reuse waters, and wastes which are not discharged into state waters. *(Boulder County, Colo.)*

■ **watchman dwelling** *(See caretaker's residence)*

■ **water bodies** Permanently or temporarily flooded lands which may lie below the deepwater boundary of wetlands. Water depth is such that water, and not the air, is the principal medium in which prevalent organisms live, whether or not they are attached to the bottom. The bottom may sometimes be considered nonsoil or the water may be too deep or otherwise unable to support emergent vegetation. Water bodies include rivers, streams, creeks, sloughs, drainageways, lakes, and ponds. *(Portland, Ore.)*

■ **water-dependent use** Referring to uses or portions of a use that cannot exist in any other location and is dependent on the water by reason of the intrinsic nature of its operations. Examples of water-dependent uses may include ship cargo terminal loading areas, ferry and passenger terminals, barge loading facilities, ship building and dry docking, marinas, aquaculture, float plane facilities, and sewer outfalls. *(Renton, Wash.)*

■ **water-enjoyment use** Referring to a recreational use or other use facilitating public access to the shoreline as a primary characteristic of the use; or a use that provides for recreational use or aesthetic enjoyment of the shoreline for a substantial number of people as a general characteristic of the use and which, through the location, design, and operation, ensures the public's ability to enjoy the physical and aesthetic qualities of the shoreline. In order to qualify as a water-enjoyment use, the use must be open to the general public and the shoreline-oriented space within the project must be devoted to the specific aspects of the use that fosters shoreline enjoyment. Primary water-enjoyment uses may include, but are not limited to, parks, piers and other improvements facilitating public access to the shorelines of the state; and general water-enjoyment uses may include, but are not limited to, restaurants, museums, aquariums, scientific/ecological reserves, resorts/hotels, and mixed-use commercial/office, provided that such uses conform to the above water-enjoyment specifications and the provisions of the Shoreline Master Program. *(Renton, Wash.)*

■ **water-related use** Use or portion of a use that is not intrinsically dependent on a waterfront location, but whose economic viability is dependent upon a waterfront location because: A. A functional requirement for a waterfront location such as the arrival or shipment of materials by water or the need for large quantities of water, or B. The use provides a necessary service supportive of the water-dependent commercial activities and the proximity of the use to its customers makes its services less expensive and/or more convenient. Examples include manufacturers of ship parts large enough that transportation becomes a significant factor in the products cost, professional services serving primarily water-dependent activities, and storage of water-transported foods. Examples of water-related uses may include warehousing of goods transported by water, seafood processing plants, hydroelectric generating plants, gravel storage when transported by barge, oil refineries where transport is by tanker, and log storage. . . . *(Renton, Wash.)*

■ **water supply system** The system of pipes, structures, and facilities through which a water supply is obtained, treated, and sold or distributed for human consumption or household use, if such system has at least 15 service connections or regularly serves at least 25 households. *(Boulder County, Colo.)*

■ **water supply system, individual** The water service pipe, the water distribution pipes and the necessary connecting pipes, fittings, control valves, and all appurtenances in or adjacent to the building or premises. *(Gurnee, Ill.)*

■ **water supply system, public** All property involved in a water utility, including land, water sources, collection systems, dams and hydraulic structures, distribution systems, and other appurtenances, pumping stations, treatment works, and general properties, or any parts thereof. *(Gurnee, Ill.)*

■ **water table** The upper limit of the portion of the soil that is completely saturated with water. The seasonal high-water table is the highest level to which the soil is saturated, as may be indicated by mottling (soil color patterns). *(Illinois Department of Public Health)*

The upper surface of the zone of saturation. *(State of Vermont)*

■ **water taxi** *(See ferry and excursion boats and water taxis)*

■ **water taxi station** The provision of passenger loading and unloading facilities from water craft. Ticket purchasing, restaurants, and retail stores shall be permitted as accessory activities if the facility is located in a district that permits those uses. *(Nashville and Davidson County, Tenn.)*

■ **water treatment plant** The facility or facilities within the water supply system which can alter the physical, chemical, or bacteriological quality of the water. *(Boulder County, Colo.)*

■ **watercourse** Natural or once naturally flowing (perennially or intermittently) water including rivers, streams, and creeks. Includes natural waterways that have been channelized, but does not include manmade channels, ditches, and underground drainage and sewage systems. *(California Planning Roundtable)*

A channel in which a flow of water occurs, either continuously or intermittently, and in the latter, with some degree of regularity. Such flow must be in a definite direction and cover a prescribed area. Watercourses may be either natural or artificial, and both may occur either on the surface or underground. *(Naperville, Ill.)*

■ **watercourse, artificial** A surface or underground watercourse constructed by man. *(Naperville, Ill.)*

■ **watercourse, natural** A surface or underground watercourse created by natural forces and conditions. *(Naperville, Ill.)*

■ **watercourse, underground** A geological formation which contains water moving in a known direction and defined channel. *(Naperville, Ill.)*

■ **waterfront** The land/water edge and the immediately adjacent property providing access to it. *(Rock Hall, Md.)*

Land or section of town/city fronting on a body of water. *(Green Bay, Wis.)*

■ **waterfront lot** A lot any portion of which is offshore of or abuts upon the ordinary high-water mark or mean high-water mark. *(Seattle, Wash.)*

■ **waterfront, marine-boat zone**  Regulates waterfront development involving a mixture of water-oriented uses–personal and tourist pleasure boating, and commercial fishing from boats, not ships, light-industrial in character; and land-based intense commercial and recreational uses and boat-related services and sales where the potential for development attracts the public for its nautical ambience and amenity. (The Zoning Report)

■ **waterfront, port-ship zone**  Regulates development on a waterfront involving the transfer of freight and cargo between sea- and river-going ships, and may be a port of call for passenger ships; the zone is heavy industrial in character. (The Zoning Report)

■ **waters**  All surface waters, including all waters of the territorial sea, tidewaters, all inland waters of any river, stream, brook, pond or lake, and wetlands. (Newport, R.I.)

■ **waters of the [jurisdiction]**  Those waters including: 1. All open, free, nontidal, waters, such as lakes, ponds, rivers, streams, and canals. 2. All freshwater wetlands. (Southwest Florida Management District)

■ **watershed**  The total area above a given point on a watercourse that contributes water to its flow; the entire region drained by a waterway or watercourse that drains into a lake, or reservoir. (California Planning Roundtable)

A land area, also known as a drainage area, which collects precipitation and contributes runoff to a receiving body of water or point along a watercourse. (Grand Traverse County, Mich.)

■ **watershed-based zoning**  Achieves watershed protection goals by creating a watershed development plan, using zoning as the basis (flexible density and subdivision layout specifications), that falls within the range of density and imperviousness allowable for the watershed to prevent environmental impacts. Watershed-based zoning usually employs a mixture of zoning practices. (Smart Growth Network)

■ **waterway**  Any body of water, including any creek, canal, river, lake or bay, or any other body of water, natural or artificial, except a swimming pool or ornamental pool located on a single lot. (Rock Hall, Md.)

■ **waterway setback**  A building setback of 50 feet from the bulkhead line or ordinary high-water mark whichever provides the greater landward distance. (Green Bay, Wisc.)

■ **way**  A street, alley, or other thoroughfare or easement permanently established for passage of persons or vehicles. (Rapid City, S.D.)

■ **wedding chapel, commercial**  An establishment that primarily provides the facilities and services for weddings on a commercial basis. This definition does not include churches and similar congregations where weddings are an ancillary use. (Hermosa Beach, Calif.)

■ **well**  A hole or shaft sunk into the earth to tap an underground supply of water. (Schaumburg, Ill.)

■ **wellfield**  A tract of land that contains a number of existing or proposed wells for supplying water as specified in the wellfield protection maps. (Broward County, Fla.)

*Commentary*: *This definition and many others related to wellfields and the topic of wellhead protection can be found in PAS Report No. 457/458, A Guide to Wellhead Protection.*

■ **wellfield area of contribution**  Area of the aquifer where groundwater flow is diverted to a pumping well due to a lowering of the water table. (Connecticut Department of Environmental Protection)

■ **wellfield recharge area**  The area from which groundwater flows directly to the wellfield area of contribution. (Connecticut Department of Environmental Protection)

■ **wellhead protection area**  The critical portion of a three-dimensional zone surrounding a public well or well field, through which water will move towards and reach such well or well field. (New Shoreham, R.I.)

■ **wetland**  Those areas that are inundated and saturated by surface or groundwater at a frequency and duration sufficient to support, and that under normal circumstances do support a prevalence of vegetation typically adapted for life in saturated soil conditions, including swamps, marshes, bogs, and similar areas. (Bucks County, Pa.)

■ **wetland, artificially created**  Wetlands created from non-wetland sites through purposeful, legally authorized human action, such as irrigation and drainage ditches, grass-lined swales, canals, detention facilities, wastewater treatment facilities, farm ponds, and landscape amenities. (Redmond, Wash.)

■ **wetland buffer or wetland buffer zones**  Areas that surround and protect a wetland from adverse impacts to its functions and values. (Renton, Wash.)

■ **wetland, coastal**  Any salt marsh bordering on the tidal waters of this state, whether or not the tide waters reach the littoral areas through natural or artificial water courses, and such uplands contiguous thereto, but extending no more than 50 yards inland therefrom, as the director shall deem reasonably necessary to protect those salt marshes. (Newport, R.I.)

■ **wetland compensation project**  Actions necessary to replace project-induced wetland and wetland buffer losses, including land acquisition, planning, construction plans, monitoring, and contingency actions. (Renton, Wash.)

■ **wetland compensatory mitigation**  Replacing project-induced wetland losses or impacts, and includes, but is not limited to, wetlands restoration and creation. (Renton, Wash.)

■ **wetland creation**  Actions performed to intentionally establish a wetland at a site where it did not formerly exist. (Renton, Wash.)

■ **wetland, disturbed**  Wetlands meeting the following criteria: (1) characterized by hydrologic isolation or hydrologic alterations such as diking, channelization, and/or outlet modification; and (2) with severe soils alterations such as the presence of large amounts of fill, soil removal, and/or compaction of soils. *(Renton, Wash.)*

■ **wetland, emergent** A regulated wetland with at least 30 percent of the surface area covered by erect, rooted herbaceous vegetation as the uppermost vegetative strata. *(Renton, Wash.)*

■ **wetland enhancement** Actions performed to improve the functioning of an existing wetland but that do not increase the area of the wetland. *(Renton, Wash.)*

■ **wetland, forested** A vegetation community with at least 20 percent of the surface area covered by woody vegetarian (trees) greater than 20 feet high. *(Renton, Wash.)*

■ **wetland, freshwater** Includes, but is not limited to, marshes; swamps; bogs; ponds; rivers; river and stream floodplains and banks; areas subject to flooding or storm flowage; emergent or submergent plant communities in any body of fresh water including rivers or streams and that area of land within 50 feet of the edge of any bog, marsh, swamp, or pond. *(Newport, R.I.)*

Freshwater swamps, marshes, bogs, and similar areas, other than forested wetlands, which are: (1) of 10 or more contiguous acres; or of less than 10 contiguous acres and adjacent to a surface water body, excluding any river, stream, or brook such that in a natural state, the combined surface area is in excess of 10 acres; and (2) inundated or saturated by surface or ground water at a frequency and a duration sufficient to support, and which under normal circumstances do support, a prevalence of wetland vegetation typically adapted for life in saturated soils. Freshwater wetlands may contain small stream channels or inclusions of land that do not conform to the criteria of this definition. *(Gorham, Maine)*

■ **wetland, in-kind compensation** To replace wetlands with substitute wetlands whose characteristics closely approximate those destroyed or degraded by a regulated activity. *(Renton, Wash.)*

■ **wetland, isolated** Those regulated wetlands that are: (1) outside of and not contiguous to any 100-year floodplain of a lake, river, or stream; and (2) with no contiguous hydric soil or hydrophytic vegetation between the wetland and any surface water. *(Renton, Wash.)*

■ **wetland margin** Transitional area extending from the outer limit of the wetland. *(Bucks County, Pa.)*

■ **wetland, newly emerging** (1) Wetlands occurring on top of fill materials; and (2) Wetlands characterized by emergent vegetation, low plant species richness, and used minimally by wildlife. *(Renton, Wash.)*

■ **wetland, nontidal** *(See wetland)*

■ **wetland, off-site compensation** To replace wetlands away from the site on which a wetland has been impacted by a regulated activity. *(Renton, Wash.)*

■ **wetland, on-site compensation** To replace wetlands at or adjacent to the site on which a wetland has been impacted by a regulated activity. *(Renton, Wash.)*

■ **wetland restoration** Actions performed to re-establish wetland functional characteristics and processes that have been lost by alterations, activities, or catastrophic events within an area that no longer meets the definition of a wetland. *(Renton, Wash.)*

■ **wetland, scrub-shrub** A regulated wetland with at least 30 percent of its surface area covered by woody vegetation less than 20 feet high at the uppermost strata. *(Renton, Wash.)*

■ **wetland, tidal** *(See wetland, coastal)*

■ **wharf** *(See also dock; pier)* Any structure built or maintained for the purpose of providing a berth place for vessels. *(Riverhead, N.Y.)*

■ **white goods** *(See also waste, bulky)* Inoperative and discarded refrigerators, ranges, water heaters, freezers, and other similar domestic and commercial large appliances. *(Alamance County, N.C.)*

■ **wholesale establishment** An establishment or place of business primarily engaged in selling and/or distributing merchandise to retailers; to industrial, commercial, institutional, or professional business users, or to other wholesalers; or acting as agents or brokers and buying merchandise for, or selling merchandise to, such individuals or companies. This is not considered a general commercial use. *(Santa Monica, Calif.)*

■ **wholesale establishment with warehouse** The display, storage, and sale of goods to other firms for resale, as well as activities involving significant movement and storage of products or equipment, including truck terminal or bus servicing facilities, motor freight transportation, moving and storage facilities, warehousing, and storage activities. *(Martin County, Fla.)*

■ **wilderness areas** Uncultivated and unimproved areas that are not readily accessible. *(California Planning Roundtable)*

■ **wildlife** Animals or plants existing in their natural habitats. *(California Planning Roundtable)*

■ **wildlife habitat** *(See also habitat protection area; preserve)* An area characterized by wildlife that forage, nest, spawn, or migrate through in search of food or shelter. *(Renton, Wash.)*

Lands that contain significant food, water, or cover for native terrestrial and aquatic species of animals. Examples include forests, fields, riparian areas, wetlands, and water bodies. *(Portland, Ore., which uses the term "fish and wildlife habitat areas")*

Areas that, because of climate, soils, vegetation, relationship to water, and other physical properties, have been identified as of critical importance to maintenance of wildlife species. *(Yakima County, Wash.)*

■ **wildlife refuge** *(See also habitat protection area; preserve)* An area maintained in a natural state for the preservation of both animal and plant life. *(California Planning Roundtable)*

■ **wind energy conversion system (WECS)** A machine that converts the kinetic energy in the wind into a usable form (commonly known as a wind turbine or windmill). The WECS includes all parts of the system except the tower and the transmission equipment. *(California Energy Commission)*

A machine by which mechanical energy supplied by the wind is changed to electric energy. *(Boulder County, Colo., which uses the term "wind-powered electric generator")*

■ **wine-tasting room** A facility in which wine products grown or processed on the owner's property may be tasted and sold. *(Merced, Calif.)*

■ **working waterfront** *(See waterfront definitions)*

■ **workplace** The place of employment, base of operation, or predominant location of an employee. *(Alameda County, Calif.)*

■ **workplace use** The combination of a variety of businesses, from office to research and development to light industry to warehousing, located in structures built with open floor plans, so as to leave most interior improvements to the tenants to design to their needs. *(California Planning Roundtable)*

■ **wrecker service** *(See motor vehicle wrecker service)*

■ **xeriscaping** *(See also landscaping definitions)* A set of garden design and landscape maintenance principles that promote good horticultural practices and efficient use of water. The term xeriscape is a registered trademark of the National Xeriscape Council and means water-conserving, drought-tolerant landscaping. *(Oviedo, Fla.)*

Landscaping characterized by the use of vegetation that is drought-tolerant or a low water use in character. *(Temecula, Calif.)*

■ **yacht, boat, and beach clubs** Institutional uses classified as either private clubs or community clubs that consist of structures and related grounds and/or moorage used for social and recreational purposes related to pleasure boating and/or swimming, the use of which is primarily restricted to members and their guests. *(Seattle, Wash.)*

■ **yachting organization** The crew, support staff, and families of a yacht temporarily housed in the city for the

America's Cup Race, any race sponsored by a local yacht club, organized by a national sailing organization, including related training. *(Newport, R.I.)*

■ **yard** An open space at grade between a building and the adjoining lot lines, unoccupied and unobstructed by any portion of a structure from the ground upward, except as otherwise provided herein. In measuring a yard for the purpose of determining the width of a side yard, the depth of a front yard, or the depth of the rear yard, the minimum horizontal distance between the lot line and the main building shall be used. *(Jefferson County, Colo.)*

An open space, on a lot with a building and bounded on one or more sides by such building, such space being unoccupied and unobstructed from 30 inches above the ground upward, except as otherwise specified in the district. A yard satisfying the yard requirement for one building shall not satisfy the yard requirement for another building. *(Multnomah, Ore.)*

such yard is the shortest horizontal distance between the front lot line or proposed front street line and the nearest point of the building or any enclosed portion thereof. For a corner lot in a residential zone defined by two street lines connected by a third line having a length of less than 50 feet (commonly known as a "truncation"), the front yard must be measured from the front lot line, not from the truncation line. *(Montgomery County, Md.)*

■ **yard, interior side** A side yard located immediately adjacent to another zoning lot or to an alley separating such side yard from another zoning lot. *(PAS Report No. 322, The Language of Zoning)*

■ **yard measurement** In measuring a yard, the building line shall be deemed to mean a line parallel to the lot line drawn through the point of a building or the point of a group of buildings nearest to such lot line. This measurement shall be taken at the right angles from the building line to the nearest lot line. *(St. Charles, Mo.)*

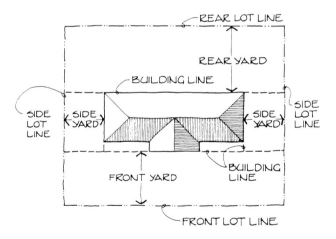

■ **yard, front** A yard extending across the full width of the lot, the depth of which is the minimum horizontal distance between the front lot line and a line parallel thereto on the lot. *(Multnomah County, Ore.)*

Open space extending across the full width of a lot between the front lot line or the proposed front street line and nearest line of the building or any enclosed portion thereof. The depth of

■ **yard, rear** Open space extending across the full width of lot between the rear line of the lot and the nearest line of the building, porch, or projection thereof. The depth of such yard is the shortest horizontal distance between the rear lot line and the nearest point of the building. When the rear lot line is less than 10 feet long or if the lot comes to a point at the rear, the depth of rear yard is measured to an assumed rear lot line, as defined under "lot line, rear." *(Montgomery County, Md.)*

A yard extending across the full width of a lot and lying between a rear lot line of the lot and the nearest point of the building. *(Rye, N.Y.)*

■ **yard sale** *(See garage sale; rummage sale)*

■ **yard, side** A yard between any building and the side lot line, extending from the front yard to the rear yard, or front lot line to rear lot line where no front yard or rear yard is required. The width of the required side yard shall be measured horizontally from the nearest point of the side lot line to the nearest part of the building. *(Multnomah County, Ore.)*

Open space between the side lot line, and the side street line or the proposed side street line, if such line falls within the lot, and the nearest line of the building, porch or projection thereof, extending from the front yard to the rear yard, or in the absence of either such yards to the front lot line or rear lot line. The width of a side yard is the shortest distance between the side lot line and the nearest point of the building, porch, or projection. For a corner lot in a residential zone defined by two street lines connected by a third line having a length of less than 50 feet (commonly known as a "truncation"), the side yard must be measured from the side street line, not from the truncation line. *(Montgomery County, Md.)*

■ **yard trash** *(See also waste, yard)* Solid waste solely consisting of vegetative matter resulting from landscaping maintenance, including grass clippings. *(Alamance County, N.C.)*

■ **youth hostel** A place where travelers may stay for a limited duration, as recognized by the International Hostel Association. *(Fairbanks North Star Borough, Alaska)*

■ **zipper lot** *(See lot, zipper)*

**zero lot line** A detached single-family unit distinguished by the location of one exterior wall on a side property line. *(California Planning Roundtable)*

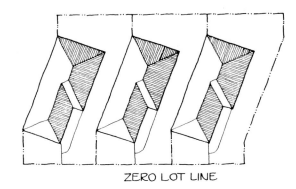

ZERO LOT LINE

A planned arrangement of buildings which touch lot lines, thereby providing zero yard on that side. *(El Paso, Tex.)*

A planned unit development in which a structure is sited on two or fewer lot lines with no yard, permitting site design flexibility while increasing the quantity of usable open space on the lot. *(Conyers, Ga.)*

A common lot line on which a wall of a structure may be constructed. *(Austin, Tex.)*

■ **zone or zoning district** Any section or sections of the city for which the regulations governing the use of land and the use, density, bulk, height, and coverage of buildings and other structures are uniform. *(Staunton, Va., which uses the term "district")*

A specifically delineated area or district in a municipality within which regulations and requirements uniformly govern the use, placement, spacing, and size of land and buildings. *(Siskiyou County, Calif.)*

Any zone as shown on the city's zoning map for which there are uniform regulations governing the use of buildings and premises or the height and area of buildings. *(Scottsdale, Ariz.)*

(1) An area of a city or county that has a unique character identifiable as different from surrounding areas because of distinctive architecture, streets, geographic features, culture, landmarks, activities, or land uses. (2) A portion of the territory of a city or county within which uniform zoning regulations and requirements apply; a zone. *(California Planning Roundtable)*

*Commentary: We have opted to list various specific zones or zoning districts by the name of the zone. So, you will find "floating zone," "holding zone," "interim zone," "overlay zone," "planned zoning district," "transitional zone," and "underlying zoning district" alphabetized under their names.*

■ **zoning** The division of a city or county by legislative regulations into areas, or zones, which specify allowable uses for real property and size restrictions for buildings within these areas. Also, a program that implements policies of the General Plan. *(California Planning Roundtable)*

A police power measure in which the community is divided into districts or zones within which permitted and special uses are established as are regulations governing lot size, building bulk, placement, and other development standards. *(Sacramento, Calif.)*

*Commentary: We have opted to list various specific types of zoning the name of the type. So, you will find "aesthetic zoning," "airport zoning," "areawide zoning," "as-of-right zoning," "conditional zoning," "cumulative (pyramidal) zoning," "density zoning," "Euclidean zoning," "exclusionary zoning," "existing use zoning," "incentive zoning," "inclusionary zoning," "performance zoning," and "spot zoning" alphabetized under their names.*

■ **zoning administrator** Generally, the local official responsible for granting zoning permits and, following a determination by the zoning board, for special permits and variances. Decisions of the official usually are appealable. In some places, the term is used to mean the hearing examiner. *(PAS Report No. 322, The Language of Zoning)*

■ **zoning amendment**    A change in the wording, context, or substance of this title or a change in the zoning or district boundaries of the official zoning map, to be made a part of this title. *(West Des Moines, Iowa)*

■ **zoning certificate**    A document signed by the zoning officer, as required by this zoning code, which acknowledges that a use, structure, building, or lot either complies with or is legally nonconforming to the provisions of this zoning code or is an authorized variance or modification therefrom. *(Newport, R.I.)*

■ **zoning code** *(See also **unified development code**)*    The duly approved, enacted, and amended ordinance that controls and regulates land use in the city. *(Maryland Heights, Mo.)*

An ordinance enacted by the city council pursuant to [state law] that sets forth regulations and standards relating to the nature and extent of uses of land and structures, which is consistent with the comprehensive plan of the city, which includes a zoning map, and complies with the provisions of [state law]. *(Newport, R.I.)*

■ **zoning enforcement officer** *(See also **code enforcement**)*    The officer designated by the [jurisdiction] as the officer responsible for enforcing and administering the requirements of the ordinance. *(McHenry County, Ill.)*

■ **zoning lot**    A lot or portion thereof within a single zoning development district, except as permitted under planned development or joint use approval shall be considered and treated as one zoning lot. *(Maui County, Hawaii)*

■ **zoning map**    A map that graphically shows all zoning district boundaries and classifications within the city, as contained within the zoning code, which is signed by the community development director and on file in the planning department. *(Escondido, Calif.)*

The map adopted as an ordinance by the municipality that delineates the extent of each district or zone established in the zoning ordinance. *(Grand Forks, N.D.)*

The map or maps that are a part of this zoning code and that delineate the boundaries of all mapped zoning districts within the physical boundary of the city. *(Newport, R.I.)*

■ **zoning permit**    A document signed by the zoning officer, as required in this chapter, as a condition precedent to the commencement of a use or the erection, construction, reconstruction, restoration, alteration, conversion, or installation of a structure or building, which document acknowledges that such use, structure, or building complies with the provisions of this chapter or an authorized variance therefrom. *(Siskiyou County, Calif.)*

Written approval by the zoning administrator that is required before commencing any construction, reconstruction, alteration of any building or other structure or before establishing, extending, or changing any use on any lot. *(Nashville and Davidson County, Tenn.)*

■ **zoo**    An area, building, or structures which contain wild animals on exhibition for viewing by the public. *(Cecil County, Md.)*

■ **zoo, private**    Any lot, building, structure, enclosure, or premises whereupon or wherein are kept by any person, other than a municipal corporation, the United States, the state, or any political subdivision thereof, two or more wild animals, whether such keeping is for pleasure, profit, breeding or exhibiting, and including places where two or more wild animals are boarded, kept for sale or kept for hire. *(Carlsbad, Calif.)*